SQL: Access to SQL Server

SUSAN SALES HARKINS AND MARTIN W.P. REID

Apress™

SQL: Access to SQL Server

ISBN (pbk): 1-893115-30-5

Printed and bound in the United States of America 12345678910

Editorial Directors: Dan Appleman, Peter Blackburn, Gary Cornell, Jason Gilmore, Karen Watterson

Technical Reviewer: Russell Sinclair

Managing Editor: Grace Wong

Project Manager: Doris Wong

Copy Editor: Tom Gillen

Production Editor: Kari Brooks

Compositor: Impressions Book and Journal Services, Inc.

Illustrator: Kurt Krames

Indexer: Valerie Robbins

Cover Designer: Tom Debolski

Marketing Manager: Stephanie Rodriguez

Distributed to the book trade in the United States by Springer-Verlag New York, Inc.,175 Fifth Avenue, New York, NY, 10010

and outside the United States by Springer-Verlag GmbH & Co. KG, Tiergartenstr. 17, 69112 Heidelberg, Germany.

In the United States, phone 1-800-SPRINGER, email `orders@springer-ny.com`, or visit `http://www.springer-ny.com`.

Outside the United States, fax +49 6221 345229, email `orders@springer.de`, or visit `http://www.springer.de`.

For information on translations, please contact Apress directly at 901 Grayson Street, Suite 204, Berkeley, CA 94710.

Phone 510-549-5930, fax: 510-549-5939, email `info@apress.com`, or visit `http://www.apress.com`.

To the child or grandchild who refuses to put me in a nursing home
and takes care of me in my old age.
—Susan Sales Harkins

For my wife Patricia—who made it all possible and who kept everything going
while I was at the keyboards—and for my children: Aine, Liam, Maeve, Emer,
Roisin, and our new addition as yet unborn. Finally to my parents,
William and Sarah Reid, who struggled for all of us.
—Martin W.P. Reid

Contents at a Glance

Contents

Foreword

THE ROAD TO MICROSOFT ACCESS enlightenment has many steps.

You see, Microsoft has built Access as a deceptively friendly database program. You can use it right out of the box, relying on the database wizards to create entire databases. You can treat a blank datasheet like a spreadsheet and just type in data, and Access will figure out how to save it for you. You can build forms with the Form wizard, reports with the Report wizard, and then just start banging data into the thing.

This is where the journey starts. The beginning database user doesn't have to know anything about tables and fields, let alone such tricky concepts as normalization or joins. And, for many users, that's enough. After all, the first thing that a database has to do is store your data so that you can find it again.

However, sooner or later, many users (and most developers) will start wondering what lies underneath the wizards and other user interface tools. That's when they start down the long road to enlightenment. The usual starting point is the Database window, with all its interesting objects. And discovering the Design view of forms and reports gives the developer the power to customize the output of the wizards. Understanding how tables, queries, and relationships work together to extract data brings more powerful insights.

From there, most Access developers continue their travels with one of the object models (DAO or ADO) and the VBA programming language. Soon, they're making the program jump through hoops, satisfied that they understand Access in depth.

But, as I said, the road has many steps. If your own journey went from the user interface to the Access objects to VBA and DAO, you've missed one of the most rewarding stretches of the trip: I refer, of course, to the SQL capabilities that are built into Access.

As you'll learn from Susan and Martin, SQL stands for *Structured Query Language*, a more-or-less standard way to work with relational data. If you've ever looked at a query in SQL view, you've seen SQL. And, if you're like far too many Access developers, you may have just wondered what it was good for and then gone on to something else.

If that's the case, the authors invite you to see how SQL works and what it's good for. As you work through this book, you'll discover that SQL provides a powerful way to define the data that you want returned from a query, as well as performs other database tasks such as defining the structure of tables. In fact, some things in Access can be done only by writing SQL statements directly. For example, you probably already know about using the Top Values property of a query to see only a portion of the query's results (for instance, say, the five most expensive products). But what if you want to see only the products that are *not* in the top five most expensive? This is where SQL comes in because you need to go beyond the graphical design tools and property settings and actually write the SQL statement to perform this query.

The answer, by the way, is to use a subquery:

```
SELECT UnitPrice FROM PRODUCTS
WHERE UnitPrice < ALL
(SELECT TOP 5 UnitPrice
FROM Products
ORDER BY UnitPrice DESC)
ORDER BY UnitPrice DESC
```

Of course, subqueries are only one of the many topics that Susan and Martin cover in this book.

But there are more reasons to learn SQL besides the fact that knowing it will make you one of the cool kids and impress all your friends. You see, the journey to Access enlightenment actually continues until you're outside of Access entirely. This paradoxical result comes about because SQL is a cross-product data language. Although the dialects differ (think of the differences between the speech of someone from Atlanta, Georgia, and someone from Boston, Massachusetts), both Access and SQL Server use SQL as their underlying data language. This means that the SQL you learn in Access will help you in working with SQL Server (as well as with other databases such as Oracle or IBM's DB2).

Beginning with Access 2000, Microsoft has made this transition much simpler by incorporating SQL Server functionality directly into Access, through the integration of the MSDE version of SQL Server with Access Data Projects. As you work through this book, you'll understand how MSDE and ADPs fit into the SQL picture. You'll learn how to "upsize" your Access application to take advantage of these new technologies, and see what you can do with your data after the upsizing process is complete.

I've been working with Access and other Microsoft technologies for almost a decade now (and with programming in general for a quarter of a century). Over that time, it's become clear to me that you learn primarily two types of things as you improve your programming skills: surface knowledge and deep knowledge.

Surface knowledge includes most of the things that you need to learn to make a particular programming language work for you. The exact syntax of the `Replace()` function in VBA, for example, is surface knowledge. Right now, knowing that is important. Ten years from now, when you've moved on to some other development platform, you won't need to devote any brain cells to remembering that syntax, any more than I can recall what I used to know of Z80 assembly language. Surface knowledge is easily supplemented by the computer; just press F1, search the index, and there it is.

Deep knowledge, on the other hand, is the stuff that you won't find in help files. For example, if you ever took a data structures course, you probably learned about hash tables. If you didn't, well, a hash table is a way to store ten pounds of stuff in a five-pound stack. The first time I ever implemented a hash table, I was programming in Pascal. Although that particular implementation is long gone on some diskette that I couldn't even read on my current PCs, the basic idea of a hash table is with me still. If the need arises, I understand how to make one work and could reimplement the idea in any language. That's deep knowledge.

For the Access developer, the first piece of deep knowledge is usually an understanding of objects, methods, and properties. I've taught hundreds of people the basics of working with objects in an Access environment. Along the way, I've watched the "aha" expression come across their faces. For a while, the syntax of creating and using objects is just a mess, something to learn by rote. But then, you suddenly grasp *why* things are designed that way, and the notion of objects starts to make its way into your deep knowledge. By now, if you've been working with objects for a while, the syntax is second nature. You don't have to concentrate on what an object represents: you can just drop it into your code and start using it.

Learning SQL is one more place for you to pick up a valuable chunk of deep knowledge. Oh, I'm not talking about the trivia of whether a particular SQL implementation uses the asterisk or the percentage symbol as a wildcard character; that's the sort of thing you can always check by hitting F1. But, as you delve into SQL, you'll realize that its use with relational databases is not purely arbitrary. It turns out that SQL is well suited for data retrieval because it was designed from the ground up to operate with sets of data. Although this book won't give you the heavyset theoretical underpinnings, it will demonstrate the power and use of SQL in Access and SQL Server. As that soaks in, you'll find that the journey was worthwhile, because Access is much easier to use when you start to think about data in the same way as the database engine does. And that's what SQL is all about.

Mike Gunderloy
Editor, Smart Access Extra
Endicott, Washington
November 2001
`http://www.larkfarm.com`

About the Authors

Susan Sales Harkins lives in Kentucky with her husband, Bill. Unlike most computer geeks, computers are not her passion, just her livelihood. Her grandchildren, whom she plays with all week while everyone else is working, are her passion. When time allows, she's a quilter and a backyard birdwatcher. Susan's first exposure to personal computers was in the early 1980s, when the accounting firm she was working for purchased one personal computer for a firm of 150 employees, and at a price of $5,000. It was slow, but the line to use it was long. Her personal interest eventually led her to a career in computer training and development.

Martin W.P. Reid is currently employed at The Queens University of Belfast, where he is responsible for staff and student computer training, teaching everything from basic Windows and Web authoring to database design. He is also employed by the faculty of Computer Science as a part-time lecturer in database design and teaches several courses using Microsoft Access for other areas in the university.

Martin particularly enjoys the contact with staff and students, and one of his biggest thrills was when two of his part-time students—who had previously never been near a database—started work as developers. It was a real pleasure watching them learn both inside and outside the class.

Martin is married with five children (four girls and one boy) with a sixth baby due in February of 2002. He credits his wife, Patricia, with keeping the whole show on the road while he plays with databases.

About the Technical Reviewer

RUSSELL SINCLAIR is the owner of Synthesystems, a consulting firm that specializes in custom development using SQL Server, Visual Basic, and Microsoft Access. He is also the Senior Systems Architect with Questica, a company that creates software for custom-design manufacturers.

Russell is the author of *From Access to SQL Server* (Apress, ISBN 1-893115-240) and is a Contributing Editor to *Smart Access Newsletter*, for whom he has also written numerous articles. He is an avid sailor, and probably spends too much time on the Internet playing *Half-Life*. He lives in Toronto, Canada, with his fiancée and two cats.

Acknowledgments

Thanks to the Apress folks for their patience, professionalism, and especially for having faith in the topic, and to the AccessD (`www.databaseadivsors.com`) folks for all their great advice and help over the years. If someone on that list can't solve your problem, it can't be solved. —*Susan Sales Harkins*

I would like to thank Susan Harkins for asking me to join this project (it was hard work but fun); Russell Sinclair for his super advice and guidance; Doris Wong for her patience; Tom Gillen for his work on my grammar; Arthur Fuller for his assistance, help, and proofreading; and the members of the AccessD list for advice, testing, and guidance. Many other people helped in one way or another, and I thank you all. —*Martin W.P. Reid*

CHAPTER 1

Structured Query Language

From Inception to Now

ONCE UPON A TIME, 64KB came in a piano crate, not on a small chip, and maintaining and manipulating data was expensive. Memory wasn't the only problem: software was in its infancy, and simple tasks such as storing and indexing files required lots of support staff. As data grew, so did the need for better ways to maintain and manipulate that data. This need gave birth to the inexpensive hardware and efficient software we take for granted today.

Part of this evolution involved the methods for data storage and retrieval. Early databases relied on the flat-file format, in which all data was stored for each record in one large table. Of course, this arrangement led to redundancy and required lots of memory. A major goal during this period was to solve the problem of redundant data.

In 1970, Dr. E. F. Codd, an IBM researcher, published an article on relational database theory, and this article set the stage for the relational database model we use today. The article outlined a method for using relational calculus and algebra to store and retrieve data—large amounts of data—easily and efficiently. In a nutshell, this theory stored information in "tables" and allowed users to interact with the data using English commands. As a result, IBM introduced a new research group known as System/R.

The goal of this new group was to create a relational database system based on Codd's theory. A prototype was put into use in several organizations, and System/R eventually evolved into SQL/Data System (SQL/DS), which later found its real potential as DB2. The System/R project ended in 1979, but the viability of the relational data model was irrefutable.

Before ending the System/R project, IBM implemented a support language for System/R's multitable and multiuser access called Structured English Query Language, or SEQUEL. This early product was pronounced *sequel.* Eventually, the product became known and pronounced as *SQL* (*S-Q-L*). You may find people that still refer to it as *sequel,* but they have usually been working with the language for a long time.

The end result of ten year's worth of research and development work is now known as Structured Query Language (SQL), which has become the industry standard for relational databases. Today, dozens of vendors provide SQL for every environment, from the desktop PC to large mainframes.

Standards

During the late 1970s and throughout the 1980s, competitors came and went. Some, like Oracle, are still present, but most either went the way of the dinosaur or they realized that SQL was the future and adapted and adopted SQL as their own query language. Eventually, SQL became the industry standard, and today many versions of SQL are available.

The American National Standards Institute (ANSI) took notice and began work to create a standard definition for SQL. ANSI is a privately run, not-for-profit organization that coordinates voluntary standardization of the U.S. computer industry. You can learn more about this organization at `http://www.ansi.org`. The current standard is based mostly on the original IBM work with a lot of additions. ANSI eventually adopted SQL as the standard language for relational database management systems. This standard has also been adopted by the International Standards Organization (ISO) and the United States government.

> **NOTE** *A European standard for SQL does exist. Known as X/OPEN, these standards support a UNIX-based environment. These standards play a vital role in the European market, but they are very different from the ANSI standards used throughout the U.S. industry.*

ANSI published its first SQL standard—SQL-86—in 1986. Subsequent updates (SQL-92 and SQL-99) were published in 1992 and 1999, respectively. Incremental parts are published as new technologies and functionality emerge.

You can download electronic copies of the standards from ANSI's Electronic Standards Store at `http://webstore.ansi.org`. Or, you can purchase hard copies (although very expensive) from American National Standards Institute, 1819 L Street, NW Suite 600, Washington, DC 20036.

The three standards are listed in Table 1-1 with their common names.

Table 1-1. ANSI Standards for SQL

VERSION	COMMON NAME	AVAILABLE
ANSI X3.135-1986	SQL-86	Hardcopy only
ANXI X3.135-1992	SQL-92	Online
ANSI X3.135-1999	SQL-99	Online

The Many Dialects

Although SQL is the accepted standard, SQL is available in many dialects, all of which are unique to their vendors. In fact, it's safe to say that SQL is available, in some form, for every important computer platform. Most of these dialects agree on simple data retrieval commands, such as SELECT. However, differences develop as the products add customized functionality. These differences are known as *vendor-specific extensions.* Because hundreds of database products support SQL, many different dialects are in use, and there's little hope that SQL will ever evolve into just one dialect.

Even products made by the same vendor (Microsoft in this case) use different dialects of SQL. Access doesn't really have an SQL dialect of its own. Access relies on Jet SQL, and SQL Server Desktop Engine and SQL Server 2000 both use Transact-SQL (T-SQL). This book focuses on Jet SQL and T-SQL.

Furthermore, this book limits its focus to Jet SQL and T-SQL in the Microsoft products Access, SQL Server Desktop Engine (MSDE), and SQL Server 2000, and using SQL with these products. Jet SQL extensions aren't supported via the query design graphic interface (Query Design window). You can access extensions only by using ADO code and OLEDB providers. Table 1-2 compares SQL tasks in both MS dialects.

Table 1-2. Differences Between Jet SQL and Transact-SQL (T-SQL)

FEATURE/KEYWORD	JET SQL	JET SQL EXTENSIONS	T-SQL
JOIN in UPDATE	○	○	∅*
JOIN in DELETE	○	○	∅*
DELETE with multiple tables	○	○	∅
Subquery in UPDATE/SET	∅	∅	○
DISTINCTROW	○	○	∅
TOP	○	○	○
TRANSFORM	○	○	∅
SELECT INTO	○	○	○
CREATE DOMAIN	∅	∅	○
ALTER DOMAIN	∅	∅	○
DECLARE CURSOR	∅	∅	○
FETCH	∅	∅	○
CREATE ASSERTION	∅	∅	○
DROP ASSERTION	∅	∅	○
UNION	○	○	○
UNION JOIN	∅	∅	○
FULL OUTER JOIN	∅	∅	○
PIVOT	○	○	∅
COMPUTE	∅	∅	○
FOR BROWSE	∅	∅	○
OPTION	∅	∅	○
ORDER BY	○	○	∅ (in views)
WITH OWNER ACCESS	∅	○	∅
GRANT	∅	○	○
LOCK	∅	○	○
FIRST	○	○	∅
LAST	○	○	∅
PIVOT	○	○	∅

Table 1-2. Differences Between Jet SQL and Transact-SQL (T-SQL) (continued)

FEATURE/KEYWORD	JET SQL	JET SQL EXTENSIONS	T-SQL
CREATE VIEW	∅	○	○
CHECK	∅	○	○

○ Supported

∅ Not supported

* Can be done in T-SQL if you use a second FROM clause in the form

```
UPDATE tblX Set X=Y
FROM tbl1, tbl2, etc.
```

This book deals with using Jet SQL or T-SQL in Access, SQL Server Desktop Edition, and SQL Server. Knowing how each product responds to SQL will help you create efficient solutions using the best product for each project.

CHAPTER 2

An Introduction to Using Jet SQL in Access

Learn How Access Takes Advantage of Jet SQL

THERE ARE FOUR TYPES of Jet SQL users in Access:

- Those who are completely oblivious to its existence and subsequently don't know Access is using Jet SQL.
- Those who know Jet SQL exists but don't know anything about it.
- Access users who can manipulate Jet SQL statements in Access and/or Visual Basic for Applications (VBA), the programming language that comes with Access (and Office) code.
- Developers who know more than one version of Jet SQL and use it in Access and beyond.

Access uses SQL every time you run a query. (From here on, references to SQL mean Jet SQL, unless otherwise noted.) You create questions using the Query Design window, and, when you run that query, SQL converts your question into the format that the Microsoft Jet database engine (or Jet) can understand. You just don't realize it's happening because Access and SQL work together seamlessly.

Queries aren't the only time SQL steps into the picture. Access relies on SQL to build reports and to populate control lists and forms. You'd be surprised to learn just how often SQL is at work behind the scenes. Almost anytime you make a task-oriented request—whether you're running a query or populating a form—SQL goes to work.

Building Access Queries

Certainly, the most obvious and consistent user of SQL is the Access query, which is simply a stored question or request. SQL converts every query before sending it on to Jet, and the types of requests you make will depend on the purpose of your database. Access provides several different query types, which we'll introduce in this chapter. Later chapters are devoted to learning the SQL syntax for each. The different query types are:

- A *Select* query retrieves and groups data and displays the results of expressions. Select queries are probably the most common.
- A *Crosstab* query summarizes data and then categorizes those summarized values.
- *Action* queries restructure or modify data. The four types of Action queries are Delete, Update, Append, and Make-Table.
- *SQL-Specific* queries must be executed via SQL commands. The SQL-Specific queries are Union, Pass-Through, Data-Definition, and Subquery. SQL queries can't be expressed graphically in the Query Design window, with the exception of some subqueries. (You can learn more about subqueries in "Creating and Using Subqueries," in Chapter 11.)

> **NOTE** *If you're familiar with Access, you may be wondering why Parameter queries aren't in the list. Parameter queries prompt you for additional information, which the query then uses to restrict its results. However, most Select and Action queries can also be a parameter query, and so they're not really a specific type of queries in the same category as those in the list.*

Using the Design Grid

Access provides a number of wizards that create some simple and unique queries for you, but most users prefer to build queries from scratch in the design grid. (See Figure 2-1.) You may know the window as the QBE, Query Builder, or Query Design grid, but, throughout this book, we'll refer to the entire window as the Query Design window. The upper pane displays a field list for each data source (tables and queries). The bottom pane, or design grid, as we'll call it, determines the data and calculated results that the query returns. The design grid includes the following cells:

- *Field* cells identify each field that the query considers in an expression or display.
- *Table* cells identify the field's data source.
- The *Sort* cell specifies a sort order—ascending, descending, or not sorted—for each field.
- The *Show* cell determines whether the field is displayed in the results. You can specify criteria in a field but not display that field in the resulting recordset.
- *Criteria* cells contain an expression for limiting the query's results.
- An *Or* cell is a type of Criteria cell that allows you to specify more than one condition, but the entry has to meet only one condition to be included in the results.

Figure 2-1. The design grid provides a graphical interface for creating queries.

Adding a Table or Query to the Query Design Window

The first step to creating a query is to specify the data source(s). You can do so either before opening the Query Design window or from inside the window. When opening the window with a specified data source:

1. Select the data source in the Database window.

2. Choose Query from the Insert menu. Alternately, choose Query from the New Object button's drop-down list. (You'll find this tool on the Database toolbar.) Then, click on OK in the New Query dialog box to open the query design grid, complete with a field list for the specified data source, as shown in Figure 2-2.

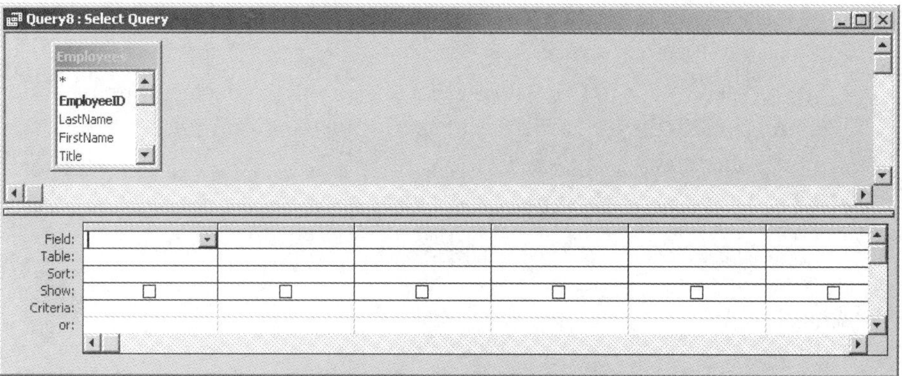

Figure 2-2. You can specify a query's data source before opening the Query Design window.

A drawback of this method is that you can specify only one data source, but you can add a data source inside the query design grid by following these four steps:

1. Click on the Show Table button on the Query Design toolbar, or choose Show Table from the View menu. Either method displays the Show Table dialog shown in Figure 2-3.

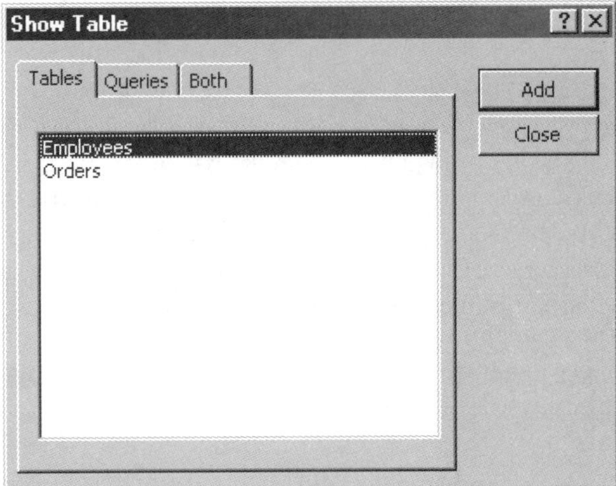

Figure 2-3. Select a table or query in the Show Table dialog to add it to the query.

2. Then, click on a tab to display all the tables, queries, or both.

3. Select a table and click on the Add button to add a field list of the selected object to the upper pane of the Query Design window. Alternately, you can simply double-click on the table or query.

4. Click on Close to close the dialog and return to the Query Design window.

The Query Design window in Figure 2-4 displays more than two field lists. There's also a join (or relationship) line between the two lists, which indicates that the two tables are related. Specifically, the line points to the related fields (the primary and foreign key fields) in both tables. (For more information on relationships, read Chapter 3, "An Introduction to Relational Database Theory.")

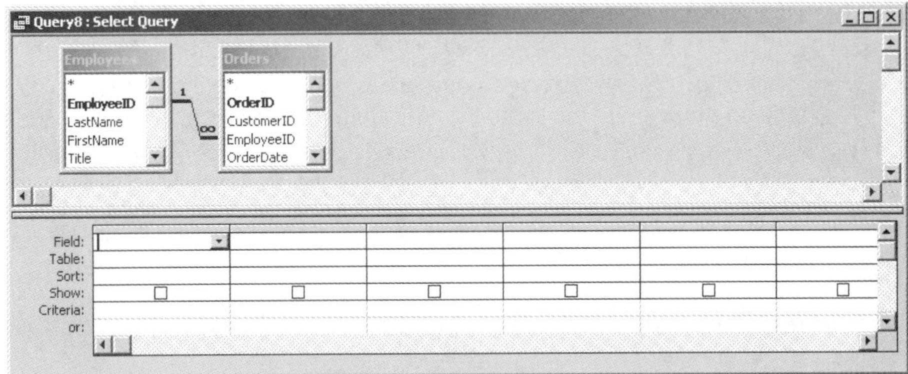

Figure 2-4. The line between the two tables indicates a relationship.

Adding a Field to the Design Grid

After specifying the appropriate data sources, you need to indicate which fields you want to include in your query by adding those fields to the design grid. Just because you add a field doesn't mean the query will display it. Fields are often used as part of a criteria expression, and the entries aren't always displayed in the query's results. You can add a field to the design grid in five ways:

- Drag the field from the field list to a Field cell.
- Double-click on a field in the field list to add that field to the first empty Field cell.
- Select a Field cell and type the field name yourself. (This isn't the preferred method because you could make typographical errors.) Be sure to specify the appropriate table in the Table field if the query has more than one data source and that source contains duplicate field names.
- Select a field name from a Field cell's drop-down list. Be sure to specify the appropriate table in the Table field if the query has more than one data source and that source contains duplicate field names.
- Drag the asterisk character from the field list to a Field cell to include all the fields in the query.

> **TIP** *When dragging fields to the design grid, you can save time by dragging a block of fields instead of dragging them one at a time. To drag a contiguous block of fields, select the first field, hold down the Shift key, and then click on the last field. Access will highlight the first, last, and all the fields in between. When adding noncontiguous fields, click on the first field, hold down the Ctrl key, and then click on the remaining fields. To select all of the fields, double-click on the field list's title bar. Drag the highlighted block to the design grid and Access adds them in the order in which they appear in the field list. This isn't all there is to creating a query. You can specify a field's sort order and add expressions that limit the results of the query or calculate new values.*

Viewing SQL Statements

The quickest way to learn SQL is to simply review the SQL equivalent of your queries. The Query Design window is the graphical interface we use to create an

Access query, but you can see the SQL translation of a query by choosing SQL View from the View button's drop-down list to open the SQL window. Figure 2-5 shows the same query in the Query Design window and the SQL window. The SQL window offers a number of benefits besides viewing the SQL equivalent of your query:

- You can copy SQL statements to a VBA module for use in code. Use the Query Design window to create the query, and then copy the SQL statement from the SQL window to the VBA module to avoid typos and other syntax errors that might occur if you write the statement yourself.
- You can create SQL statements that have no graphical representation and therefore can't be built in the Query Design window (SQL-Specific queries).
- The SQL window supplies very specific error messages, so it's a good place to debug SQL statements that are used elsewhere.

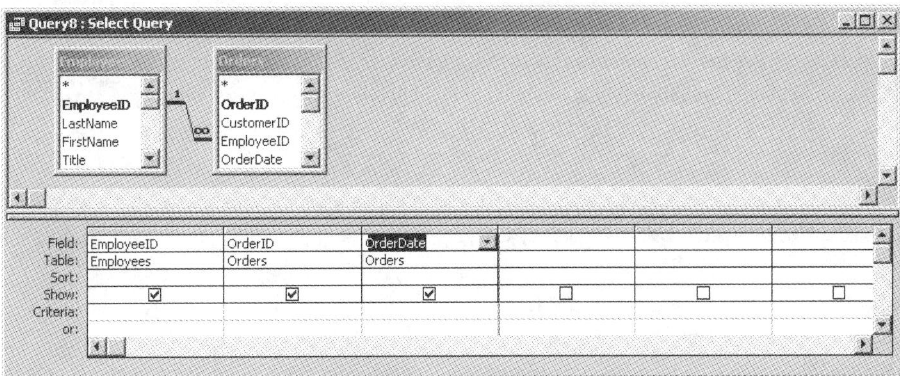

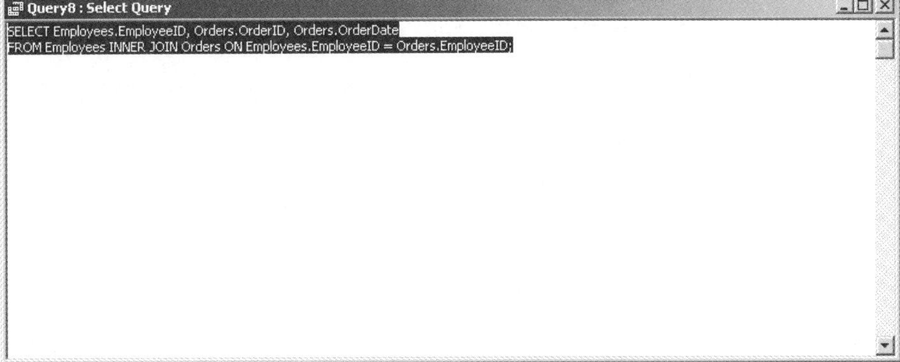

Figure 2-5. The SQL window displays a query's equivalent SQL statement. The window in the top figure is the familiar Query Design window, and the SQL window is shown in the bottom figure.

How Access Uses SQL

Knowing that SQL is translating your data requests is only part of the package. Often, a task is made much more simple by substituting an SQL statement for a traditional data source or including an SQL statement in a VBA procedure. The main benefit is flexibility and functionality. SQL statements can produce results that you can get only from a query. You can use a fixed query to populate a form, report, or control, but using the equivalent SQL statement reduces the number of fixed queries in your application, which can be an important issue in a large application.

> *It can be difficult to maintain a large number of queries, but many people are under the impression that Access stores only the SQL statement that you put into the record source. However, if you look at the hidden queries in the MDB database, you will find that all of your SQL statements for forms, reports, combos, and list boxes are actually stored as standard queries with an odd naming convention.*
>
> *Designing forms in this way is often considered "bad form," but it does make the database window a little less cluttered. (I tend to do a bit of both.) The important thing is that it makes no difference in performance.*
>
> Russell Sinclair, author of *From Access to SQL Server* (Apress)

Specifying a Data Source

The Northwind.mdb sample file that comes with Access often uses SQL statements instead of fixed queries as the Row Source for controls. Figure 2-6 shows the Orders form open in Design view. You can see that the Row Source property for the EmployeeID control is an SQL statement (even though you can't see the entire statement) because the setting begins with a SELECT clause.

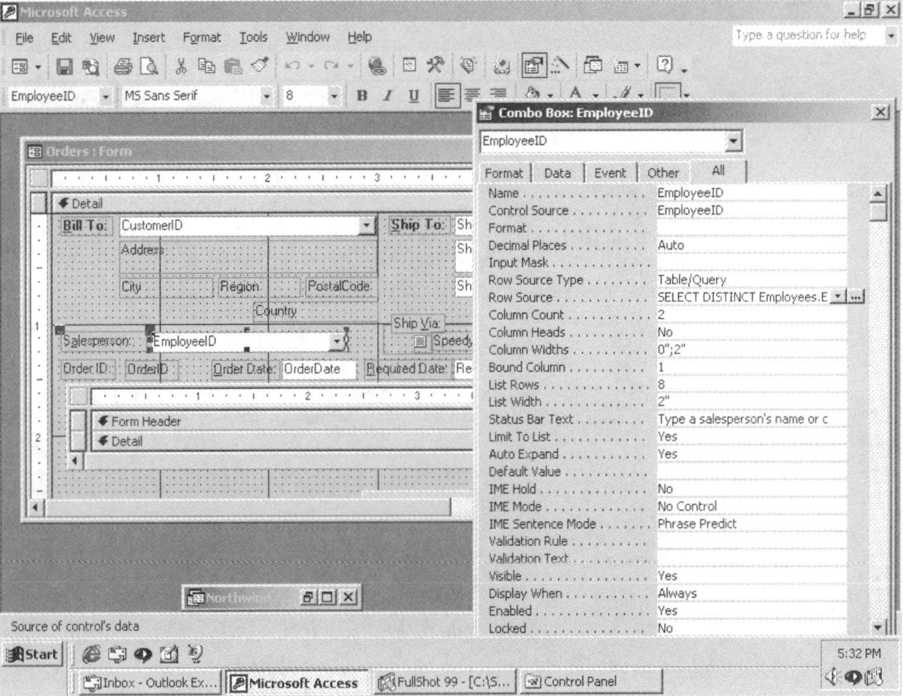

Figure 2-6. Open the Orders form in Design view.

> **TIP** *Anytime you need to see a complete property setting, simply select the property field and press* `Shift+F2` *to open that setting (expression) in the Zoom window.*

To see the entire statement, select the Row Source property field and then click on the Builder button (the button with the eclipses just to the right of the field that appears once you select the field). Doing so launches the SQL Statement: Query Builder. The resulting window is a Query Design window that you can modify just as you would a regular query. Notice that the design grid already contains the fields that SQL needs to retrieve data and populate the control, as shown in Figure 2-7. You can adjust the settings via the builder window instead of trying to rewrite the SQL statement.

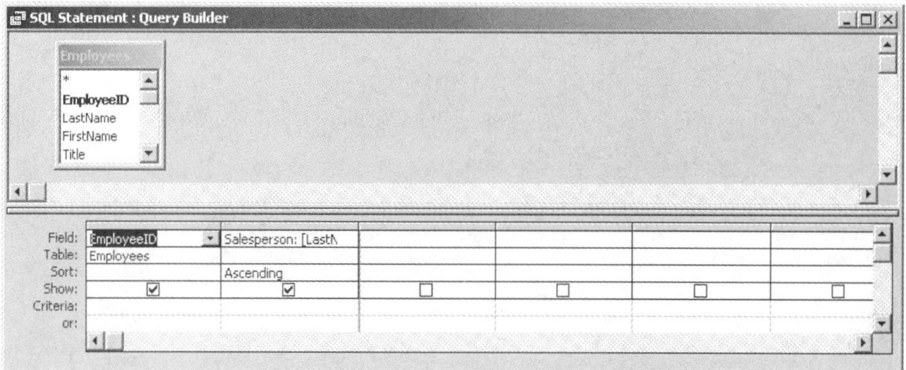

Figure 2-7. Click on the Builder button to launch the SQL Statement: Query Builder.

> **TIP** *The SQL Statement: Query Builder can be launched from any form or report's Control Source property or from a combo or list box control's Row Source property. Simply select the field, and, if the builder's available, Access displays the Builder button to the right of the field.*

The query concatenates the LastName and FirstName fields from the Employees table (with a comma and a space between the two) to display a list of employee names. To see the equivalent SQL statement, shown in Figure 2-8, choose SQL View from the View button's drop-down list. If you compare this statement to the one displayed in the Row Source field, you'll find that they're the same. The result is the control shown in Figure 2-9.

Figure 2-8. Open the SQL window to view the EmployeeID control's SQL statement.

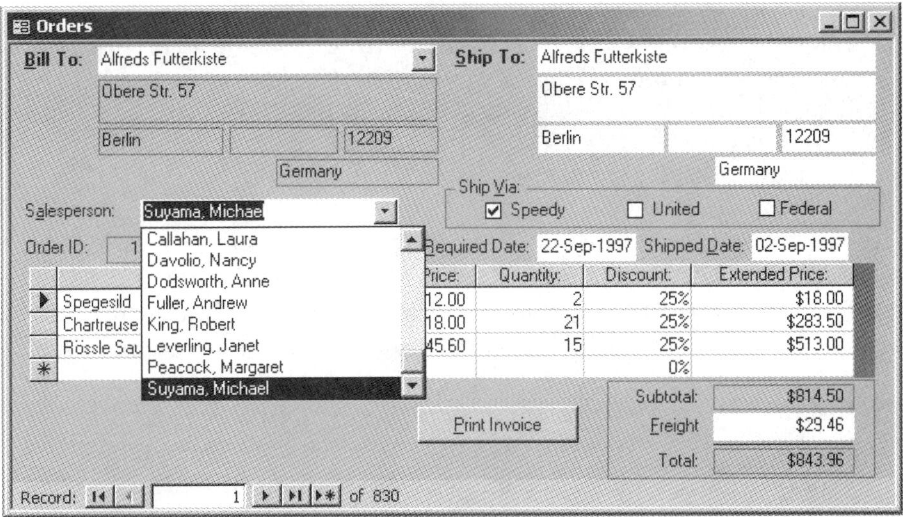

Figure 2-9. The Row Source property's SQL statement populates the control with a list of employee names.

In addition, if you choose Datasheet View from the View button's drop-down list, you can see the results of the query in Datasheet view. You can jump back and forth between the builder, the SQL statement, and the results until the statement is correct. Then, you close the builder and save your changes when prompted. The control's Row Source property will automatically update accordingly to reflect any changes you make.

Omitting Fixed Queries

Using SQL to populate a control is a fairly common practice. What you might not see as often is SQL statements used to populate a form or report. Many developers use fixed queries. Replacing a fixed query with an SQL statement adds a layer of protection. Because there's no fixed query object in the Database window, a user must know how to open the form or report and alter the Record Source property to change the data source for a form or report. Using SQL statements as a form or reports record source means someone is much less likely to modify the source your form or report is based on in such a way that your object stops working correctly.

> **TIP** *Earlier versions of Jet had to optimize an SQL statement each time you ran it; as a result, fixed queries were faster than SQL statements. This is no longer the case, however, and SQL statements are now executed just as quickly as fixed queries when used as a Record Source property.*

The forms and reports in the Northwind sample database use fixed queries, so we'll use the SQL window to copy a query's SQL statement to the dependent form's Record Source property, thus eliminating the need for the fixed query. First, we need to know which query is the form's data source. To determine the form's data source, open the form in Design view. Then, double-click on the Form Selector (the gray square at the intersection of the horizontal and vertical rulers) to open the form's Properties window. Figure 2-10 shows the Orders form's Properties window. As you can see, the Record Source property is a query named Orders Qry.

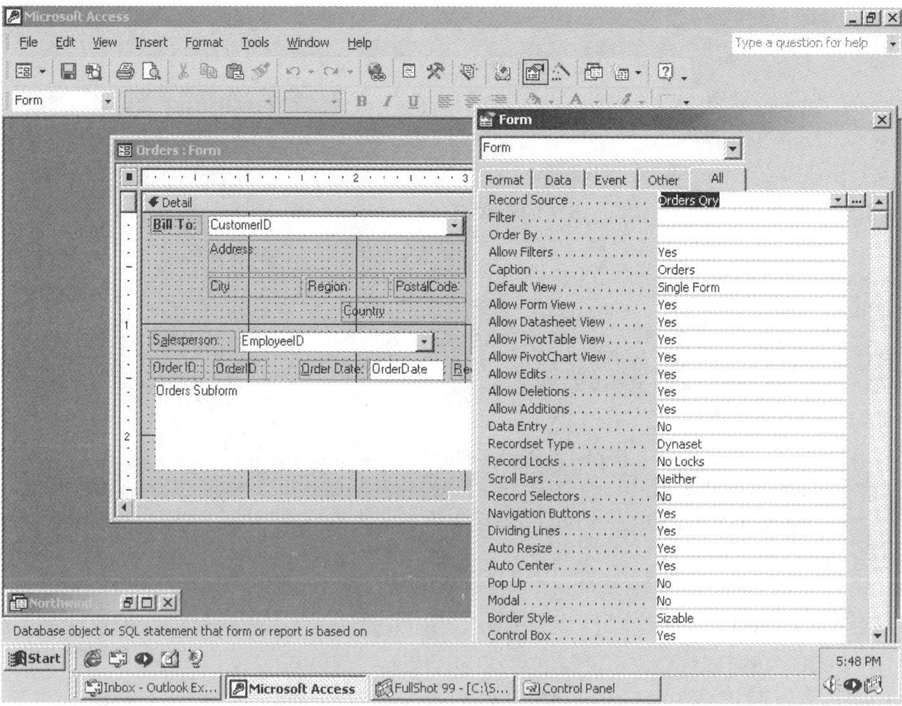

Figure 2-10. The Orders form is populated by the Orders Qry query.

Next, we need to open the Orders Qry query, copy its SQL statement to the clipboard, and paste it into the form's Record Source property field. To do so:

1. Without closing the form in question, display the Database window (press F11), and then click on the Queries shortcut in the Database window's Object bar.

2. Select Orders Qry and then click on Design on the Database Window toolbar.

3. In Design view, choose SQL View from the View button on the Query Design toolbar.

4. Highlight the entire SQL statement, including the semicolon (;) at the end.

5. Press `Ctrl+C` to copy the SQL statement to the clipboard.

6. Close the query. Don't save the query if prompted.

7. After copying the SQL statement to the clipboard, you're ready to paste it into the form's Record Source property field. To do so, simply return to the form's Properties window (in Design view), highlight the current setting of the Record Source property, and press `Ctrl+V` to replace that setting with Orders Qry's SQL statement.

8. Click on the View button to see the form in Form view; you'll find that the form responds in exactly the same manner as the original that used Orders Qry to retrieve its recordset.

Built-in Functions

Some built-in functions use SQL WHERE clauses as arguments, which we'll review in Chapter 5, "Retrieving Data." For example, the **DAvg()** function calculates the average of a set of values in a specified set of records. The syntax for the **DAvg()** function is

```
DAvg(expression, domain[, criteria])
```

where *expression* identifies the field you're averaging, *domain* identifies the data source, and *criteria* is a string that specifies limitations on *expression*, and is often an SQL WHERE clause, without the keyword WHERE. To calculate the average unit price of all products sold where the discount value is less than ten percent, you might use a function similar to

```
DAvg("[UnitPrice]","[Order Details]", "[Discount] < .1")
```

Functions that accept WHERE clauses as arguments are as follows:

- **DAvg()**
- **DCount()**
- **DFirst()**
- **DLast()**
- **DLookup()**
- **DMax()**
- **DMin()**
- **DstDev()**
- **DstDevP()**
- **DVar()**
- **DvarP()**

Although you're not creating an entire SQL clause, writing these arguments should be easier once you understand SQL's syntax.

Executing SQL with VBA

Most of this book will examine SQL statements without consideration for executing those statements. When using a query or populating a form, report, or control, you don't manually execute the statements; instead, Access executes the statement when you run the query or activate the object in question. In contrast, you can control how and when an SQL statement is executed by executing that statement via VBA.

Using RunSQL

As with so many Access tasks, there's more than one way to execute an SQL statement in VBA. The DoCmd object's RunSQL method is the VBA equivalent of the RunSQL macro action and takes the form

```
DoCmd.RunSQL sqlstatement[, usetransaction]
```

where *sqlstatement* is a string expression that equals a valid SQL statement for an action or data-definition query and *usetransaction* is the value True or False. True is the default and includes the query in a transaction. A transaction wraps a series of changes: either all are made or none are made, but a transaction won't allow any modifications to be made if even one can't be completed. (You can learn more about data-definition queries in Chapter 8, "Creating and Modifying Tables.")

The maximum length of the *sqlstatement* argument is 32,768 characters. However, the RunSQL method won't work with an ordinary SELECT statement. RunSQL works with the following SQL statements:

- INSERT INTO
- DELETE
- SELECT INTO
- UPDATE
- CREATE TABLE
- ALTER TABLE
- DROP TABLE
- CREATE INDEX
- DROP INDEX

Still working in the Northwind.mdb sample file, let's assume you want to change the term "Sales Representative" in the Employees table's Title field to "Account Executive". You could run a fixed query, but we're going to show you how to accomplish this change using VBA's RunSQL method. The key is to start with the Query Design window. Whenever possible, let Access write as much of your SQL statement as possible by using the query design interface and then copying the query's equivalent SQL statement from the SQL window to a VBA module. You may be proficient at SQL, but we all make occasional mistakes, which we can usually avoid by copying the SQL statement and limiting how much of the statement we enter ourselves. Now, let's create that query.

The procedure shown in Listing 2-1 executes an UPDATE SQL statement using the DoCmd object's RunSQL method. Specifically, this statement will change every occurrence of the string "Sales Representative" in the Employees table's Title field to "Account Executive". To create this procedure the easy way, follow these steps:

1. In the Database window, click on the Tables shortcut and then highlight Employees.

2. Choose Query from the New Object button's drop-down list, and then click on OK in the New Query dialog box.

3. Choose Update Query from the Query menu.

4. Add the Title field to the query design grid. Use one of the methods described earlier in this chapter in "Adding a Field to the Design Grid." In this case, double-clicking on Title in the field list may be the most efficient choice.

5. Enter "Account Executive" in the Update To field and "Sales Representative" in the Criteria cell, as shown in Figure 2-11. In most queries, you could click on Datasheet View on the View menu to check the results of the query, but an Update query isn't as accommodating. Datasheet view displays each field that's about to be updated, and, in this context, that's only somewhat helpful.

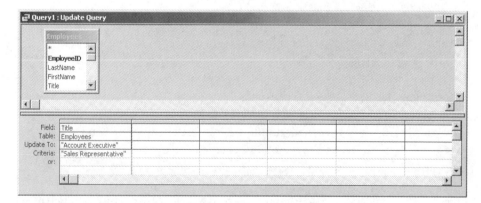

Figure 2-11. Create an Update query in the Query Design window.

6. Choose SQL View from the View button to view the query's equivalent SQL statement. The statement is already highlighted, so press `Ctrl+C` to copy the statement to the clipboard.

7. Launch the Visual Basic Editor (VBE) by pressing Alt+F11.

8. Open the module you want to run the SQL statement from, or open a new module by choosing Module from the Insert menu.

9. Enter the procedure shown in Listing 2.1. Type the `DoCmd.RunSQL` statement, enter a space and double quotes ("), and then press `Ctrl+V` to paste the statement right into your procedure. Type closing double quotes at the end of the statement. If VBA wrapped the statement, position the cursor at the beginning of the wrapped line and press Backspace to pull the line up to the preceding line until the statement is all on one line. Or, you can add a line-continuation character and modify the quotes around the text as shown in Listing 2-1.

10. VBA will still complain because Access has used double quotes to delimit the two strings, "Account Executive" and "Sales Representative." Replace each set with single quotes (').

11. Make sure the cursor is somewhere inside the procedure, and then click on the RunSub/UserForm button (or press F5) to execute the procedure. Click on Yes in the resulting confirmation message. Then, click on the View Microsoft Access button on the Standard menu and open the Employees table. As you can see in Figure 2-12, each "Sales Representative" entry has been changed to "Account Executive". Save the module as basRunSQLExecute if you created a new module for your function.

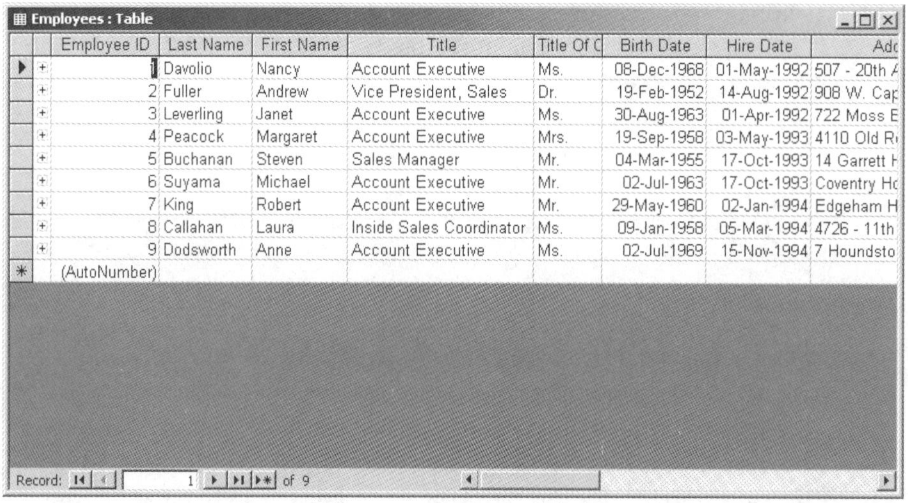

Employees : Table

Employee ID	Last Name	First Name	Title	Title Of C	Birth Date	Hire Date	Adc
1	Davolio	Nancy	Account Executive	Ms.	08-Dec-1968	01-May-1992	507 - 20th A
2	Fuller	Andrew	Vice President, Sales	Dr.	19-Feb-1952	14-Aug-1992	908 W. Cap
3	Leverling	Janet	Account Executive	Ms.	30-Aug-1963	01-Apr-1992	722 Moss E
4	Peacock	Margaret	Account Executive	Mrs.	19-Sep-1958	03-May-1993	4110 Old R
5	Buchanan	Steven	Sales Manager	Mr.	04-Mar-1955	17-Oct-1993	14 Garrett H
6	Suyama	Michael	Account Executive	Mr.	02-Jul-1963	17-Oct-1993	Coventry Hc
7	King	Robert	Account Executive	Mr.	29-May-1960	02-Jan-1994	Edgeham H
8	Callahan	Laura	Inside Sales Coordinator	Ms.	09-Jan-1958	05-Mar-1994	4726 - 11th
9	Dodsworth	Anne	Account Executive	Ms.	02-Jul-1969	15-Nov-1994	7 Houndsto
(AutoNumber)							

Record: 1 of 9

Figure 2-12. The DAO RunSQL method executes an Update query.

Listing 2-1. Execute SQL Using the RunSQL Method

```
Function RunSQLUsingRunSQL()
DoCmd.RunSQL "UPDATE Employees SET Employees.Title = 'Account Executive'" _
    & "WHERE (((Employees.Title)='Sales Representative'));"
End Function
```

NOTE *Typically, developers use Function to denote procedures that return a value and Sub to denote procedures that perform a task. Throughout this book, you may find procedures defined as Function when you might think Sub is more appropriate. We use Function because many of our examples use this method instead of using actual events to trigger an event procedure.*

Using the Execute Method

The Execute method is more complicated, but with that complexity comes a great deal of flexibility. You can use this method with more than one object, but, for our purposes, we'll show you how to use it with the Database object in the Data Access Objects (DAO) library and the Connection object in the ActiveX Data Objects (ADO) library.

> **NOTE** *The Execute method is part of the data object libraries, not Access or VBA. Therefore, you must add a reference to either the Data Access Object or the ActiveX Data Object library to use this Execute method. For more information on using the Execute method, read "Using Execute" later in this chapter.*

Data Access Objects

As long as you're working with local data, you can still work with DAO. In this example, we'll show you how to run an update SQL query using the DAO Execute method.

> **TIP** *Select queries don't perform any kind of action other than retrieving data. Therefore, there's not much reason to execute them in VBA. Executing an SQL statement in the context of VBA generally performs some kind of action, rather than creating a recordset of data that you can manipulate afterward. When you need to run a Select query, it's best to do so by filling a Recordset object. That way you can actually manipulate the resulting recordset via the Recordset object's methods.*

If you created the example in the previous section, you can add the procedure in Listing 2-2 to the same module by copying and pasting the SQL statement and then running the procedure. If you're just starting, complete steps 1 through 8 in the previous example, and then follow these three steps:

1. Enter the procedure in Listing 2-2, up to and including the db.Execute statement. Then, enter a space and double quotes ("). Next, press `Ctrl+V` to paste the statement right into your procedure. Type closing double quotes at the end of the statement. If VBA wrapped the statement, position the cursor at the beginning of the second line and press Backspace to pull the line up to the first line, so the statement is all on one line. Or, insert a continuation character (_). Watch out for the closing quote that VBA may try to add to each line as you're readjusting them.

2. Because ADO is the default, we must add a reference to the DAO library. To do so, choose References from the Tools menu. In the References dialog, locate and check the Microsoft DAO 3.6 Object Library item, as shown in Figure 2-13, and click on OK. It's not enough to just highlight the library; you must check it as well.

> **NOTE** *DAO is the default data object library in Access 97 and earlier versions.*

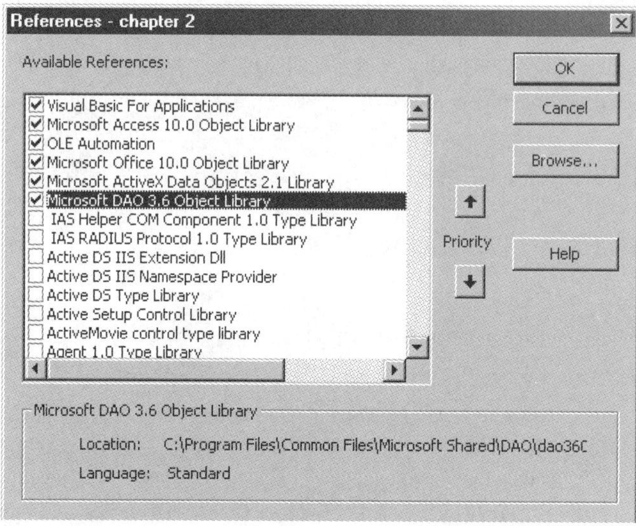

Figure 2-13. Reference the DAO library.

3. Repeat steps 10 through 11 in the previous exercise.

Listing 2-2. This Procedure Uses the DAO Execute Method to Run an SQL Statement

```
Function RunSQLUsingDAOExecute()
Dim db As DAO.Database
Set db = CurrentDb()
db.Execute "UPDATE Employees SET Employees.Title = 'Account Executive'" _
    & "WHERE (((Employees.Title)='Sales Representative'));"
Set db = Nothing
End Function
```

Admittedly, this is a very simple example, but that's what we wanted. More than likely, you wouldn't run a one-time update from VBA. However, you might want to create a generic procedure that accepts arguments, like the one in Listing 2-3 if you update large amounts of data often.

Listing 2-3. This Generic Procedure Passes Arguments

```
Function RunSQLUsingDAOExecuteWithArg(fld As String, _
    changeto As String, crit As String)
Dim db As DAO.Database
Dim strSQL As String
Set db = CurrentDb()
strSQL = "Update Employees SET Employees." & fld
strSQL = strSQL & " = '" & changeto & "'"
strSQL = strSQL & " WHERE Employees." & fld
strSQL = strSQL & " = '" & crit & "'"
strSQL = strSQL & ";"
Debug.Print strSQL
db.Execute strSQL
Set db = Nothing
End Function
```

You can use the procedure in Listing 2-3 to return the values in the Title field to their original values. To do so, add the procedure to a module, open the Immediate window by pressing `Ctrl+G` (if necessary), enter the statement

```
?RunSQLUsingDAOExecuteWithArg("Title","Sales Representative","Account Executive")
```

and then press Enter. VBA will pass the three argument values to the procedure, which will then build the following SQL statement string:

```
Update Employees SET Employees.Title = 'Account Executive' WHERE
Employees.Title = 'Sales Representative';
```

The `db.Execute` statement then runs the SQL statement, which includes the argument values. If you wanted to increase the functionality even further, you could also pass the name of the table. This example updates Text fields, as you can pass only strings.

> **TIP** *You may have noticed that we explicitly declared the Database object using the DAO library prefix. That's because DAO isn't the default in Access 2002 (or Access 2000). Now that there's more than one data object library available, we recommend that you explicitly identify which library you're referencing for better readability. In addition, if both libraries should be referenced, there would be no confusion which library VBA needs to call.*

ADO

ADO doesn't include a Database object; when using ADO, you'll use the Connection object's Execute method. The SQL statement is essentially the same, as you can see from Listing 2-4. The main difference is the way in which the two procedures connect to the data source: DAO uses the Database object, and ADO uses the Connection object. If you've already created the DAO procedure from the previous section, simply add the procedure in Listing 2-4 to the same module. If not, follow the instructions for copying an SQL statement from the SQL window to a VBA module in the "Using RunSQL" section, but use the procedure in Listing 2-4. Listing 2-5 is the ADO equivalent of the argument-passing procedure shown in Listing 2-3.

Listing 2-4. Executing an SQL STATEMENT via the ADO Execute Method

```
Function RunSQLUsingADOExecute()
Dim cnn As ADODB.Connection
Set cnn = CurrentProject.Connection
cnn.Execute "UPDATE Employees SET Employees.Title = 'Account Executive'" _
    & "WHERE (((Employees.Title)='Sales Representative'));"
End Function
```

Listing 2-5. Use the ADO Alternative to Pass Arguments

```
Function RunSQLUsingADOExecuteWithArg(fld As String, _
    changeto As String, crit As String)
Dim cnn As ADODB.Connection
Dim strSQL as String
Set cnn = CurrentProject.Connection
strSQL = "Update Employees SET Employees." & fld
strSQL = strSQL & " = '" & changeto & "'"
strSQL = strSQL & " WHERE Employees." & fld
strSQL = strSQL & " = '" & crit & "'"
strSQL = strSQL & ";"
Debug.Print strSQL
cnn.Execute strSQL
End Function
```

Debugging Tricks

The SQL window doesn't display just SQL statements. Once you're familiar with the environment, you'll find that this window has a couple of hidden talents, such as:

- You can build SQL statements in the Query Design window and then copy the statement to a VBA module.
- You can debug SQL statements in the SQL window by copying them from the VBA module to the SQL window and running them there.

We've already shown you how to create an SQL statement in the Query Design window for use in a VBA statement (in the section titled "Using RunSQL"). You definitely have the advantage because Access creates an equivalent SQL statement for every query. Simply build the query as you normally would. You might not be able to create the complete statement, but the Query Design window will start you out with a valid statement. Once you've gone as far as you can in the Query Design window, open the SQL window and copy the SQL statement to a VBA module. There, you can tweak the statement as necessary. Even the experts use this trick because, as we've said, knowing SQL isn't enough: you must also be a competent typist. And, frankly, the query design grid can create the statement faster than most of us can type it.

It's fair to assume that most of the time you'll fine-tune SQL statements that you copy from the SQL window to a module by concatenating literal values and variables. Unfortunately, doing so opens the door to errors, and the VBA error messages aren't very helpful when it comes to SQL statements. When errors do occur, you can rely on the SQL window to help you find the error faster than you can find it yourself. (You can learn about concatenating literal values and variables in the section "Concatenating Literal Values and Variables" in Chapter 4.)

Assign the SQL statement to a string variable and include the `Debug.Print` statement directly following the definition statement. That way, VBA prints the evaluated statement to the Immediate window. You can then copy the evaluated statement from the Immediate window to the SQL window and run it from there. For some reason, the error messages that the SQL window displays are more meaningful and more accurately help you pinpoint the actual error.

You might be wondering why you can't just copy the SQL statement directly from the module. You can, but most of the time your SQL statements will include concatenated variables and literal values. You can't run such a statement in the SQL window. In contrast, the statement that VBA prints in the Immediate window contains the evaluated version of your statement, with no variables.

Now, let's look at an example, still using the Northwind.mdb sample file. Enter the DAO procedure in Listing 2-6 in a module; the ADO version is in

Listing 2-7. This procedure fills a Recordset object with one record: the employee with the oldest value in the HireDate field from the Employees field.

Listing 2-6. The Debug.Print Statement Prints the Evaluated SQL Statement in the Immediate Window

```
Function DebugDAOEx1(fld As String, tbl As String)
Dim db As DAO.Database
Dim rst As DAO.Recordset
Dim strSQL As String
Set db = CurrentDb()
strSQL = "SELECT TOP 1 * FROM " & tbl & " ORDER BY " & tbl & fld & ";"
Debug.Print strSQL
Set rst = db.OpenRecordset(strSQL)
rst.Close
db.Close
Set db = Nothing
Set rst = Nothing
End Function
```

Listing 2-7. The ADO Version Also Uses the Print.Debug Statement

```
Function DebugADOEx1(fld As String, tbl As String)
Dim cnn As ADODB.Connection
Dim rst As New ADODB.Recordset
Set cnn = CurrentProject.Connection
Dim strSQL As String
strSQL = "SELECT TOP 1 * FROM " & tbl & " ORDER BY " & tbl & fld & ";"
Debug.Print strSQL
rst.Open Source:=strSQL, ActiveConnection:=cnn
rst.Close
Set rst = Nothing
End Function
```

After entering one of the procedures in Listings 2-6 and 2-7, open the Immediate window by pressing Ctrl+G if necessary and enter either

```
?DebugDAOEx1("HireDate", "Employees")
```

or

```
?DebugADOEx1("HireDate","Employees")
```

When you do, VBA returns the error message shown in Figure 2-14. Chances are you'll see this error message frequently, but it isn't all that helpful. You'll learn through experience that this error almost always means that there's a typo in the statement, but that's not a great clue. Click on End to clear the error message.

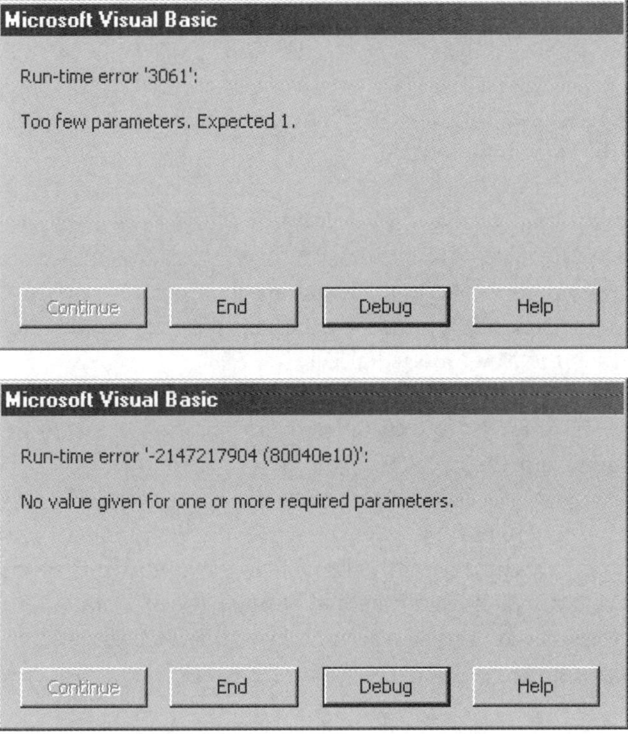

Figure 2-14. The DAO SQL statement returns the error on the top; ADO returns the error on the bottom.

> **TIP** *When using DAO, be sure to update the references by choosing References from the Tools menu, checking the Microsoft DAO 3.6 Object Library item, and click on OK.*

This is where the `Debug.Print` statement comes in handy. We can copy the evaluated statement from the Immediate window to the Query Design window and run it there to get a better idea of what's wrong with the statement:

1. First, copy the SELECT statement from the following line:

   ```
   strSQL = "SELECT TOP 1 * FROM " & tbl & " ORDER BY " & tbl & fld & ";"
   ```

   Be sure to omit the "strSQL =" component, because you want to copy just the SQL statement.

2. Return to the Database window by clicking on the Database window icon on the taskbar or clicking on the View Microsoft Access button on the Standard toolbar. In the Database window, click on the Queries shortcut, click on New on the Database Window toolbar, and then click on OK in the New Query dialog box.

3. Close the Show Table window and click on the View button, which will automatically display SQL.

4. Press `Ctrl+V` to paste the SQL statement into the SQL window and run the query by clicking on the Datasheet View item or the Run button. Access returns an error message because the SQL statement isn't valid: you forgot about the concatenated variables. Click on OK to clear the error message.

5. You need the evaluated version of your SQL statement, so return to the Visual Basic Editor's Immediate window by clicking on the appropriate icon on the Windows taskbar. Highlight the evaluated SQL statement, as shown in Figure 2-15, and press `Ctrl+C` to copy the statement to the clipboard.

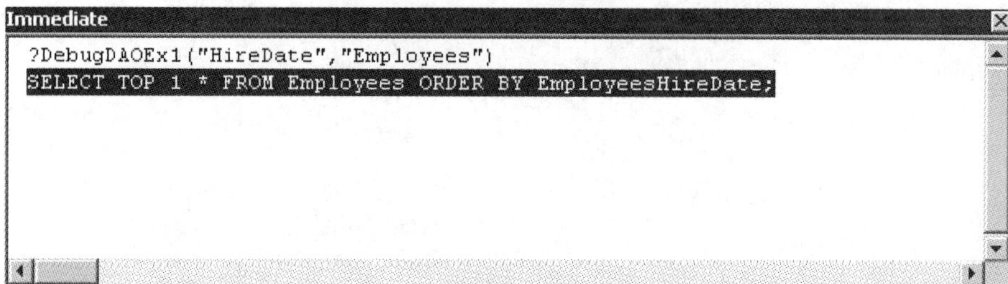

Figure 2-15. The `Debug.Print` *statement prints the evaluated SQL statement in the Immediate window.*

6. Return to the SQL window. If you open a new SQL window, simply press `Ctrl+V` to paste the evaluated statement. If you returned to the previous window, highlight the existing statement and then press `Ctrl+V` to replace the old statement with the evaluated version.

7. Now, click on the Run button to run the query, and Access returns the parameter prompt shown in Figure 2-16, which points right to the EmployeesHireDate reference. Because Access can't find this reference, we know it must be incorrect. It's easy to find this mistake with such a good pointer: it's missing the period (dot) identifier. It should be Employees.HireDate. Not only is this error easy to find, it's easy to fix. Simply replace the statement in your code with the following statement:

   ```
   strSQL = "SELECT TOP 1 * FROM " & tbl & " ORDER BY " & tbl & "." & fld
   & ";"
   ```

   The new component `& "."` concatenates the period character (.) between the name of the table and the field.

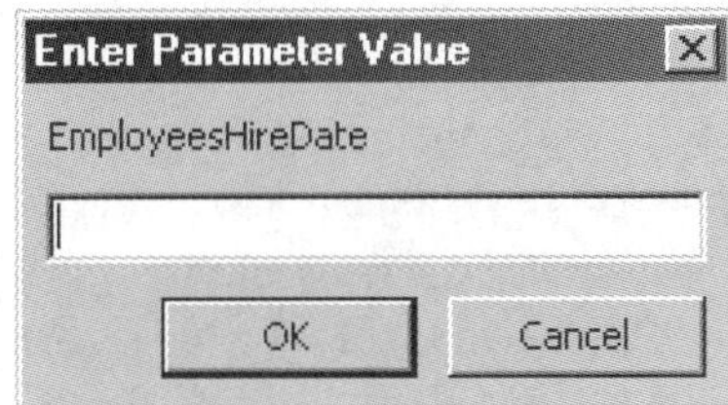

Figure 2-16. The incorrect SQL statement returns this prompt when run in the SQL window.

8. After updating the statement, run the procedure from the Immediate window again. It should now run without errors.

The corrected DAO procedure is in Listing 2-8; the correct ADO procedure is in Listing 2-9.

Listing 2-8. The Correct Version Includes a Concatenated Period Character

```
Function DebugDAOEx1(fld As String, tbl As String)
Dim db As DAO.Database
Dim rst As DAO.Recordset
Dim strSQL As String
Set db = CurrentDb()
strSQL = "SELECT TOP 1 * FROM " & tbl & " ORDER BY " & tbl & "." & fld & ";"
```

```
Debug.Print strSQL
Set rst = db.OpenRecordset(strSQL)
rst.Close
db.Close
Set db = Nothing
Set rst = Nothing
End Function
```

Listing 2-9. The Correct ADO Version Includes a Concatenated Period Character and Is Shorter Than the DAO Version

```
Function DebugADOEx1(fld As String, tbl As String)
Dim cnn As ADODB.Connection
Dim rst As New ADODB.Recordset
Set cnn = CurrentProject.Connection
Dim strSQL As String
strSQL = "SELECT TOP 1 * FROM " & tbl & " ORDER BY " & tbl & "." & fld & ";"
Debug.Print strSQL
rst.Open Source:=strSQL, ActiveConnection:=cnn
rst.Close
Set rst = Nothing
End Function
```

It's a good habit to assign SQL statements to string variables and include a `Debug.Print` statement immediately following that final definition statement. You never know when you'll make an error writing a statement, and you'll want these tools available when you need them. Adding them after the fact takes extra time and can add to your frustration.

CHAPTER 3

An Introduction to Relational Database Theory

There Is No Substitute for a Good Design

A PROPERLY DESIGNED relational database is a flexible and powerful management tool, and a proper design requires knowledge of relational database theory. Unfortunately, many users undertake the business of creating an Access database with little knowledge of how Access really works. Even those who understand relational database theory often skip the planning phase, which can be the deathblow to an application before it's even in use.

A badly designed database is apt to produce anomalies, which are errors that occur while modifying, updating, adding, or deleting data. Besides being a nuisance to the user, these errors can undermine the integrity of your data. On the other hand, a properly normalized and designed database is easy to use, effective, and easily accepts new features to expand functionality.

> *The number one design mistake most developers make is to put too much focus on interface design or program flow. As much as possible, data storage and integrity should be independent of the interface, allowing multiple interfaces to be developed.*
>
> Gary Ray, Application Developer

Before we launch into the actual discussion of theory, let's review a few terms that may be new to you:

- *Database*: A collection of persistent data
- *Relational database*: A collection of persistent data stored in multiple but related tables

- *Relational Database Management System (RDBMS)*: An integrated system of related data and the tools necessary to support the management of that data
- *Table*: A collection of related data that's stored in rows and columns
- *Field*: A column within a table that equals the smallest unit of data in the database
- *Record*: A row within a table, composed of fields, and containing related data for one complete entity or data unit
- *Scheme*: A table's field names, as a set
- *Primary key*: A value that uniquely identifies each record
- *Foreign key*: A primary key value in a related table (Foreign key values aren't unique within that table.)
- *Relation*: In the relational model, a relation is simply a table. In Access, we refer to an association between two tables as a relation.

The Rules of Normalization

A relational database eliminates redundancy by storing data in multiple tables. Relationships (also known as associations) among these tables allow you to join tables and pull the data together as necessary. Let's look at a quick example. When entering orders, you don't want to repeat the customer's full name and address for every order entered into your application. Doing so would consume resources unnecessarily. With today's powerful systems, saving a bit of memory by reducing the amount of data may not seem like a priority, but redundant data can be a large drain on performance across a network. Instead, you enter a unique value that identifies the customer that also relates each order record to its appropriate customer. When you need the customer's address for a particular order record, you simply relate the order and customer information tables on the field that contains the unique identifying value.

One of the first steps to implementing a relational database design is to normalize your tables. (First, you need to study the application's purpose and divide the data into tables.) Technically, normalization is the process of creating table schemes according to a fixed set of rules. There are currently seven rules. We'll look at the first four, which are really constraints known as *normal forms*:

- *First normal form (1NF)*: All fields must be atomic, meaning that the data can't be divided further. More specifically, this rule states that there can be no multivalued items or repeating groups. In addition, you must add a primary key.

- *Second normal form (2NF)*: First, the table must meet 1NF. Then, all fields within a table must describe the primary key value and be fully dependent upon that key. Any non-key value that doesn't fully support (describe) all values in a key should be removed.

- *Third normal form (3NF)*: The table must first satisfy 1NF and 2NF. You must remove any value that describes any non-key value. In other words, all fields must be mutually independent.

- *Boyce-Codd normal form (BCNF)*: There must be no possibility of dependent fields. This subrule was added to 3NF to compensate for its inadequacies. You may find many applications that are not normalized to BCNF, but that still perform efficiently.

First Normal Form (1NF)

This first step toward normalization is often the simplest: you divide the data until you can subdivide no more. A person's name is the perfect example. Typically, we think of a name as one piece of data, until we need to store that name. You might start out with a table scheme:

```
Table A: {Name,Address,City,State,ZIP,Phone}
```

First normal form requires that we subdivide each field into the smallest possible unit. The Name field can be broken down into the first name, the last name, and possibly the middle initial. Storing the name as one entry makes searching and sorting more difficult than it needs to be. Storing the name in the order of last name, first name resolves some of these problems—at least until the first name becomes an issue. There's just no easy away around it: you need to store the last and first names separately:

```
Table A: {FirstName,LastName,Initial,Address,City,State,ZIP,Phone}
```

Sometimes the decision isn't so clear, and there are no hard and fast rules—only guidelines—to point the way. For instance, a street address that includes the number and the street may or may not be atomic. Your needs should be the deciding factor. If you'll need to manipulate your records by street number or by street names, consider storing the components separately:

```
Table A: {FirstName,LastName,Initial,StreetAddress,StreetName,
  City,State,ZIP,Phone}
```

Next, think of each entry as a lone entry. In other words, don't store a list of related items in the same field. Rather, store only one item and create a record for each. First normal form requires that each item be a lone entry, and accommodating this rule often leads to a related table. You wouldn't store all of a person's phone numbers in one field. Instead, you'd create a second table, which lists each phone number as a single record and relates each record to the original table by including the order's unique identifying value in both tables:

```
Table A: {PersonID,FirstName,LastName,Initial,StreetAddress,StreetName,
  City,State,ZIP}
Table B: {Phone,PersonID}
```

In this case, you might have multiple records with the same PersonID value but different Phone entries. It's not unusual at all to end up with a few more tables at the end of this phase than when you started.

The Right Keys

The next step requires that we give each table a primary key. Earlier, we defined these two terms:

- *Primary key*: A value that uniquely identifies each record
- *Foreign key*: A primary key value in a related table (Foreign key values don't have to be unique.)

There's much more to the concept than just unique values. In fact, if you mention primary keys in a group of database developers, you better step back because it's a topic that's sure to spark a heated debate.

> *The number one mistake made by most developers is the use of "natural keys" for primary keys.*
>
> Gustav Brock, VP Development, Copenhagen

The issue isn't whether to use keys; you have to if you're working with related data. Rather, the issue is determining proper candidates for keys. The two schools of thought are:

- Use the data to create keys, or
- Use a unique value (or set of values) that is separate from the data.

The challenge when working with a primary key based on data is finding a field or a combination of fields where the data is unique. For example, let's try to create a primary key from the data fields in Table A. You might lean toward using the LastName field as a primary key, but last names are seldom unique. Even adding the FirstName field doesn't guarantee a unique value. Many people share the same first and last names. About the only way to base a primary key on data in Table A would be to include the LastName, FirstName, StreetAddress, and StreetName fields. Chances are you won't run into any people using the same first and last names living at the same address. The problem is, however, that it's not completely impossible, just highly improbable. Therefore, exceptions should be the rule when it comes to primary keys. For this reason, you'll find most developers don't rely on data to create what's known as a "natural" primary key.

CAUTION *Primary keys are indexed automatically. In addition, assigning a primary key to data fields automatically eliminates the possibility of entering duplicate data because primary keys must be unique values. You might forget about preventing duplicate values in your non-key fields when using AutoNumbers (or similar expressions) as your primary key. Be sure to assign a unique index to your data fields where necessary to avoid duplicates when you use AutoNumber fields as your primary key.*

At the risk of sparking a debate, we recommend that you use the AutoNumber (or some other unique expression) for primary key fields instead of relying on data fields. The AutoNumber data type automatically stores a unique value for each record as it's added. By default, a set of AutoNumber values starts with the value 1 and are sequentially incremented by 1.

TIP *To assign a primary key, open the table in Design view, select the row or rows that comprise the primary key candidate, and click on the Primary Key button on the Table Design toolbar.*

> *A couple of years ago, I wrote an application to track changes for a large newspaper. The business rules involved route numbers, rate codes (denoting various service types), and either zero or one change per business day. The company representatives told me these rules hadn't changed for 20 years and would never change.*
>
> *So, in well-intentioned ignorance, I developed the app using a natural key based on the combination of route number, rate code, and current date.*
>
> *Within days of deploying the app people were screaming that they could no longer enter multiple changes per day. Turns out the people in the know had no idea what the users were really doing. It then came as no surprise to me when, within six months, they also changed the route number scheme and rate code scheme that "would never change."*
>
> *I learned my lesson then. I'll never again use natural keys. Even the best of intentions and years of stability in a system can't predict the future with any certainty. Just when you think you've got a permanent situation, it changes.*
>
> Ron Allen

> **CAUTION** *Many applications use Social Security numbers as a natural key. This decision can have a negative affect on your data because our unique Social Security numbers often have duplicates, even though they're not supposed to. We recommend you never use Social Security numbers as a natural key. Even when duplicates aren't a problem, using Social Security numbers can cause snags. Not every one wants to share their Social Security numbers and, by law, they don't have to (in most circumstances). In addition, not everyone has a Social Security number. Then, you have to deal with confidentiality problems as someone could break into your system and steal those numbers for criminal activity.*

The process of choosing a primary key is made easier if you can further identify each field as an identity or informational field. An identity field identifies the record in some way—these are usually primary key fields. Informational fields disclose some attribute about the entity stored in that record. For instance, in our previous scheme, PersonID is clearly an identity field because it stores a unique value that identifies the person (entity) stored in that record. On the other hand, LastName is clearly an informational field because it shares (or describes) some attribute about the person identified by the PersonID value.

As long as an informational field relates to the identity field, you're on the right track. Our previous example

```
Table A: {PersonID,FirstName,LastName,Initial,StreetAddress,StreetName,
  City,State,ZIP}
```

meets this requirement: each field shares some attribute about the person identified by the PersonID value.

The PersonID field will be Table A's primary key field, so Table A is normalized to the First normal form. Table B doesn't appear to have a primary key candidate because all of the fields have the potential to repeat values. (Two people could have the same phone number if they're living together and sharing the same phone, and each person could have more than one phone.) We could create a multifield primary key based on both the Phone and PersonID fields. The table does have a foreign key, though: PersonID). Keep in mind that a foreign key is simply another table's primary key field and can be duplicated. Instead of relying on a natural, multifield key, we'll add a new field—PhoneID—as the primary key. At this point, the two table schemes are as follows:

```
Table A: {PersonID,FirstName,LastName,Initial,StreetAddress,StreetName,
  City,State,ZIP}
Table B: {PhoneID,Phone,PersonID}
```

Second Normal Form (2NF)

After satisfying First normal form, you're ready to take on Second normal form. There doesn't appear to be any Second normal form violations: all non-key values fully describe or otherwise support the primary key value. But what happens if we add a Yes/No field that denotes whether the person has a fax number? The dependency of this new field

```
Table A: {PersonID,FirstName,LastName,Initial,StreetAddress,StreetName,
  City,State,ZIP,Fax}
```

on the PersonID value isn't as obvious as in the other fields because Fax really shares information about that person's phone lines, and not the person (the value in PersonID). At first, you might consider adding this field to the phone table (Table B). What you'll probably find, though, is that a Yes/No field that identifies whether a phone number is a fax number isn't particularly useful in this context. What this table really needs is a value, similar to those in Table 3-1, that identifies the type of phone. When you enter each phone number, you'll also identify the type of phone by entering a code value.

Table 3-1. Phone Codes

PHONE DESCRIPTION	CODEID
Business phone	1
Home phone	2
Fax	3
Cell	4

At this point, Table B's scheme grows by an additional field.

```
Table B: {PhoneID,Phone,PersonID,CodeID}
```

Adding the CodeID field to Table B presents a new problem. How will you know what the codes represent? The solution is a new table

```
Table C: {CodeID,Description}
```

and its field dependencies are easy to check. Description definitely shares information about CodeID, the identity field—we've found the new table's primary key:

```
Table C: {CodeID,Description}
```

At this point, we have the following three tables. All are normalized to the Second normal form because all have a primary key, all fields are the smallest unit possible, and all fields fully support the primary key:

```
Table A: {PersonID,FirstName,LastName,Initial,StreetAddress,StreetName,
  City,State,ZIP}
Table B: {PhoneID,Phone,PersonID,CodeID}
Table C: {CodeID,Description}
```

Third Normal Form (3NF)

After normalizing a table to the Second normal form, you're ready to remove fields that describe non-key fields. Third normal form states that no field can depend on another field. Technically, you must remove any value that describes a non-key value. The easiest way to find violations of the Third normal form is to change the data in any given field. If an entry in another field needs to be modified because of that change, then you've got a Third normal form violation.

Although our previous example has no violations, we can create one. Let's assume that you want to add a field named StreetComplete that combines the StreetAddress and StreetName fields:

```
{PersonID,FirstName,LastName,Initial,StreetAddress,StreetName,
  StreetComplete,City,State,ZIP}
```

The modification seems innocent enough, but what happens when you change a StreetAddress or a StreetName value? Suddenly, the StreetComplete value is invalid, and it's up to you to remember to correct that value. This is the very situation that Third normal form avoids. You don't need to store the combined value: use an expression that concatenates the two components when the combined value is needed.

Boyce-Codd Normal Form (BCNF)

Redundant data can still occur, even if all your tables are correctly normalized to the Third normal form, which ensures that a table has no dependent fields. Boyce-Codd normal forms goes a step further by requiring that there be no possibility of a dependency. For example, in Table A, the ZIP value depends on the City and StreetName values (and even the StreetAddress value in some cases). If we know the ZIP code for a particular street, we know the ZIP code for any other record that shares the same StreetName value, even if we don't have the City value. In this case, we could create another table for the City and State fields using the schemes:

```
Table A: {PersonID,FirstName,LastName,Initial,StreetAddress,StreetName,ZIPID}
Table D: {ZIPID,ZIP,City,State}
```

> **CAUTION** *It is possible for two cities to have the same ZIP code, so the Boyce-Codd normal form example is appropriate only in theory. You probably won't want to apply it to a working solution. In addition, it would be impractical to store all the ZIP codes for the entire country if your database stores only a few hundred records. The moral of this tip is that some rules are meant to be broken.*

Do you notice a problem with this arrangement? All we really did was move the problem to another table, because now the possibility of dependency exists in Table D:

- ZIP is still dependent on city and state.
- State is dependent upon city.
- City could be dependent upon state.

Fully implementing BCNF could mean a number of additional tables to accommodate addresses. This is where most developers part ways with normalization because, in Access, this much normalization can adversely affect performance. Imagine having to pull together three or more tables just to get a complete address.

Creating Relationships

It's safe to assume that the data you need to analyze, manipulate, and view won't all be in the same table, if you've normalized those tables. That's why relationships are important to this discussion. In Access, you'll use relationships to pull all the data together when you need it. You'll encounter three types of relationship possibilities:

- one-to-one
- one-to-many
- many-to-many

In this section, we'll review these three types of relationships.

One-to-One Relationships

This uncommon relationship relates lone records. A matching record in both related tables isn't necessary, but there can be only one when there is a match. What you may find is that most one-to-one relationships are forced by business rules, and that they change as needs expand. For instance, a teacher may have only one aide, or he or she may have no aide at all. In that case, you'd have a one-to-one relationship. However, if someday the budget allows more aides, your database will need to accommodate that change. You'll find few one-to-one relationships that flow naturally from the data itself.

One-to-Many Relationships

The one-to-many relationship is probably the most common. The *one* table may have many matching records in the *many* table. However, the records in the many table can relate to only one record in the one table. In other words, a customer may have many orders, but each order belongs to only one customer. Furthermore, you can't have any order in the many table that doesn't relate to a customer in the one table. Such a record is known as an *orphan*, and orphans are considered an anomaly. (Access allows orphans, so it's your job to avoid them by properly relating your tables.)

> **NOTE** *Orphans are also known as a* dangling reference. *The requirement that each foreign key value match a primary key value in the related (one or parent) table is known as a* referential constraint. *We'll learn more about constraints in Chapter 8 (in the section "Adding a CONSTRAINT Clause").*

Many-to-Many Relationships

A many-to-many relationship can be a bit of a pain because in Access, you must create a third table to accommodate the relationship. This is because one table can contain many records for each record in the second table, and there is no way to represent this in a relational database without creating a linking table. For instance, a specific order could relate to many products in a products table, and each product could, in turn, be a part of none, any, or even all orders in the orders table.

What you end up with is three tables: the orders table, the products table, and a third table that contains the primary key from both tables. This third table should have a one-to-many relationship with both tables. Each record in the new table will relate to only one record in both original tables, but both of the original tables may have many records that relate to a record in the new table.

About Joins

A *join* is a type of rule that further defines a relationship by determining which records are selected or acted upon. Some documents refer to two types of joins: inner and outer. We'll be looking at the three types of joins that Access supports:

- Inner (equi-join, natural join, and 0-join)
- Left Outer
- Right Outer

Inner Join

An inner join is usually the simplest to grasp. In an inner join, a query returns only those records from both tables that have a matching value in the related fields (primary and foreign key fields). The word both is a key element in understanding this rule. Consider the phone list example from earlier in this chapter. Using an inner join, a query based on Table A and Table B will return only those persons from Table A who also have a phone number listed in Table B. Figure 3-1 illustrates this relationship graphically as two intersecting circles. The resulting query returns the records that intersect (join) in the middle.

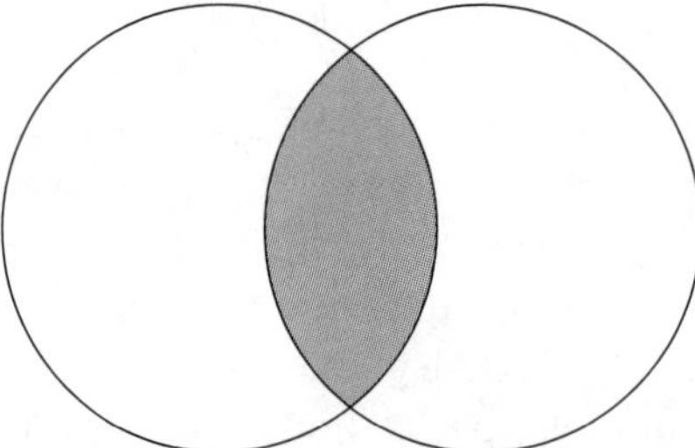

Figure 3-1. Think of an inner join as two intersecting circles.

Left Outer

Outer joins contain all the records from one side of a relationship and only those records from the second table that match the related field. In the case of a left outer join, the query returns all the records in the one table. In other words, a record is returned even if there are no matching values in the related field. The circles in Figure 3-2 illustrate this relationship. Notice that the left circle is completely shaded, indicating that the query returns all the records. The intersection is also completely shaded, which means that the query returns records from the many table where the two circles intersect: the many table contains a matching value in the related field.

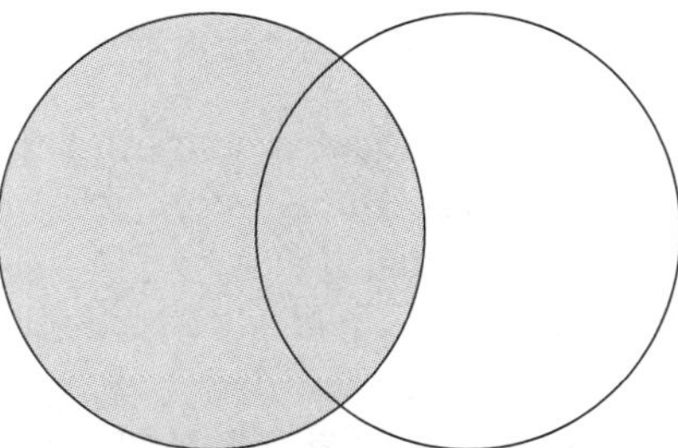

Figure 3-2. Left outer joins return all the records from the one table.

Right Outer

As you might expect, the right outer join returns all the records from the many table and only those records from the one table where the related field contains a matching value, as illustrated in Figure 3-3.

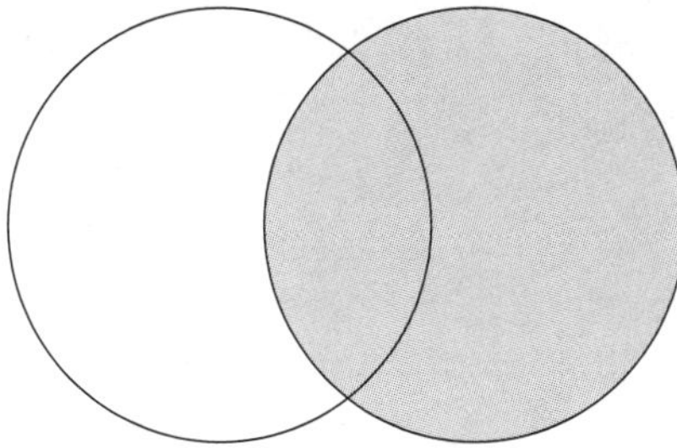

Figure 3-3. A right outer join includes all the records from the many table.

> **NOTE** *You may be wondering where the terms* left *and* right *came from in reference to joins. Originally, in diagrams, the one table was always on the left and the many table was always on the right.*

Creating Permanent Relationships

By its nature, Access always thinks in relational terms and joins tables by default. You can turn off this behavior, but you probably won't want to unless you have a specific reason for doing so. When creating a query, Access automatically joins tables if either of the following conditions exists:

- Both tables contain a field of the same name and data type, with one exception. Access will relate an AutoNumber field to a Long Integer field (Number). At least one of the fields must be a primary key. Primary keys are indicated by bold type in the field list, which makes them easy to spot.
- A permanent relationship exists in the Relationships window.

> **TIP** *You can create a relationship between fields yourself if they are the same data type. The name doesn't matter in this case. Simply drag a primary key field from one field list to the other.*

On those rare occasions when you don't want Access to control relationships, turn off this feature by pulling down the Tools menu, choosing Options, clicking on the Tables/Queries tab, and deselecting the Enable AutoJoin option, as shown in Figure 3-4. Keep in mind that disabling this feature affects only unrelated tables. Access still gives precedence to permanent relationships established via the Relationships window. (We'll review the Relationships window in the next section.)

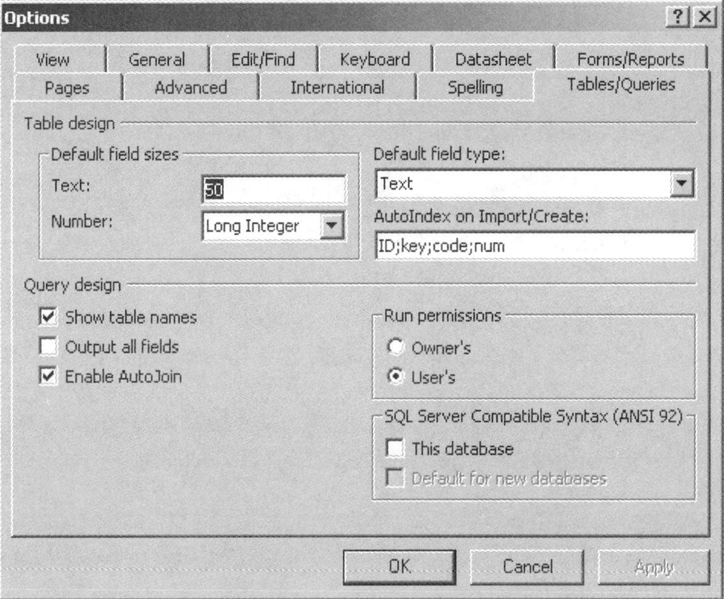

Figure 3-4. Uncheck the AutoJoin option when you want more control over relationships.

NOTE *You'll see the words* temporary *and* permanent *applied to relationships throughout this section. Permanent relationships are created and deleted only in the Relationships window. Temporarily joining two tables in the Query Design window affects only that query. If two tables are permanently related and you delete the join line between the two tables in the Query Design window, Access disables that join for the current query only. Access won't delete the permanent relationship that exists between the two tables. To permanently delete a relationship, you must do so in the Relationships window and then save the changes.*

Using the Relationships Window

The Relationships window displays permanent relationships between the tables in a database. This graphical representation of the relationships won't include temporary relationships manually created in queries. Figure 3-5 shows the relationships for the Northwind.mdb sample file that comes with Access. To open this window, simply open the Northwind database and then click on the Relationships button on the Database toolbar.

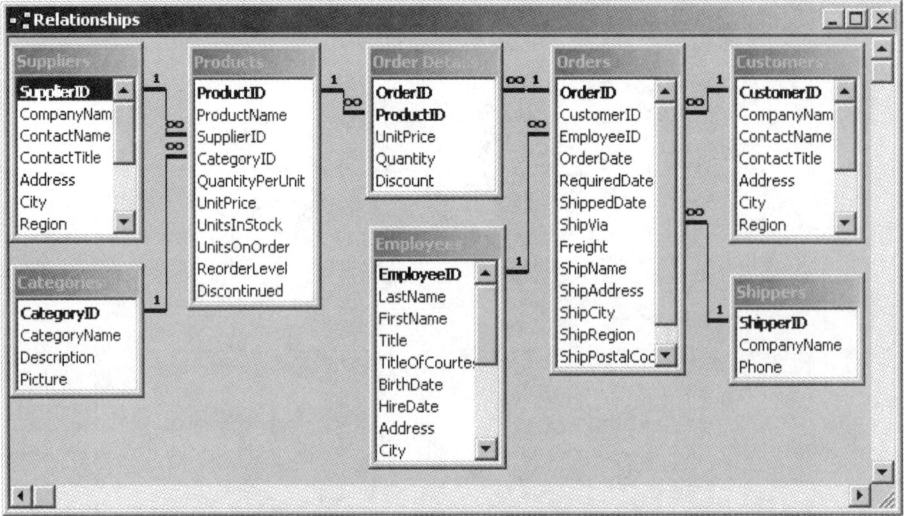

Figure 3-5. The Relationships window displays a graphical representation of the relationships between tables.

Now, let's create a few relationships between the tables in our ongoing name and phone list. First, create the three tables shown in Figure 3-6. The three primary key fields—PersonID, PhoneID, and CodeID—are all AutoNumber fields. That means the two foreign key fields in Table B, PhoneID, and CodeID must be Number fields.

To create a permanent relationship between Table A and Table B from our phone list example:

1. Open the Relationships window by clicking on the Relationships button on the Database toolbar.

2. Click on the Show Table button (on the Relationships toolbar) if necessary (the Show Table dialog box may already be open), and then add all three tables to the window by double-clicking on each in the Show Table dialog box (shown in Figure 3-7). Alternately, select the table or query and then click on Add. Click on Close to return to the Relationships window.

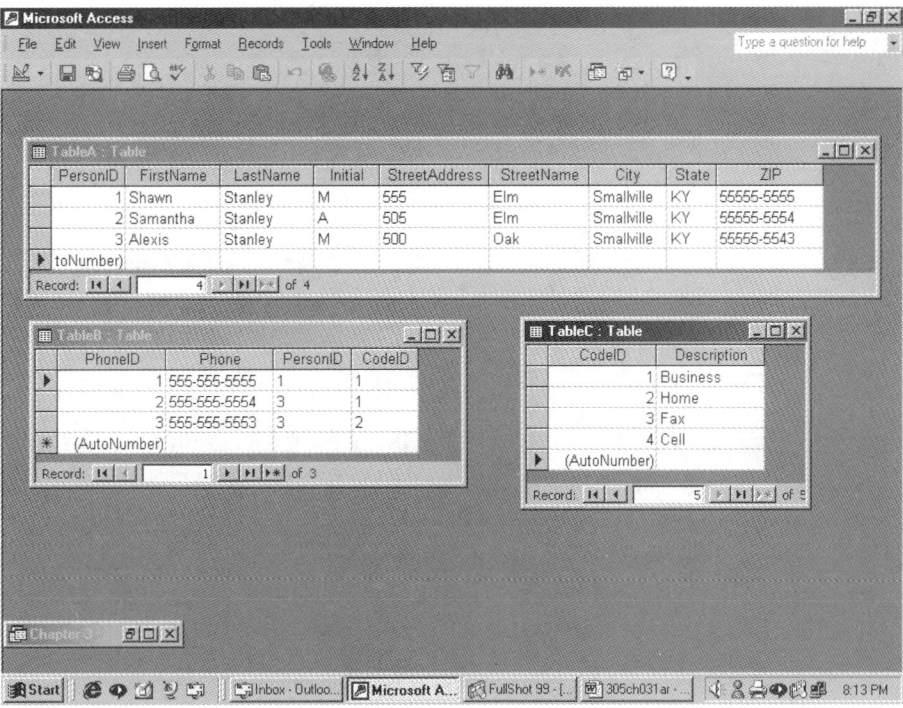

TableA : Table

PersonID	FirstName	LastName	Initial	StreetAddress	StreetName	City	State	ZIP
1	Shawn	Stanley	M	555	Elm	Smallville	KY	55555-5555
2	Samantha	Stanley	A	505	Elm	Smallville	KY	55555-5554
3	Alexis	Stanley	M	500	Oak	Smallville	KY	55555-5543
toNumber)								

TableB : Table

PhoneID	Phone	PersonID	CodeID
1	555-555-5555	1	1
2	555-555-5554	3	1
3	555-555-5553	3	2
(AutoNumber)			

TableC : Table

CodeID	Description
1	Business
2	Home
3	Fax
4	Cell
(AutoNumber)	

Figure 3-6. We'll create a few relationships between these tables.

> **CAUTION** *A well-designed application can grow to include new features and functionality without ever changing the original relationships. You may add new ones, but you'll seldom need to change a relationship. If you need to change relationships in a working application, we recommend that you be careful because it's difficult to anticipate all the future repercussions.*

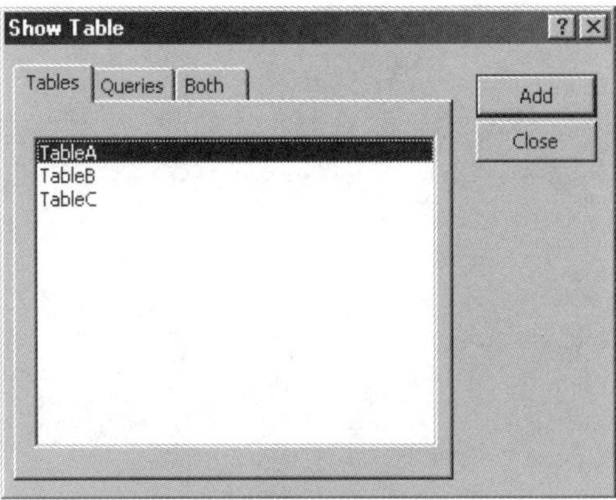

Figure 3-7. Add tables to the Relationships window via the Show Table dialog box.

> **TIP** *To see relationships for a particular table, select that table and click on the Show Direct Relationships button on the Relationships toolbar. To display all the relationships defined in the database, click on the Show All Relationships button. If you've deleted a table from the Relationships table, but that table has relationships, clicking on either button redisplays it.*

3. Drag a primary key field from one field list to another. For example, drag PersonID in the Table A field list (notice that it's in bold to indicate its primary key status) to PersonID in Table B. Access converts the mouse pointer into a small icon that resembles a field list item. When you release the field item, Access displays the Edit Relationships dialog box shown in Figure 3-8. The dialog box lists the tables and the fields on which the relationship will be based. In this case, that's the PersonID field in both Table A and Table B. Also notice that Access displays the kind of relationship you're dealing with (one-to-many) and displays that type in the Relationships Type control at the bottom of the dialog box.

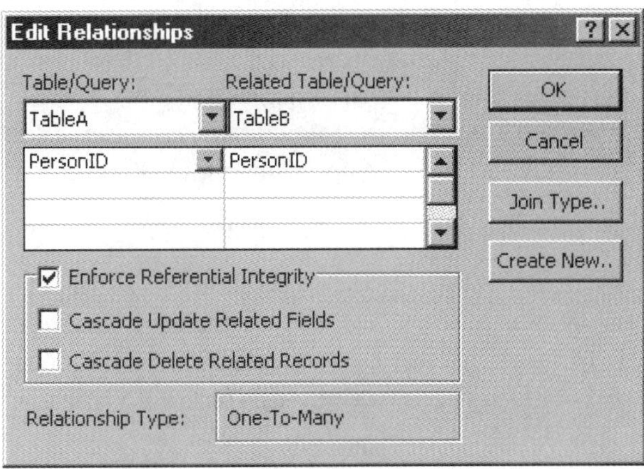

Figure 3-8. Choose a relationship or join type.

4. Click on the Join Type button and choose one of the options in the dialog box shown in Figure 3-9. The default option is 1: Only include rows where the joined fields from both tables are equal. The other two options represent the left outer and right outer joins, respectively. (We'll discuss join types in more detail later in this chapter.) We don't want to change the default join, so click on OK to return to the Edit Relationships dialog box.

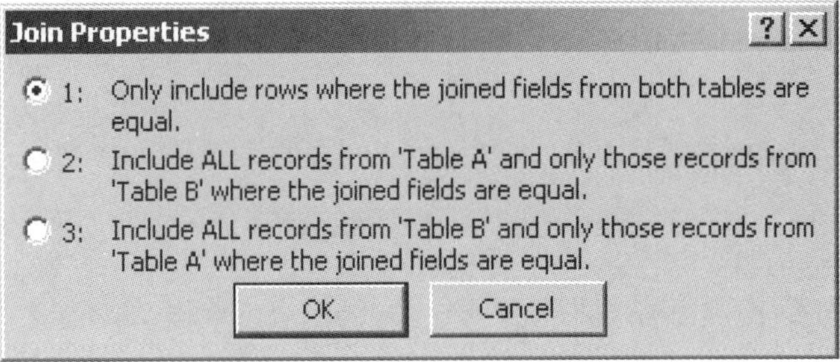

Figure 3-9. There are three types of joins.

5. If you want to enforce referential rules, click on the Enforce Referential Integrity option and then select the appropriate level of force that you wish to imply. *Referential integrity* is a set of predefined rules by which the relationship enforces that values in a foreign-key field match a primary key value in the related table. The Cascade Update Related Fields updates foreign key values in related tables when you change a primary key value. Likewise, Cascade Delete Related Fields deletes related records when you delete a primary key record. Note that the delete

option deletes records, not values. A primary key value can't be null, so you can't delete just the value. Enabling the delete option ensures that you don't leave orphan records when you delete a record from a *parent* table. By *parent*, we mean the related table containing the orphan record's primary key value. Check the Enforce Referential Integrity option.

6. Click on Create to close the dialog box and create the relationship between the two tables, which is indicated by the join line, shown in Figure 3-10. You can learn a great deal about the relationship from the join line. For example, the infinity sign represents the many table, which in this case is Table B. The 1 symbol next to Table A identifies it as the one table. The presence of these symbols is also a clue: it means that the relationships enforce referential integrity. A line with no symbols indicates a relationship that doesn't enforce referential integrity.

7. Repeat steps 3 through 6 to create a similar relationship between the CodeID fields in Table B and Table C.

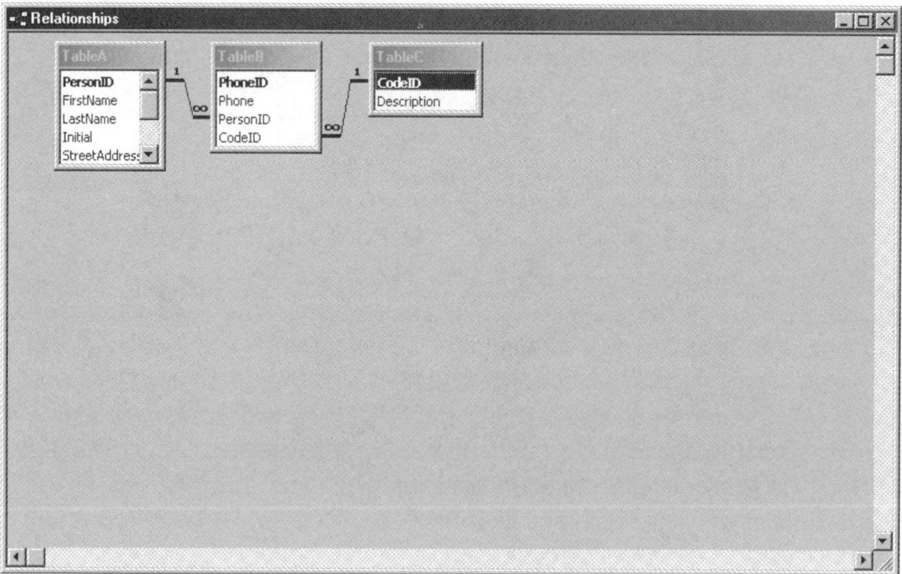

Figure 3-10. You can learn a great deal from a relationship from the join line.

> **TIP** *Printing the Relationships window is a quick and easy way to document your application's relationships. To do so, open the Relationships window by clicking on Relationships on the Database toolbar. Then, choose Print Relationships from the File menu. Access will create a report, which you can save and print like any other report.*

When you check the Enforce Referential Integrity option, Access applies rules that protect the *integrity* of your data. Specifically, these rules ensure that the relationships between your tables are valid and that they remain valid as you update, add, and delete data. However, a few conditions must be met before you can use this option:

- The parent field in the relationship must be a primary key or have a unique index.
- The fields must be of the same data type.
- The related tables must be in the same database. You can't enforce integrity rules outside of the current database.

When referential integrity is enabled, Access follows a set of strict rules to maintain the relationships. A one record, or parent record, must exist in the one table before you can add a related record to the many table. For instance, in our previous phone list example, if John Smith isn't in Table A, you can't add a phone for John Smith to Table B. Doing so would require a PersonID value for John Smith, and none exists. In addition, you can't delete a parent record in the one table until you delete all the child records in the many table. (A child record refers to a foreign key entry in a related table.)

As we mentioned, if you select the Cascade Update Related Fields option, Access updates corresponding foreign key values automatically when making changes to a primary key value. When this option isn't selected, you can't change a primary key value if related records exist, and referential integrity is enabled. You must change the foreign key values first. Cascade Delete Related Records is similar. If you delete a record from the one side of a relationship, Access also deletes related child records in the many table. (When referential integrity is disabled, you can change and delete primary key values, without consideration for foreign key values.)

Now that you're familiar with the types of relationships, let's put that information to work. Let's suppose that you want to create a list of phone numbers for each person listed in Table A that has a business number listed in Table B (from our previous examples). To accomplish this task, you'll need information from two tables:

```
Table A: {PersonID,LastName,FirstName}
Table B: {PhoneID,Phone,PersonID,CodeID}
```

An Access query based on these two tables and related on the PersonID field—primary key in Table A and foreign key in Table B—would list only those records from both tables in which the contents of the PersonID field match. (That's because Access relationships default to an inner join, which you learned about in a previous section.) To limit the results to only business numbers, you'd limit the CodeID field with a criteria expression, most likely a specific CodeID value.

You would need all three tables if you want to identify the phone number type (CodeID):

```
Table A: {PersonID,LastName,FirstName}
Table B: {PhoneID,Phone,PersonID,CodeID}
Table C: {CodeID,Description}
```

In this case, you end up with two inner joins. The first would be identical to that listed above: between Table A and Table B. After returning the records from Table A and Table B only where the PersonID value matches, the query would also include the Description value for each record where the CodeID value matches in both Table B and Table C.

It might be clearer if we express this with real data. Let's suppose Alexis Stanley has two phone numbers, Shawn Stanley has one, and Samantha Stanley has none (see Figure 3-6). The query shown in Figure 3-11 would return a list that included Alexis and Shawn, but not Samantha, as shown in Figure 3-12.

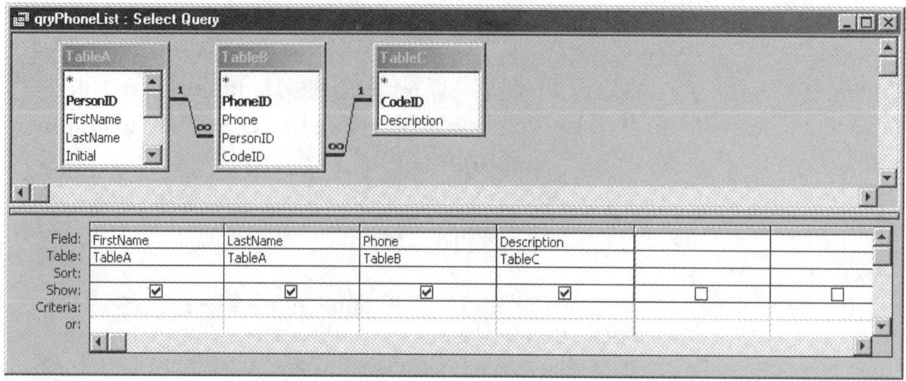

Figure 3-11. The default inner join returns only those record that have matching values in the related fields.

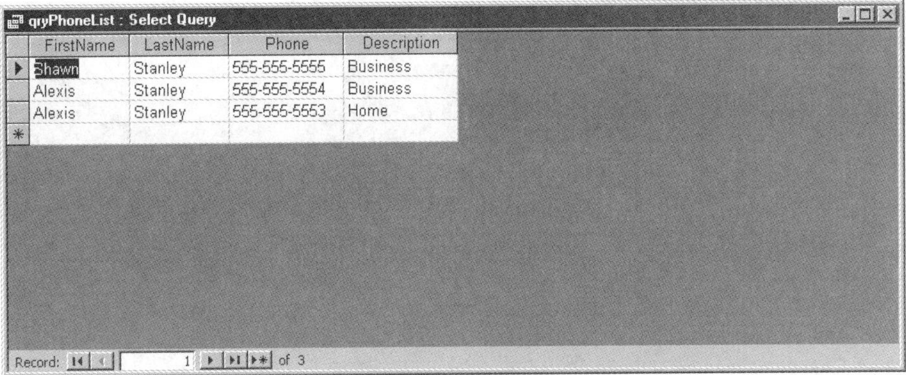

Figure 3-12. The query returns only those people with a phone number in Table B.

Changing the default join can have a major impact on the query's results. For instance, a left outer join on Table B and Table C and a right outer join on Table B and Table C return all the records, as shown in Figure 3-13. To make this change, follow these steps:

1. Open the previous query in Design view.
2. Right-click on the join line between Table A and Table B, and choose Join Properties from the resulting submenu shown in Figure 3-14.
3. Select the second option in the Join Properties dialog box, as shown in Figure 3-15, and click on OK.
4. Repeat steps 2 and 3 for the relationship line between Table B and Table C. Except this time, choose the third option in step 3.
5. Run the query.

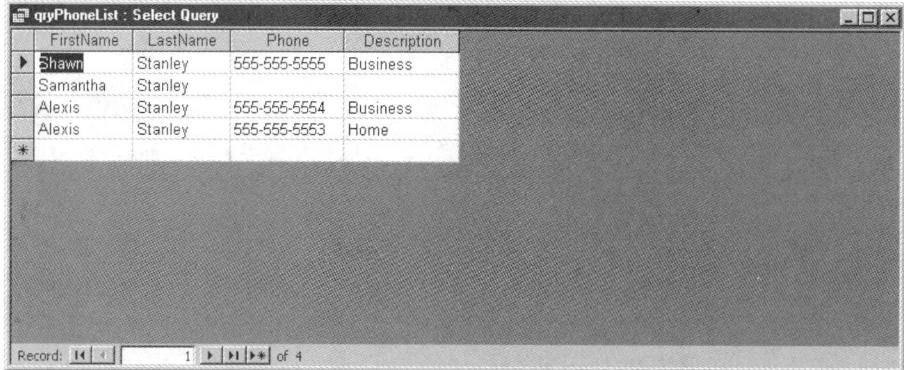

qryPhoneList : Select Query

FirstName	LastName	Phone	Description
Shawn	Stanley	555-555-5555	Business
Samantha	Stanley		
Alexis	Stanley	555-555-5554	Business
Alexis	Stanley	555-555-5553	Home

Record: 1 of 4

Figure 3-13. Changing the join type returns a complete list of names, regardless of whether the person has a phone number in Table B.

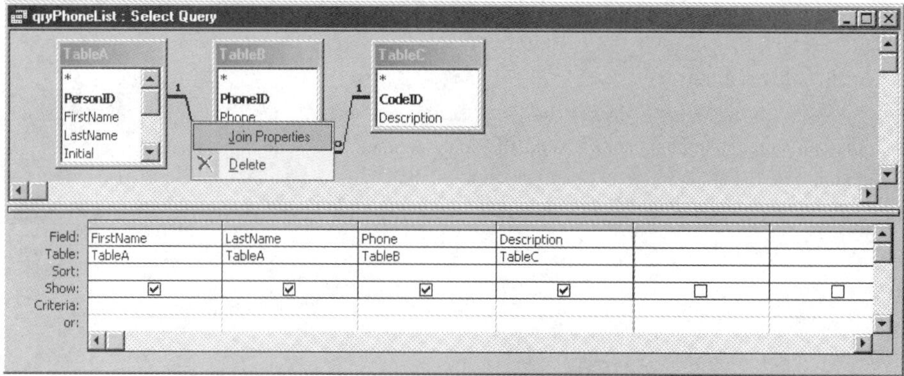

Figure 3-14. Choose Join Properties from the submenu.

Join Properties

Left Table Name: Table A
Right Table Name: Table B
Left Column Name: PersonID
Right Column Name: PersonID

- 1: Only include rows where the joined fields from both tables are equal.
- 2: Include ALL records from 'Table A' and only those records from 'Table B' where the joined fields are equal.
- 3: Include ALL records from 'Table B' and only those records from 'Table A' where the joined fields are equal.

OK | Cancel | New

Figure 3-15. Select the second join option.

Without relationships, a query based on more than one table or query still returns records, but the result will be meaningless in most cases. In a manner of speaking, relationships limit the query results. The limits imposed depend on the type of join: inner, right outer, or left outer.

> **TIP** *A Cartesian product (or cross product) is the result of a query based on multiple tables where no relationship exists. Access joins every record in each table with every record in every other table. In other words, a query based on two unrelated tables, both with ten records, would return 100 records.*

They're Everywhere!

The evidence of relationships is everywhere in your Access applications. Open a table in Datasheet view and check the left-most column. Is there a column of plus signs (+)? If so, then that data is related to data in another table. Click on the plus sign to the left of a record to see the related records in what's known as the subdatasheet. Even the subdatasheet can have a subdatasheet. Another example is a subform; have you ever used the Form wizard to create a main form/subform? If so, the wizard relied on existing relationships to determine which fields to link in order to display the appropriate data. You may not realize it, but Access is depending on relationships all the time.

Self-Join

The self-join is a bit unusual in that it combines records from the same table, creating a relationship to itself. Technically, it's not a join type because a self-join can be any of the three types of joins—but we call it a self-join. They're not common, but they are exactly the right tool when needed. To illustrate this unique join, let's expand on our phone list example just a bit and add an EmergencyContact field to Table A. Then, enter the new contact values shown in Figure 3-16, and save the changes.

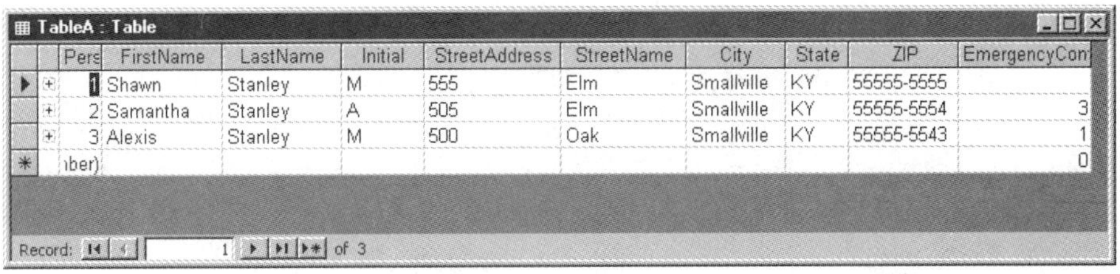

TableA : Table

	Pers	FirstName	LastName	Initial	StreetAddress	StreetName	City	State	ZIP	EmergencyCon
+	1	Shawn	Stanley	M	555	Elm	Smallville	KY	55555-5555	
+	2	Samantha	Stanley	A	505	Elm	Smallville	KY	55555-5554	3
+	3	Alexis	Stanley	M	500	Oak	Smallville	KY	55555-5543	1
*	ıber)									0

Record: 1 of 3

Figure 3-16. Add the EmergencyContact field to Table A.

Now, create a query based on Table A per the following steps:

1. Click on the Tables shortcut in the Database toolbar, select Table A, choose Query from the New Object button's drop-down list, and then click on OK in the New Query dialog box.

2. Click on Show Tables on the Query Design toolbar. In the Show Tables dialog box, click on the Tables tab, select Table A, and click on Add. Click on Close to close the Show Tables dialog box.

3. Right-click on the Table A_1 field list, choose Properties from the resulting shortcut menu, and change the Alias property from Table A_1 to Emergency, as shown in Figure 3-17. Changing the Alias property isn't necessary, but it removes some of the confusion of working with two copies of the same table.

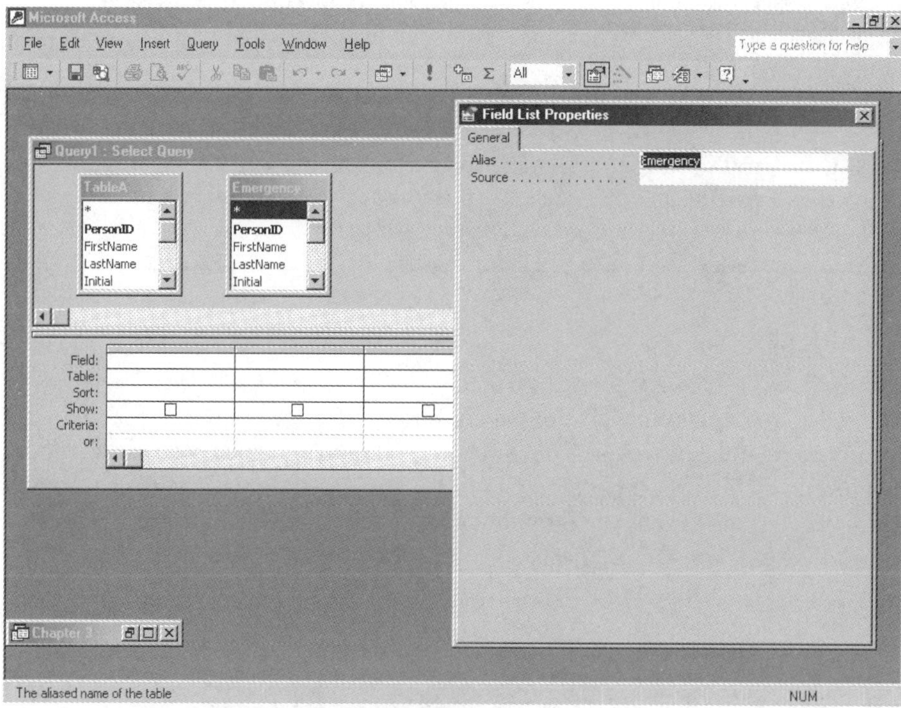

Figure 3-17. Change the Alias property.

TIP *The field list doesn't always display the entire table name in its title bar. When this is the case, you can use the Alias property to display a shorter name. Doing so doesn't change the underlying table's name.*

4. Create the relationship by dragging the EmergencyContact field from Table A's field list to the PersonID field in the Emergency field list.

5. Add the FirstName and LastName fields from Table A to the design grid.

6. Add the expression

```
EmgyContact: Emergency.FirstName & " " & Emergency.LastName
```

to the next Field cell, as shown in Figure 3-18. At this point, the query returns the records shown in Figure 3-19, which is incomplete because we also need the emergency contact's phone number.

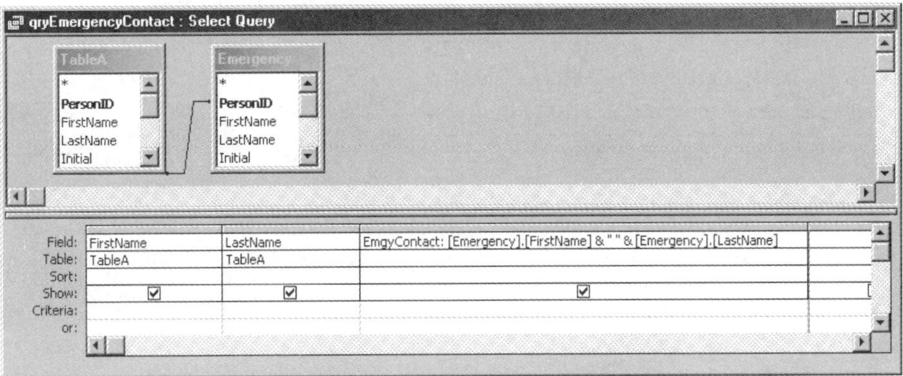

Figure 3-18. Add the EmgyContact expression to the design grid.

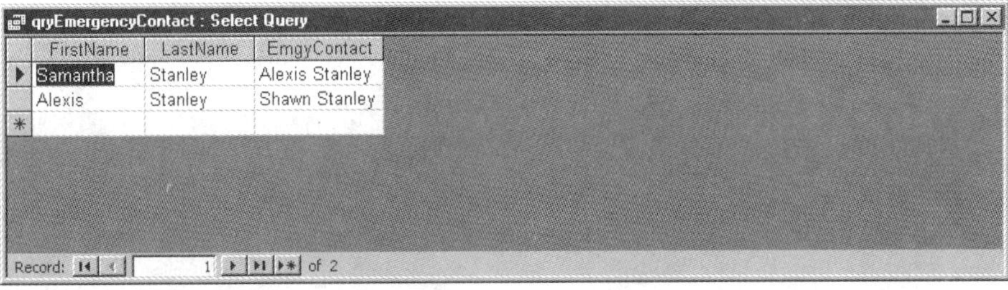

Figure 3-19. This query doesn't display a phone number for the emergency contact.

7. If you ran the query in the last step, return to Design View. Click on the Show Tables button and add Table B and Table C, and then close the Show Tables dialog box.

8. Because there's a permanent relationship between Table A and Table B, the query inherits it. For this query, you'll need to delete that relationship, so select the join line between Table A and Table B and press Delete. Be careful not to select the join line between Emergency and Table A. (You can move the field lists if necessary.)

9. Add the Phone field from Table B and the Description field from Table C, as shown in Figure 3-20.

10. Run the query, which returns the list shown in Figure 3-21.

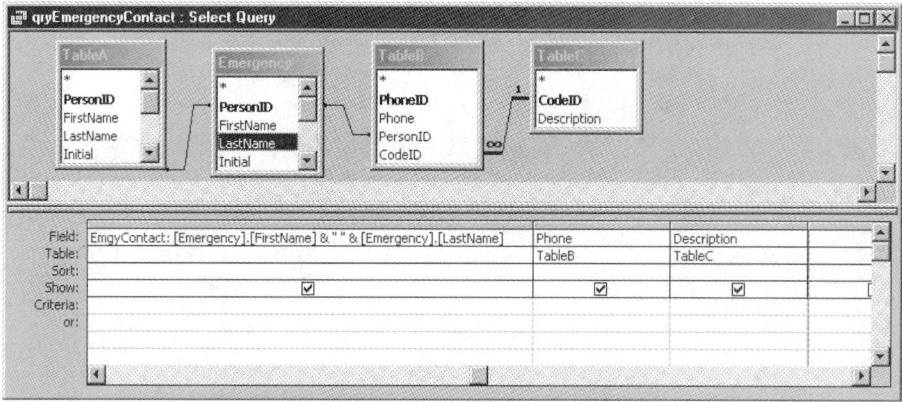

Figure 3-20. Add fields from Table A and Table B.

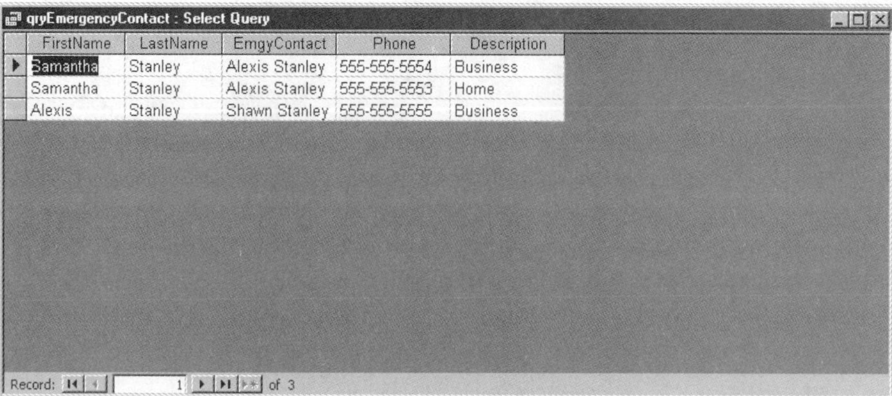

Figure 3-21. The query returns contact names and numbers.

Samantha Stanley is listed twice because her emergency contact, Alexis Stanley has two phones listed, and the query lists both. In addition, did you notice that the query didn't return a record for Shawn Stanley? That's because he doesn't have an emergency contact (or at least we don't have that information yet.) To include him in the list anyway, change the first join, an INNER JOIN to a RIGHT JOIN. The second join is an INNER JOIN, change it to a LEFT JOIN. Then, the final join is another INNER JOIN; change it to a LEFT JOIN. You could do so the hard way by right-clicking on the join lines between the tables and modifying the options in the Edit Relationships dialog box. Or, you can open the SQL window by choosing SQL View from the View button's drop-down list and simply overwriting the existing joins, as we've done in Figure 3-22. The results of changing the joins are shown in Figure 3-23. This time Shawn Stanley is listed, even though the contact and phone information is missing.

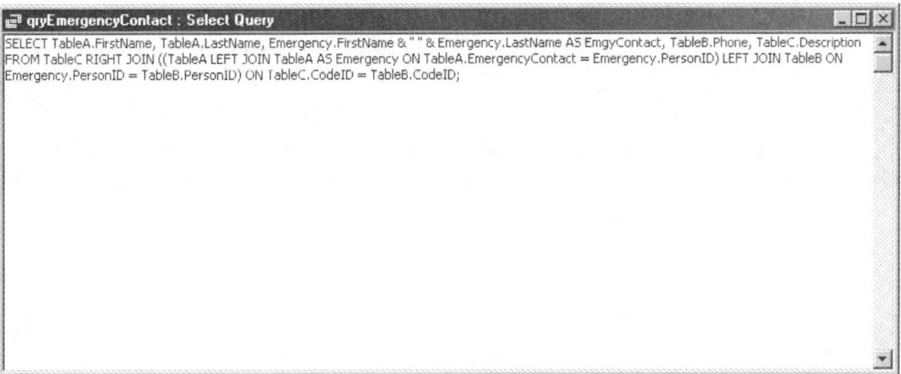

Figure 3-22. Use the SQL window to modify the query.

qryEmergencyContact : Select Query

FirstName	LastName	EmgyContact	Phone	Description
Shawn	Stanley			
Samantha	Stanley	Alexis Stanley	555-555-5554	Business
Samantha	Stanley	Alexis Stanley	555-555-5553	Home
Alexis	Stanley	Shawn Stanley	555-555-5555	Business

Record: 1 of 4

Figure 3-23. A left outer join includes every record in Table A.

So Where's Referential Integrity Fit In?

In the last section, you learned just enough about referential integrity to make you dangerous. That's why we're starting off this final section with a strong recommendation that you use referential integrity. However, we don't recommend that you enable either of the cascading options permanently. It's usually best if you turn on the option when you need it, use it, and then turn it off again. Changing data—and especially deleting it—can have far-reaching repercussions and careful consideration should always be given before proceeding with changes and deletions. When either cascading option is turned on, that option's corresponding action will warn you that you're about to change or delete records. We are so used to seeing these warnings that we often don't ever read them: we just click on OK and go on our merry way. If you end up changing or deleting records you really hadn't intended to, it's too late. That's why we recommend you keep both cascading options turned off. Doing so forces you to consider the impact that your actions will have before you take that final step. By all means, turn on the options and use them to your advantage, when you need them. But don't leave them on permanently as you can't undo the damage once it's done.

Another point worth making early on is that an AutoNumber primary key renders the update cascade useless. The cascade update option updates foreign key values when you change a primary key value. If your primary key is an AutoNumber field, you can't change those values. Consequently, the cascade update option will never be used.

With just the Enforce Referential Integrity option enabled (refer to Figure 3-8), the relationship between a primary and foreign key table will do the following:

- Forbid you to enter a foreign key value before a matching primary key value in a related table exists
- Forbid you to delete a primary key value if there are matching foreign key values in a related table
- Forbid you to modify a primary key value if a matching foreign key value exists in a related table

In this context, when we use the term *primary* and *foreign key* value, we're referring to the entire record, not just the value.

> **TIP** *Earlier in this chapter, we talked about the 1 and the infinity signs as they pertain to a join. They also tell you about referential integrity. If the symbols aren't visible, you know with a quick glance that referential integrity isn't enabled for that relationship.*

Let's see how all these rules apply to our name and phone tables. Open Table B and try to enter a new record using the PersonID value 4. Doing so produces the error message shown in Figure 3-24. Click on OK to clear the message. Then, press the Esc key to delete the unsaved record.

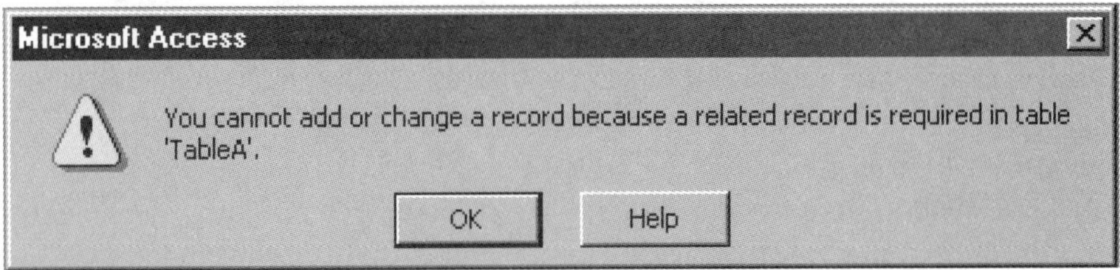
Microsoft Access
You cannot add or change a record because a related record is required in table 'TableA'.
OK
Help

Figure 3-24. Entering a new phone record at the wrong time will produce this error.

The problem is that there is no PersonID value of 4. Remember, in Table B, the PersonID field is a foreign key and relates to the PersonID primary key field in Table A. Until that table contains a primary key value of 4, you can't enter a phone record using that value in the foreign key field.

Let's try another one. Open Table A and try to delete the record for Shawn Stanley. Doing so produces the error message shown in Figure 3-25. Click on OK to clear the message. Similarly to the previous example, you can't delete a record from Table A when a phone record in Table B exists for that person.

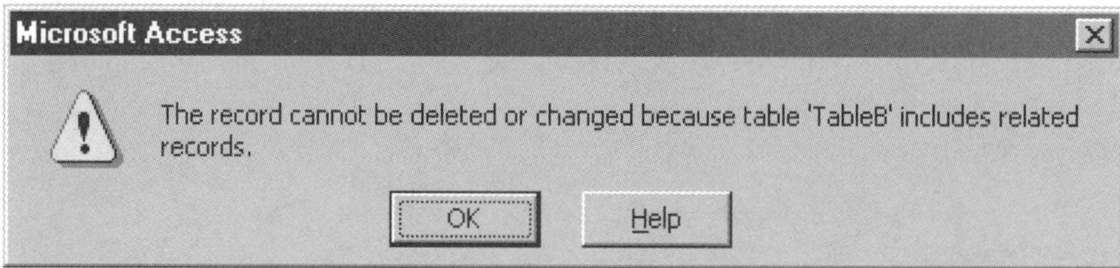

Figure 3-25. Deleting a record from Table A will produce this error if a phone record exists for that person.

None of our primary key fields are based on natural data, so we can't see referential integrity at work in this case. Just remember that you can't modify a primary key value if a foreign key value exists in a related table.

Using Cascade Options

Referential integrity has some built in flexibility in the way of cascade options, which we've already discussed briefly. When referential integrity is enabled, Jet will ignore changes or deletions to primary key values where related foreign key values are involved. The cascade options take referential integrity a step further, making all the necessary updates or deletions to avoid orphans. In other words, Jet allows the change or deletion, but also updates all dependent values accordingly:

- Changing a primary key value with the Cascade Update Related Records option enabled will also update any foreign key values in any related table, accordingly.
- Deleting a primary key value with the Cascade Delete Related Records option enabled will also delete any foreign key values in any related table, accordingly.

> **TIP** *Before turning on either cascade option, be sure to review all the joins carefully. A cascade task not only works for the tables in the current relationship, but the cascade will ripple through all the relationships—both direct and indirect.*

No cascade option allows you to enter a foreign key value before the primary key value exists in a related table. In these cases, you will still need to enter the primary key value before entering any foreign key values.

Now, let's see how enabling the Cascade Delete Related Records option affects updates and deletions in our name and phone tables. First, we have to enable the option:

1. Open the Relationships window by clicking on the Relationships button on the Database window.

2. Right-click on the join line, select Edit Relationships, and then enable the Cascade Delete Related Records option, as shown in Figure 3-26.

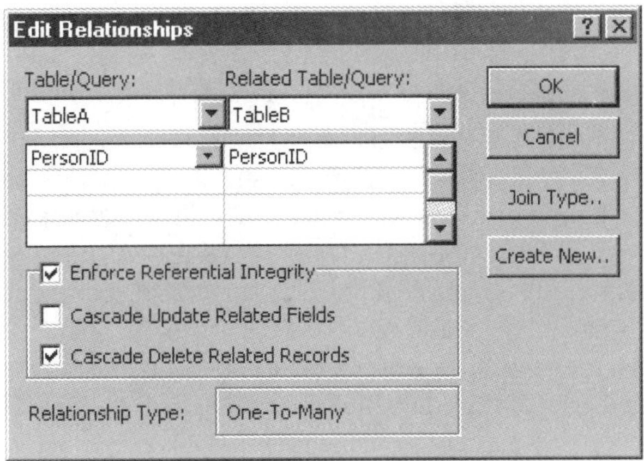

Figure 3-26. Enable the Cascade Delete Related Records option.

3. Click on OK and close the Relationships window.

Open Table A and try to delete the record for Shawn Stanley. Doing so will display the message shown in Figure 3-27. Click on Yes to delete the record for Shawn Stanley. (Clicking on No cancels the delete task.) Next, open Table B, and, as you can see in Figure 3-28, the phone record for Shawn Stanley (1) is gone. Jet deleted the record you intended and the related foreign key value in Table B.

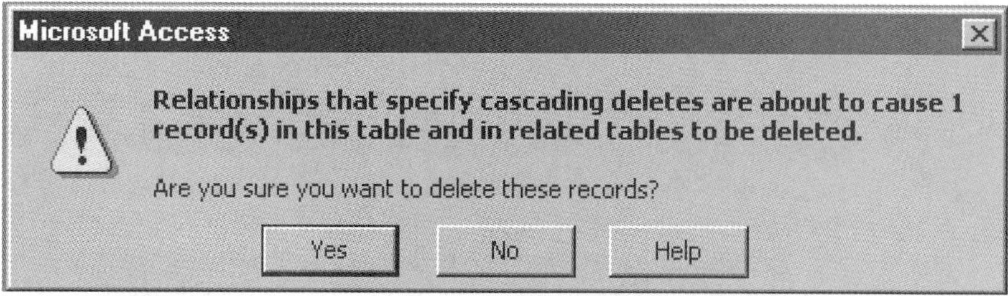

Figure 3-27. The cascade update option displays this error message if you try to delete a primary key value when foreign key values exist in a related table.

TableB : Table

	PhoneID	Phone	PersonID	CodeID
▶	2	555-555-5554	3	1
	3	555-555-5553	3	2
*	(AutoNumber)		0	0

Record: 1 of 2

Figure 3-28. Jet deleted the foreign key value from Table B.

All of our tables use AutoNumber primary keys, so we can't show you how the Cascade Update Related Records option works. You can't change an AutoNumber value; therefore, the option is useless in our example database. This arrangement may seem to conflict with the need for referential integrity, but it really doesn't. The truth is, you'll probably never need to change an AutoNumber value used as a primary key, and so losing the cascade update option is a moot point.

Referential integrity is a powerful feature, and a database must enforce referential integrity to meet the relational model. However, its power also makes it dangerous when misused, so don't underestimate it. Enable referential integrity to protect the integrity of your data. But use the cascade options wisely—only when needed. Don't permanently enable them. A relational database is a complicated beast, but normalized tables, relationships, and referential integrity used wisely can make the difference between a functioning and efficient application and a piece of junk.

CHAPTER 4

SQL Grammar

Learn SQL's ABCs

IT ISN'T ENOUGH TO KNOW that Jet SQL's churning away behind the scenes while you work. To realize the real benefits of having this hitchhiker on board, you need to be able to speak, read, and write SQL. Don't be intimidated by the prospect of learning SQL—the language is simple and straightforward. In addition, many large databases (Microsoft SQL Server, Oracle and Sybase) use SQL as their primary language, so learning to use Jet SQL in Access now may be to your advantage later. As we learned in Chapter 1 ("Structured Query Language"), SQL's been around for a while, and it's cropping up all over the place, so a working knowledge of any SQL dialect is definitely a good skill to acquire.

The SQL language comprises keywords, and the key to using SQL successfully is to know how to arrange these keywords in the proper order. An SQL statement can potentially contain many pieces, but you don't have to use all the components in every SQL string. In fact, you will rarely use them all in one statement. However, knowing what's available and the syntax that SQL requires is critical.

At this point, you'll need to be familiar with a few terms:

- A *keyword* is an individual string (word) that has a meaning unique to the Jet engine.

- A *clause* is any portion of an SQL statement that begins with a keyword and includes arguments.

- An SQL *statement* is a complete string that can be interpreted and executed by the Jet engine. You'll often see the term used in reference to keywords, but, technically, *statement* refers to the entire string—all keywords, arguments, and so on.

SQL consists of a long list of keywords that you combine into different types of clauses. Those simple clauses are then combined to create entire statements. In a nutshell, you combine several SQL keywords to create a statement that retrieves data or modifies data or an object.

Statement Structure

Most SQL statements have the same basic syntax. Each statement will include at least two keywords and a few arguments in the form

```
action fieldlist FROM datasource [WHERE clause] [ORDER BY clause];
```

where *action* identifies the type of task that the SQL statement will effect. The *fieldlist* argument identifies the fields that will be retrieved or modified. The *datasource* argument identifies the table or query in question. The WHERE and ORDER BY clauses allow you to limit and group the retrieved data; these clauses are optional. Every statement won't follow this exact form, but this particular form is the cornerstone of the SQL language.

In addition to performing actions on data, an SQL statement can also modify the structure of database objects. These types of statements will, as a general rule, have fewer clauses. For the most part, the SQL statement indicates an action and identifies the data or object that SQL will act upon.

Common SQL Keywords

The following table is a list of some of the more common SQL keywords.

KEYWORD	TYPE	DESCRIPTION	ACCESS QUERY TYPE
SELECT	Action	Retrieves data	Select
UPDATE SET	Action	Modifies existing data	Update
DELETE	Action	Deletes records	Delete
INSERT INTO	Action	Inserts records into an existing table	Append
SELECT INTO	Action	Copies an existing table's structure and data to a new table	Make Table
ALL	Limits	Predicate that specifies all the fields in a datasource	N/A
DISTINCT	Limits	Predicate that returns unique values in the specified field(s)	N/A
DISTINCTROW	Limits	Predicate that returns unique records	N/A
FROM	Information	Specifies the data source	N/A
WHERE	Limits	Argument is a conditional expression that limits records	N/A
GROUP BY	Display	Argument combines similar values into one record	Totals
HAVING	Display	Argument determines which grouped records are displayed	N/A
ORDER BY	Display	Argument determines sort order	N/A

The Action Keyword Cornerstone—SELECT

Every statement consists of a few keywords. They define the statement's action (or task) and any parameters. By far, the most common SQL action keyword is SELECT, which retrieves data and uses the form

```
SELECT fieldlist FROM tablelist
```

The SELECT keyword identifies the action expected from the Jet engine: to select data. The arguments *fieldlist* and *tablelist* identify the fields that Jet will retrieve data from and the table that contains those fields, respectively. You can substitute a specific list of fields with the asterisk (*), which will retrieve all the fields in the table.

> **CAUTION** *Don't use reserved keywords to name objects in your database. Doing so could confuse the Jet engine, which will then return ambiguous errors.*

Now, let's look at the rest of the keywords used with the SELECT keyword. First, there's the FROM keyword, which combined with *tablelist* creates a clause that identifies the data source. Now, open the Northwind.mdb sample file and let's try a simple example in the SQL window:

1. First, click on the Queries shortcut in the Database window, click on New on the Database Window toolbar, and then click on OK in the New Query dialog box.

2. In the resulting Query Design window, close the Show Tables and dialog box, and then click on the View button (which should default to SQL View).

3. Enter the simple SELECT statement

   ```
   SELECT * FROM Employees;
   ```

   as shown in Figure 4-1.

4. Click on the Run button to see the query's results, which is identical to the Employees table because you've just retrieved all the fields in the Employees records without limiting the records in any way.

Figure 4-1. Enter this simple SELECT statement in the SQL window.

> **TIP** *When entering an SQL statement into the SQL window, you can break the statement and go to a new line anywhere. If a source name contains an illegal character (such as a space character), enclose the reference in square brackets ([ ]). In addition, the semicolon (;) isn't necessary. Access will add it for you.*

Limiting Fields

Returning all the fields is inefficient unless you really need all the data. To limit the results, specify the fields instead of using the asterisk (*) using the form

```
SELECT field1, field2, field3 . . .
FROM table;
```

For instance, the statement

```
SELECT LastName, FirstName, Title
FROM Employees;
```

returns the LastName, FirstName, and Title fields from the Employees table.

Limiting Records with Predicates

The ALL predicate returns all records, and it isn't used in basic Select statements because that's the default. For instance,

```
SELECT LastName, FirstName, Title
FROM Employees;
```

and

```
SELECT ALL LastName, FirstName, Title
FROM Employees;
```

return the same records. You'll not find much use for this predicate until we get into more-complicated queries, such as the UNION query, which we discuss in "Using UNION Queries" in Chapter 10 ("Advanced Manipulation Techniques").

To limit the results to unique values you have two choices: the DISTINCT and DISTINCTROW predicates. The DISTINCT predicate limits the results to unique values in a specific field. For instance, the statement

```
SELECT *
FROM [Order Details];
```

returns all the records in the Order Details table. To limit the resulting query to unique order numbers, you'd use the statement

```
SELECT DISTINCT OrderID
FROM [Order Details];
```

You must remember to specify the field (or fields) you're limiting to unique values—the predicate works with the field list as a whole. Don't try to use the DISTINCT predicate with the asterisk.

> **TIP** *The DISTINCT predicate is useful when populating combo and list box controls with unique entries from a particular field for selection purposes. For example, you could use the DISTINCT predicate to limit a long list of names, cities, or countries to a unique listing.*

Limit the results to unique records by using the DISTINCTROW predicate. You can use this predicate with the asterisk because Jet reduces the results to only those records that are completely unique. Individual entries can be repeated in the same field, but no record can be duplicated.

The TOP predicate returns a number or percentage of records, beginning with the first record. For instance, the phrase

```
SELECT TOP 10
```

would return the first ten records instead of the entire queryset, regardless of the number of records that meet any other conditional criteria (a WHERE clause). The phrase

```
SELECT TOP 10 PERCENT
```

would return the first ten percent of qualifying records. If the query would otherwise return 200 records, the additional TOP predicate would limit the results to only 20 records (10 percent of 200).

Working with External Data

The FROM clause specifies the table from which you want to retrieve data; it usually refers to a native table. (By *native*, we mean a table that's in the active database.) You can use the IN clause to specify external tables that aren't linked. Use the form

```
FROM table IN pathdatabasename
```

For instance, to retrieve data from a table named tblEmployee in a database file named Personnel, you might use the statement

```
FROM tblEmployee IN "c:\hr\personnel.mdb"
```

You can also reference Access tables using the form

```
FROM pathdatabasename.table
```

When working with foreign data, use the form

```
FROM product;DATABASE=path;.table
```

The ODBC form is

```
FROM ODBC;connectstring;.table
```

Adding Clauses

Predicates don't limit the query by criteria. For that you'll need a WHERE clause. You'll probably use WHERE and ORDER BY clauses more often than the others listed in the table in the earlier sidebar. The WHERE clause restricts the data, and the ORDER BY clause determines how Jet sorts the retrieved data.

Let's suppose you want to limit the employee records (from the Employees table) to only those employees who live in Seattle. The statement

```
SELECT *
FROM Employees
WHERE City="Seattle";
```

would limit the results to only those records in which the City field contained the string "Seattle". Now let's further suppose you want to sort those results by the employees' last names. Adding an ORDER BY clause would do the trick:

```
SELECT *
FROM Employees
WHERE.City="Seattle"
ORDER BY LastName;
```

You can also group records and limit those groups by adding a GROUP BY and HAVING clause in the form

```
SELECT *
FROM table
WHERE field = wherecriteria
GROUP BY groupbycriteria
HAVING groupcriteria
ORDER BY field;
```

We'll review the GROUP BY and HAVING keywords in the section "Using GROUP BY to Create Groups" in Chapter 7 ("Grouping and Summarizing Data").

NOTE *In an effort to keep things simple in this introductory chapter, our examples use the syntax of* field = value. *As queries become more complex, you may need to specify the table or query in the form* table.field. *In fact, if you create a query in the Query Design window and then view it in the SQL window, you'll see that Jet includes the table references automatically. If your query is based on only one table or query, you don't need to enter the table reference. However, when you're working with multiple tables or queries and a fieldname occurs in more than one of those sources, you must include the table reference, so Jet will know to which field you're referring.*

Adding Joins

We learned about joins in Chapter 3 ("An Introduction to Relational Database Theory"). Now, let's learn how to add them to an SQL statement. Remember, you must reference more than one table or the same table twice (as is the case with a self-join). First, let's look at the syntax for an inner join:

```
SELECT *
FROM onetable INNER JOIN manytable ON primarykeyfield = foreignkeyfield
```

The statement

```
SELECT Orders.OrderID, Orders.CustomerID, [Order Details].UnitPrice
FROM Orders INNER JOIN [Order Details] ON Orders.OrderID = [Order
Details].OrderID;
```

creates a join on the OrderID field in the Orders and Order Details table. As a result, the resulting query identifies each item ordered by the purchasing customer and the item's price, as shown in Figure 4-2.

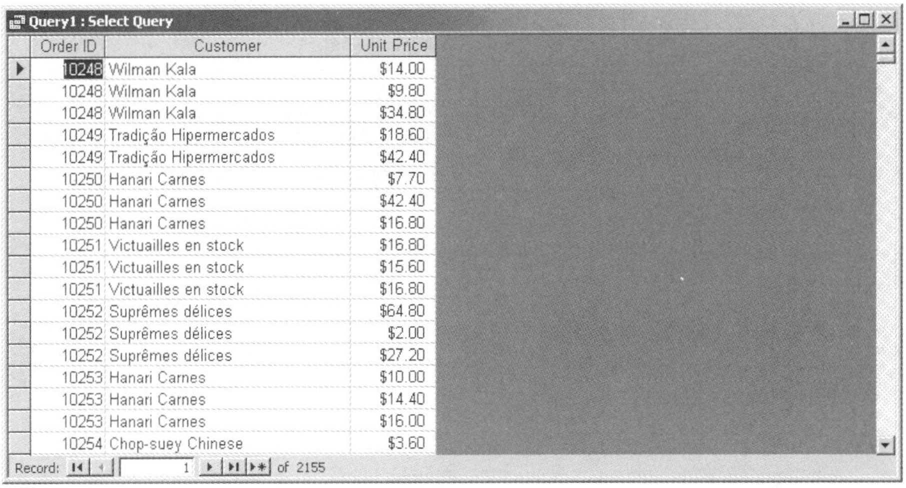

Query1 : Select Query

Order ID	Customer	Unit Price
10248	Wilman Kala	$14.00
10248	Wilman Kala	$9.80
10248	Wilman Kala	$34.80
10249	Tradição Hipermercados	$18.60
10249	Tradição Hipermercados	$42.40
10250	Hanari Carnes	$7.70
10250	Hanari Carnes	$42.40
10250	Hanari Carnes	$16.80
10251	Victuailles en stock	$16.80
10251	Victuailles en stock	$15.60
10251	Victuailles en stock	$16.80
10252	Suprêmes délices	$64.80
10252	Suprêmes délices	$2.00
10252	Suprêmes délices	$27.20
10253	Hanari Carnes	$10.00
10253	Hanari Carnes	$14.40
10253	Hanari Carnes	$16.00
10254	Chop-suey Chinese	$3.60

Record: 1 of 2155

Figure 4-2. A join makes it possible to return data from multiple tables.

You need to consider a few guidelines when adding a join to an SQL statement:

- You can nest joins.
- An inner join may contain an outer join (nested); an outer join may not contain an inner join.
- You can add a join to an SQL statement even if a permanent relationship doesn't exist.

Concatenating Literal Values and Variables

Running an SQL statement from VBA often requires concatenating literal values or variables. Errors result from the simplest delimiting mistakes and can be difficult to debug if you're looking for a syntax or logic error. Fortunately, the rules are clear and easy to apply when embedding literal values and variables in an SQL string:

- Enclose all strings in quotation marks (" " and ' ').
- Enclose all dates in pound signs (#).
- Don't delimit values or variables.

Rely on these three rules whether you're working with literal values or variables.

Let's look at a few quick examples. All strings must be delimited with single or double quotes. For instance, to find all records that belong to a specific employee, you might use the expression

```
SELECT * FROM Employees WHERE LastName = "Buchanan"
```

or

```
SELECT * FROM Employees WHERE LastName = 'Buchanan'
```

Omitting the delimiters as follows:

```
SELECT * FROM Employees WHERE LastName = Buchanan
```

forces the Jet engine to treat the string "Buchanan" as a variable and return an error—unless of course there is such a variable (which would be a whole new problem).

You must delimit a date with the pound sign (#), in the form

```
#5/15/01#
```

Jet recognizes that the string enclosed by the # character is a Date/Time data type and that we're using the U.S. date format M/D/Y. Omitting the delimiters will force Jet (or Access or VBA) to interpret the string as an expression, which in this case would return the value 0.333333333333333. When concatenating values, you don't need any delimiters: you simply enter the value.

Embedding Strings

Nothing's ever as simple as applying one rule in Access: additional concerns always cloud the issue. Delimiting, or embedding strings in an SQL string, is no exception. You must enclose a string in quotation marks. Of course, you must follow some rules for using either the single or double quotation marks as delimiters:

- A delimited string can't contain a lone quotation mark of the same type as the delimiting character.
- If you must include a quotation mark of the same type, you must enter two, three, and even four, depending on the exact use.
- A string delimited with a double quotation mark can contain a single-quotation mark and vice versa.

Table 4-1 applies these rules to the OpenForm method, which requires that the WHERE clause be enclosed in double quotation marks. Not knowing (or following) these three rules can create havoc.

Table 4-1. Delimiting a where *Argument*

EXAMPLE	RESULT
DoCmd.OpenForm "Employees", , , "LastName = Buchanan"	VBA interprets Buchanan as a variable because there are no delimiters. VBA will display a parameter prompt when it can't find a variable named Buchanan.
DoCmd.OpenForm "Employees", , , "LastName = "Buchanan" "	Breaks rule 1 by inserting a lone quotation mark of the same type as the delimiter, and returns a syntax error.
DoCmd.OpenForm "Employees", , , "LastName = ""Buchanan"""	Example of rule 2 solution but isn't very readable because of all the quotation marks.
DoCmd.OpenForm "Employees", , , "LastName = 'Buchanan'"	Example of rule 3 and is the preferred method.
DoCmd.OpenForm "Employees", , , "LastName = 'O'Buchanan'"	Breaks rule 1, and returns a syntax error. The simplest solution to this problem is to concanate the name to the field reference as follows: "LastName=" & "O'Buchanan" & """"

Concatenating String Variables

The procedure in Listing 4-1 passes the string stored in the variable name to the OpenForm method's *where* argument, which uses an SQL WHERE clause (without the WHERE keyword). This function will open the form (empty) and then display a parameter prompt because VBA can't find the variable name.

Listing 4-1. No Concatenation

```
Function OpenFormToName1(name As String)
DoCmd.OpenForm "Employees", , , "LastName = name"
End Function
```

The problem isn't really just a delimiting mistake this time. You must concatenate, or combine, the variable to the rest of the WHERE clause. You might try the procedure shown in Listing 4-2, but it won't work either. VBA still interprets the value of name as a variable instead of using the variable's value in the WHERE string.

Listing 4-2. Missing Delimiters

```
Function OpenFormToName2(name As String)
DoCmd.OpenForm "Employees", , , "LastName = " & name
End Function
```

Listing 4-3 concatenates the variable and correctly delimits the variable's value. Because you're delimiting the name variable with single quotation marks, you could run into trouble if one of the names contains a single quotation mark, such as O'Buchanan.

Listing 4-3. Concatenation and Delimiters

```
Function OpenFormToName3(name As String)
DoCmd.OpenForm "Employees", , , "LastName = '" & name & "'"
End Function
```

Using the OpenForm Procedures

Here's how to enter and run each of the procedures in Listing 4-1, 4-2, and 4-3. First, open the Visual Basic Editor by pressing `Alt+F11` or clicking on the Code button on the Database toolbar. Then, choose Module from the Insert menu and enter a procedure. To run the procedure, open the Immediate window (if necessary) by pressing `Ctrl+G` and enter the statement

```
?OpenFormToNamex("Buchanan")
```

where *x* indicates the sequential number at the end of each function name. VBA opens the form and displays the record(s) for Buchanan.

> **CAUTION** *You may see the plus sign (+) used as a concatenation operator. It's still supported, but only for backward compatibility. We recommend you not use this operator because it slows things down. (This slowdown results from VBA (or Jet) having to determine whether you're using the sign as a mathematical operator before it can perform a concatenation task.)*

The Chr() Alternative

There is one way to include a lone single or double quotation mark in a string delimited with the same character: use the **Chr()** function. Specifically, the **Chr(34)** function returns the double quotation mark, and the **Chr(39)** character returns the single quotation mark. VBA interprets the result of the **Chr()** function as a string, not as a delimiter, even though we can use it that way. To use this method for delimiting, simply concatenate a **Chr()** function on either side of the literal value or variable. Following our OpenForm method example, you'd use the procedure in Listing 4-4.

Listing 4-4. The Chr() Function as a Delimiter

```
Function OpenformToNameChr(name As String)
Dim strSQL As String
DoCmd.OpenForm "Employees", , , "LastName = " & Chr(34) & name & Chr(34)
End Function
```

> **NOTE** *Because WHERE clauses are a large part of the SQL language, you might try the Chr() in your SQL statements, but they tend to slow down queries.*

CHAPTER 5

Retrieving Data

An Introduction to Jet SQL's Data Query Language

SQL PERFORMS TWO FUNCTIONS: It manipulates data and modifies the structure of database objects. Data Manipulation Language (DML) is the SQL terminology that manages the actual data. In other words, DML retrieves and modifies data in a variety of data-oriented tasks:

- Retrieve data from the database
- Add new records to an existing table or tables
- Modify existing records
- Delete existing records

> **NOTE** Data Manipulation Language (DML) *is the term used to refer to those SQL statements that manipulate or act upon data. Using DML, you can retrieve, add, modify, and delete data, but you can't alter the structure of an object.*

In this chapter, we'll discuss how to retrieve data using SQL's Data Manipulation Language (DML). For the most part, that involves using SELECT statements to retrieve data. Chapter 6 will review SQL DML statements and syntax for modifying data.

The SELECT Statement

In Chapter 4 ("SQL Grammar"), we introduced you to the SELECT statement, which is SQL's most basic and probably the most often used statement. Most applications are built around retrieving data for viewing, analyzing, and even updating, so it's little wonder the SELECT statement is used the most.

> **NOTE** *The word* statement, *in general reference to SQL keywords, refers to the entire task-related string, not just the keyword. For instance, SELECT * FROM Employees is an SQL statement and SELECT is the keyword.*

In its simplest form, the SELECT statement retrieves data using the form

```
SELECT fieldlist
FROM datasource;
```

where *fieldlist* is the asterisk character (*) or a comma-separated list of the fields you want to retrieve and *datasource* identifies the table or query in which the data is stored. For instance, the statement

```
SELECT *
FROM Employees;
```

would retrieve all the fields and all the records from the Employees table. On the other hand,

```
SELECT LastName, FirstName, Title, ReportsTo
FROM Employees;
```

would retrieve only the LastName, FirstName, Title, and ReportsTo fields for all of the records in the Employees table, ignoring any other fields that the table might contain. To test this SQL statement via the Access SQL window (using Northwind, the sample database that comes with Access):

1. Click on the Queries shortcut on the Object bar in the Database window. Click on New on the Database toolbar, and then click on OK in the New Query dialog box.

2. In the Query Design window, click on the Close button in the Show Tables dialog box, and then choose SQL View (the default) from the View button to open the SQL window.

3. Enter the statement

   ```
   SELECT LastName, FirstName, Title, ReportsTo
   FROM Employees;
   ```

   as shown in Figure 5-1.

> **TIP** *For optimum performance, list only the fields you really need to see. Displaying extraneous data slows your query. If you want to retrieve all of the fields, the asterisk is more efficient than naming each field individually.*

4. Click on the Run button to view the results shown in Figure 5-2.

> **NOTE** *SQL ignores white space (hard returns and extra spaces); you can break a line anywhere you want or add multiple spaces where one would suffice. You can even enter the statement as a single line. We're breaking the lines into clauses for easy reading.*

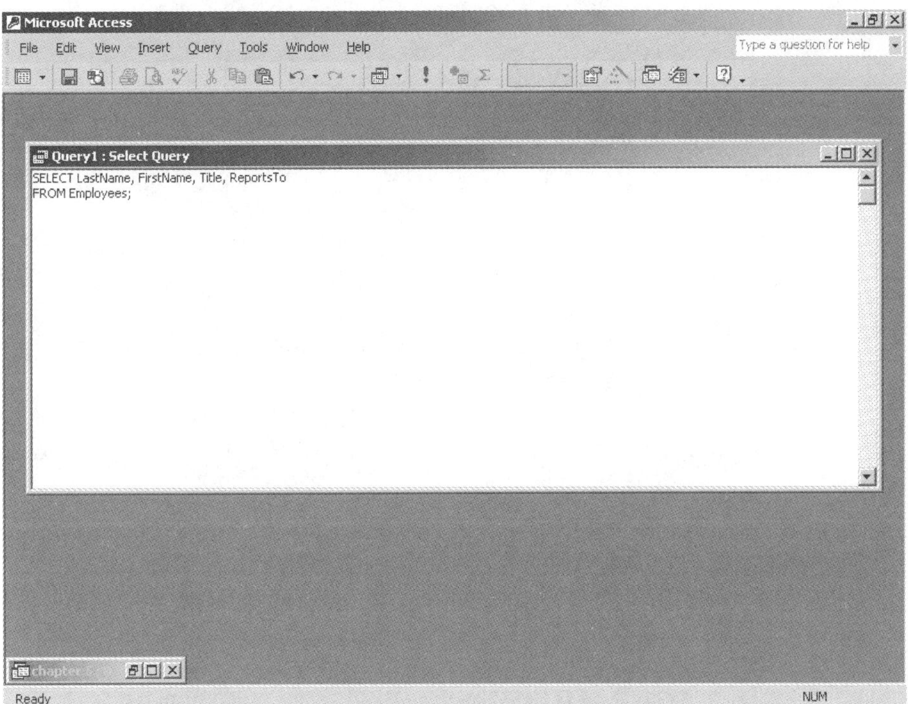

Figure 5-1. This SQL statement retrieves data from the LastName, FirstName, Title, and ReportsTo fields.

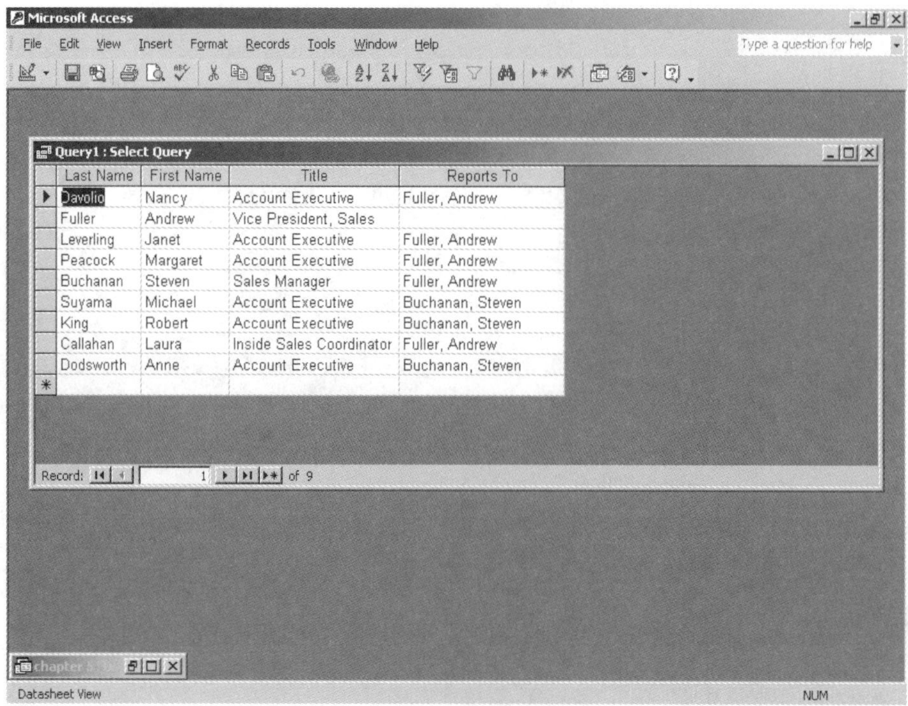

Last Name	First Name	Title	Reports To
Davolio	Nancy	Account Executive	Fuller, Andrew
Fuller	Andrew	Vice President, Sales	
Leverling	Janet	Account Executive	Fuller, Andrew
Peacock	Margaret	Account Executive	Fuller, Andrew
Buchanan	Steven	Sales Manager	Fuller, Andrew
Suyama	Michael	Account Executive	Buchanan, Steven
King	Robert	Account Executive	Buchanan, Steven
Callahan	Laura	Inside Sales Coordinator	Fuller, Andrew
Dodsworth	Anne	Account Executive	Buchanan, Steven

Figure 5-2. SQL retrieves all the records from Employees, but only four fields from each record.

The previous example is the SELECT statement's simplest form, and SELECT has much more to offer. The complete syntax for the SELECT statement is

```
SELECT predicate fieldist
FROM table
WHERE condition
GROUP BY field
HAVING condition
ORDER BY field;
```

As you can see, this statement is flexible enough to handle most any data retrieval needs you might have. The Jet engine searches the specified table(s), retrieves the appropriate columns, and then selects only those rows that meet the conditions. Once the data is retrieved, Jet groups and sorts the resulting rows appropriately. (We'll cover sorting in "Sorting the Results of a SELECT Statement" later in this chapter.)For specific instructions and examples for using GROUP BY and HAVING, read "Using GROUP BY to Create Groups" and "Using HAVING" in Chapter 7.

NOTE *A SELECT statement will not change or modify existing data in any way.*

Using the AS Keyword to Create an Alias

Like a Select query, the SQL statement uses field names as the corresponding column's header text. Field names don't always provide helpful clues to determining the purpose of the data they contain. This is especially true when internal naming conventions dictate the name of a field. For instance, you might end up with an obscure field name such as fldtxt101 instead of EmployeeID. (We recommend you use descriptive names.) Or, you may inherit an application that uses unusual (or no) naming conventions. When field names aren't descriptive, you can use the AS keyword to specify a string that SQL will display as the column header instead of the field name. The column headings in our previous example are descriptive enough, but let's suppose you wanted to change them, without changing the actual name of the field. You could use the AS keyword as follows:

```
SELECT LastName AS [Employee's Last Name], FirstName AS [Employee's First Name],
  Title, ReportsTo AS [Reports To]
FROM Employees;
```

If you run this statement, you'll find it doesn't have the expected results: SQL seems to ignore the AS keywords and the alias. That's because these fields have a Caption property set in the Employees table, and you can't modify a (Jet) user-defined property using SQL.

The only way around this problem is to delete the Caption settings in the underlying table. (In this case, that's the Employees table.) Although deleting the setting should have limited repercussions, you should consider this behavior when using it.

CAUTION *The Field object's Name property (DAO and ADO) returns the field name, right? Not always. If you use the AS keyword to set an alias in an SQL statement, the Name property will return the alias, not the underlying field name or even the field's Caption property setting.*

Beyond AS

Bound objects inherit an alias defined by the AS keyword. To illustrate this behavior, let's populate the same list box with two different SQL statements—one with and one without the AS keyword. To build the form, follow these steps:

1. Choose Form from the Insert menu on the Database toolbar, and click on OK in the New Form dialog box.
2. If the toolbox isn't already open, click on the Toolbox button on the Form Design toolbar.
3. Add a list box control to the form. The control should be approximately two inches wide and one inch deep.
4. Double-click on the control to open the Properties sheet (if necessary).
5. Name the new control lstASExample.
6. Enter the following SQL statement as the control's Row Source property

   ```
   SELECT LastName AS Name, Title AS Position
   FROM Employees;
   ```

7. Change the Column Count property to 2.
8. Change the Column Heads property to Yes.
9. Click on the View button to see the control, shown in Figure 5-3 in Form view.

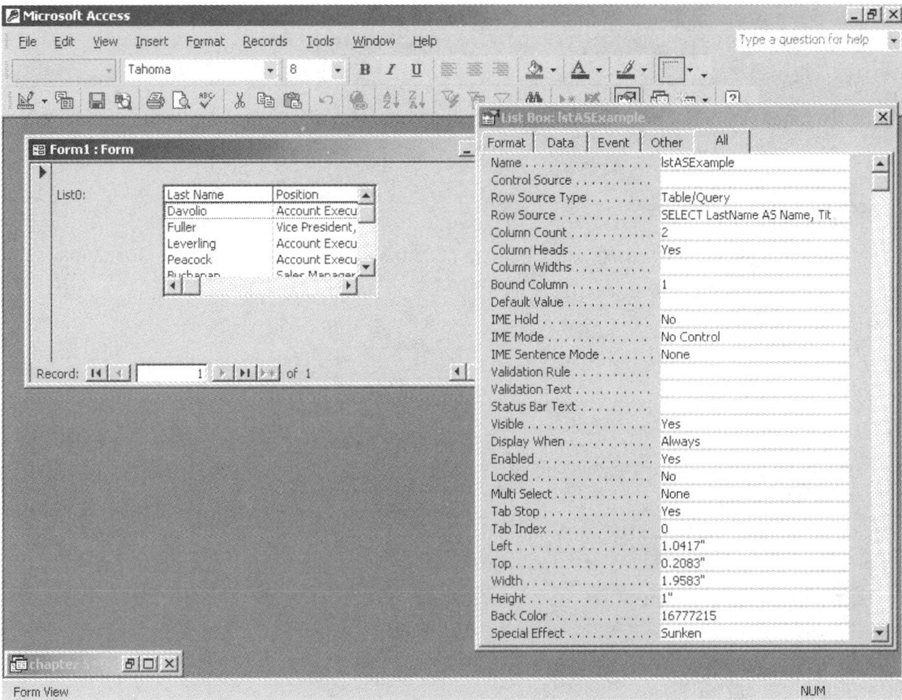

Figure 5-3. The control doesn't display both aliases as column headings.

> **NOTE** *The Properties sheet (or window) may remain open (as we've shown in Figure 5-3), if you have the form's Allow Design Changes property set to All Views (which is the default). If Access closes the Properties window when you switch to Form view, don't worry: your form's Allow Design Changes property is probably set to Design View Only. Viewing the Properties window can be useful during the development of your application, but you should set the property to Design View Only before the application actually goes into production.*

Only one of the columns displays the alias that we specified. The Title column displays the alias "Position", but the LastName column displays that field's Caption property—Last Name (with a space)—instead of the alias we specified, "Name".

> **CAUTION** *VBA's ItemData property will return the specified index value for a list box of the combo box's bound column. For instance, ItemData(0) returns the first item in the list. In our example, you might expect ItemData(0) to return Davolio, because that's the first item in the list. However, it doesn't because our control's Column Heads property is set to Yes. When this is the case, the 0 index value starts with the column heading, and not the first item in the list. Therefore, ItemData(0) would return Last Name, not Davolio. To get Davolio, you'd use ItemData(1). VBA treats the column heading as just another item in the list.*

Limiting the SELECT Results

Seldom will you want to retrieve all the records in the underlying data source. Typically, you'll limit the results by specifying a condition that each record must meet to be included in the query's results (creating a subset of the underlying records).

The SQL WHERE clause accepts a conditional expression in the form

```
SELECT listfield
FROM datasource
WHERE criteriaexpression
```

where *criteriaexpression* is the condition that a record must meet to make it to the result set. A WHERE clause can contain up to 40 conditional expressions, which you combine using the logical operators AND and OR. (We'll discuss these operators more in the "The Scoop on AND and OR" section in this chapter.)

> **NOTE** *The SQL WHERE clause corresponds to the Criteria and Or cells in the Query Design window.*

Still working with the Northwind sample file that comes with Access, let's suppose you want to see only those employees that work in London. The SELECT statement

```
SELECT *
FROM Employees
WHERE City = 'London';
```

returns only the four London employees, as shown in Figure 5-4. (For specific information on delimiting literal values and variables, see the "Concatenating Literal Values and Variables," section in Chapter 4.)

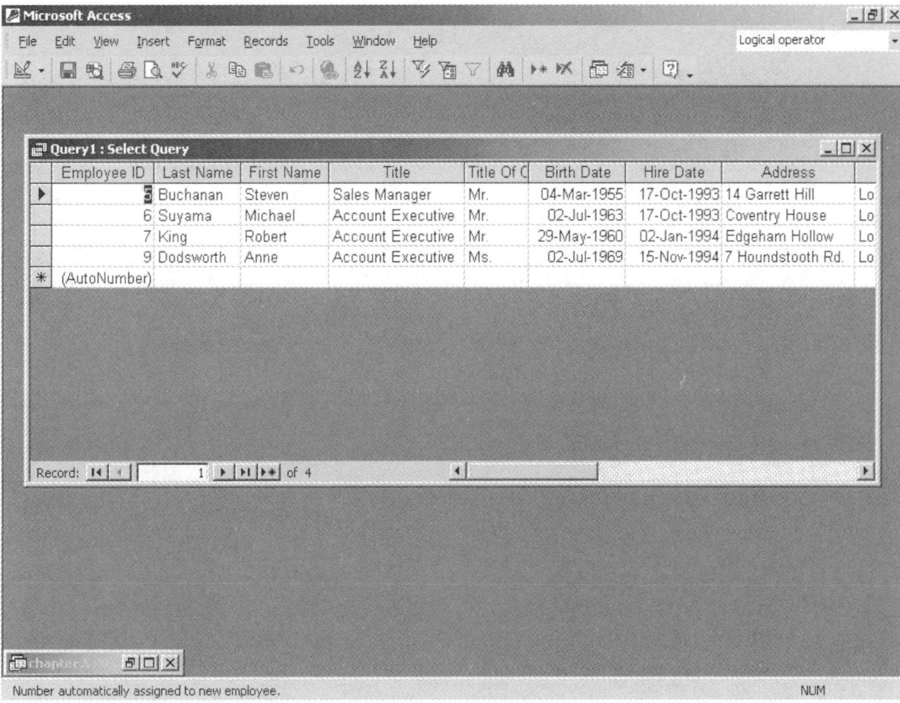

Figure 5-4. The WHERE clause limits the query's results to only those records in which the City field contained the string "London".

Complex Expressions That Limit Results

A WHERE clause's conditional expression can be as simple as an existing value. We showed you such an example in the last section. On the other hand, the expression can be much more complex and include operators and operands. The key to working with complex expressions is to properly delimit the values and variables.

The example in the last section restricted the query to a single, literal value—a city. This is one of the simplest ways to restrict data. Now, let's try something a little more difficult. Let's suppose you want to review only the orders (Orders table in Northwind) that were shipped during a specific time period. To do so:

1. Open a blank query by clicking on the Queries shortcut on the Object bar in the Database window, clicking on New on the Database Window toolbar, and then clicking on OK in the New Query dialog box.

2. Click on Close in the open Show Tables dialog box and click on the View button, which defaults to SQL View.

3. Enter the SQL statement

```
SELECT * FROM Orders WHERE ShippedDate BETWEEN #1/1/96# AND #12/31/96#;
```

4. Click on Run on the Query Design toolbar to see the results shown in Figure 5-5.

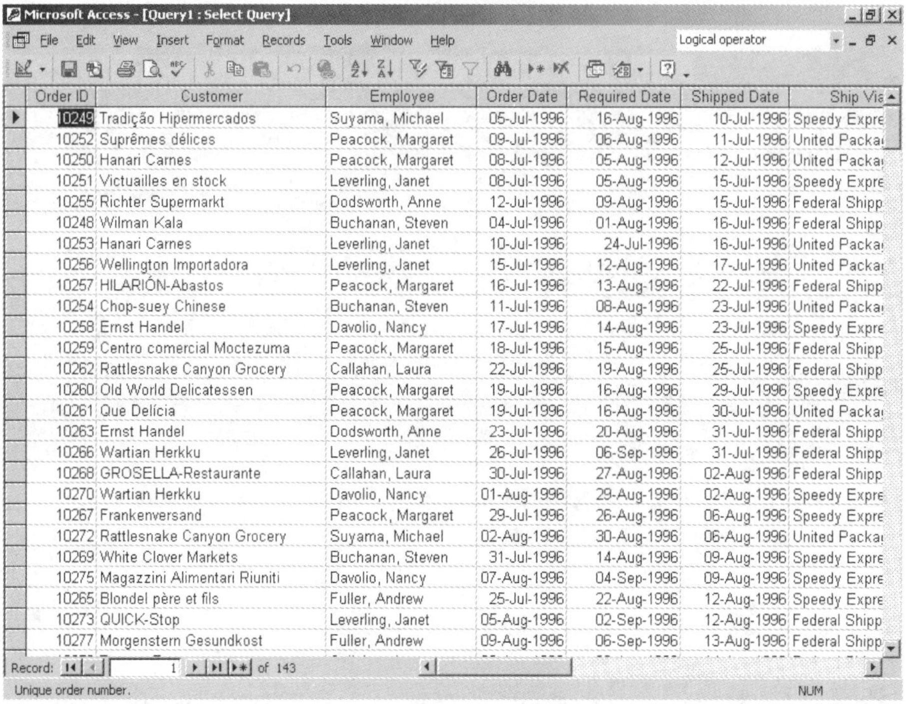

Microsoft Access - [Query1 : Select Query]

Order ID	Customer	Employee	Order Date	Required Date	Shipped Date	Ship Via
10249	Tradição Hipermercados	Suyama, Michael	05-Jul-1996	16-Aug-1996	10-Jul-1996	Speedy Expre
10252	Suprêmes délices	Peacock, Margaret	09-Jul-1996	06-Aug-1996	11-Jul-1996	United Packa
10250	Hanari Carnes	Peacock, Margaret	08-Jul-1996	05-Aug-1996	12-Jul-1996	United Packa
10251	Victuailles en stock	Leverling, Janet	08-Jul-1996	05-Aug-1996	15-Jul-1996	Speedy Expre
10255	Richter Supermarkt	Dodsworth, Anne	12-Jul-1996	09-Aug-1996	15-Jul-1996	Federal Shipp
10248	Wilman Kala	Buchanan, Steven	04-Jul-1996	01-Aug-1996	16-Jul-1996	Federal Shipp
10253	Hanari Carnes	Leverling, Janet	10-Jul-1996	24-Jul-1996	16-Jul-1996	United Packa
10256	Wellington Importadora	Leverling, Janet	15-Jul-1996	12-Aug-1996	17-Jul-1996	United Packa
10257	HILARIÓN-Abastos	Peacock, Margaret	16-Jul-1996	13-Aug-1996	22-Jul-1996	Federal Shipp
10254	Chop-suey Chinese	Buchanan, Steven	11-Jul-1996	08-Aug-1996	23-Jul-1996	United Packa
10258	Ernst Handel	Davolio, Nancy	17-Jul-1996	14-Aug-1996	23-Jul-1996	Speedy Expre
10259	Centro comercial Moctezuma	Peacock, Margaret	18-Jul-1996	15-Aug-1996	25-Jul-1996	Federal Shipp
10262	Rattlesnake Canyon Grocery	Callahan, Laura	22-Jul-1996	19-Aug-1996	25-Jul-1996	Federal Shipp
10260	Old World Delicatessen	Peacock, Margaret	19-Jul-1996	16-Aug-1996	29-Jul-1996	Speedy Expre
10261	Que Delícia	Peacock, Margaret	19-Jul-1996	16-Aug-1996	30-Jul-1996	United Packa
10263	Ernst Handel	Dodsworth, Anne	23-Jul-1996	20-Aug-1996	31-Jul-1996	Federal Shipp
10266	Wartian Herkku	Leverling, Janet	26-Jul-1996	06-Sep-1996	31-Jul-1996	Federal Shipp
10268	GROSELLA-Restaurante	Callahan, Laura	30-Jul-1996	27-Aug-1996	02-Aug-1996	Federal Shipp
10270	Wartian Herkku	Davolio, Nancy	01-Aug-1996	29-Aug-1996	02-Aug-1996	Speedy Expre
10267	Frankenversand	Peacock, Margaret	29-Jul-1996	26-Aug-1996	06-Aug-1996	Speedy Expre
10272	Rattlesnake Canyon Grocery	Suyama, Michael	02-Aug-1996	30-Aug-1996	06-Aug-1996	United Packa
10269	White Clover Markets	Buchanan, Steven	31-Jul-1996	14-Aug-1996	09-Aug-1996	Speedy Expre
10275	Magazzini Alimentari Riuniti	Davolio, Nancy	07-Aug-1996	04-Sep-1996	09-Aug-1996	Speedy Expre
10265	Blondel père et fils	Fuller, Andrew	25-Jul-1996	22-Aug-1996	12-Aug-1996	Speedy Expre
10273	QUICK-Stop	Leverling, Janet	05-Aug-1996	02-Sep-1996	12-Aug-1996	Federal Shipp
10277	Morgenstern Gesundkost	Fuller, Andrew	09-Aug-1996	06-Sep-1996	13-Aug-1996	Federal Shipp

Record: 1 of 143

Unique order number.

Figure 5-5. A total of 143 orders were shipped in 1996.

TIP *Nulls can have far-reaching effects when you're restricting data. If a conditional field is null, Jet will exclude it from the results. That's because null doesn't equal anything—it can't satisfy any condition, other than Is Null. For instance, the simple expression WHERE* `fld < 10 OR fld <= 10` *should return every value in fld, but it won't return a Null value. That row would be missing from your result set. Adding an Is Null operator as an OR criteria will return Null values and those that actually meet the condition. For example, the expression WHERE* `fld < 10 OR fld <= 10 OR fld Is Null` *will return all values from fld.*

What Are Operators and Operands?

Operators are the mathematical, comparison, logical, and concatenation symbols in an expression. Operands are the values—literal, variables, references, and functions—that you want evaluated by the operators. Table 5-1 lists the operators that are available to you in SQL.

Table 5-1. The Operators in SQL

TYPE	SIGN	DESCRIPTION
Mathematical	+	Addition
Mathematical	-	Subtraction
Mathematical	-	Changes the sign of an operand
Mathematical	*	Multiplication
Mathematical	/	Division
Mathematical	\	Integer division
Mathematical	^	Exponentiation (not supported by SQL Server)
Mathematical	MOD	Returns the remainder of division by an integer (% in T-SQL)
Comparison	=	Equals
Comparison	>	Is greater than
Comparison	<	Is less than
Comparison	>=	Is greater than or equal to
Comparison	<=	Is less than or equal to
Comparison	<>	Is not equal to
Comparison	IS	Compares two object reference variables
Comparison	LIKE	Compares string values by character
Logical	IN	Compares a value to a list of values.
Logical	OR	Meets any one condition
Logical	AND	Meets all conditions

Table 5-1. The Operators in SQL (continued)

TYPE	SIGN	DESCRIPTION
Logical	BETWEEN	Falls between two extremes and is inclusive of both ends
Logical	NOT	Negates the logical result of an expression

> **NOTE** *Integer division returns the integer portion of the result. Any decimal portion is truncated. The MOD operator returns the remainder of a division without the integer portion of the division result.*

The Scoop on AND and OR

Often, limits depend on more than one field. In this case, you can use the AND and OR operators to define multiple conditions. The AND operator forces a comparison to meet all the conditions, whereas the OR operator allows a comparison to meet just one condition. All conditional expressions in an AND expression must evaluate to True to be included in the query's results. In contrast, only one conditional expression must evaluate to True for that record to be included in an OR's results. For example, the following statement would return all the records shipped in 1996 by Speedy Express:

```
SELECT * FROM Orders WHERE ShippedDate Between #1/1/96# AND #12/31/96# AND
  ShipVia =1 ;
```

as you can see in Figure 5-6. This example actually contains two AND operators, so don't get them confused. The component `ShippedDate Between #1/1/96# AND #12/31/96#` states the first condition, and the component `ShipVia =1` expresses the second condition. We're using the AND operator to combine these two conditions. The AND operator between the two dates provides a mechanism by which we can include several values in one condition.

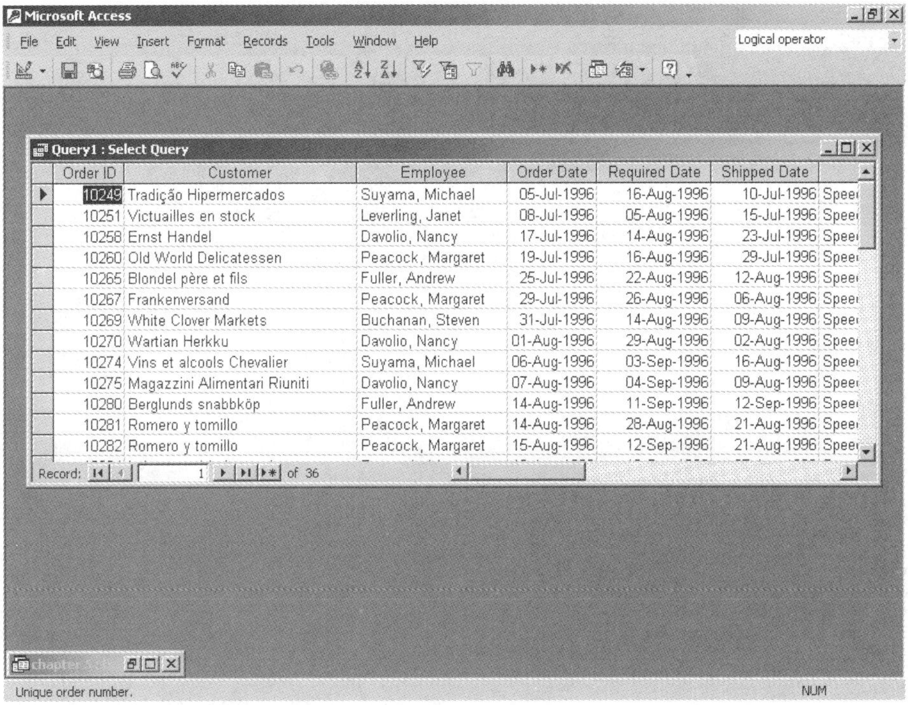

Figure 5-6. A total of 36 orders meet both conditions.

First, Jet evaluates the ShippedDate and if the conditional expression `Between #1/1/96# AND #12/31/96# AND ShipVia=1` evaluates to True. If the ShipVia value is 2, that conditional expression is False. Consequently, the AND expression returns False, because one of the conditions is False (isn't met), and Jet excludes the record from the results. If both conditions evaluate to True, Jet includes the record.

Now, change the AND operator to an OR operator:

```
SELECT *
FROM Orders
WHERE ShippedDate Between #1/1/96# AND #12/31/96# OR ShipVia =1 ;
```

Make sure you change the right AND operator (the one between the two conditions, and not the AND operator between the two dates). As you can see in Figure 5-7, the result is very different: 356 orders meet one condition or the other but not necessarily both. The OR operator requires that only one conditional expression be True to be included in the query results.

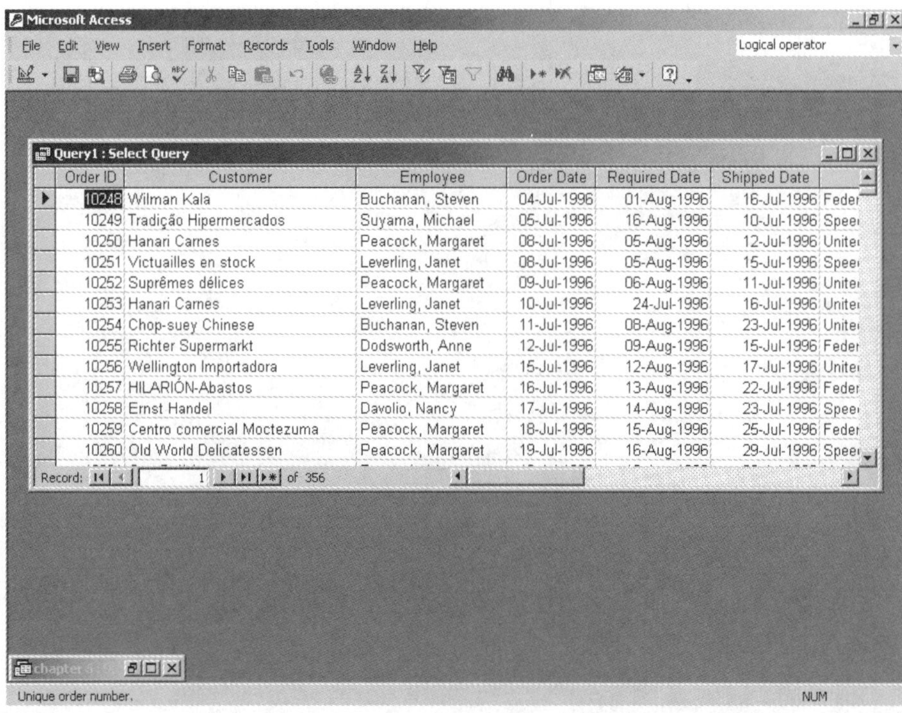

Order ID	Customer	Employee	Order Date	Required Date	Shipped Date	
10248	Wilman Kala	Buchanan, Steven	04-Jul-1996	01-Aug-1996	16-Jul-1996	Feder
10249	Tradição Hipermercados	Suyama, Michael	05-Jul-1996	16-Aug-1996	10-Jul-1996	Spee
10250	Hanari Carnes	Peacock, Margaret	08-Jul-1996	05-Aug-1996	12-Jul-1996	Unite
10251	Victuailles en stock	Leverling, Janet	08-Jul-1996	05-Aug-1996	15-Jul-1996	Spee
10252	Suprêmes délices	Peacock, Margaret	09-Jul-1996	06-Aug-1996	11-Jul-1996	Unite
10253	Hanari Carnes	Leverling, Janet	10-Jul-1996	24-Jul-1996	16-Jul-1996	Unite
10254	Chop-suey Chinese	Buchanan, Steven	11-Jul-1996	08-Aug-1996	23-Jul-1996	Unite
10255	Richter Supermarkt	Dodsworth, Anne	12-Jul-1996	09-Aug-1996	15-Jul-1996	Feder
10256	Wellington Importadora	Leverling, Janet	15-Jul-1996	12-Aug-1996	17-Jul-1996	Unite
10257	HILARIÓN-Abastos	Peacock, Margaret	16-Jul-1996	13-Aug-1996	22-Jul-1996	Feder
10258	Ernst Handel	Davolio, Nancy	17-Jul-1996	14-Aug-1996	23-Jul-1996	Spee
10259	Centro comercial Moctezuma	Peacock, Margaret	18-Jul-1996	15-Aug-1996	25-Jul-1996	Feder
10260	Old World Delicatessen	Peacock, Margaret	19-Jul-1996	16-Aug-1996	29-Jul-1996	Spee

Figure 5-7. The OR expression returns 356 records.

NOTE *A fixed query—one you create in the Query Design window and save as an Access object—can take a substantial performance hit if you add expressions. If a query containing expressions is slow, try moving the expressions to the bound form or report. There's always a tradeoff when dealing with expressions, and, depending on how you use the bound object, there's no guarantee that this arrangement won't be worse. For instance, a form that must continually calculate one or more complex expressions may be more annoying than a form that's slow to populate and display initially, but otherwise updates quickly.*

Early versions of the Jet engine ran SQL statements significantly slower than fixed queries, but enhancements to version 3.5 have improved performance. You should now notice no difference between a fixed query and an SQL statement used as a data source.

Understanding How OR Really Works

The OR operator can be a bit tricky when combined with the NOT operator. The key is to understanding how the OR operator works and just when the NOT operator negates its results. Consider the following statement:

```
SELECT *
FROM Orders
WHERE NOT(ShipCountry = 'France') OR NOT(ShipCountry = 'Austria');
```

You might think that this statement returns all records except those that have either France or Austria in the ShipCountry field. However, this statement returns all the records. Jet's doing its job; the expression is the problem.

When you run the query, the Jet engine checks the contents of the ShipCountry field and, if that entry equals France, the conditional expression `ShipCountry = 'France'` is True, which the NOT operator then negates to False. Because the second conditional expression `ShipCountry = 'Austria'` is False, the NOT operator negates that to True. Because the second conditional expression now equals True, Jet includes the record in the results, even though the entry is France. Likewise, if the entry is Austria, one of the conditional expressions ultimately evaluates to True, so Jet includes the record in the results.

The problem is with the number of NOT operators used. When working with the OR operator, you'll want just one NOT operator that negates the results of the OR expression, not each conditional expression in the OR expression. The correct statement

```
SELECT *
FROM Orders
WHERE NOT(ShipCountry = 'France' OR ShipCountry = 'Austria');
```

evaluates both conditional expressions and then negates that result to either True or False. So, if the ShipCountry entry is France, the first conditional expression is True and the second is False. Consequently, the OR expression returns True because one of the conditions is met. Then, the NOT operator negates that result to False so Jet doesn't include the record in the query's results.

Including Wildcards

Wildcards can lend a bit of flexibility when a complete entry isn't known because Jet has more opportunities to match an entry. Table 5-2 lists the wildcards that SQL supports. Combine these wildcards with the LIKE operator.

Table 5-2. Wildcards Supported by SQL

CHARACTER	DESCRIPTION	OLE DB AND ADO EQUIVALENT
*	Matches any character or block of characters in that position	%
?	Matches any single character in that position	_
#	Matches any single digit (0-9)	N/A
[*list*]	Specifies a range of characters	(*list*)
[!*list*]	Specifies any single character not in *list*	(^*list*)

For example, the asterisk (*) represents any character or block of characters in a specific position. So, let's suppose you want to return a list of all the contacts that are managers (in the Northwind Customers table). You could enter a list of the specific types of managing titles, but the * wildcard is simpler. To find all managers:

1. Open a blank query by clicking on the Queries shortcut in the Database window, clicking on New on the Database Window toolbar, and then clicking on OK in the New Query dialog box.

2. Close the Show Tables dialog box and click on the View button, which automatically defaults to SQL view.

3. In the SQL window, enter the statement

   ```
   SELECT *
   FROM Customers
   WHERE ContactTitle LIKE '* Manager';
   ```

4. Run the query to return the records shown in Figure 5-8. The second word in each ContactTitle entry is "Manager". However, this statement would not match a lone entry of "Manager" because of the space between the asterisk and the string "Manager". If you want to match all entries, use the statement

   ```
   WHERE ContactTitle LIKE '*Manager'
   ```

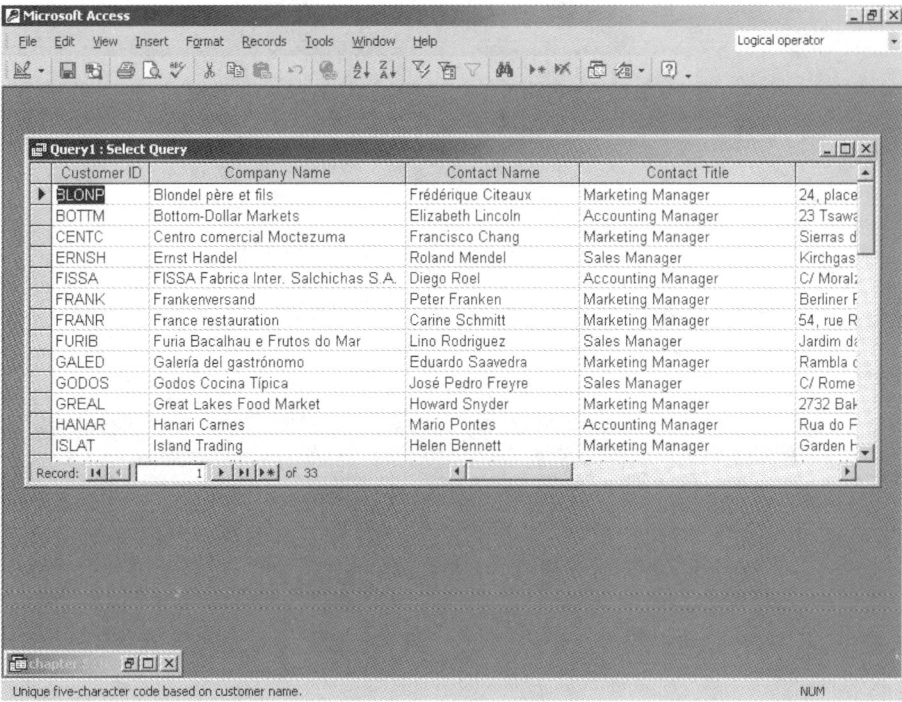

Figure 5-8. A total of 33 customer contacts have the string "Manager" in their titles.

The ? character matches a single character in that position. This is a great tool to use when an entry includes a special character that you can't easily reproduce. For instance, the customer Comércio Mineiro includes a diacritical accent: the special character é. If you enter Comercio Mineiro as the search string, Jet returns nothing because Jet knows the difference between e and é. Under these circumstances, the ? wildcard can be your best friend. Open a blank query using steps 1 and 2 in the last example, and then enter the SQL statement

```
SELECT *
FROM Customers
WHERE CompanyName LIKE 'Com?rcio Mineiro';
```

Running the query returns the one record shown in Figure 5-9.

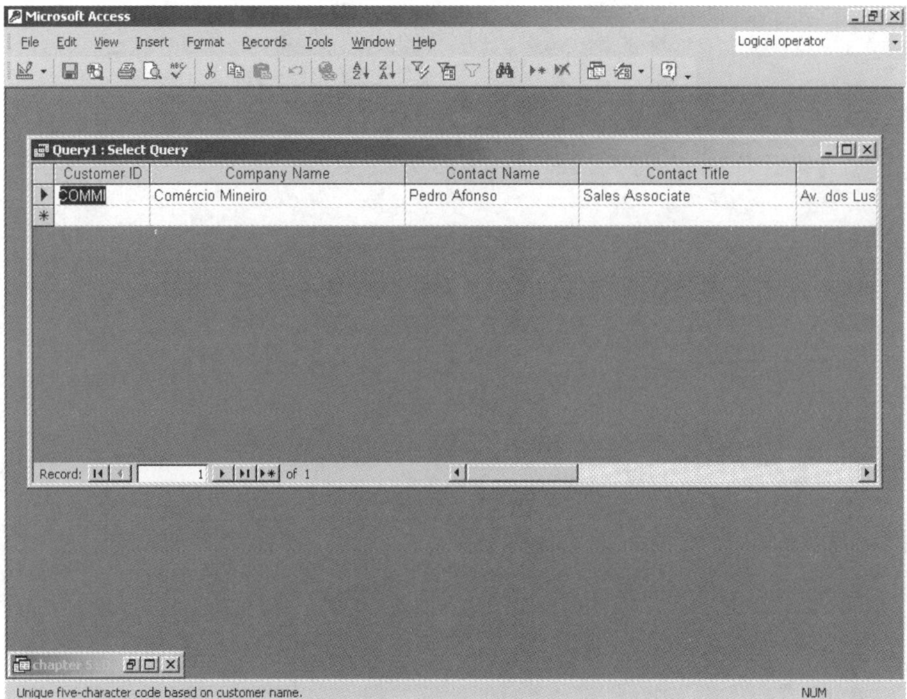

Figure 5-9. Using the ? wildcard, you can return entries that contain special characters.

In this case, the clause

```
WHERE CompanyName LIKE 'Com*';
```

would return the same result set, but that won't always be the case. Sometimes you will need a more exclusive match.

> **NOTE** *The # character works just like the ? wildcard character, except it's limited to representing digits (0 through 9) instead of any character.*

When searching for a series of characters, use the [ ] wildcard in one of the following forms

"first-last"
"value1,value2"
"first1-last1,first2-last, . . . "
"first1-last1,value1, . . . "

where the *first* and *last* variables refer to the first and last values in a series and the *value* variables refer to individual values. For instance, the following statement

```
SELECT *
FROM Customers
WHERE CompanyName LIKE '[A-C]*';
```

will return all the customers that begin with the letters A, B, and C, as shown in Figure 5-10. To return all the companies that start with any letter other than A, B, or C, you'd use the clause

```
WHERE CompanyName LIKE '[!A-C]*';
```

Microsoft Access

Query1 : Select Query

Customer ID	Company Name	Contact Name	Contact Title	
ALFKI	Alfreds Futterkiste	Maria Anders	Sales Representative	Obere Str. 5
ANATR	Ana Trujillo Emparedados y helados	Ana Trujillo	Owner	Avda. de la
ANTON	Antonio Moreno Taquería	Antonio Moreno	Owner	Mataderos
AROUT	Around the Horn	Thomas Hardy	Sales Representative	120 Hanove
BERGS	Berglunds snabbköp	Christina Berglund	Order Administrator	Berguvsväge
BLAUS	Blauer See Delikatessen	Hanna Moos	Sales Representative	Forsterstr. 5
BLONP	Blondel père et fils	Frédérique Citeaux	Marketing Manager	24, place Kl
BOLID	Bólido Comidas preparadas	Martín Sommer	Owner	C/ Araquil, 6
BONAP	Bon app'	Laurence Lebihan	Owner	12, rue des
BOTTM	Bottom-Dollar Markets	Elizabeth Lincoln	Accounting Manager	23 Tsawass
BSBEV	B's Beverages	Victoria Ashworth	Sales Representative	Fauntleroy C
CACTU	Cactus Comidas para llevar	Patricio Simpson	Sales Agent	Cerrito 333
CENTC	Centro comercial Moctezuma	Francisco Chang	Marketing Manager	Sierras de C
CHOPS	Chop-suey Chinese	Yang Wang	Owner	Hauptstr. 29
COMMI	Comércio Mineiro	Pedro Afonso	Sales Associate	Av. dos Lus
CONSH	Consolidated Holdings	Elizabeth Brown	Sales Representative	Berkeley Ga

Record: 1 of 16

Unique five-character code based on customer name. NUM

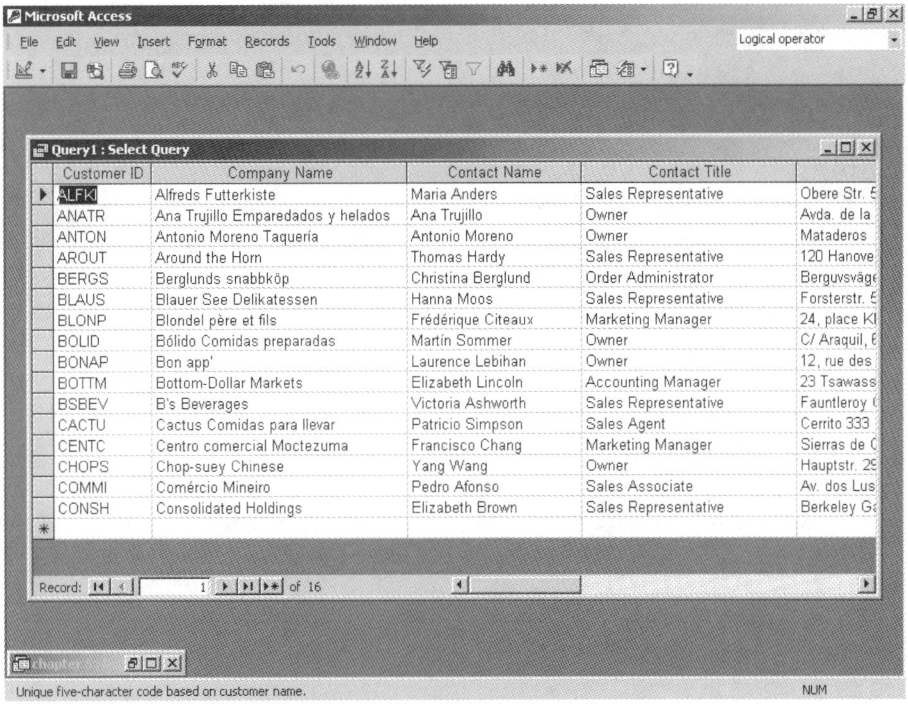

Figure 5-10. A total of 16 companies begin with the letters A, B, or C.

The [ ] wildcard handles more complex lists. For instance, the phrase

```
WHERE CompanyName Like '[A-C, X-Z]*';
```

would return all the companies that start with the letters A, B, C, X, Y, and Z. The phrase

```
WHERE CompanyName Like '[!A-C, X-Z]*';
```

would return all the companies that begin with any letter other than A, B, C, X, Y, and Z.

A series can consist of just one letter. We can easily add any character to this combination by simply inserting the additional value. The phrase

```
WHERE CompanyName Like '[!A-C, Q, X-Z]*';
```

would return all the companies that begin with any letter other than A, B, C, X, Y, Z, and Q.

The [ ] wildcard has one more trick up its sleeve: you can add a literal character to the beginning of the series in the form

```
WHERE CompanyName Like 'c[A-C]*';
```

In this case, the statement would return all the companies that begin with the letters ca, cb, and cc. Adding the ! character would return everything but those same entries.

*If your Access application has the potential to be upsized to SQL Server, you can save yourself a lot of work where wildcards are concerned. SQL Server's equivalent * wildcard is the % character. Part of upsizing will include replacing all the * wildcard characters in your code with the % character—unless you plan ahead.*

Define a compiler argument in the form

```
#IF CON_SQL = True Then
  Const conAllWildcard = "%" 'for SQL
#ELSE
  Const conAllWildcard = "*" 'for Jet
#END IF
```

Then, all you have to do is set the CON_SQL to True or False, appropriately.

Arthur Fuller, Lead Developer,
ETS Escape Routes, Inc., artful@cgocable.net

Using Wildcards in DAO and ADO Code

You might expect the data object libraries to support the same wildcards, but they don't. That's because DAO and ADO adhere to different SQL standards. You can read more about these standards in Chapter 1 ("Structured Query Language"). Both libraries accept wildcards, just not the same wildcards. (See Table 5-2.)

The procedures in Listing 5-1 and 5-2 both pass a variable in an SQL statement that's then used to create a Recordset object. The `Debug.Print` statement then prints the recordset in the Immediate window. The value passed should be a single alpha character or a series of them. The SQL statement then concatenates that value with the * (DAO) and % (ADO) wildcard characters to return values from the LastName field that begin with the passed value.

Listing 5-1. DAO * Wildcard

```
Function WildcardsDAO(chrs As String)
Dim db As DAO.Database
Dim rst As DAO.Recordset
Dim strSQL As String
Set db = CurrentDb
strSQL = "SELECT LastName FROM Employees " & _
    "WHERE LastName Like '" & chrs & "*'" & ";"
Debug.Print strSQL
Set rst = db.OpenRecordset(strSQL)
Do Until rst.EOF
    Debug.Print rst.Fields(0)
    rst.MoveNext
Loop
End Function
```

Listing 5-2. ADO % Wildcard

```
Function WildcardsADO(chrs As String)
Dim rst As New ADODB.Recordset
Dim cnn As ADODB.Connection
Dim strSQL As String
Set cnn = CurrentProject.Connection
strSQL = "SELECT LastName FROM Employees " & _
    "WHERE LastName Like '" & chrs & "%'" & ";"
Debug.Print strSQL
rst.Open strSQL, cnn
Do Until rst.EOF
    Debug.Print rst.Fields(0)
    rst.MoveNext
Loop
End Function
```

To run the procedures:

1. Launch VBE by pressing `Alt+F11`, insert a module by choosing Module from the Insert menu, and enter the procedures shown in Listing 5-1 and 5-2.

2. Choose References from the Tools menu and check Microsoft DAO 3.6 Object Library in the References dialog and click on OK. (Otherwise, the DAO example will return an error.)

3. In the Immediate window, enter the statement

   ```
   ?WildcardsDAO("D")
   ```

   and VBA will print the text shown in Figure 5-11 in the Immediate window. The first Debug statement prints the evaluated SQL string. Then, the procedure prints the contents of the first (and in this case only) field for all records in the recordset. Because we passed the letter D, the procedure returns the strings Davolio and Dunsworth.

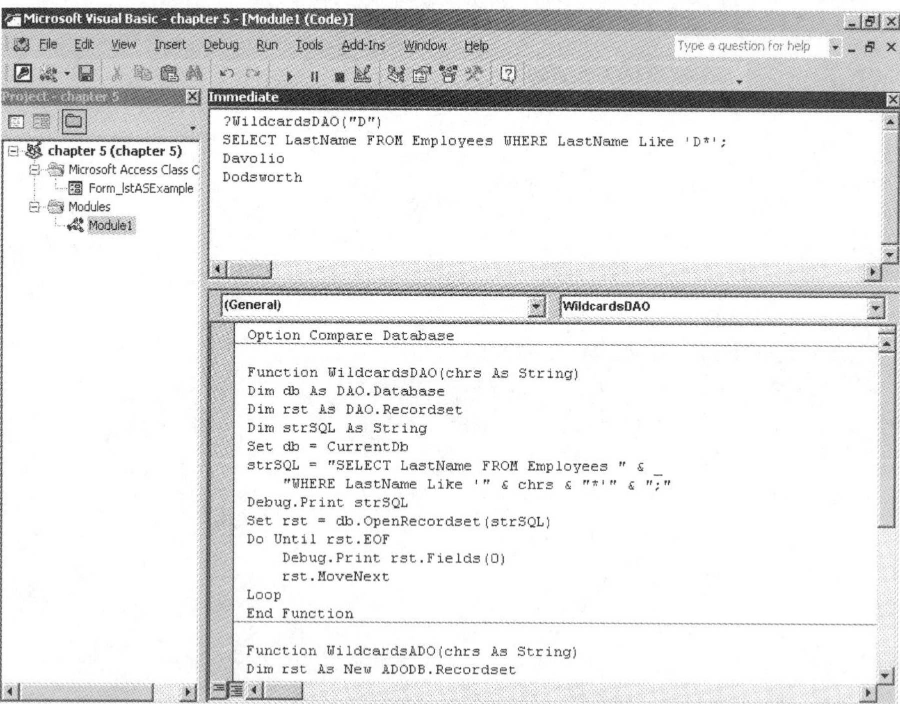

Figure 5-11. The DAO procedure prints matching records in the Immediate window.

4. Now run the statement

```
?WildcardsADO("D")
```

and VBA returns the same results (except for the slight difference in the evaluated SQL string), as shown in Figure 5-12, using the % wildcard character.

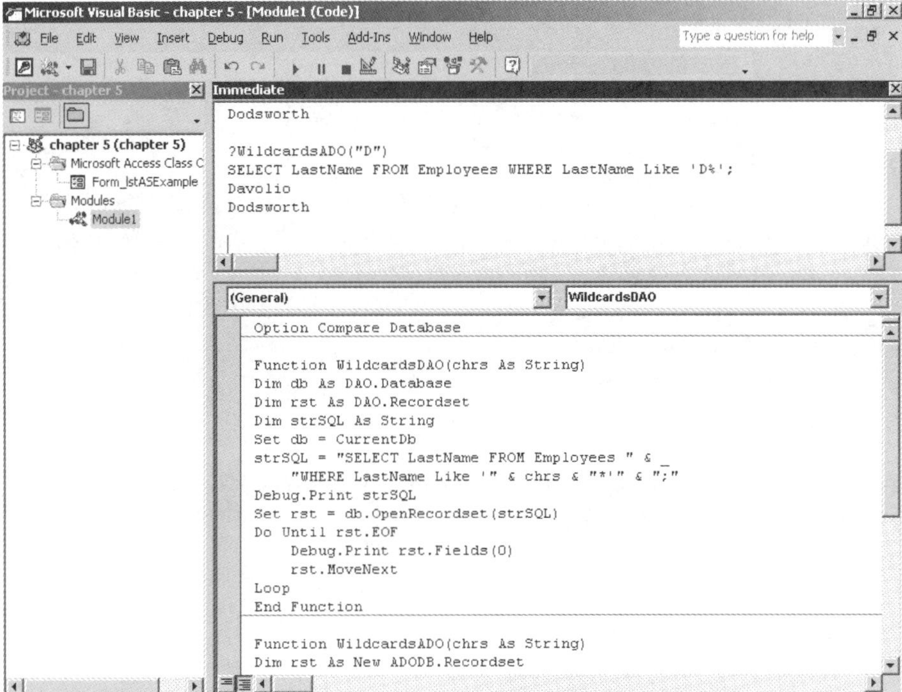

Figure 5-12. The ADO procedure also returns matching records.

5. Try substituting the % character in WildcardADO()'s SQL string with the * character and running the procedure again. The procedure won't produce an error, but neither will it print any matching data. That's because the recordset is empty: ADO doesn't recognize the * wildcard string and tries to match the literal string "D*" and thus returns an empty set.

Sorting the Results of a SELECT Statement

Sorting in a table or query is easy: you just click on Sort Ascending or Sort Descending on the appropriate toolbar. You can bring the same order to the results of an SQL statement including an ORDER BY clause. Specifically, the clause

```
ORDER BY fld ASC
```

sorts in ascending order, and the clause

```
ORDER BY fld DESC
```

sorts in descending order.

You can sort the query's results by any field in the underlying data source; the field does not need to be included in the query's results. To illustrate this flexibility, the statement

```
SELECT CompanyName, ContactName
FROM Customers
ORDER BY ContactName
```

returns CompanyName and ContactName data and sorts the results by the ContactName. In contrast, the statement

```
SELECT CompanyName, ContactName
FROM Customers
ORDER BY Country
```

returns the same data but sorts it by Country, even though that field isn't included in the query's results. Figure 5-13 shows the results of this query. As you can see, the sort order isn't obvious because the Country field isn't included in the results.

> **NOTE** *You can sort on a Text, Numeric, or Date/Time field.*

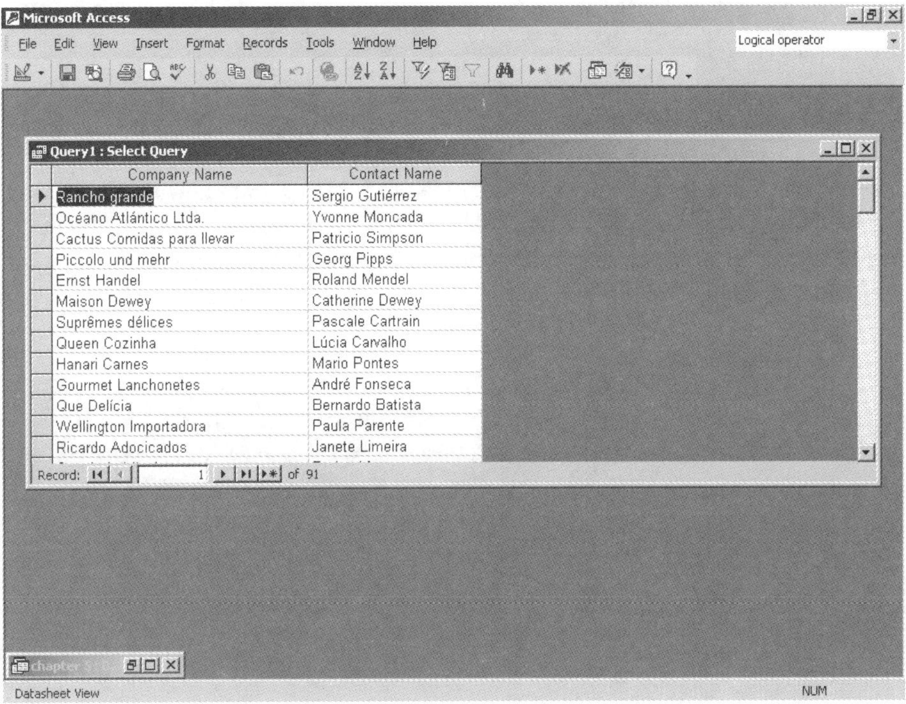

Figure 5-13. The sort order isn't obvious because the sort field isn't included in the results.

None of the above examples include the ASC or DESC argument. That's because ascending order is the default. You can add the ASC argument for readability, but it isn't necessary. To force a descending sort, you must include the DESC argument in the form

```
SELECT CompanyName, ContactName
FROM Customers
ORDER BY Country DESC
```

Specifying the sort order by fieldname is only one way to specify the sort order; SQL also accepts an integer that represents the field's position. Country is the ninth column from the left, so the clause

```
ORDER BY 9 DESC
```

is the equivalent of

```
ORDER BY Country DESC
```

SQL accepts multiple fields in the sort order and sorts the fields in order of precedence from left to right. The clause

```
ORDER BY LastName, FirstName
```

sorts by LastName first, then sorts the FirstName entries that fall within a specific group of LastName entries. For example, Bob Smith, Anne Smith, and Jill Sadler would sort as Jill Sadler, Anne Smith, and Bob Smith. Anne and Bob are sorted by their first names within the Smith group.

> **CAUTION** *Specifying a field's position instead of its name in a sort task has limited value because the value isn't self-documenting, whereas the field name is. We recommend that you use this particular syntax only when the field's position takes precedence over the field's name. We mention the form only because it's available, not because we necessarily recommend it.*

Using SELECT Statements in SQL Objects

Until now, this chapter has been full of rules and simple examples. Now it's time to apply these rules to Access objects. We'll keep the objects themselves as simple as possible so the objects don't distract from the techniques. In this section, we'll show you how to use SQL statements to populate forms, controls, reports, and even enhance lookup fields.

Let's look at a simple form example that uses a WHERE clause to limit a form's recordset to employees in a specific city. The form gets the limiting criteria via a list box, which uses a SELECT statement. To get started, use the AutoForm wizard to create the simple employees form, shown in Figure 5-14 and which we named frmWHEREExample.

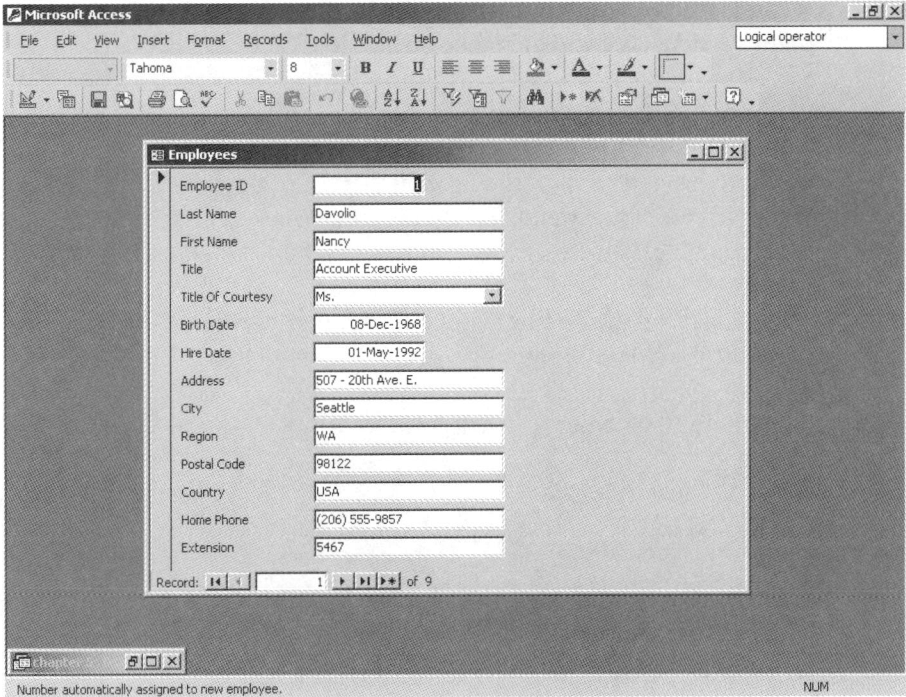

Figure 5-14. This form will filter the form's underlying recordset using the SQL WHERE clause.

To simplify our example, we deleted all the controls below the Extension control. You can use this form to follow our example, or you can use the Employees form in the Northwind database. However, the Northwind version is very busy, and you might find it easier to work with our simpler form. Just remember to update your references accordingly throughout the following instructions:

1. Open frmWHEREExample (or Employees from the Northwind database) in Design view.
2. Open the form's Header section by choosing Form Header/Footer from the View menu.
3. If necessary, click on the Toolbox button to open the Toolbox and add a list box control to the new Header section. The list box should be approximately two inches wide and one inch deep. You'll probably need to enlarge the Header section by pulling the Detail section's title bar down a bit. (Hover the mouse pointer over the top border of the Detail

section's title bar until the mouse pointer converts to the double-arrow pointer. Then, click and drag the title bar down and release.)

4. We moved the label component above the control and entered the string "View Employee:" as the label's Caption property. We also applied the Bold font property to the label. Although none of this step is critical to the success of the overall technique, it does make the control more readable.

5. Double-click on the list box to open the Properties window and name the control lstWHEREExample.

6. Enter the SQL statement

   ```
   SELECT DISTINCT LastName
   FROM Employees
   ```

   as the control's Row Source property. The DISTINCT predicate limits the list to unique values (which isn't necessary in this case, but should be included in case that should change: you could acquire a new employee that shares the same last name as a current employee). To learn more about the DISTINCT predicate, read the section "Limiting Records with Predicates" in Chapter 4.

7. Next, click on the Code button on the Form Design toolbar to open the VBE to your form's module.

8. Enter the event procedure in Listing 5-3, as shown in Figure 5-15.

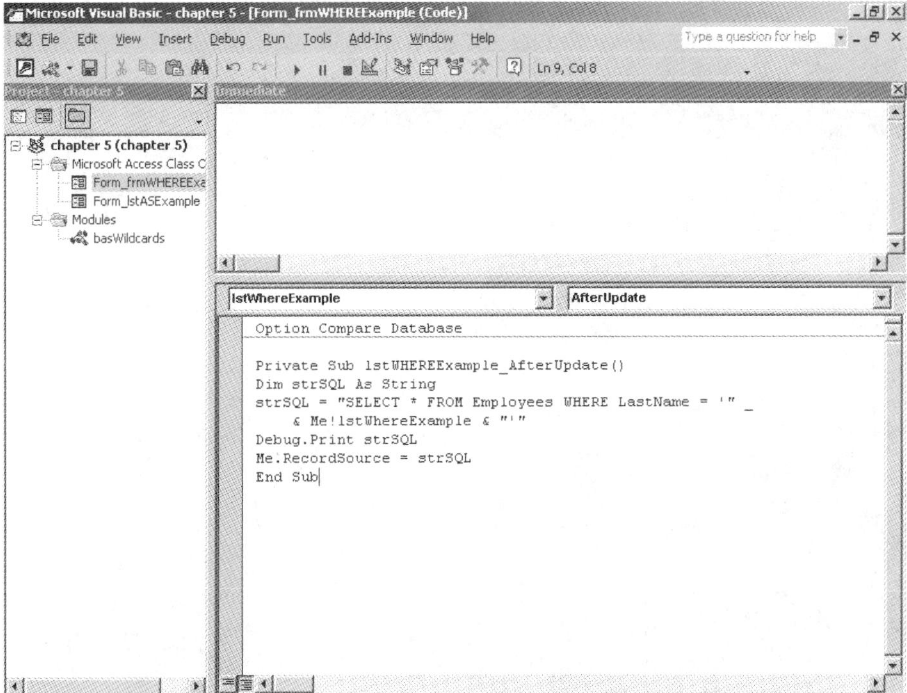

Figure 5-15. The AfterUpdate procedure filters the form's recordset.

9. Click on the View Microsoft Access button on the VBE's standard toolbar or click on the appropriate icon on the Windows taskbar to return to the employees form.

10. Click on the View button to open the form in Form view.

11. Select any employee in the list box and watch the form's Detail section update its contents. Figure 5-16 shows the result of clicking on Fuller, and the navigational toolbar displays the number of records in the filtered set (1).

12. Be sure to save your changes before closing frmWHEREExample. (We named our modified form frmWHEREExampleComplete.)

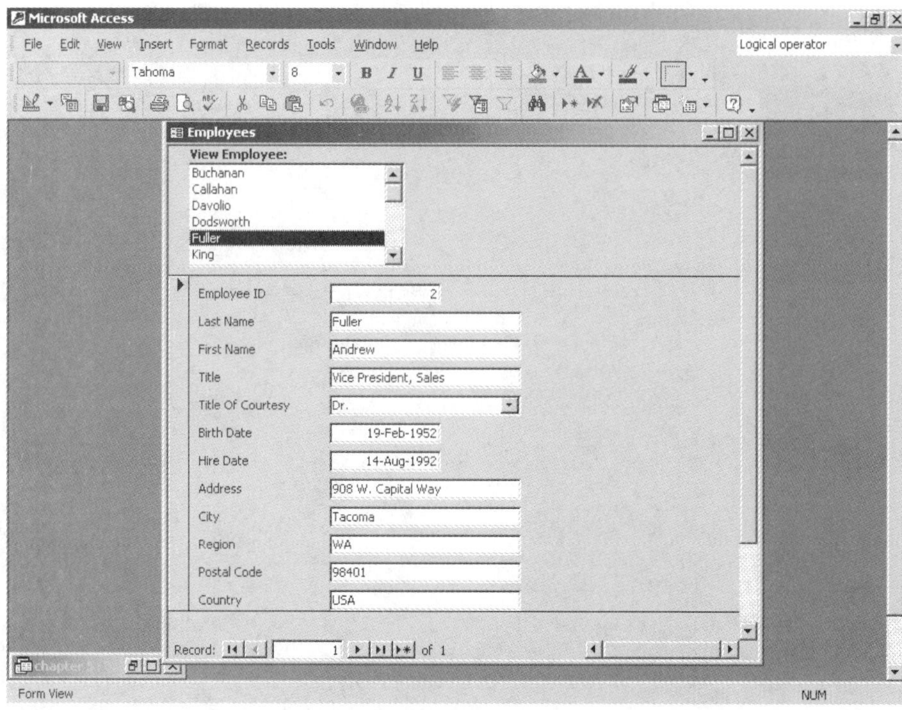

Figure 5-16. The form displays the employee information for Fuller.

Listing 5-3. AfterUpdate Event Procedure

```
Private Sub lstWHEREExample_AfterUpdate()
Dim strSQL As String
strSQL = "SELECT * FROM Employees WHERE LastName = '" _
    & Me!lstWHEREExample & "'"
Debug.Print strSQL
Me.RecordSource = strSQL
End Sub
```

Are you wondering how the form works? Clicking on an item in lstWHEREExample (the list box you added to the form's header) triggers that control's After Update event. After declaring the strSQL variable, the second line in the control's event procedure builds the SELECT SQL statement, including the concatenated WHERE criteria—the selected item in the list box. The `Debug.Print` statement is a debugging shortcut that you can learn about in the "Debugging Tricks" section of Chapter 2. The final statement replaces the form's current Record Source property with the SQL SELECT statement, which repopulates the form with the appropriate records. In this case, that's any record in which the LastName field contains the same string as the selected item in the list box (Fuller). Keep in mind that the control equals the contents of the bound column, and not necessarily the selected item. This will become more obvious in the subsequent examples.

Be Careful How You Use DISTINCT

In step 6 of the exercise in the last example, you used the SQL statement

```
SELECT DISTINCT LastName
FROM Employees
```

to populate the list box with a unique list of last names from the Employees table. Using DISTINCT can get you into trouble if you don't understand how it works. You must remember that the DISTINCT predicate works with all the fields listed, not just the one that immediately follows the keyword. Consequently, adding fields to the SELECT clause can affect the way in which SQL applies the DISTINCT predicate. (For basic information on the DISTINCT predicate, read "Limiting Records with Predicates" in Chapter 4.)

Let's find out what happens when we duplicate a last name in the Employees table. To do so, just open the Employees table and enter "Fuller" and "Mandy" as the last and first name entries, respectively, of a new record. (You won't need any other data for our example.) Close the table and open frmWHEREExample (the one you created in the last section). The list still displays just one item for Fuller. However, this time, when you select Fuller from the list, the form displays a filtered set of two records, as shown in Figure 5-17: one for Andrew and one for Mandy. To see Mandy's record, just click on the Next record button on the navigational toolbar.

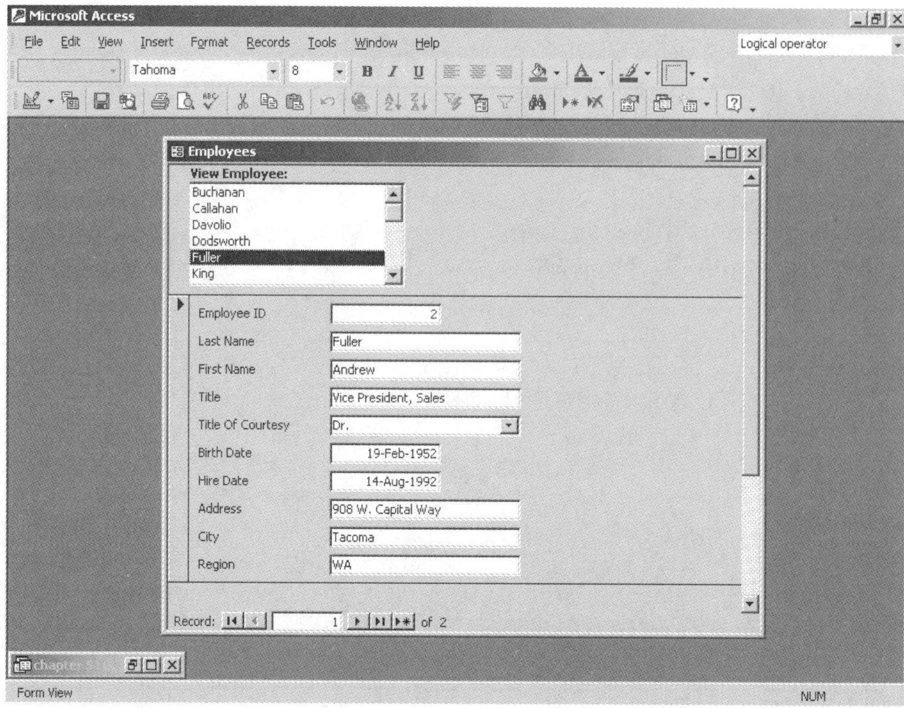

Figure 5-17. The form filters the underlying records and displays two records: one for Andrew and one for Mandy.

There's an alternative to this approach: add the first name to the control's list. Remember, Jet applies the DISTINCT predicate to all the fields, which means SQL will eliminate only those records in which the first name and the last name are both duplicated. To make this modification:

1. Work with the frmWHEREExample (or frmWHEREExampleComplete) or copy it and work with the copy. Our solution is presented in frmWHEREExampleDistinct.

2. Open the form in Design view and double-click on lstWHEREExample (the list box in the Header section). Click on the Builder button to the right of the Row Source property to open the SQL Statement: Query Builder. The builder already has the current SQL statement displayed in graphic terms. Add the FirstName field to the design grid, as shown in Figure 5-18. Close the builder and save the changes when prompted.

NOTE *The DISTINCT clause is already part of the SQL statement, and Jet retains it when you add the FirstName field to the design grid.*

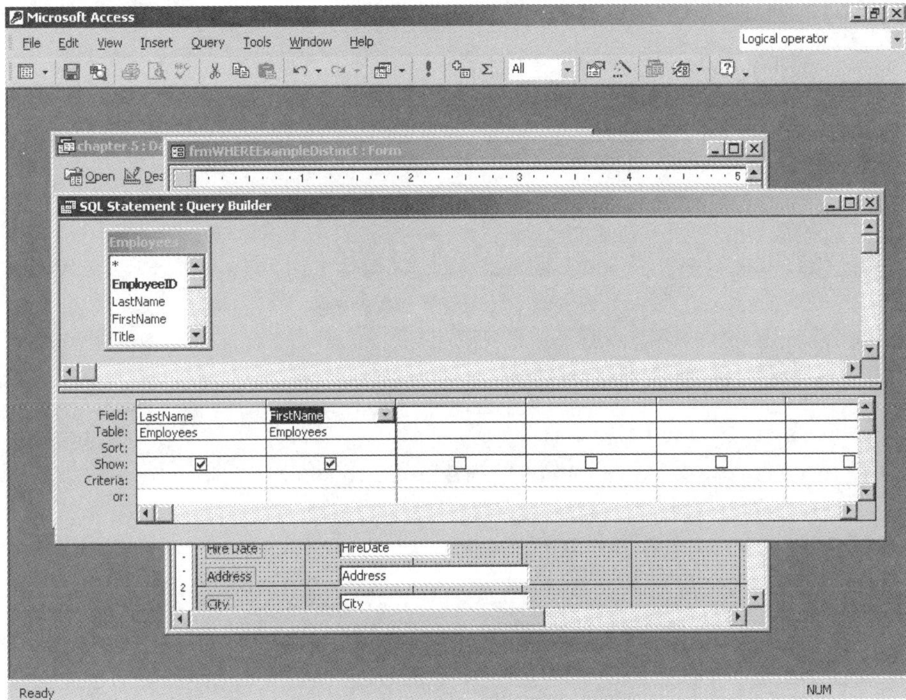

Figure 5-18. Modify the query in the Query Builder.

3. Change the Column Count property to 2.

4. Click on the View button to see the modified control, shown in Figure 5-19 in Form view. The control now displays an item for both Andrew and Mandy.

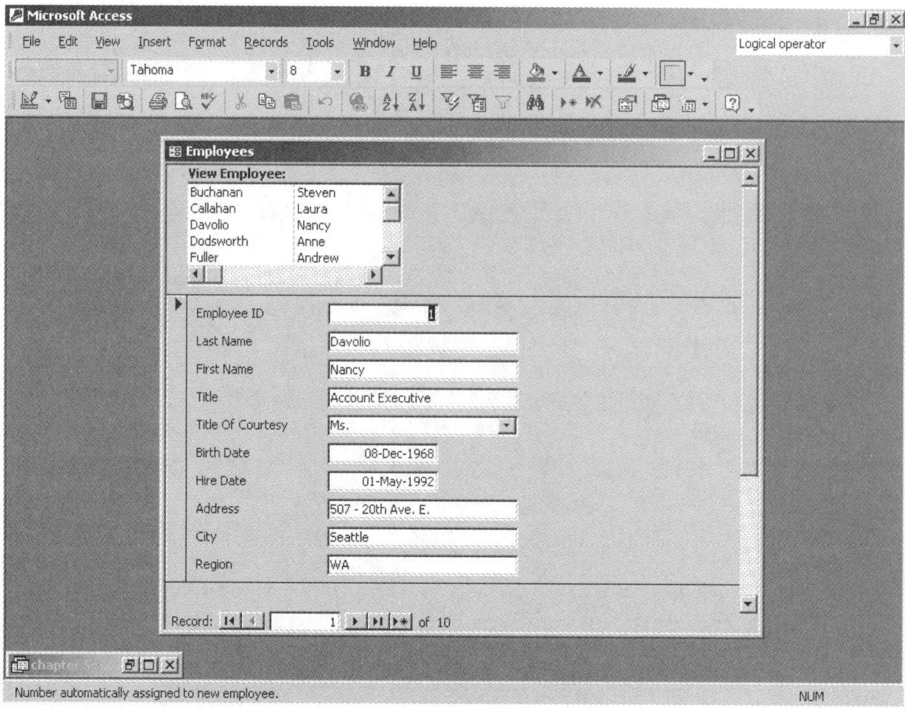

Figure 5-19. Andrew and Mandy Fuller are both listed.

> **TIP** *You don't have to switch back and forth between Design and Form view because you can update properties in Form view. In Design view, make sure the form's Allow Design Changes property is set to All Views. Then, leave the Properties window open when you return to Form view. Make changes and watch the form update automatically.*

The changes you just made update only the display of the control. The procedure in Listing 5-3 still filters the underlying recordset only by the contents of the LastName field. Replace the control's AfterUpdate event procedure with the one in Listing 5-4. This procedure uses both names to filter the underlying recordset.

Listing 5-4. lstWHEREExample_AfterUpdate

```
Private Sub lstWHEREExample_AfterUpdate()
  Dim strSQL As String
  Dim strLast As String
  Dim strFirst As String
  Dim strCriteria As String
  strLast = Me!lstWhereExample.Column(0)
  strFirst = Me!lstWhereExample.Column(1)
  strCriteria = "LastName = '" & strLast & "" _
    & " AND FirstName = '" & strfirst & "'"
  strSQL = "SELECT * FROM Employees WHERE " & strCriteria
  Debug.Print strSQL
  Me.RecordSource = strSQL
End Sub
```

Add a Little Concatenation

Although the list box in the last example is functional, we can certainly make it better by concatenating the last and first names into a format that's more familiar: first name, space character, and then last name. To make this change:

1. Return the form to Design view and double-click on lstWHEREExampleDistinct, or work directly with the Properties window in Form view. (We're working with a copy of frmWHEREExampleDistinct that we named frmWHEREExampleConcatenation.)

2. Click on the Builder button to the right of the Row Source property to open the Query Builder.

3. Enter the expression

   ```
   Name: FirstName & " " & LastName
   ```

   in the third Field cell, as shown in Figure 5-20. (Access will add the brackets.)

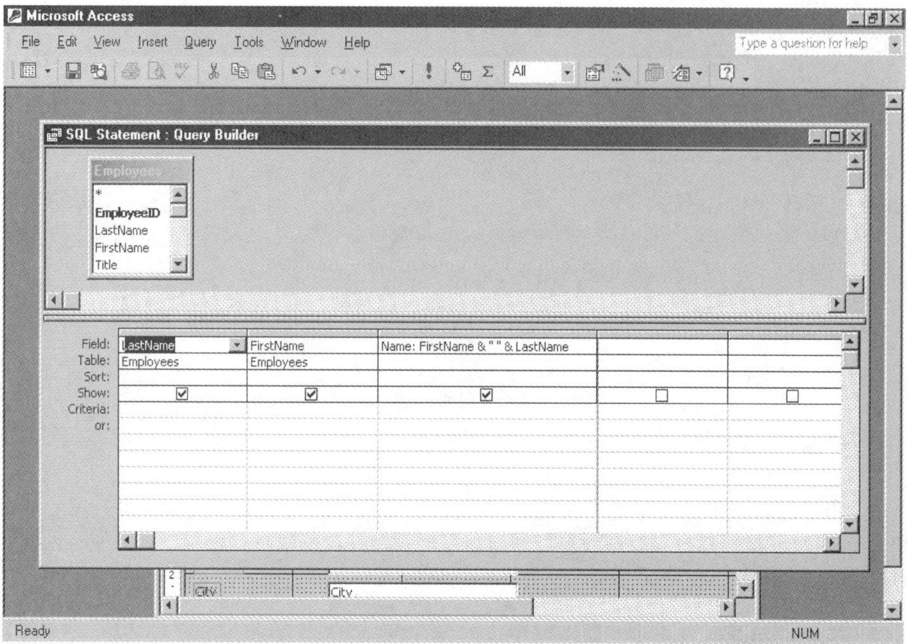

Figure 5-20. The Name expression concatenates the first and last name values.

4. Close the builder and save your changes.

5. Change the Column Count property to 3 and reset the Column Widths property to 0";0";1".

6. If you're working in Design view, click on the View button to return to Form view. The modified control (shown in Figure 5-21) displays the names in a more readable format and displays an item for Andrew and Mandy. The DISTINCT predicate is still hard at work. If you enter a second record for Mandy Fuller, the control will display only one.

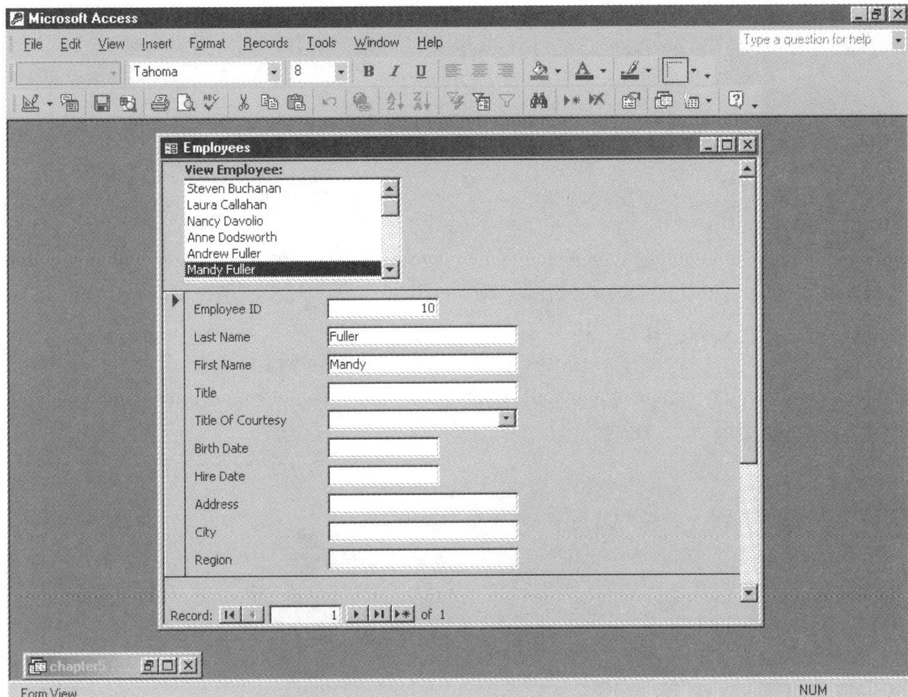

Figure 5-21. Now the names are listed by first names and then last names.

ORDER BY in the Sort

Although not exhibited by our current example, you could be confronted with one last problem: the DISTINCT predicate forces a sort—from left to right. That's because Jet assigns a temporary (internal) index to help compare field entries to prevent duplicates. The first column just happens to be bound to the LastName field, so the resulting list is sorted in a familiar manner. But this might not always be the case. Fortunately, you can add an ORDER BY clause to sort the resulting list by any field. For instance, the following statement would sort the list by the LastName and then the FirstName field:

```
SELECT DISTINCT LastName, FirstName, FirstName & " " & LastName AS Name
FROM Employees
ORDER BY LastName, FirstName
```

If you make this change to the control's Row Source property, you won't see any change. That's because the control currently sorts Arthur Fuller before Mandy Fuller as a result of the DISTINCT predicate's forced sort in search of duplicates. Not every SQL statement will use the DISTINCT predicate, and then you'll need the ORDER BY clause for sorting.

Updateable Queries

Sometimes you retrieve data to view or analyze what's there. Often, you'll want to modify that data in some way. For instance, you may need to change a client's address and phone number or update an employee's base salary. Most of the time, you'll simply open a bound form, find the appropriate record, and update the data. Have you ever tried to update data and received the error message "This recordset is not updateable"? If you expected Access to accept the change, this message may present a mystery.

> **NOTE** *Don't confuse the term* updateable query *with the SQL UPDATE statement or the Access Action Update query. Right now, we're mainly concerned with Select queries that retrieve data and save subsequent changes to that data to the data source.*

When you use a query to present data that you then plan to update, you need to follow specific rules. The query may still reject updates due to incorrect data types or validation rules. These rules apply to both SELECT statements and fixed Select queries.

- A query based on a single table is updateable, provided that:

  The query contains no aggregate functions or refers to a query that contains an aggregate function.

  The query's Unique Values property is set to No.

  The query doesn't include a GROUP BY clause.

- A query based on multiple tables with one-to-one relationships is updateable provided that the three conditions specified above are also met.

- A query based on more than one table or query with a valid join. When this arrangement results in a one-to-many relationship, you can change data on either side as long as you don't violate referential integrity constraints, and provided that the three conditions specified above are also met.

Updating data in a one-to-many relationship is generally allowed, but you may run into a problem now and again. When this happens, you can try the following suggestions:

- If you can't update the foreign key, enable cascading updates between the related tables.
- If a new record fails to display the foreign key value in Datasheet view, add the foreign key field to the query.
- If you can't edit the foreign key value after updating data in the one table, save the record. Then, you should be able to edit data in the many table.

NOTE *There are two types of aggregate functions: domain aggregates and SQL aggregates. Domain aggregates are used by VBA, and SQL aggregates are used in an SQL statement. Although they aren't interchangeable, you can use both in a calculated control. You'll run into both with updateable queries as fixed queries accept domain aggregates, and, of course, you'll use SQL aggregates in SQL statements. To learn more about SQL aggregates, read Chapter 7 ("Grouping and Summarizing Data").*

You can read more about controlling referential integrity and constraints using SQL in Chapter 9 ("Manipulating Relationships and Indexes").

The following queries are not updateable:

- Crosstab, SQL Pass-Through, and Union queries
- Multitable queries based on three or more tables among which there is a many-to-one-to-many relationship.
- Totals view

Even though a query may meet all the conditions and should be updateable, it may reject changes. Other factors beyond the updateable query must be considered. First, you must have permission to update the underlying data source. Similarly, a table may be read-only. If this is the case, Access won't let you update the data. You'll need to consult your network administrator to resolve these two issues. A third reason involves networked applications: a user may have a record locked, temporarily. Generally, you can resume your update as soon as the record is unlocked.

Updateable Clues

You can quickly tell with a glance whether a query is updateable. Simply open the query in Query Datasheet view, and look for a blank row at the bottom of the datasheet. If there's no blank row, it's not an updateable query—at least, you can insert new records—but you may be dealing with a non-updateable query. If you're working with a bound form, check the navigational toolbar at the bottom of the form. If the New Record button is disabled, you may not be working with an updateable query. Similarly, if the New Record command is disabled, you may be dealing with a query that can't be updated. To check, pull down the Edit menu, and choose Go To.

A disabled button or menu command doesn't automatically indicate that the query isn't updateable. Both can be disabled in other ways. The query may be updateable, but other settings may prevent you from altering the underlying data.

Updateable Queries in an Access Project or Data Access Page

If you're working in an Access Project or with a Data Access Page, the rules are a little different:

- A query based on a single table or join must have a primary key constraint, unique constraint, or a unique index.
- A view or stored procedure that contains a join is read-only.
- A query that contains a one-to-many relationship accepts changes only to the many side.

SELECT in Lookup Fields

A lookup task is one that refers to a field or table of data and returns a value based on coordinates that refer to specific positions or values within that field or table. A lookup task might return the third value from the fourth row in a particular table. Or, it might match a value in one field and return the corresponding value in the field immediately to the right.

Lookup fields display a value other than the value that they store. For instance, the field may display an employee's name, but actually store that employee's primary key value. Those primary key values may be critical to normalization, but they're not much help to most of us when we're viewing data. The employee's name means something to you, whereas that employee's primary key value is just a number. You could memorize all the primary key values, but that's not an efficient use of your time or abilities.

You can create a lookup field at the table level and bound controls will inherit the lookup field's properties. This is the real benefit of the feature. However, some developers avoid using lookup fields because of the confusion they can cause for the user who's unfamiliar with the feature. You may choose not to use the feature, but you should know that it exists and how to spot it in action; doing so can save you a lot of troubleshooting and aggravation if you should encounter them.

> *". . . people think Access lookup fields are somehow implemented at the database engine level. They're not. They're implemented at the Access level, with user-defined properties of the field that specify the lookup table and other lookup properties. As far as Jet (or, in Access 2002, SQL Server) is concerned, there is absolutely no difference between a lookup field and another field of the same basic data type. All the database engines do with the user-defined properties is store them.*
>
> *Access itself uses the lookup information in datasheets to display the other side of the lookup (but you don't let your users get to raw datasheets, right?) and on forms and reports to come up with the default properties of controls based on the field. So as far as I'm concerned, lookup fields are just a device to enable faster and more consistent GUI design, and I don't see anything wrong with them."*
>
> Mike Gunderloy, Lark Group, Inc., (`http://www.larkfarm.com`)

At this point, you might be wondering just why lookup fields are in a chapter about SQL SELECT. Lookup fields depend on SQL SELECT to display values other than the value that the field actually stores. Now, let's go explore a lookup field in the Products table in the Northwind sample database. The first field, OrderID, is the table's primary key field and the result of an AutoNumber data type. The fourth field, Category, identifies the product by its category. Notice that the field is actually a drop-down text box, as shown in Figure 5-22.

> **NOTE** *If you enter or modify data in Datasheet view, you can use the lookup field's drop-down list to enter data instead of typing the value yourself. Typically, entering and modifying data at the table level is frowned upon. Most developers tend to deny table-level access to users, and instead guide users to enter and modify data via data entry forms. Because controls inherit lookup field properties, a control bound to a lookup field will include a drop-down list that displays the appropriate values. This is one argument for using lookup fields: avoiding the development work involved in creating a comparable combo or list box in a data entry form. Access does the work automatically.*

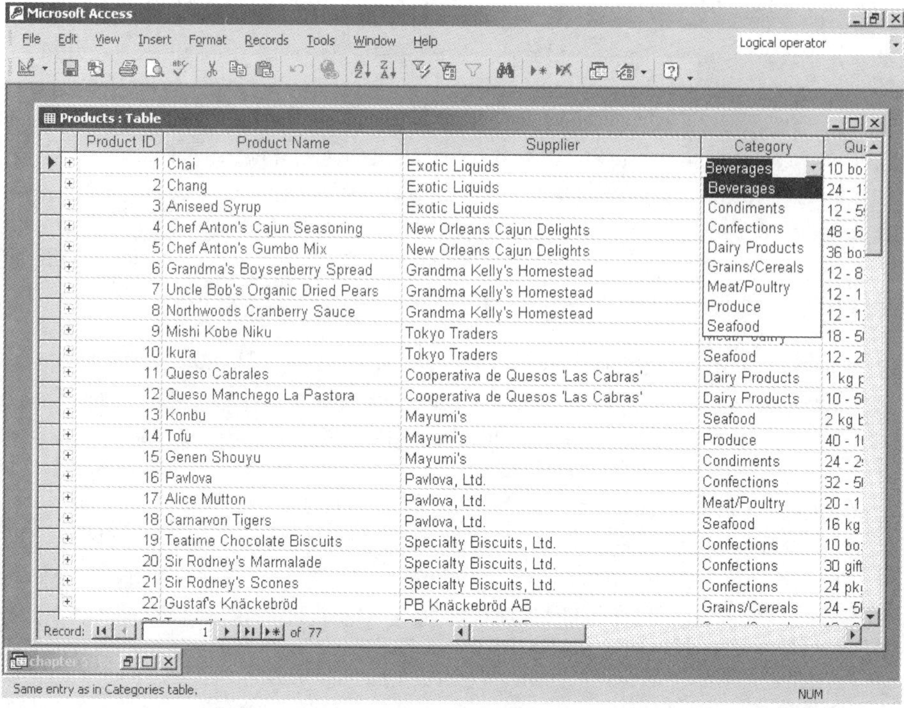

Figure 5-22. Select the appropriate customer from the field's drop-down list.

You might think that the Category field actually stores the category's name (description), but it doesn't, and your first clue is the drop-down list. When you encounter a drop-down list at the table level, it's an indication that the field is really a lookup field. Open the table in Design view (click on the View button on the Table Datasheet toolbar) and select the CategoryID field, as shown in Figure 5-23. (The CategoryID and Category fields are one and the same. The Caption property takes precedent in Datasheet view.) Although the Category field displays text, the field is obviously a numeric field. That's your second clue that you're dealing with a lookup field.

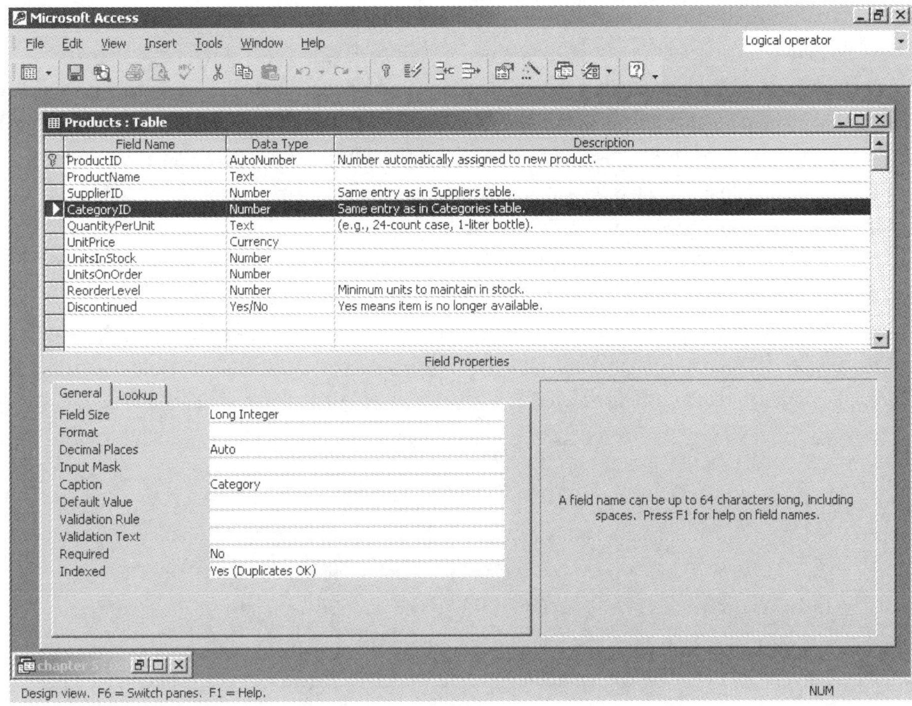

Figure 5-23. The Category field is actually a numeric field.

To learn more about the field's lookup properties, click on the Lookup tab in the Field Properties pane. The Row Source property contains a SELECT statement, which defines the content's of the field's drop-down list. Specifically, the CategoryID field's SELECT statement is

```
SELECT Categories.CategoryID, Categories.CategoryName
FROM Categories
ORDER BY Categories.CategoryName;
```

As a result of this statement, the field displays a unique list of CategoryID and CategoryName values from the Categories table, and sorts both lists by the CategoryName values. But the field displays only the CategoryName values. (See Figure 5-24.) The DISTINCT predicate isn't necessary because CategoryID is a primary key value, and primary key values must be unique.

> **NOTE** *You can review the lookup field's entire Row Source property (the SQL statement above) in the Zoom window by selecting the Row Source field and then pressing* `Shift+F2`.

Take a look at the remaining properties. The Column Count property is 2, but the Column Widths property is 0" This means that the first column—CategoryID—is hidden, which explains the single column in the drop-down list. But how do you explain the field's data type and the fact that it stores a number and not the text shown in the drop-down list? The Bound Column's property is 1, which means that the control is bound to the first column, the CategoryID column (a Numeric field), and not the values displayed in the drop-down list.

Lookup controls are used throughout Access applications: combo and list boxes are abundant. Lookup fields simply extend that functionality to the table level. Some developers may disapprove of the feature, but users lacking the expertise to create multicolumn list and combo boxes can rely on their usefulness by creating them at the table level in the guise of lookup fields.

Creating a Lookup Field

Access includes a wizard that can create lookup fields quickly and easily. You can also create them yourself by simply clicking the Lookup tab and entering the appropriate SELECT statement and setting the remaining properties. If you're really good at SQL, you may find the manual method quicker than the wizard. The wizard creates two types of lists:

- *Lookup list*: a list based on existing values in a table or query
- *Value list*: a fixed list that you enter

Northwind tables are full of lookup fields, which means that we can't show you how to create one without deleting one first, because there are no lookup field candidates that aren't already lookup fields. For that reason, let's delete the CategoryID lookup field properties in the Products table. To do so:

1. Open the Products table in Design view, select the CategoryID field, and then click on the Lookup tab in the Field Properties pane.
2. Select Text Box from the Display Control field's drop-down list. The affected field will no longer display the items in the drop-down list as each record's entry, but instead will display the stored value, as determined by the bound control.
3. View the table in Datasheet view by clicking the View button on the Table Design toolbar and saving the change you just made to the table. As you can see in Figure 5-24, the field displays the actual CategoryID values, and not the category's corresponding name or description.

4. You must delete the relationship between the two fields before you can run the Lookup wizard. Close the Products table and then click on the Relationships button on the Database toolbar. Select the join line between Products and Categories and press Delete. Click on the Yes button in the resulting confirmation message. Close the Relationships window and save the change.

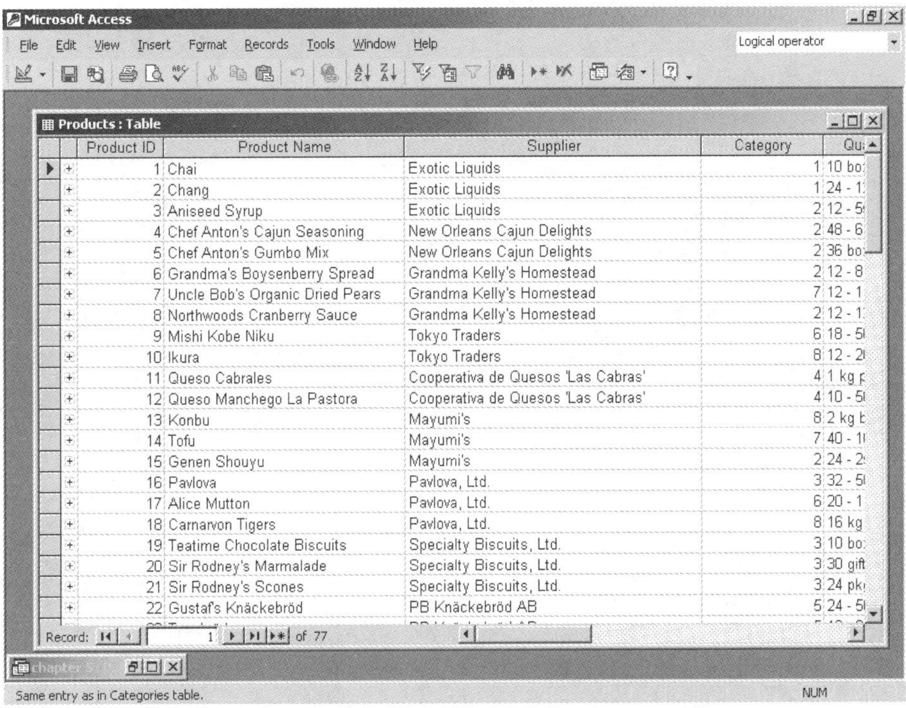

Product ID	Product Name	Supplier	Category
1	Chai	Exotic Liquids	1
2	Chang	Exotic Liquids	1
3	Aniseed Syrup	Exotic Liquids	2
4	Chef Anton's Cajun Seasoning	New Orleans Cajun Delights	2
5	Chef Anton's Gumbo Mix	New Orleans Cajun Delights	2
6	Grandma's Boysenberry Spread	Grandma Kelly's Homestead	2
7	Uncle Bob's Organic Dried Pears	Grandma Kelly's Homestead	7
8	Northwoods Cranberry Sauce	Grandma Kelly's Homestead	2
9	Mishi Kobe Niku	Tokyo Traders	6
10	Ikura	Tokyo Traders	8
11	Queso Cabrales	Cooperativa de Quesos 'Las Cabras'	4
12	Queso Manchego La Pastora	Cooperativa de Quesos 'Las Cabras'	4
13	Konbu	Mayumi's	8
14	Tofu	Mayumi's	7
15	Genen Shouyu	Mayumi's	2
16	Pavlova	Pavlova, Ltd.	3
17	Alice Mutton	Pavlova, Ltd.	6
18	Carnarvon Tigers	Pavlova, Ltd.	8
19	Teatime Chocolate Biscuits	Specialty Biscuits, Ltd.	3
20	Sir Rodney's Marmalade	Specialty Biscuits, Ltd.	3
21	Sir Rodney's Scones	Specialty Biscuits, Ltd.	3
22	Gustaf's Knäckebröd	PB Knäckebröd AB	5

Figure 5-24. The CategoryID field now displays the actual stored values: the CategoryID values.

Now, we're ready to re-create the lookup field. To execute the Lookup wizard:

1. Open the Products table in Design view.

2. Open the CategoryID field's Data Type drop-down list, and select Lookup Wizard (the last item on the list).

3. Select the "I want the lookup column to look up the values in a table or query" option, and click on Next. When you want to create a value list, you'll select the "I will type in the values that I want" option. (The wizard uses the term *lookup column,* whereas we use the term *lookup field.*)

4. In the next window, select the table or query that contains the lookup values. In the case of our example, select Categories, as shown in Figure 5-25. To choose a query, be sure to select the Queries option in the View section, or click on the Both option to see both tables and queries in the same list. Click on Next to continue.

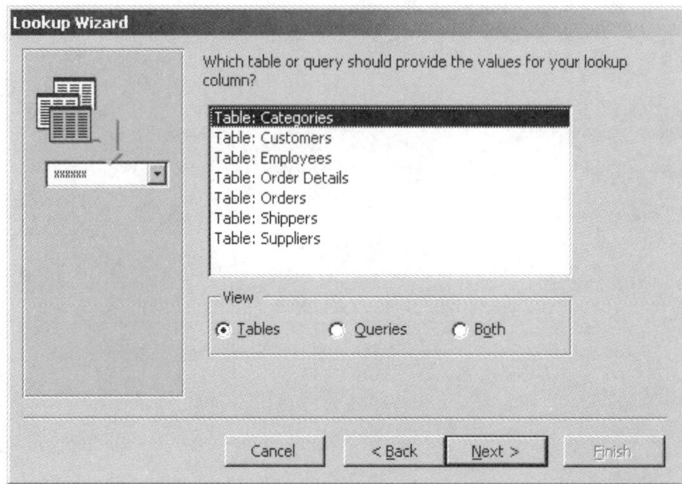

Figure 5-25. Choose the Categories table.

5. Next, select the actual fields that contain the lookup values. We've selected CategoryID and CategoryName, as shown in Figure 5-26. To move a field from the Available Fields control to the Selected Fields control, simply double-click on it in the Available Fields control. Or, select the field and click on the > button. Normally, the Available Fields control lists all of the fields in the table or query. Because a lookup field already exists (but is currently disabled), the wizard defaults to the existing properties, but this behavior doesn't create a problem for our example. Click on Next to continue.

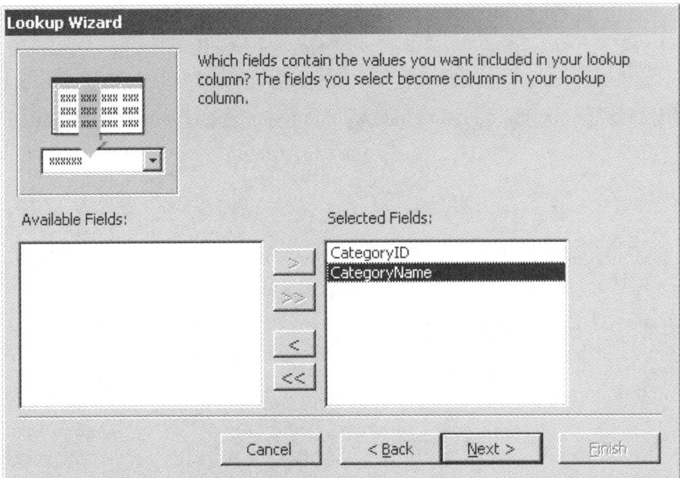

Figure 5-26. Add CategoryID and CategoryName to the Selected Fields control.

6. The wizard will display the lookup field's items, as shown in Figure 5-27. As you can see, the wizard hides the primary key field by default. If you'd rather display the primary key values, simply uncheck the Hide Key Column option. We recommend that you don't do this unless you have specific reasons for displaying the primary key field. When you're ready to continue, click on Next.

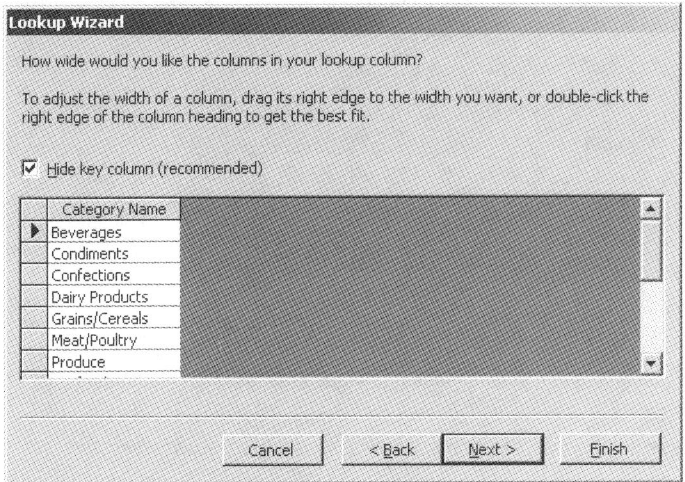

Figure 5-27. The wizard displays the lookup values.

7. In the final window, enter a name for the lookup field, or accept the wizard's default (which is what we chose) and click on Finish.

8. Click on Yes to save the table. The results are the same as the original lookup field. We didn't change any properties; we just showed you how to create the field.

> **CAUTION** *If you find it necessary to reestablish a relationship to build a lookup field, be sure to reset the referential integrity settings because the wizard won't do so. The wizard sets only the basic relationship.*

You could enter the list of categories yourself and forego the table altogether, and, in this next example, we'll show you how to do so. However, we don't advocate this approach. We're simply using the example to show you how to create a value list; we're not suggesting that you use this technique to rid your application of lookup tables. In fact, we recommend that you don't. Lookup tables are a vital resource in many applications, and, in most cases, the application refers to these values for a number of reasons. We suggest that you use a value list (in lieu of a table) only when you're certain that you will not need the values for any other purpose, and even then we're not sure it's a great idea. Simply put, we don't recommend value lists, but we'll show you how to create one:

1. Refer to the exercise just before the last to disable the existing lookup field on the CategoryID field in the Products table.

2. Open the CategoryID field's Data Type drop-down list, and select Lookup Wizard (the last item on the list).

3. Select the "I will type in the values that I want" option, and click on Next.

4. In the resulting window, change the 1 to 2 in the Number of Columns control.

5. Then, enter the CategoryID values and descriptions listed in Table 5-3. Be sure to press the Tab key between each entry. (Pressing Enter displays the next window.) When the list is complete, click on Next.

Table 5-3. Value List

CATEGORYID	CATEGORYNAME
1	Beverage
2	Condiments
3	Confections
4	Dairy products
5	Grains/cereals
6	Meat/poultry
7	Produce
8	Seafood

6. Select Col1 from the Available Fields list to identify the field that contains the values you want the field to actually store. Click on Next.

7. In the final window, enter a name for the lookup field, or accept the wizard's default (which is what we chose) and click on Finish.

8. Click on Yes to save the table. The results are the same as the original lookup field. We didn't change any properties; we just showed you how to create the field.

This time, examine the Lookup properties carefully, because you'll notice a number of differences. First, the Row Source property is a value list. Specifically, the Row Source property is

```
1;"Beverages";2;"Condiments";3;"Confections";4;"DairyProducts";
  5;"Grains/Cereals";5;"Meat/Poultry";6;"Produce";7;"Seafood"
```

Before, this property was a SELECT statement. In addition, the Column Widths property is 1";1", which means the field will display both lists, not just one.

Enhancing a Lookup Field

Lookup fields display descriptive text instead of a field's underlying value. For instance, a field may store a unique identifying value, say an employee number, but the field displays the employee's name. Access uses SQL statements to display the contents of a lookup field, which has a Row Source property just like a combo or list box control. Simply open a table that contains a lookup field in Design view, select the field in question, and then click on the Lookup tab in the Field Properties pane. For instance, the EmployeeID field in the Orders table contains the following SQL statement as its Row Source property:

```
SELECT DISTINCTROW Employees.EmployeeID, [LastName] & ", " & [FirstName] AS
Name
FROM Employees
ORDER BY Employees.LastName, Employees.FirstName;
```

The `[LastName] & ", " & [FirstName] AS Name` is similar to our last example and displays the first and last name. The difference is that this component displays the last name first. In addition, the ORDER BY clause sorts by both the LastName and the FirstName fields.

If, however, you added Mandy Fuller to the Employees table twice, as we discussed in the last section, the lookup field will now display two items for "Fuller, Mandy". If you really have two employees by that name, that's probably what you'll want, but you'd also want to display additional information to distinguish one from another. If you change the Column Widths properties to display both the EmployeeID and the concatenated results of the above expression, the field also displays the EmployeeID field. This may or may not matter. If it does, you could rearrange the order of the fields, adjust the Bound Column property (to follow the new position of the EmployeeID field), and reset the Column Widths property, so that the field displays both columns. The resulting SQL statement might resemble the following:

```
SELECT DISTINCTROW [LastName] & ", " & [FirstName] AS Name,
  [Employees].[EmployeeID]
FROM Employees
ORDER BY [Employees].[LastName], [Employees].[FirstName];
```

Or, you might prefer to leave the field order alone and add the ReportsTo column to the display. You can modify a lookup field's SQL statement to enhance the display in any number of ways. The important thing to remember is to make sure that the Bound Column always matches the underlying value you want to store.

Keep in mind that any change you make to a lookup field will be inherited by any bound controls.

CHAPTER 6

Modifying Data

Using Jet SQL's Data Manipulation Language to Change Existing Data

SELECT QUERIES THAT ARE BUILT in the Query Design window have equivalent SQL statements, which you can use to populate controls, forms, and reports via object properties and VBA code. Action queries also have equivalent SQL statements, which you'll usually combine with VBA or ADO (or DAO) to run action queries programmatically.

> **NOTE** *Chapter 2 ("An Introduction to Using Jet SQL in Access") has two sections on executing SQL statements programmatically: "Executing SQL with VBA" and "Using the Execute Method."*

Modifying data is a routine part of most data entry tasks. You'll usually work via a data entry form that's been populated with an updateable recordset. (To learn about updateable recordsets, read "Updateable Queries" in Chapter 5.) That recordset may be the result of a bound table, query, or even a SELECT statement, which you learned about in Chapter 5. You could open each record and modify it individually, but doing so wouldn't be efficient if there's a better alternative. When dealing with large groups of records, one of the Action queries listed in Table 6-1 might be a better solution.

Table 6-1. Action Queries

SQL	DESCRIPTION	ACCESS EQUIVALENT	RECORDSET EQUIVALENT
UPDATE SET	Modifies existing data	Update query	Edit
DELETE:	Deletes records	Delete query	Delete
INSERT INTO	Appends records into an existing table	Append query	AddNew
SELECT INTO	Copies an existing table's structure and/or data to a new table	Make-Table query	NA

TIP *You can't undo an Action query, whether you're working through the SQL window or the Query Design window. Before running such a query, run it as a Select query and review the results. If those results aren't what you expected, you can adjust the query and try again. Repeat this step as many times as necessary to make sure the query affects just the right records in just the way you intend. We also recommend that you create a backup of a table before running an update query against it. Thus, you can always revert to the original (backup) if the query returns unexpected results.*

In addition, SQL queries aren't the only way to complete these updating tasks. You can also use Recordset objects, which many people find easier to use. However, in most cases, they are slower than an equivalent query.

Almost always, an SQL DML statement (an Action query in this case) is more efficient than looping through the records in an ADO Recordset object. Depending on the amount of data you're updating, a Recordset construct can take much longer to complete as the equivalent SQL statement. This won't always be the case, but we recommend that—whenever you're considering using a recordset to update, insert, or delete data—that you compare your recordset solution to its equivalent SQL statement. We think that the SQL statement will outperform a Recordset object almost all of the time.

Changing Existing Data with UPDATE

Updating tasks (modifying existing data) are common and probably best handled via data entry forms. After displaying the appropriate record, you make changes as necessary and save those changes. You might make just one change, or you might change many records within the same session. However, the changes would most likely be unique to each record: adding information you've just acquired, correcting mistakes, and updating data that has changed.

> **NOTE** *To avoid actually changing the data in your copy of Northwinds, we suggest you make a copy of each table and execute each example against the copy. Or, import the tables into a blank database and confine your examples to the imported tables.*

> **CAUTION** *We also recommend that you always create a backup copy of any table you're about to alter with an Action query* before *you run the SQL statement. In this way, you can always return to the contents of the original table if the query has unexpected or unwanted results.*

Occasionally, you may need to make the same modification to a group of records. For instance, the United States Post Office might add a new ZIP code to a region that affects a number of your employees or customers. Or, management might decide to change a particular employee classification title. The reasons for updating a group of records are as unique as your application. When you need to make the same modification to multiple records, don't change each individual record when an SQL UPDATE statement will do the work for you.

The SQL UPDATE statement uses the following syntax:

```
UPDATE datasource
SET col = expression;
```

where *datasource* identifies the table (or query) that contains the data you're updating, *col* identifies the field affected, and *expression* evaluates to the new entry. For instance, the simple statement

```
UPDATE Products
SET UnitPrice = UnitPrice + (UnitPrice * .01)
```

increases the UnitPrice of each item in the Products table by one percent.

> **CAUTION** *You can't use a subquery in a SET clause. Jet doesn't support this construct.*

The simple form shown in Figure 6-1 asks for a little information from you and then builds the appropriate SQL string to increase or decrease the UnitPrice value by a certain percentage. We won't give you complete instructions for building the form, but Table 6-2 lists the controls and the nondefault property settings. (This form, frmUPDATEEx1, is in the download file at `http://www.apress.com`.)

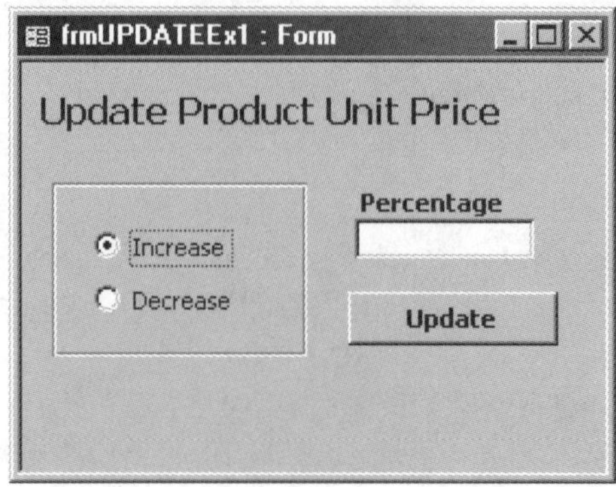

Figure 6-1. We'll use this form to modify the existing UnitPrice values in the Products table.

Table 6-2. frmUPDATEEx1

CONTROL	PROPERTY	SETTING
Option Group	Name	fraOptions
	Default Value	1
Option Button	Name	optIncrease
	Option Value	1
Option Button	Name	OptDecrease
	Option Value	2
Text Box	Name	txtPercentage
Command Button	Name	cmdUpdate
	Caption	Update

To use the form, simply select one of the options: Increase (the default) or Decrease. Then, enter the value by which you want to increase or decrease the UnitPrice values, and then click on the Update button. Doing so executes the code shown in Listing 6-1. The first six lines declare and define variables. The next two lines

```
bytOptions = frmOptions
strOperator = Choose(bytOptions, "+", "-")
```

identify the mathematical operator, which in this simple example will be the plus sign or the minus sign (+ or -). The next statement

```
dblPercent = txtPercentage * 0.01
```

converts the value you enter as an integer to a percentage value by multiplying it by 0.01. You can skip this step if you want to force the user to enter a decimal value. Because most people visualize percentage values as integers—1%, and not 0.01—we added this functionality for convenience.

Now, we get to the heart of the form's purpose: building the SQL statement that will update the UnitPrice values. Specifically, the statement

```
strSQL = "UPDATE Products SET UnitPrice = UnitPrice " & strOperator & _
    " (UnitPrice * " & dblPercent & ");"
```

concatenates the operator and value and then assigns the result to a String variable named strSQL. The `Debug.Print` that immediate follows simply prints the evaluated string to the Immediate window for debugging purposes. Finally, the statement

```
cnn.Execute strSQL
```

executes the actual update query and changes each UnitPrice appropriately.

Listing 6-1. cmdUpdate_Click()

```
Private Sub cmdUpdate_Click()
    Dim cnn As ADODB.Connection
    Set cnn = CurrentProject.Connection
    Dim bytOptions As Byte
    Dim strOperator As String
    Dim dblPercent As Double
    Dim strSQL As String
    bytOptions = frmOptions
    strOperator = Choose(bytOptions, "+", "-")
    dblPercent = txtPercentage * 0.01
    strSQL = "UPDATE Products SET UnitPrice = UnitPrice " & strOperator & _
        " (UnitPrice * " & dblPercent & ");"
    Debug.Print strSQL
    cnn.Execute strSQL
End Sub
```

At this point, let's use the form to increase the UnitPrice values by one percent, to create the SQL statement we discussed earlier. First, you might want to open Products and review a few of the UnitPrice values, so you can compare the results when you're done. For instance, the values for the first three products—Chai, Chang, and Aniseed Syrup—are $18.00, $19.00, and $10.00, respectively. Because the Increase option is the default, you need only enter the value 1 in the Percentage control, and then click on the Update button. Then, open Products and review the UnitPrice values. The prices of the first three products are now $18.18, $19.19, and $10.10, as shown in Figure 6-2.

Products : Table

Category	Quantity Per Unit	Unit Price	Units In Stock	Units On Order	Reorder Level	Discontinued
Beverages	10 boxes x 20 bags	$18.18	39	0	10	☐
Beverages	24 - 12 oz bottles	$19.19	17	40	25	☐
Condiments	12 - 550 ml bottles	$10.10	13	70	25	☐
Condiments	48 - 6 oz jars	$22.22	53	0	0	☐
Condiments	36 boxes	$21.56	0	0	0	☑
Condiments	12 - 8 oz jars	$25.25	120	0	25	☐
Produce	12 - 1 lb pkgs.	$30.30	15	0	10	☐
Condiments	12 - 12 oz jars	$40.40	6	0	0	☐
Meat/Poultry	18 - 500 g pkgs.	$97.97	29	0	0	☑
Seafood	12 - 200 ml jars	$31.31	31	0	0	☐
Dairy Products	1 kg pkg.	$21.21	22	30	30	☐
Dairy Products	10 - 500 g pkgs.	$38.38	86	0	0	☐
Seafood	2 kg box	$6.06	24	0	5	☐
Produce	40 - 100 g pkgs.	$23.48	35	0	0	☐
Condiments	24 - 250 ml bottles	$15.66	39	0	5	☐
Confections	32 - 500 g boxes	$17.62	29	0	10	☐
Meat/Poultry	20 - 1 kg tins	$39.39	0	0	0	☑
Seafood	16 kg pkg.	$63.13	42	0	0	☐
Confections	10 boxes x 12 pieces	$9.29	25	0	5	☐
Confections	30 gift boxes	$81.81	40	0	0	☐
Confections	24 pkgs. x 4 pieces	$10.10	3	40	5	☐

Record: 1 of 77

Figure 6-2. We used an SQL statement to increase the UnitPrice values in the Products table by one percent.

> **NOTE** *The Access query equivalent to SQL's UPDATE statement is the Update query. The Update To cell equates to the* expression *argument in the SET clause. The Recordset object equivalent to an UPDATE statement is the Edit method.*

Limiting the Records Updated

Seldom will you change all the records in the data source. More often than not, the change will be limited to a specific group of records, which you can isolate using the WHERE clause in the following form:

```
UPDATE datasource
SET col = expression
WHERE criteria;
```

In other words, you want Jet to make certain changes to records that meet the conditional requirements in *criteria*.

Continuing with our previous example, let's suppose you don't want to change the prices of all your products. You want to increase the prices for only those products that are currently less than or equal to $20. In this case, you'd use the following statement:

```
UPDATE Products
SET UnitPrice = UnitPrice + (UnitPrice * .01)
WHERE UnitPrice <= 20;
```

If UnitPrice is less than or equal to 20, Jet replaces the existing entry in the UnitPrice field with the results of the expression `UnitPrice + (UnitPrice * .01)`. Any UnitPrice entry that's greater than 20 is left alone. In all likelihood, you might use the statement

```
UPDATE Products
SET UnitPrice = UnitPrice + (UnitPrice * .01)
WHERE UnitPrice <= 20 And Discontinued = False;
```

to avoid updating products that you no longer handle, as indicated by the Discontinued value of True. Only current products, or those with the value False in the Discontinued field, will be updated if the UnitPrice is $20 or less. In truth, preparing to update prices would probably be an extensive process, because you can't change the prices on previously quoted orders that haven't been closed out yet. But, once you had the kinks worked out, the SQL statement that would update product prices would be fairly simple.

The form in Figure 6-3 illustrates adding a WHERE clause to limit the affected records. (This form, frmUPDATEEx2 is in the download file at `http://www.apress.com`.) This time, we'll add a WHERE clause to the SQL statement before running it via the Execute method. Table 6-3 lists the additional controls and nondefault properties, and Listing 6-2 shows the enhanced code.

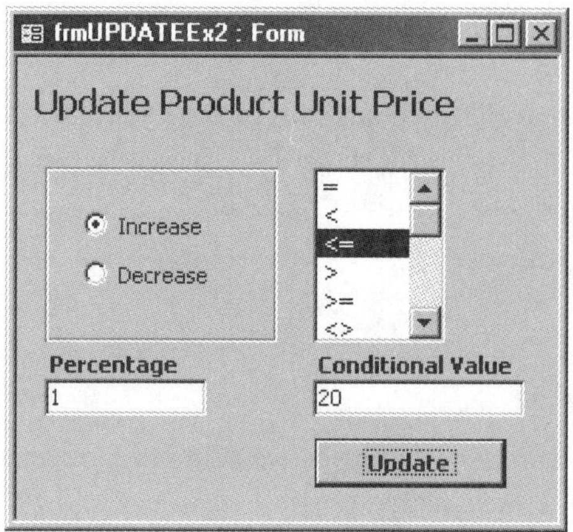

Figure 6-3. This form adds a bit of flexibility to the first one by allowing you to specify conditions.

Table 6-3. frmUPDATEEx2

CONTROL	PROPERTY	SETTING
List Box	Name	lstOperator
	Value	Row Source Type
	"=";"<";"<=";">";">=";"<>"	Row Source
Text Box	Name	txtValue

Listing 6-2. Accommodating enhanced tasks.

```
Private Sub cmdUpdate_Click()
    Dim cnn As ADODB.Connection
    Set cnn = CurrentProject.Connection
    Dim bytOptions As Byte
    Dim strOperator As String
    Dim dblPercent As Double
    Dim strSQL As String
    Dim strWHERE As String
    Dim strWHEREOperator As String
    Dim intValue As Integer
    bytOptions = frmOptions
    strOperator = Choose(bytOptions, "+", "-")
    dblPercent = txtPercentage * 0.01
    strWHEREOperator = lstOperator
    intValue = txtValue
    strWHERE = " WHERE UnitPrice " & strWHEREOperator & txtValue & _
        " AND Discontinued = 0"
```

```
    Debug.Print strWHERE
    strSQL = "UPDATE Products SET UnitPrice = UnitPrice " & strOperator & _
        " (UnitPrice * " & dblPercent & ")" & strWHERE & ";"
    Debug.Print strSQL
    cnn.Execute strSQL
End Sub
```

For the most part, the form and code work the same as our earlier example except for the addition of the `strWHERE` variable which represents the WHERE clause. To use the form to execute the previous example of increasing by one percent only those UnitPrice values that are equal to or less than 20, enter the value 1 in the Percentage control, choose the <= item in the new list box, enter 20 in the Conditional Value control (see Figure 6-3), and click on the Update button. Figure 6-4 shows the changes made to the Products table.

Products : Table

Category	Quantity Per Unit	Unit Price	Units In Stock	Units On Order	Reorder Level	Discontinue
Beverages	10 boxes x 20 bags	$18.18	39	0	10	☐
Beverages	24 - 12 oz bottles	$19.19	17	40	25	☐
Condiments	12 - 550 ml bottles	$10.10	13	70	25	☐
Condiments	48 - 6 oz jars	$22.00	53	0	0	☐
Condiments	36 boxes	$21.35	0	0	0	☑
Condiments	12 - 8 oz jars	$25.00	120	0	25	☐
Produce	12 - 1 lb pkgs.	$30.00	15	0	10	☐
Condiments	12 - 12 oz jars	$40.00	6	0	0	☐
Meat/Poultry	18 - 500 g pkgs.	$97.00	29	0	0	☑
Seafood	12 - 200 ml jars	$31.00	31	0	0	☐
Dairy Products	1 kg pkg.	$21.00	22	30	30	☐
Dairy Products	10 - 500 g pkgs.	$38.00	86	0	0	☐
Seafood	2 kg box	$6.06	24	0	5	☐
Produce	40 - 100 g pkgs.	$23.25	35	0	0	☐
Condiments	24 - 250 ml bottles	$15.66	39	0	5	☐
Confections	32 - 500 g boxes	$17.62	29	0	10	☐
Meat/Poultry	20 - 1 kg tins	$39.00	0	0	0	☑
Seafood	16 kg pkg.	$62.50	42	0	0	☐
Confections	10 boxes x 12 pieces	$9.29	25	0	5	☐
Confections	30 gift boxes	$81.00	40	0	0	☐

Record: 1 of 77

Figure 6-4. The second form updates only specific UnitPrice values in the Products table, not all of them.

> **NOTE** *The example forms in this section are available for download at* `http://www.apress.com`*. These forms contain only the barebones code needed to illustrate these examples; they don't include appropriate error handling.*

Updating Multiple Fields

You're not limited to updating just one field at a time. Updating multiple fields is as simple as including additional arguments in the SET clause and separating each with a comma (,). Just make sure that any WHERE clause is appropriate for each change. The statement

```
UPDATE Products
SET UnitPrice = UnitPrice + (UnitPrice * .01), ReorderLevel =
    ReorderLevel + (ReorderLevel * .10)
WHERE UnitPrice <= 20 And Discontinued = 0;
```

increases the UnitPrice and ReorderLevel values by one percent and ten percent, respectively, for each current (not discontinued) item that's currently $20 or less.

Updating with Joins

As is the case with most SQL statements, you can work with multiple data sources (tables or queries) when updating data via an SQL UPDATE statement. For instance, our previous example updates the price and reorder level for specific products. Now, let's suppose you want to temporarily reduce the price on products with a current price of $20 or more for a specific customer: QUICK-Stop. To handle this task, you'll need to work with a join as follows:

```
UPDATE Orders INNER JOIN [Order Details] ON Orders.OrderID =
     [Order Details].OrderID
SET [Order Details].UnitPrice = UnitPrice-(UnitPrice*0.1)
WHERE Orders.CustomerID = "QUICK" AND [Order Details].UnitPrice>=20;
```

In Chapter 4's section "Adding Joins", we learned that a join takes the form

onetable `INNER JOIN` *manytable* `ON` *primarykeyfield* `=` *foreignkeyfield*

and our UPDATE example follows this form. In this example, the one table is Orders and the many table is Order Details. Also, `Orders.OrderID` is the primary key field and `[Order Details].OrderID` is the foreign key.

> **CAUTION** *You can't run an UPDATE SQL statement on a source that includes a GROUP BY clause. Such a clause would produce a summary query. In fact, if you create an Update query in the query design grid, Access disables the Totals option on the View menu.*

Avoiding UPDATE

When confronted with a task that involves making the same change to a group of existing records, you won't always need an UPDATE query. If you're changing a primary key value and the respective relationship forces cascading updates, you can change the primary key value in the one table and Access will automatically update any corresponding foreign key values in any related many tables.

You can't change a primary key value if it's based on an AutoNumber field, so this technique is limited to natural keys. If you take our advice in Chapter 3 ("An Introduction to Relational Database Theory"), you won't use natural keys. Most likely, you will use the AutoNumber data type, which renders the Cascade Update option useless, because you can't change an AutoNumber value in Access. On the other hand, cascading deletes are still viable. We'll cover this in the section "Removing Data with DELETE" later in this same chapter.

Adding New Data with INSERT INTO

Most applications collect new data on a regular basis, and adding that new data is a routine part of data entry. Occasionally, data entry isn't the most efficient solution, especially if you can add new data with a query. You might receive a disk full of data that you could analyze or add to an existing database. Or, you might want to import data from another database. To add rows of data, use the INSERT INTO statement in the form

```
INSERT INTO target
SELECT source;
```

where *target* identifies the table you're inserting the data into and *source* identifies the records that you're inserting. This form copies data from one table to another. The *source* table can be any valid SELECT statement and can even include a GROUP BY clause, a join, a WHERE clause, or a subquery.

> **CAUTION** *The INSERT INTO clause doesn't support the asterisk (*) character in the* target *argument. This is different from the other DML statements, so be careful.*

A major problematic point is that *target* must contain the same fields as *source*. The table structures themselves can differ, but the specific fields identified in both clauses must match. For instance, open the SQL window and enter the statement

```
INSERT INTO Employees
SELECT Products.*
FROM Products;
```

as shown in Figure 6-5. When you run the query, Jet returns the error message shown in Figure 6-6. Specifically, Jet tries to find the first field in Products, ProductID *(source)*, in Employees *(target)* and returns an error when there's no match.

Figure 6-5. This INSERT INTO statement will attempt to copy the records from the Products table into the Employees table.

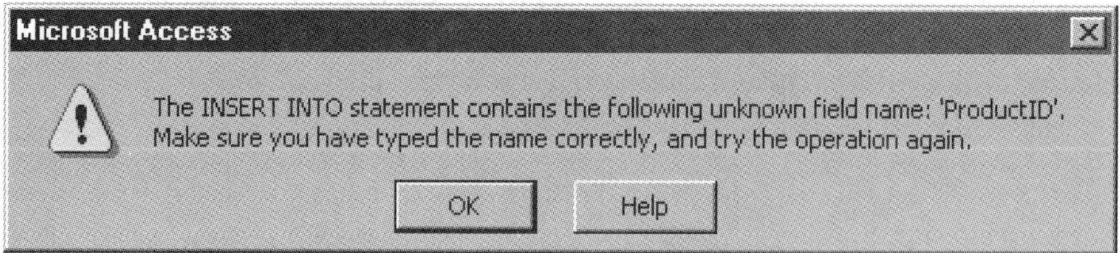

Figure 6-6. Access complains because the fields don't match.

To run a valid INSERT INTO statement, you'll need two tables that share at least some of the same field names and data types. The easiest way to accomplish this is to simply copy a table's structure and then insert data into that table. First, we need to copy a table via the following steps:

1. In the Database window, select Categories and then choose Copy from the Edit menu (or press `Ctrl+C`).

2. Choose Paste from the Edit menu (or press `Ctrl+V`).

3. Enter the name "tblCategories" and select the Structure Only option, as shown in Figure 6-7. Then, click on OK.

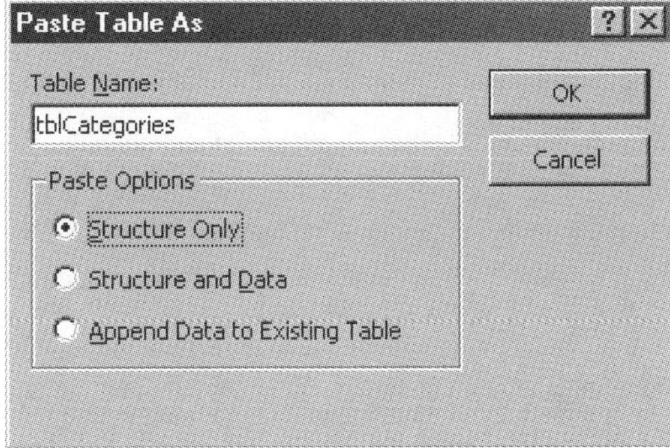

Figure 6-7. Name the new table and choose the Structure Only option.

4. Open the newly copied table, tblCategories. Figure 6-8 shows tblCategories in Datasheet view: an empty table that is structurally identical to the Categories tables.

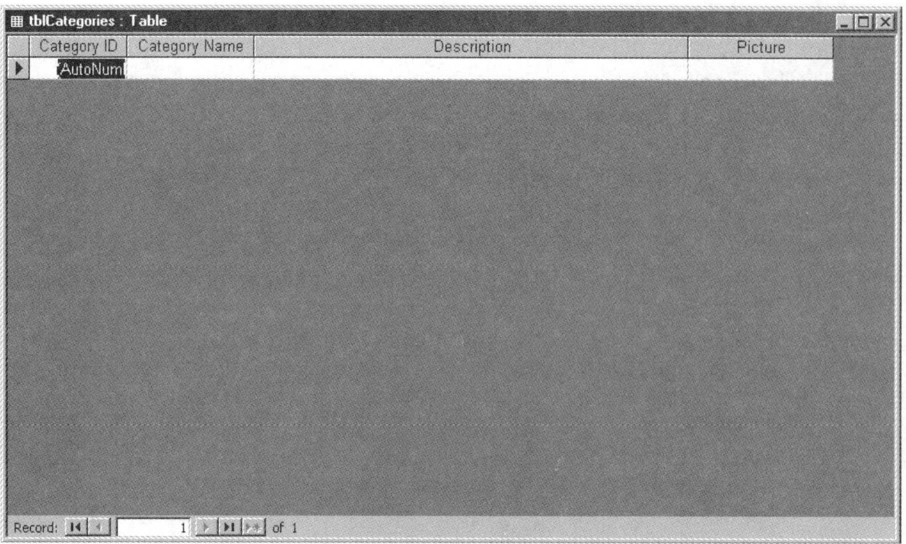

Figure 6-8. The newly copied table is empty.

> **NOTE** *We're not going to use a form example with INSERT INTO because of the complexities involved when fields don't match. Review the section "Executing SQL with VBA" in Chapter 2 ("An Introduction to Using Jet SQL in Access") and the section "Concatenating Literal Values and Variables" in Chapter 4 ("SQL Grammar") for guidelines on building an SQL string and executing it via VBA.*

To create an INSERT INTO statement to copy records from the Categories table into tblCategories:

1. Open the SQL window and enter the statement

```
INSERT INTO tblCategories
SELECT Categories.*
FROM Categories;
```

2. Run the query, and Jet returns the informational message shown in Figure 6-9. Click on Yes to append eight records. (Clicking on No cancels the append task.)

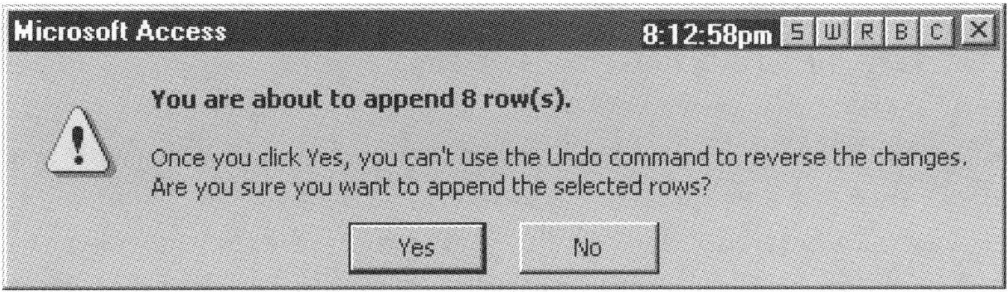

Figure 6-9. Jet tells you how many records you're appending to the target *table.*

3. Return to the Database window and open tblCategories, which is now identical to Categories in all ways except name, as it now contains the same data.

> **CAUTION** *You can't use the Undo command (on the Edit menu) to delete records you append using an INSERT INTO statement.*

We mentioned earlier that the table structures must match, but that's not entirely true. To be specific, *target* must contain every field specified in the SELECT statement. In other words, if you deleted the Picture field in tblCategories and tried to run the above query, Jet would complain because it wants to insert field data into tblCategories but cannot find an appropriate field. If you delete Picture from Categories, Jet will not care about the discrepancy and will complete the append task. Jet doesn't return an error when there's no data to copy, but it does complain when it can't find a field to hold the data it wants to copy.

Inserting a Single Row of Data

The INSERT INTO statement has a second form, which facilitates inserting a single row of data. The syntax is

```
INSERT INTO target (col1, col2, col3, . . . )
VALUES (value1, value2, value3, . . . );
```

The *colx* column references are optional, but they allow you a bit more flexibility because you can specify individual fields and the value with which you intend to update each field. If you omit the column references, you must include a value for each field in *target*. When including the column references, the order of those references must match the order in the table definition (Design view). You must include the primary key field (unless you're using an AutoNumber field) and any other fields into which you intend to insert data.

You might not find many uses for this particular syntax, but it's helpful for appending data via an unbound form. Some developers actually prefer unbound forms to bound forms because they believe that sharing data and controlling updates are easier. You'll find developers who disagree, but a discussion of unbound forms is a bit off the topic and well beyond the scope of this chapter.

The code shown in Listing 6-3 uses the INSERT INTO statement to add a single record to the Northwind Shipping table.

Listing 6-3. INSERT INTO

```
Private Sub cmdSave_Click()
    Dim cnn As ADODB.Connection
    Dim strSQL As String
    Dim strName As String
    Dim strPhone As String
    Set cnn = CurrentProject.Connection
    strName = Chr(39) & Me!txtCompanyName & Chr(39)
    strPhone = Chr(39) & Me!txtPhone & Chr(39)
    strSQL = "INSERT INTO Shippers (CompanyName, Phone) " _
        & "VALUES (" & strName & ", " & strPhone & ");"
    Debug.Print strSQL
    cnn.Execute strSQL
    Set cnn = Nothing
End Sub
```

We don't have to worry about the ShipperID value because that's an AutoNumber data type. As soon as the code inserts the new data, Access will issue a value for that field. The code in Listing 6-3 is attached to cmdSave's Click event.

Figure 6-10. The Save button's Click procedure executes an SQL INSERT INTO statement.

As is, this form would be used strictly for data entry because you can't browse or modify existing data. After entering a value for both fields, you'd click on the Save button. If you don't click on that button, Access will not copy the values to the Shipping table. Unlike a bound form, you can display data without saving the data to an underlying table.

Enter data into both controls, as shown in Figure 6-11, and click on Save to execute the Click event procedure shown in Listing 6-3. After declaring and defining a few variables, the statements

```
strName = Chr(39) & Me!txtCompanyName & Chr(39)
strPhone = Chr(39) & Me!txtPhone & Chr(39)
```

delimit the two values you just entered with the single apostrophe character ('). If you're passing a numeric value, you can skip this step. When passing a date value, use the pound sign delimiter (#). The next statement

```
strSQL = "INSERT INTO Shippers (CompanyName, Phone) " _
    & "VALUES (" & strName & ", " & strPhone & ");"
```

builds the SQL statement by concatenating the values you entered into the form into the SQL string. Then, the Recordset object's Open method executes the SQL statement in the statement

```
rst.Open Source:=strSQL, ActiveConnection:=cnn
```

At this point, you can open the Suppliers table to see the newly added record, shown in Figure 6-12.

Figure 6-11. Enter data into the INSERT INTO example form.

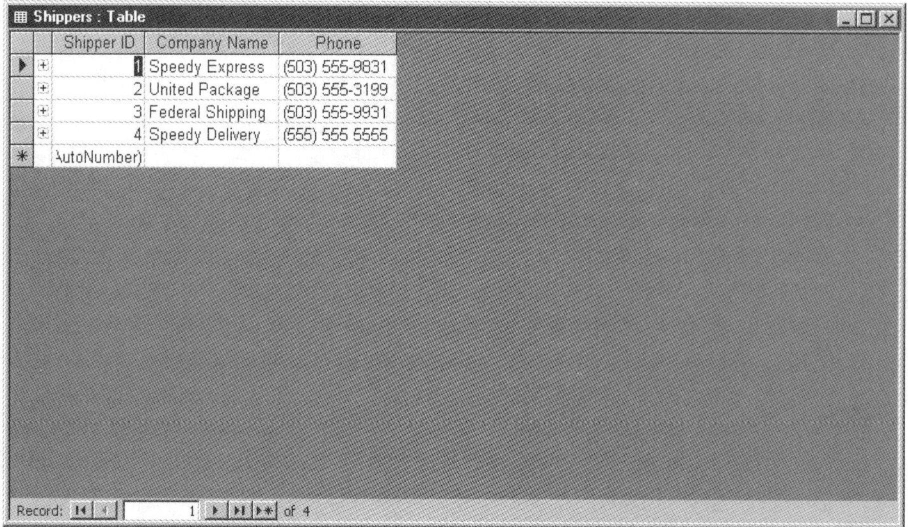

Shipper ID	Company Name	Phone
1	Speedy Express	(503) 555-9831
2	United Package	(503) 555-3199
3	Federal Shipping	(503) 555-9931
4	Speedy Delivery	(555) 555 5555
(AutoNumber)		

Figure 6-12. Our example form used an INSERT INTO statement to add a new record to the Suppliers table.

> **NOTE** *The form for this example, frmINSERTINTOEx is available for download at* `http://www.apress.com`. *Like most of our examples, we've kept it simple on purpose, but, as such, it contains no error handling. For instance, it permits duplicate records and doesn't force any particular format for the phone number value.*

Removing Data with DELETE

Deleting records isn't really a controversial topic, but you'll find some developers turn a bit green at the idea of dumping perfectly good data. Even so, SQL allows you to delete records.

> **CAUTION** *There's one thing to keep in mind when working with a DELETE statement: SQL deletes the entire record, not individual entries.*

The SQL alternative to the Delete query is the DELETE statement, which takes the following form:

```
DELETE list
FROM table
```

where *table* identifies the table that contains the data from which you're deleting data. The *list* argument is fairly obscure and unnecessary, because DELETE works on entire records, not fields. However, you could specify a *list* argument, perhaps for readability and documentation purposes.

The simplest delete task would remove all the data from a table. For example, the statement

```
DELETE
FROM tblEmployees
```

would leave `tblEmployees` blank. A DELETE statement won't delete the table: it just deletes the data in the table. You could restate this task using the statement

```
DELETE tblEmployees.*
FROM tblEmployees
```

You might even see this statement take the following form:

```
DELETE tblEmployees.Salary
FROM tblEmployees
```

Because the *list* argument specifies a single field, you might get the mistaken idea that SQL will delete only the data from the Salary field. Don't fall into this trap, as SQL will delete the entire record, even if you specify a single field in the *list* argument.

TIP *To delete data from a single field, run an UPDATE query and specify Null as the Set value. For example, following the Salary example, you'd use the statement*

```
UPDATE Employees
SET Employees.Salary = Null;
```

You can't delete the contents of a field if the Required property is set to Yes, or if the field is indexed. Even a validation rule can prevent this type of update task.

Like most statements, you can limit the DELETE task by adding a WHERE clause in the form

```
DELETE list
FROM table
WHERE condition
```

The following statement would delete all the discontinued items from the Northwind Products table:

```
DELETE Products.Discontinued
FROM Products
WHERE Products.Discontinued=-1;
```

Adding Subqueries to DELETE

Once you start adding conditions to a delete task, things can get complicated fast. You can use the data in one table to determine which rows are deleted in a related table by adding a subquery to the WHERE clause (or joins in the FROM clause). For instance, let's suppose you want to delete inactive customers. Specifically, you want to delete customers that haven't ordered anything since December 31, 1996.

The Northwind Customers table doesn't contain any kind of data that would alert you as to that customer's status. The only way you could determine whether the customer is currently ordering from you is to review the Orders table. Furthermore, a simple SELECT using the criteria `<=#12/31/96#` returns only those orders that were placed on or before December 31, 1996. But those same customers may have ordered since then. Any criteria you try specifically on the order date field will return order date information, not customer information.

The trick is to delete the customer information in the Customers table, based on the order date in the Orders table. You'll need a subquery for this. Specifically, the statement

```
SELECT CustomerID
FROM Orders
WHERE OrderDate >=#1/1/1997#
In (SELECT CustomerID FROM Orders WHERE OrderDate >=#1/1/1997#);
```

will return the CustomerID entries from the Orders table where the OrderDate entry is greater than or equal to January 1, 1997. In this context, *greater than* means any date after January 1, 1997. The problem is, we don't want to delete these records: we just want to know which customers aren't included among these records. The solution is the following statement, which uses the previous SELECT statement as a subquery:

```
DELETE
FROM Customers
WHERE Customers.CustomerID Not
In (SELECT CustomerID FROM Orders WHERE OrderDate >=#1/1/1997#);
```

The IN operator uses the results of the subquery, which retrieves the CustomerID value of each order that falls on or after January 1, 1997, as its argument. Then, the NOT operator searches for any CustomerID values listed in the Customers table that are not in the results of the subquery. When a value isn't found in the subquery's results, it is then deleted from the Customers table. Let's run this example and see what happens:

> **TIP** *In the accompanying exercise, you'll delete records from the Northwind Customers table. You'll probably want to work with a copy of that table instead of the original. In addition, whenever you modify a table, it's a good idea to save a backup of the table first. That way you can always return to the original table if the query has an undesired or unexpected result.*

1. Open the SQL window by clicking on Queries on the Object bar in the Database window and then clicking on New in the Database Window toolbar. Click on OK in the New Query dialog box.

2. In Design view, click on the Close button on the Show Tables dialog box.

3. Click on the View button (which defaults to SQL View) to open the SQL window.

4. Enter this statement:

   ```
   DELETE
   FROM Customers
   WHERE Customers.CustomerID Not
   In (SELECT CustomerID FROM Orders WHERE OrderDate >=#1/1/1997#);
   ```

5. You may want to see which records Jet will delete before it actually commits the act. The easiest way to do this is to substitute the SELECT * clause for the DELETE in the SQL window and then run the query. When

you're ready to actually delete the records, replace the first SELECT keyword with DELETE. In this case, the SELECT query returns the following CustomerID values: CENTC, FISSA, and PARIS (as shown in Figure 6-13).

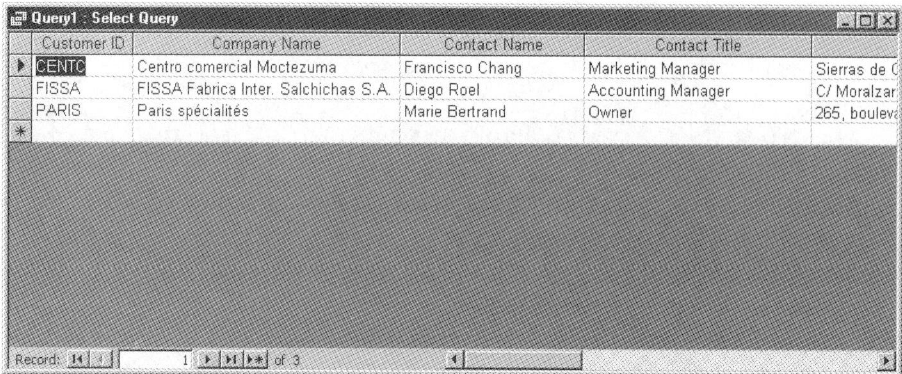

Figure 6-13. Three customers haven't placed an order since January 1, 1997.

6. Click on the Run button on the Query Design toolbar.

7. Access will display the number of records you're about to delete, as shown in Figure 6-14. In this case, Jet will delete three records. You can click on No to cancel the action, but click on Yes to continue.

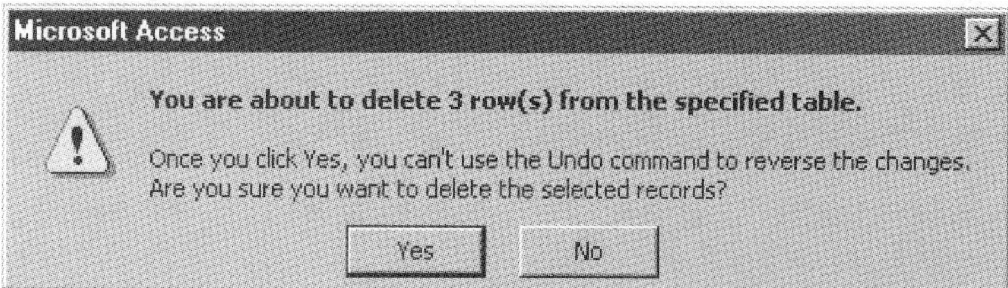

Figure 6-14. Jet tells you how many records meet the conditions and will be deleted.

8. Next, the Jet warns you that it can't delete one of the customer records due to a key violation, as shown in Figure 6-15. Click on Yes to continue. Then, open the Customers table and look for CENTC, FISSA, and PARIS. CENTC's record is still intact, but Jet did successfully delete the other two.

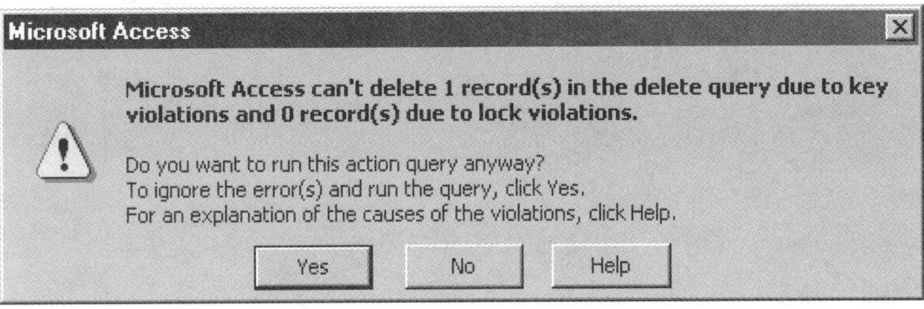

Figure 6-15. Jet can't delete all the records.

TIP *More than likely, you won't want to delete customer records, even if they're inactive. Consider adding an additional field and flagging the record as inactive or even archiving the data if you really want to remove it from the active customer table. In this way, you'll have access to the data should the customer suddenly start ordering again.*

You're probably wondering why Jet refused to delete the customer record for CENTC. The message mentioned a key violation, but the message is a little misleading. This customer has a record in the Orders table, and deleting it would violate referential integrity rules that are currently in place. (If you'd like to review referential integrity, see "So Where's Referential Integrity Fit In?" in Chapter 3.) Let's review the relationship between the Customers and Orders table:

1. Click on the Relationships button on the Database toolbar.

2. Right-click on the join line between the Customers and Orders tables, and then choose Edit Properties to display the dialog box shown in Figure 6-16. Currently, the Enforce Referential Integrity option is enabled, so Jet won't delete a record from a one table (Customers) when a many record exists (Orders).

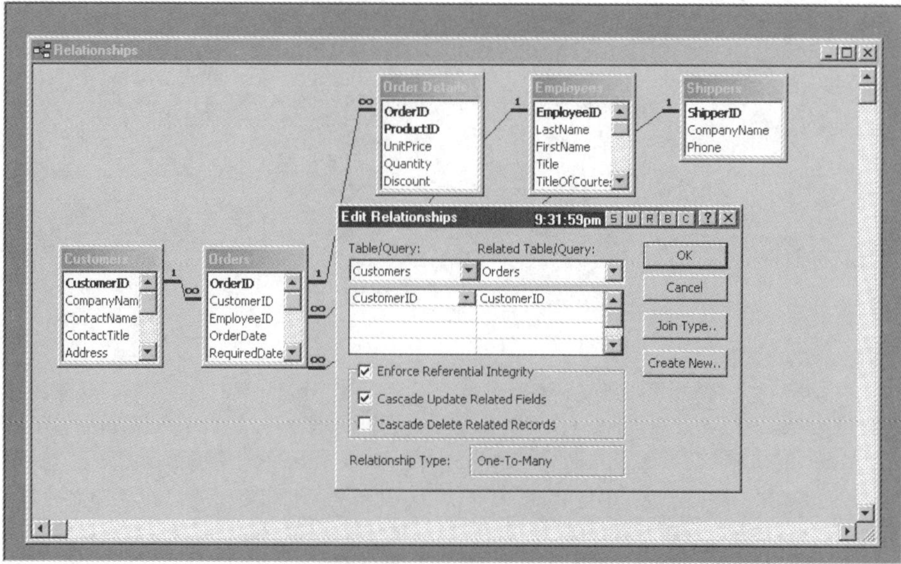

Figure 6-16. The Edit Relationships dialog box displays referential rules.

Enforcing Cascading Deletes

Enabling the Cascade Delete Related Records option (in Figure 6-16, this option isn't checked), you can avoid the problem of an incomplete delete task, which we just experienced in our last exercise. In addition, you can delete related many records (child records) by simply deleting the one (or parent) record in the one table.

First, let's clean up the Customers table. We have two options. First, we can manually delete the many records (in this case, that's the one record for CENTC in the Orders table), and then delete the record for CENTC in the Customers table. Or, second, we can enforce cascading deletes and let Jet do it for us. To choose this second option:

1. Repeat steps 1 and 2 from the last exercise.

2. In the Edit Relationships dialog, select the Cascade Delete Related Records option.

3. Click on OK.

4. Return to the earlier DELETE query and run it again. First, Access displays a message similar to the one shown earlier in Figure 6-14. This time, however, Access deletes only one record (because you've already deleted the records for FISSA and PARIS).

5. Click on Yes to complete the delete task. Now, open the Customers table to confirm that Jet really deleted the record for CENTC.

> **TIP** *It's a good idea to check Referential Integrity settings before running an update or delete task that includes a join. As we've stated before, if you're using AutoNumber primary keys, cascading updates are a moot point, but, as we've shown in this last exercise, cascading deletes can save you additional work if you prepare properly. However, we also recommend that you not leave this option on permanently. Turn it on when you need it, and then turn it off.*

Avoiding DELETE

Now let's look at a situation in which you can actually avoid DELETE. Let's suppose you want to delete the company with ID ALFKI because it's gone out of business. Because cascading deletes is enabled, you can delete the record for ALFKI in the Customers table and Jet automatically deletes any child records in the Orders table (or any related table where cascading deletes is enabled). Because the cascading delete option is already enabled (step 2 of the last exercise), the task is very simple:

1. First, open the Customers table and click on the plus sign (+) to the left of the record for ALFKI to expand the subdatasheet for that record, which displays six orders for this customer: 10643, 10692, 10702, 10952, 10835, and 11011. Next, expand the subdatasheets for each order to display the actual items in each order, as shown in Figure 6-17. We can't display the entire hierarchy, but, by scrolling, you learn that the orders have the following number of products:

   10643 has 3

   10692 has 1

   10702 has 2

   10835 has 2

   10952 has 1

   11011 has 2

TIP *If subdatasheets aren't available, select the table for which you want to display subdatasheets, pull down the Insert menu, and then choose Subdatasheets. In the Insert Subdatasheet dialog, select the table or query that contains the related records you want to display. Then, if necessary, set the Link Child Fields and Link Master Fields settings. (Most of the time, Access does a good job of selecting the appropriate fields.) Click on OK to close the dialog, and Access should display plus signs (+) to the left of each record. Click on a plus sign to expand the subdatasheet for a record.*

Customer ID	Company Name	Contact Name	Contact Title	
ALFKI	Alfreds Futterkiste	Maria Anders	Sales Representative	Obere Str. 57

Order ID	Employee	Order Date	Required Date	Shipped Date	Ship Via	Freight	
10643	Suyama, Michael	25-Aug-1997	22-Sep-1997	02-Sep-1997	Speedy Express	$29.46	Alfreds

Product	Unit Price	Quantity	Discount
Rössle Sauerkraut	$45.60	15	25%
Chartreuse verte	$18.00	21	25%
Spegesild	$12.00	2	25%
*	$0.00	1	0%

Order ID	Employee	Order Date	Required Date	Shipped Date	Ship Via	Freight	
10692	Peacock, Margaret	03-Oct-1997	31-Oct-1997	13-Oct-1997	United Package	$61.02	Alfreds

Product	Unit Price	Quantity	Discount
Vegie-spread	$43.90	20	0%
*	$0.00	1	0%

Order ID	Employee	Order Date	Required Date	Shipped Date	Ship Via	Freight	
10702	Peacock, Margaret	13-Oct-1997	24-Nov-1997	21-Oct-1997	Speedy Express	$23.94	Alfreds

Product	Unit Price	Quantity	Discount
Aniseed Syrup	$10.00	6	0%
Lakkalikööri	$18.00	15	0%
*	$0.00	1	0%

Order ID	Employee	Order Date	Required Date	Shipped Date	Ship Via	Freight	
10835	Davolio, Nancy	15-Jan-1998	12-Feb-1998	21-Jan-1998	Federal Shipping	$69.53	Alfreds

Product	Unit Price	Quantity	Discount
Raclette Courdavault	$55.00	15	0%
Original Frankfurter grüne Soße	$13.00	2	20%
*	$0.00	1	0%

Order ID	Employee	Order Date	Required Date	Shipped Date	Ship Via	Freight	
10952	Davolio, Nancy	16-Mar-1998	27-Apr-1998	24-Mar-1998	Speedy Express	$40.42	Alfreds

Product	Unit Price	Quantity	Discount

Record: 1 of 3

Figure 6-17. ALFKI has six records.

2. Next, open the Relationships window by pressing F11 to return to the Database window and clicking on Relationships on the Database toolbar, and then check the existing relationships. You're looking for relationships that exist between the Customers and Orders table and any other tables, other than the one between the two tables. In other words, is either Customers or Orders related to any other tables? As you can see in Figure 6-18, a relationship exists between Orders and Order Details. Relationships also exist between the Orders table and the Employees Shippers tables, but those won't be affected by a delete task.

> **TIP** *Before embarking on any update or delete task, regardless of how you initiate it, you should always check the relationships between the tables involved. In addition, make sure that the affected tables don't have other relationships that might be affected by the modifying task if the relationship enforces cascading updates or cascading deletes (or doesn't enforce either, as the case may be). An update or delete can have far-reaching results that you never anticipated.*

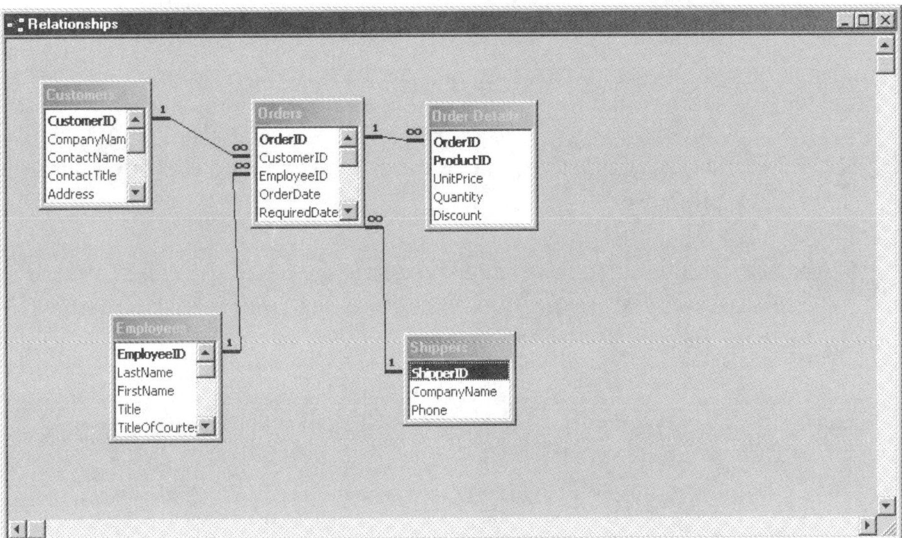

Figure 6-18. There's a relationship between Orders and Order Details.

3. Double-click on the join line between the two tables (Orders and Order Details) to learn more about the relationship. From the Edit Relationships dialog, shown in Figure 6-19, we learn that there's a one-to-many relationship based on the OrderID fields and that referential integrity is turned on.

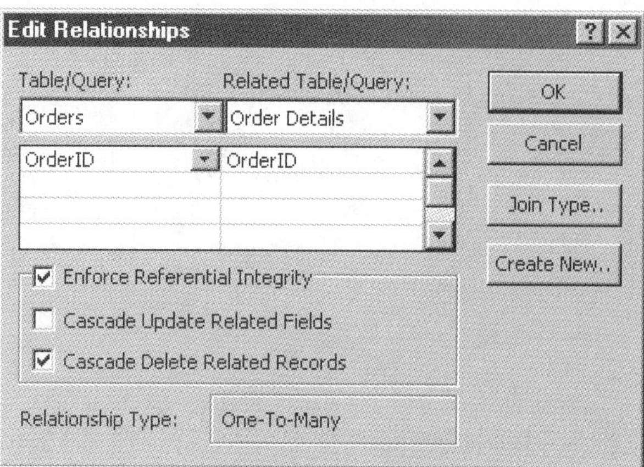

Figure 6-19. This one-to-many relationship enforces referential integrity.

4. Select the Cascade Delete Related Records option, and click on OK. (Ours is already on.)

5. Now, open the Customers table and delete the record for ALFKI. Access will warn you that you're about to delete related records, as shown in Figure 6-20.

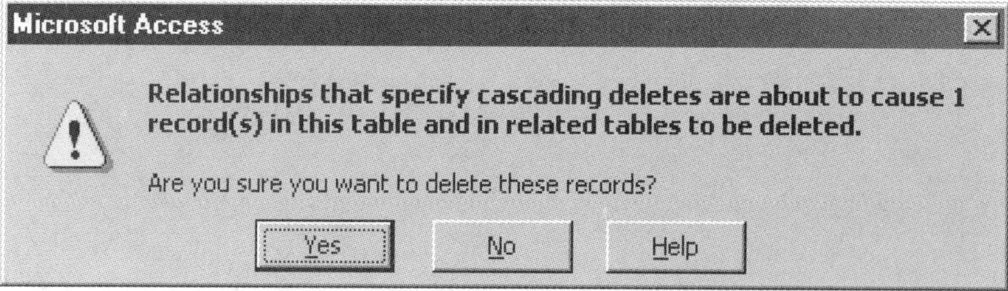

Figure 6-20. Access warns you that deleting this record will delete related records.

6. Click on Yes to complete the task.

7. Open the Orders table and scroll down to order number 10643. As you can see in Figure 6-21, the record is gone. As you continue to scroll, you will find that all the orders for ALFKI are now gone. When we deleted the ALFKI record in Customers, cascading deletes forced Jet to delete related records in the Orders table. Access deleted every record in the Orders table where the CustomerID value equaled ALFKI.

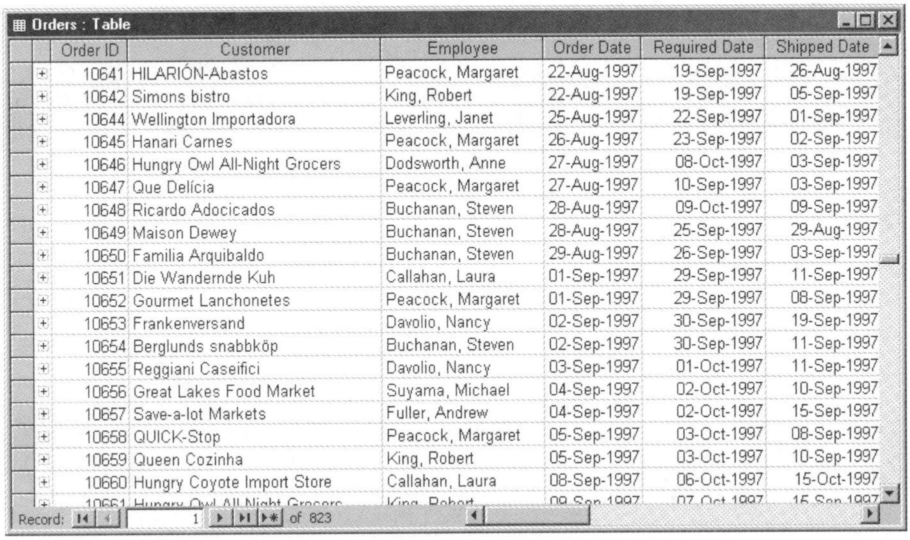

Orders : Table

Order ID	Customer	Employee	Order Date	Required Date	Shipped Date
10641	HILARIÓN-Abastos	Peacock, Margaret	22-Aug-1997	19-Sep-1997	26-Aug-1997
10642	Simons bistro	King, Robert	22-Aug-1997	19-Sep-1997	05-Sep-1997
10644	Wellington Importadora	Leverling, Janet	25-Aug-1997	22-Sep-1997	01-Sep-1997
10645	Hanari Carnes	Peacock, Margaret	26-Aug-1997	23-Sep-1997	02-Sep-1997
10646	Hungry Owl All-Night Grocers	Dodsworth, Anne	27-Aug-1997	08-Oct-1997	03-Sep-1997
10647	Que Delícia	Peacock, Margaret	27-Aug-1997	10-Sep-1997	03-Sep-1997
10648	Ricardo Adocicados	Buchanan, Steven	28-Aug-1997	09-Oct-1997	09-Sep-1997
10649	Maison Dewey	Buchanan, Steven	28-Aug-1997	25-Sep-1997	29-Aug-1997
10650	Familia Arquibaldo	Buchanan, Steven	29-Aug-1997	26-Sep-1997	03-Sep-1997
10651	Die Wandernde Kuh	Callahan, Laura	01-Sep-1997	29-Sep-1997	11-Sep-1997
10652	Gourmet Lanchonetes	Peacock, Margaret	01-Sep-1997	29-Sep-1997	08-Sep-1997
10653	Frankenversand	Davolio, Nancy	02-Sep-1997	30-Sep-1997	19-Sep-1997
10654	Berglunds snabbköp	Buchanan, Steven	02-Sep-1997	30-Sep-1997	11-Sep-1997
10655	Reggiani Caseifici	Davolio, Nancy	03-Sep-1997	01-Oct-1997	11-Sep-1997
10656	Great Lakes Food Market	Suyama, Michael	04-Sep-1997	02-Oct-1997	10-Sep-1997
10657	Save-a-lot Markets	Fuller, Andrew	04-Sep-1997	02-Oct-1997	15-Sep-1997
10658	QUICK-Stop	Peacock, Margaret	05-Sep-1997	03-Oct-1997	08-Sep-1997
10659	Queen Cozinha	King, Robert	05-Sep-1997	03-Oct-1997	10-Sep-1997
10660	Hungry Coyote Import Store	Callahan, Laura	08-Sep-1997	06-Oct-1997	15-Oct-1997
10661	Hungry Owl All-Night Grocers	King, Robert	09-Sep-1997	07-Oct-1997	15-Sep-1997

Record: 1 of 823

Figure 6-21. Jet forced cascading deletes and deleted all the related records for ALFKI in the Orders table.

8. Now, open the Order Details table and search for records for orders 10643, 10692, 10702, 10952, 10835, and 11011. There won't be any. For each record in Orders, there may be many related records in Order Details. If you delete a record in Orders without deleting related records from Order Details, you create orphan records: many records that relate to no primary key value in the one table. Remember when we turned on cascading deletes for the relationship between the Orders and Order Details table in step 4? By enforcing cascading deletes, Jet deletes records related to orders 10643, 10692, 10702, 10952, 10835, and 11011.

TIP *Used correctly, cascading deletes is a great tool. We caution you to use it with discretion and to always back up tables before running any kind of delete (or modifying) task, just in case. In addition, we recommend that you turn the feature on when it's needed and then turn it off, rather than leaving it on permanently.*

Creating New Tables with SELECT INTO

Copying a table probably isn't the most common task, but it's still something you may need to do from time to time. One possible motive for creating a table is performance: if a form or report is based on a complex query or contains too many calculated controls, you can improve performance by copying the results of all those complicated equations to a table and then base the object on the table. Or, you may need to create a copy of data for historical purposes. Exporting data is also a good reason for creating a table. Crosstab queries can be another problem as you can't update or export them; you may find it easier to create a table from the Crosstab query and work with the table.

The best way to copy a table when a copy task won't do is to run a Make-Table query, an Access Action query. SQL's equivalent—the SELECT INTO statement—creates a new table by copying rows from one table to another.

The SELECT INTO statement uses the form

```
SELECT * INTO newtable
FROM table;
```

where *newtable* is the name of the table you're creating and *table* identifies the data source from which you're copying records. This syntax will copy all the fields and existing records in *table* to a new table named *newtable*, without making any changes to *table*. You simply have a new copy of *table*, without its primary keys, indexes, and Caption properties.

NOTE *The SELECT INTO statement won't copy the original table's primary key, indexes, or column and table properties (beyond the default properties assigned to all tables). In addition, the SELECT INTO statement defaults to field names and ignores any Caption properties in the source table.*

Like most SQL statements, SELECT INTO is very flexible. For instance, you can limit the fields added to the new table by specifying fields in the SELECT clause in the form

```
SELECT col1, col2, col3, . . . INTO newtable
FROM table;
```

You can also limit the actual data that's copied by adding a WHERE clause in the form

```
SELECT col1, col2, col3, . . . INTO newtable
FROM table
WHERE condition;
```

You can even determine the order of the copied records by including an ORDER BY clause in the form

```
SELECT col1, col2, col3, . . . INTO newtable
FROM table
WHERE condition
ORDER BY colx;
```

The field specified by *colx* does not have to be part of the new table. In other words, you can reorganize the data by the contents of a field that's not included in the new table.

> **TIP** *A SELECT INTO statement will replace an existing table if one exists, but it will warn you first. However, Jet deletes the existing table before it actually creates the new one, so, if something goes wrong, you can't fall back on the existing table. It's a good idea to always make a copy of the existing table before running the SELECT INTO statement if you're replacing an existing table.*

Now, let's look at a simple example of INSERT INTO and use it to create a copy of the Order Details table (in Northwind.mdb):

1. Open the SQL window and enter the statement

   ```
   SELECT * INTO tblOrderDetailsCopy
   FROM [Order Details];
   ```

2. Click on Run in the Query Design toolbar. Access will display the information message shown in Figure 6-22. The message tells you how many records the query will copy to the new table. In this case, we're copying all the records.

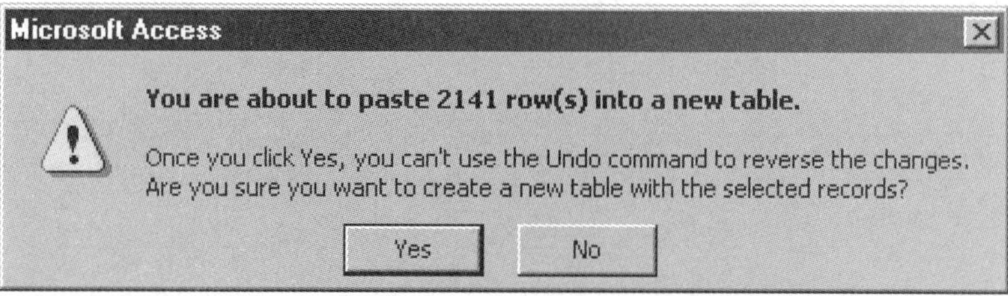

Figure 6-22. Click on Yes to confirm the SQL task.

3. Click on Yes to confirm the task and create the new table named tblOrderDetailsCopy. If you like, return to the Database window and check for the new table. Open it and examine the contents: the data matches that in the Order Details table. If you open the new table in Design view, as shown in Figure 6-23, you'll see that the table doesn't contain a primary key field or any indexes. In addition, none of the fields have a Caption property—even though three of the fields (OrderID, ProductID, and UnitPrice) in the Order Details table do. Close the table before you continue because leaving it open will create an error later in step 6.

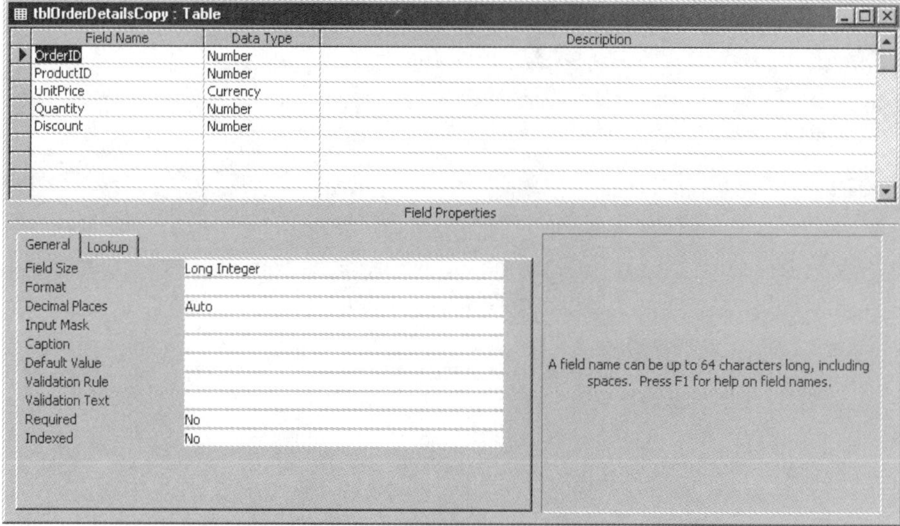

Figure 6-23. The new table doesn't contain a primary key field or any indexes.

4. Now, return to the SQL window and replace the previous statement with

```
SELECT OrderID INTO tblOrderDetailsCopy
FROM [Order Details]
ORDER BY ProductID;
```

5. Run the query, and Access displays the error message shown in Figure 6-24, warning you that the existing copy of tblOrderDetailsCopy will be deleted before you continue.

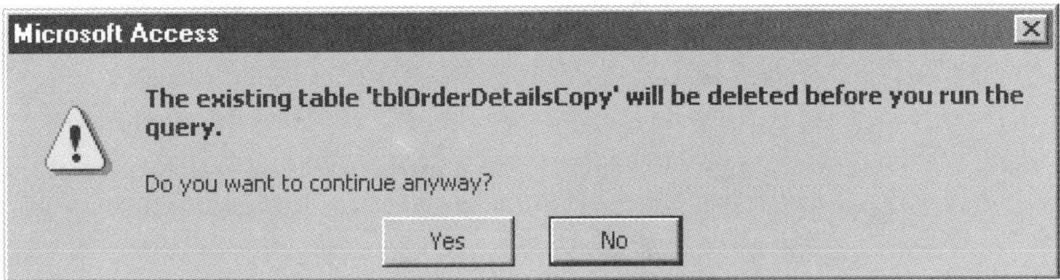

Figure 6-24. Access warns you that the table already exists and will be deleted.

6. Click on Yes to continue, and Access will display the same error message shown in Figure 6-22. (If you opened tblOrderDetailsCopy in Design view in step 3, click on OK and close tblOrderDetailsCopy and run the query again.)

7. Click on Yes when Access displays the number of records that the current task will copy.

8. Open tblOrderDetailsCopy. This time, you'll find that Jet copied only the OrderID field and that those entries aren't in OrderID order: they're in order of the ProductID field, which we didn't copy to the new table.

Copying an Empty Recordset

In our previous examples, we copied data to the new table that we created using INSERT INTO. You can create the table without copying any data using a WHERE clause in the form

```
SELECT * INTO newtable
FROM table
WHERE FALSE;
```

For instance, the statement

```
SELECT * INTO tblOrderDetailsCopy
FROM [Order Details]
WHERE FALSE;
```

bases a new table named tblOrderDetailsCopy on the existing table Order Details. However, because no record can meet the FALSE condition, no record is copied to the new table.

TIP *The data you need isn't always in the active database or project; fortunately, you can get that data in a number of ways. You can use a VBA function procedure (user-defined function) that grabs the data you need or you can create a link to the data you need. The simplest way may be a Select query using the following form:*

```
SELECT fldlist
INTO table
IN 'completepathtodatasource'
FROM table
```

Bypassing INSERT INTO

If a table already exists, INSERT INTO will simply overwrite it. When including the WHERE FALSE clause, the task is redundant because there's no data to copy. When this is the case, you might consider using the following procedure, which bypasses the INSERT INTO task only when the table already exists. Be sure to reference the Microsoft ADO Extension 2.1 for DLL and Security library.

```
Function INSERTINTOADOXEx(tbl As String, newtbl As String)
Dim cat As New ADOX.Catalog
Dim strSQL As String
Set cat.ActiveConnection = CurrentProject.Connection
On Error Resume Next
DoCmd.SetWarnings False
If cat.Tables.Item(newtbl).Name = "" Then
    strSQL = "SELECT * INTO " & newtbl & " FROM " & _
        tbl & " WHERE FALSE;"
    Debug.Print strSQL
    DoCmd.RunSQL strSQL
```

```
End If
    On Error GoTo 0
    DoCmd.SetWarnings True
End Function
```

Adding Error Handling

In step 6 of the previous example, you found that Jet wouldn't copy over an open table if you failed to close tblOrderDetailsCopy in step 3. When you're running a query in the SQL window, this error isn't a big deal: you simply clear the error message, close the table, and try again. Of course, you'd want to inhibit this message if you were creating a custom application for inexperienced users. Actually, if you're running this query via code, you'll want to avoid the error altogether.

The function in Listing 6-4 inhibits error and warning messages during an INSERT INTO task. First, the function declares and defines the variable strSQL, which equals a fairly generic INSERT INTO statement. You'll pass the *table* and *newtable* arguments when you call the function. The `DoCmd.SetWarnings` statement turns off the warning messages we saw in our earlier examples. The `On Error Resume Next` statement doesn't keep an error from occurring when *newtable* is open: it just inhibits any error messages and allows VBA to continue. To avoid losing data in the event of an error, the SelectObject and Rename methods create a copy of *newtable* if it exists, and `On Error` inhibits an error if it doesn't. The Close method closes the table if it's open, and `On Error` inhibits the would-be error message if it isn't. Then, the `On Error GoTo 0` resets the `On Error`. After running the INSERT INTO statement, the code resets the SetWarnings property. Now, you can run the INSERT INTO statement, without worrying whether the table is open or clearing any warning messages to continue.

Listing 6-4. INSERTINTOEx()

```
Function INSERTINTOEx(tbl As String, newtbl As String)
Dim strSQL As String
strSQL = "SELECT * INTO " & newtbl & " FROM " & _
    tbl & ";"
Debug.Print strSQL
DoCmd.SetWarnings False
On Error Resume Next
DoCmd.SelectObject acTable, newtbl
DoCmd.Rename newtbl & "copy", acTable, newtbl
```

```
DoCmd.Close acTable, newtbl
On Error GoTo 0
DoCmd.RunSQL strSQL
DoCmd.SetWarnings True
End Function
```

TIP *You can use the INSERT INTO statement with any valid SELECT statement that produces a recordset. That includes the GROUP BY clauses, joins, Union queries, and subqueries. (You can learn more about UNION queries in "Using Union Queries" in Chapter 10 ("Advanced Manipulation Techniques").*

CHAPTER 7

Grouping and Summarizing Data

Using Jet SQL Aggregates and Clauses to Group and Summarize Data

IF YOU WORK WITH DATABASES on a regular basis, you'll probably often run into the term *aggregate*. In regards to databases, an aggregate is simply a set or group of records. Hence, *to aggregate data* means to group or summarize it. You can use Jet SQL to aggregate in one of two ways:

- by grouping data using a GROUP BY clause, or
- by summarizing data using SQL aggregate functions.

You might think of summarizing and grouping data as the same function, and—although the results are somewhat similar—these results are not the product of the same task. Generally, a group simply sorts like data together. For instance, you may want to group all employees by their department or supervisor. On the other hand, a summary includes an analysis, which can be as simple as a set of subtotals that are based on grouped data. For example, you may want to count employees, subtotaling them by departments or supervisors and then displaying a total that includes all employees. In the second example, you could even omit the actual data and just display the subtotals and total.

Because *aggregate* means "to group," including summarized data in this category may cause a bit of confusion. Generally, summarized data is grouped, but this isn't always the case. Similarly, grouped data doesn't always analyze (summarize) the grouped data. So, you need to remember that grouping and summarizing are two distinct functions, even though both require that the data be grouped in some fashion. Sometimes you benefit from combining both, and sometimes you just need one or the other.

Summarizing Data

Using SQL aggregate functions, you can quickly obtain totals for an entire table or a specific group of records (a subset). The figure shown in Figure 7-1 is a report of employees (from the Employees table in Northwinds) that also summarizes the data by returning the number of employees in the table. To summarize the data, we added an SQL aggregate function—**=Count([LastName])**—to the report's Footer section. A quick glance at the report's footer is all we need to glean the number of employees (nine). Figure 7-2 shows the report in Design view.

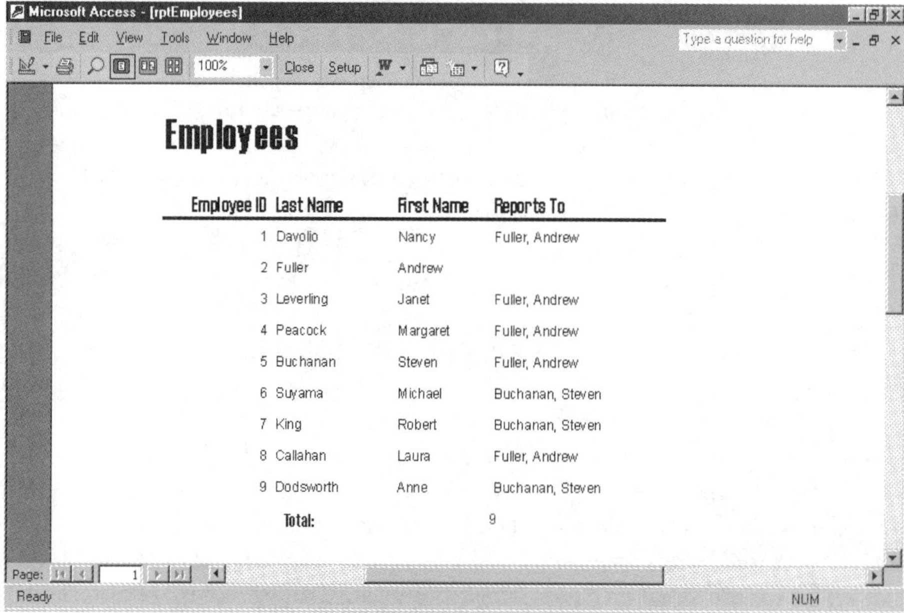

Figure 7-1. An SQL aggregate function summarizes the employee data by returning the number of employees in the report.

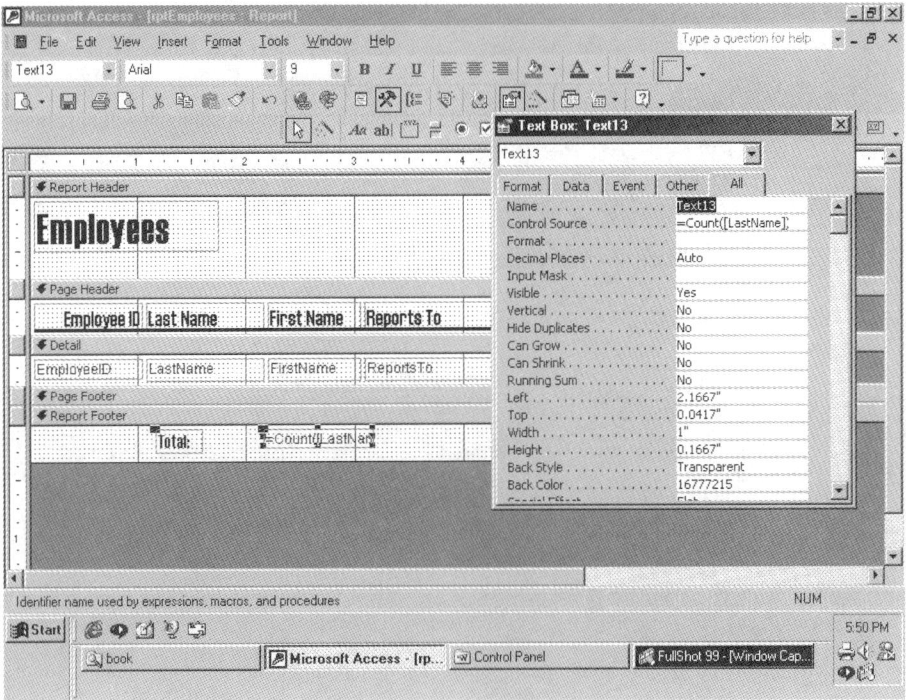

*Figure 7-2. The **Count()** function is in the report's Footer section.*

Handling Null Values

Null values can affect the result of an aggregate function. For instance, in our current example, we count the entries in the LastName field. Let's suppose that you don't want to know the number of actual personnel, but the subordinate employees instead. The distinction between the two is Andrew Fuller, who has no entry in the ReportsTo field. Upon closer inspection of Mr. Fuller's employee information in the Employees table, we see that he's the head honcho—specifically, the Vice President of Sales. You might not want to include him in your count. When a case like this arises, you can usually just reconsider the field that you're referencing in your aggregate. Here, we can change the function to calculate the ReportsTo field instead—**=Count([ReportsTo])**—which returns the value 8, instead of 9. Refer to Table 7-1, later in this section, to see which aggregates consider Null values.

Now, let's suppose that you want to group your employees by their supervisors. You don't need to add anything to the report; you just need to rearrange it. Specifically, add a group, based on the ReportsTo field, to the Detail section and then open a header and footer for the new group. Move the ReportsTo field to the

ReportsTo Header section (the group's header) and then move the **Count()** function to the ReportsTo Footer section (the group's footer), as shown in Figure 7-3. Figure 7-4 shows this report in print preview.

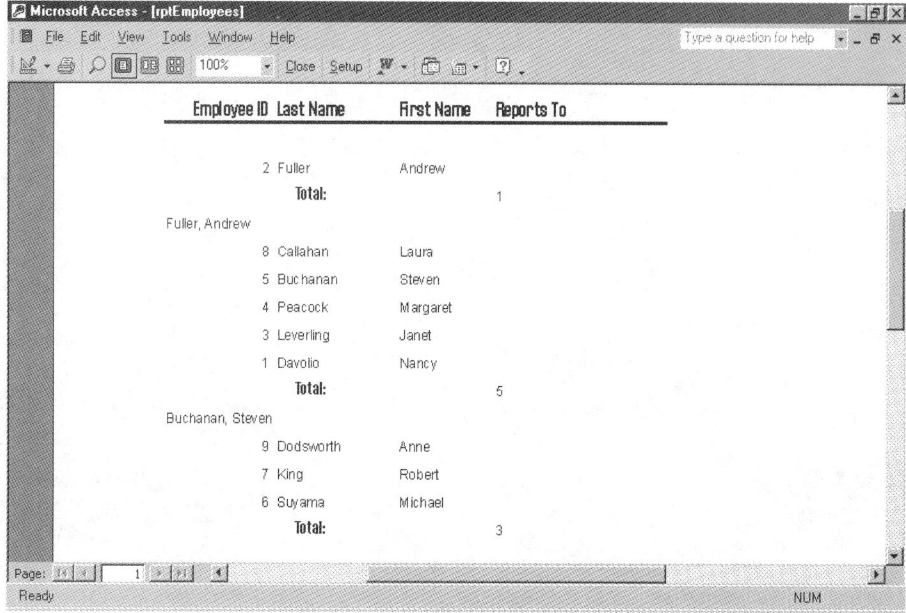

Figure 7-3. A summarizing report in Print Preview

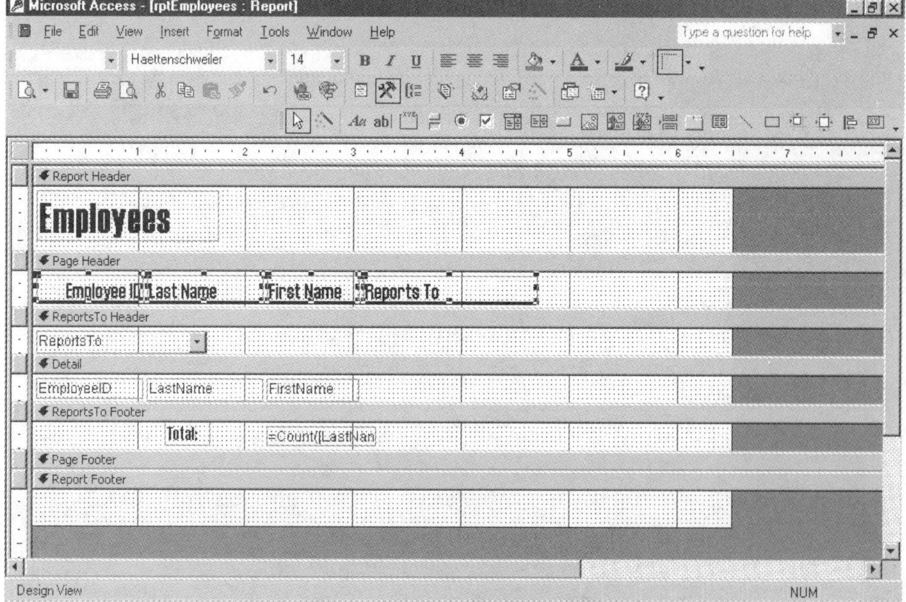

Figure 7-4. We added a group and subtotals to our previous report.

If you're not familiar with reports, use these step-by-step instructions to modify the report:

1. Select the Detail section's title bar and then click on the Sorting and Grouping button on the Report Design toolbar, or choose Sorting and Grouping from the View menu.
2. Choose ReportsTo from the Field/Expression drop-down list.
3. Change both the Group Header and Group Footer properties to Yes, as shown in Figure 7-5. Close the Sorting and Grouping dialog.

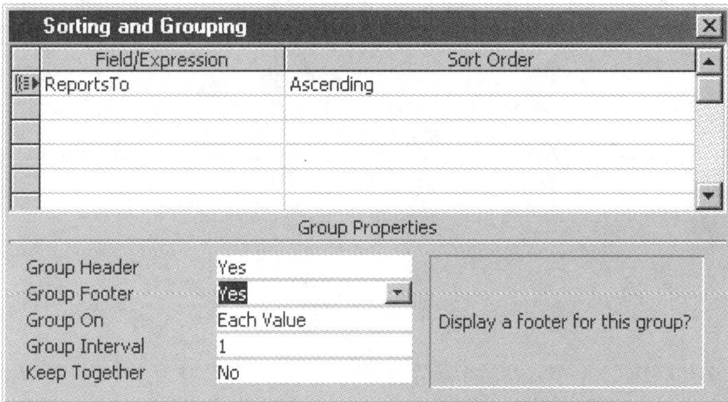

Figure 7-5. Modify the Sorting and Grouping properties.

CAUTION *In our example report, the ReportsTo controls display the supervisors' names and not their identification numbers because the ReportsTo field in the Employees table is a lookup field. (You can learn more about lookup fields in "SELECT in Lookup Fields" in Chapter 5.) If you use the grouping feature in the Report wizard, the report won't inherit the lookup properties of the ReportsTo field.*

Rules for Using SQL Aggregates in Group Sections

Adding an overall total, as shown in Figure 7-6, is easy. Simply copy the **Count()** function in the ReportsTo Footer section to the ReportsTo Footer section. You may be wondering here how the same function can calculate different results. It can because SQL aggregates consider only the data in the current report section.

In other words, in a group, the **Count()** function includes only the data in a particular group; in the report's footer, it includes all the data in the report.

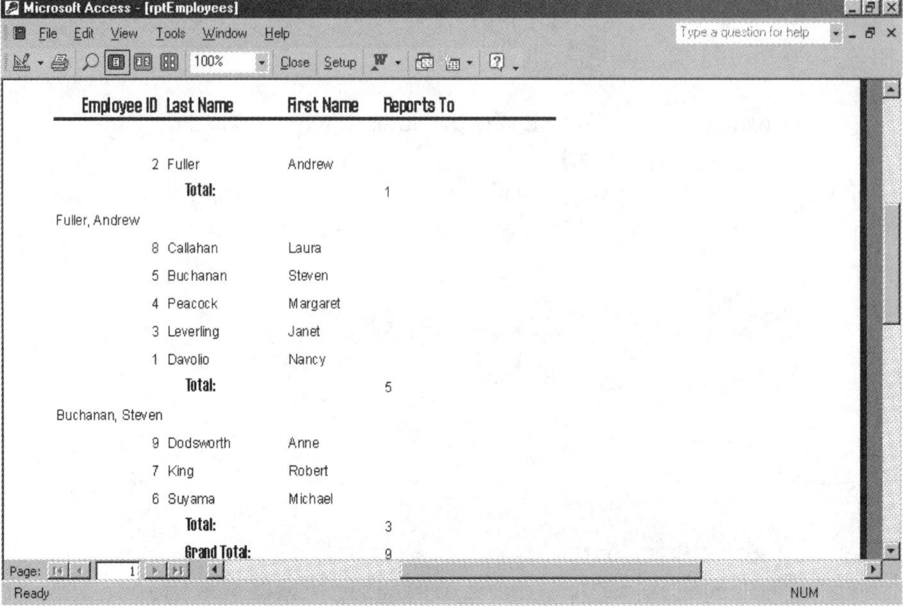

*Figure 7-6. This report uses a **Count()** function to also return the total number of employees.*

As we just demonstrated, where you locate the function makes quite a difference. Use the following guidelines when adding SQL aggregate functions to a report:

- An aggregate in a group header or footer considers only the values in the specified field for each group.
- An aggregate in the Report header or footer uses all the values in the specified field throughout the entire report.
- An aggregate in the Page header or footer returns an error.
- An aggregate placed in the Detail section returns an overall total, similar to the same function placed in a report's header or footer.

Presenting the SQL Aggregate Functions

In Access, you'll encounter two types of aggregate functions: domain and SQL. Domain aggregates are used in VBA, but they shouldn't be included in an SQL statement. SQL aggregates are the VBA equivalents, and you'll include these in your SQL statements. Table 7-1 lists the SQL aggregates. The main difference between the two aggregates is that an Access domain aggregate can be limited by criteria, and an SQL aggregate can't. The domain aggregates accept an argument that's the equivalent of a WHERE clause without the WHERE keyword. (For more information on how to create a WHERE clause, read "Concatenating Literal Values and Variables" in Chapter 4 and "Limiting the SELECT Results" in Chapter 5.)

> **TIP** *SQL aggregates accept only one argument, which can be a reference to a field (column) or an expression that refers to a field. In this context, we prefer to use the term* field *rather than* column, *because doing so emphasizes the rule that the argument must be a field. When working with reports, this can be a bit confusing because some users tend to think of report controls and fields as one and the same. They aren't. The field is the underlying data source that actually contains the data (in a table or query), and a control is the object that displays that data in the report. A control often has the same name as the underlying field, and this can also cause confusion. In fact, we recommend that you rename controls created by any of the report wizards. (The wizard defaults to the underlying field name when naming the control.) But, when you rename a control, don't make the mistake of using the control's name in an SQL aggregate function, because it won't always work. Use the name of the underlying field (the data source) whenever possible.*

Table 7-1. SQL Aggregate Functions

FUNCTION*	USE	CONSIDERS NULL	ACCESS/VBA EQUIVALENT	T-SQL
Avg*(fld)*	Mean or average	No	**DAvg()**	Avg
Count*(fld)*	Counts the number of non-Null values in fld	No	**DCount()**	Count
Count*(*)*	Counts the total number of rows	Yes	**DCount(*)**	Count
Sum*(fld)*	Sums the values in fld	No	**DSum()**	Sum
Min*(fld)*	Returns the smallest value in fld	No	**DMin()**	Min
Max*(fld)*	Returns the largest value in fld	No	**DMax()**	Max
First*(fld)*	Returns the value in the first row	Yes		
Last*(fld)*	Returns the value in the last row	Yes		
StDev*(fld)*	Returns sample standard deviation for fld	No	**DStDev()**	StDev
StDevP*(fld)*	Returns population standard deviation for fld	No	**DStDevP()**	StDevP
Var*(fld)*	Returns sample variance for fld	No	**DVar()**	Var
VarP*(fld)*	Returns population deviation for fld	No	**DVarP()**	VarP

*The *fld* argument can either be an expression or refer to an actual column.

> NOTE *SQL doesn't limit you to its own SQL aggregate functions. You can also use user-defined functions or VBA functions. However, doing so can slow things down if you're working through an ODBC or OLE DB connection. That's because Jet must send the Jet-compatible portion of your query to the server for evaluation and then calculate the non-SQL portion locally.*

Aggregates in Queries

Our previous aggregate examples have used reports, and we've completely bypassed the SQL window. You don't need a report to group data. For instance, let's suppose that you want to know the total number of orders and the smallest and largest freight bill for shipping those orders. If you don't need to view the dependent data, you can skip the report and use a quick query. The following steps are to create the necessary SQL statement:

1. Select the Orders table (in Northwind) in the Database window, choose Query from the Insert menu, click on OK, and then choose SQL View from the View button.

2. In the SQL window, enter the statement:

```
SELECT Count(OrderID) AS TotalOrders, Min(Freight) AS SmallestFreight,
    Max(Freight) AS LargestFreight
FROM Orders;
```

3. Click on the Run button to see the results shown in Figure 7-7.

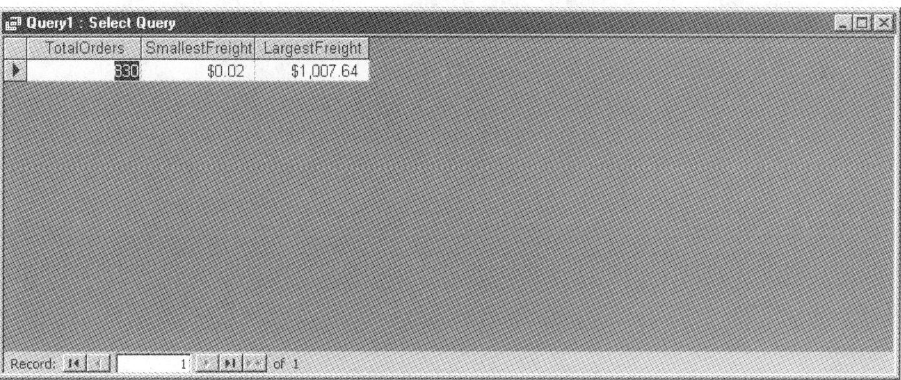

Figure 7-7. Aggregate functions return all three values in this query.

If you're more comfortable interpreting queries in Design view, take a look at the above query, shown in Figure 7-8 in Design view; the SQL aggregates appear as calculated columns in Design view. The thing to keep in mind is that each column is on its own in this setup. Although you're referring to the same data source, each aggregate function refers to a different field: the **Count()** expression returns the total number of entries in the OrderID field; the **Min()** expression returns the smallest value in the Freight field; and, similarly, the **Max()** expression returns the largest value in the Freight field. There's no dependency or relationship among these expressions.

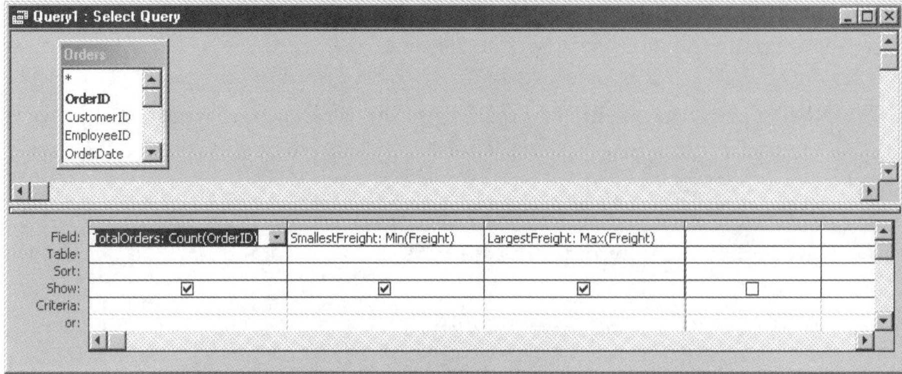

Figure 7-8. Aggregate functions return all three values in this query.

> **NOTE** *You can't include data and summarized values in the same Select query. However, you can display summary values along with the data, in a Union query. You'll find this technique in Appendix A.*

Using GROUP BY to Create Groups

When you need a bit more than quick totals, use the GROUP BY clause to define data groups. The Access query equivalent is the Totals query, which isn't a query type but rather a specialized view of the data. These queries can be difficult to work with, but the key is to include only those columns that define a group or summarize data for a group. In other words, you can't include extraneous data when grouping records.

> **TIP** *Jet groups Null values in a GROUP BY field; it doesn't eliminate those Null values from the result set. On the other hand, most SQL aggregate functions don't evaluate those Null values. See Table 7-1 to see just which functions consider Null values. When Null values are a possibility, be sure to consider them in your expressions to avoid erroneous data.*

Now, let's suppose that you want to group the orders by their order date, but you want to see only the minimum and maximum freight cost and the number of orders. You can do so by adding a GROUP BY clause to a SELECT statement in the following form:

```
SELECT list
   FROM table
GROUP BY list
```

(Notice that we're back to the SQL view in the Query Design window.) The GROUP BY *list* can reference columns, calculated fields, or constants. However, *list* can't reference an aggregate function, which means that you can't just add a GROUP BY clause to the earlier SQL statement that we used in the previous section ("Aggregates in Queries"). Instead, you must add only the column (or columns) that defines the group. In this case, that's OrderDate. Then, you can add the GROUP BY clause as follows:

```
SELECT OrderDate, Count(OrderID) AS TotalOrders, Min(Freight) AS SmallestFreight,
    Max(Freight) AS LargestFreight
FROM Orders
GROUP BY OrderDate;
```

In Design view, shown in Figure 7-9, you can clearly see the Totals aggregates:

- The Group By aggregate in the OrderDate column defines the group.
- The Count aggregate counts the number of records in each group.
- The Min aggregate returns the smallest value from the Freight field for each group (based on the OrderDate value).
- The Max aggregate returns the largest value from the Freight field for each group.

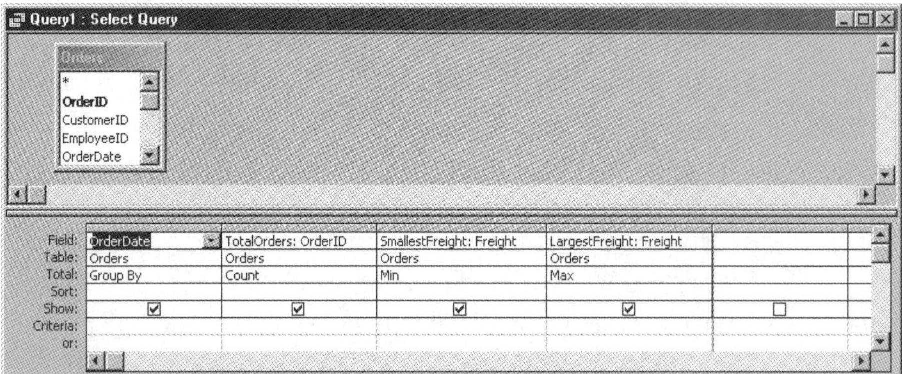

Figure 7-9. Design view displays the SQL aggregates as Totals aggregates.

> **NOTE** *The Jet can't group on Memo or OLE Object fields, so don't include these fields in a GROUP BY clause. In addition, you don't need to specifically refer to a field in the SELECT clause to group by it. As long as the field is a valid field in the data source, you can omit referring to it in the SELECT clause, but still group by that field by adding it to the GROUP BY clause. If, however, you refer to a field in the SELECT clause, you must also refer to it in the GROUP BY clause or in an aggregate function.*

Regardless of whether you build this query in the SQL window or Design view, the results, shown in Figure 7-10, are the same. Each date is displayed only once, despite the number of orders placed on that date: there's your group. The minimum and maximum freight values for each day are often the same, when there's only one order for that date. The TotalOrders column displays the number of orders for each group, or date. On July 8, 1996, there were two orders. The smaller order of the two costs $41.34 to ship, and the larger costs $65.83. (When we say *smaller* or *larger*, we're referring only to the order's shipping weight of the order and not the final cost of the items in the orders.)

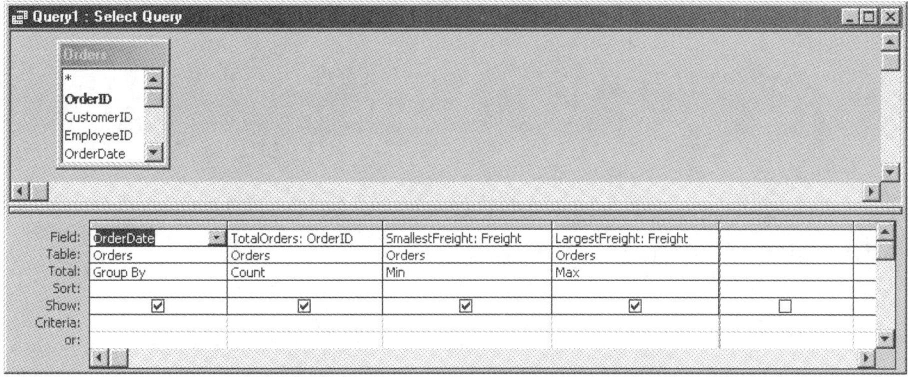

Figure 7-10. The SQL aggregates return results based on the records in each group.

CAUTION *Avoid using too many fields in GROUP BY clauses because adding extra grouping levels slows the query.*

Limiting Grouped Data

You can limit the results of a grouped query in two ways. As in any SELECT query, you can include a WHERE clause, which Jet applies before it groups the records. In addition, you can further limit the grouped results by adding a HAVING clause, which is applied to only the results after the grouping and any aggregation have taken place. In a nutshell, the WHERE clause eliminates records that you don't want in the group. The HAVING clause then further filters grouped records based on information about that group.

Using WHERE

The WHERE clause limits the results of a SELECT query, and we've seen several examples of its use in chapters 5 and 6. To a WHERE clause, the GROUP BY is inconsequential because Jet compares data and eliminates records that don't meet the WHERE condition before it groups the records. We can illustrate this point by limiting the previous example to return only those orders that occurred after January 1, 1997. To do so, you'd include a WHERE clause because you're limiting the data returned by the SELECT query (OrderDate) as follows:

```
SELECT OrderDate, Count(OrderID) AS TotalOrders, Min(Freight) AS SmallestFreight,
    Max(Freight) AS LargestFreight
FROM Orders
WHERE OrderDate > #1/1/1997#
GROUP BY OrderDate;
```

You can see that we've added a Criteria expression in Design view, shown in Figure 7-11. Remember, a Criteria expression in the query design grid is the equivalent of an SQL WHERE clause. The only difference between this SQL statement and the one from our previous example is the WHERE clause: notice the WHERE aggregate in the OrderDate column's Total field. The results are shown in Figure 7-12. As you can see, Jet returns only those records in which the OrderDate value is greater than January 1, 1997. Then, the GROUP BY clause returns a unique record for each OrderDate value from the resulting recordset.

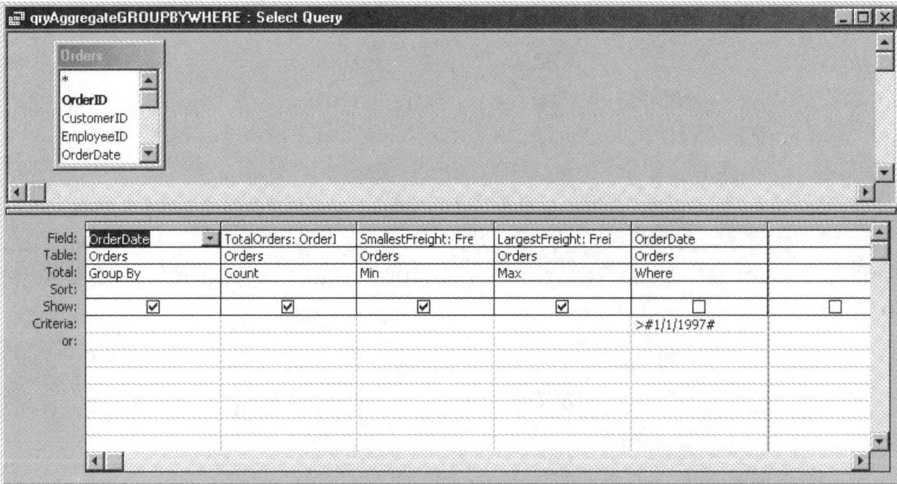

Figure 7-11. The SQL WHERE clause is equivalent to the Criteria expression in the query design grid.

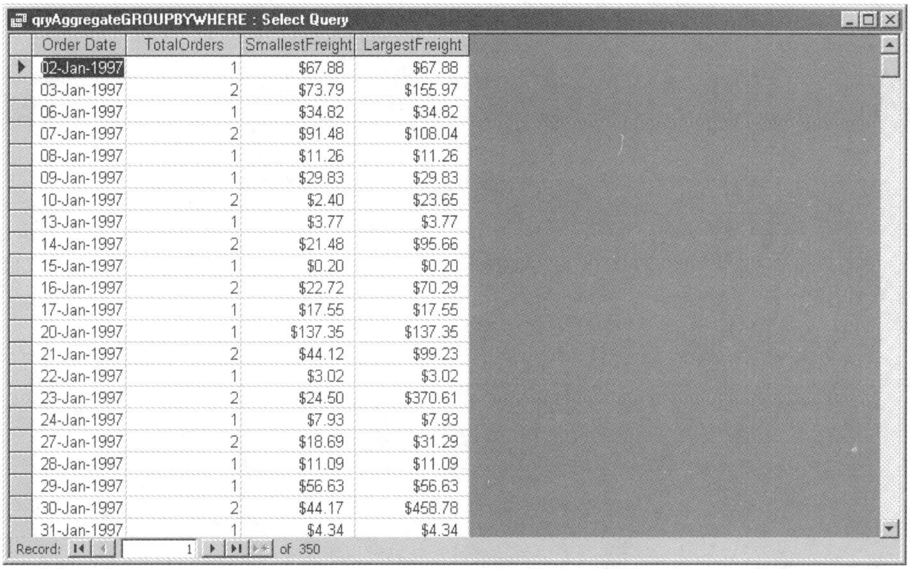

qryAggregateGROUPBYWHERE : Select Query

Order Date	TotalOrders	SmallestFreight	LargestFreight
02-Jan-1997	1	$67.88	$67.88
03-Jan-1997	2	$73.79	$155.97
06-Jan-1997	1	$34.82	$34.82
07-Jan-1997	2	$91.48	$108.04
08-Jan-1997	1	$11.26	$11.26
09-Jan-1997	1	$29.83	$29.83
10-Jan-1997	2	$2.40	$23.65
13-Jan-1997	1	$3.77	$3.77
14-Jan-1997	2	$21.48	$95.66
15-Jan-1997	1	$0.20	$0.20
16-Jan-1997	2	$22.72	$70.29
17-Jan-1997	1	$17.55	$17.55
20-Jan-1997	1	$137.35	$137.35
21-Jan-1997	2	$44.12	$99.23
22-Jan-1997	1	$3.02	$3.02
23-Jan-1997	2	$24.50	$370.61
24-Jan-1997	1	$7.93	$7.93
27-Jan-1997	2	$18.69	$31.29
28-Jan-1997	1	$11.09	$11.09
29-Jan-1997	1	$56.63	$56.63
30-Jan-1997	2	$44.17	$458.78
31-Jan-1997	1	$4.34	$4.34

Record: 1 of 350

Figure 7-12. Jet processes a WHERE clause before grouping the data specified in a GROUP BY clause.

Using HAVING

Sometimes you'll want to limit the results of your query by comparing the results of an aggregate. For instance, let's suppose that you don't want to limit the records by the OrderDate, but rather by the number of records in each group. For example, you might want to group all the records, but eliminate those that have only one order in the group. In this case, you'd include the HAVING clause as follows:

```
SELECT OrderDate, Count(OrderID) AS TotalOrders, Min(Freight) AS SmallestFreight,
    Max(Freight) AS LargestFreight
FROM Orders
GROUP BY OrderDate
HAVING Count(OrderID) > 1;
```

In Design view, shown in Figure 7-13, you see only the Criteria expression in the TotalOrders field. You can't really tell that the Criteria expression is part of a HAVING clause. The key to knowing whether you're dealing with a WHERE or HAVING clause is the data source. If the field is a data field, such as OrderDate, then the Criteria expression is the equivalent of a WHERE clause. When the Criteria is executed against an aggregate function, such as **Count()**—as shown in

Figure 7-13—SQL uses a HAVING clause. This is one of the two main distinctions between the two clauses. (The other is that the two clauses are applied at different times, which we've already discussed.) Figure 7-14 displays the results of the HAVING clause example. The TotalOrders column contains values greater than 1.

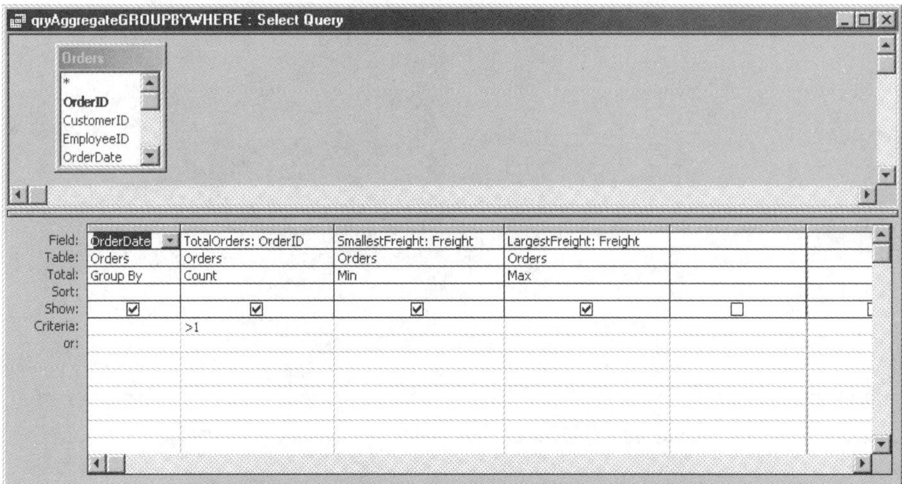

Figure 7-13. The Criteria expression is the equivalent of a HAVING clause.

qryAggregateGROUPBYWHERE : Select Query

Order Date	TotalOrders	SmallestFreight	LargestFreight
08-Jul-1996	2	$41.34	$65.83
19-Jul-1996	2	$3.05	$55.09
01-Aug-1996	2	$4.54	$136.54
14-Aug-1996	2	$2.94	$8.98
27-Aug-1996	2	$6.40	$79.70
09-Sep-1996	2	$17.68	$45.08
20-Sep-1996	2	$17.52	$24.69
03-Oct-1996	2	$3.43	$34.57
16-Oct-1996	2	$10.19	$12.75
29-Oct-1996	2	$26.78	$166.31
11-Nov-1996	2	$64.19	$162.33
22-Nov-1996	2	$131.70	$183.17
26-Nov-1996	2	$30.54	$71.97
28-Nov-1996	2	$10.14	$13.55
03-Dec-1996	2	$0.45	$1.17
05-Dec-1996	2	$3.94	$124.12
09-Dec-1996	2	$20.39	$22.21
12-Dec-1996	2	$7.99	$35.03

Record: 1 of 254

Figure 7-14. The HAVING clause eliminated records whose TotalOrders value wasn't greater than 1.

> **NOTE** *A HAVING clause can contain up to 40 expressions linked by logical operators, such as AND and OR.*

Combining WHERE and HAVING

It's possible to use the WHERE and HAVING clauses together. Following our previous example, you could limit the SELECT set to those orders made after January 1, 1997, and having more than one order per day. To do so, you'd simply use both the WHERE and HAVING clauses from our previous examples, as follows:

```
SELECT OrderDate, Count(OrderID) AS TotalOrders, Min(Freight) AS SmallestFreight,
    Max(Freight) AS LargestFreight
FROM Orders
WHERE OrderDate > #1/1/1997#
GROUP BY OrderDate
HAVING Count(OrderID) > 1;
```

In Design view, shown in Figure 7-15, both Criteria expressions are present. The results, shown in Figure 7-16, contain only those records whose OrderDate value is greater than January 1, 1997, and in which the TotalOrders value is greater than 1.

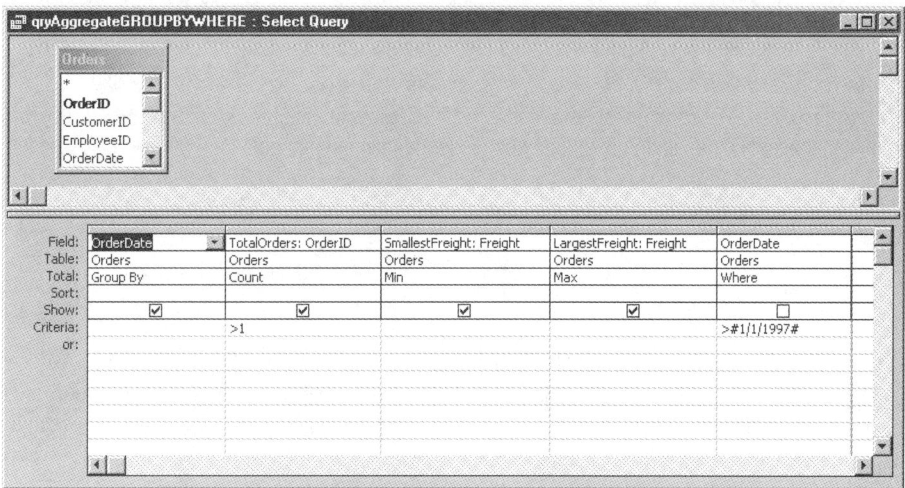

Figure 7-15. You can use both the WHERE and HAVING clause in one statement.

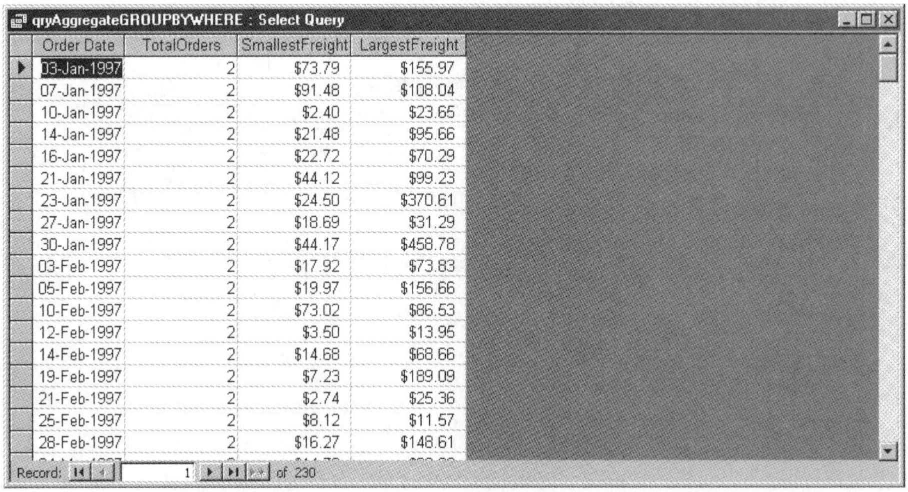

qryAggregateGROUPBYWHERE : Select Query

Order Date	TotalOrders	SmallestFreight	LargestFreight
03-Jan-1997	2	$73.79	$155.97
07-Jan-1997	2	$91.48	$108.04
10-Jan-1997	2	$2.40	$23.65
14-Jan-1997	2	$21.48	$95.66
16-Jan-1997	2	$22.72	$70.29
21-Jan-1997	2	$44.12	$99.23
23-Jan-1997	2	$24.50	$370.61
27-Jan-1997	2	$18.69	$31.29
30-Jan-1997	2	$44.17	$458.78
03-Feb-1997	2	$17.92	$73.83
05-Feb-1997	2	$19.97	$156.66
10-Feb-1997	2	$73.02	$86.53
12-Feb-1997	2	$3.50	$13.95
14-Feb-1997	2	$14.68	$68.66
19-Feb-1997	2	$7.23	$189.09
21-Feb-1997	2	$2.74	$25.36
25-Feb-1997	2	$8.12	$11.57
28-Feb-1997	2	$16.27	$148.61

Record: 1 of 230

Figure 7-16. We've eliminated old records and limited the results to those dates that have more than one order.

> **NOTE** *If you have trouble remembering when Jet applies each clause, the statement itself offers a clue. The WHERE clause is positioned before the GROUP BY clause, and Jet applies it before it groups the SELECT's results. The HAVING clause follows the GROUP BY clause, and Jet applies the HAVING clause to the grouped results of the SELECT.*

Working with Multiple Criteria

In the last section, we combined both the WHERE and HAVING clauses, which gives the illusion of working with multiple criteria—but only to an extent because Jet omits data at different points. You may need to specify multiple criteria to either a WHERE or a HAVING clause, and doing this can be a bit tricky when combined with the GROUP BY clause. We've already stated the problem: you can't include extraneous columns in a GROUP BY clause. (By *extraneous*, we mean any column not being grouped.) Sometimes this limitation can force you to modify your solutions. We've already reviewed multiple criteria in a WHERE clause. For more information on that subject, see "Complex Expressions That Limit Results" in Chapter 5.

In this section, we'll show you some problems that you can expect to encounter when working with multiple criteria in a HAVING clause. First, let's look at a simple GROUP BY clause that returns the total freight cost for each postal code region in the Orders table:

```
SELECT ShipPostalCode, Sum(Freight) AS SumOfFreight
FROM Orders
GROUP BY ShipPostalCode;
```

Figure 7-17 shows the results. We've included only the two fields that are absolutely necessary—ShipPostalCode and Freight—to determine these subtotals. The first row totals orders for which the ShipPostalCode field is null. (Refer to Table 7-1 for more information on Null values and aggregates.) Figure 7-18 shows this same query in Design view.

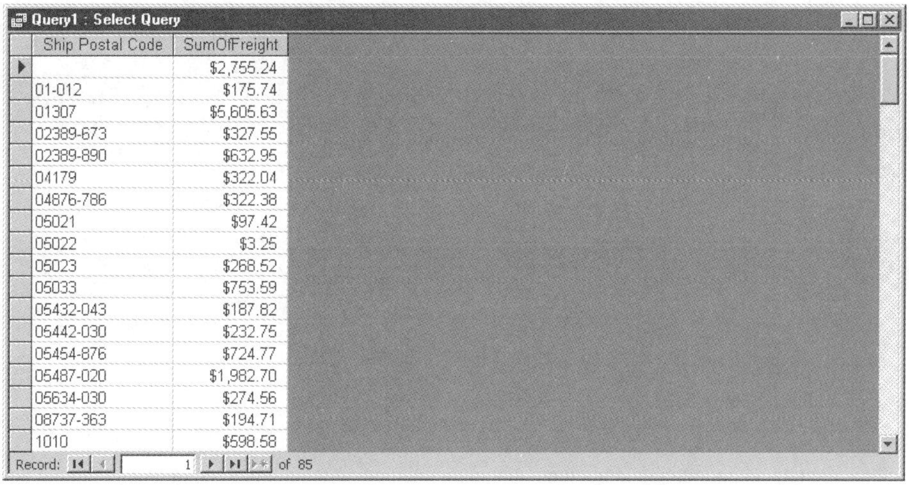

Query1 : Select Query

Ship Postal Code	SumOfFreight
	$2,755.24
01-012	$175.74
01307	$5,605.63
02389-673	$327.55
02389-890	$632.95
04179	$322.04
04876-786	$322.38
05021	$97.42
05022	$3.25
05023	$268.52
05033	$753.59
05432-043	$187.82
05442-030	$232.75
05454-876	$724.77
05487-020	$1,982.70
05634-030	$274.56
08737-363	$194.71
1010	$598.58

Record: 1 of 85

Figure 7-17. The SQL GROUP BY clause produces this simple subtotaled list of freight costs.

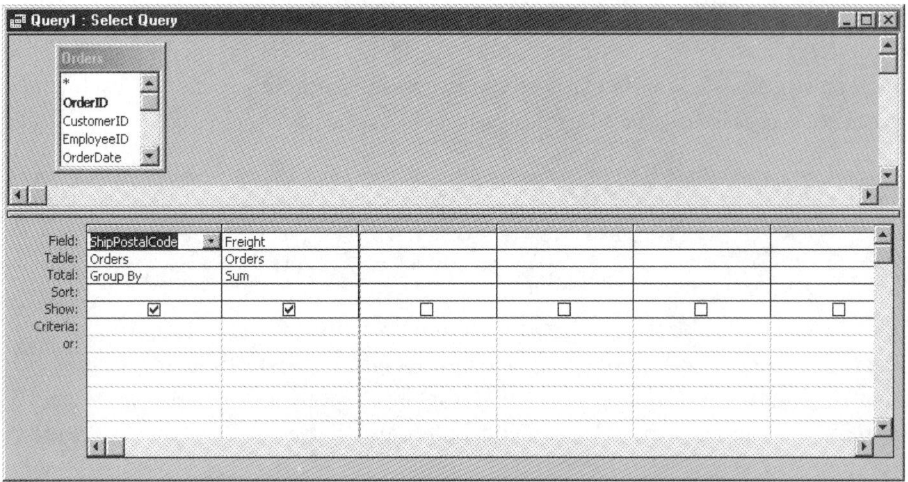

Figure 7-18. Design view shows the graphic representation of our GROUP BY clause.

Now, let's complicate the picture by limiting the subtotals to two particular codes. (You could limit them by more than two codes, but we're going to use just two to keep the example simple.) For example, let's calculate the total freight costs for two postal code regions in Brazil: 04876-786 and 02389-890. To do this, we'll add a HAVING clause that specifies more than one criteria using the OR operator:

```
SELECT ShipPostalCode, Sum(Freight) AS SumOfFreight
FROM Orders
GROUP BY ShipPostalCode
HAVING ShipPostalCode ="04876-786" OR
  ShipPostalCode = "02389-890";
```

Figure 7-19 shows the results of this query, and Figure 7-20 shows the query in Design view. As you can see, we have just two subtotals—one for each of the postal codes specified in the HAVING clause.

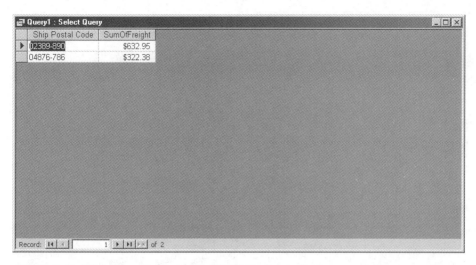

Figure 7-19. Multiple criteria in the HAVING clause limit our previous query to just two postal code regions.

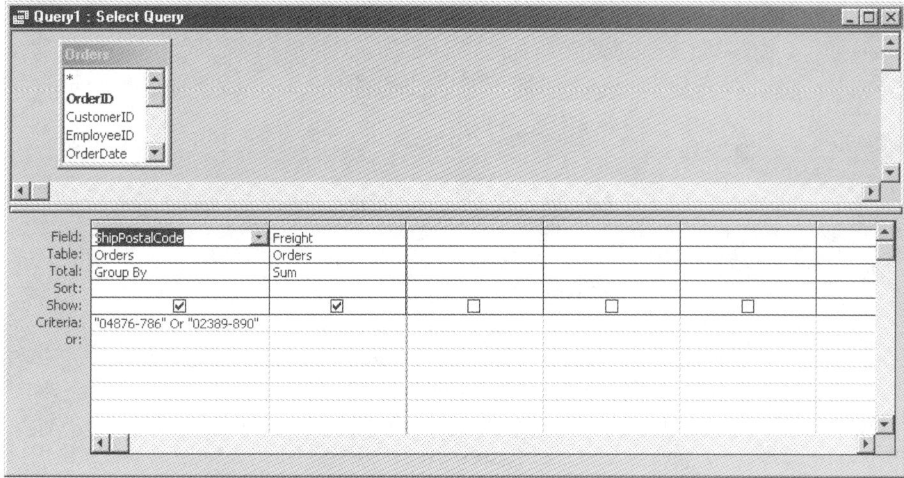

Figure 7-20. Design view shows the graphic representation of our multiple HAVING clause criteria.

This isn't the only way to express this particular solution, however. You could also specify the multiple criteria in the WHERE clause using the statement

```
SELECT ShipPostalCode, Sum(Freight) AS SumOfFreight
FROM Orders
WHERE ShipPostalCode ="04876-786" OR
  ShipPostalCode="02389890"
GROUP BY ShipPostalCode;
```

The graphical equivalent is shown in Figure 7-21. Keep in mind that the WHERE and GROUP BY criteria are seldom as interchangeable as they are in this example. In this particular case, you can use the Expression aggregate instead of the Where aggregate, as shown in Figure 7-21. The SQL equivalent of the Expression aggregate is the same as the multiple HAVING clause: the SQL statement doesn't change; only the way Access displays it in the Query Design window changes.

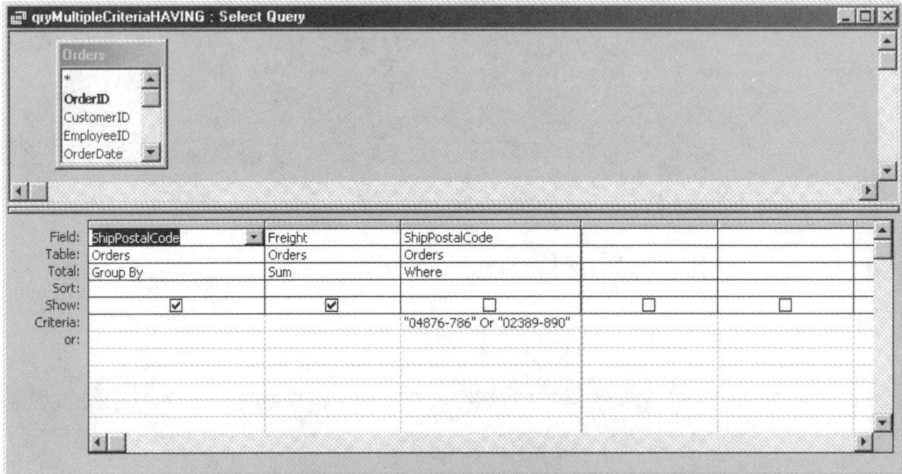

Figure 7-21. In this case, the Where and Expression options are interchangeable.

Expression and Where Aggregate Options Aren't Interchangeable

In the accompanying example, you're able to use the Expression and Where aggregate options (Access, not SQL) interchangeably. This unusual circumstance isn't normal by any means. The Expression option creates a calculated field that includes an aggregate function: the HAVING clause is always specific to an aggregate by way of the GROUP BY clause. In contrast, the Where option specifies criteria for a field you're not using to define a group.

If you do run into a situation in which the two are interchangeable, the Where option is usually the better choice because Where reduces the records before the aggregation, which improves performance.

We can still further complicate our GROUP BY example. Let's suppose that you want one freight cost total for both postal codes. As long as your query includes a GROUP BY clause on the ShipPostalCode field, you can't return just one total for two different codes. Instead, you must eliminate the ShipPostalCode from the GROUP BY clause. You might be wondering how we can group by a particular field without including it in a GROUP BY clause. In this particular situation, the solution is to summarize the Freight field and use the postal codes as criteria. The result is the following SQL statement:

```
SELECT Sum(Freight) AS SumOfFreight
FROM Orders
HAVING ShipPostalCode="04876-786" Or ShipPostalCode="02389-890";
```

Figure 7-22 shows the results of this statement. As you can see, this statement returns a single value: the total freight cost for all orders shipped to the postal code regions 04876-786 and 02389-890. Figure 7-23 shows the equivalent query in Design view. The aggregate rule still applies: the HAVING clause limits the SUM aggregate in the SELECT clause.

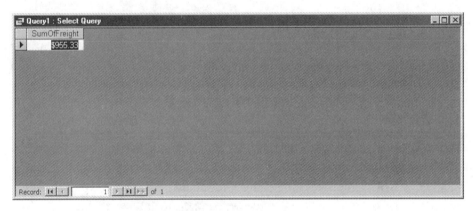

Figure 7-22. By moving the aggregate to the SELECT statement, we can eliminate the GROUP BY clause.

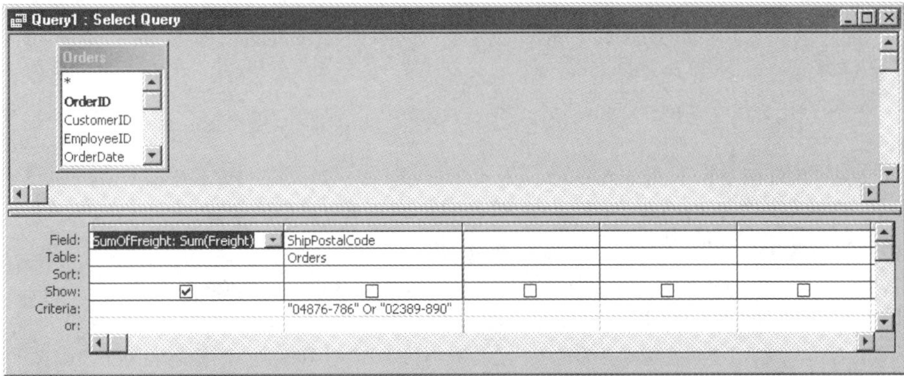

Figure 7-23. Design view shows how the HAVING clause limits the SUM aggregate.

Creating Crosstab Queries

Although a Crosstab query could be considered a complex Select query, it's also a summarized view of your data, and that's why we're including it in this chapter on aggregating data. Basically, a Crosstab query groups summarized data by categories. On that note, it's really more of a Totals query (or view) than a Select query.

All Crosstab queries have three components: one column heading, one or more row headings, and one summary field. These components are arranged in such a manner as to display a great deal of data in a relatively small area. To create a Crosstab query, use the TRANSFORM statement in the form

```
TRANSFORM aggregate
SELECT statement
PIVOT column
```

where *aggregate* is one of the SQL aggregate functions discussed in the earlier section "Presenting the SQL Aggregate Functions," and *column* is the pivot column that will become the column heading. The *SELECT statement* is any valid SELECT with a GROUP BY clause. The SELECT statement specifies the crosstab's row heading, and the PIVOT clause identifies the column headings.

Access includes a wizard—the Crosstab Query wizard—that walks you through the process of creating a Crosstab query. Although the wizard is a means to an end, you may find that the method we're about to show you—tweaking a GROUP BY query—is more predictable. Of course, this method assumes a certain amount of SQL knowledge. If you feel intimidated, try the following examples anyway; you may find that just working through these examples clears up some of the mystery surrounding the Crosstab query and maybe even SQL itself.

When using this method, look for two things in your SELECT statement:

- At least two GROUP BY clauses
- No HAVING clause

The TRANSFORM statement uses at least one of the GROUP BY fields as its column heading. In addition, the TRANSFORM statement doesn't support the HAVING clause. When restricting data by the results of an aggregate, base the Crosstab query on a GROUP BY query that includes the aggregate's HAVING clause.

Now, let's suppose that you want to build a Crosstab query that totals the number of orders by day and employee. You can start with the following GROUP BY query:

```
SELECT OrderDate, EmployeeID, Count(OrderID) AS TotalOrders
FROM Orders
GROUP BY OrderDate, EmployeeID;
```

Figure 7-24 shows the results of this query. Notice that there are two GROUP BY fields: OrderDate and EmployeeID. As a result, the query counts the total number of orders per employee for each order date. Although the query is adequate, the visual impact is lessened because dates are repeated when more than one employee has an order on the same day. A crosstab would summarize the data so that you could quickly summarize dates and employees.

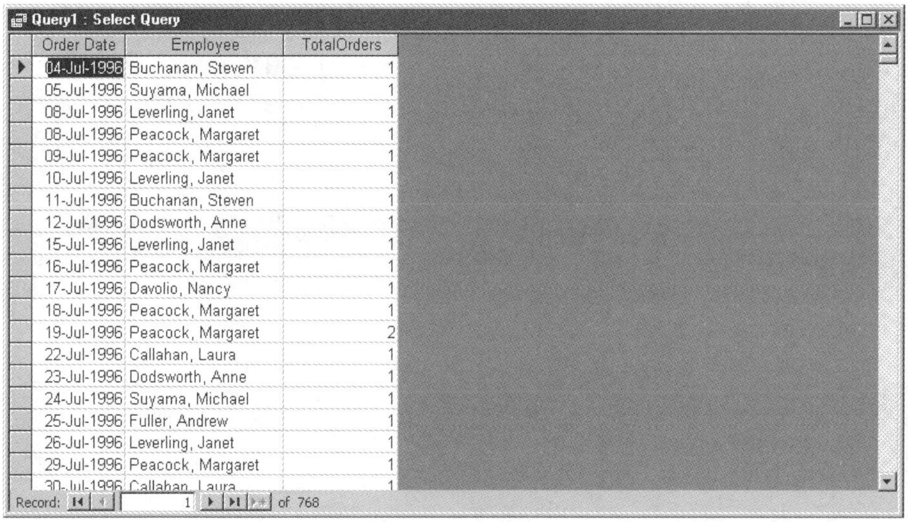

Query1 : Select Query

Order Date	Employee	TotalOrders
04-Jul-1996	Buchanan, Steven	1
05-Jul-1996	Suyama, Michael	1
08-Jul-1996	Leverling, Janet	1
08-Jul-1996	Peacock, Margaret	1
09-Jul-1996	Peacock, Margaret	1
10-Jul-1996	Leverling, Janet	1
11-Jul-1996	Buchanan, Steven	1
12-Jul-1996	Dodsworth, Anne	1
15-Jul-1996	Leverling, Janet	1
16-Jul-1996	Peacock, Margaret	1
17-Jul-1996	Davolio, Nancy	1
18-Jul-1996	Peacock, Margaret	1
19-Jul-1996	Peacock, Margaret	2
22-Jul-1996	Callahan, Laura	1
23-Jul-1996	Dodsworth, Anne	1
24-Jul-1996	Suyama, Michael	1
25-Jul-1996	Fuller, Andrew	1
26-Jul-1996	Leverling, Janet	1
29-Jul-1996	Peacock, Margaret	1
30-Jul-1996	Callahan, Laura	1

Record: 1 of 768

Figure 7-24. The TotalOrders field counts the number of orders for employee, per day.

Once you have the data grouped appropriately, open the query's SQL window and make the following changes:

1. Add a TRANSFORM clause before the SELECT statement using the aggregate function that you want to summarize. In this case, that's the **Count()** aggregate.

2. Delete the aggregate from your SELECT clause.

3. Add a PIVOT clause to the end of the statement using one of the GROUP BY fields as the argument. Move the field that appropriately specifies the crosstab's column heading. In this case, that's the EmployeeID field. The

remaining GROUP BY field becomes the row heading, and you can have more than one row heading.

4. Delete the field that you just moved to the PIVOT clause from the GROUP BY clause. Following our example, the result is the statement

```
TRANSFORM Count(OrderID) AS TotalOrders
SELECT OrderDate
FROM Orders
GROUP BY OrderDate
PIVOT EmployeeID;
```

The resulting query, shown in Figure 7-25, displays a list of unique dates in the first column and the EmployeeID values as the column headings across the top. The summarized values are the total number of orders for the corresponding date (row) for the corresponding employee (column).

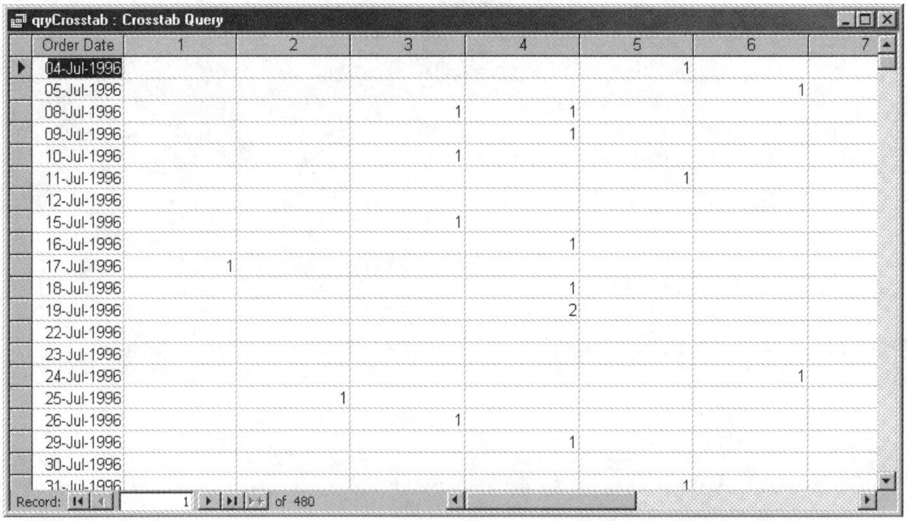

qryCrosstab : Crosstab Query

Order Date	1	2	3	4	5	6	7
04-Jul-1996					1		
05-Jul-1996						1	
08-Jul-1996			1	1			
09-Jul-1996				1			
10-Jul-1996			1				
11-Jul-1996					1		
12-Jul-1996							
15-Jul-1996			1				
16-Jul-1996				1			
17-Jul-1996	1						
18-Jul-1996				1			
19-Jul-1996				2			
22-Jul-1996							
23-Jul-1996							
24-Jul-1996						1	
25-Jul-1996		1					
26-Jul-1996			1				
29-Jul-1996				1			
30-Jul-1996							
31-Jul-1996					1		

Record: 1 of 480

Figure 7-25. The intersection of a row and column displays the total number of orders placed by the employee represented by that column on the date represented by that row.

Adding a JOIN to TRANSFORM

> **NOTE** *Changing the column heading text isn't the only reason for adding a JOIN clause to a TRANSFORM statement. You may legitimately need the JOIN to include in an aggregate function or a GROUP BY clause.*

The TRANSFORM query (crosstab) shown in Figure 7-25 has one problem: the column headings display the EmployeeID values (the primary key) and not the employee's name. Technically, this is correct, but the primary key values don't help you much unless you've memorized them all. Displaying the employee's name would be more helpful.

A JOIN in the FROM clause solves this problem. Specifically, you add a JOIN clause that returns the LastName entry for each employee and then refer to that LastName field in the PIVOT clause as follows:

```
TRANSFORM Count(OrderID) AS TotalOrders
SELECT OrderDate
FROM Employees INNER JOIN Orders ON Employees.EmployeeID = Orders.EmployeeID
GROUP BY OrderDate
PIVOT LastName;
```

> **TIP** *Be sure to include the table identifier when multiple data sources contain fields with the same name as we did in the accompanying example. If there's no JOIN, you don't need to worry about these identifiers as much. This example is the first time in this chapter that we've explicitly referred to the data source in this manner.*

Figure 7-26 shows the query in Design view and Figure 7-27 shows the results of the query. You could further enhance the display by including the employees' first names by substituting the PIVOT clause with:

```
PIVOT FirstName & " " & LastName;
```

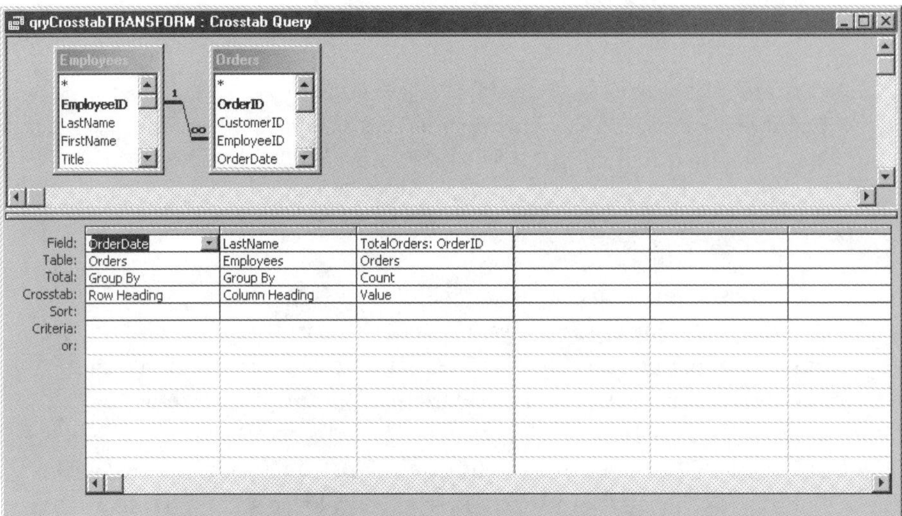

Figure 7-26. Our changes are reflected in the query design grid.

qryCrosstabTRANSFORM : Crosstab Query

Order Date	Buchanan	Callahan	Davolio	Dodsworth	Fuller	King	Leverli
04-Jul-1996	1						
05-Jul-1996							
08-Jul-1996							
09-Jul-1996							
10-Jul-1996							
11-Jul-1996	1						
12-Jul-1996				1			
15-Jul-1996							
16-Jul-1996							
17-Jul-1996			1				
18-Jul-1996							
19-Jul-1996							
22-Jul-1996		1					
23-Jul-1996				1			
24-Jul-1996							
25-Jul-1996					1		
26-Jul-1996							
29-Jul-1996							
30-Jul-1996		1					
31-Jul-1996	1						

Record: 1 of 480

Figure 7-27. Now, the column headings display the employees' last names.

Specifying Column Headings

In the last section, we showed you how to use a JOIN to display meaningful column headings in a crosstab's results. You might not need to resort to a JOIN because the PIVOT clause supports predicates—the IN predicate to be precise. You'll find this useful when you want to display alternate text in the column headings, but a JOIN isn't adequate. Unfortunately, the IN predicate isn't dynamic like the JOIN solution, by which we mean that it doesn't update automatically.

Our last example isn't a candidate for the IN predicate because the EmployeeID field is a Number field, and we want to display text. The data type of the PIVOT field must match the IN predicate's list. So, let's suppose that you have a crosstab that uses the abbreviated form of the day of the week (sorted alphabetically): Fri, Mon, Sat, Sun, Thu, Tue, and Wed. You could improve the display by including the IN predicate in the PIVOT clause as follows:

```
PIVOT dayoftheweekfield IN("Mon","Tue","Wed","Thur","Fri","Sat","Sun")
```

> **TIP** *When using this technique, just be sure that the IN arguments exactly match the column headings. If they don't, SQL simply drops that column from the display.*

Limiting Column Headings

You can use the IN predicate to limit the columns. To best illustrate this technique, we'll use the Orders TRANSFORM that we've been working on. Suppose we want to limit the display of that crosstab to just a few employees instead of all of them. Specifically, the following statement would display only the data pertinent to Nancy Davolio (EmployeeID value 1), as shown in Figure 7-28.

```
TRANSFORM Count(OrderID) AS TotalOrders
SELECT OrderDate
FROM Employees INNER JOIN Orders ON Employees.EmployeeID=Orders.EmployeeID
GROUP BY OrderDate
PIVOT LastName IN ("Davolio");
```

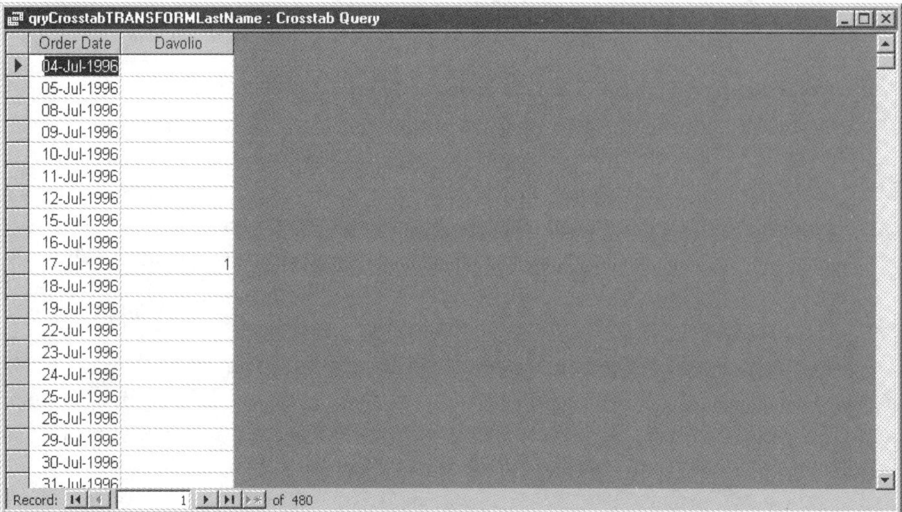

Figure 7-28. The crosstab displays only the column for Nancy Davolio.

> **NOTE** *Don't confuse the PIVOT SQL clause with the new Access 2002 PivotTable view. The PIVOT clause specifies the field (or expression that evaluates to a field) that serves as the column heading in a Crosstab query. A PivotTable is an Office Web component that displays table data in a specialized view (as a pivot table).*

When using this technique remember these three guidelines:

- The argument (in this case the string Davolio) must match exactly.
- The IN predicate accepts multiple items. Each needs to be separated by a comma (,).
- The data type of the IN predicate's argument list must match the PIVOT field's data type.

> **NOTE** *Transact-SQL (T-SQL) doesn't support TRANSFORM or PIVOT clauses. Thus, the Upsizing wizard can't translate an MDB file's Crosstab query when you upsize that file to an ADP project of SQL Server. You'll have to rewrite the Crosstab using a T-SQL view, function, or stored procedure. You can learn more about upsizing Crosstab queries in Chapter 17.*

CHAPTER 8

Creating and Modifying Tables

An Introduction to SQL's Data Definition Language

CHAPTERS 5, 6, AND 7 INTRODUCED YOU to Data Manipulation Language (DML), which is SQL's data management terminology. In those chapters, you learned to manipulate the data stored in your database. DML's sibling, Data Definition Language (DDL), manages the objects in a database—specifically, the tables, indexes, and relationships, as defined below.

- A table is a collection of related data that's stored in rows and columns (records and fields, respectively).
- An index defines how Jet arranges and sorts the data that's stored in tables.
- A relationship determines how tables are related to one another (through the use of primary and foreign key values).

In this chapter, we'll review the three statements that create and modify tables: CREATE TABLE, ALTER TABLE, and DROP. For more-detailed information on DDL and indexes and relationships, read Chapter 9. (For basic information on tables, relationships, and primary and foreign key values, read the Chapter 3 sections "Creating Relationships" and "The Right Keys."

Creating Tables

Table Specifications

When creating a new table, keep the following specifications in mind:

- Table name is limited to 64 characters.
- Field names are limited to 64 characters.
- Each table can contain up to 255 fields. (SQL Server tables can contain 1,024 columns.)
- Each table is limited in size to 2GB minus the space needed for system objects (because the default size of the database is also 2GB).
- A Text field can contain up to 255 characters.
- A Memo field can contain up to 1GB if entered programmatically, or 65,535 if entered manually.
- An OLE Object field is limited to 1GB.
- Each table can have up to 32 indexes.
- Each index can contain up to 10 fields

Most of the time, you create tables manually, during the early days of an application's life. However, some applications require new tables (usually temporary tables for housing temporary data or defining temporary relationships). When you need to create tables programmatically, use SQL's CREATE TABLE statement.

Creating a new table using SQL involves a minimum of three tasks:

- Name the table.
- Name the fields.
- Define a data type for each field.

Fortunately, the CREATE TABLE statement allows for all three of these tasks. To create a table, use the syntax

```
CREATE TABLE tblname
(fldname1 type, fldname2 type, fldname3 type, . . . )
```

where *fldnamex* identifies each field by name, and *type* specifies *fldnamex's* data type. When *type* is a Text field, be sure to specify the field's length (the Field Size property) using the form

```
fldname Text(50)
```

Otherwise, SQL defaults to 255 characters. It's good programming practice to explicitly define field lengths to save on resources (albeit not much). Table 8-1 lists SQL data types and lists the appropriate *type* keyword for each Jet data type. (We've omitted SQL Server data types that have no corresponding type in Jet.) As you review this table, you'll notice that the Jet reserved keyword for each data type closely resembles the corresponding Access data type. They don't, however, always match exactly, so be careful to use the proper keyword.

> **TIP** *When a field name contains a space character, you must enclose the field name in square brackets ([ ]).*

Table 8-1. SQL Data Types

SQL SERVER	ACCESS	STORAGE SIZE	DESCRIPTION	JET RESERVED WORD (DDL)*
text(fieldsize)	Text	2 bytes per character	0 to a maximum of 2.14 gigabytes	LONGTEXT
image	OLE Object	As required	0 to a maximum of 2.14 gigabytes (OLE objects)	LONGBINARY
bit	Yes/No	1 byte	Integers 0 or 1 (Yes/No)	BIT
tinyint	Number, Byte Field Size	1 byte	An integer value between 0 and 255	BYTE, TINYINT (OLEDB/ADO**)
smallint	Number, Integer Field Size	2 bytes	A short integer between -2^15 through 2^15-1	SHORT
int	Number, Long Field Size	4 bytes	A long integer between -2^31 through 2^31-1	LONG
money	Currency	8 bytes	A scaled integer between -2^63 through 2^63-1	CURRENCY
datetime	Date/Time	8 bytes	A date or time value between the years 100 and 9999	DATETIME
real	Number, Single Field Size	4 bytes	A single-precision floating-point value with a range of -3.40E+38 through 3.40E+38	SINGLE
float	Number, Double Field Size	8 bytes	A double-precision floating-point value with a range of -1.79E+308 through 1.79E+308	DOUBLE, DOUBLE PRECISION (OLEDB/ADO**)
decimal (precision,scale)	Number, Decimal Field Size	17 bytes SQL Server; 14 bytes Access	An exact numeric data type that holds values from -10^-28 to 10^28-1	DECIMAL
counter, autoincrement	AutoNumber, Long Field Size	4 bytes	A long integer between -2,147,483,648 and 2,147,483,647	COUNTER, AUTOINCREMENT

*Use these SQL reserved keywords when specifying a field's data in a CREATE TABLE statement.

**Available only through code that you can't execute using the SQL window interface.

Specifying Null

Similarly to specifying a field's data type, you can specify that the field not accept a Null value by including NOT NULL. Simply include the NOT NULL combination after the *type* argument in the form

```
CREATE TABLE tblname
(fldname1 type NOT NULL,
fldname2 type NOT NULL,
fldname3 type NOT NULL, . . . )
```

to eliminate Null values in a field. If you omit NOT NULL, Jet accepts a Null value.

What about Nulls?

A Null value means the value is unknown, not that the value doesn't exist. For instance, you might leave a fax field for a new customer blank because you don't know the fax number. Later, you can update the record with the appropriate number. If you learn the customer doesn't have a fax, then you might make a more appropriate entry such as "N/A," rather than leaving the field "Null". Some developers prefer not to leave fields null once it's known that the data doesn't exist.

Often, too many Null values point to an unnormalized table. For example, the above phone scenario requires a table with a field that's specifically designated for just fax numbers. Most likely, you'd also have specific fields for other phone types, such as office, home, cellular, and so on. But this arrangement isn't the most efficient. Instead, consider a table with three fields: a foreign key value that relates the phone to the corresponding customer, a phone number type value, and the phone number. The phone number type value might be a simple list of values, such as 1, 2, and 3, for business, fax, and home, respectively. You enter a record for each phone number and identify that number by phone type—entering only the records you need and eliminating Null values for phone types that don't apply to a particular customer.

NOTE *Microsoft ADO Extensions for DDL and Security (ADOX) offers an alternative to the SQL CREATE TABLE statement. Although ADOX requires more code, the results are more flexible because ADOX is compatible with other database engines via OLE DB providers.*

The CREATE TABLE function is much more flexible than the basic form indicates. Table 8-2 lists additional features. Although there's more, we'll leave referential integrity and foreign keys for Chapter 9 ("Manipulating Relationships and Indexes").

Table 8-2. CREATE TABLE Extensions

DESCRIPTION	KEYWORD	SYNTAX*	EXAMPLE	EXPLANATION	AVAILABLE
Add a default	DEFAULT	CREATE TABLE *table* (*col coltype* [CONSTRAINT *conname contype*], *col coltype* [DEFAULT *defaultvalue*])	CREATE TABLE tblCustomers (CustomerID LONG CONSTRAINT ndxPK PRIMARY KEY, Contact TEXT DEFAULT Harkins)	Creates a table named tblCustomers, defines a primary key field named CustomerID and a Text field named Contact and sets Contact's default value to "Harkins"	ADO
Add a check constraint	CHECK	CREATE TABLE *table* [CONSTRAINT [*name*]] CHECK (*condition*)	CREATE TABLE tblCustomers (CustomerID LONG, ContactID BYTE, CONSTRAINT ndxContactID CHECK(ContactID BETWEEN 1 AND 15))	Creates a table named tblCustomers and defines a primary key field named ContactID and a BYTE field named ContactID and applies a CHECK CONSTRAINT to ContactID, which rejects any entry but the values 1 through 15	ADO
Define compression mode	WITH COMP	CREATE TABLE *table* (*col coltype* WITH COMP [NOT NULL])	CREATE TABLE tblCustomers (CustomerID LONG CONSTRAINT ndxPK PRIMARY KEY, Contact TEXT(50) WITH COMP)	Sets the Unicode Compression property for the Contact field to Yes in a new table named tblCustomers	ADO

> **NOTE** *The Microsoft Jet Engine (since 4.0) stores all TEXT data types in the Unicode two-byte character representation format, replacing the multi-byte character set (MBCS) format in previous versions. Although Unicode requires more space per character, TEXT columns can be defined to automatically compress the data when possible by setting the Unicode Compression property to Yes (for that field).*

Adding a CONSTRAINT Clause

The CONSTRAINT clause creates or deletes a constraint and works with CREATE TABLE (and ALTER TABLE, which we'll discuss later). A constraint is simply a rule that limits the values that you can enter into a field and preserves the integrity and consistency of your data. Although a constraint is similar to an index, they aren't the same. (An index is a dynamic cross-reference of one or more fields that permits faster data retrieval.) Table 8-3 lists and defines the types of constraints, but we won't deal with all of them in this chapter. (For more information on the PRIMARY KEY and FOREIGN KEY constraints, read the section "About Jet Indexes" in Chapter 9.)

Table 8-3. Constraints

CONSTRAINT	DESCRIPTION
PRIMARY KEY	A primary key uniquely identifies each record. All values in the primary key field must be unique. The field cannot contain any Null values, and each table can contain only one primary key, although the primary key can comprise multiple fields.
FOREIGN KEY	A foreign key relates to a primary key in a related table. The corresponding primary key values can be duplicated in a foreign key field, and a foreign key field can contain Null values.
UNIQUE	A unique index means that no two records in the current table have the same value in the index field. You can apply a unique index to multiple fields. In this case, the combined values in all the included fields must be unique, but a single field within the multiple field index can contain duplicate values.
NOT NULL	This constraint won't allow Null values in a field. It's the equivalent of setting a field's Required property to Yes.
CHECK	Check constraints limit values. They're the Jet equivalent to validation rules. If you name the constraint, you can use the name only once because each constraint name must be unique. You must remove the CHECK CONSTRAINT before Jet allows you to delete a table created with the CHECK CONSTRAINT clause. CHECK constraints are available through only the OLE DB provider using ADO: you can't apply a CHECK constraint through the SQL window.

For more information on CONSTRAINTS, read Chapter 9.

Beyond the type of constraint, which we just discussed, you can apply a constraint in one of two ways:

- You can apply a constraint to a single field. This arrangement is known as a *single-field* or *column-level* constraint. The constraint is specified when you declare the field.
- You can apply a constraint to two or more fields. These are known as *multi-field* or *table-level* constraints.

When adding a constraint to a single field, use the following syntax:

```
CREATE TABLE tbl
      (fldname1 type. . . .
      fldname2 type
CONSTRAINT ndxname ndxtype)
```

where *ndxname* identifies the index, and *ndxtype* specifies the index type. The CONSTRAINT clause needs to follow the field to which the constraint applies.

For example, the following statement creates a table named tblCustomers with two fields: CustomerID (the primary key field) and CustomerName:

```
CREATE TABLE tblCustomers
      (CustomerID INTEGER PRIMARY KEY, CustomerName TEXT(50))
```

Primary key fields are automatically indexed, but, because you didn't assign a name using the *ndxname* argument, Jet assigns one internally. You can gain a bit more control by including a CONSTRAINT clause as follows:

```
CREATE TABLE tblCustomers
(CustomerID INTEGER CONSTRAINT ndxCustomerID PRIMARY KEY,
      CustomerName TEXT(50))
```

This statement allows a bit more flexibility because you know how to reference the constraint—ndxCustomerID—if modifications are necessary later.

To apply a constraint to more than one field, use the syntax

```
CREATE TABLE tbl
      (fldname1 type,
      fldname2 type,
CONSTRAINT ndxname ndxtype (fldname1, fldname2, . . . ))
```

The following statement creates a table similar to the one in our previous example. The only difference is that the ndxCustomerID constraint is applied to both fields, instead of just the CustomerID field:

```
CREATE TABLE tblCustomers
      (CustomerID INTEGER,
      CustomerName TEXT(50),
CONSTRAINT ndxCustomerID PRIMARY KEY (CustomerID, CustomerName))
```

> **NOTE** *Chapter 9 goes beyond the simple task of assigning primary and unique constraints. In it, you'll learn how to use the CONSTRAINT clause to create table and field constraints as they pertain to relationships and cascading updates and deletes.*

Avoiding a CREATE TABLE Error

If you try to create a table that already exists, Jet returns an error. However, you don't need a complex error-handling scheme. The code shown in Listing 8-1 executes the previous DDL example using ADO. After defining the strSQL variable and before the code actually executes the DDL SQL statement, an On Error Resume Next statement handles the error produced by the Close and DeleteObject methods when tblCustomers is open or doesn't exist. If tblCustomers is open, the Close method closes it; if tblCustomers exists, the DeleteObject method deletes it.

Listing 8-1. CreateTableDDL()

```
Function CreateTableDDL()
Dim cnn As New ADODB.Connection
Dim strSQL As String
Set cnn = CurrentProject.Connection
strSQL = "CREATE TABLE tblCustomers " & _
"(CustomerID INTEGER, CustomerName TEXT(50)," & _
"CONSTRAINT ndxCustomerID PRIMARY KEY (CustomerID, CustomerName))"
On Error Resume Next
DoCmd.Close acTable, "tblCustomers"
DoCmd.DeleteObject acTable, "tblCustomers"
On Error GoTo 0
cnn.Execute strSQL
End Function
```

> **NOTE** *If you're not familiar with creating and executing procedures in Access, read the section "Executing SQL with VBA" in Chapter 2.*

Modifying a Table's Structure

Once a table exists, you can modify it by adding or removing fields and indexes. Whether you created the table through the Access table designer or by a CREATE TABLE statement, you can use an ALTER TABLE statement to modify the schema of an existing table to add or delete a new field or constraint. Although useful, the ALTER TABLE statement has a few limitations: it isn't a multifaceted solution (it simply adds or deletes), and it doesn't have the capacity to change an existing field's definition. However, the ALTER TABLE statement has several specific functions, as listed in Table 8-4.

> **NOTE** *Always approach a table-altering task with great care because altering a table's structure can destroy data. For instance, if you change a field's data type, the Jet engine may truncate existing data, or even delete data in order to meet the new data type's limitations. In addition, you could break that table's relationships.*

Table 8-4. Functions of the ALTER TABLE Statement

DESCRIPTION	KEYWORD	SYNTAX*	EXAMPLE	EXPLANATION	AVAILABLE
Add a field	ADD COLUMN	ALTER TABLE *table* ADD [COLUMN] *col type*[(*size*)] [CONSTRAINT *conname contype*]	ALTER TABLE tblCustomers ADD COLUMN Contact Text(50) CONSTRAINT ndxContact UNIQUE	Modifies the existing table tblCustomers by adding a new Text field with a Field Size property of 50 named Contact and applying a unique index named ndxContact to that field	SQL view and ADO

(continued)

Table 8-4. Functions of the ALTER TABLE Statement (continued)

DESCRIPTION	KEYWORD	SYNTAX*	EXAMPLE	EXPLANATION	AVAILABLE
Add a field with a default value	ADD COLUMN	ALTER TABLE *table* ADD [COLUMN] *col type*[(*size*)] [CONSTRAINT *conname contype*] [SET DEFAULT *defaultvalue*	ALTER TABLE tblCustomers ADD COLUMN Contact Text(50) CONSTRAINT ndxContact UNIQUE DEFAULT abc	Modifies the existing table tblCustomers by adding a new Text field with a Field Size property of 50 and setting its Default Value property to abc	ADO
Change a field's data type**	ALTER COLUMN	ALTER TABLE *table* ALTER [COLUMN] *col newtype*[(*size*)]	ALTER TABLE tblCustomers ALTER COLUMN Contact TEXT(25)	Changes the existing field, Contact, in tblCustomers to a Text field and limits the Field Size property to 25	SQL view and ADO
Add a default value	ALTER COLUMN	ALTER TABLE *table* ALTER [COLUMN] *col newtype*[(*size*)] [SET DEFAULT *defaultvalue*	ALTER TABLE tblCustomers ALTER COLUMN Contact SET DEFAULT abc	Sets a default value of "abc" for the existing field Contact in tblCustomers	ADO
Delete a default value	ALTER COLUMN	ALTER TABLE *table* ALTER [COLUMN] *col* DROP DEFAULT	ALTER TABLE tblCustomers ALTER COLUMN Contact DROP DEFAULT	Deletes an existing default value setting from the Contact field in tblCustomers	ADO
Add a constraint	ADD CONSTRAINT	ALTER TABLE *table* ADD CONSTRAINT *conname contype* (*col1, col2, . . .*)	ALTER TABLE tblCustomers ADD CONSTRAINT ndxContact UNIQUE (Contact)	Adds a unique constraint to the existing field Contact in tblCustomers	SQL view and ADO
Delete a constraint	DROP CONSTRAINT	ALTER TABLE *table* DROP CONSTRAINT *conname*	ALTER TABLE tblCustomers DROP CONSTRAINT ndxContact	Deletes an existing constraint named ndxContact	SQL view and ADO

(continued)

Table 8-4. Functions of the ALTER TABLE Statement (continued)

DESCRIPTION	KEYWORD	SYNTAX*	EXAMPLE	EXPLANATION	AVAILABLE
Delete a primary key constraint	DROP CONSTRAINT	ALTER TABLE *table* DROP CONSTRAINT PRIMARY KEY	ALTER TABLE tblCustomers DROP CONSTRAINT PRIMARY KEY	Deletes the primary key field from tblCustomers	SQL view and ADO
Drop a field	DROP COLUMN	ALTER TABLE *table* DROP [COLUMN] *col*	ALTER TABLE tblCustomers DROP COLUMN Contact	Deletes an existing field named Contact from tblCustomers	SQL view and ADO
Change compression mode	WITH COMP	ALTER TABLE *table* ALTER COLUMN *col coltype* WITH COMP	ALTER TABLE tblCustomers Contact TEXT(50) WITH COMP	Modifies the Unicode Compression property for the Contact field to Yes in an existing table named tblCustomers	ADO

*Brackets ([ ]) indicate an optional argument.

**You can't alter an existing column's data to a COUNTER data type if the column already contains data.

> **TIP** *You can't rename a column (field). Instead, you must remove the field using the DROP COLUMN clause and then re-create it using the new name. Keep in mind that, when you run the DROP COLUMN clause against the field, you'll be deleting the data as well as the field. If you want to preserve the data, copy the data to a temporary field, delete and re-create the field, and then copy the data from the temporary field to the newly created field. Or, add the new field, and copy the data from the old field to the new field using an UPDATE statement. Then, delete the old (original) field.*

You know what a statement task does when you write it, and including optional keywords such as COLUMN in the ALTER TABLE statement may seem like an unnecessary nuisance. However, consider the maintenance developer that must add some new feature to the application six months or a year later. He or she may not be as familiar with SQL as you are. Adding that single keyword makes the code's purpose obvious: it adds a field to a table. Without the COLUMN keyword, the developer may have to spend additional time deciphering the code.

Making your code more readable doesn't require much of your time, and it can save time and frustration down the road.

Where's the Semicolon?

You may have noticed that we omitted the semicolon in our sample statements throughout this chapter. Whether the semicolon is necessary is the subject of some controversy because you can run a statement in the SQL window or code without it. In fact, if you include the semicolon at the end of a SET DEFAULT or DEFAULT statement, Jet incorrectly adds the actual semicolon character to the default value. For instance, if the statement specifies the string "abc" as the default value and you include the semicolon at the end of the clause (statement), Jet actually sets the property to "abc;" instead of "abc".

Because Jet seems to run fine without the semicolon, you may choose to exclude it, because Jet will add it for you. To illustrate this point, if you omit the semicolon from a simple SQL statement run by the SQL window, Jet will execute the statement correctly. If you save the query and reopen it in the SQL window, you will see that the Jet added the semicolon for you. However, it's perfectly safe for you to omit the semicolon from SQL statements.

Avoiding an ALTER TABLE Error

Attempting to alter a table can return a variety of errors, as listed below. If you're running these DDL statements programmatically, you'll want to allow for these errors and handle them appropriately:

- Before altering a table, you should make sure it's closed. If you run an ALTER TABLE statement on an open table, Jet returns an error.
- You can't use ADD COLUMN to add a field that already exists.
- You can't delete a field if a constraint exists on that field. You first must delete the constraint using DROP CONSTRAINT. Then delete the field using DROP COLUMN.
- If you attempt to delete a field, table, or constraint that doesn't exist, Jet will return an error.
- You must remove a CHECK CONSTRAINT before you can remove the table to which it applies.

The procedure shown in Listing 8-2 has simple but effective error handling for all of these possibilities. If you attempt to modify a table that's open, Jet will return an error. Therefore, you should always make sure that the table in question is closed before executing the DDL statement. That's the task of these three lines:

```
On Error Resume Next
DoCmd.Close acTable, "tblCustomers"
On Error GoTo 0
```

If the table is opened, the Close method closes it. If the table's closed, the Resume Next argument skips the error. The GoTo 0 argument in the third line resets the On Error statement. The next problem is the error returned when you attempt to add a field that already exists. The generic errHandler routine simply displays the appropriate error description in a message box. Depending on your situation, error handlers can be very sophisticated, but a short, simple routine such as this can be helpful in alerting the user to two things: the task wasn't completed and why it wasn't. In this case, it displays the internal description, so it will be specific to the error, even if you change the SQL string.

Listing 8-2. AlterTableDDL()

```
Function AlterTableDDL()
Dim cnn As New ADODB.Connection
Dim strSQL As String
Set cnn = CurrentProject.Connection
strSQL = "ALTER TABLE tblCustomers ADD COLUMN Contact Text(50) " & _
    "CONSTRAINT indContact UNIQUE"
On Error Resume Next
DoCmd.Close acTable, "tblCustomers"
On Error GoTo errHandler
cnn.Execute strSQL
Exit Sub
errHandler:
MsgBox Err.Description, vbOKOnly, "Can't complete task"
End Function
```

Using DROP

The Jet DROP statement can be used to delete a table or index. Using the form

```
DROP INDEX index ON table
```

deletes an index, where *index* identifies the index by name. Similarly, you can delete a table using the form

```
DROP TABLE table
```

New extensions offer additional forms of DROP that delete views, procedures, users, and groups, which are beyond the scope of this chapter.

CHAPTER 9

Manipulating Relationships and Indexes

Advanced SQL's Data Definition Language Topics

CHAPTER 8 CONCENTRATES ON creating and modifying tables using SQL, but creating the table is only part of the process. It stands to reason that you'll also need to specify relationships between any tables that you create. Fortunately, Access does a good job of managing and enforcing relationships between tables and manipulating indexes.

Using the Relationships window, you can manually create permanent relationships between tables. However, using Jet SQL, you can add the appropriate primary and foreign key fields using the CONSTRAINT clause. Then, Access takes over, automatically creating a relationship when you join the two tables in a query. In this chapter, we'll show you how to enhance relationships by enforcing referential integrity and using cascading updates and deletes.

> **NOTE** *For more information on the CONSTRAINT clause, see "Adding a Constraint Clause" in Chapter 8 ("Creating and Modifying Tables"). The rules for automatically creating relationships between two tables are listed in "Creating Permanent Relationships" in Chapter 3 ("An Introduction to Relational Database Theory"). You can learn about referential integrity and cascading options in "So Where's Referential Integrity Fit In?" also in Chapter 3.*

Enforcing Referential Integrity

Chapter 3 briefly mentioned referential integrity, but there's a lot more to say on the subject. In fact, to qualify as a relational database management system, a database system must enforce referential integrity. As you can see, it's an important topic and deserves a more thorough discussion than was allocated in Chapter 3.

Integrity refers to a set of rules that maintains relationships and, through these relationships, the dependability of your data. Integrity rules are of two types:

- *Entity*: Entity integrity states that each row must be uniquely identified. You can infer from this rule that each table must have a primary key and that a primary key value can't be a Null value.

- *Referential*: Referential integrity states that a foreign key value must either have a matching primary key value in a related table, or be a Null value.

I think computers have only one mission, and that is to make life easier for all—including developers. Thus, whenever you can get the computer to do the dirty work, do so; and maintaining referential integrity is one such area.

Gustav Brock, Cactus Data ApS, gustav@cactus.dk

Why You Need Referential Integrity

The most important aspect of any application is the dependability of its data. If the data's not right, the application is useless. One way to protect data integrity is to limit the data that users can enter and how and when they can modify and delete existing data. One way to protect your data is to take advantage of referential integrity options. Enforcing referential integrity means three things:

- You can't enter a new record if the foreign key value doesn't have a matching primary key value in the related table.

- You can't delete a record if the primary key value matches foreign key values in a related table.

- You can't modify a record's primary key value if matching foreign key values exist in a related table.

A Few Rules

You can't enforce referential integrity in every relationship. Three conditions must be met to enforce referential integrity:

- The related fields must either be a primary key field in one of the tables or have a unique index.
- The related fields must be the same data type with one exception. You can relate a Number and an AutoNumber field.
- The related tables must be in the same database. You can't enforce referential integrity between linked tables.

Cascading Options

Enforcing referential integrity protects your data by limiting when you can enter, delete, and modify data. Cascading options add flexibility by allowing you to enter, delete, and modify without violating referential rules. These options do so by making two assumptions, so you really need to be careful when applying these options. These assumptions are:

- If you update a primary key value, you want to update all matching foreign key values.
- If you delete a primary key value, you want to delete all matching foreign key values.

> **NOTE** *If you use AutoNumber data types to create primary key values, the cascading update option is useless. That's because you can't modify a primary key value; therefore, there will be no need for Jet to automatically update foreign key values for you.*

These cascading options aren't turned on by default. When you turn them on, Jet makes these two assumptions and makes decisions for you by updating and deleting foreign key values when you update or delete a primary key value. There's no option for adding orphan records. In other words, if you try to add a foreign key value before a matching primary key value exists in the related table, Jet will reject the entry (as long as referential integrity is turned on). There is no cascading option that will automatically create and add a primary key value.

> **NOTE** *SQL Server 2000 supports cascading options; earlier versions don't. As long as you upsize an MDB file to SQL Server 2000, cascades should remain intact. Read "Table Relationships," in Chapter 17 ("Upsizing Directly from Access").*

Enabling Cascading Options

Use the CONSTRAINT clause to enable cascading options using the ON UPDATE CASCADE or ON DELETE CASCADE keywords in an ALTER TABLE or CREATE TABLE statement. In addition, you must apply these keywords to the foreign key in the form

```
CREATE TABLE tbl
(fld1, fld2, . . . ,
CONSTRAINT conname, PRIMARY KEY, (fld1, . . . ),
CONSTRAINT conname, FOREIGN KEY (fld)
REFERENCES reftbl [(fld1, . . . )]
action)
```

where *reftbl* [(*fld1*, . . .)] identifies the related table and field(s) that contains *tbl*'s foreign key values (in an existing table). The *action* keywords are identified in Table 9-1.

Table 9-1. ON UPDATE Actions

ACTION	EXPLANATION
ON UPDATE CASCADE	Updates foreign key values when you modify a primary key value.
ON DELETE CASCADE	Deletes foreign key values when you delete a primary key value.
ON UPDATE NO ACTION*	You can't change the value of a primary key if it's referenced in the foreign key table (*reftbl*).
ON DELETE NO ACTION*	You can't delete a primary key value if it's referenced in the foreign key table (*reftbl*).
ON UPDATE SET NULL**	Sets a foreign key value to NULL if you update the matching primary key value.
ON DELETE SET NULL**	Sets a foreign key value to NULL if you delete the matching primary key value.

*This is the default setting and you don't need to set it, but including it does improve readability.
**Extensions available only via ADO code since Access 2000.

NOTE *You can't modify an existing relationship. First, you must delete a relationship and then re-create it. Use the DROP CONSTRAINT clause to remove a relation in the form*

```
ALTER TABLE tbl DROP CONSTRAINT relation
```

where relation *identifies the relationship. If you assign the name using code, you already know the name. When you're dealing with a relationship that was created manually, the Jet engine combines both table names, listing the primary key table first.*

An Example

You can run the CREATE statement in the SQL window, but it doesn't support the cascading option actions. Therefore, we'll need ADO to create tables when referential integrity is included in the task. The code in Listing 9-1 creates two new tables, tblStudent and tblPhone.

Listing 9-1. CascadingEx1

```
Function CascadingEx1()
    Dim cnn As ADODB.Connection
    Dim strSQL As String
    Set cnn = CurrentProject.Connection
    strSQL = "CREATE TABLE tblStudent" _
      & "(StudentID AUTOINCREMENT, LastName TEXT(25), " _
      & "FirstName TEXT(15), " _
      & "CONSTRAINT PK PRIMARY KEY (StudentID)) "
    Debug.Print strSQL
    On Error Resume Next
    DoCmd.Close acTable, " tblStudent "
    DoCmd.DeleteObject acTable, " tblStudent "
    cnn.Execute strSQL
    On Error GoTo 0
    strSQL = "CREATE TABLE tblPhone" _
      & "(PhoneID AUTOINCREMENT, PhoneNo TEXT(10), PhoneType LONG, " _
      & "StudentID LONG, " _
      & "CONSTRAINT PK PRIMARY KEY (PhoneID), " _
      & "CONSTRAINT FK FOREIGN KEY (StudentID) " _
      & "REFERENCES tblStudent " _
      & "ON DELETE CASCADE)"
```

```
    Debug.Print strSQL
    On Error Resume Next
    DoCmd.Close acTable, "tblPhone"
    DoCmd.DeleteObject acTable, " tblPhone "
    cnn.Execute strSQL
    On Error GoTo 0
End Function
```

To create this procedure, open the Visual Basic Editor (VBE), insert a new module, and enter the function shown in Listing 9-1. To run it, make sure that the cursor is inside the function text, and click on the Run Sub/UserForm button on the VBE's standard toolbar.

After creating the two tables, open them both in Design view (as shown in Figure 9-1) to see both designs and check for the primary keys. Next, open the relationships window, right-click on the join line between the two tables, and choose Edit Relationships to see the result of the ON DELETE CASCADE clause in the Edit Relationships dialog box (shown in Figure 9-2). That statement turned on the Cascade Related Records option.

> **NOTE** *The sections "Creating Tables" and "Modifying a Table's Structure" in Chapter 8 ("Creating and Modifying Tables") discuss the CREATE TABLE and ALTER TABLE statements, respectively.*

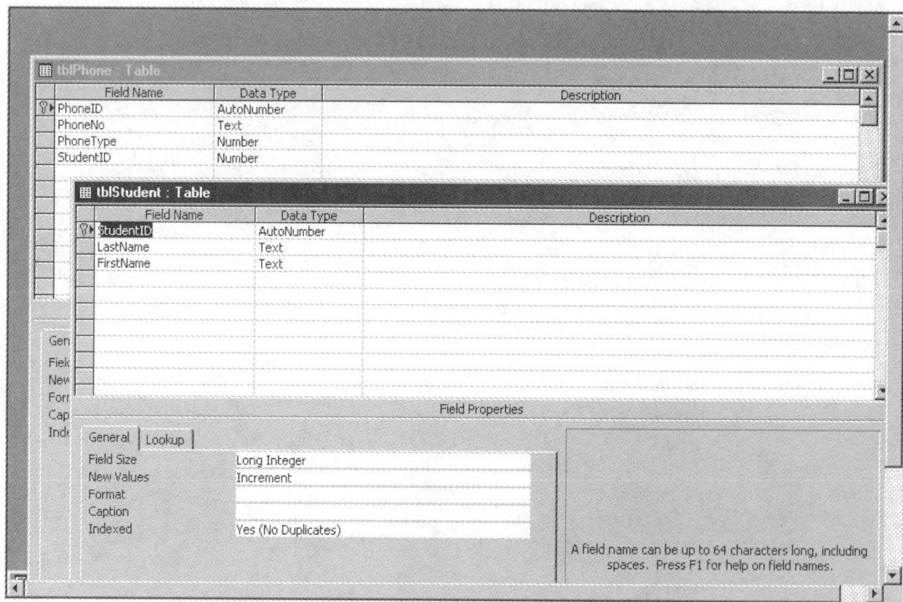

Figure 9-1. We used VBA and ADO to create these two tables.

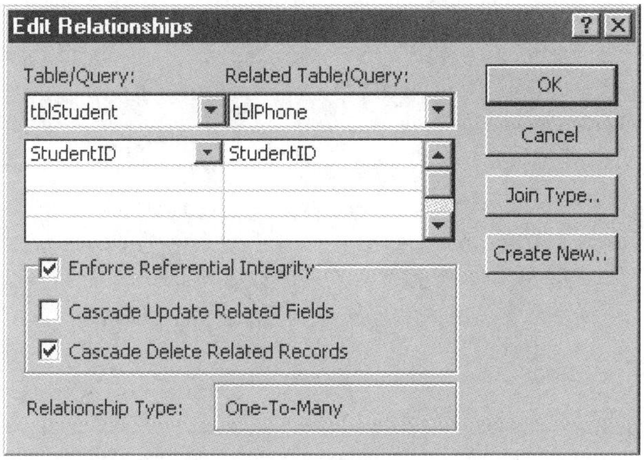

Figure 9-2. The relationship between tblStudent and tblPhone enforces the Cascade Delete Related Records options.

NOTE *To learn why we included the Debug.Print statement, read "Debugging Tricks," in Chapter 2 ("An Introduction to Using Jet SQL in Access").*

The error-handler we use in Listing 9-1 is discussed in "Avoiding a CREATE TABLE Error," in Chapter 8 ("Creating and Modifying Tables").

The first SQL statement creates the tblStudent table:

```
CREATE TABLE tblStudent
(StudentID AUTOINCREMENT, LastName TEXT(25), FirstName TEXT(15),
CONSTRAINT PK PRIMARY KEY (StudentID))
```

The second statement then creates tblPhone, and specifies and then relates StudentID in tblPhone as its foreign key value and turns on the cascading delete options:

```
CREATE TABLE tblPhone
(PhoneID AUTOINCREMENT, PhoneNo TEXT(10), PhoneType LONG, StudentID LONG,
CONSTRAINT PK PRIMARY KEY (PhoneID),
CONSTRAINT FK FOREIGN KEY (StudentID)
REFERENCES tblStudent
ON DELETE CASCADE)
```

WARNING *Use cascading delete (ON DELETE CASCADE) with great care. In fact, you might not want to turn it on permanently at all, choosing instead to turn it on when you need it and then turning it back off until it's needed again. The problem is that it's just too easy to delete a record when you really didn't mean to. Although Jet warns us, we are so used to these confirmation and warnings messages that we often click on OK without considering what the consequences might be. Deleting data seriously degrades the dependability of your data, and you can't undo a delete.*

Setting Referential Integrity

You can set referential integrity manually via the Relationships window. To do so:

1. Open the Relationships window by clicking the Relationships button on the database toolbar.
2. Right-click on the appropriate join line.
3. Select Edit Properties from the resulting submenu.
4. Check the Enforce Referential Integrity option.
5. The Cascade Delete Related Records option is the equivalent of the ON DELETE CASCADE SQL option. The Cascade Update Related Records option is the equivalent of the ON UPDATE CASCADE SQL option.

Now, let's add some data and see how referential integrity options limit your data entry opportunities. First, open tblPhone and try to enter a phone record. Enter any value in the StudentID field. When you try to save the record, Jet displays the error message shown in Figure 9-3. That's because there's no matching primary key value in tblStudent. (StudentID is the foreign key in tblPhone and the primary key in tblStudent.) Click on OK to clear the message. (You'll have to click on OK twice to clear subsequent warnings.)

> **TIP** *The system table MSysRelationships contains a field for each relationship in the szRelationship column. To "unhide" a system table so you can view the information, choose Options from the Tools menu. Then, click the View table and check the Systems Object option. Alternately, run the documenter to create a report of relationships. To do so, choose Analyze from the Tools menu, select Documenter from the resulting submenu, click the All Object Types tab, check the Relationships object, and click on OK.*

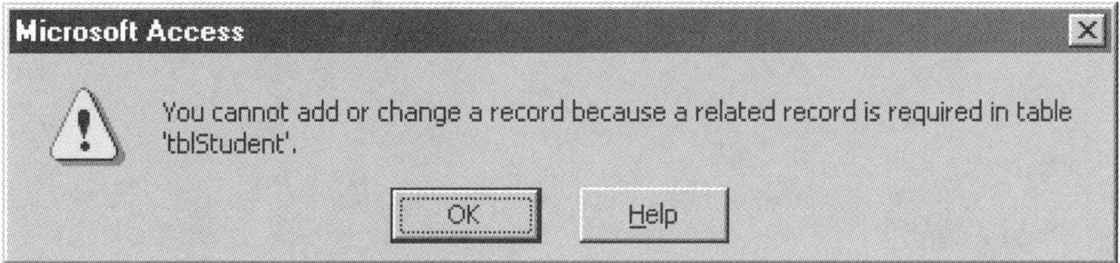
Microsoft Access
You cannot add or change a record because a related record is required in table 'tblStudent'.
OK
Help

Figure 9-3. Jet returns an error when you try to enter a foreign key value before entering the primary key value.

Open tblStudent and enter a few records, as shown in Figure 9-4. Then, reopen tblPhone and enter a few phone records using only existing StudentID value from tblStudent, as shown in Figure 9-5.

tblStudent : Table

StudentID	LastName	FirstName
1	Stanley	Alexis
2	Harkins	Susan
3	Reid	Martin
(AutoNumber)		

Record: 3 of 3

Figure 9-4. Enter a few primary key records in tblPhone.

tblPhone : Table

PhoneID	PhoneNo	PhoneType	StudentID
2	5555555555	1	1
3	5551234567	2	1
4	5555551234	1	2
(AutoNumber)			

Record: 4 of 4

Figure 9-5. Use only existing primary key values from tblPhone as the foreign key values in PhoneID.

You're ready to see the cascading delete option in action. With data in both tables, open tblStudent and try to delete the first record. When you do, Jet displays the message (shown in Figure 9-6) informing you that deleting the primary key value will also force Jet to delete a related foreign key value in a related table. In this case, the StudentID value 1 relates to two phone records: PhoneID values 2 and 3. Click on Yes to continue the delete task. Return to or open tblPhone to confirm that both records for Alexis Stanley are gone, as shown in Figure 9-7.

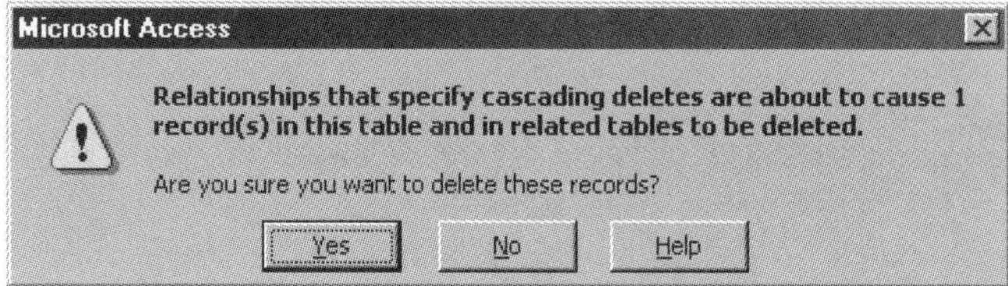

Figure 9-6. Jet warns you that the current delete task will also delete a related record.

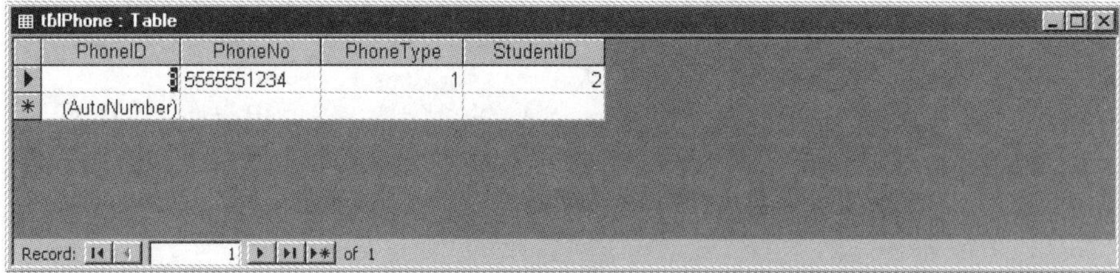

PhoneID	PhoneNo	PhoneType	StudentID
3	5555551234	1	2
(AutoNumber)			

Figure 9-7. The cascading delete option forced Jet to delete the related records.

> **NOTE** *If tblPhone is open when you execute the delete task, Jet will display #Deleted values in the appropriate fields. Simply close and reopen the table to clear those values.*

Cascading updates work in similar fashion, but, because we used AutoNumber fields as our primary key, we can't use them. At first, you might see this as a negative side effect, but in truth it is a positive one. Most likely, you'll have no need to update a primary key value if you use an AutoNumber field, thus rendering the whole topic moot.

> **NOTE** *You can use the Data Access Objects (DAO) Relation object or the ActiveX Data Object Extensions for DLL and Security (ADOX) library to create and manipulate relationships. Neither offers more functionality, just an alternative method. In fact, SQL offers the ability to customize the AutoNumber seed and increment values, which you can't do using the Relation object. If SQL Server may be in your application's future, you'll probably find the SQL statements the least trouble when converting. As a side note, you can also use ADOX to customize an AutoNumber field. For more information on ADO and ADOX, read Appendix B.*

About Jet Indexes

Considering the huge job that indexes perform, it's difficult to find a good definition for them. A simplistic definition of an index is a lookup table (usually a separate file) that stores key values and pointers to each entry in the index field. Technically, that definition applies to a nonclustered index, which is the only type Jet supports.

> **NOTE** *SQL Server offers clustered and nonclustered indexes. For more information on SQL Server indexes, read "Indexes" in Chapter 17 ("Upsizing Directly from Access").*

The reason you use an index is clearer: an index finds and sorts data quickly. Without an index, data is stored in no particular order, beyond the order in which you entered it. As a consequence, Jet must view the entire table to find data. This process is called a *table scan*, and requires that Jet view each record in the data.

> **NOTE** *The term* index *is also used to identify the position of a particular element, in respect to a particular set of elements. For instance, an array contains a number of values, and each value within the set has an index number, which identifies it uniquely.*

An index allows Jet to find data without scanning the entire table. In this context, an index is simply a list of values with a pointer to each row in the table that contains that particular value. This list of values is sorted, which makes it easy for the Jet engine to find a particular value and then return only those rows indicated by the pointers in the index.

WARNING *Despite that fact that an index is sorted, don't assign an index simply to sort a table by a particular column. Doing so can have unexpected results because an index sort is an internal process and won't necessarily return the type of sort you need. An index is not a dependable sort mechanism.*

When to Use Indexes

Jet automatically assigns indexes to primary keys and to foreign keys if referential integrity is enforced. To assign an index manually:

1. Open the table in Design view.
2. Select the field you want to index.
3. Choose one of the following settings from the Indexed property:
   - Yes (Duplicates OK)
   - Yes (No Duplicates)
4. The No option is the default, and indicates that there is no index on the field.

In addition, the PRIMARY KEY, FOREIGN KEY, and UNIQUE constraint types apply indexes. (For more information on these constraint types, read "Adding a CONSTRAINT Clause" in Chapter 8.)

Don't get slap-happy and start assigning indexes to all your fields thinking that you'll improve the performance of your application. Indexes actually decrease performance when used incorrectly. Every time you alter a table by updating, deleting, or inserting data, Jet refers to the index and then sorts the index accordingly, and that takes time. (You won't see this sorting take place in Datasheet view.) If you consider indexing a field, do so only if that field meets all of the following conditions:

- The field's data type is Text, Number, Currency, or Date/Time.
- You plan to frequently search and or sort records.
- The field contains mostly different values.

> **TIP** *If you're not sure whether to add an index, let Performance Analyzer give you some advice. First, remove all the indexes from the table. (Don't delete the primary key.) Then, run the analyzer by choosing Analyze from the Tools menu, and then selecting Performance from the resulting submenu. Click on the Tables tab, check the table you're analyzing, and then click on OK. Chances are that, if the analyzer doesn't suggest an index, you don't need it.*

Creating Fast Foreign Keys

Jet automatically indexes a foreign key. Specifically, when you create a relationship that enforces referential integrity, Jet creates an index on the foreign key field. Most of the time, you'll want to retain that index. However, an index occasionally has a negative effect on performance if the key has a number of duplicate values. When this is a possibility, consider creating what's known as a fast foreign key—an unindexed key. To do so, include the NO INDEX keyword in the following form:

```
CONSTRAINT conname, FOREIGN KEY NO INDEX (fld)
REFERENCES reftbl [(fld1, . . . )]
```

If you omit the NO INDEX keyword, Jet will apply an index.

> **NOTE** *The NO INDEX keyword isn't supported in the SQL window; you need ADO code to execute a SQL statement that uses this keyword.*

Avoid Duplicate Indexes

Jet will automatically index a foreign key value when you enforce referential integrity, even if an index already exists. When this happens, you end up with duplicate indexes, which aren't a problem. However, a duplicate index does count toward the limit of 32 indexes per table. We recommend that you don't include the INDEX clause when also using the CONSTRAINT clause to define a primary and or foreign key.

Creating a Multiple Field Index

A single index can consist of more than one field. Generally, you'll do so when combined data from more than one field can uniquely identify a record. (It's very similar to the process of using multiple fields in a natural data primary key field—only the purposes differ.) To create a multifield index:

1. Open the table in Design view.
2. Click on the Indexes button on the table design toolbar to open the Indexes dialog box.
3. Enter a name for the index in the Index Name cell.
4. Choose the first field in the index from the Field Name cell's drop-down list.
5. Select a sort order from the Sort Order cell's drop-down list.
6. In the next row, choose the second field in the index from the Field Name cell's drop-down list. (Don't enter a new name for the index; you're still entering fields for the same index.)
7. Repeat steps 5 and 6 as many times as necessary to add all the fields to the index. Figure 9-8 shows a multifield index by the name of Name, based on the LastName and FirstName fields.

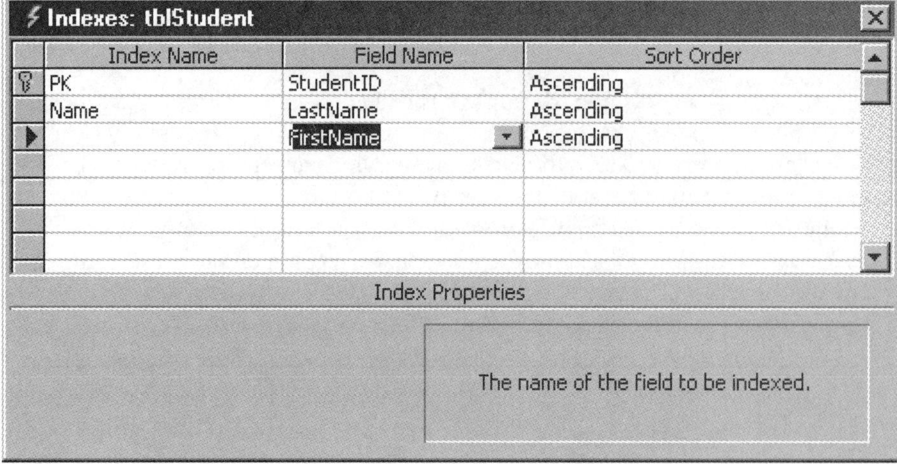

Figure 9-8. Create multifield indexes in the Indexes dialog box.

Using SQL to Set an Index

In the section "Adding a CONSTRAINT Clause" in Chapter 8 ("Creating and Modifying Tables"), we determined that the CONSTRAINT clause defines a rule that limits the type of data you can enter. The PRIMARY KEY, FOREIGN KEY, UNIQUE, and NOT NULL constraints all require an index (which Jet defines automatically), so you might think of these constraints as indexes, although they aren't. (Remember, the FOREIGN KEY constraint requires that you enforce referential integrity to force an index.)

In addition to using the CONSTRAINT clause, you can also use the CREATE INDEX statement to add an index to an existing table. Use the form

```
CREATE INDEX indexname
ON tbl (fld1, . . . )
WITH indextype
```

where *indexname* is the index's name, all indexes must have a name, and *tbl* and *fld1* identifies the field(s) that compose the key. Table 9-2 lists the different *indextype* arguments.

Table 9-2. Indextype Arguments

INDEX TYPE KEYWORD	DESCRIPTION	TABLE DESIGN EQUIVALENT
PRIMARY	Creates a primary key index	Primary Key
DISALLOW NULL	Doesn't allow Null values	Required property set to Yes
IGNORE NULL	Allows Null values, but Jet doesn't index them	N/A
UNIQUE	Doesn't allow duplicate values	Indexed property set to Yes (No Duplicates)

NOTE *SQL Server uses the NOT NULL index, not the DISALLOW NULL. You may want to watch for this when upsizing an Access MDB file to SQL Server.*

Returning an Index Name

Every index must have a name. When you create an index manually (in Table Design view), Access assigns a name internally, even though you probably don't realize it. If the index is a primary key index, Access names the index Primary Key. Otherwise, Access uses the name of the column as the index name. We recommend that you follow this convention when using SQL to assign an index.

When using SQL to create an index, it's easy to document that index's name by specifying the name in the SQL statement. You'll need DAO code to determine the name of those indexes that Access names for you (when you define an index manually). Following the previous conventions, it's easy enough to guess at the name, but you might as well let the following function do the work for you to avoid any kind of human error:

```
Function FindIndex(tbl As String)
    Dim db As DAO.Database
    Dim tdf As DAO.TableDef
    Dim idx As DAO.Index
    Set db = CurrentDb
    Set tdf = db.TableDefs(tbl)
    For Each idx In tdf.Indexes
        Debug.Print idx.Name
    Next
End Function
```

Simply pass the name of the table to the function, and then view the VBE Immediate window for a list of all the index names in the table. In actual code, you'll probably assign the name of the index to a variable.

NOTE *You can't set an index to a Memo, Hyperlink, or OLE Object field.*

Now, let's use SQL to add an index to tblPhone. To do so, make sure tblPhone is closed, and then run the following statement in the SQL window:

```
CREATE UNIQUE INDEX Phone
ON tblPhone (PhoneNo, PhoneType)
WITH DISALLOW NULL
```

This statement adds an index named Phone, based on the PhoneNo and PhoneType fields. The UNIQUE keyword creates an index that prohibits duplicate entries in the combined fields. This means that you could duplicate the phone number or the phone type entry; you just can't duplicate both entries. In addition, we included the WITH DISALLOW NULL clause so neither field will allow Null values. Access doesn't update the table's properties, but that's because we created a multifield index. That's why it's always important to check the Indexes dialog box when seeking information on a table's indexes. As you can see in Figure 9-9, information about the multifield index we just added to tblPhone can be found in the Indexes dialog box.

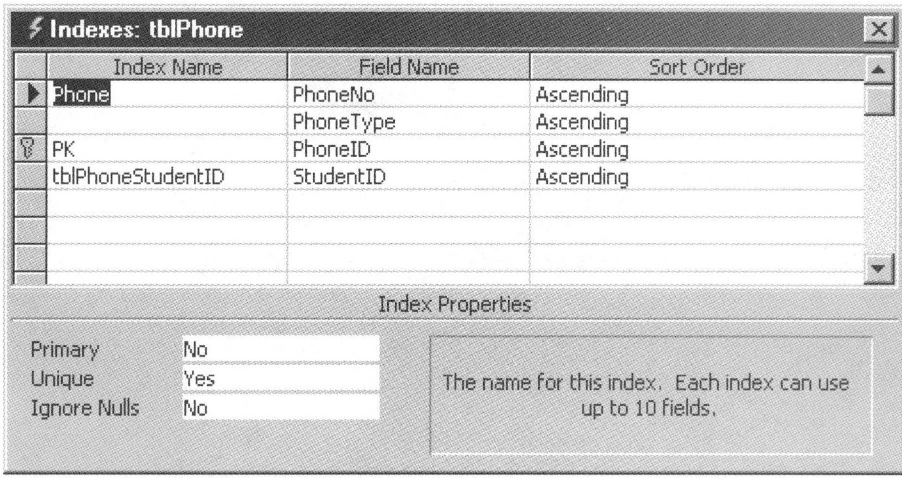

Figure 9-9. Check the Indexes dialog box for information on multifield indexes.

Dropping an Index

You can use the ALTER TABLE or DROP statement to delete an index from a table. Use either of two forms:

```
ALTER TABLE tbl
DROP CONSTRAINT indexname
```

or

```
DROP INDEX indexname ON tbl
```

Open the SQL window and run the following statement to delete the Phone index in tblPhone:

```
ALTER TABLE tblPhone
DROP CONSTRAINT Phone
```

> **NOTE** *You can't remove an indexed field until you remove its index. In addition, you can't delete an index if it's involved in a relationship. You must first delete all the relationships in which that index is a part, and then Jet will allow you to delete the index. Use the DROP CONSTRAINT clause to remove a relation or index.*

Indexes are a complex subject, and they can improve performance or drastically undermine it. In this section, we've attempted to introduce the subject and show you how to create, manipulate, and delete indexes using SQL.

CHAPTER 10

Advanced Manipulation Techniques

Beyond the DLL and DDL Basic Tasks

SQL ISN'T LIMITED TO JUST RETRIEVING and manipulating data. SQL can perform a number of more complex tasks, such as security and transaction processing. In addition, SQL-specific queries, even when performing simple tasks, can be complicated because you must create and execute them as SQL statements; you can't duplicate them in the query design window.

In truth, each of these topics deserves a chapter of its own. In particular, transaction processing and security can be a huge undertaking. Our coverage of these topics isn't comprehensive. We'll limit our discussions to the interaction between SQL and each topic. There's a lot to know about security and transaction processing; in this chapter you'll learn how SQL applies to these subjects.

SQL-Specific Queries

A few powerful query types can be executed only via the SQL window (or ADO). You can't duplicate them in the query design window. These are known as *SQL-specific queries,* and three queries are of this type: Union, Data Definition, and Pass-Through. In this section, we'll review these three query types:

- *Union*: These queries combine result sets that have similar structures.
- *Pass-Through*: These queries send SQL statements to an ODBC database server without passing the query through the Jet engine first.
- *Data-Definition*: These queries create, delete, and alter tables and queries.

Subqueries are also considered an SQL-specific type, but we cover subqueries in "Creating and Using Subqueries" in Chapter 11 ("Queries: The Sequel").

Using Union Queries

The UNION statement is really an operator, not a statement in the same sense as most SQL statements and clauses, although Access executes the operator as it does any other SQL statement. A UNION query combines records from two tables and produces a read-only recordset. To run a UNION query, use the form

```
select1 fldlist
UNION
select2 fldlist
```

where *select1* and *select2* represent two compatible tables or queries. Just as in a SELECT clause, you can replace *fldlist* with an asterisk (*) to include all the fields in the data source. In addition, the SELECT clause can include any valid joins. The most important condition is that, for the queries to be compatible, the field order must be identical in both recordsets because Access matches the field by order, not by name.

You can't include an OLE-object field in a Union query, unless you include the ALL predicate, in the following form:

```
select1 fldlist
UNION ALL
select2 fldlist
```

Omitting the ALL predicate in a Union query that also specifies an OLE-object field produces an error. By default, Jet deletes duplicate records from a Union query, which requires a bit of behind-the-scenes sorting. Because an OLE-object field can't be sorted, Jet returns an error. The ALL predicate avoids the problem by including all records. If you must limit the results, run the Union query first, and then run a second query to limit those results.

The ALL Predicate Eliminates Sort

By default, a Union query sorts its results by the values in the first column, even if there's no ORDER BY clause. That's because Union queries include an implicit DISTINCT, which omits duplicate records. To find duplicates, Jet must sort the records.

If you want the results to include all records, including duplicates, add the ALL predicate to the UNION keyword, in the form UNION ALL. Doing so will eliminate the sort in the results. This may or may not be a problem.

You can still sort the results; they just won't be automatic. The easiest way to sort is to simply include an ORDER BY clause. Or, when there are more than two SELECT statements, position the UNION ALL clause in the first set. If only one of the remaining UNION statements doesn't contain the ALL predicate, Jet will sort the results.

NOTE *It can be easy to confuse a Union and Append query because they both combine records from different tables. The distinguishing quality is that the Union query combines records from two tables into a new recordset separate from the data sources. An Append query adds records from one table to another existing table.*

Let's suppose that you want to combine employee, customer, and supplier address information to create one large address list. (We'll use the appropriate tables from the Northwind sample database.) The following statement doesn't work because the number of columns in each resulting recordset doesn't match:

```
SELECT LastName, FirstName, Address, City, Region, PostalCode, Country
FROM Employees
UNION
SELECT CompanyName, Address, City, Region, PostalCode, Country
FROM Customers
UNION
SELECT Companyname, Address, City, Region, PostalCode, Country
FROM Suppliers
```

Fortunately, the solution is simple once you review the different fields. The name entity comprises only one field—CompanyName—for both Customers and Suppliers. On the other hand, the Employees name entity requires two fields: LastName and FirstName. We can fix this problem quickly by simply concatenating the LastName and FirstName fields into one field. Remember, Access doesn't care whether the field names match—only that the recordsets have the same number of fields and that the field data types match, field by field. The following statement concatenates the two fields and creates a valid UNION statement:

```
SELECT LastName & " " & FirstName, Address, City, Region, PostalCode, Country
FROM Employees
UNION
SELECT CompanyName, Address, City, Region, PostalCode, Country
FROM Customers
UNION
SELECT Companyname, Address, City, Region, PostalCode, Country
FROM Suppliers
```

The resulting recordset, shown in Figure 10-1, includes 129 records: 9 from Employees, 91 from Customers, and 29 from Suppliers.

> **WARNING** *Jet doesn't care if the field names in the SELECT clauses match, but the data type must be compatible. If the data types don't match, Jet chooses the data type that's most compatible to both. For instance, if one field is an Integer and the other a Long Integer, the resulting column will be a Long Integer, because Long Integer can accommodate all existing data in both fields, whereas Integer might not. If you combine text and numbers, Jet returns a Text column, which could have far-reaching repercussions.*

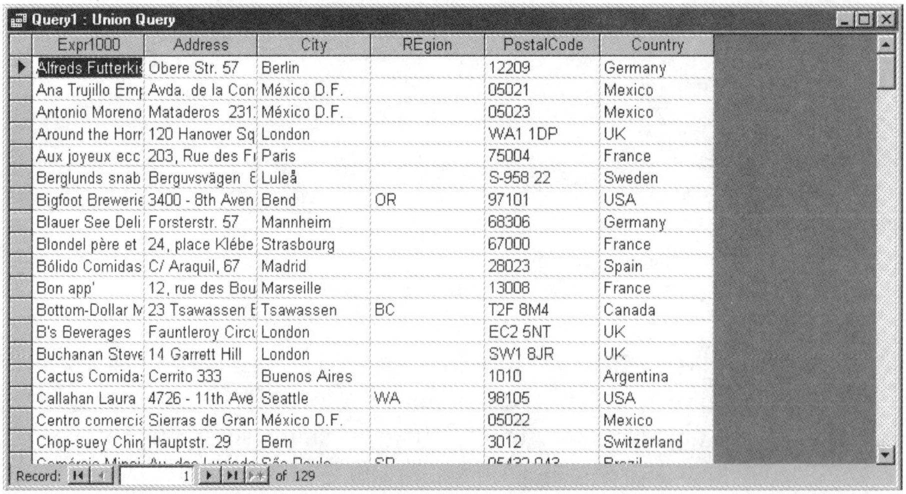

Query1 : Union Query

Expr1000	Address	City	REgion	PostalCode	Country
Alfreds Futterki:	Obere Str. 57	Berlin		12209	Germany
Ana Trujillo Emp	Avda. de la Con	México D.F.		05021	Mexico
Antonio Moreno	Mataderos 231:	México D.F.		05023	Mexico
Around the Horr	120 Hanover Sq	London		WA1 1DP	UK
Aux joyeux ecc	203, Rue des Fr	Paris		75004	France
Berglunds snab	Berguvsvägen 8	Luleå		S-958 22	Sweden
Bigfoot Brewerie	3400 - 8th Aven	Bend	OR	97101	USA
Blauer See Deli	Forsterstr. 57	Mannheim		68306	Germany
Blondel père et	24, place Klébe	Strasbourg		67000	France
Bólido Comidas	C/ Araquil, 67	Madrid		28023	Spain
Bon app'	12, rue des Bou	Marseille		13008	France
Bottom-Dollar M	23 Tsawassen E	Tsawassen	BC	T2F 8M4	Canada
B's Beverages	Fauntleroy Circu	London		EC2 5NT	UK
Buchanan Steve	14 Garrett Hill	London		SW1 8JR	UK
Cactus Comida:	Cerrito 333	Buenos Aires		1010	Argentina
Callahan Laura	4726 - 11th Ave	Seattle	WA	98105	USA
Centro comercia	Sierras de Gran	México D.F.		05022	Mexico
Chop-suey Chin	Hauptstr. 29	Bern		3012	Switzerland

Record: 1 of 129

Figure 10-1. The UNION query returns 129 address records.

Notice that the first field in the resulting recordset is named Expr1000. Generally, Access uses the column names from the first SELECT clause to name the new fields, but the first field is a calculated field and has no alias. Access has automatically assigned it the alias Expr1000. We can add an AS clause to resolve this problem:

```
SELECT LastName & " " & FirstName AS Name, Address, City, Region,
  PostalCode, Country
FROM Employees
UNION
SELECT CompanyName, Address, City, Region, PostalCode, Country
FROM Customers
UNION
SELECT Companyname, Address, City, Region, PostalCode, Country
FROM Suppliers
```

The SELECT clause will apply the alias "Name" to the first column in the first recordset. As a result, the resulting recordset will use Name as its field name, as shown in Figure 10-2.

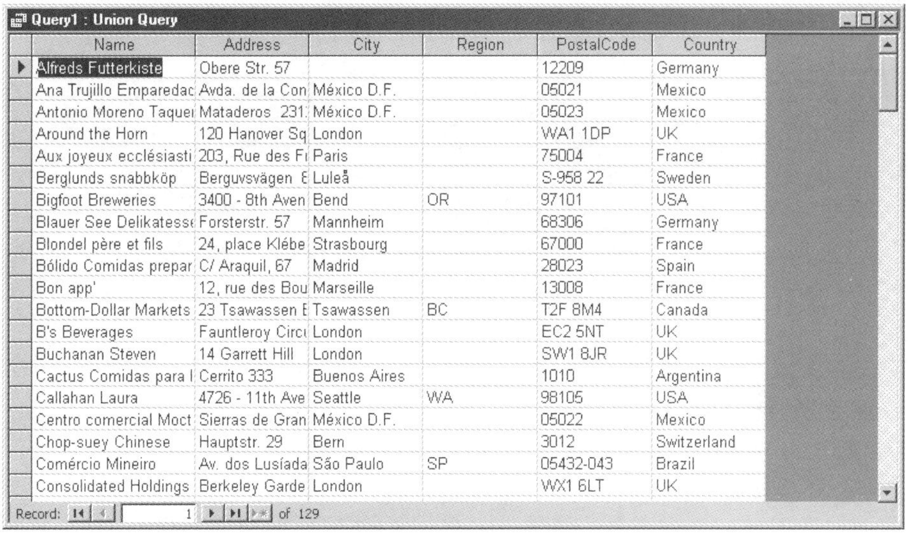

Query1 : Union Query

Name	Address	City	Region	PostalCode	Country
Alfreds Futterkiste	Obere Str. 57			12209	Germany
Ana Trujillo Emparedac	Avda. de la Con	México D.F.		05021	Mexico
Antonio Moreno Taquei	Mataderos 231:	México D.F.		05023	Mexico
Around the Horn	120 Hanover Sq	London		WA1 1DP	UK
Aux joyeux ecclésiasti	203, Rue des Fı	Paris		75004	France
Berglunds snabbköp	Berguvsvägen 8	Luleå		S-958 22	Sweden
Bigfoot Breweries	3400 - 8th Aven	Bend	OR	97101	USA
Blauer See Delikatesse	Forsterstr. 57	Mannheim		68306	Germany
Blondel père et fils	24, place Klébe	Strasbourg		67000	France
Bólido Comidas prepar	C/ Araquil, 67	Madrid		28023	Spain
Bon app'	12, rue des Bou	Marseille		13008	France
Bottom-Dollar Markets	23 Tsawassen E	Tsawassen	BC	T2F 8M4	Canada
B's Beverages	Fauntleroy Circı	London		EC2 5NT	UK
Buchanan Steven	14 Garrett Hill	London		SW1 8JR	UK
Cactus Comidas para l	Cerrito 333	Buenos Aires		1010	Argentina
Callahan Laura	4726 - 11th Ave	Seattle	WA	98105	USA
Centro comercial Moct	Sierras de Gran	México D.F.		05022	Mexico
Chop-suey Chinese	Hauptstr. 29	Bern		3012	Switzerland
Comércio Mineiro	Av. dos Lusíada	São Paulo	SP	05432-043	Brazil
Consolidated Holdings	Berkeley Garde	London		WX1 6LT	UK

Record: 1 of 129

Figure 10-2. Add an alias to solve field name conflicts.

> **TIP** *Normally, the UNION operator omits duplicate records from its results. To include all records, even duplicates, add the ALL predicate to the UNION clause in the form*
>
> ```
> select1
> UNION ALL
> select2
> ```
>
> *If you know there are no duplicates, but there's a lot of data, adding the ALL predicate can improve performance because the ALL predicate allows Jet to skip the comparison step.*

Sorting

Like most queries, you can sort the results by adding an ORDER BY clause. To do so, use the form

```
select1
UNION
select2
ORDER BY fld
```

where *fld* identifies the sort field. For instance, let's sort the address list from the previous example by the Name field. To do so, you'd add the ORDER BY clause as follows:

```
SELECT LastName & " " & FirstName AS Name, Address, City, Region, PostalCode,
  Country
FROM Employees
UNION
SELECT CompanyName AS Name, Address, City, Region, PostalCode, Country
FROM Customers
UNION
SELECT Companyname AS Name, Address, City, Region, PostalCode, Country
FROM Suppliers
ORDER BY Name
```

Note that only one ORDER BY clause is required for the entire UNION statement. This clause should come after the last SELECT statement in the UNION.

Adding an ALL Option to a Control List using UNION

Combo and list box controls offer choices: you simply select an item from the control's list. Although you can select all the items in a list box (but not a combo box) if you set the control's Multi Select property to Extended, dealing with the selected results would be awkward. Perhaps the best solution is to use the UNION operator to add an ALL item to the control's list.

Remember, the UNION operator doesn't care if the field names match, only that the fields match in number and data type. Therefore, you can add an ALL item to most any single column list using the form

```
SELECT fldlist FROM tbl
UNION SELECT "(All)"
FROM tbl
```

In this case, *tbl* must be the same data source. You're simply adding a new row to the list without actually referring to data in the data source; the "(All)" string acts as the data.

To illustrate this unique use of the UNION operator, open a blank form, add a combo box, and enter the following statement as that control's Row Source property:

```
SELECT CategoryName
FROM Categories
UNION SELECT "(ALL)"
FROM Categories
```

The resulting combo box is shown in Figure 10-3. The UNION SELECT operator returns a unique, and consequently sorted, list.

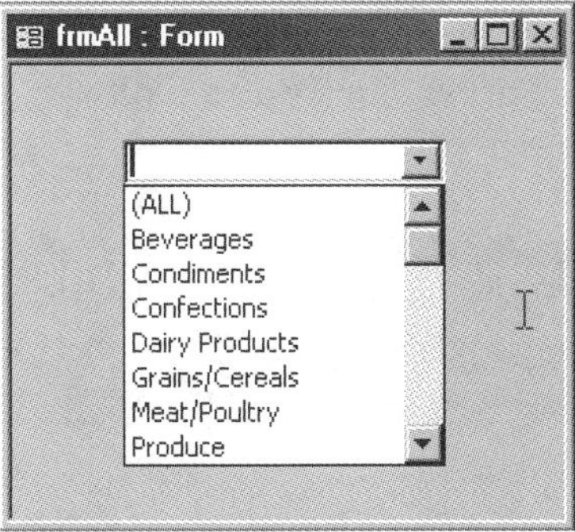

Figure 10-3. Use UNION to add an ALL item to a control's list.

The parentheses enclosing the ALL string aren't necessary, but they force Access to sort the ALL item to the top of the list. That's because the ASCII value of the opening parentheses (() is 40 and the ASCII value of the letter A is 65. Regardless of the text enclosed by the parentheses, Access displays the enclosed item first. You can use this technique to add any number of unique items to a control's list.

TIP *When a list is based on more than one field, you must add a pseudo column to the UNION SELECT clause for each column. For instance, to add the CategoryID to the previous example's list, you'd use the statement*

```
SELECT CategoryID, CategoryName
FROM Employees
UNION SELECT "","(ALL)"
FROM Employees
```

If you want to add an ALL item to both columns, you'd use the clause

```
UNION SELECT "(ALL)","(ALL)"
```

Using Pass-Through Queries

Pass-through queries allow you to work directly with foreign data on a server, instead of linking to the table. These queries bypass Jet, which translates a query into a format that the foreign data source can interpret. Occasionally, Jet can't interpret the SQL, and that's when Pass-Through queries come to the rescue. These queries are sent uninterpreted to the defined ODBC data source. This means that you'll need to be familiar with the exact SQL dialect used by the server database. The one disadvantage to the Pass-Through query is that its results are read-only. In addition, they're a bit limited in that you can't use VBA or Jet functions, either built-in or user-defined.

NOTE *Pass-Through queries work only with relational data. To access data in a flat-file format, you'll need OLE DB (and that means code).*

To create a Pass-Through query, open the query design window without specifying any tables. Then, choose SQL Specific from the Query menu. Next, choose Pass-Through from the resulting submenu. This adds three new properties to the query, which we've listed in Table 10-1. You can't create a Pass-Through query in the SQL window; you must access it through the Query menu.

Table 10-1. The Three Properties of the Pass-Through Query

PROPERTY	DESCRIPTION	DEFAULT
ODBC Connect Str	Specifies the ODBC connection string	ODBC;
Returns Records	Determines whether the query returns records	Yes
Log Messages	Set to Yes, this property will log warning and informational messages to a local table.	No

The default setting for the ODBCConnectStr is ODBC;, which causes Jet to prompt you for a connection string. The ODBC Connection String Builder creates a more appropriate string. To create a Pass-Through query:

1. Open a blank query design window by clicking on the Queries shortcut on the Object bar in the database window, clicking New on the Database Window toolbar, and click on OK in the New Query dialog box. Then, close the Show Table dialog box without adding any tables or queries.

2. Choose SQL Specific from the Query menu, and then select Pass-Through.

3. Enter the appropriate SQL statement.

4. To see the Properties dialog box, click on the Properties button.

5. To set a specific connection string, access the builder by selecting the ODBC Connect Str property. As a result, Access will display the builder button to the right of the property field (the ellipses character). Clicking this button launches the builder.

6. Run the query. If you skipped the previous step, Jet will prompt you for a connection string.

About Data-Definition Queries

Chapters 8 and 9 offer an in-depth discussion about Data-Definition queries, so we won't repeat the information here. These statements allow you to create and alter tables. You can execute a Data-Definition query from the SQL window or you can open a blank query, close the Show Table dialog box, choose SQL Specific from the Query menu, and then select Data Definition. There's little difference between the two.

Applying Security

Security can easily be set in Access by choosing Security from the Tools menu, but all the work is done by Jet. This means that you can set security options using SQL. More specifically, you can set security using DDL. You may find some resources that refer to SQL statements that manage security as Data Control Language (DCL).

In Access (Jet), security comes on two levels: share and user. A simple password is all that's needed to establish the share level, but the user level is much more complex because it establishes groups and users and gives permission to each group and user to perform specific tasks in the database. There's a lot to learn about user-level security beyond the SQL statements that control it, and this won't be a comprehensive look at security. Instead, we'll stick to SQL's participation.

> **NOTE** *All SQL security statements must be executed through Jet using ADO and OLE DB. You can't execute security via the SQL window.*

Setting Share-Level Security

Assigning a password to a database is easily accomplished using the ALTER DATABASE statement. First, open the database in exclusive mode. To do so:

1. Access the Open dialog box (from the File menu).
2. Choose Open Exclusive from the Open button's drop-down list, as shown in Figure 10-4.

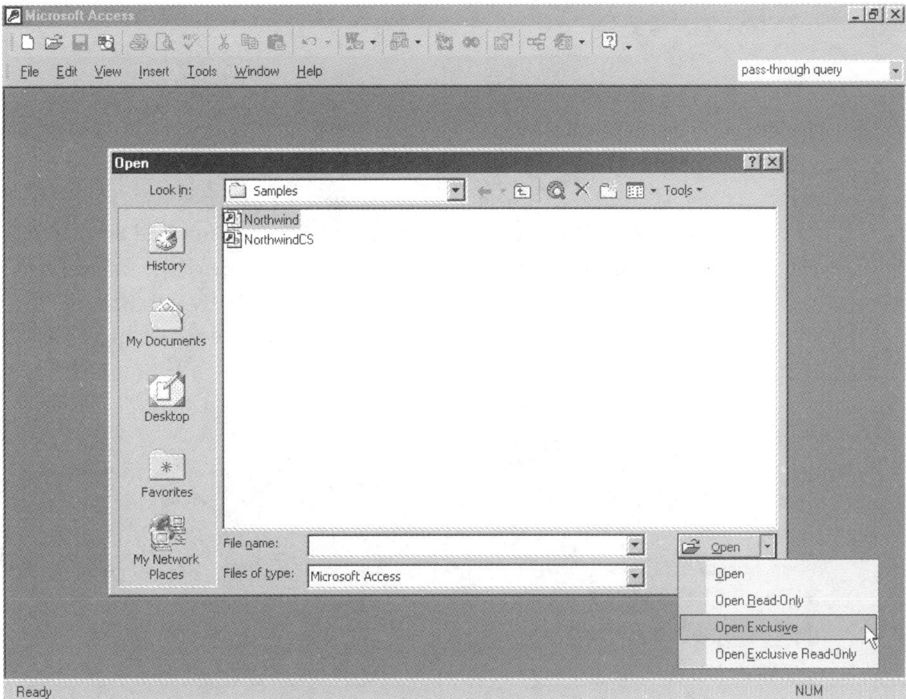

Figure 10-4. Choose Open Exclusive from the Open button's drop-down list to open a database in exclusive mode.

While the database is open in exclusive mode, run the ALTER DATABASE statement in the form

```
ALTER DATABASE PASSWORD new old
```

(using ADO and OLEDB) where *new* is a new password and *old* is an old password. The two password arguments allow you to change an existing password.

To set a password the first time, use the form

```
ALTER DATABASE PASSWORD new NULL
```

Likewise, to remove a password without setting a new one, use the form

```
ALTER DATABASE PASSWORD NULL old
```

Setting User-Level Security

User-level security requires an administrator who grants permission to individuals to view and modify an application's data and its objects. Every time Jet runs, it searches for the workgroup information file (called system.mdw by default and residing in the Office subdirectory where you installed Microsoft Office), which contains settings that determine who can do what while working in Access. If you're working with a single-user system with no security settings, Jet still refers to this file and its settings, even though you may not realize it. By default, this file contains one user named Admin who has full access to all Access features, files, data, and objects. The security's in place; it's just not restricting Admin (you).

> **NOTE** *User-level security is a huge subject that's well beyond the scope of this book. In this section, we'll supply the SQL commands for programmatically controlling security. If you don't know the ins and outs of user-level security, we recommend you read "Securing Access Databases," Chapter 18 in* Microsoft Office 2000/Visual Basic Programmer's Guide. *Chapter 18 is available online at* `http://msdn.microsoft.com/library/default.asp?url=/library/en-us/odeopg/html/deovrsecuringyourdatabasewithaccess.asp`. *In addition, the Microsoft Access Security FAQ, available online at* `http://support.microsoft.com/support/kb/articles/Q207/7/93.ASP`, *is an excellent resource for learning how to apply user-level security to an Access database. Applying security incorrectly could permanently lock your database, so don't practice or experiment on working or development files.*

From this point on, much about user-level security will be assumed. We'll list the necessary steps to apply user-level security, and, where appropriate, we will list and define any equivalent SQL statements that you'll use to programmatically control security at this step.

Step 1–Log on and create a new administrative user account for yourself

1. Open any Access database.
2. Choose Security from the Tools menu.
3. Select User and Group Accounts from the resulting submenu.

4. Click on the Change Logon Password tab.

5. Enter the same password in the New Password and Verify text boxes, click on Apply, and then click on OK.

6. Quit Access and open the database you want to secure.

7. Log on using the Admin user account and the password you just assigned in step 5.

> **NOTE** *There's no equivalent SQL statement. You must complete step 1 manually.*

Step 2—Adding a new admin account from which you'll secure the file

1. Choose Security from the Tools menu.

2. Select User And Group Accounts from the resulting submenu.

3. Click on the Users tab.

4. Click on New and enter the new username and personal identification value.

5. Click on OK to add the new user account.

6. Select Admins in the Available Groups list and click on the Add button to add your new administrator account to the Admins group. (All members of the Admins group have access to the user-level security system.)

7. Remove Admin from the Admins group, now that you're done with it. Choose Admin from the Name drop-down list and then select Admins in the Member Of list box, and click on Remove.

8. Click on OK and quit Access.

9. Open the database you want to secure, logging on using the administrator username you just created in step 4. (You don't have a password for this account yet.)

10. Assign a password for the new administrator username by choosing Security from the Tools menu, clicking on User And Group Accounts from the resulting submenu, and clicking on the Change Logon Password tab. Enter the same password in the New Password and Verify controls.

The second step of the process can be tackled using SQL. Table 10-2 lists the many syntax forms for the SQL CREATE USER and DROP USER SQL statements you'll need to add, delete, and modify User and Group accounts.

Table 10-2. CREATE USER and DROP USER Syntax

SYNTAX	EXPLANATION
CREATE USER *username password*	Creates a new user account and assigns a password for that user
CREATE USER *username1 password1, username2 password2, . . .*	Adds more than one user account at the same time. Separate each user and his or her password with a comma.
CREATE USER *username password pid*	Adds the user account using a personal identification value (PID)
DROP USER *username*	Deletes the user account
DROP USER *username1, username2, . . .*	Drops several user accounts at the same time

Step 3–Running the Access Security Wizard

1. Open the database and log on to the appropriate workgroup information file.

2. Launch the wizard by choosing Security from the tools menu. Then, select User-level Security Wizard from the resulting submenu.

3. Accept the default option, Modify My Current Workgroup Information File, and click on Next.

4. By default, the wizard secures all the objects in the database. To remove security for a particular object, click on the appropriate Class tab and uncheck the individual objects. Click on Next.

5. To add a group and its permissions to the current workgroup information file, check a predefined group. (See Table 10-3 for a list of predefined groups.) When you select a group, the wizard updates the permissions in the Group permissions control to the right of the group list. Click on Next.

6. For the most part, you'll retain the default option (No, The Users Group Should Not Have Any Permissions). All members of the Users group have full permissions for all objects, so be careful when assigning the Yes, I Would Like to Grant Some Permissions To the Users Group option. Doing so will allow anyone with a copy of Access to have the same permissions as those you assign to your Users group. Click on Next.

7. Add new users by selecting <Add New User> and entering a username and password. Then, click on the Add This User To The List button. Click on Next.

8. Now you can assign or remove users to groups currently in the workgroup information file. With the default option (Select A User And Assign The User To Groups) selected, open the Group Or User name drop-down list, select the name you entered as your administrator (fourth step of step 1) and select all the security groups. Continue to add users to groups as needed. Be sure to choose only the security groups that are appropriate for each user.

9. Retain the backup name and location, unless you have a specific reason for changing them, and click on Finish.

10. Print the resulting report. You can't save it, but you can export it by closing it and then saving it as a Snapshop file (.snp).

Table 10-3. Predefined Groups

GROUP	PERMISSION LEVEL
Full Permissions	Full permission on all database objects, but can't assign permissions to other users
Project Designers	Full permissions to edit data and all objects other than tables and relationships
Full Data Users	Full permission to edit data, but can't alter the design of any database object
Read-Only Users	Can read all data, but can't add data or alter the design of any object
Update Data Users	Can view and update data, but can't insert or delete data, nor alter the design of any object
New Data Users	Can read and insert data, but can't delete or update data nor alter the design of any object
Backup Operators	Can open the database exclusively for backup and compacting, but can't see any objects

NOTE *When creating or changing security, be sure to write down all usernames, passwords, and PID'S and then store the list and a copy of the report in a secure place. Also, be sure to store a copy of the backup file and SNP version of the report in a secure folder or on CD and store it in a secure location. Delete the backup file and the SNP report from any local folders, so unauthorized users can't access them.*

When using SQL to programmatically control security, use the many clauses and syntax forms listed in Table 10-4.

Table 10-4. ADD USER and DROP USER Syntax

SYNTAX	EXPLANATION
ADD USER *username* TO *group*	Add a user account to an existing group.
ADD USER *username1, username2* TO group	Add more than one user account to the same group.
DROP USER *username* FROM group	Remove a user account from a group. Removing a user from a group doesn't remove the user account. To delete a user account, see DROP USER syntax in Table 10-5.
DROP USER *username1, username2* FROM group	Remove more than one user account from the same group.
ALTER USER *username* PASSWORD *new old*	Change the password for an existing user account.
GRANT *privilege* ON *object objectname* TO *user*	Allow a user or group to perform specific type of action in regards to database objects. See Table 10-5 and 10-6 for *privilege* arguments and *object* keywords. The *user* argument can be a user or group account.
REVOKE *privilege* ON *object objectname* FROM *user*	Revokes specified permission on named object for a user or group account.

TIP *Be sure to add all users to the default group, Users. Those users who aren't included in the Users group don't have Read privileges to Jet tables.*

Table 10-5. Privilege Arguments

ARGUMENT	APPLIES TO	EXPLANATION
SELECT	Tables, objects, containers	User can read data and design of table, object, or container.
DELETE	Tables, objects, containers	User can delete data from a specific table, object, or container.
INSERT	Tables, objects, containers	User can insert new data.
UPDATE	Tables, objects, containers	User can update data.
DROP	Tables, objects, containers	User can delete table, object, or container.
SELECTSECURITY	Tables, objects, containers	User can view permissions for a specific table, object, or container.
UPDATESECURITY	Tables, objects, containers	User can change permissions for a specific table, object, or container.
UPDATEIDENTITY	Tables	User can change the values in auto-incremental columns.
CREATE	Tables, objects, containers	User can create a new table, object, or container.
SELECTSCHEMA	Tables, objects, containers	User can view design of a specific table, object, or container.
SCHEMA	Tables, objects, containers	User can modify the design of a specific table, object, or container.
UPDATEOWNER	Tables, objects, containers	User can change the owner of a specific table, object, or container.
ALL PRIVILEGES	All	User has all permissions for all objects and the database.
CREATEDB	Database	User can create a new database.
EXCLUSIVECONNECT	Database	User can open a database in exclusive mode.
CONNECT	Database	User can open a database.
ADMINDB	Database	User can administer a database.

Table 10-6. Object Arguments

KEYWORD	EXPLANATION
TABLE	Applies to any table in the database.
OBJECT	Applies to forms, queries, reports, macros, views, and procedures.
CONTAINER	Tables, relationships, forms, or reports. Permissions are inherited by new objects of the same type.
DATABASE	Implies the current database, and is seldom needed in explicit form.

> **NOTE** *This section doesn't do complete justice to the subject of user-level security. Rather, this section serves to introduce you to the appropriate SQL statements that you can use to programmatically control security.*

Transactional Processing

In a perfect world, you execute a command and Jet obeys—no errors, no problems. Error handling is one way to protect an application from imperfections. Transaction processing is another. Whereas error handling catches very specific problems, transaction processing deals with a larger picture. Specifically, if anything gets in the middle of the task, cancel it. In other words, one action balances another. If one process can't be completed, all actions are cancelled, not just the one that can't be completed.

> **NOTE** *SQL Desktop Edition and SQL Server 2000 have an advantage over Access and Jet when it comes to transaction processing. Using Jet, you'll need Visual Basic for Applications (VBA)—the programming language that supports Office—because Jet doesn't support transaction processing. Both SQL Desktop Edition and SQL Server 2000 fully support transaction processing. The SQL engine maintains an activity log and, during recovery, automatically reverts to the most recent and stable version.*

Let's use your checking account to illustrate transaction processing. First, you deposit your paycheck in the bank, dividing it between your checking and savings account. Now, let's assume that the bank correctly deposits a percentage of your deposit to your savings account, but something goes wrong and the remainder of that deposit isn't credited to your checking account. The unpleasant result is bounced checks.

Transaction processing prevents this type of error by balancing one action against the other. Processing one task without the other produces an error, and, as a result of that one error, all transactions are cancelled in a process known as *rolling back*, undoing a completed task. In SQL terms, a transaction is a group of SQL statements that must be completed successfully as a group or not at all.

The first step is to mark the beginning of a transaction with the BEGIN TRANSACTION statement. Next, you include the transaction code, statements that perform the actual tasks. You also include the ROLLBACK TRANSACTION and COMMIT TRANSACTION statements to direct the flow appropriately. If there's an error, the ROLLBACK TRANSACTION cancels all the work. If no errors are encountered, the COMMIT TRANSACTION statement saves all the changes.

In a nutshell, Jet maintains a log of completed transactions. If there's an error, Jet refers to the log and returns everything to the state of the last completed transaction (undoing all changes during the current processing cycle). If there's no error, Jet updates the log by adding a newly completed transactions item. Transaction processing can be applied to your application in a number of ways, but the simplest is to capture an error and direct the flow accordingly, as follows:

```
Dim cnn As ADODB.Connection
Set cnn = CurrentProject.Connection
On Error GoTo RollBackSub
  cnn.Execute "BEGIN TRANSACTION"
  cnn.Execute task1
  cnn.Execute task2
  . . . and so on
  cnn.Execute "COMMIT"
  On Error GoTo 0
  Exit Function
RollBackSub:
cnn.Execute "ROLLBACK"
```

Transactional processing is a complex yet powerful subject. Don't try to initiate transactional processing based on what little you've learned in this section. We're introducing you only to the SQL language you may encounter when working with transactional processing. A solid understanding of what's going on behind the scenes is required to successfully apply transactional processing.

CHAPTER 11

Queries: The Sequel

When a Simple Query Isn't Enough

MOST SQL SOLUTIONS INVOLVE one SELECT or ACTION statement, but sometimes a more complex approach is needed. Subqueries, also known as *subselects*, and Parameter queries are both appropriate solutions in the right situations. A subquery combines two queries by embedding a SELECT statement within another. A subquery isn't necessarily any faster than two fixed queries, but, once you start executing queries programmatically, you may find that subqueries are a bit easier to work with because you'll need to execute only one query instead of two. In addition, some developers actually find subqueries easier to write once they're familiar with the syntax.

Parameter queries are a flexible solution for those tasks that limit the same field to different values. Instead of hard-coding a specific criteria expression into the query, you enter what's known as a *parameter expression*. When you execute the query, Access prompts you for more-specific criteria. This means you can use the same query to limit the data in a variety of ways.

However, prompting users for criteria has some unique problems, and, in the end, you may decide Parameter queries are just too unstable. In fact, many developers don't use them. Basically, it's difficult to ensure that the user enters only appropriate responses to the parameter prompt. A simple typo can result in erroneous data or no data at all, and, unless the user realizes his or her mistake, it may go unnoticed. We're including Parameter queries in this section because, when you execute queries with parameters in code, you have much more control over the values of the parameters.

Creating and Using Subqueries

Almost all of our examples until now have relied on a single statement, whether it's a SELECT statement or an Action query. A single statement is adequate most of the time, but a complicated problem occasionally requires a complex solution. A subquery combines two queries; specifically, a subquery is a SELECT statement within another SELECT statement or Action query. Thus, the results of the embedded SELECT become part of the search condition for the main query.

You can think of a subquery as a type of filter, because, most of the time, you add a subquery to a WHERE clause—basing the query's results on values returned by the subquery. The filtered results can be obtained by applying one of the following comparisons:

```
WHERE value or expression [NOT] IN (SELECT statement)
WHERE fld ANY|SOME|ALL (SELECT statement)
WHERE [NOT] EXISTS (SELECT statement)
WHERE fld comparison operator (SELECT statement)
```

Replacing Nested Queries with One Subquery

Subqueries can be awkward to write, and so many people opt to run Nested queries instead. A Nested query is one query based on another, and sometimes a Nested query is the best or only solution. Once you're familiar with subqueries, you may find them easier to write than Nested queries. Keep in mind that not every Nested query can be rewritten as a subquery.

> **NOTE** *Don't try to rewrite all your Nested queries to improve performance because there won't be any noticeable difference, if any at all.*

A common use of subqueries is to display extraneous data in a Totals query. Normally, you'd have to use a Nested query to display additional data about a particular record along with the results of an aggregate. For example, let's suppose you want to display the most recent order and the employee who took the order. You could use a Totals query to display the most recent order, but you can't add the employee field because doing so adds another group, which changes the grouped results.

Perhaps the easiest solution is to build a Totals query that returns the customer and the most recent order using the following query:

```
SELECT Max(OrderDate) AS MostRecent
FROM Orders
```

This query returns the results shown in Figure 11-1; Figure 11-2 shows the graphic representation of this statement. (You could also state this query as a Totals query (view) using the Max aggregate.) We'll continue working with this example throughout this section, so save the query as qryMax.

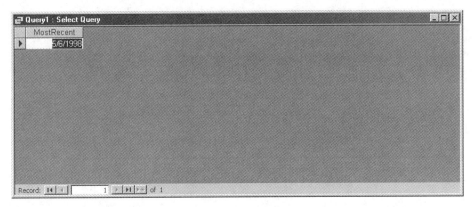

Figure 11-1. The Max aggregate returns the most recent order.

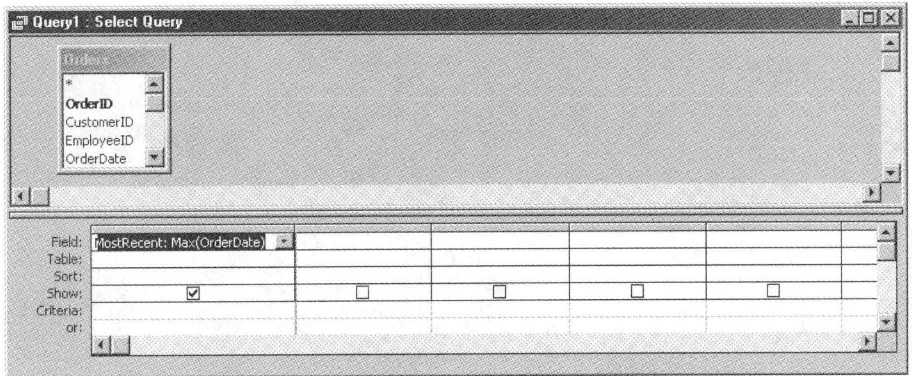

Figure 11-2. The query design window shows an aggregate expression that returns the most recent OrderDate value.

Next, the query shown in Figure 11-3 is based on the previous query and the Orders table. The SQL statement for this query is as follows:

```
SELECT qryMax.MostRecent, Orders.EmployeeID
FROM qryMax INNER JOIN Orders ON qryMax.MostRecent = Orders.OrderDate;
```

Jet returns the most recent date from the first query, qryMax, and the EmployeeID value that matches that value. In this case, there are four, as shown in Figure 11-4. Save the second query as qryMaxExtra.

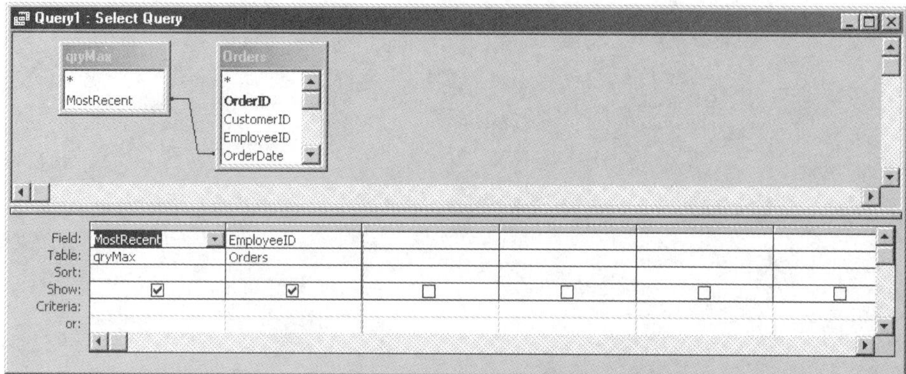

Figure 11-3. This query is based on the first query and the Orders table.

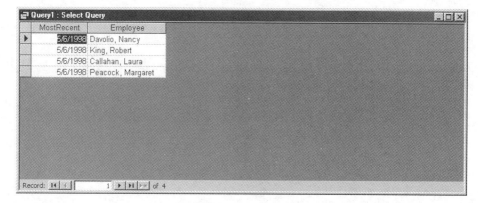

Figure 11-4. There happens to be more than one order for the date returned by the first query.

Combining the Nested Queries

When you have Nested queries as shown in the previous example, you can often replace them with one using a subquery. The first query becomes the subquery in the second query—after a bit of tweaking. It's not as difficult as it sounds, but it isn't an intuitive process. Let's combine the two Nested queries above into a subquery arrangement:

1. Open the first query (qryMax) in SQL view. Highlight the SQL text and then press Ctrl+C to copy it to the clipboard.

2. Open the second query in the SQL window and add the WHERE keyword in the appropriate spot, as shown in Figure 11-5.

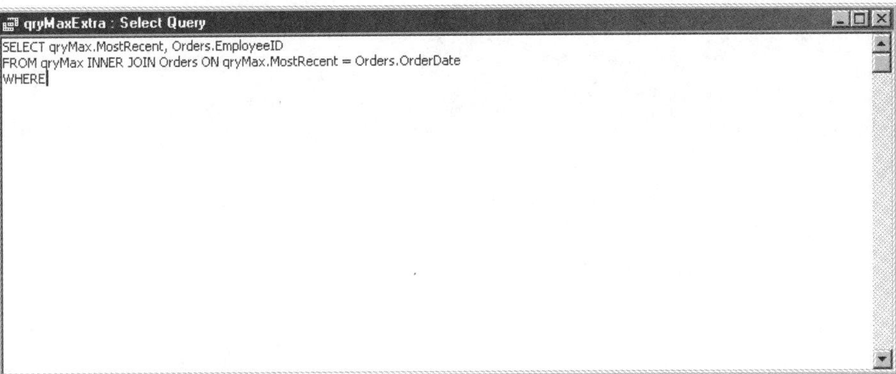
SELECT qryMax.MostRecent, Orders.EmployeeID
FROM qryMax INNER JOIN Orders ON qryMax.MostRecent = Orders.OrderDate
WHERE

Figure 11-5. Add the WHERE keyword in the appropriate position.

3. Then, paste the first SELECT statement beneath the WHERE clause. (The SELECT won't always be the WHERE condition, but it usually is.) Enclose the copied SELECT statement in parentheses, as shown in Figure 11-6.

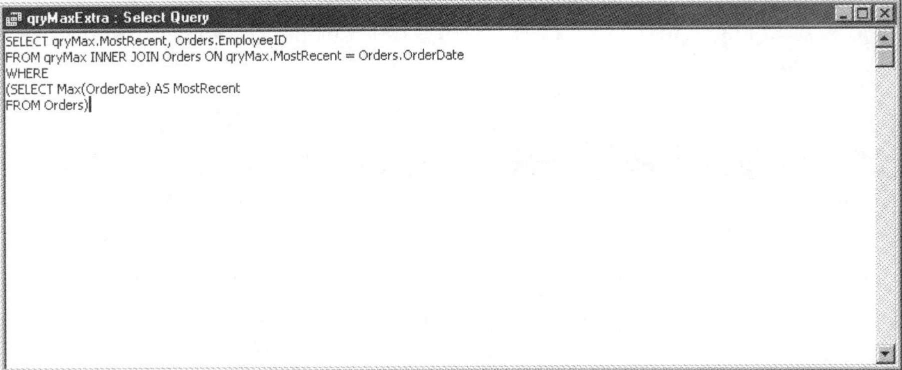
SELECT qryMax.MostRecent, Orders.EmployeeID
FROM qryMax INNER JOIN Orders ON qryMax.MostRecent = Orders.OrderDate
WHERE
(SELECT Max(OrderDate) AS MostRecent
FROM Orders)

Figure 11-6. Paste the SELECT statement beneath the new WHERE clause and enclose it in parentheses.

4. Replace all the references to qryMax and MostRecent in the main query's SELECT statement, as shown in Figure 11-7 with the corresponding table and field names. In this case, the table is Orders and the field name is OrderDate. You can usually simply erase the references to the query fields.

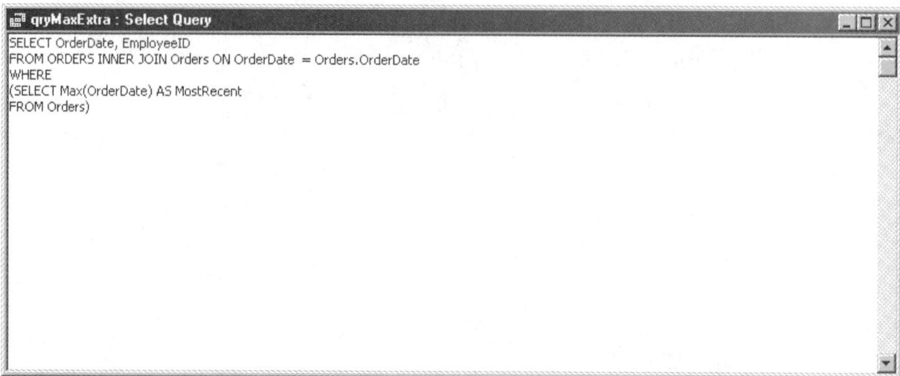

Figure 11-7. Update references in the main query.

5. If there's a join, you may need to delete it, as the subquery usually restates the search criteria specified in the join.

6. Add the first part of the equality expression to the WHERE clause. In this case, we want to match the values in OrderDate that are returned by the subquery. The IN predicate handles this particular condition, as is the case in Figure 11-8.

Figure 11-8. Complete the conditional expression of the WHERE clauses.

7. Run the query. Often, the first try returns unseen errors, which you can correct once Jet pinpoints them with an error message.

DELETE Revisited

A subquery can be added to any SELECT or action query. The subquery solution we used in the section "Adding Subqueries to DELETE," in Chapter 6 used a subquery to determine which customer records to delete. In Chapter 6, we viewed this subquery from the perspective of the Action query. Now, let's review it as a subquery.

First, let's restate the problem: how to delete inactive customers from the Customers table. In this case, *inactive* means any customer that hasn't placed any order since January 1, 1997. The solution is to limit a query to all orders placed on or after January 1, 1997. Then, use that query as a subquery in a DELETE query that limits the customer records to those that aren't included in that subquery.

Let's use the previous method to break this problem down into two different queries and then combine them. First, the following query returns a list of orders placed on or after January 1, 1997:

```
SELECT CustomerID
FROM Orders
WHERE OrderDate >=#1/1/1997#
```

Save the query as qryOrderDate. Figure 11-9 shows the query in design view, and Figure 11-10 shows the results.

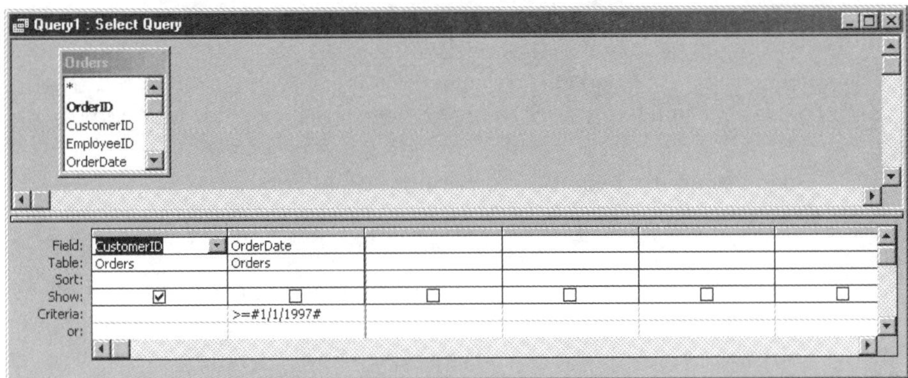

Figure 11-9. The criteria expression `>=#1/1/1197#` *limits the OrderDate field.*

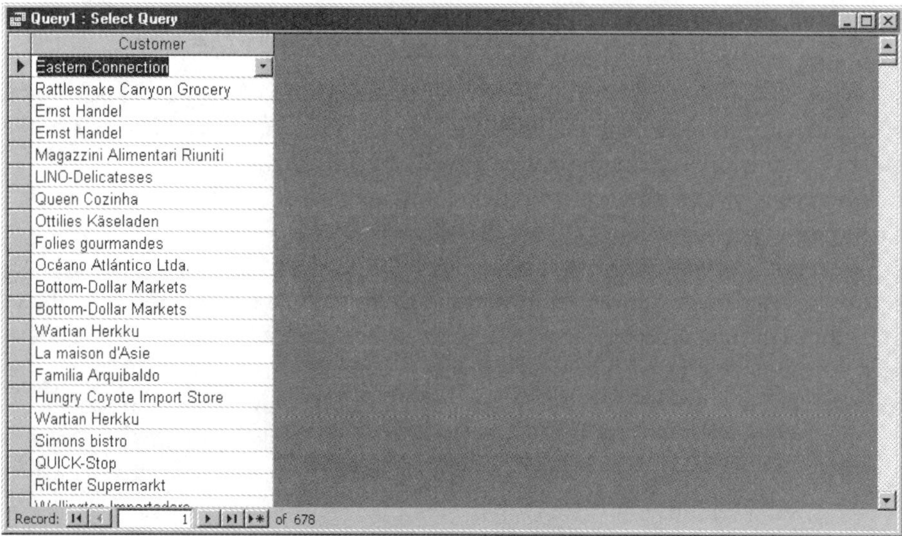

Figure 11-10. A total of 678 orders have been placed since January 1, 1997.

In this particular example, you won't actually combine two queries, as you did before because executing the DELETE statement

```
DELETE *
FROM Customers
```

would delete all the records from the Customers table. Saving this query as a fixed query could prove dangerous. Deleting a table full of customer data isn't the kind of mistake you really want to make. Now, let's create the subquery:

1. Open `qryOrderDate` in the SQL window. Highlight the SELECT statement and copy it to the clipboard by pressing Ctrl+C. Close the query.

2. Create a new, unbound query and open it to the SQL window. Enter the DELETE statement shown above, but enter it as a SELECT statement. You don't want to delete any records just yet.

3. Add a WHERE clause just below, as shown in Figure 11-11.

Figure 11-11. Add a WHERE clause to the DELETE statement.

4. Complete the first part of the WHERE clause's conditional expression, as shown in Figure 11-12. Remember, we're looking for all the customers that aren't in the results of the subquery.

Figure 11-12. Add the conditional components to the WHERE clause.

5. Finally, paste the SELECT query beneath the WHERE conditional expression by pressing Ctrl+V. Then, enclose it in parentheses, as shown in Figure 11-13.

Figure 11-13. Enclose the subquery in parentheses.

6. Run the query and check the results, shown in Figure 11-14. If all is well, return to the SQL window, replace the first SELECT keyword with the DELETE keyword, and run the query again.

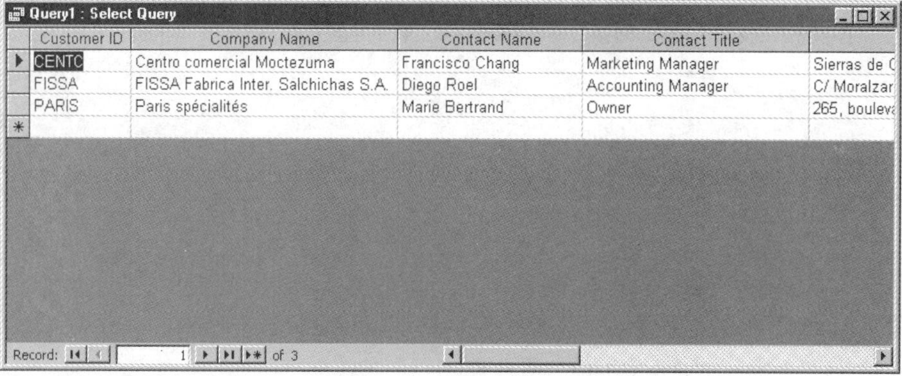

Customer ID	Company Name	Contact Name	Contact Title	
CENTC	Centro comercial Moctezuma	Francisco Chang	Marketing Manager	Sierras de C
FISSA	FISSA Fabrica Inter. Salchichas S.A.	Diego Roel	Accounting Manager	C/ Moralzar
PARIS	Paris spécialités	Marie Bertrand	Owner	265, bouleva

Figure 11-14. The SELECT query provides a peek at the results.

NOTE *Before running any Action query, be sure to make a backup of the table to be modified. That way you can return to the original data in the query if you choose. If you decide to run the DELETE query in this example, be sure to first carefully review the section in Chapter 6 for additional information on referential integrity rules.*

Using EXISTS

The EXISTS predicate compares values against rows in a subquery. If the subquery returns at least one row, the result of the EXISTS statement will be True; if the subquery doesn't return any rows, the result of the EXISTS statement will be False. For example, the following statement returns a product that hasn't been ordered:

```
SELECT ProductID, ProductName
FROM Products
WHERE NOT EXISTS
(SELECT * FROM [Order Details] WHERE ProductID = Products.ProductID)
```

In other words, Jet checks every ProductID in the Order Details table against the ProductID values in the Products table. If a ProductID value isn't found in the Order Details table, Jet returns that value.

All products have been ordered, so, if you run this query, Jet returns an empty recordset. You can get the query to return a record by deleting a product from the Order Details table:

1. Make a copy of the Order Details table and name it Order Details Copy.
2. Open the Order Details Copy table, sort it by Product, and delete the five records for Mishi Kobe Niku.
3. Replace the [Order Details] component in the above subquery with [Order Details Copy].
4. Run the query to see the results shown in Figure 11-15.

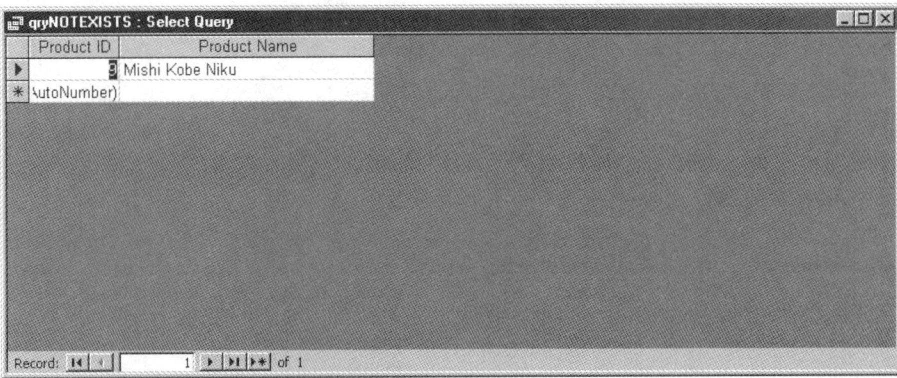

Figure 11-15. The NOT EXISTS predicate finds missing values.

Column Selects

A special type of subquery, known as a *column select*, replaces a column in a SELECT clause's field list with another SELECT statement. This technique has a user-defined function flavor to it because, most of the time, the replacing SELECT statement uses an expression to return a value. For example, let's suppose you want to know which products have or haven't been ordered, but, instead of possibly displaying an empty recordset (as was the case above), you want to accompany each item with a simple "yes" or "no" string. The following statement returns each item and identifies whether that item has been ordered:

```
SELECT ProductID, ProductName,
   Iif(EXISTS(SELECT * FROM [Order Details] WHERE ProductID = Products.ProductID),
    "Yes", "No") As [Ordered Status]
FROM Products
```

This query produces the results shown in Figure 11-16. You can add as many columns as you like this way, just as long as the results of the subquery can be appropriately applied to each record.

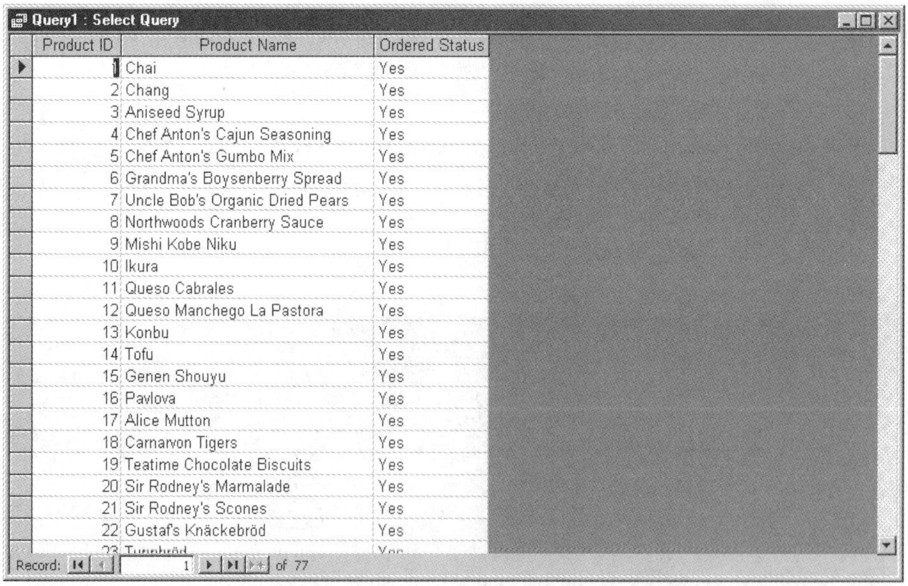

Query1 : Select Query

Product ID	Product Name	Ordered Status
1	Chai	Yes
2	Chang	Yes
3	Aniseed Syrup	Yes
4	Chef Anton's Cajun Seasoning	Yes
5	Chef Anton's Gumbo Mix	Yes
6	Grandma's Boysenberry Spread	Yes
7	Uncle Bob's Organic Dried Pears	Yes
8	Northwoods Cranberry Sauce	Yes
9	Mishi Kobe Niku	Yes
10	Ikura	Yes
11	Queso Cabrales	Yes
12	Queso Manchego La Pastora	Yes
13	Konbu	Yes
14	Tofu	Yes
15	Genen Shouyu	Yes
16	Pavlova	Yes
17	Alice Mutton	Yes
18	Carnarvon Tigers	Yes
19	Teatime Chocolate Biscuits	Yes
20	Sir Rodney's Marmalade	Yes
21	Sir Rodney's Scones	Yes
22	Gustaf's Knäckebröd	Yes

Record: 1 of 77

Figure 11-16. This subquery adds a column to the results.

Using Subqueries When a Dynamic Solution Is Needed

Subqueries can be used to query the same table, which is especially helpful if you're missing a key piece of data. For instance, let's suppose that you want to return all the products that are priced lower than Chocolade (a product name), but you don't know the current price for Chocolade. If you did, you could run the following query:

```
SELECT ProductName, UnitPrice
FROM Products
WHERE UnitPrice < 12.75
```

Not knowing the actual price of Chocolade isn't that big of a deal because you can simply look it up. But what if the price is subject to change? Entering the literal price means that you'd have to also remember to update the query or code. In this case, the following subquery might be a more efficient choice, even if you know the current price:

```
SELECT ProductName, UnitPrice
FROM Products
WHERE UnitPrice <
(SELECT UnitPrice FROM Products
WHERE ProductName = "Chocolade")
```

Both queries return the same results, shown in Figure 11-17. Choose the first for a one-time solution; use the subquery for a more permanent and dynamic solution.

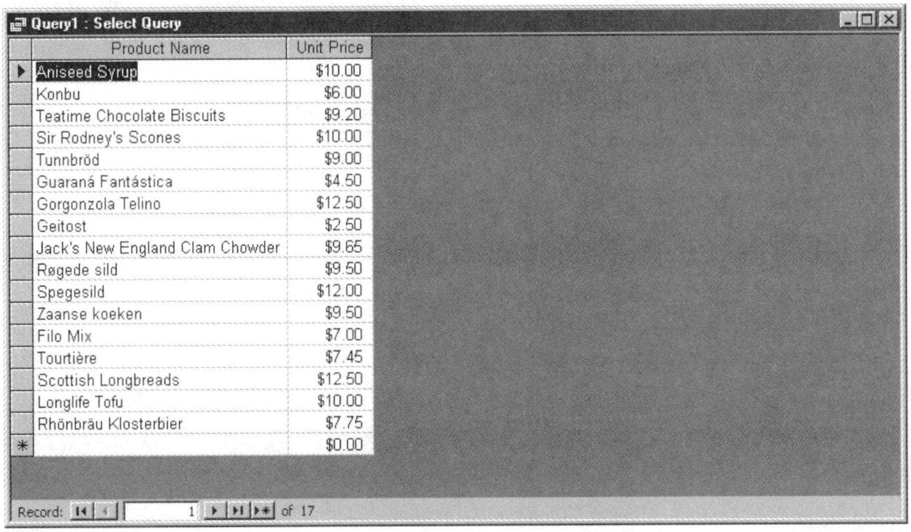

Query1 : Select Query

Product Name	Unit Price
Aniseed Syrup	$10.00
Konbu	$6.00
Teatime Chocolate Biscuits	$9.20
Sir Rodney's Scones	$10.00
Tunnbröd	$9.00
Guaraná Fantástica	$4.50
Gorgonzola Telino	$12.50
Geitost	$2.50
Jack's New England Clam Chowder	$9.65
Røgede sild	$9.50
Spegesild	$12.00
Zaanse koeken	$9.50
Filo Mix	$7.00
Tourtière	$7.45
Scottish Longbreads	$12.50
Longlife Tofu	$10.00
Rhönbräu Klosterbier	$7.75
*	$0.00

Record: 1 of 17

Figure 11-17. A subquery can provide a dynamic solution.

Parameter Queries

Flexibility can be the key to efficient solutions (especially with queries), and limiting the records using fixed criteria isn't always the best way to approach a query task. Occasionally, you need a more dynamic solution, and that's where parameter queries can make a big difference.

A parameter query prompts you for criteria before running the query. For example, the query shown in Figure 11-18 shows a typical parameter query in the query design window. In this example, the query returns the total sales amount for a particular salesperson. When you execute the query, Access displays a parameter prompt and you should respond by entering an appropriate value. In this case, that would be an employee's identification value (EmployeeID), such as 1, as shown in Figure 11-19, and then click on OK. Figure 11-20 shows the results: a single record for one of the employees.

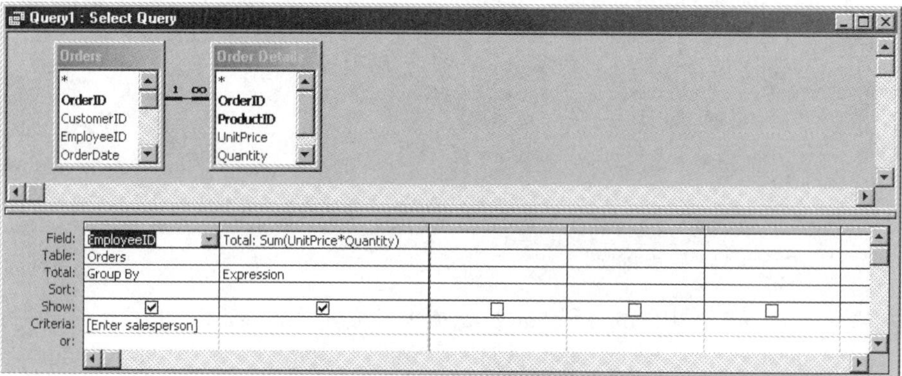

Figure 11-18. This parameter query prompts you for a specific salesperson.

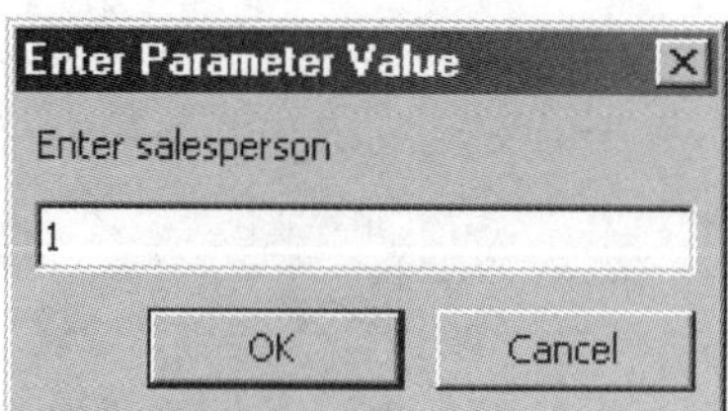

Figure 11-19. Enter criteria when prompted.

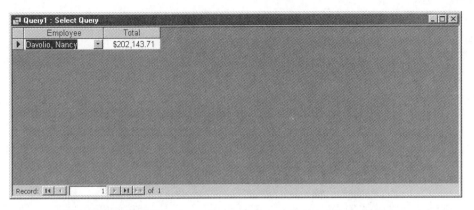

Figure 11-20. We can limit the query's results by entering a literal value as criteria.

Most parameter queries are just SELECT queries that limit the results using a WHERE or HAVING clause. The difference is that, instead of using an expression or literal value in the clause's conditional component, SQL refers to the criteria expression. For instance, the above query's SQL statement is as follows:

```
SELECT Orders.EmployeeID, Sum([UnitPrice]*[Quantity]) AS Total
FROM Orders INNER JOIN [Order Details] ON Orders.OrderID =
  [Order Details].OrderID
GROUP BY Orders.EmployeeID
HAVING Orders.EmployeeID=[Enter salesperson]
```

The HAVING clause uses the condition expression:

```
Orders.EmployeeID=[Enter salesperson]
```

The right side of the equals sign refers to the parameter expression that we saw earlier in Figure 11-18, instead of a literal value or an expression that returns a value.

Setting a Parameter's Data Type

When running the above query, you must know that the query expects a value instead of an actual name. (The EmployeeID field displays a name instead of a value because it's a lookup field.) If you enter a name as text, Access returns an empty recordset. If you don't know why, you might assume that the employee in question has no sales to report, and that would be incorrect. One way to protect from this type of error is to specify a parameter's data type. To specify a data type, add a PARAMETER clause before the SELECT statement. The following statement defines the [Enter salesperson] parameter as a Byte data type:

```
PARAMETERS [Enter salesperson] Byte;
SELECT Orders.EmployeeID, Sum([UnitPrice]*[Quantity]) AS Total
FROM Orders INNER JOIN [Order Details] ON Orders.OrderID =
  [Order Details].OrderID
GROUP BY Orders.EmployeeID
HAVING Orders.EmployeeID=[Enter salesperson];
```

> **NOTE** *You can also define a parameter's data type via the query design window. To do so, copy the parameter expression to the clipboard by highlighting it and pressing Ctrl+C. Then, choose Parameters from the Query menu. In the resulting Query Parameters dialog box, press Ctrl+V to copy the parameter expression to the Parameter column. Then, select a data type from the Data Type column's dropdown list, and click on OK.*

Now, run the above query and enter "Nancy Davolio" instead of her corresponding employee value of 1. When you do so, Access displays the error message shown in Figure 11-21 instead of an empty recordset. Run the query a second time and enter 1. This time the query returns the expected result.

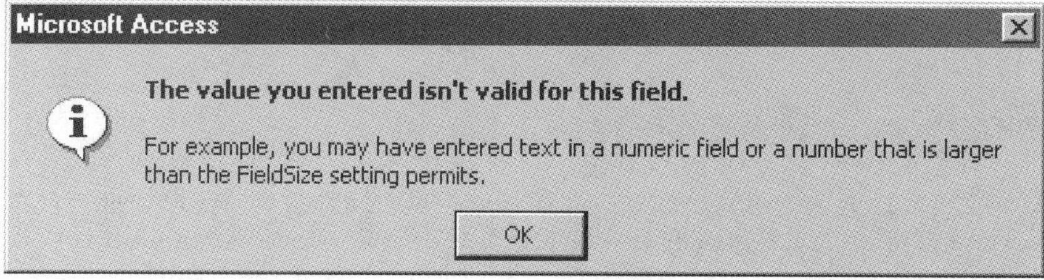

Figure 11-21. Access displays a generic error message if you enter the wrong data type in response to the parameter prompt.

Avoiding Nulls

In the above examples, we always responded to the parameter prompt by entering some kind of value, even if it was inappropriate. If you fail to enter a value, Access may return an empty recordset, as shown in Figure 11-22. Here, instead of entering a value, we left the prompt empty, and clicked on OK.

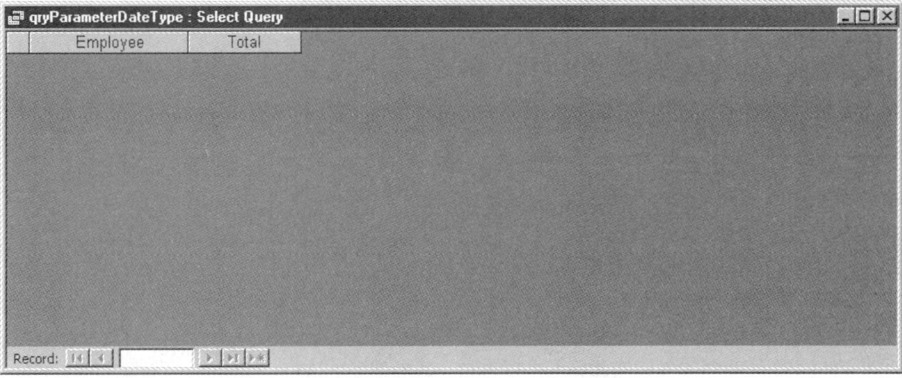

Figure 11-22. Ignoring the parameter prompt returns an empty recordset.

Did you expect to see all the records? It's a logical expectation because, normally, a query returns all the records in the data source (in the absence of any limiting criteria). You might expect the same of a parameter query. However, Access doesn't interpret an empty parameter as the absence of criteria. Instead, Access interprets the empty parameter as a Null value, and you may end up with nothing.

The solution is to add a LIKE operator to the parameter expression in the form

```
HAVING fld Like [parameter] & "*"
```

The asterisk is a wildcard character, which Access simply adds to the parameter expression. Using our previous example, change the HAVING clause to

```
HAVING Orders.EmployeeID LIKE [Enter salesperson] & "*"
```

Then, run the query and enter the value 1. The parameter expression evaluates to 1* and returns the results shown earlier in Figure 11-20.

> **NOTE** *You can read about wildcards in the section "Including Wildcards" in Chapter 5.*

This solution has one limitation: the query returns any employee whose number merely begins with the value 1. This includes EmployeeID values 11, 100, and 1234, just to name a few. So, if you really want to return just one record, this solution doesn't work.

However, it does solve the original problem of returning an empty recordset, when you really meant to return all the records. Run the query and click on OK, leaving the parameter prompt empty. Access evaluates the parameter expression as *, instead of NULL, and returns all the non-null records, as shown in Figure 11-23.

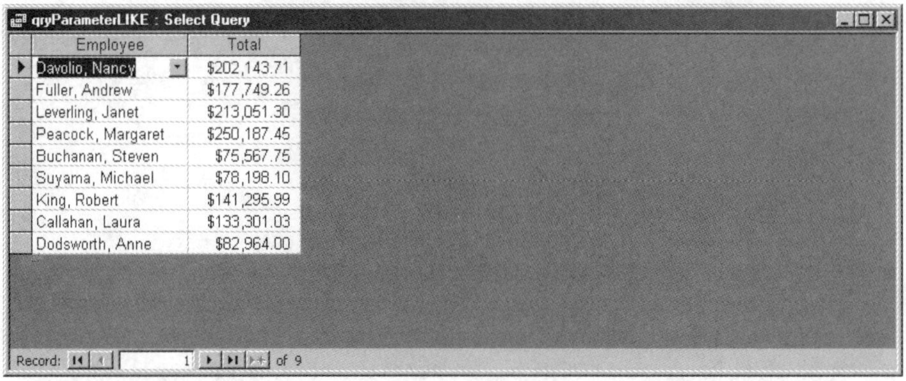

qryParameterLIKE : Select Query

Employee	Total
Davolio, Nancy	$202,143.71
Fuller, Andrew	$177,749.26
Leverling, Janet	$213,051.30
Peacock, Margaret	$250,187.45
Buchanan, Steven	$75,567.75
Suyama, Michael	$78,198.10
King, Robert	$141,295.99
Callahan, Laura	$133,301.03
Dodsworth, Anne	$82,964.00

Record: 1 of 9

Figure 11-23. Adding the LIKE operator returns all records if you ignore the parameter prompt.

This solution has one more problem, and that's the reaction of Access when there really is a Null value. Let's suppose that you want to use a Parameter query to search for orders going to a particular city. You want to negate the Parameter query by returning all the records, which would include any Null values. To accommodate both conditions:

1. The first thing we have to do is create a Null value in the City field of the Customers table. Open the Customers table and delete the first City value (Berlin).

2. Run the following query

```
SELECT.CompanyName, City, OrderID
FROM Customers INNER JOIN Orders ON Customers.CustomerID =
  Orders.CustomerID
WHERE City = [Enter City]
```

   If you ignore the parameter prompt, Access returns an empty recordset.

3. Run the query and enter the string "Berlin". Again, the query returns an empty recordset because we deleted the only Berlin record (not necessarily the only Berlin customer, but the only Berlin customer with an order).

4. Modify the WHERE clause to the following:

```
WHERE City Like [Enter City] & "*"
```

5. Run the query and ignore the parameter prompt to return all the records. However, notice in Figure 11-24 that the query doesn't return any of the order records for Alfreds Futterkiste. (That's the Berlin customer.) Then, run the query again, entering the string "Berlin". This time, the query result is empty, because there is no such record. Run the query a third time using the string "Ber." Several records have a City value beginning with the string "Ber."

qryParameterLIKEISNULL : Select Query

Company Name	City	Order ID
Ana Trujillo Emparedados y helados	México D.F.	10308
Ana Trujillo Emparedados y helados	México D.F.	10625
Ana Trujillo Emparedados y helados	México D.F.	10759
Ana Trujillo Emparedados y helados	México D.F.	10926
Antonio Moreno Taquería	México D.F.	10365
Antonio Moreno Taquería	México D.F.	10507
Antonio Moreno Taquería	México D.F.	10535
Antonio Moreno Taquería	México D.F.	10573
Antonio Moreno Taquería	México D.F.	10677
Antonio Moreno Taquería	México D.F.	10682
Antonio Moreno Taquería	México D.F.	10856
Around the Horn	London	10355
Around the Horn	London	10383

Record: 1 of 824

Figure 11-24. Alfreds Futterkiste is missing from our list.

6. Modify the WHERE clause to the following:

```
WHERE Customers.City Like [Enter City] & "*" OR [Enter city] Is Null
```

7. Run the query one last time and ignore the parameter query. This time, the OR expression includes Null values, so the query returns records for Alfreds Futterkiste as shown in Figure 11-25.

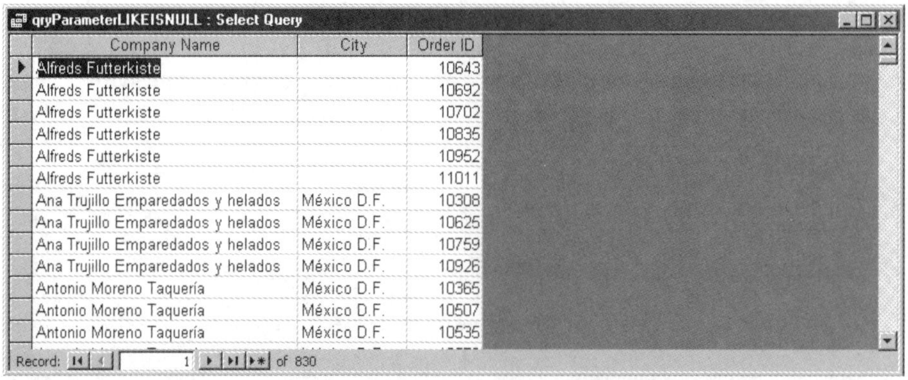

qryParameterLIKEISNULL : Select Query

Company Name	City	Order ID
Alfreds Futterkiste		10643
Alfreds Futterkiste		10692
Alfreds Futterkiste		10702
Alfreds Futterkiste		10835
Alfreds Futterkiste		10952
Alfreds Futterkiste		11011
Ana Trujillo Emparedados y helados	México D.F.	10308
Ana Trujillo Emparedados y helados	México D.F.	10625
Ana Trujillo Emparedados y helados	México D.F.	10759
Ana Trujillo Emparedados y helados	México D.F.	10926
Antonio Moreno Taquería	México D.F.	10365
Antonio Moreno Taquería	México D.F.	10507
Antonio Moreno Taquería	México D.F.	10535

Record: 1 of 830

Figure 11-25. Adding "Is Null" to the expression includes Null values in the query's results.

Working with Multiple Parameters

A query allows more than one criteria expression, and, similarly, a parameters query allows more than one parameter expression. You'll apply these multiple parameters in one of two ways:

- as one expression joined by an AND or OR operator, usually multiple parameters based on the same field, or
- as separate expressions based on more than one field.

Querying records for date values that fall within a specific time period is a good example of using more than one parameter in one expression. For instance, the following query prompts you for two dates (a beginning date and an ending date) and returns records wherein the ShippedDate value falls within the two dates:

```
PARAMETERS [Enter beginning date] DateTime, [Enter ending date] DateTime;
SELECT OrderID, ShippedDate, ShippedDate
FROM Orders
WHERE ShippedDate Between [Enter beginning date] And [Enter ending date]
```

When you run this query, Access runs two parameter prompts, not just one. Enter a date into both, as shown in Figure 11-26, to express a specific time period. Specifically, the expression in the WHERE clause evaluates to

```
WHERE ShippedDate Between #8/1/97# And #8/31/97#
```

As you can see in Figure 11-27, this example returns shipped orders for the month of August, 1997. Viewing the query in the query design window (shown in Figure 11-28) clearly shows that the parameters are included in just one expression.

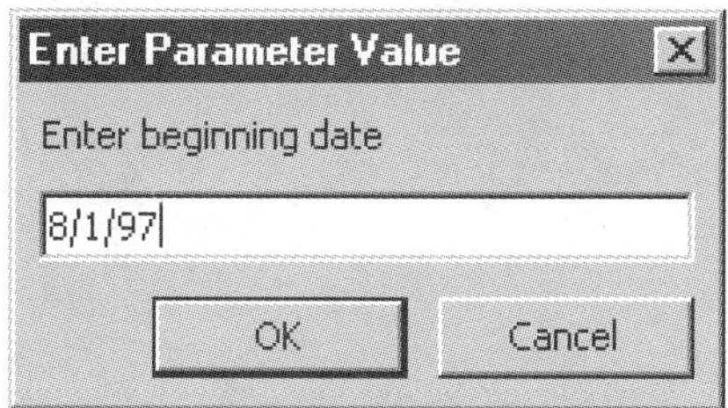

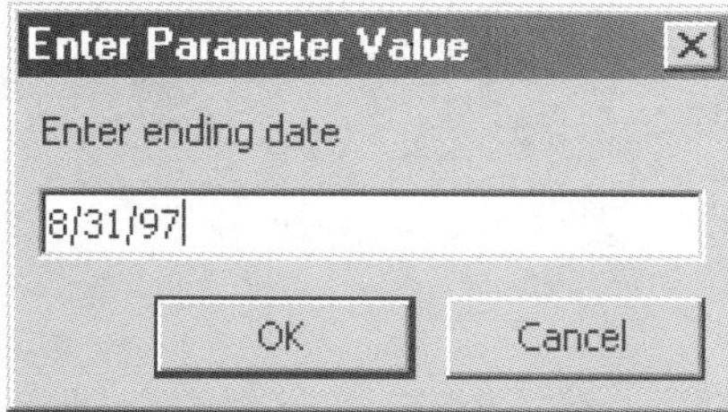

Figure 11-26. This query matches dates during the time period expressed by the two parameter values.

Query1 : Select Query

Order ID	Shipped Date	Shipped Date
10608	01-Aug-1997	01-Aug-1997
10611	01-Aug-1997	01-Aug-1997
10612	01-Aug-1997	01-Aug-1997
10613	01-Aug-1997	01-Aug-1997
10614	01-Aug-1997	01-Aug-1997
10617	04-Aug-1997	04-Aug-1997
10616	05-Aug-1997	05-Aug-1997
10610	06-Aug-1997	06-Aug-1997
10615	06-Aug-1997	06-Aug-1997
10619	07-Aug-1997	07-Aug-1997
10603	08-Aug-1997	08-Aug-1997
10618	08-Aug-1997	08-Aug-1997
10621	11-Aug-1997	11-Aug-1997
10622	11-Aug-1997	11-Aug-1997
10596	12-Aug-1997	12-Aug-1997
10623	12-Aug-1997	12-Aug-1997
10593	13-Aug-1997	13-Aug-1997
10620	14-Aug-1997	14-Aug-1997
10625	14-Aug-1997	14-Aug-1997
10631	15-Aug-1997	15-Aug-1997

Record: 1 of 36

Figure 11-27. We returned shipped orders for the month of August, 1997.

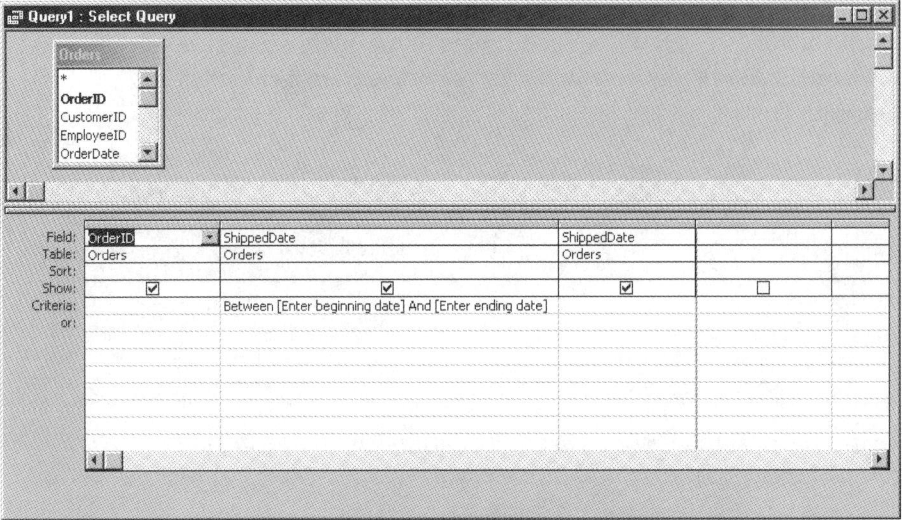

Figure 11-28. Both parameters are in one expression.

Now let's look at the following query, which includes a third parameter based on the CustomerID field. This query limits the records to a specific time period and customer using an AND operator. Figure 11-29 shows this query in design view, where you can more easily discern two different parameter expressions.

```
PARAMETERS [Enter customer] Text, [Enter beginning date] DateTime,
      [Enter ending date] DateTime;
SELECT OrderID, CustomerID, ShippedDate, ShippedDate
FROM Orders
WHERE CustomerID=[Enter customer] AND ShippedDate Between
      [Enter beginning date] AND [Enter ending date]
```

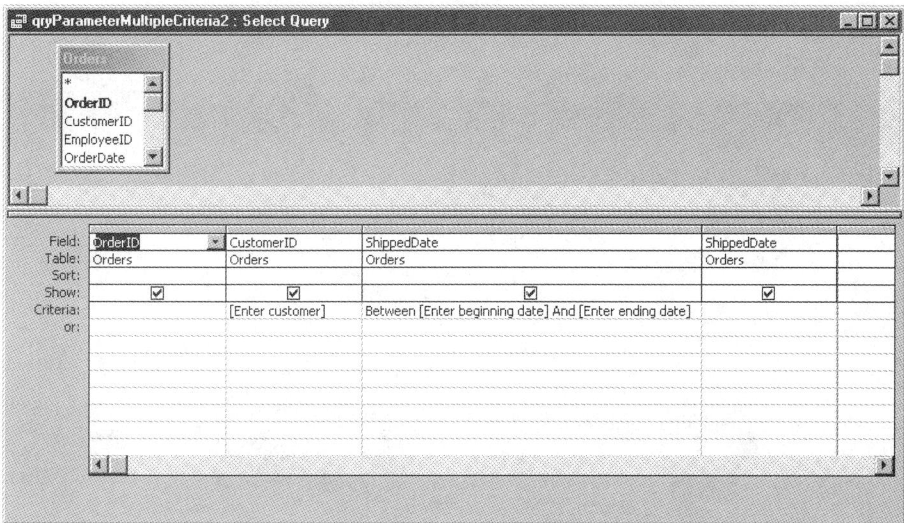

Figure 11-29. Two fields contain parameter expressions.

Running the report displays the two parameter prompts shown in Figure 11-26, plus another (shown in Figure 11-30). Positioning the [Enter customer] parameter first in the PARAMETERS clause forces Access to display that prompt first. The results are shown in Figure 11-31 and include only those records ordered by Ernst Handel and shipped during August, 1997.

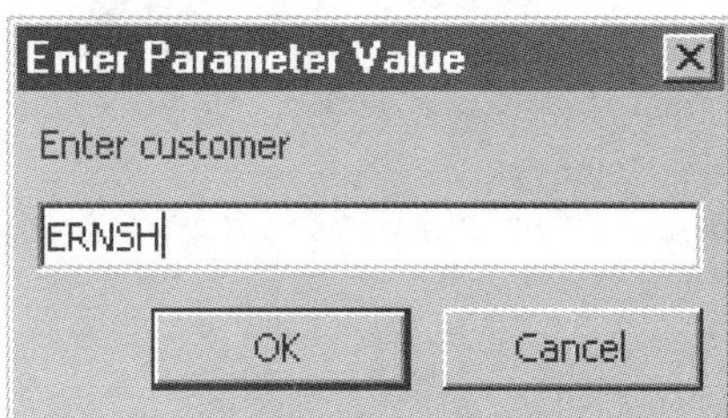

Figure 11-30. We added a third parameter prompt to the query.

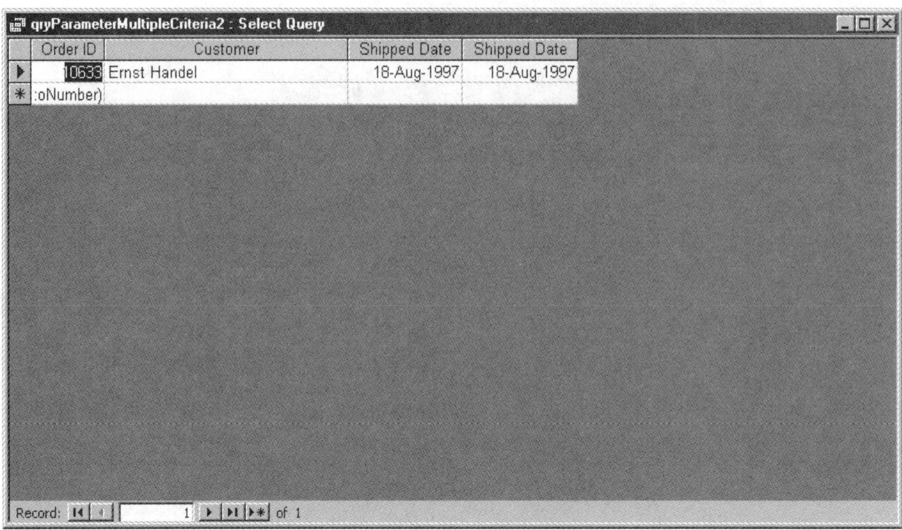

Figure 11-31. The third parameter limits the records to a particular customer.

Specifying a Default Value for a Parameter

Technically, you can't specify a default value for a parameter, but you can trick Access into using one. A default value can save a lot of unnecessary data entry if you use the same criteria more often than any other. For instance, you might query for a particular customer or region more often than any other. When this is the case, the default comes in handy, because you don't have to enter anything. The default value is already there, and clicking on OK executes the query using the default value as the criteria.

The secret to accomplishing this task is to use the Eval() and InputBox() functions together in the form

```
Eval("InputBox(""prompt"", ""title"", ""defaultvalue"")")
```

Simply enter an expression in this form in lieu of a parameter expression. For example, let's suppose that you query the Orders table for shipped orders for different customers, but most of the time you're checking the shipped orders for Ernst Handel. The following query displays an input box using ERNSH as the default value:

```
SELECT CustomerID, EmployeeID, ShippedDate
FROM Orders
WHERE CustomerID=Eval("InputBox(""Enter a customer:"",""CustomerQuery"",
      ""ERNSH"")")
```

Figure 11-32 shows the same query in design view.

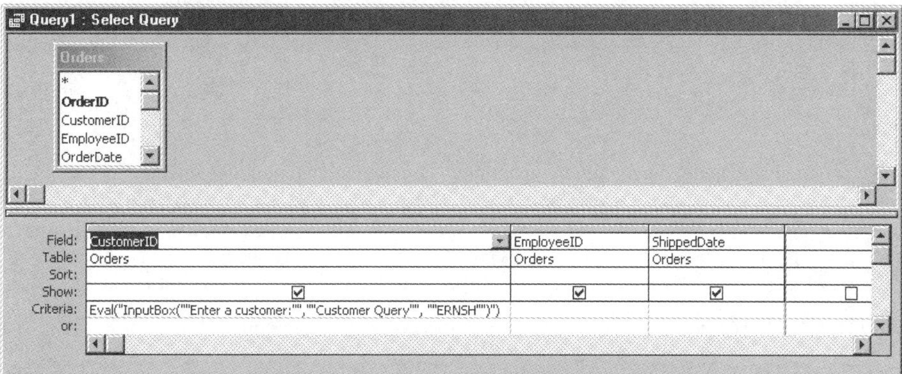

Figure 11-32. The Criteria expression displays an input box.

Run the query, and Access displays the input box shown in Figure 11-33. You can accept the default value and click on OK to return the results shown in Figure 11-34, or you can overwrite the default value and click on OK to change the results.

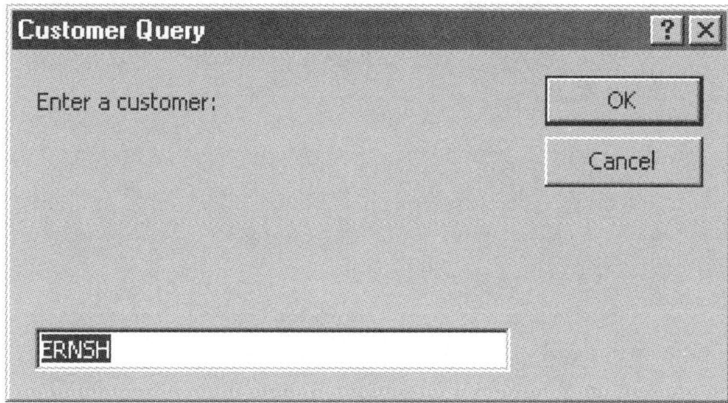

Figure 11-33. The input box displays a default value.

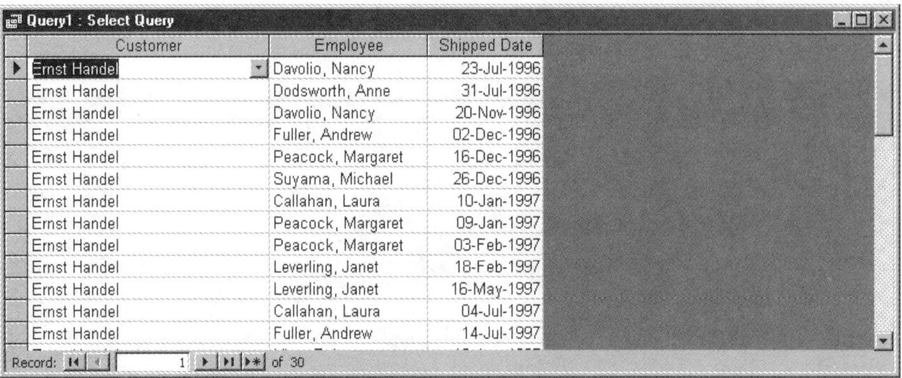

Query1 : Select Query

Customer	Employee	Shipped Date
Ernst Handel	Davolio, Nancy	23-Jul-1996
Ernst Handel	Dodsworth, Anne	31-Jul-1996
Ernst Handel	Davolio, Nancy	20-Nov-1996
Ernst Handel	Fuller, Andrew	02-Dec-1996
Ernst Handel	Peacock, Margaret	16-Dec-1996
Ernst Handel	Suyama, Michael	26-Dec-1996
Ernst Handel	Callahan, Laura	10-Jan-1997
Ernst Handel	Peacock, Margaret	09-Jan-1997
Ernst Handel	Peacock, Margaret	03-Feb-1997
Ernst Handel	Leverling, Janet	18-Feb-1997
Ernst Handel	Leverling, Janet	16-May-1997
Ernst Handel	Callahan, Laura	04-Jul-1997
Ernst Handel	Fuller, Andrew	14-Jul-1997

Record: 1 of 30

Figure 11-34. The default value, ERNSH, returns these records.

NOTE *You probably don't see the Eval() function very often, as its task is specialized: the Eval() function evaluates a string expression and allows the query to evaluate and execute the InputBox() function. Without Eval(), this trick isn't possible.*

CHAPTER 12

An Introduction to the SQL Server 2000 Desktop Engine

When You're Ready for a More Powerful Engine

MICROSOFT ACCESS (JET) IS a powerful relational database, and, as such, it provides a useful tool for those needing a desktop database. Many need more. Microsoft markets SQL Server Desktop Engine as an alternative to Jet for those instances when you need a database server that can be easily distributed and installed, and you don't want to spend a lot of money. The SQL Desktop engine (known as MSDE 1.0 in Office 2000) is a data engine that's based on core SQL Server technology. Basically, you're getting the full-blown SQL Server engine with some limitations (which we'll discuss later). In this chapter, we'll view just what SQL Desktop is and who it services. Along the way, we'll compare Access, SQL Desktop, and SQL Server features and requirements.

SQL Desktop has much in common with the full version of SQL Server. In this chapter, you'll see many references to other sections within the book. We apologize for this but felt that SQL Desktop Engine warranted inclusion. For many developers, the desktop engine will be the entry path to the full SQL Server and there is little information available.

> **NOTE** *When discussing table and form properties, the information and details can equally be applied to the full SQL Server 2000 database. Much if not all of the information provided in this chapter applies equally when you are working with the full version of SQL Server 2000.*

The Future of Access and SQL Server 2000 SQL Desktop Engine

There is some worry among Access users that Microsoft is pruning Access and will eventually eliminate it in lieu of SQL Server or .NET. Many see SQL Desktop as a negative purveyor of this plan rather than as a positive move to increase the number of flexible solutions to more users. It's impossible to divine Microsoft's intentions, but Access is a powerful desktop database and as such, will probably be with us for a long time as a desktop database application. However, what we probably won't see is an improved version of Jet. Anything said on this subject is speculation, but let's do speculate:

- All client/server applications are good candidates for SQL Desktop, but that doesn't mean all client/server applications must or should convert to SQL Desktop. It just means that you may have, in Desktop, a more efficient (and free) alternative to your current arrangement.

- Regardless of your application's current status, anyone wanting to apply new database engine technologies to their applications should become familiar with SQL Desktop. If and when Microsoft does decide to forego improvements to Jet in lieu of newer technologies, you'll be in the proverbial catbird seat. We don't want to add to the industry gossip that Microsoft is dropping its support of Jet, but, at some point, Microsoft probably will cease to improve and enhance Jet. Many developers suspect that Microsoft has no plans to improve Jet or ODBC. Although we have no definitive word from Microsoft sources, we are also of this opinion. Learning SQL Desktop and therefore SQL Server, and being prepared, is a good idea.

Whether you believe that SQL Desktop is a marketing strategy to introduce Access users to SQL Server 2000 or advanced notice that Jet has evolved as far as it's going to, one thing is still certain: SQL Desktop is a valuable tool for a few Access users in the right circumstances.

What Is the SQL Desktop Engine?

SQL Desktop offers you, as an Access user, a choice between Jet or SQL Server. Using SQL Desktop Engine, you can connect an Access application to the SQL Server engine—specifically, the SQL Server 2000 SQL Desktop Engine—by way of ADP (Access Data Projects) files or by creating the tables on SQL Desktop Engine and linking to them from within an ADP. In a simple client/server setup, you can think of Access Data Projects as an interface (front-end) to the more efficient SQL

Server 2000 engine. You're still using Access technology to develop the interface. Reaping all the Rapid Application Development (RAD) techniques of Access, but you're manipulating your data with a faster, more powerful engine (than Jet). To run SQL Desktop, you need one of the following operating systems:

- Windows 95/98 (Windows security features not supported)
- Windows Me (Windows Security features not supported)
- Windows 2000 Professional
- Windows NT 4.0 Workstation
- Windows 2000/NT Server

NOTE *MSDE 1.0 will run on Windows 95, but SQL Desktop (MSDE 2000) won't. You'll need Office XP Developer Engine to create a runtime version of an ADP application. If you're working with Access 97 applications or earlier, stick with Jet.*

In addition, you must have Access 2000 or 2002 installed. Here are a few specifics about SQL Desktop:

- ADP files use SQL Server tables.
- ADP files store front-end application objects (forms, reports, and so on) in the ADP document file (docfile).
- ADP files don't contain queries. Select Queries are stored as views, and Action queries are replaced by stored procedures. All such objects are stored in the desktop engine. (For more information on views and stored procedures, read Chapters 14 and 16. Also see Chapter 17, "Upsizing Directly from Access.")
- There's no Table or Query Design window. These are replaced with the da Vinci windows, which are similar in function to the Access design windows. But the Design New Query dialog box still uses the word *Query*. (Perhaps Microsoft should consider changing *Query* to *Stored Procedure*.) See Chapters 13, 14, and 15 for an overview of using the graphical design tools when working through some examples.

- User-defined functions (UDFs) are new to SQL Server 2000 and SQL Desktop Engine. UDFs are discussed in Chapter 16.
- ADPs don't support Jet or Data Access Objects (DAO). DAO is optimized for use with the Jet engine. With SQL Server, it is recommended that you use OLE DB and ADO. Appendix B offers an introductory discussion of ADO and ADOX. Perhaps the most important issue for us is that the SQL Desktop engine uses Transact-SQL (T-SQL) and not Jet SQL. Chapter 15 provides an overview of T-SQL.
- Database operations occur on the server rather than on the client as with Access.

Major Limitations

Several significant differences are found between SQL Desktop Engine and the full-blown version of SQL Server 2000. First, there's the issue of current users, or more specifically, concurrent users. The SQL Desktop engine is "optimized" for five users. In other words, up to five users can expect performance similar to SQL Server 2000. Any more than five and performance slips significantly. *Optimized* is a Microsoft marketing term that really means the limit is by design. Chapter 13 provides an overview of each of the available SQL Server versions.

SQL Desktop and Concurrent Users

Don't let the five-user limit scare you off. We've heard many reports of systems successfully using ADP projects with many more than five users. Concurrent users constitute an actual transaction, not a connection to the server. In other words, a person who is connected but isn't active does not count as one of the five users. On the other hand, one user can consume all five user spots by trying to process concurrent actions.

SQL Desktop concurrent user throttling is looked after by a process called *Target Benchmark Users (TBU)*. The TBU is set within SQL Desktop, and, when the number of concurrent threads exceeds this limit, each additional thread or process is delayed until active threads fall back within limits. There is some discussion over the actual number to which the TBU is set. Microsoft documentation states five, although some developers have claimed that it is actually eight.

TBU does not concern itself with users but rather the execution threads that are created by each user when they connect to the database and perform some action. If a user is connected to the database but is inactive, then TBU is not activated. It is also possible for a single user to make multiple active connections to the database, and in this way TBU could start affecting other users.

The biggest problem with TBU (other than its existence) is that no messages are passed to the client that the limit has been reached and that further batches are being "slowed down." However, there is a command—DBCC CONCURRENCYVIOLATION—that can assist you in discovering how batches are performing. To run DBCC CONCURRENCYVIOLATION:

1. Click on Start (on the Task bar), and then choose Run.

2. Type "OSQL –E" if using integrated security mode. Otherwise you will be required to enter a username and password.

3. At the prompt, type "DBCC CONCURRENCYVIOLATION(DISPLAY)".

4. Click on Go.

The output from this is fairly cryptic. For instance, the following readout:

```
Concurrency violations since 2001-11-24 02:30:00.093
1 2 3 4 5 6 7 8 9
5 6 7 8 9..........
```

indicates that there was one occasion when the system was five batches over the limit, two times when it was six times over the limit, three times when it was seven times over the limit, and so on. We can quickly ascertain that the number of simultaneous connections to the server are slowing things down. It's at this point (when you receive readings similar to these) that you may need to reexamine your application and perhaps consider a move up to the full server.

The second important limitation is the size of the database. SQL Server 2000 is capable of handling terabytes of data (these large databases are known as *very large databases*, or *VLDBs*), whereas the SQL Desktop is limited to two gigabytes of data minus the system tables. However, there is no limit to the number of SQL Desktop databases you can have on an instance of the server.

The graphical management tools (and additional applications installed with SQL Server)—in particular Enterprise Manager—are not available with SQL Desktop. System management is performed either via command-line tools (ISQL) or by using code.

> **NOTE** *One of the drawbacks when using SQL Desktop is the lack of a user interface. Access developers (although fully capable of using code) are used to managing their systems via a graphical interface. Perhaps if Microsoft had made the Enterprise Manager available with SQL Server, more developers would be willing to try it.*

These limits are by design and protect Microsoft's interest in SQL Server 2000, and that's not necessarily a bad thing. It's just good business for Microsoft. You get a lot for free, so, if these limitations aren't a problem, you have a powerful and free alternative to Jet.

Who Should Use the SQL Desktop Version

It might be easier to answer this question if we first eliminate those that won't use SQL Desktop, such as the average Access user. Access can handle a number of business needs, and many Access users and developers will never even install SQL Desktop. By *average user,* we mean those developers and casual users who run networked and single-user applications in Access with no problems. Access adequately handles the solution, and there are no plans in the near future to drastically change it. You probably don't need SQL Desktop if:

- You're using Access 97 or earlier.
- You have more than five simultaneous users.
- You have limited resources.
- You have limited funds for training personnel and need a database that's easy to use.

Keep in mind that things change. Businesses grow and so do the applications that support them. It's impossible to determine right now that you will never need to convert your applications to SQL Server.

> **NOTE** *The organization I currently work for is beginning the process of transferring all Access databases to SQL Server. One of the main reasons for this is the increase in users and the stability of SQL Server. There will be no further development of Microsoft Access databases on a corporate basis. Access will be used solely as the front end to SQL Server.*

In addition, Access users with a client/server application should consider SQL Desktop if they'd like a more stable environment, better performance, and have five or fewer concurrent users.

> **NOTE** *A database could have hundreds of users, but not all users will be generating activity on the database at any given point in time. Concurrent users are those users who are actively generating some system activity. So, even though you have many users, you may still have only a limited number of concurrent users at any given time.*

SQL Desktop is a real boon to the SQL Server developer who needs to distribute a runtime application. Doing so using SQL Server directly is difficult because it involves complex licensing issues; SQL Desktop solves this dilemma. Similar to the Developer's Toolkit, which helps you create a runtime version of an Access file, SQL Desktop embeds its database engine into an application, so you can install that SQL Server solution on non-SQL Server systems. It's an easy and inexpensive solution to a long-time problem, and that in itself makes SQL Desktop a valuable addition to the database solutions arena.

Desktop Engine may also be useful for staff who are out of the office and who need the power of SQL Server to work with data while on the road. They can then upload the new data upon return.

Although not as apparent as other uses, SQL Desktop is also a valuable training tool to anyone who wants to learn about SQL Server but who doesn't possess the software. In this capacity, SQL Desktop could help someone decide whether SQL Server is the right solution for his or her needs, once Access no longer meets them. Some of the areas in which SQL Desktop will outperform Microsoft Access (all versions) include:

- *Backup:* More-extensive backup is available, including backing up database transactions.
- *Security:* SQL Desktop can use Windows 2000 Integrated Security. (See Chapter 18 for an overview of SQL Server security.)
- *Transaction logs:* SQL Desktop will record and maintain a history of database transactions. The system can be restored to a specific point in time if required.
- *Compatibility:* Objects can be transferred without modification to the full version of SQL Server.
- *Dynamic locking:* The server will automatically choose the optimal locking method to use.

> **NOTE** *The second part of the book looks at each of these areas in some detail.*

New to SQL Desktop

Most of the changes to SQL Desktop are enhancements that make the SQL Desktop environment more compatible with Access. In this way, we feel Microsoft is attempting to lure more Access developers into the world of SQL Server by allowing them to take advantage of SQL Server's performance from within the Access environment.

Access 2002 comes with a new service provider named Client Data Manager (CDM). The CDM is a new OLE provider, which is designed exclusively for Access 2002. It deals with the back end (Jet or SQL Server) and your front-end objects. One of its main design purposes was to make working with SQL Server easier for Access developers. One of the best features is that you no longer need to use the Uniquetables property to "mark" a single table as updateable. Using the CDM, we can create one to many forms, and now both ends of the relationship are updateable. In addition, we are now able to use field defaults directly from the server rather than having to use the form default property as with Access 2000.

Access users should find the development environment in SQL Desktop more similar to Access than MSDE 1.0 was. As a result, SQL Desktop inherits some of the new features available in SQL Server 2000:

- *Extended properties:* SQL Desktop and SQL Server 2000 now support many Jet features that were neglected in earlier versions: lookup fields, subdatasheets, master-child relationships, data validation messages, and input masks.

- *Functions:* SQL Desktop now allows user-defined functions. You'll use functions to return specific values, execute nested queries, return recordsets, and return a new Table data type. Chapter 16 discusses UDFs.

- *Updateable views and functions:* These are the equivalent of updateable queries (queries based on related tables that can be updated via the query). Don't confuse these with the SQL Update query. Chapter 14 looks at views in some detail.

- *Referential integrity:* SQL Desktop now supports cascading updates and deletions.

Differences between SQL Desktop and SQL Server 2000

Given that the SQL Desktop engine is really SQL Server 2000, you might expect to find that all of the features and tools in SQL Server 2000 are also available in SQL Desktop, but that's not the case. The most important differences were mentioned briefly in "Major Limitations" earlier in this chapter. Table 12-1 is a feature comparison between SQL Desktop and SQL Server 2000.

Table 12-1. Comparison of SQL Desktop and SQL Server 2000

FEATURE/ISSUE	SQL DESKTOP	SQL SERVER 2000
Database size	2GB	Limited by the amount of physical storage space
Users	5	Hundreds (thousands with the Enterprise Edition)
Instances	1 for running 1.0 and 2000 on same system	16
English query (a natural-language query general tool)	N/A	Included
Analytical services (OLAP)	N/A	Included
Data mining	N/A	Included
Enterprise Manager (management tool)	N/A	Included
Query Analyzer (management tool)	N/A	Included
Books Online (documentation)	N/A (but can be downloaded)	Included

Installing the SQL Desktop Version

If you upgrade from Office 2000 to Office XP, the installation process won't automatically upgrade MSDE 1.0 to SQL Desktop (MSDE 2000). In fact, MSDE 1.0 will be left completely intact until you manually upgrade it. After reviewing what's new to SQL Desktop in the "New to SQL Desktop" section earlier in this chapter, you'll probably decide to upgrade MSDE 1.0 to SQL Desktop.

Upgrading

If you're upgrading from MSDE 1.0 to SQL Desktop, you have two options:

- Uninstall the earlier version and then install SQL Desktop.
- Use the Upgrade option while installing SQL Desktop.

To uninstall MSDE 1.0 or SQL Server 7.0:

1. Open the control panel.
2. Select the Add/Remove Programs tool.
3. Highlight MSDE 1.0 or SQL Server 7.0 in the Add/Remove Programs dialog box.
4. Click on Remove (Add/Remove in Windows 98).

Once you've uninstalled the previous version, installing SQL Desktop is easy. Just locate the setup.exe program on the Microsoft Office XP CD-ROM, and double-click on it. (Alternately, click on the taskbar's Start button, choose Run, and then enter the command line

```
X:\MSDE2000\setup.exe
```

where *X* represents the designation of your CD-ROM drive. The dialog box shown in Figure 12-1 indicates that SQL Desktop Engine is being installed.

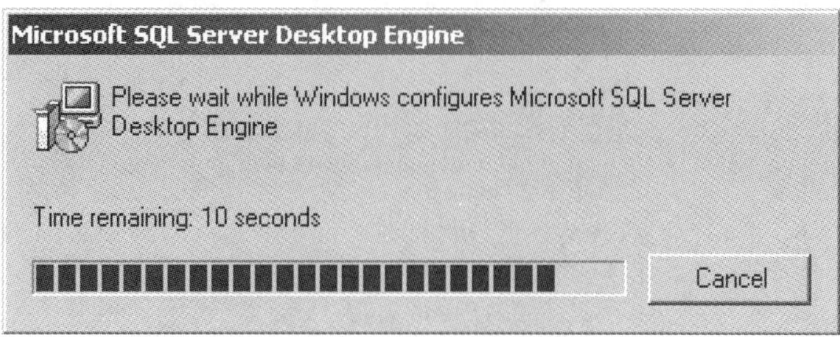

Figure 12-1. Installing SQL Desktop: This dialog box follows the installation progress of SQL Desktop Engine.

The other option is to upgrade MSDE 1.0, which you should do if you're currently using MSDE 1.0. The easiest way to upgrade is to use the UPGRADE installation option. Specifically, add the UPGRADE=1 switch using the command-line method we just discussed. Microsoft offers the capability to control the installation process to a small degree. Specifically, you can add instructions to the command line to

- Specify destination folders.
- Determine an SQL Server instance name.
- Upgrade from SQL Server 7.0.
- Set SQL Server logon security mode.
- Create a log file for installation troubleshooting.
- Add a reinstallation switch.

The different installations settings are listed in Table 12-2.

Table 12-2. Installation Options

OPTION	SYNTAX*	DESCRIPTION	SPECIAL NOTE
?	/?	Displays a list of setup switches.	
i	/i packagefile	Specifies the name of the Windows Installer installation package file (an MSI file) to be used to install an instance of the SQL Server 2000 SQL Desktop Engine.	For more information on package files, visit `http://msdn.microsoft.com/library/default.asp?url=/library/en-us/distsql/distsql_58dv.asp`.
SETTINGS	/SETTINGS inifilename	Identifies an INI file that specifies the installation options. Don't use this option with command-line options.	
TARGETDIR	/TARGETDIR ="drive:\path\"	Identifies where the executable files are installed.	
DATADIR	/DATADIR ="drive:\path\"	Identifies the folder where the SQL Server system is built.	
INSTANCENAME	/INSTANCENAME ="INSTANCENAME" (INSTANCENAME must be in all caps with no spaces.)	Allows SQL Desktop to run on same system with an earlier version of MSDE (1.0) or SQL Server (7.0).	MDAC 2.5 clients don't recognize the INSTANCENAME option. For more information, read the "Resolving Connectivity Problems" section in "Configuring SQL Server 2000 SQL Desktop Engine" available online at `http://support.microsoft.com/support/kb/articles/Q301/4/13.ASP`.
X	/x packagename	Similar to i, but used during the installation process.	
L	/L* [filename] (/L*v [filename])	Creates an error log file named *filename*.	Adding *v* to the switch creates a verbose log. The *filename* argument is optional.

(continued)

Table 12-2. Installation Options (continued)

OPTION	SYNTAX*	DESCRIPTION	SPECIAL NOTE
qn	/qn	Runs setup with no user interface.	
qb	/qb	Runs setup with basic user interface (progress dialogs).	

*Microsoft documentation shows all switches preceded by the / character, but it's our experience that it isn't always needed.

Aid Troubleshooting by Creating an Installation Log File

The installation process can create an error log to document problems that occur during the installation process. To create this log, simply add the /L * setup switch. (See Table 12-1.) For instance, the following statement would create an error log file named DE.txt at C:\:

```
X:\MSDE2000\Setup.exe /L* C:\DE.txt
```

After installing SQL Desktop, simply open DE.txt in Notepad to review any error messages.

Installing SQL Desktop from the Office XP CD-ROM

The setup files are located in the MSDE2000 Folder on the XP CD-ROM. The following information refers to a clean install to an MS Windows 2000 server.

Double-click on the setup file to begin the process, and then sit back and wait. With this setup, there are no screens, no Next buttons, and no multiple system restarts. Figure 12-2 shows the final stage in the initial setup. When you restart your system, you should see SQL Server Service Manager in the task bar. Figure 12-3 shows the new icon. (It's the one on the far right.) Open Service Manager by double-clicking on it. Figure 12-4 shows Service Manager.

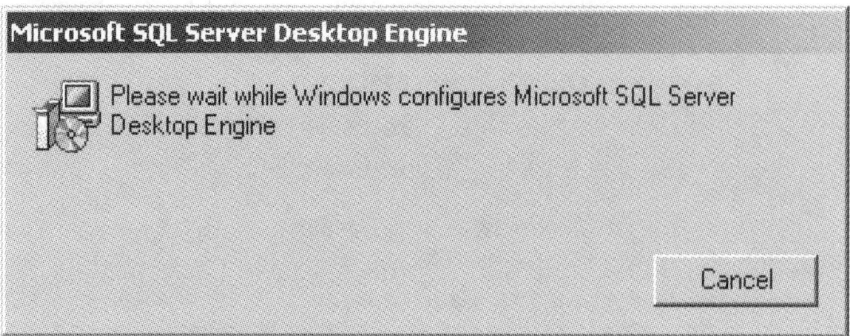

Figure 12-2. Final stage of setup

Figure 12-3. SQL icon in the system tray

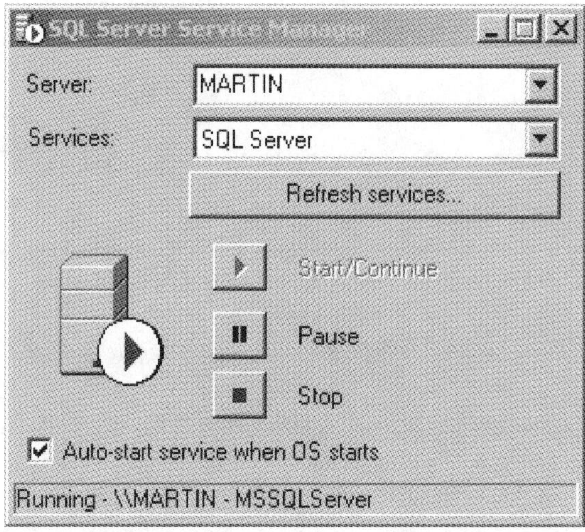

Figure 12-4. SQL Server Service Manager

Note that we checked the box to ensure that SQL Server starts as the PC boots. Make sure you also do so to avoid manually starting the service each time you work with the server. This is the same Service Manager as found in the full version of SQL Server 2000. As you can see, very little is involved in the installation of SQL Desktop, which is a nice change!

NOTE *Windows 95/98 and ME users will be restricted to using TCP/IP for connections to the server. Other network libraries (such as Named Pipes) are not available with these operating systems.*

Getting Acquainted with the SQL Desktop Environment

Because the second part of this book deals with SQL Server 2000 and Access Data Projects, we won't look at working with the desktop edition in great detail. Many of the functions and techniques are identical to working with the full version of SQL Server 2000 and are covered in Chapters 13 through 19.

It's time to actually open an ADP file, otherwise known as an Access project. The NorthwindCS.adp file is the ADP equivalent of the Northwind.mdb file—the sample database that's been shipped with Access for years. To install NorthwindCS:

1. After installing the SQL Desktop engine, open NorthwindCS.adp, which you should find in the Program Files\Microsoft Office\Office10\Samples subfolder. You can also select the project from the main Access Help menu: select Help, choose Sample Databases, and then select Northwind Sample Access Project.

2. Figure 12-5 shows the Database window, which is similar to the MDB Database window. The Queries item in the Object bar is new to SQL Desktop 2000, replacing Views and Stored Procedures in MSDE 1.0 (Access 2000). You should note a few differences between the project Database window and the MDB Database window. First, the queries list in the Database window includes views, functions, and stored procedures. Second, the Database Diagrams item permits you to add and maintain relationships—similar to the Relationships window in an MDB file—but this item offers many additional facilities once you move into Access Data Projects, including the ability to actually create and amend table structures.

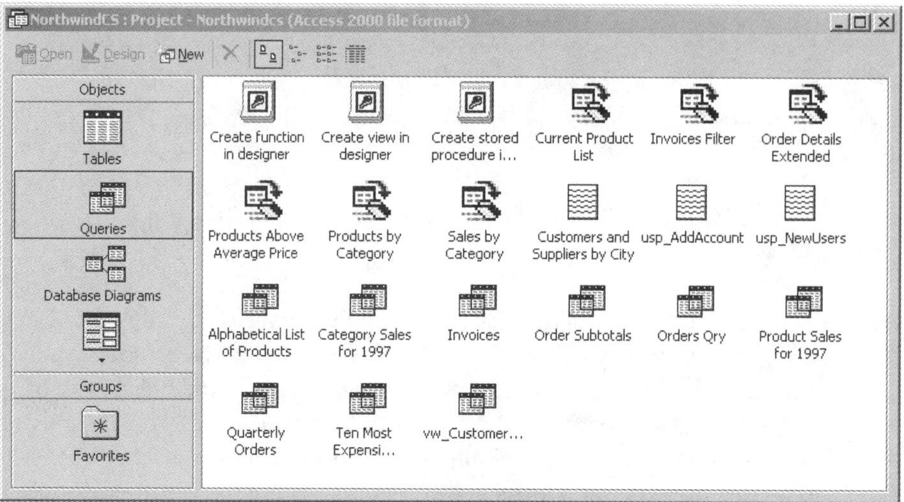

Figure 12-5. Database window

SQL Desktop Tables

SQL tables look just like Access tables in Datasheet view, but Table Design view is considerably different. In addition, the property names aren't always the same. Figure 12-6 shows a table in the project designer (the equivalent of the Access Design view). In SQL Desktop, this environment is called the da Vinci MS Design Tools. Table 12-3 compares the table properties.

> **NOTE** *The terms* field *and* column *aren't necessarily interchangeable. However, you'll often find that SQL Server uses the term* column *to refer to what is commonly called a* field *in Access.*

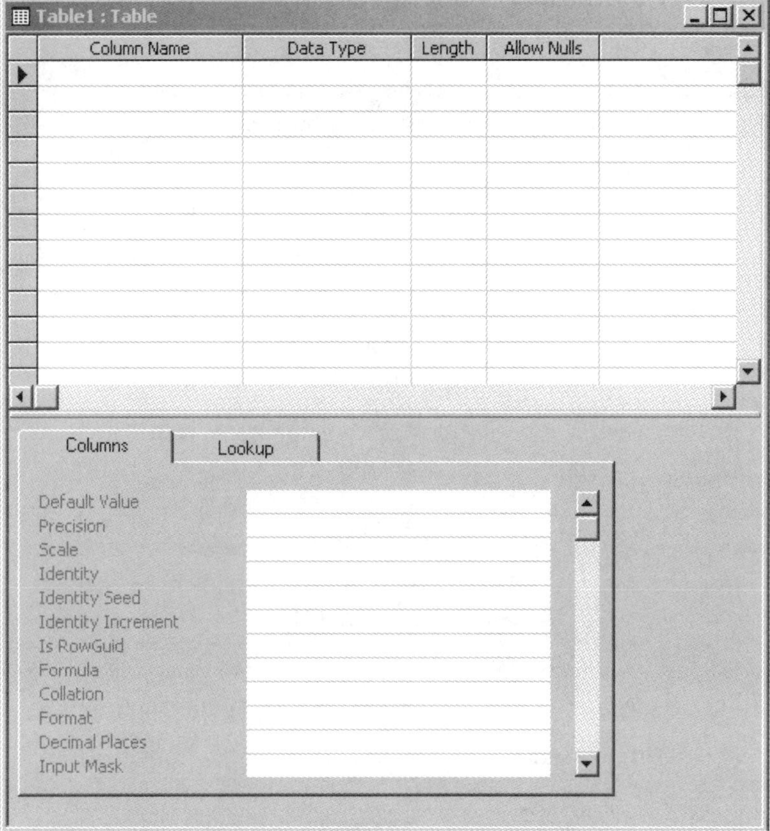

Figure 12-6. Table Design view

The project designer is very different from the Access Design view environment.

Table 12-3. Comparison of SQL Server 2000 and Jet Table Properties

ACCESS	SQL DESKTOP	DESCRIPTION OF PROPERTY	DEFAULT
Field Name	Column Name	The column's (field's) name	
Data Type	Data Type and Field Size	Combines Jet's Data Type and Field Size properties	
Field Size	Length	Determines the size of a character column (text field)	
Required	Allow Nulls	When selected, allows Null values, which is the opposite of setting the Required property to Yes	

(continued)

Table 12-3. Comparison of SQL Server 2000 and Jet Table Properties (continued)

ACCESS	SQL DESKTOP	DESCRIPTION OF PROPERTY
Description	Description	Describes a column's (field's) values or purpose
Default Value	Default Value	Automatically enters a specific value for each new record
Numeric and Decimal data types	Precision	Specifies total number of digits for a column (field)
Numeric and Decimal data types	Scale	Specifies the total number of digits for the decimal portion of any value
AutoNumber data type and Increment as the New Values property	Identity	Returns a unique value for each record
Seed (only available in Jet SQL)	Identity Seed	Sets the starting value of an Identity column (field)
Increment (only available in Jet SQL)	Identity Increment	Determines the incremental value between each identity value
N/A	Is RowGridRowGuid	Specifies that the row contain a GUID (globally unique identifier) Although not restricted to replication, that's its primary use.
N/A	Formula	Expression for creating a computed value
N/A	Collation	Sets the sorting order for character columns (text fields)
Format	Format	Set column (field) display
Decimal Places	Decimal Places	Settings of 0 to 6, which determines the number of digits that following the decimal point (formatting only)
Input Mask	Input Mask	Displays a formatting string during data entry that guides and limits the user to enter valid data

> **NOTE** *The Lookup properties are the same in both Access and SQL Desktop.*

Access 2002 and Security

One of the major problems with SQL Desktop is the lack of a user interface to manage the database. Enterprise Manager, a graphical tool for managing your SQL Server installation, is not supplied with SQL Desktop. As a result, managing databases and users is slightly more complicated and requires the use of stored procedures or code. You are encouraged to read Chapter 18, "Security Issues," in conjunction with this section. Security is a serious issue and one that you should understand before attempting any of the examples here.

> **NOTE** *Enterprise Manager is available with the Office XP Developer CD-ROM. It is also possible to install the Evaluation Edition of SQL Server to take advantage of the Enterprise Manager. However, at the time of writing, the licensing issues from this approach are unclear. It appears that when your evaluation period for SQL Server 2000 expires the Enterprise Manager tools remain fully functional.*

Access 2002 also permits you to activate the "sa" default user account on SQL Desktop. This is the highest-level account within the database. The "sa" account has all privileges on all database objects and should be handled with care. See Chapter 18 for a discussion of this account.

We will use the NorthwindCS.adp file that comes with Office XP to demonstrate setting the "sa" account.

> **NOTE** *When installing on Windows 98 or Windows ME, the default is to use SQL Server Authentication. On NT or Windows 2000, the default security mechanism is Windows Authentication. In this case, the Windows administrators user group is automatically added to the server as system administrators. This group can be removed once installation is complete.*

To enable the "sa" account:

1. Select Server Properties from the View menu to see the server properties shown in Figure 12-7.

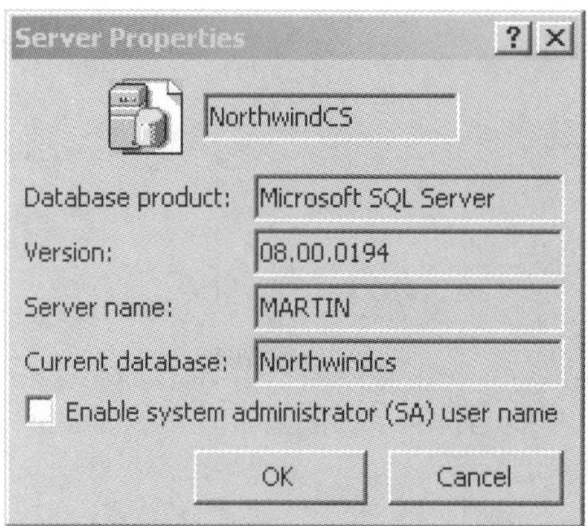

Figure 12-7. SQL server properties

2. Check the Enable System Administrator (SA) username. Figure 12-8 shows the resulting message. Make sure you read it and do as it says. The default setup creates the sa login with a blank password. The first thing we need to do is to create a password for this user. When you click on OK to create the sa account, you will be prompted to enter a password. Leaving the sa account password blank is a serious breach of server security, and at some point you will regret having done so.

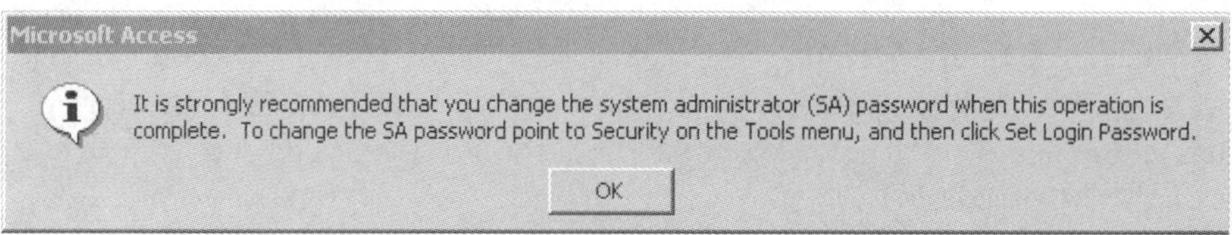

Figure 12-8. The sa login security warning

3. Leave the password blank for the moment, and click on OK.

To add a password for the "sa" account:

1. From the main menu, select Tools.
2. Select Security.
3. Select Set Login Password from the security menu. Figure 12-9 shows the resulting Set Password dialog box.

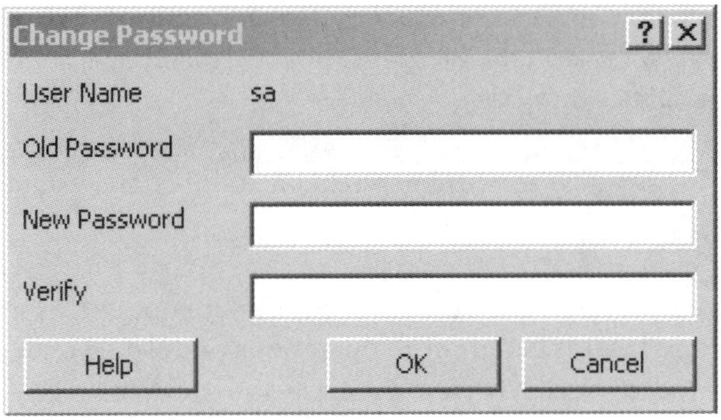

Figure 12-9. Setting the system administrator password

4. Leave the Old Password box blank, and enter a new password for the account.

5. Enter the password again.

6. Click on OK to complete the security setup for the account.

> **TIP** *Do not under any circumstance leave the sa account with a blank password.*

Database Files

When working with Access, we are used to working with a single database file, but, once you make the move to SQL Desktop, this is no longer the case. For example, with the Northwind project, you are dealing with at least two files. Both of which are vital to the operations of your database.

> **WARNING** *Whatever you do, don't mess with these files when the database is open (or closed for that matter). Don't move them, don't delete them, and don't touch them. Remember, this is no longer Microsoft Access: you cannot simply copy a data file and then reopen it somewhere else. This is the world of SQL Server, and things are different.*

The files we are concerned with are Northwindcs.mdf and Northwindcs.ldf. You'll find these two files in the Program Files/Microsoft SQL Server/MSSQL/Data subfolder:

- Northwindcs.mdf is the primary data file for the database, similar to a MDB file.
- Northwindcs.ldf contains the transactions for your database. The transaction log contains details of all operations performed on your database. If you ever need to recover your database, the transaction log is vital if you want to recover the system to a particular point in time. Figure 12-10 shows the MDF and LDF files associated with a new install of SQL Desktop.

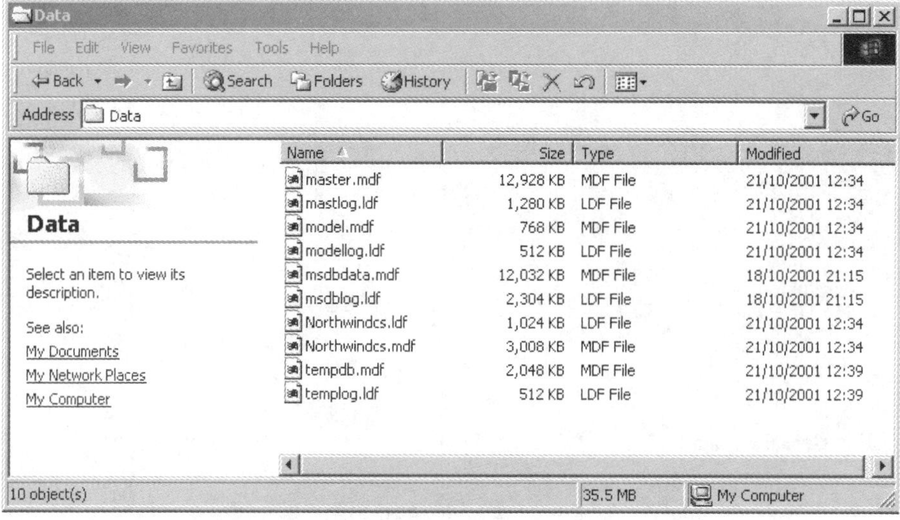

Figure 12-10. New data and transaction files

> **NOTE** *Backup is discussed in Chapter 17. It is in this area that the lack of Enterprise Manager is sorely missed. Enterprise Manager contains several graphical tools that make backing up an SQL Server Database very easy.*

If you do need to move your database, two system stored procedures are used: Sp_detach_db to detach the database from SQL Server, and sp_attach_db to reattach the database from its new location. In most cases, you will detach and attach the MDF data file and the LDF transaction log file.

For example, I have created a new SQL Desktop ADP called NorthwindAttach. It is located in the folder F:\ADPs\NorthwindAttach.adp. We can move the database files to C:\Program File\Microsoft Office\ Microsoft SQL Server/MSSQL/Data. To do so, you can execute sp_detach_db and sp_attach_db from the command line. The stored procedure can also be executed within a stored procedure created in Access 2002. (See SQL Server Books Online for a full description of the process that's required to detach and detach data files.) The syntax for the commands is as follows:

```
Sp_detach_db @dbname = 'NorthwindAttach'
```

To attach the database files in their new location, run the following stored procedure:

```
Sp_attach_db @dbname = 'NorthwindAttach'
@filename1= ' F:\ADPs\copy\NorthwindAttach.mdf'
@filename2 = 'F:\ADPs\copy\NorthwindAttach.ldf'
```

Forms in Access Data Projects

You will also notice, in addition to the changes in the design of tables, that the database forms have changed. You will have new properties available, but some old friends will also make a welcome appearance. Table 12-4 shows some of the most interesting form properties available with SQL Server.

Table 12-4. ADP Form Properties

PROPERTY	COMMENT	PROPERTY TYPE
Max Records	The maximum number of records that will be retrieved by the form.	Data
Server Filter	Used to specify a subset of records used by the form.	Data
Server Filter by Form	The form will open in Server Filter by Form mode.	Data
Unique Table	Uniquely identifies a table for update. Used with views, stored procedures when multiple tables are used.	Data
Input Parameters	Used to pass values to and from the form.	Data
On Dirty	Enables you to run a macro or VBA before a record is modified.	Event
On Undo	Macro or VBA than can run before changes to records are undone.	

When you open a form in an ADP, pay close attention to the navigation bar because two new options are available. (Look at the right-hand side of the navigation bar.) When the form is loading, notice one of the buttons on the bar will turn red. This indicates that records are downloading from the server. Users can actually stop the download by clicking the button while it is red. Beside this button is another, which when clicked opens a dialog box where the user can limit the number of records returned to the form. The default is 10,000. Figure 12-11 shows the dialog box with the default of 10,000 records.

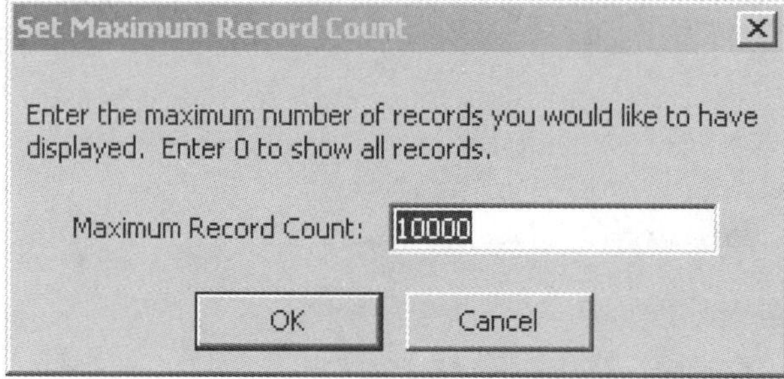

Figure 12-11. Setting the record downloads for a form

The MAX Records property can also be set using the standard form properties for an individual form. To set this property for an individual form:

1. Select the Form Group in the Database window.

2. Select the Customer form.

3. Click on Design on the menu. The Customer form will open in Design view.

4. Select View from the main menu.

5. Select Properties.

6. In the Properties dialog box, click on the Data tab. You may then enter the Max Records property. Figure 12-12 shows the Customer form with the Max Record property set to 100.

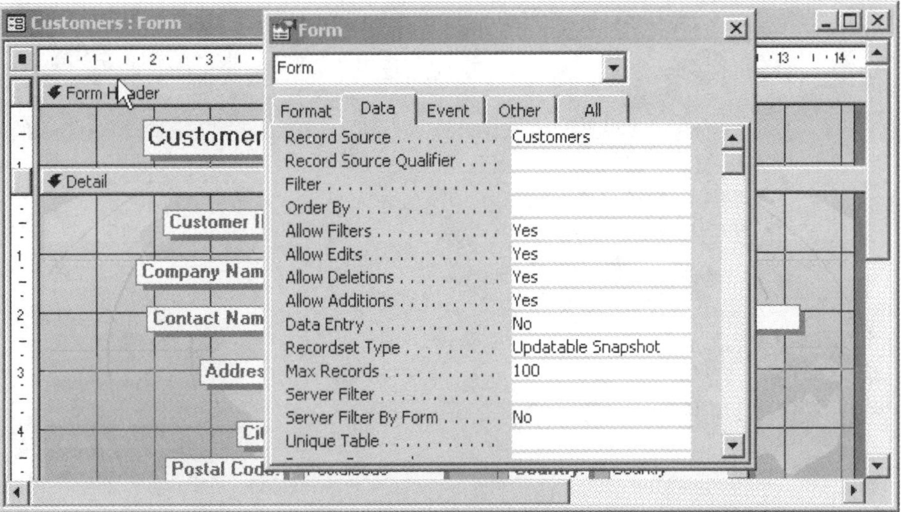

Figure 12-12. Customer form Max Records property

We can also set the default value for this property for all databases:

1. Select Tools from the main menu.
2. Select Options.
3. In the Options dialog box, click on the Advanced tab. Figure 12-13 shows the advanced properties.

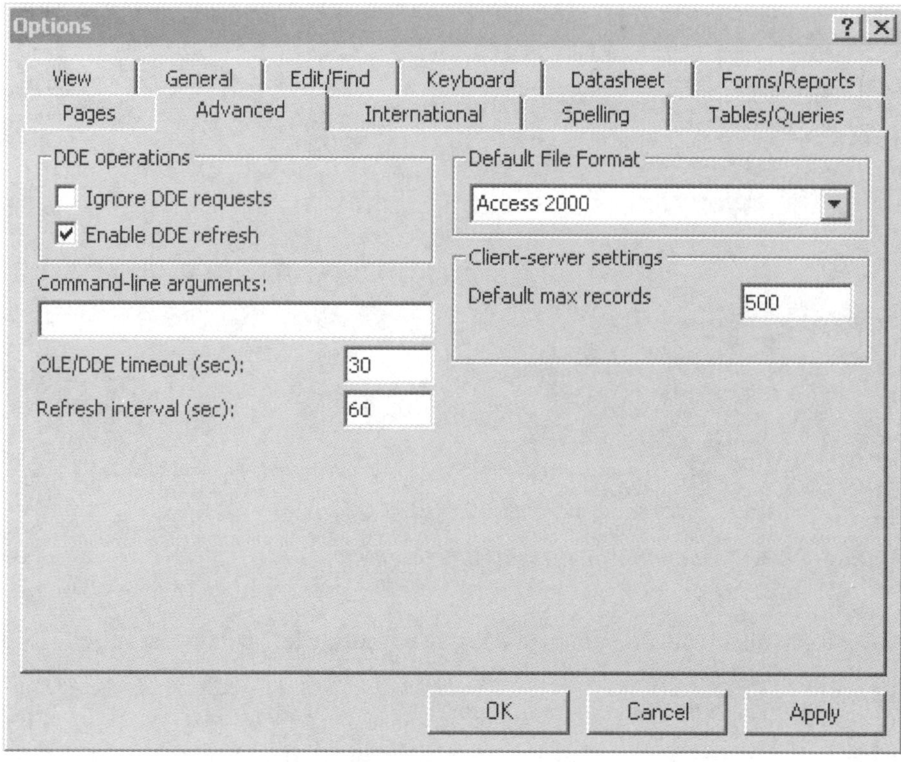

Figure 12-13. Display advanced options

4. Change the default property to 100 (or whatever value is appropriate for your needs).

Changing the default properties will not affect existing forms. All new forms will, however, pick up the new default Max Records property.

We can also use ADO to supply a value to the Max Records property. For example, the following code is the Open event for a copy of the Customers form:

```
Dim cnn as ADODB.Connection
Dim rst as ADODB.Recordset
Set cnn =CurrentProject.AccessConnection
Set rst = New ADODB.Recordset
 With rst
     Set .ActiveConnection = cnn
     .Source = "SELECT * FROM Customers"
     .LockType = adLockOptimistic
     .CursorType = adOpenKeyset
```

```
        .MaxRecords = 10
        .Open
    End With
        'Set the form's Recordset property to the ADO recordset
        Set Me.Recordset = rst
        Set rst = Nothing
        Set cnn = Nothing
```

The existing record source is removed from a copy of the existing Customer form. The code populates the form with the records and sets the Max Records value to 10. Note that, in this case, the property applies to only the record set we are opening, not to any form in the Access project.

To create the unbound Customer form:

1. Select the Customer form in the Database window.
2. Using the right mouse button, select Copy.
3. Using the right mouse button, select Paste.
4. Paste a copy of the form as CustomersMax.
5. Open the new form in Design view and remove the Customer table as the record source. (Select View, Properties from the main Access menu.)
6. Click on the Event tab.
7. Select the OnOpen property field.
8. Click on the ellipses button to the right of the property text box.
9. Select Code Builder from the dialog (if prompted). You are now in the VBA development environment.

> **TIP** *A quick way to get to the VBA editor is to press F7 when the cursor is in any of the form properties. This will immediately open the VBA editor.*

10. Enter the preceding ADO code between the procedure stub created by Access.
11. Close the VBA editor. (Select File, and then choose Return to Microsoft Access.)

12. Close and save the form.

13. Open the form as normal. You should have access to at most ten customer records.

This chapter introduced you to SQL Server Desktop Engine (MSDE 2000). We have seen how to install the engine and upgrade from MSDE 1.0. Many of the topics also apply to SQL Server, and, in the second part of this book, much of what you have seen here is discussed in detail mainly from an SQL Server perspective.

It is our view that SQL Desktop will be widely used by developers as a test-bed, a free tool that will be used to teach yourself SQL Server before you take the leap into the world of client/server and SQL Server 2000. For those reasons, we would recommend SQL Desktop to developers mainly because it is free, and, as a teaching tool for SQL Server, it has no comparison. Remember that the SQL Server database engine is not Microsoft Access. You are entering a new world, and much of what you will find there is fun. Hopefully, the second part of this book will assist you in the exploration of that world and get you started on the journey towards client/server database development.

CHAPTER 13

Introduction to SQL Server

Meet the Beast

SEVERAL FLAVORS OF SQL SERVER are currently in use today: version 6.5, version 7, and the new Microsoft SQL Server 2000. This section will look at the newest member of the MS database server family, examining some of the features of the software and how you access them.

So what is SQL Server? Think of Microsoft Access; add several hundred (or thousand) users, gigabytes of data, high levels of security, and you're almost there. SQL Server—the major Microsoft Relational Database Management System (RDBMS)—is often called "Access' Big Brother". It is Microsoft's flagship RDBMS product and one of the most popular commercial DB systems in use. Its popularity as a Web database is also rising mainly due to its tight integration with Internet Information Services version 5 (IIS5) and the Windows 2000 operating system.

In the next few chapters, we hope to remove some of the fear you may have in working with the "monster database." By the end of this section, however, you should be capable of

- installing SQL Server
- working with Enterprise Manager
- backing up and maintaining your work
- working with T-SQL (SQL Server's version of SQL)
- analyzing your queries for performance
- using stored procedures
- setting up basic database security

- getting your data to the Web
- using basic XML within SQL Server2000 and Access 2002

> **NOTE** *This is not meant to be an exhaustive resource or document on SQL Server and Access 2002. Books Online should be your first port of call, followed closely by the Microsoft SQL Server Web site.*

History of SQL Server

Moving from what to me was the familiar interface of MS Access to SQL Server was intimidating, to say the least. However, many of the functions and day-to-day operations of the database can still be performed using the familiar graphical user interface beloved by Access developers. Using Access Data Projects, we have a similar means of working with the database engine. Within SQL Server, we have other graphical tools including Enterprise Manager. Some of the problems with Access 2000 (described later) have been resolved in Access 2002. Most of all your skills in design, table construction, and querying and programming in DAO, ADO, and VBA will prove invaluable. Not that there isn't still a lot to learn, but your skills in these are directly transferable to SQL; it's just that you will be working on a grander scale.

The history of the development of SQL Server makes interesting reading and deals with the relationship between many of the biggest players in the relational database world: Microsoft, IBM and Sybase.

In 1987, OS/2 was released following an agreement between Microsoft and IBM. Closely following this initial release, IBM released a high-end version of OS/2 that contained a small workgroup database called OS/2 Database Manager, which was intended to work with IBM's DB2 database product.

Microsoft, realizing that the high-end OS/2 operating system with bundled database would soon absorb the market for their joint "lower" version, decided to enter into a development agreement with Sybase, mainly to bundle its database product DataServer with OS/2 in the hope of capturing some of the operating system market from IBM. The main database in use however, particularly in the PC marketplace, was Ashton-Tate's dBase.

The wonderful marketers at Microsoft struck again and persuaded Ashton-Tate to "certify" its database as Ashton-Tate/Microsoft SQL Server. This, of course, was an attempt to take the dBase market. So here we have a database product, licensed from Sybase being "trademarked" by Microsoft competitor Ashton-Tate. What can one say about the business skill of the executives at Microsoft! In 1988, the first beta version of what would become SQL Server was released at a vastly reduced rate for developers, as usual.

One of the major advances during this period was Sybase's granting permission to the Microsoft SQL programmers to view and finally work with database source code. The final bit of the jigsaw puzzle fell into place in late 1991 when Windows 3.1 was released, and many users, rather than move to OS/2, went straight onto Windows 3.1.

SQL Server and Access 2002

How Does It Fit?

Many Access developers have wondered for some time what direction Microsoft is pushing Access in. (Many of us are still wondering.) With this release, we can see two obvious pushes: the Internet and using Access as the application development tool for SQL Server. Access Data Projects have moved out of being a stage one technology and we believe they now have a place as a RAD application for SQL Server back ends. The inclusion of XML in both SQL and Access 2002 positions both systems well for the future growth of this technology and its use on the Web. Out in the field, more and more professional Access developers are moving into developing SQL Server back ends to their databases.

So will Access still have a place? In our view, Access will continue to fulfill the database role for the small business or small local workgroup. Larger systems and the push to have data available on the Internet will leave many of you with no option but to hit the keyboard and start using SQL Server. The main problem will be how many of our smaller business customers can afford the change being forced onto them by Microsoft.

SQL Server 2000 Editions

Several "editions" of SQL Server 2000 are available: Enterprise Edition, Standard Edition, Developer Edition, SQL Server 2000 Desktop, and CE Edition.

Enterprise Edition

This is the full version of the server that is available as a 120-day evaluation download from Microsoft. (I have this version installed for this section.) This free download provides you with an opportunity to "touch and feel" before purchase. This is the top-of-the-line edition and can be used for a large Web site, online transaction processing, and data warehouse solutions. Enterprise Edition supports up to 64GB of memory and up to 32 processors.

Standard Edition

Standard Edition is the version that most users will have and need. I have chosen to use the Enterprise version simply because it was free and downloadable from Microsoft. The Standard Edition is aimed at small to medium business users who do not need the additional features of Enterprise Edition. Standard Edition can use up to 2GB of RAM and up to four processors.

Developer Edition

Developer Edition is similar in all ways to the full Enterprise Edition. The main restriction is that it can be used only for development and testing; the license does not allow its use in a production environment.

SQL Server 2000 Desktop

This is the edition that replaces MSDE (version one). It is still commonly referred to by Access developers as *MSDE.* No graphical client tools are provided with this edition, but OSQL is provided as a command-line utility.

> **NOTE** *OSQL permits you to execute T-SQL statements, stored procedures, and scripts from the command line. OSQL is started from within the operating system. Select Start|Run, and type "OSQL" into the Run dialog box to start the command-line interface.*

The graphical tools such as Enterprise Manager are not included. However, you can use various techniques including SQL-DMO, ADO, OLEDB, and so on to manage an instance of Desktop Edition. Chapter 12 looks at installation of the Desktop Edition.

> **NOTE** *If you interact in any way with a full SQL Server 2000 installation, then a client access license (or processor license) is required.*

It is worth noting that severe restrictions are placed on the performance of the Desktop SQL Server; that is, they are "fixed" so that performance drops depending on the number of concurrent threads accessing the database. Is this, as has been suggested, a teaser to get you to upgrade to SQL Server, perhaps? See Chapter 12 for a discussion on MSDE.

CE Edition

This is a version of SQL Server designed for handheld devices. To be honest, we have not used this version, and so our experience is limited (to say the least). CE Edition supports the following features:

- Compatible with SQL Server 2000 SQL
- 32 indexes per table
- Support for NULL
- Transaction support
- DDL
- DML
- SELECT: SET Functions (aggregates), INNER/OUTER JOIN, SUBSELECT, and GROUP BY and HAVING

One important deficiency is that stored procedures are not supported.

Types of Installation

Three main types or options are available when installing SQL Server:

- Typical
- Minimum
- Custom

The typical installation is the most commonly used and should suit most readers of this section. It is the default install in which most of the common features of SQL Server will be installed. Over the years from SQL Server 6, Microsoft has made the installation a lot friendlier. The typical install will suit most people, and it provides most of the required functionality. For those readers who would like to see what is actually installed, try the custom install. Be careful with your choices here and remember to take a few notes particularly about any items with which you may not be familiar. You can always look them up later using Books Online.

If your system is short on disk space and processing power, you might choose to install with the minimum option. Some of the basic features of SQL Server, such as Books Online, will not be installed. Books Online is without doubt essential to your learning curve with SQL Server, and you should install them if at all possible. (If required, Books Online can also be run from the installation CD-ROM.) They may also be downloaded or viewed directly from the Microsoft MSDN Web site.

Custom installation is recommended for advanced users of SQL Server because it allows you to change many of the default options. For many of you just beginning the move to SQL Server, the default or typical installation should provide all the features you require. Additional options can be installed as your experience with the software grows. However, we offer a few words of warning: in a production environment, the default settings may leave your system vulnerable to outside access (hacking). There is no substitute for experience and planning the installation *before* you put the CD-ROM into the drive. This is of particular importance if you intend to use SQL Server as the basis for a Web-based application.

Installing SQL Server 2000

I should begin by saying that my installation of SQL Server 2000 to test for this section was perhaps one of the easiest installations I have ever performed. Comprehensive guidelines for the hardware and software requirements for SQL Server 2000 are available for download at `http://msdn.microsoft.com/library/psdk/sql/in_overview_74vn.htm`. Like all software installations, we should consider several things before loading the CD-ROM.

Hardware Requirements

Table 13-1 shows the minimum hardware and software requirements for SQL Server 2000.

Table 13-1. Minimum SQL Server 2000 Requirements

EDITION	OPERATING SYSTEM	MEMORY	DISK SPACE
Enterprise and Standard	Microsoft Windows NT Service Pack 5 (SP5), Microsoft Windows NT Server 4.0 Enterprise Edition with SP5 or later, Microsoft Windows 2000 Server, Microsoft Windows 2000 Advanced Server, and Microsoft Windows 2000 Datacenter Server	64MB	95MB–270MB
Developer Edition	As above but on Windows 2000 Pro	64MB	270MB
Desktop	As Standard and Enterprise but additionally on Microsoft Windows 98, Microsoft Windows Millennium Edition, Windows 2000 Professional	64MB with Windows 2000, 32MB for other OS	44MB

NOTE *The Evaluation Edition of SQL Server 2000 also runs on Windows 2000 Professional. Don't forget to get SP1 as well as the evaluation copy. (Service Pack 2 is now available for download from the Microsoft SQL Server Web site (*`http://www.microsoft.com/sql`*). Remember, for production, SQL Server is an industrial-strength database, and, as such, it requires an industrial-strength server operating system such as Windows 2000 Server.*

Before You Install

The following issues should be addressed before you begin the install process:

- Make sure your system meets the basic hardware/software requirements.
- Ensure that you have read all the installation documents before starting. How many of us have ever just loaded the CD-ROM and clicked on Install, only to run into trouble later?

- Ensure that you have sufficient permissions on the installation target server. The best case is that you are a member of the system administrators group for the computer (for Windows 2000 and NT computers). You may run into problems with the installation if you do not have sufficient rights to update system files as required by SQL Server.
- Make sure all possible services that could try to connect to the server or that use ODBC (including IIS) are stopped.
- Stop all antivirus utilities. Remember to restart them once the installation has been completed.

Installing the Monster

As we have already stated, a standard install of SQL Server is fairly simple. I am going to install the Evaluation Edition of SQL Server because many of you may use this to get to grips with the technology.

Figure 13-1 shows the initial screen, which opens when the install CD-ROM is inserted.

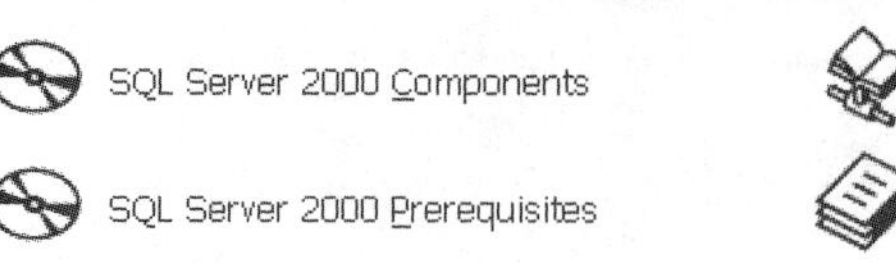

Figure 13-1. Installation screen

Five options are available:

- SQL Server Components
- SQL Server Prerequisites
- Browse Setup/Upgrade Help
- Read the Release Notes
- Visit Our Web Site

Most of these options are fairly self-explanatory, and we won't go into any details. However, take the time to read or scan the release notes. The Browse Setup/Upgrade Help option is also worth looking at because it provides a lot of useful information. It is also vital to visit the Microsoft SQL Server Web site to check that your operating system is up to date and that all required service packs have been applied.

SQL Server Components

Figure 13-2 shows the screen from which you'll install components. The components available are:

- Install Database Server (this is SQL Server 2000)
- Install Analysis (for analysis and data warehousing)
- Install English Query (provides the ability to ask questions of the database in plain English)

> **NOTE** *Given the breadth of SQL Server 2000, we will look at just installing Database Server in this chapter. Books Online and the Microsoft Web site will provide you with additional information on English Query and Analysis Services.*

Figure 13-2. Server components

Select Install Database Server to begin the process. Figure 13-2 shows the next screen. SQL Server 2000 permits you to install multiple instances of the server on a single system. Click on Next on the introduction screen. Figure 13-3 shows the screen from which you'll choose a computer name.

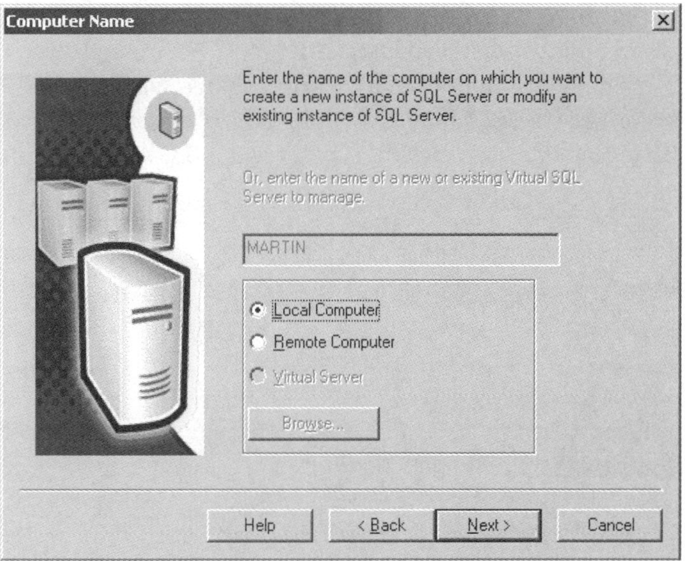

Figure 13-3. Choosing a computer name

If you are installing the server to the local computer, the option to enter a computer name is disabled. If this is the case, click on Next to proceed. If the installation is to take place on a remote computer or virtual server (virtual servers will be available in a clustering environment), the Computer Name option is enabled. Should this be the case, enter the name of the computer and click on Next.

The installation selection screen then offers you three options:

- *Create a new instance of SQL Server or install client tools:* This option permits you to install the full database server, or you may install the client tools only (that is, install the user interface to SQL Server). In this case, only Enterprise Manager and Query Analyzer will be installed. Figure 13-4 shows the screen with Create a New Instance selected. Multiple instances of the server are useful for testing or hosting multiple database-driven Web sites.

- *Upgrade, remove, or add components to an existing instance of SQL Server:* Unless you have an existing installation of SQL Server, this option is inactive. When available, however, the option does exactly as stated and allows you to add, remove, or upgrade an existing instance of the server.

- *Advanced options:* This option permits you to work with the more advanced options when installing SQL Server. For example, you can create an installation file that is used to perform an unattended installation of the server, you can repair damaged SQL Server registry entries, or you can work with server clustering. Many of these options are outside the scope of this book.

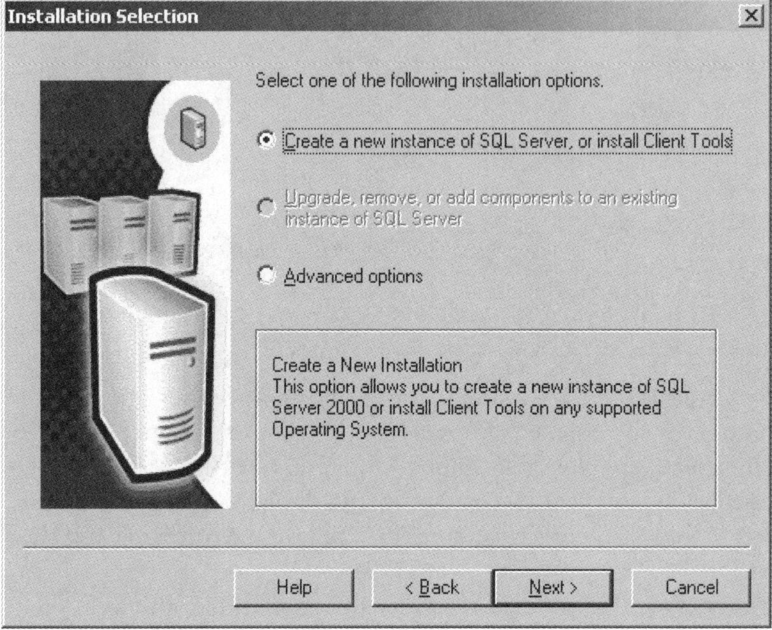

Figure 13-4. Installation selection

You will then be prompted for your name and company. Enter these details and click on Next to continue to the license agreement. Click on Yes if you agree. (Clicking on No stops the installation process.) You will then be required to select an installation definition. See Figure 13-5. Three types of installation are available:

- Client Tools Only
- Server and Client Tools
- Connectivity Only

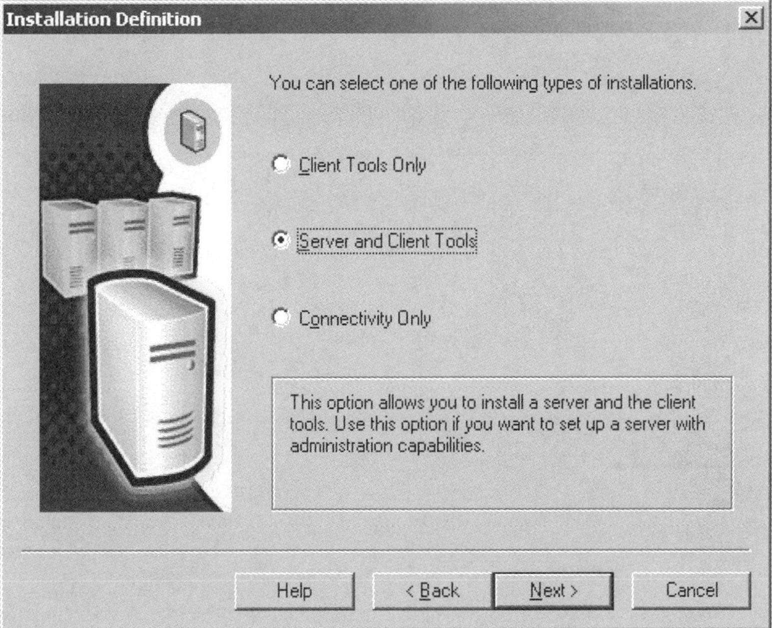

Figure 13-5. Installation definitions

Because we are installing the full server, select Server and Client Tools and click on Next.

NOTE *To install Client Tools only, select the Client Tools Only option and click on Next. Or follow the same process to install the third option, Connectivity Only. In this case, you will install only the Microsoft Data Access components and network libraries.*

You will be asked to enter a name for this instance of SQL Server. If this is a second instance of the server, the name you enter must be unique. (If this is the first instance of the server being installed, it is not necessary to enter a server name.) Click on Next.

Figure 13-6 shows the instance name screen with a name for this particular instance of the server entered. Click on Next to proceed.

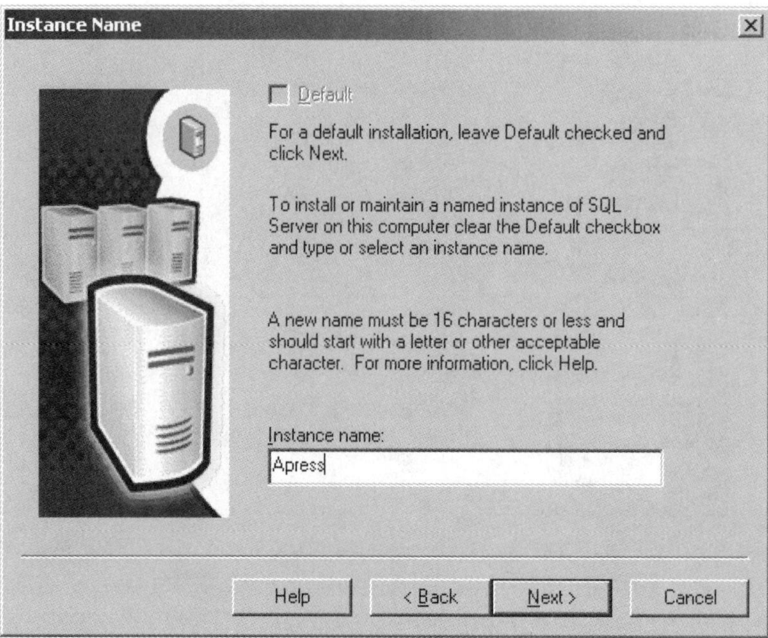

Figure 13-6. Adding an instance name

Now you get into the details of the installation. Figure 13-7 shows the setup screen. You can indicate the type of setup (typical, minimum, custom). Select the folders if you do not like the chosen default. For testing purposes and using the evaluation edition, the typical installation should be sufficient. Figure 13-7 shows the setup screen.

> **NOTE** *If you do choose to perform a custom install, you will have more control over what components and subcomponents are installed. You may want to choose this option if you require additional control over the components for your particular installation. In my case, the only additional item not included as part of the typical installation was the SQL Server code examples.*

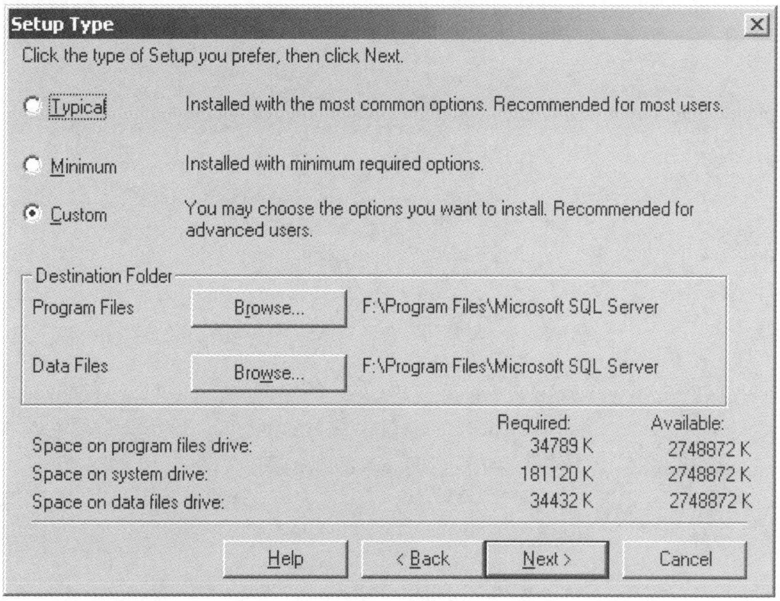

Figure 13-7. Setup type

I have selected the typical installation option. You can change the option to suit your particular preference and click on Next to enter the details on the service accounts that SQL Server will use. You can use any account here or have your network administrators create an account for SQL Server. It is probably a good idea to have a new account created solely for the use of SQL Server. Click on Next to enter one of the most important screens, that for authentication mode. Figure 13-8 shows the authentication screen.

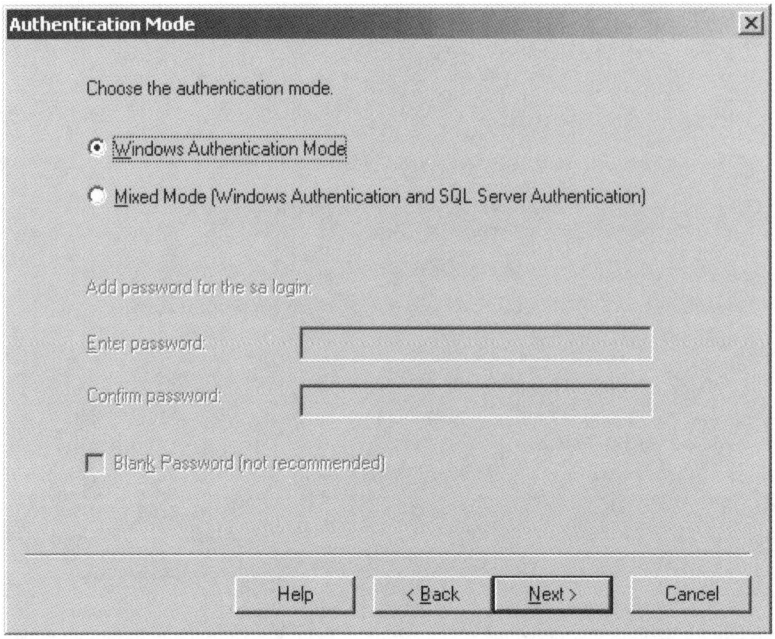

Figure 13-8. Authentication mode

This screen is used to set up security for SQL Server. Security is discussed in Chapter 18. However, if you choose to use Mixed Mode security, make sure that you create a username and password for the default sa account. Do not check the Blank Password box. There have been many reports of SQL Server installations being hacked due to the developer overlooking the fact that the default password set for the sa role is blank or installing with a blank password and then forgetting to enable it. Many textbooks also use the sa account with a blank password for demonstration purposes. Although this isn't the fault of the software vendor, it is one loophole that could be closed very easily. In our view, the Blank Password option should be disabled and a password made compulsory for the sa role when using Mixed Mode security.

Once you've entered these details into these screens, you will be prompted to click on Next to start the file copy and install SQL Server.

Overall, the installation is painless. The main thing to remember is to assign the password to the sa account if you're using Mixed Mode security.

NOTE *In addition to SQL Server 2000, several other programs are also installed, some of which you will use almost as often as the Enterprise Manager. The main programs installed include:*

- *Service Manager*
- *Query Analyzer*
- *OSQL*
- *Client Network Utility*
- *Profiler*

NOTE *To see the additional programs that have been installed, select Start|Program File|SQL Server. Programs installed will be shown in the SQL Server menu.*

Introducing Enterprise Manager

All of us are well used to managing Access databases via the Database window. SQL Server 2000 has a database window, but it is called *Enterprise Manager.* Although the Access Database window gives you access to a single database, Enterprise Manager permits access to all databases via a single interface. Enterprise Manager is used to manage databases and their associated objects. In this section, we will look at Enterprise Manager in some detail because a great part of your working day will be spent using this very useful application.

We will provide a quick overview of some of the features and look at others, such as Database Designer, in some detail. To a small degree, Database Designer equates to both Access' Database window and the Relationship window, but it offers features that most Access developers would die for. Within Access, the Relationship window is used to create relationships among tables. In SQL Server, we can use Database Designer not only to create relationships between tables but also to design entire databases. To have the same functionality using Access, we use a combination of the Database window to manage objects and the Relationship window to manage relationships. Even then, you are restricted to working with a single database file. We will look at using the Database Designer features from within SQL Server 2000 and Access 2002. Most of the features of Database Designer are available from either side of the database.

> **NOTE** *The full features of Enterprise Manager would fill (and have already) a book on their own, so, although I will try to cover some of the more useful tools and topics, please bear this in mind while reading this section.*

Microsoft Management Console

The interface that is used to manage Enterprise Manager is common to many Microsoft management tasks, and it may look familiar to those of you who have used Windows 2000 or who manage IIS5 Web sites. Figures 13-9 through 13-11 show some of the applications managed via the management console.

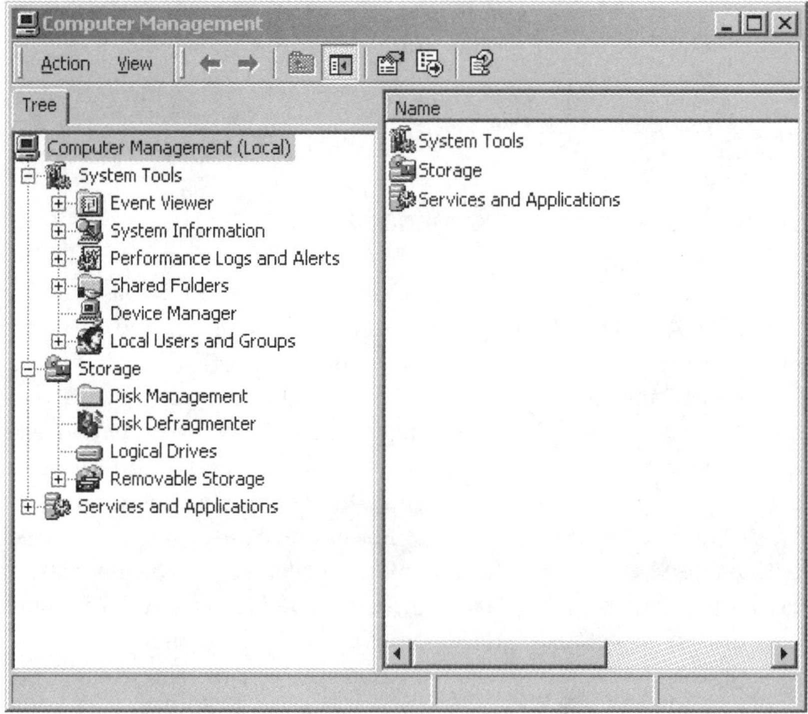

Figure 13-9. Computer management

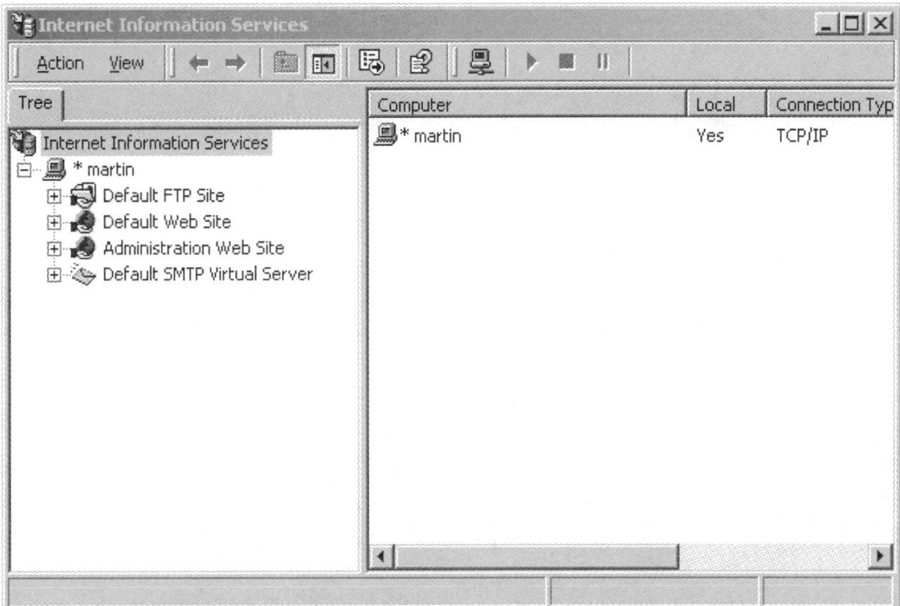

Figure 13-10. Internet services

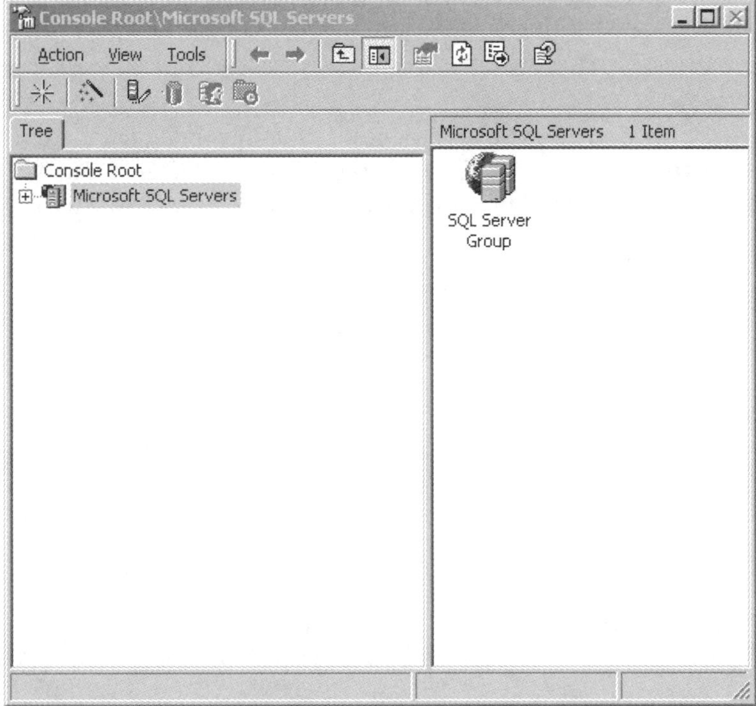

Figure 13-11. SQL Server 2000 console root

As can be seen, we are looking at the same interface to the management functionality of different applications. In this way, we have a common interface to many different management applications.

So, what's the big deal about this database window and how does it differ from our friend in Access?

For starters, one of the main differences we shall see is that, from this single point, we can manage all our databases and their objects including user security and replication. As you know, within Access we can manage (via the user interface) only the current database file that we have open. Appendix A contains a section on ADOX, which can be used to manipulate Access databases and objects via code.

Let's examine each of the options available in Enterprise Manager, starting at the top.

SQL Server Group

This is purely an administration option. The Server Group facility permits you to "group" servers together under common categories, with each group containing the databases and other objects created. Groups provide you with a way to store related projects, and, if you're like me, you need all the organizational help that the PC or server can provide. In addition, groups permit you to manage multiple servers on the network (or across the Internet for that matter). In fact, from my desk here in Belfast, I have created databases on SQL Server instances located in the United States.

We will open and examine a server group. With the server group expanded, I will open the database folder. As can be seen in Figure 13-12, all databases are exposed. We can access all objects related to a specific database by selecting the database folder and expanding it by clicking on the + symbol beside the database name. (You can also simply click on the database name.)

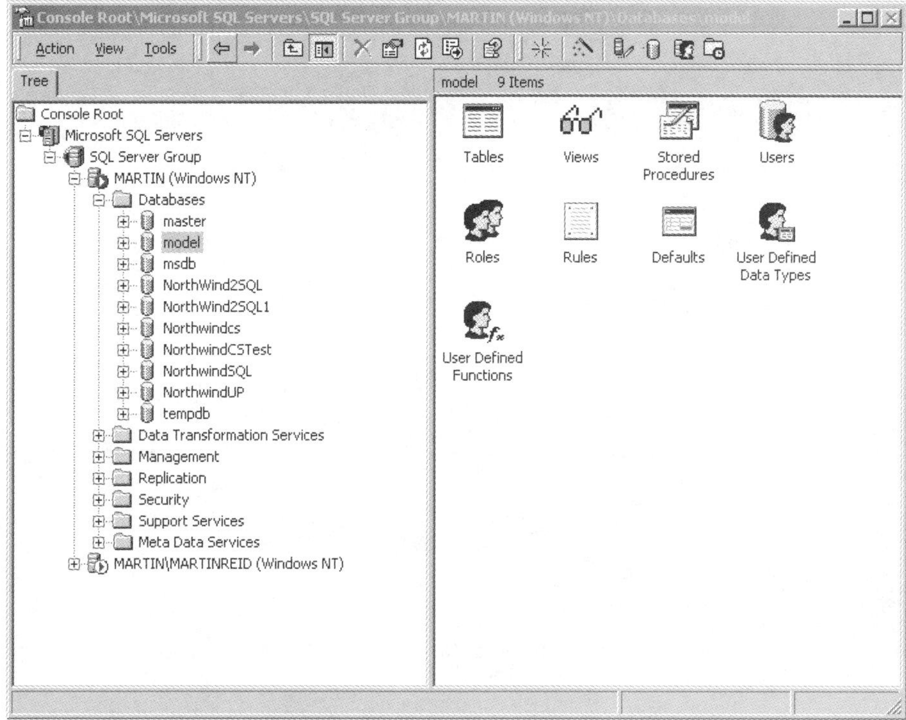

Figure 13-12. SQL server group

I will select the test database NorthwindSQL (an SQL Server database used in an Access project), and we will look at the options that are available. Once you select the database or expand the folder, additional information is provided both in the expanded folder listing and in the right-hand pane of the Enterprise Manager window. Figure 13-13 shows Enterprise Manager at this point.

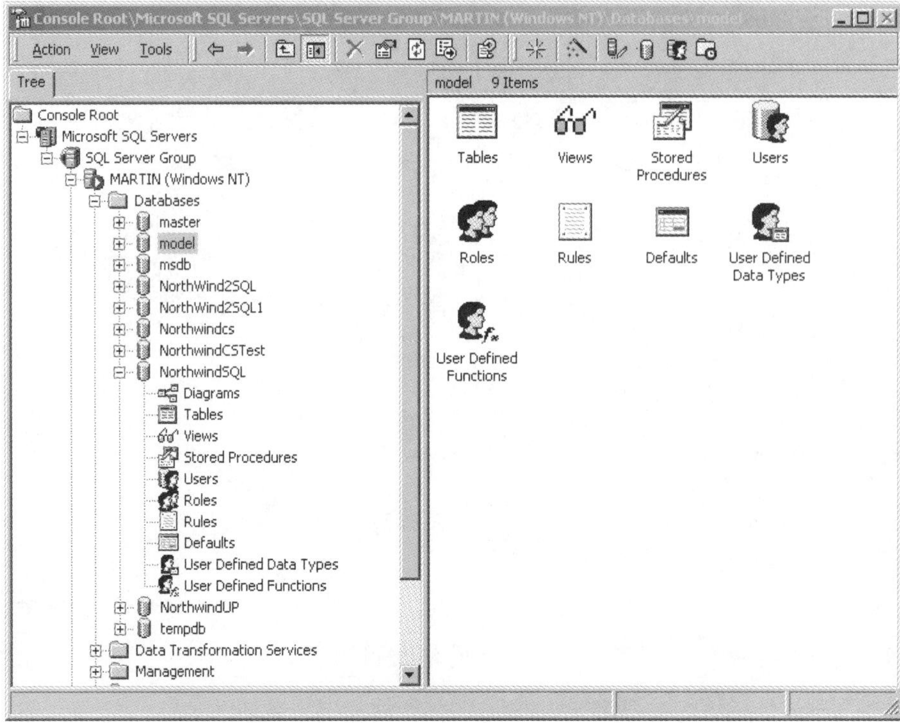

Figure 13-13. Database information

Options

The options from within the expanded database folder and the right-hand pane are identical.

We will begin with the database diagram because this should be familiar to most Access developers (even if you don't think so at this stage). One of the major advances you will find with database diagrams in SQL Server 2000 and Access Projects is the ability to create multiple diagrams for a single database, unlike Access wherein we can have only one diagram. In this way, we can break up very large database diagrams into manageable sections. We can also use the diagram to redesign the tables, add an index, completely delete (drop) the database; new to SQL Server 2000 is the availability of Cascading Delete and Update options.

> **NOTE** *All options are also available using the Action Menu option. Personally, I prefer using the right mouse button when available, but you should learn the menu options as well. In the following options, I will use the right mouse button to call up the menus where possible. As is usual with MS, there are several ways to do the same thing.*

Database Diagrams

All Access developers are familiar with using the Access Relationship window to manage relationships among our tables and other database objects. The Diagram window in SQL provides you with all of these facilities (plus much more), and you should be intimately familiar with the interface and the options it provides. We will also look at using Access 2002 to perform many of these functions, which until Access Data Projects and SQL Server 2000 had to be handled from within SQL Server. In most of the examples, I will use SQL Server 2000 and Access 2002 to demonstrate some of the features.

> **NOTE** *All of the layout details for the database diagram are held in an SQL Server system table: dtproperties.*

Using Enterprise Manager, select the NorthwindSQL database (or one of your choice), right-click over the Diagrams item and select New|Database Diagram from the shortcut menu to open the diagram window. This launches a diagram wizard, which is a little bonus because the same facility is not available within Access 2002. Figure 13-14 shows the shortcut menu.

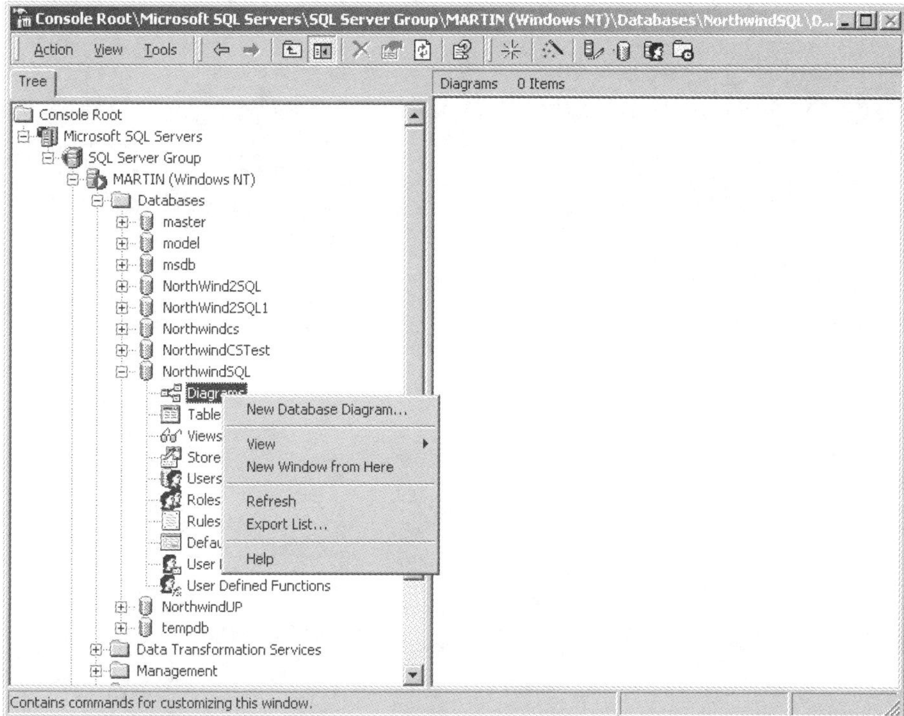

Figure 13-14. Database diagram shortcut menu

Running the Diagram Wizard

Using the wizard should be second nature to the Access community, and this one functions in the same way as the standard Access wizards with which we are familiar. Figure 13-15 shows the first wizard screen.

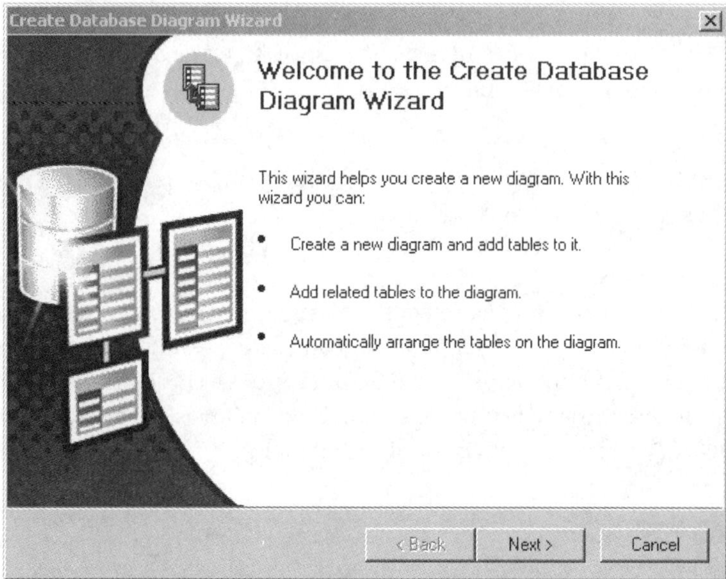

Figure 13-15. Opening the Diagram wizard screen

Simply click on Next to proceed. Figure 13-16 shows the second screen of the process.

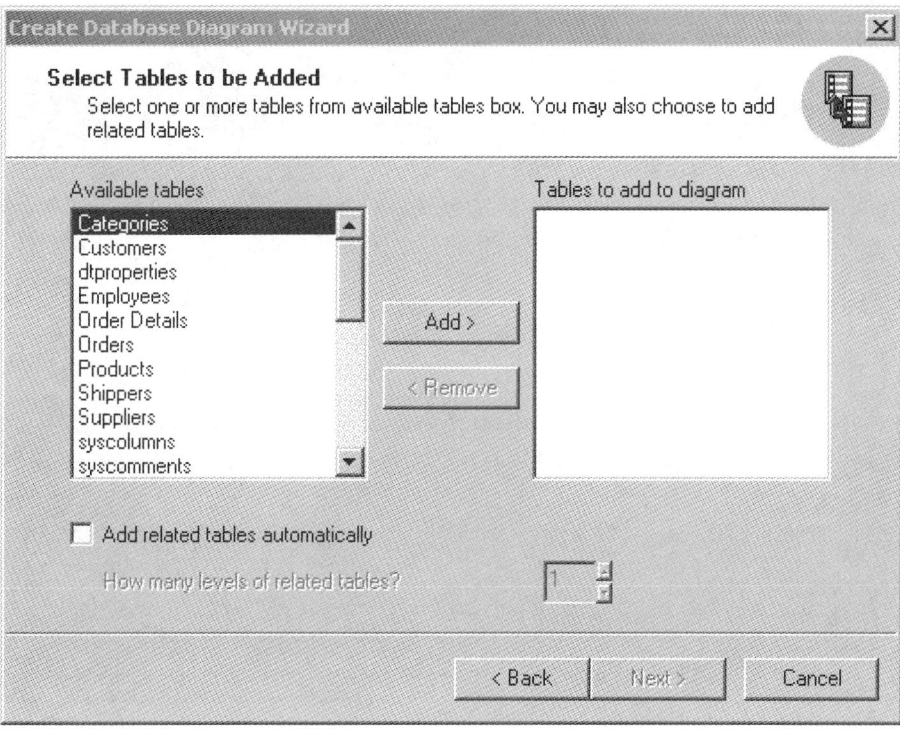

Figure 13-16. The Database Diagram wizard—Select Tables

As you can see, this is very similar to the built-in Access wizards and uses a similar technique to select and move objects for further actions. At any point in the process, we can move back to reexamine or change an option. Using the wizard, we can select individual tables or use the Shift (or Ctrl) key and click to select multiple objects to move. You will notice, however, that included in the table list are not only your production tables but all systems tables as well. Be careful when selecting tables that you select only user tables. Figure 13-17 shows the table selection.

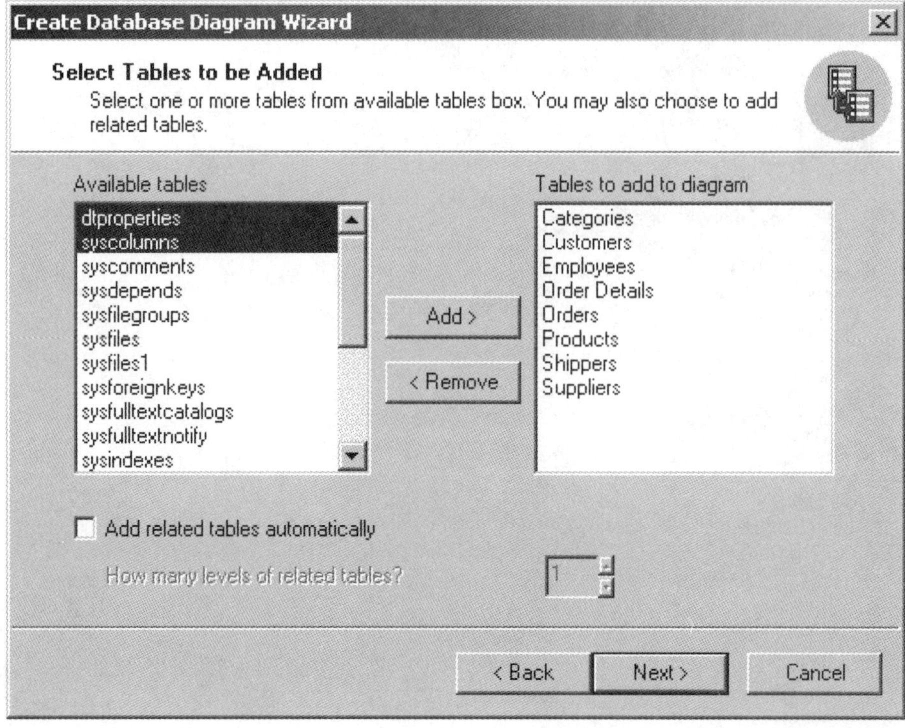

Figure 13-17. Select tables

Enterprise Manager provides an option that allows you to turn off the display of system tables. To disable the display of system tables:

1. Right-click over the server name to open the shortcut menu.
2. Choose Edit SQL Server Registration Properties.
3. In the Registered SQL Server Properties dialog box, uncheck the Show System Database and System Object checkbox.

Once you have selected the required tables (in this case I have selected all the user tables from the NorthwindSQL database), click on Next. The wizard will ask you to confirm your decision, and you simply click on Finish to generate the diagram. See Figure 13-18.

> **NOTE** *A useful feature of the wizard is the ability to transfer multiple related tables by checking the Add Related Tables Automatically checkbox. For example, if we have a relationship between the Customer and Order tables, when the Customer table is selected the Order table will automatically be included in the transfer list. It is also possible to indicate the number of related levels to include.*

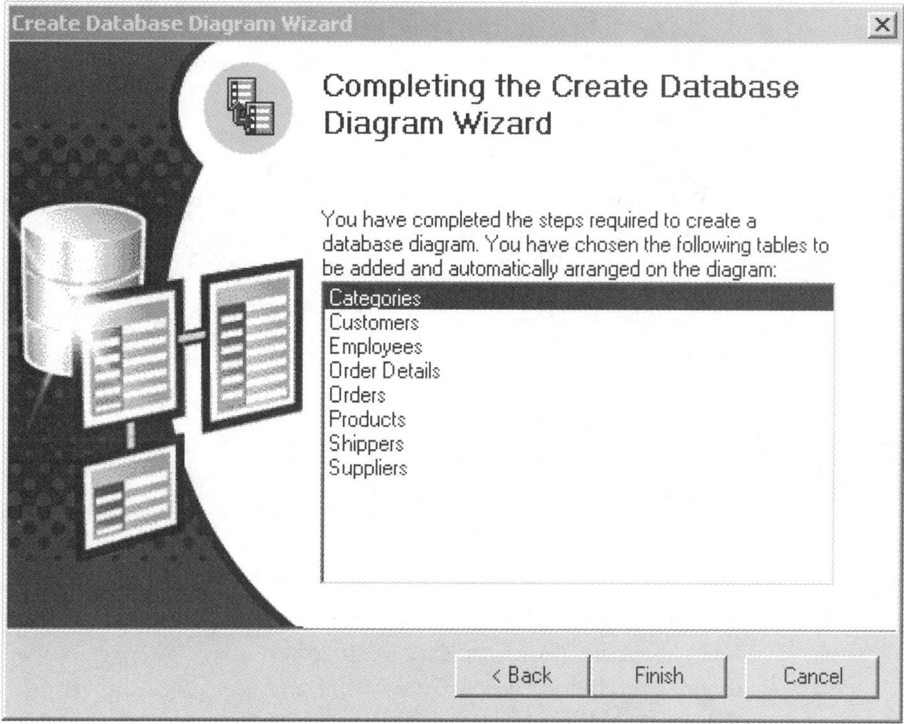

Figure 13-18. The final Diagram wizard screen

The resulting diagram (see Figure 13-19) is displayed in the window.

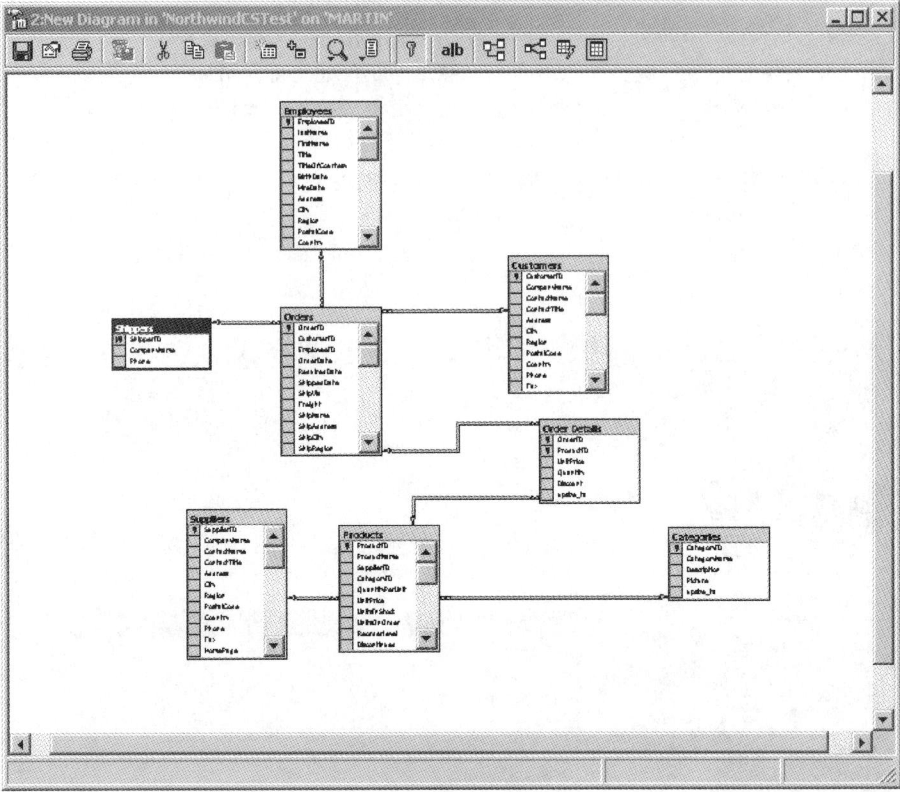

Figure 13-19. Northwind database diagram

As you can see, this is very similar to the relationship diagram in Access, but bear in mind that this tool is much more powerful and provides several features that aren't available in Access. Close and save the diagram.

Once saved, the diagram is available from within an Access 2002 project. In this case, I have rearranged the tables to make the diagram a little more readable. See Figure 13-20.

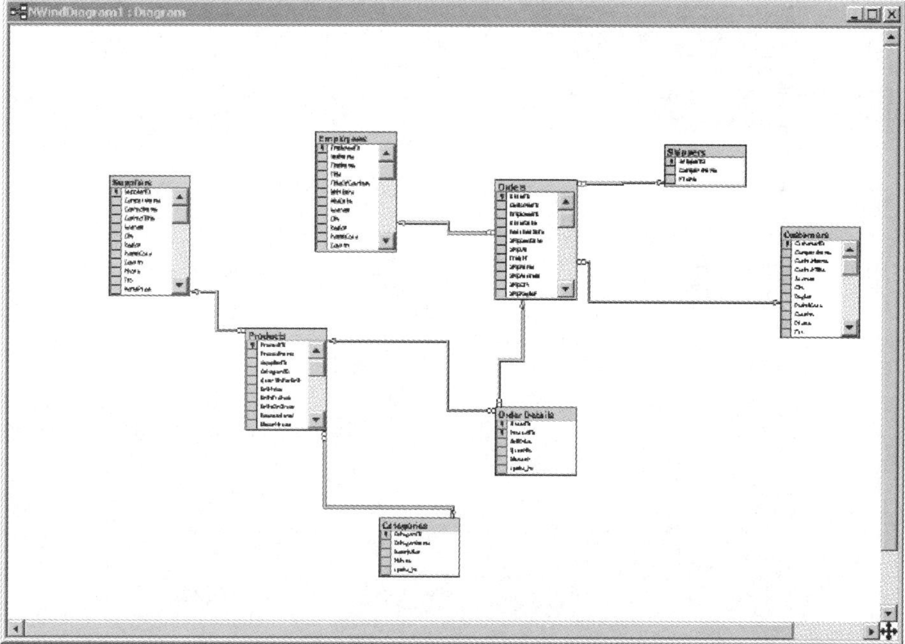

Figure 13-20. Database diagram as viewed in Access 2002

A nice feature of Access' Diagram window is the ability to move around large diagrams using the screen that's revealed by clicking on the crosshairs at the bottom-right corner of the diagram screen. The resulting screen is shown in Figure 13-21. Using this screen allows you to pan a diagram and go to any area of interest.

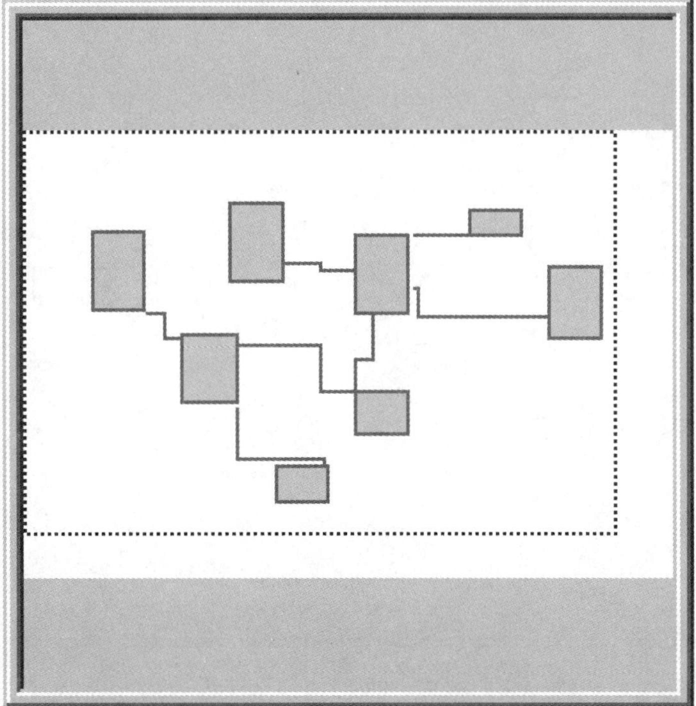

Figure 13-21. Diagram panning

The diagram shown in Figure 13-21 reveals the relationships among the tables in the Northwind database. It also allows us to do quite a bit more, which we will discuss shortly.

> **NOTE** *You may need to enlarge areas of the diagram, which you can do via the magnifying glass on the toolbar.*

The key symbol indicates the "one" end of a relationship, and the infinity (∞) symbol represents the "many" end of the relationship. Note that referential integrity has been enforced between these tables at the server. (We will discuss this later.)

> **NOTE** *One-to-many is a common relationship type found among tables and is the default relationship within Access. I am a little annoyed with texts that also state that many-to-many relationships are rare. They aren't. I have seldom designed a database or had my students do a design exercise without encountering many-to-many relationships. The only relationship you will find that is fairly uncommon is the one-to-one relationship.*

Creating Diagrams without the Wizard

We all know that at some point in database design and construction you need to get your hands dirty and dive right in. To use the full facilities of Database Designer, it is a matter of jumping in and seeing what's there. In this section, we will manually create the same diagram as previously, while adding a new table to demonstrate some of the other features that are found in this powerful tool. In this case, we will work with the designer totally from within an AccessXP Data Project.

With the NorthwindSQL database file open and using the Database window, I can simply select Database Diagrams and click on New. You can, of course, work with an existing diagram if required.

What you will see is very similar to the standard Access Relationship window, including the Show Table dialog box. But here the similarity ends. All we can do at this point is add a table (or tables) to the Design window. As with a standard Show Table dialog box, you must first select the tables and close the dialog box before you can continue with any actions. Tables can be selected by simply double-clicking the table name or selecting the table and clicking on Add. Once selected, the table is removed from the Show Table dialog box. Note that system objects are again available. See Figure 13-22.

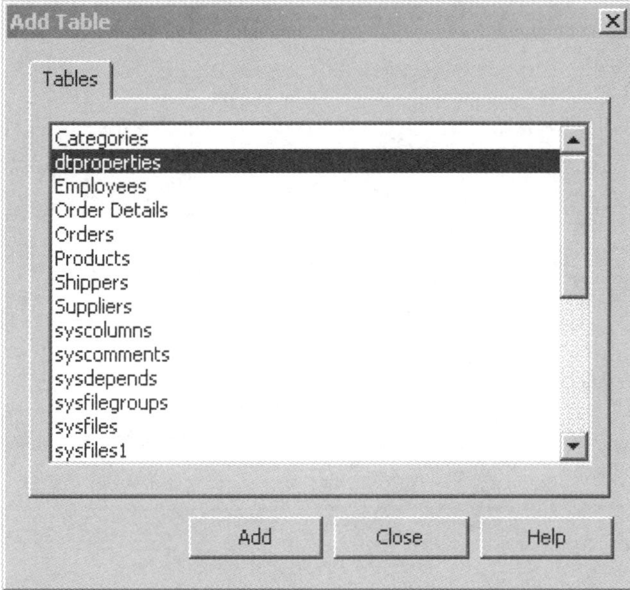

Figure 13-22. The Add Table dialog box

Once the required tables have been inserted, close the dialog box. The window now shows the tables you will be working with. (I have deleted the previous relationship created within SQL Server 2000 for this example.)

Creating a Relationship between the Customer and the Order Table

Creating the relationship is no different than creating a standard Access relationship between two tables. It is simply a matter of selecting the Primary Key field from the one side of the relationship and dragging and dropping it over the related foreign key value in the related table. Once this is done, the Create Relationship dialog box will open. Figure 13-23 shows this dialog box. In this case, I am relating the Customers and Orders tables. (You may need to delete the existing relationship to follow this example.)

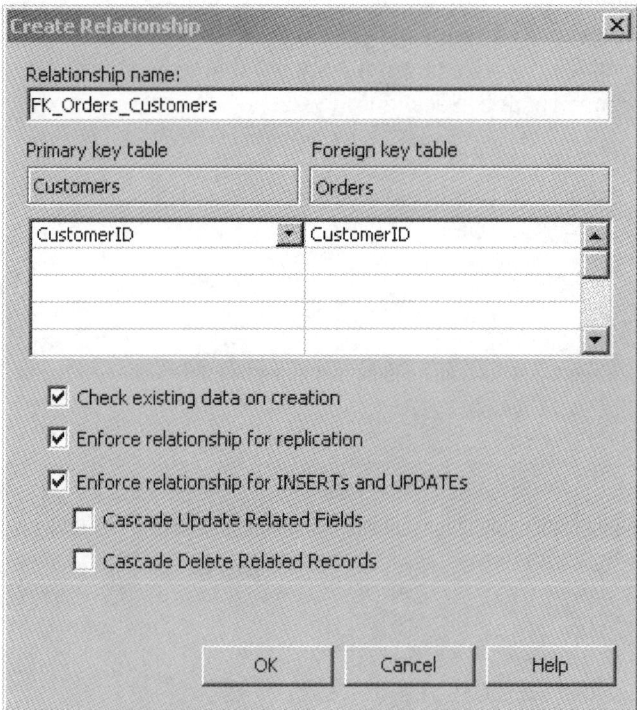

Figure 13-23. Creating a relationship

> **NOTE** *Just like as in Access, the relationship will be named, but, unlike as in Access, you have control over the relationship name when you create it via the graphical interface. To have the same control when using Access, the relationship must be created via code.*

In this case, the relationship is named FK_Orders_Customers. Just like the standard Access dialog box, the tables and related columns in the relationship are shown. By default, some additional options are preselected:

- *Check Existing Data on Creation:* Check that data currently in the table meets the constraint.
- *Enforce Relationship for Replication:* Enforces referential integrity for replication.
- *Enforce Referential Integrity for Inserts and Updates:* Ensures that data meets the requirements of the relationship when inserted or updated.

Two additional options (new with SQL Server 2000) are available: Cascade Update Related Fields and Cascade Delete Related Records. Both options are not selected by default. I have removed the check from the Check Existing . . . checkbox because none of the tables have any data. If the table contains data, checking this option will ensure that the data meets the new conditions being created.

> **NOTE** *Please observe the following facts about the Cascade Update and Cascade Delete options.*
>
> Cascade Update*: Should you change a Primary Key value, the database will automatically change all related Foreign Key values in this relationship only. The best advice I can give you is to not change Primary Key values unless you're prepared for a lot of grief and manual checking.*
>
> Cascade Delete*: This can be horrendous if used in the wrong way. Delete a record in the "one" side of a relationship, and the database will delete all the records in the "many" side. So, if you delete a customer record, all associated order records will be deleted also. The local tax offices will love you! All your historical order data just left the database in a hurry. This option needs to be used with care and planning before being implemented. In fact, some developers would never use it, preferring to manage the delete process via code. This is a slower process, but it's one that can give you more control over what is actually removed from your tables.*

Click on OK to create the relationship. As you can see in Figure 13-24, the relationships among the tables created in Access are exactly like those created earlier in SQL Server.

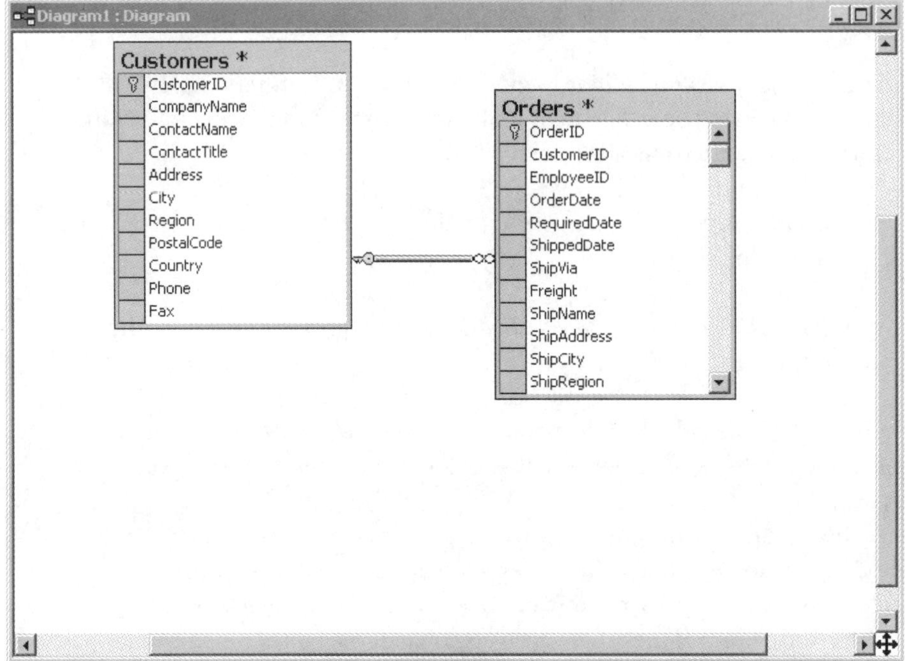

Figure 13-24. Relationships in Access 2002

So what else can this wonderful thing do? Well, if I select a table and use the right mouse button while in the designer, the shortcut menu (shown in Figure 13-25) appears.

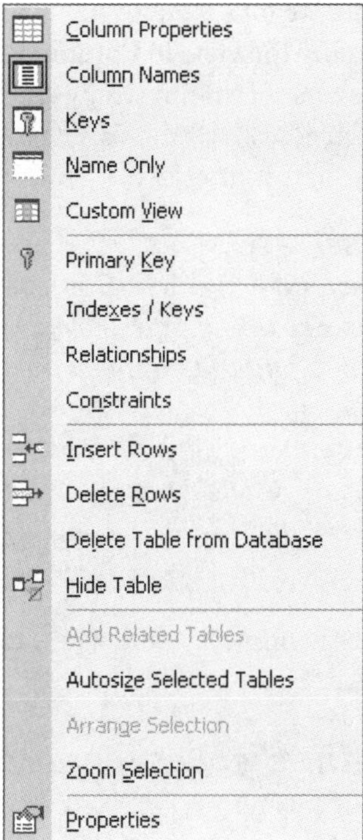

Figure 13-25. The Table shortcut menu

Some of these options can change the appearance of the tables in the designer. For example, selecting Column Properties will display the design of the table including data types. Figure 13-26 shows this change.

Customers *

Column Name	Data Type	Length	Allow Nulls
CustomerID	nvarchar	5	
CompanyName	nvarchar	40	
ContactName	nvarchar	30	✓
ContactTitle	nvarchar	30	✓
Address	nvarchar	60	✓
City	nvarchar	15	✓
Region	nvarchar	15	✓
PostalCode	nvarchar	10	✓
Country	nvarchar	15	✓
Phone	nvarchar	24	✓
Fax	nvarchar	24	✓

Figure 13-26. Column properties

It is with options like this that we take a major departure from the Access Relationship window. Changing the view to Column Properties actually permits us (with the correct permissions set) to physically change the design of the table, right in the designer within Access 2002. You can change the column name, data type, precision, and so on from this interface.

> **NOTE** *It pays to pay attention while in the Designer window. For instance, it is possible to overwrite a column name. (Select Column Names from the menu to change the view.) Figure 13-26 shows the Customers table in Column Name view. While in this view, it is very easy to amend a column name or data type (for example, if you're making multiple changes to a diagram and accidentally change a field name). When prompted to accept the changes, the accidental table change will also be saved to the database.*

We can also use the Designer window to build a new table.

Creating a Table in the Designer and Access 2002

We are going to use the Designer window to add a third table to our database to hold the contact details of our companies. It will be related to the Company table in a one-to-many relationship. (Each company can have one or more contacts.) You can use the right mouse button to open another shortcut menu and select the New Table menu option. Make sure you do not have a table selected when you click the right mouse button. See Figure 13-27, which shows the new menu options.

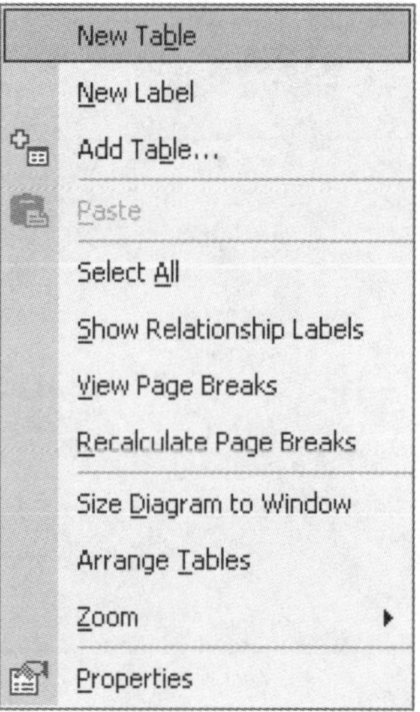

Figure 13-27. Access 2002 Short Cut Menu in the Diagram Wimdow

You will be prompted for a name for the new table. Enter the table name, in this case tblContact, and click on OK to open the Table Design window. See Figure 13-28.

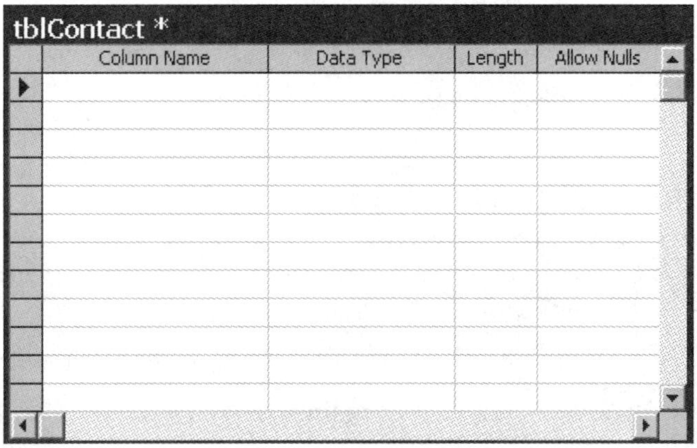

Column Name	Data Type	Length	Allow Nulls

Figure 13-28. Table Design window within the Diagram window

Here we can define the various columns required in the new table including the foreign key to the Customer table.

NOTE *Before the new table is available in the Database window, you must close and save the designer. When saving, you will be prompted to save the changes, click on Yes to commit or No to cancel all changes. It is also possible to save an SQL script of the changes to a text file. Simply click on Save to Text File to create a record of the changes. However, you will still be required to save the changes once the text file is created.*

Once the table has been defined, we can simply create the relationship between the Customer and tblContact tables as before.

One thing we can do with Access MDB files which wasn't possible in SQL Server 2000 or when using Access Data Projects is to add the same table to the Designer window twice. The ability to add a table to the window twice makes creating self-joins (recursive relationships) very easy. It is possible, however, to create a self-join using SQL Server. For example, for a staff table, each member of the staff reports to a manager. To create this relationship, the staff number of the line manager is stored with the subordinates' records. To discover who manages whom, a self-join is required. We relate the Employees table to itself. The Employees table within the Northwind Access data Project contains a field, ReportsTo. This field will contain the EmployeeID of the line manager of an individual employee. To create a self-join (that is, relate each manager to their subordinates) using Diagram Designer in Access 2002:

1. Select Database Diagrams from the Database window.
2. Click on New from the menu.
3. In the Add Table dialog box, select the Employee table.

> **NOTE** *Notice that the Employees table is removed from the list of available tables in the Add Table dialog box. As a result, it is not possible to do as you would in a standard Access relationship diagram and add the same table multiple times.*

4. Click on Add to add the table to the diagram.
5. Click on Close to close the Add Table dialog box.

   In the Diagram window, click on the Employee table to select it. The table border will turn blue indicating that the object is selected.

> **NOTE** *If you do happen to select an additional table, do not simply select the table and press Delete to remove it from the Diagram window. This will not only remove the table from the window but from the database.*

6. Click on the EmployeeID primary key, but do not release the mouse button.
7. Drag the EmployeeID down the table to the ReportsTo field and release the mouse button.

> **NOTE** *The Create Relationship dialog box will open. As with Access relationships, this dialog box gives you the opportunity to double-check the relationship details.*

8. Click on OK to save the relationship.

Viewing and Working with Properties in the Designer from Access 2002

Another major departure for Access developers is the Properties dialog box that's available within the window. Unlike as in Access, the relationship properties deal with a lot more than relationships, and we can change and enter several important properties of the tables including indexes and constraints for any table within the database.

For this example, we will look at the properties for the Customers table. To open and view properties, open an existing database diagram. The Properties dialog box is available by either right-clicking over a relationship line or by right-clicking a table and selecting Properties from the shortcut menu. Figure 13-29 shows the properties for the Northwind Customers table.

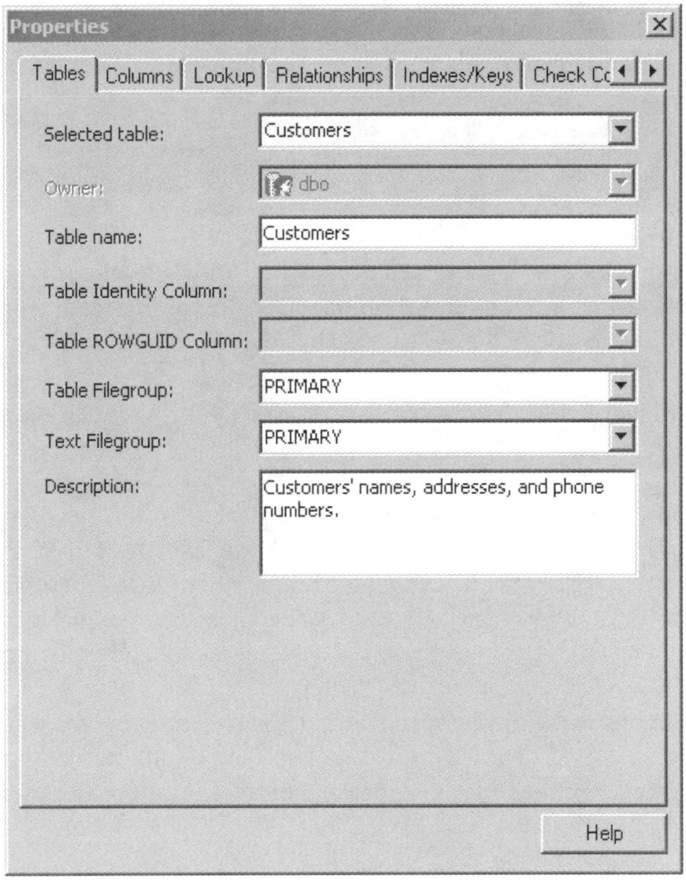

Figure 13-29. Properties of the Customer table

As can be seen, this dialog box offers several different tabs and is vastly different from the usual Access Relationships dialog box.

> **NOTE** *Clicking a blank area of the diagram when the properties dialog box is open will remove the dialog box from the screen. This results in an error message "The selected object has no editable properties. Select a different object." Simply click on the required table object to "reopen" the Table Properties dialog box.*

Tables

You can select any of the tables using the drop-down list. The table shown in the list will default to the currently selected table. All properties shown by the dialog box under the various tabs will relate to the selected table. If you then select a different table, the properties will change to reflect this.

Columns

Column properties for the selected table are available. The column can be changed using the Column Name drop-down list. Just as in Access, we can create an input mask, caption, index, or change the column definitions.

Lookup

The Lookup property can be used when we are dealing with Foreign Key values in our tables. The standard way to view a foreign key in a related table is as a numeric value, that is, the related table's Primary Key value. (For example, the CustomerID in an orders table will relate back to the customer placing the order.) Using a lookup, we can display the actual customer name rather than the CustomerID value. However, the "real" Foreign Key value is always used to maintain the relationship below the covers. To use the Lookup property, you must be in Table Design view. Then click on the Lookup Tab Column Design section of the window, and change the Display Control default from Text Box to either List or Combo Box.

This change enables the various additional options available when creating a lookup. By default, the lookup options are disabled. The options enabled include:

- *Row Source Type:* The row source for the box can be a table, view, or function. You may also choose a value list or a field list. This property works with the Row Source property. The actual row source is specified using the next option.

- *Row Source Property:* If your Row Source Type is set to Table, the drop-down list shows the tables and views available. Stored procedures are not shown in the list, but you can type in the name of a stored procedure (that does not amend records). If you're using a value list, you can enter a list of values separated by semicolons into the control (value1; value2; value3). Setting the Row Source property to Field List, you can select a table from the drop-down list.

- *Bound Column:* Once you have selected the type and row source you must indicate the bound column. This is a numeric value that represents the column in the source bound to your database table. The Bound Column option is set to Column 1 (EmployeeID).

- *Column Count:* This indicates the number of columns in the list of combo box control. Column Count is set to 2 (so that the SQL statement returns two columns).

- *Column Heads:* This is used to display the column headings in your list or combo box. Column heads are not displayed (set to No).

- *Column Widths:* This is used to set the size of the data columns in the list or combo box. This property can be set to zero to hide individual columns (that is, suppress the display of a particular column in the list or combo box).

  For example, in the Northwind ADP, the EmployeeID field within the Orders table uses a lookup value. In this case, the row source type is set to Table/Views/Functions. The row source is an SQL statement. In this case, SQL is used because we are concatenating the Employee LastName and FirstName fields. The SQL used is:

  ```
  SELECT EmployeeID LastName+ ','+FirstName
  FROM dbo.Employees
  ORDER BY LastName, FirstName
  ```

> **NOTE** *You can click on the ellipsis [. . .] button to the right of the Row Source text box to open Query Builder to create the SQL statement.*

Column widths are set to 0cm;5.07cm. Setting the first column (EmployeeID) to zero results in it being hidden from the user in the combo box. It is common practice to hide the Primary Key value with drop-down lists.

To view this feature, open the Orders table (Northwind ADP) and click in the EmployeeID field. Note that the field uses a drop-down list to display the employee name rather than the EmployeeID number.

Relationships

Details on relationships in which the Customer table participates are shown by clicking on the Relationships tab in the Property dialog. You can also create or delete relationships. Just as in Access, relationships within SQL Server are named. However, SQL Server makes renaming relationships much easier than doing so in Access. We can also set the Cascade features of the relationship via this tab.

Indexes

All indexes for the selected table are available. Just as with relationships, we can delete and create indexes within this dialog box. (We'll discuss indexes shortly.)

Check Constraints

At times during table design in Access, developers place validation rules against table fields. Constraints provide you with a similar feature in SQL Server and ADPs. So a constraint can be directly equated to an Access validation rule. The constraint will restrict the data that the user can enter, just like the validation rule.

Backing up Your Work

Most Access developers (if not all) are very familiar with the need to back up their databases. In the case of Access, this process can be fairly simple, and various techniques are used from full-blown code databases, which will automatically back up your database, to the simple act of copying a database onto a floppy disk or Zip drive. The importance of regular backup cannot be overstated. Those of us who have failed to back up and have suffered as a result will know this to be only too true. (I remember reading that there are two types of database developers: those who have suffered a major data loss and those who will.) However, creating a backup of an SQL Server database usually involves a bit more than just copying the database to a disk.

Why Back Up?

. . . because computers can fail, users can make mistakes, developers can make even bigger mistakes, data can be deliberately corrupted (for instance, by hacking), and, in some cases, a full server installation could be lost, for example, as a result of a fire or other disaster. However, hardware failure and human error account for the majority of data lost within organizations. Data within a company or organization has a value that could be expressed in monetary terms. Next to the staff, data is probably the single most important asset many companies have. Just think about the effect on a business such as Amazon.com if their main customer databases were to be lost! The company could not function. So always prepare for the possibility of losing either some or all of your system at some point in its life and remember that, unlike as in Access, we may have millions of records and you will certainly have several additional files to include in the backup process.

What Gets Backed Up?

As we have stated, backing up an Access database can involve a process as simple as copying and pasting the MDB file to a new folder. With SQL Server, the process can be simple (just backing up the data files) or complex (involving backing up both the data files and a special file—the transaction log). This log contains details of all the changes that have taken place within the database and which action or transaction made the change. We can back up both the transaction log and the database, and we can restore either or both. Remember backing up the transaction log alone backs up only those transactions that have occurred since the last backup.

Choosing to back up either the database alone or the database and transaction logs can have a dramatic effect on the state of your database should a restore be required. For example, choosing to back up the database alone will mean the loss of all transactions that have occurred since the last backup. This type of backup is very easy to create and is a simple one-step process. Restoring from a database backup is also fairly straightforward.

Choosing to back up both the database and the transaction logs will mean that you can restore the database to its exact state at the time of failure (or to be more accurate, the last backup of the transaction log). Data loss will be minimized. Of course, this depends on the transaction logs not being damaged and becoming unrecoverable. In a production environment, it would be recommended that both the database and the transaction logs are backed up. This is a decision for the business to make (with the appropriate advice), and it usually involves determining how much data it can afford to lose. For example, if we backed up the database on a weekly basis, then, in the event of a system failure, we would lose a week's worth of data. Could the company afford this?

In general, the backup schedule depends on the individual circumstances of the business or organization. In a high-availability setup, the database may be backed up on a nightly or daily basis with transaction logs being backed up on an hourly (or even quarter-hourly) basis. Under other circumstances, the database could be backed up on a weekly basis with a daily log backup.

This method can also reduce the amount of time that it takes to back up the database. The use of differential backups makes it possible to create smaller database backups that contain only the changes made to the database since the last full database backup. Using this method, you can reduce the amount of data you can lose between full database backups.

NOTE *It was and still is common practice to perform backups to tape drive. However, given the low costs of hard drives, many organizations are now backing up to disk. Using hot-swappable disks, it is possible to perform the backup and remove the disk for safekeeping. Backing up to swappable disks offers a speed improvement over backing up to tape.*

For those hardy souls amongst us, it is also possible to back up using T-SQL. The following code fragment will back up the demonstration database "NorthwindSQL" to a local folder on the same system:

```
BACKUP DATABASE NorthwindSQL TO DISK = 'C:\Backup\NWDbackup.bak
```

For the GUI lovers of Access, Enterprise Manager should meet most of your requirements for backup. Before creating the backup, however, we must first create the backup device. This device can be a disk or tape unit, or a network server (in fact, in the installation in my office, data is copied to local disk, then it is backed up to tape) or a removable media such as a Zip drive or tape unit connected to the SQL Server box. (If you are using a detachable device such as a tape unit, it must be directly connected to the server box.)

Using the Maintenance Plan Wizard

We can use the Maintenance Plan wizard to schedule an automated backup of the database and its objects. The backup can be programmed to take place on a set day and time. It is even possible for the server operator to receive an email when the job has been performed.

> **NOTE** *Before running the Maintenance Plan wizard, make sure that SQL Server Agent is running. Open the Maintenance folder and right-click over SQL Server Agent and ensure that the service is running.*

To start the Maintenance Plan wizard:

1. Right-click on the selected database and choose All Tasks|Maintenance Plan from the submenu.

2. Click on Next in the Welcome screen. You'll now see the Select Databases screen, as shown in Figure 13-30. This screen is used to select the database(s) this maintenance plan is for. In this case, the NorthwindSQL database is already selected. You may need to scroll down the list to view the selected database.

> **NOTE** *In addition to selecting individual databases for backup, we can also choose to back up all databases, all system databases, or all user databases.*

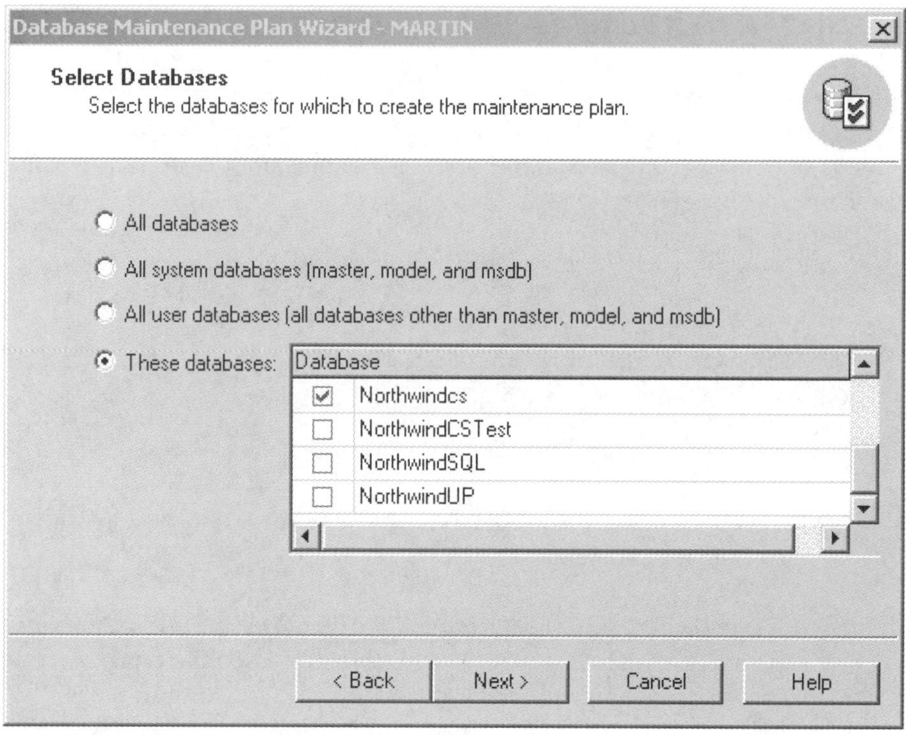

Figure 13-30. Select databases

3. If required, select the database(s) to be backed up and click on Next. The next screen allows you to set up some optimization for the database. Many of the options refer to indexes and internal methods of ensuring that they are optimized, but many of these options are beyond the scope of this chapter. For additional information on the options, simply click on the screen's Help button. Figure 13-31 shows the Database Optimization screen with some of the optimizing options selected. You can also set a schedule as to when you want these particular optimizations to be performed. Figure 13-32 shows the schedule opened via the Change button on this screen. The default is each Sunday at 1:00 AM on a weekly basis.

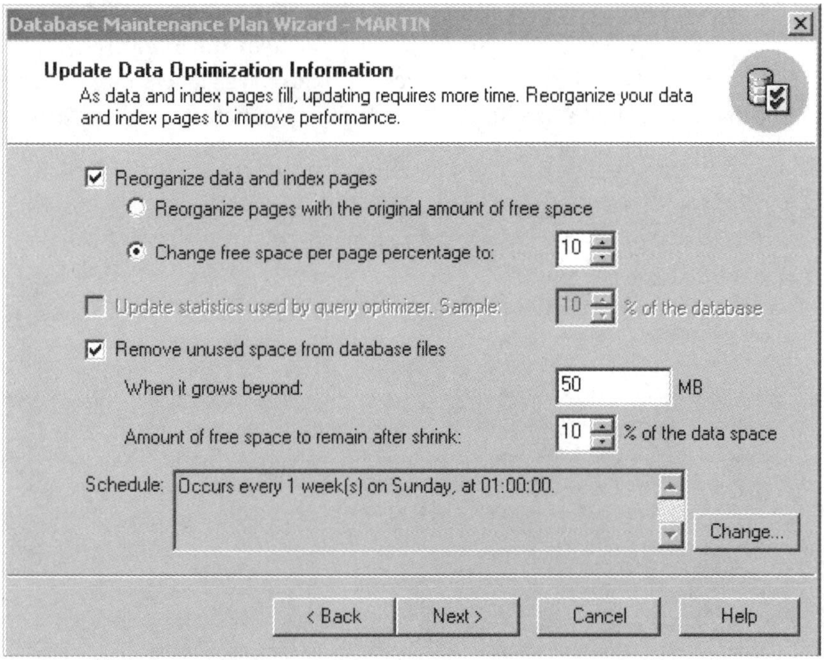

Figure 13-31. Data optimization

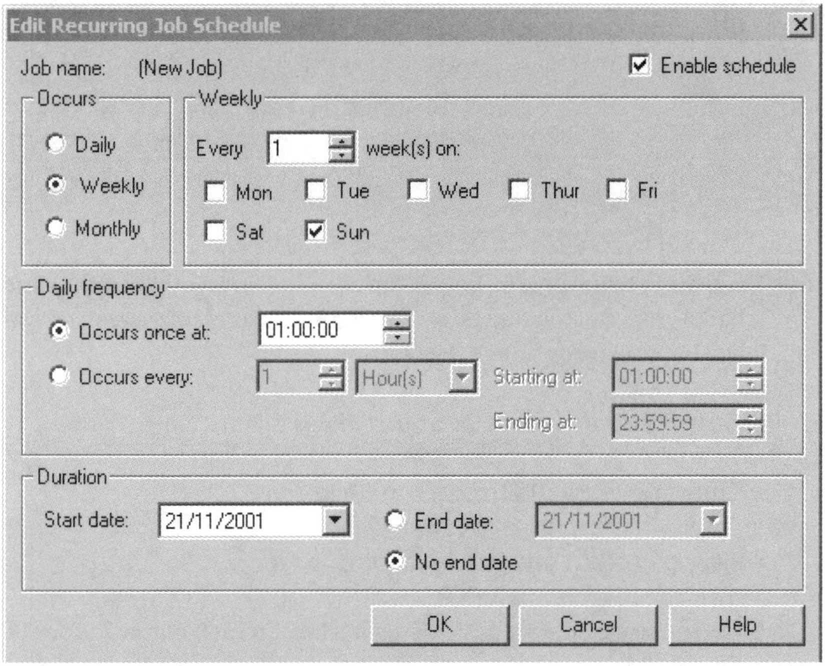

Figure 13-32. Edit recurring job schedule

4. Click on Next to display the Database Integrity screen, as shown in Figure 13-33. Again, we can set options to check the integrity of the actual database, including indexes. As before, we can also schedule this process to run at a specific time including just before we run a database backup. Click on Next.

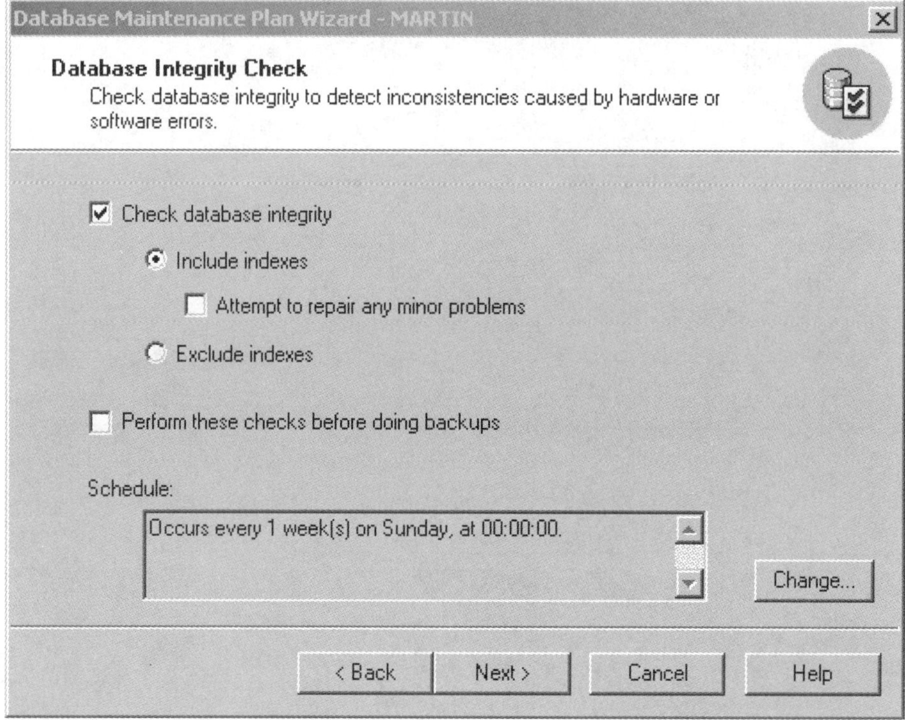

Figure 13-33. Database integrity

5. Now we get to the point: the Backup Plan screen is used to set up and schedule our database backup. Figure 13-34 shows this screen with the following backup options selected:

   - Backup the transaction log as part of this maintenance plan.
   - Verify the integrity of the backup when done.
   - Backup to disk. (You can also backup to tape.)

   As can be seen, the database will be backed up each day at 2:00 AM.

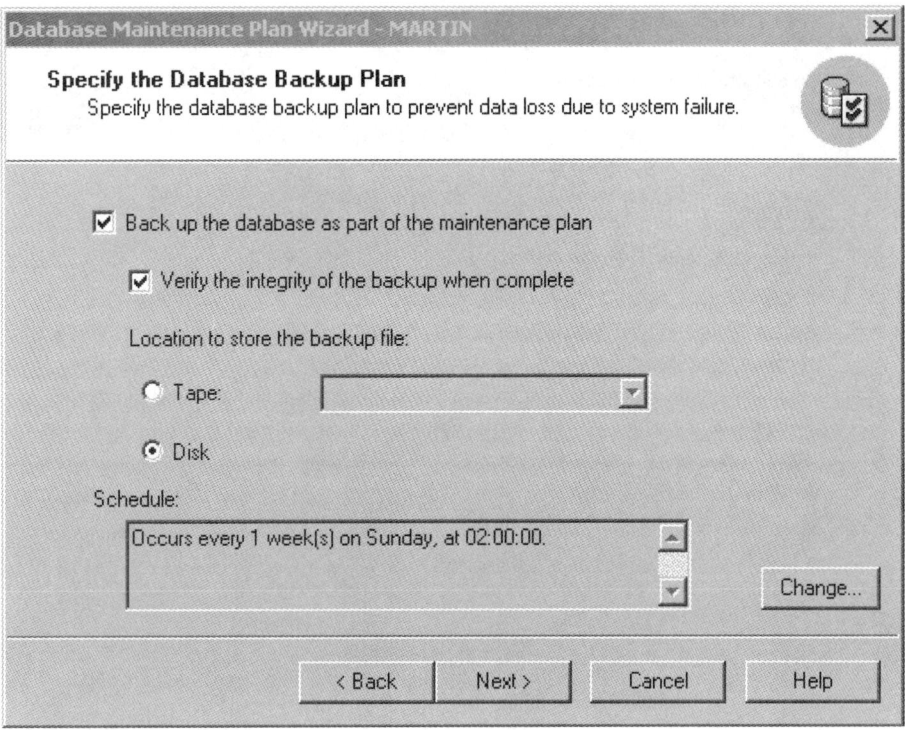

Figure 13-34. Backup plan

6. Complete the required options (including changing the schedule) and click on Next.

7. From the next screen (shown in Figure 13-35), we'll determine the database backup locations. Here we can select a folder for the files. If backing up multiple databases, we can create a subfolder for each database. We can also specify a default file extension for the backup. BAK is usually sufficient. Click on Next.

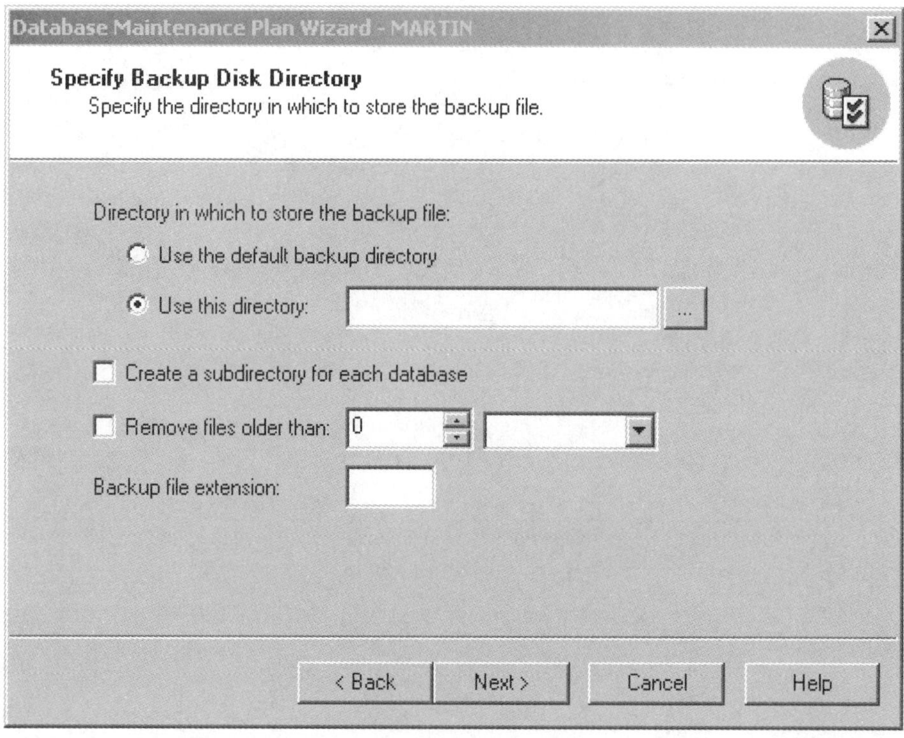

Figure 13-35. Database backup location

8. On this screen, you can set options for the transaction logs. (See the following section "Improve Query Performance with Indexes".) As with the database, we can include the transaction logs in the backup. Again, we can save the files to disk or tape. Figure 13-36 shows the transaction log backup options. Click on Next to proceed.

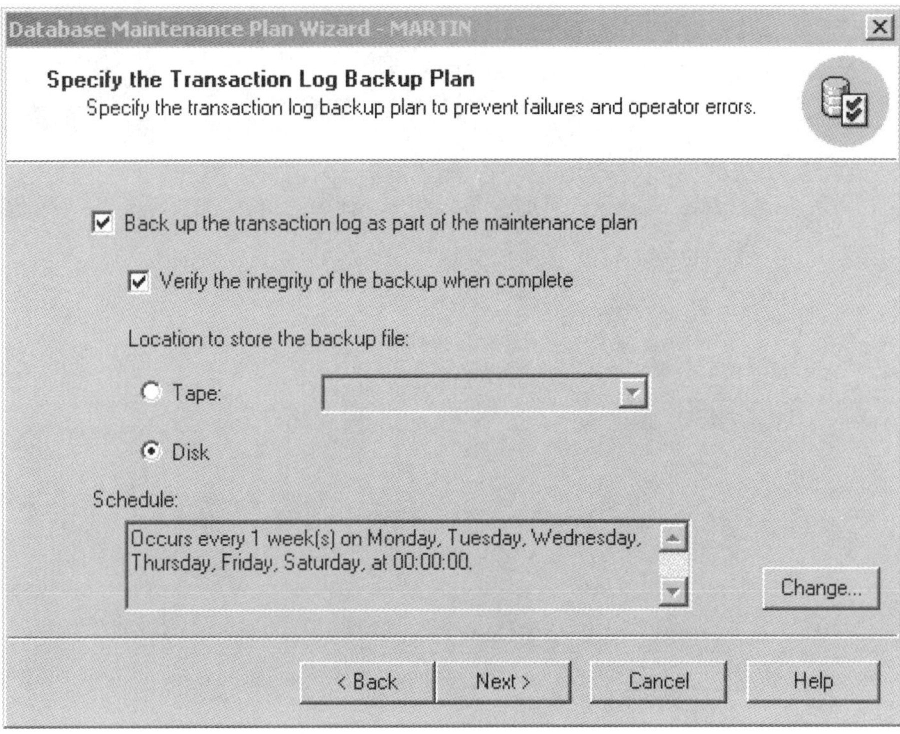

Figure 13-36. Transaction log backup options

9. The next screen (Figure 13-37) permits you to select a folder for the logs. As with a database backup, we can use subfolders to store backups. Click on Next.

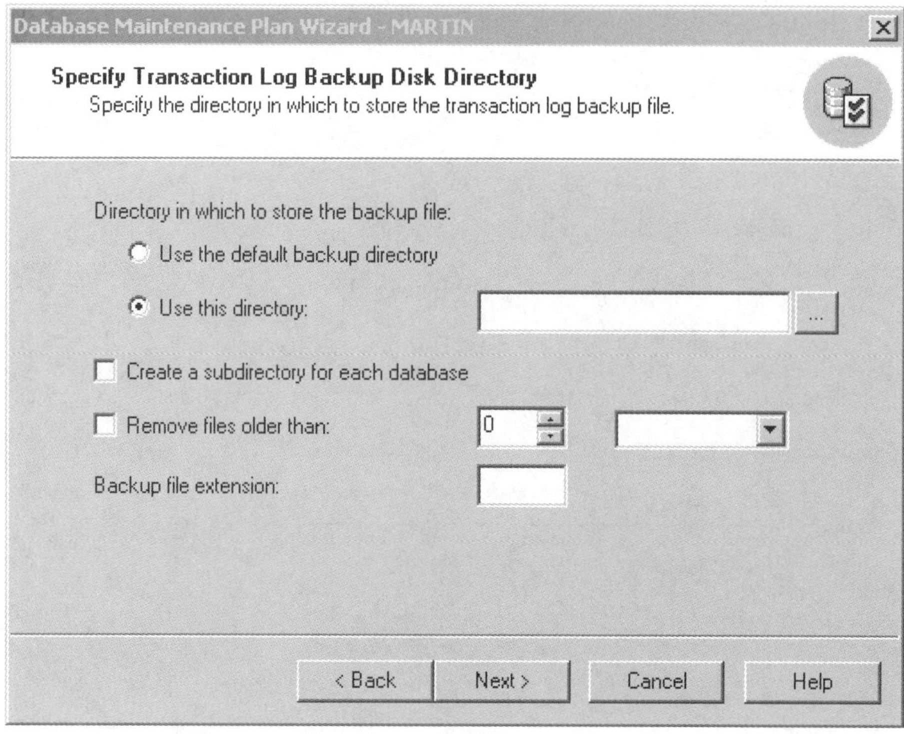

Figure 13-37. Translation log backup location

10. The next screen permits you to select a folder to store the reports that are generated by the maintenance plan. In this case, I have chosen to write the report to a text file. Note that it is also possible to have the report emailed to an operator. Figure 13-38 shows the screen with both options selected. This screen can be used to write the maintenance history report to a system table (sysdbmaintplan_history). Details on the steps taken by the plan, the results, and any error information will be included. It is important to limit the size of this table. We can use the Limit Rows in Table option to ensure that the table does not get too large. If the limit is reached, earlier rows for this plan will be deleted. Figure 13-39 shows the maintenance plan history. It is also possible to use Windows authentication to write the history to a remote server. Click on Next.

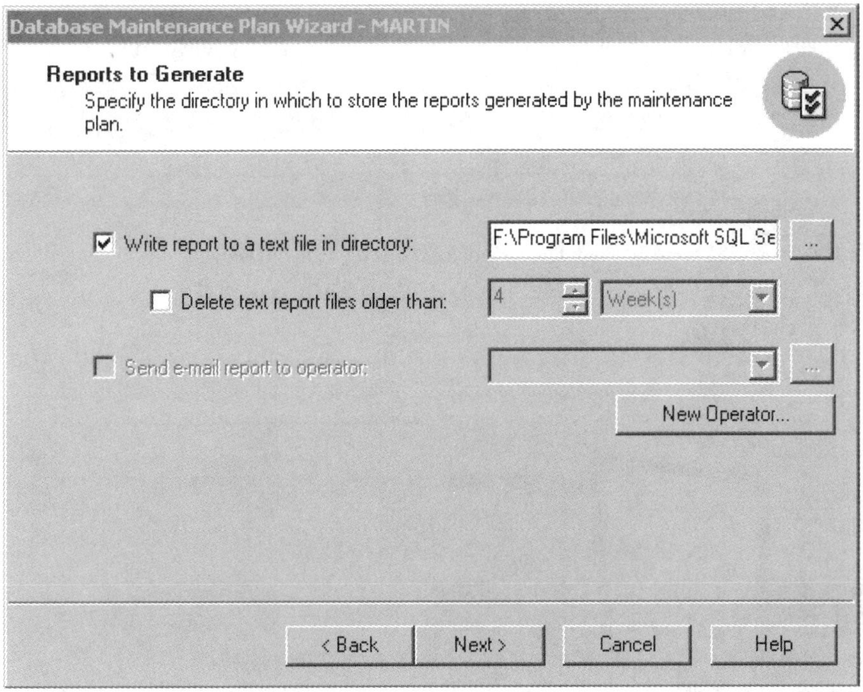

Figure 13-38. Report generation

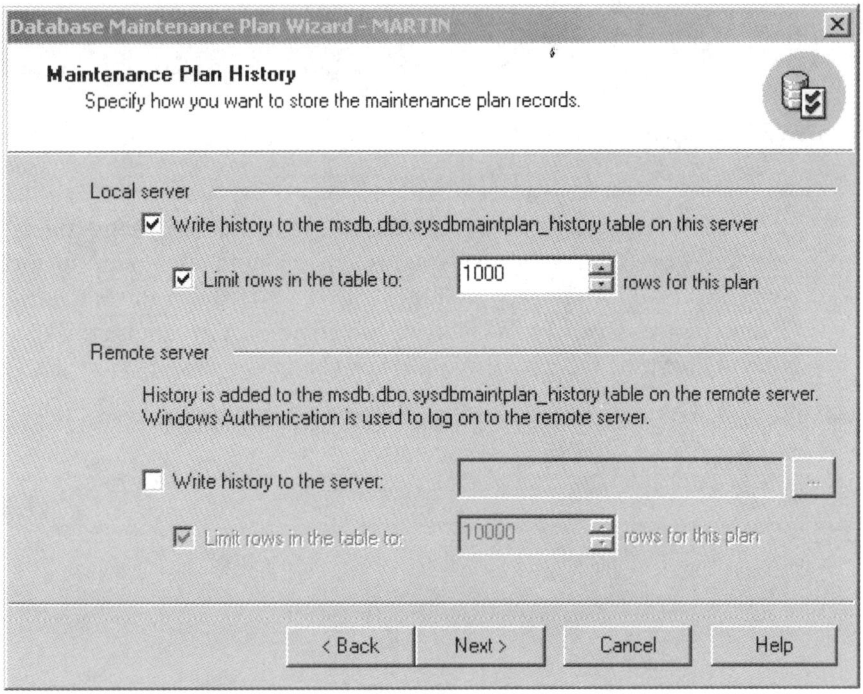

Figure 13-39. Maintenance plan history

11. The final screen (Figure 13-40) is where you can name the maintenance plan and review the actions it will perform. Give the maintenance a name and click on Finish.

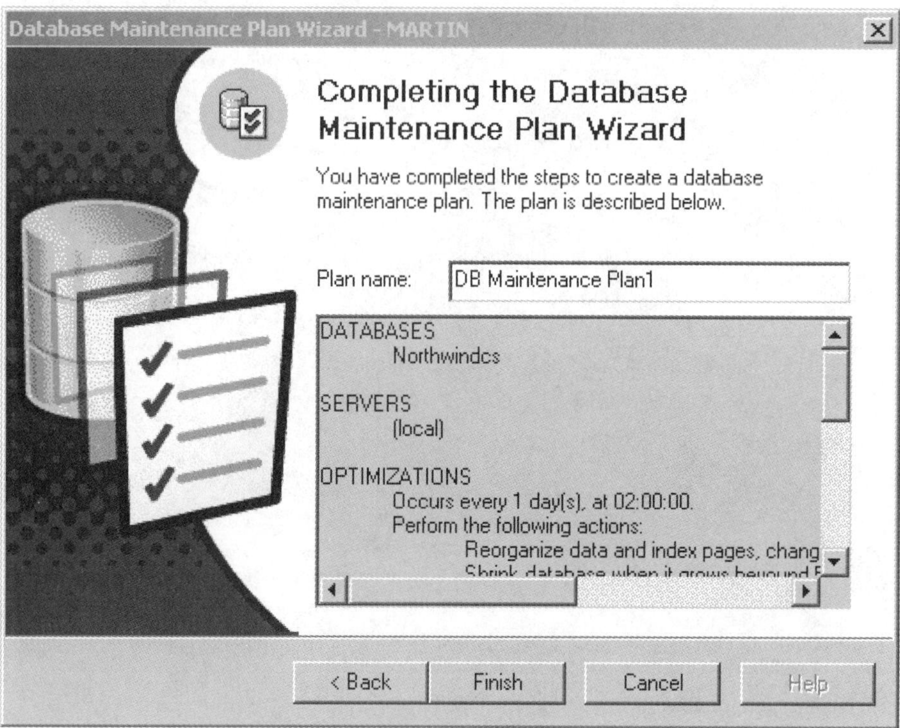

Figure 13-40. Complete the maintenance plan.

12. If all is well, you will be informed that the maintenance plan has been created. You can view the plan you just created (and other maintenance plans) using the Management folder. Figure 13-41 shows the database maintenance screen for the plan we just created. (You can use this feature to fine-tune the plan and make any changes necessary.)

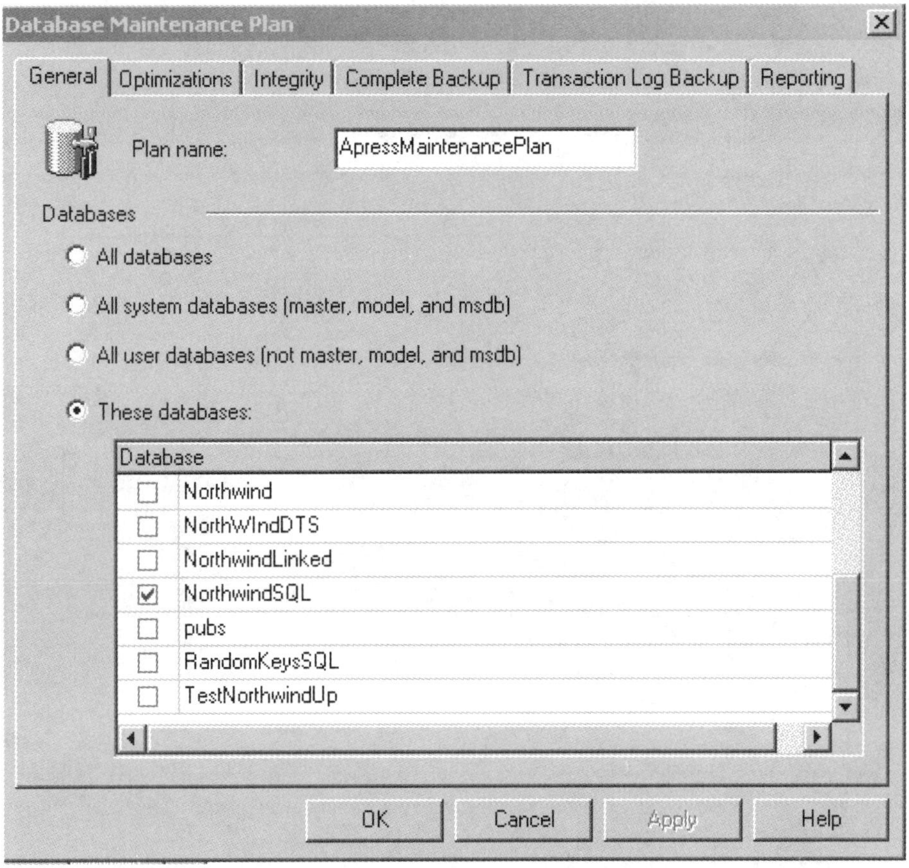

Figure 13-41. Database maintenance plan

As you have seen, the Maintenance Plan wizard is a useful tool not only for backing up the database or databases but also for overall optimization of the system.

Restoring the Database

On Monday morning, you grab your coffee, boot up the box, and discover that the #@!* database has fallen over. But you don't panic because you have all the required backups over in the mainframe room. Planning and backup have saved the day. So let's restore the database and make our users and boss happy people again.

Restoring a database can be a fairly straightforward process. When a database fails, Enterprise Manager marks it as failed, and the nice yellow color of the icon changes to a deathly gray. What a nice sight to greet you after a weekend!

First, you'll right-click on the failed database name and select All Tasks|Restore Database. Figure 13-42 shows the Restore Database screen.

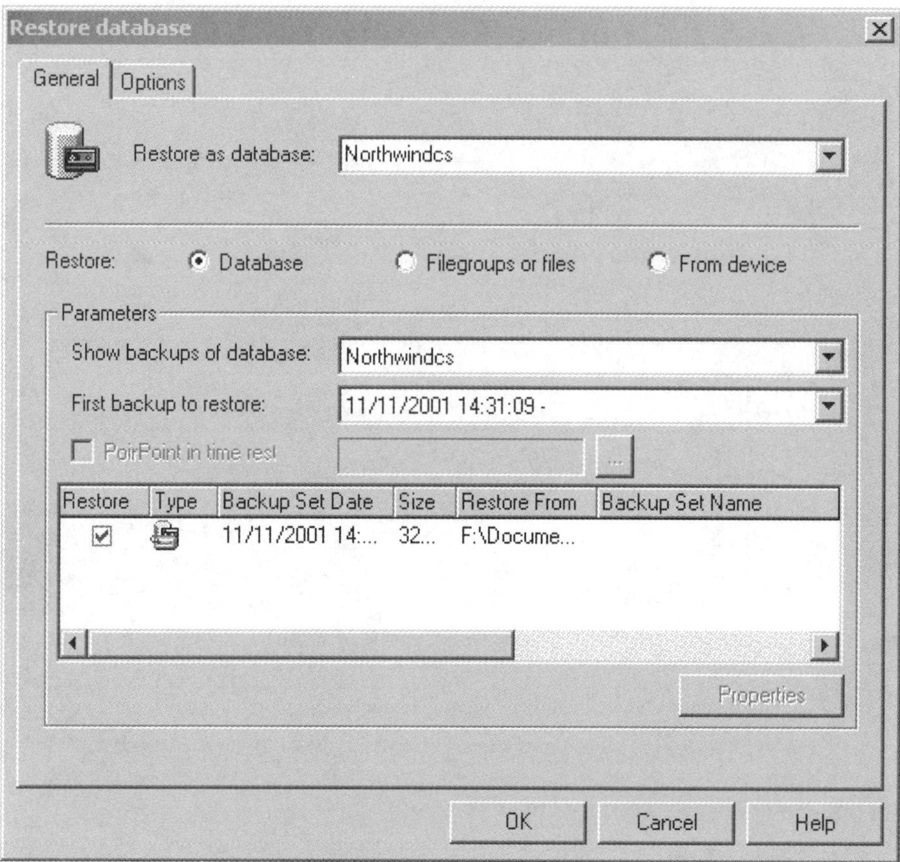

Figure 13-42. Restore database—General tab

As can be seen, the database to restore is selected. You can choose to restore another database using the drop-down list. Also included are all the backups made of this particular database. You can choose which database to restore by checking the box beside the database name.

Options Tab

Several options are available under this tab. The initial option, Leave Database Operational, should be used only when you are applying the last restore in a series. If you set the database as operational, then the additional restores that are required will not be permitted. Usually you will select the second option, Leave Database Non-operational, until you have completed the backup process.

Once all options have been set and you have double-checked everything, click on OK to start the restore process and finish that coffee while waiting. Figure 13-43 shows the Options tab with the selections.

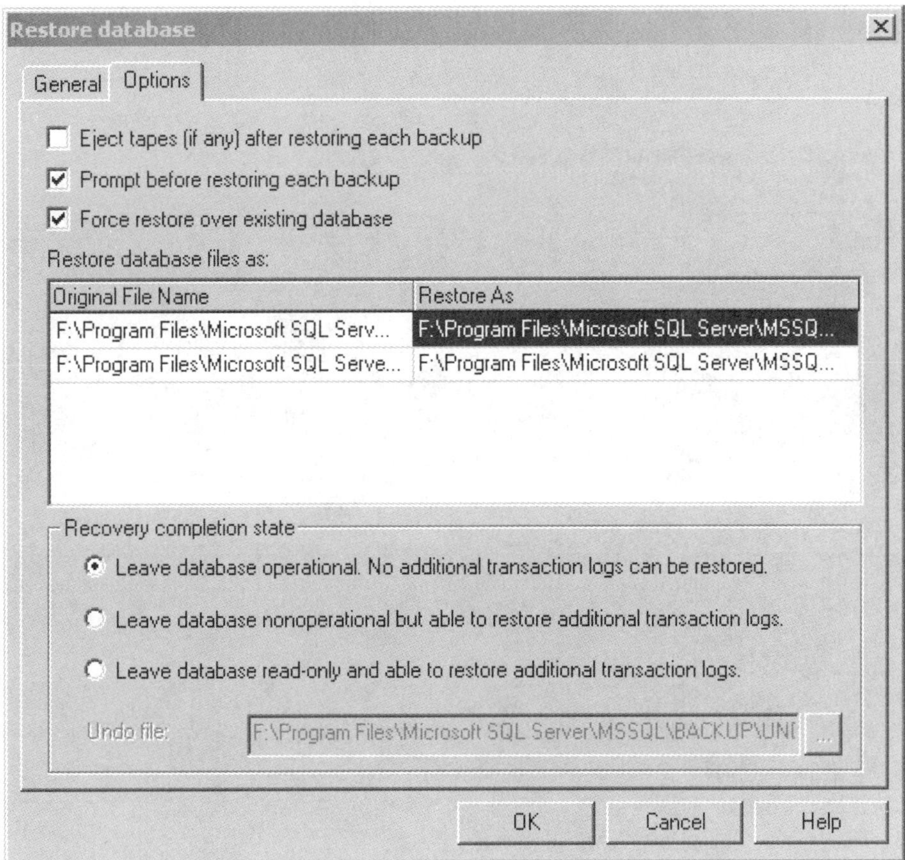

Figure 13-43. Restore options

Once the options have been selected, review them, review them again, and then click on OK to perform the restore.

Once the restore has finished its magic, check the database to ensure that it is fully functioning again.

Using MS Access 2002 to Back up an SQL Server Database

Access 2002 has a built-in backup facility. Although it's useful for small backups, I would recommend using the backup facilities within SQL Server to back up a sizeable database. The process to back up a small (very small) SQL Server Database is a simple three-step process:

1. Select Tools|Database Utilities|Backup SQL Database. Figure 13-44 shows the menu selection.

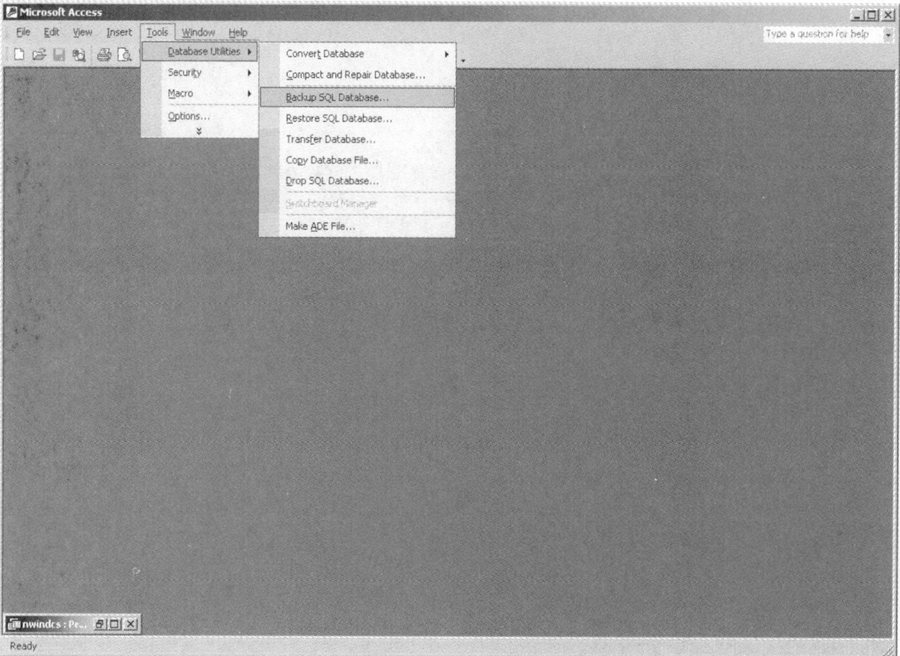

Figure 13-44. Access 2002 backup menu

2. Select a folder to save the backup to and name the backup file.

3. Click on OK to back up the database. Figure 13-45 shows the succeed message.

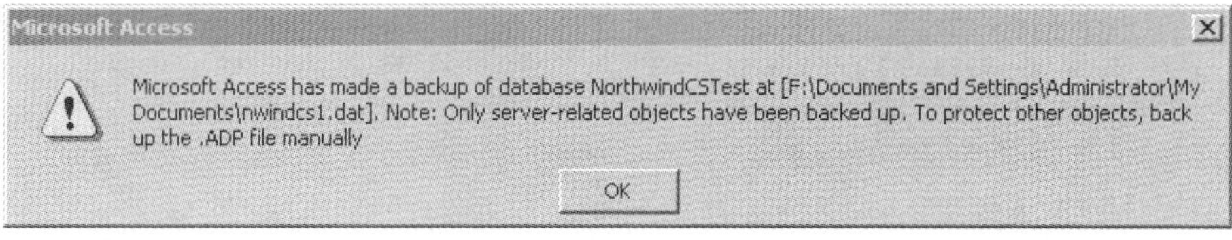

Figure 13-45. Backup successful

As we can see from the confirmation dialog box in Figure 13-45, only server-side objects have been backed up. What about objects contained within your ADP file itself? I am afraid you're on your own, and the ADP file must be backed up manually. Again, this can simply be a case of copying the ADP file to disk, Zip drive, or a local server.

> **NOTE** *We can also restore a database using Access 2002. Again, select Tools|Database Utilities|Restore SQL Database. You will be prompted to close the database and select a backup file to restore from.*

So, how useful is this feature? Not very if you're backing up a massive SQL Server database with hundreds of tables and thousands of records. Although I haven't exactly timed this, I would guess that it would take long enough to back up a substantial database that I would start looking for different backup strategies than those built into Access 2002. The Backup Database command within Access 2002 simply places a call to the SQL Server Backup Database command. This option will perform a full database backup of the specified database. Again, on a large database, this process can be slow. The following command is executed in response to calling a database backup from Access 2002. (Note that the path to your backup location will differ from that shown.)

```
BACKUP DATABASE [Northwindcs] TO DISK = N' F:\NwindBK\Northwind.dat WITH NOINT
```

The NOINT command ensures that the backup is added to previous backups, thus ensuring that they are not overwritten.

> **NOTE** *It is also possible to restore an SQL Server 2000 database that was created using the backup facility. To restore using Access 2002, select Tools|Database Utilities|Restore SQL Database. Access will warn you that the currently open database must be closed. Click on OK to continue. You will be prompted to select the backup file to use as the restore. Once the backup file has been selected, simply click on OK to restore the file. But be careful: double-clicking the backup file name will immediately run the restore command. It's easy to make an error and restore the wrong backup file.*

Database Properties

From within Enterprise Manager, we can also view properties that apply to the database as a whole. To view the properties, simply right-click on a database and select Properties from the shortcut menu. Figure 13-46 shows the Database Properties dialog box.

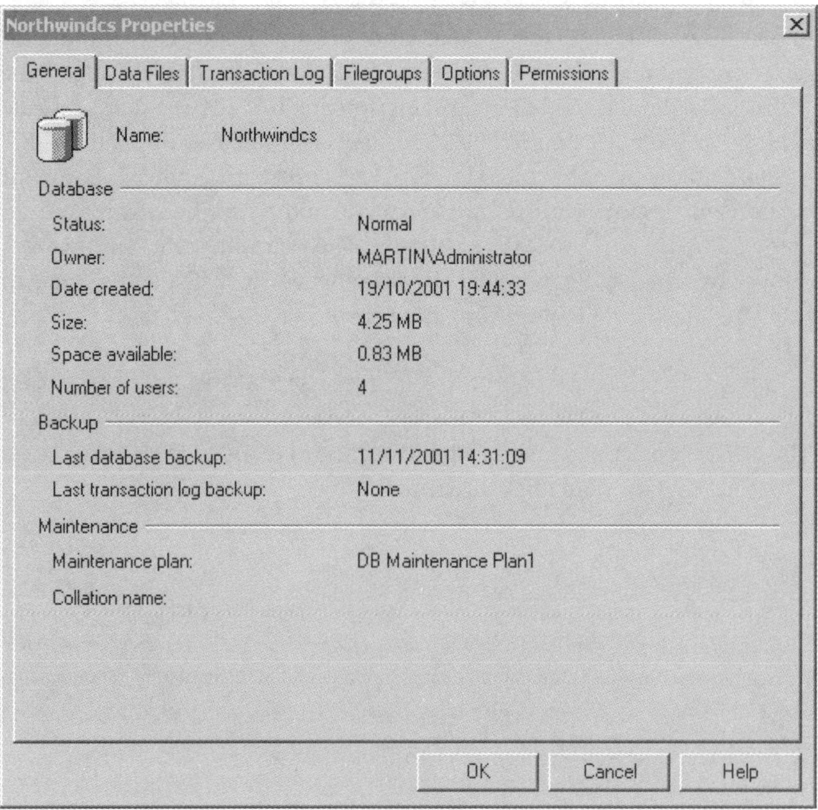

Figure 13-46. Database Properties dialog box

Table 13-2 shows the information that's available.

Table 13-2. Database Properties

TAB	DESCRIPTION
General	Information on the server, database statistics, users, last backup date, maintenance plans.
Data Files	Name and location of the data files, space allocated, information on file growth.
Transaction Log	Name and location of the transaction logs, properties of the transaction log.
Filegroups	Basic information on the database file groups.
Options	Access restrictions, recovery model, general settings, compatibility level.
Permissions	Users and groups with permissions in the current database. Permissions can also be managed from this view.

The properties can provide you with a very useful overview of your SQL Server database.

Improve Performance with Indexes

Most of us working with Access, whatever version, will have encountered indexes at one time or another. Unless really pushed, many of us tend to ignore this powerful (if limited) functionality provided by the Access DBMS. We can no longer afford to do so when developing in or against SQL Server.

It has been argued by many that it was the availability of indexing that really pushed the use of database systems. Up until the use of proper indexing, RDMS had been viewed as slow and inefficient. This statement could be true, as we shall see later. The proper use of indexes can have an especially remarkable effect on the performance of your database.

So what are indexes? What do they do? With my students, I initially start by comparing a database index to the index in a book. Before looking up a record in the table, the database checks the index, finds the page number (or record number in this case), and goes directly to the required row in the table—therefore speeding up the process of getting your data out of the system. Just think how long it would take you to find, say, a single page in a 900-page book by having to look at each individual page. The same principles apply to finding records in large tables. Without some sort of index, it could take hours to find a single record from the thousands or even millions held in a database. Of course, if things were that simple, there would be no need for this section and I would be fractionally poorer as a result.

However, before we can look at indexing in SQL Server, we must understand how data is stored on the hard drive and how the internal structure is created and managed.

When data is stored within the database, it is held on the hard drive in 8KB pages. Without indexes, these pages are totally unorganized, and chaos reigns. We bring order to this chaos by the proper use of indexing.

What Happens When There Is No Index?

Normal operations on a PC cause files to be stored, scattered over the hard drive. Database records without an index follow a similar pattern. Although not of vital importance to beginners, the following information provides useful insight into how SQL Server stores your data.

SQL Server stores data in extents, which is an 8KB data page. The main problem is that, when your data fills one extent, SQL Server simply stores new data on a new extent. However, this new extent may be stored in another area of the disk. Just think of a customer or order table: thousands of records are stored in different areas on your hard drive(s). In techno-speak, such a storage strategy is known as a *heap*, for obvious reasons. This does not mean that SQL Server searches every area of the data file for records. There is a method used to find the data, but, without the use of indexes, it can be much slower.

SQL Server has a special table, sysindexes, that records information about all tables in the database, whether indexed or not. However, nonindexed tables are treated in a different way: they are recorded within the sysindexes table as having an index identifier of zero. Another special value, the FirstIAM column tells the server where the first index allocation map page is in the database. The IAM is used to tell SQL where the various extents are stored on the disks.

So what's the problem? Each time SQL needs to find an extent, it must refer back to the IAM to find the location of the next extent. This process of referring back to the IAM is known as a *table scan.* So do we use indexes on everything? The short answer is no. Storing data in heaps is actually acceptable for small tables, and performance may indeed be faster than using an index. However, larger tables should always be indexed; indeed, to upsize your Access 2002 database, each table should have a unique primary key index.

Which Type of Index to Use

Working with indexes in Access 2002 is a fairly straightforward process: you select a field or fields and choose Create Index. In SQL Server, things are slightly different. A number of different index types are available, and choosing the correct type will affect the performance of your database.

Clustered Indexes

The idea of a clustered index is very simple; data is stored in a predefined order based on the constraints imposed by the index. For example, if we created a clustered index on customer surname, all records would be sorted by surname in A–Z order on the hard drive. As a result of this ordering, each table can have only one clustered index. How does this improve speed? Well, consider the following query:

```
SELECT Surname, Forename, Address1
FROM Customers
WHERE Surname = X
```

Using a clustered index on the surname increases the speed of the query because all records are stored in surname order, which results in fewer page reads. The customers with surname *X* will either all be on the same page or on sequential pages. For example, unlike searching a heap, there is no continual referring back to the IAM. Clustered indexes are particularly well suited for searching ranges of data, such as:

```
SELECT X, Y, Z
FROM TABLE
WHERE Value 1 is Between VALUE 2 AND VALUE 3
```

Nonclustered Indexes

Unlike a clustered index, this type of index does not point directly at the data. In this case, a key is held that points to the actual data rows. You can have multiple nonclustered indexes per table. If you fail to specify the index type when creating an index, then the index defaults to nonclustered.

Unique Index

Columns that contain unique data can have a unique index created on them. However, this feature is not to be used for integrity, that is, checking a value is unique. Use constraints or triggers for this. However, using triggers for this purpose can be slow.

> **NOTE** *When you create a unique index, you can also set Ignore Duplicate Key to "Yes". In this way, if you are doing a large insert, all valid records will be inserted. Only those records causing duplicates will be rejected. Without this option, all records would be rejected.*

Index Wizards

SQL Server Enterprise manager provides some methods to assist you in managing and optimizing indexes. Two wizards are available: the Create Index wizard and the Index Tuning wizard. Of these, the Index Tuning wizard is the more useful because it will take a representative workload for your database and suggest ways in which the indexes can be managed to improve performance. (Look under Tools|Wizards to view these tools.)

> **NOTE** *Before using the Index Tuning wizard, you will be required to run and save a database trace using the SQL Server Profiler tools. This is to allow the wizard to see how the database is being used with a proper workload. Sample databases like Northwind do not contain sufficient data to see the tools operate at their full potential.*

This chapter provided you with an overview of SQL Server 2000 and Access 2002. We had an overview of Enterprise Manager, database diagrams, and a brief introduction to backup and restore procedures. Some of the new features regarding indexing were also introduced. In following chapters, we will look at some of these features in greater detail.

CHAPTER 14

SQL Server Views

Looking through the Window

MANY ACCESS DEVELOPERS will be unfamiliar with the concept of a database view even though they may have been using the Access equivalent for many years. It is common practice to build Access queries and to use those queries as the record source for other Queries or SQL statements. You can think of a view as something similar but in this case a lot more powerful. Chapter 15 also discusses views and contains further examples including creating and populating a view using ADO.

Because creating views is a fairly simple process we shall begin by looking at the syntax used. The syntax for CREATE VIEW statements is:

```
CREATE VIEW [ < database_name > . ] [ < owner > . ]
 view_name [ ( column [ , . . . n ] ) ]
[ WITH < view_attribute > [ , . . . n ] ]
AS
select_statement
[ WITH CHECK OPTION ]

< view_attribute > ::=
    { ENCRYPTION | SCHEMABINDING|VIEW_METADATA}
```

Table 14-1 shows the arguments used with the CREATE VIEW statement.

Table 14-1. CREATE VIEW Arguments

ARGUMENT	COMMENTS
View_Name	Not surprisingly, this is the name of the view. In Access 2002, the name will be prefixed with the owner (for example, dbo in my case).
Column	Column names as assigned in the SQL SELECT statement.
AS	The actions the view will perform.
Select_Statement	The SQL statement used to define the view.
WITH CHECK OPTION	This is very useful and will prohibit you from inserting data via the view, which would invalidate the view's WHERE clause.
WITH ENCRYPTION	Encrypts the view definition within the SQL Server system tables.
SCHEMABINDING	Protects the definition of the view. Changes to the base tables the view is based on will fail. For instance, you cannot drop a table that has a view based on it without dropping the view first.
VIEW_METADATA	See following discussion on inserting data via views.

Working with Views

The code that follows is a standard SQL statement, in which a WHERE clause is used to restrict the data returned:

```
Select data From
Table
Where
Field = City
```

This query will return data for the city as defined in the WHERE clause. We can then use this query as the basis for preparing other queries bearing in mind the restricted data available. For example:

```
Select
Something
From
The Query
```

We are treating the query as if it were another table in the database but this time without extraneous information. A view works in much the same way; that is, it will create specific content when executed on the server and we can then build SELECT statements to hit the view.

Think of a view as a window into the table data. We can choose either to show some of the data in a table or tables or to restrict the fields available in the view. Remember, the view does not hold any data. Your data is still stored within the tables used by the view. However, with several restrictions, it is still possible to add, insert, and delete the table data using a view.

There are some differences between views, tables, and queries. Indexed views are stored within the database in the same way as a table. SQL treats an indexed view just as if it were a table, but a standard view is not treated in this way. Only the view definition is stored in the database. In addition, views have the following restrictions:

- Views cannot contain an ORDER BY clause. However, we can circumvent this restriction by using the TOP PERCENTAGE statement. (This is discussed in Chapter 15.)
- Views cannot be parameterized. (Again, see Chapter 15.)
- Views cannot be used with temporary tables. (Surprise!)

Advantages of Views

Views provide us with another tool, which can be used both to present data to the end user and to assist us in its management. A view can be much more flexible than a table, and this flexibility is but one of the many advantages that they offer the developer. Views also provide increased security because they permit us to limit direct access to the database tables. We can hide system complexity from our end users, presenting them with a simplified view of the database structure. Using views can also make the use of third-party query tools less complex for the user. With T-SQL, we can create complex views that can be used by the end users with these query tools without understanding the complex statements underlying their structure. Views can also help improve the performance of your database particularly when we are moving data across the network to the clients.

Let's look at some of these advantages in a little more detail.

Security

Rather than give users permissions at the table level, we can assign permissions to a view or views. For example, one of the previous systems I worked on held data on business clients, and some of this data was confidential accounting information that was not available to all staff members. In this case, a view was used to permit the majority of the staff to access the nonconfidential data. Other staff members—those with appropriate permissions—could then see the confidential accounting data. At times, users may require access to specific accounting information, such as accounting ratios. Again, this information could be provided via a restricted view. In this way, the detailed accounting information could be hidden while still providing the required data. For example, in the Northwind ADP I have created a table to store data on directors' bonuses.

To permit staff members to view directors' contact details but hide their current bonus payments, I have created a view called View_Directors. The "View" prefix is used simply for this example, and you may want to hide the fact that users are retrieving data using a view and omit the "View" portion of the object name. The full syntax for creating this view is:

```
CREATE VIEW [View_Directors]
AS
SELECT
DirName,DirAddress,DirTown,DirPostcode,DirPhone,DirEmail,DirFax
FROM
tblDirectors
```

Permission to access the view can now be given to users or groups without giving away details of the directors' bonuses this year. Those staff members who need to see the bonus data can either use another view containing the bonus data or be given direct access to the table or a stored procedure providing the data.

Another nice feature with security is that we can permit a user to access the view without granting specific access to the underlying table. Let's try it and see what happens. For this example, we are going to create a view of the Northwind Customers table. We will create a form to be used to enter new records only. The twist here is that the user will not have any permissions directly on the Customers table, but they will have access to the view. Details on how to create the view follow in later examples. (For an overview of security, see Chapter 18.)

The user for this example has been given permission to access the database, but no table permissions have been granted. The user has been given permission (SELECT and INSERT) to access the view, vw_Customer. This view simply permits the user to view existing records. The INSERT permission should enable them to add new records to the table via the view. The SQL for the view is shown below. (SELECT * is considered bad form by many developers. However, it can prove useful when developing the database, saving you from re-creating the view SQL each time you adjust a table. When selecting from tables, you will generally select only those columns that are required.)

```
CREATE VIEW dbo.vw_Customer
AS
SELECT dbo.Customers.*
FROM dbo.Customers
```

In Access 2002, a simple data entry form has been created using the form wizard and the newly created view used as the form's record source. Figure 14-1 shows the form. One thing should be apparent immediately: even though the user has been given permission to insert records in SQL Server 2000, they are unable to do so in Access 2002 via the form. Note that the Add New Record form buttons are unavailable as are the menu option to add a new record. If we choose the tables group in the database window, no tables are available. The tables question is easy to answer: we didn't give permission on any database tables.

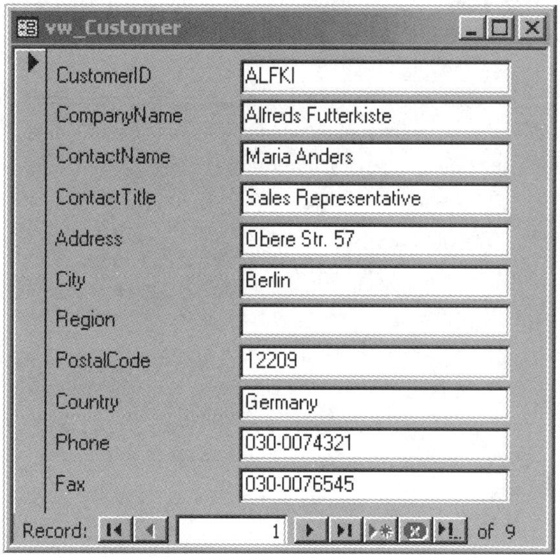

Figure 14-1. Input form based on SQL Server view

So what's going on?

This simple question took up some considerable time in debate and testing between several experienced Access developers and was only solved by the intervention of Mike Gunderloy, a developer and author with many years' experience in, among other things, Microsoft Access development. Despite the documentation available, which implies that you can update data via views without granting explicit permissions on the underlying table to the user, it was impossible to achieve in Access 2002 or Access 2000 ADPs. So what's the answer? To use a view in an ADP and permit the user to enter new records but without granting permissions on the underlying table, we need to change one of the View properties. You must be logged into the server as a system admin user to save the changes to the View properties. From the database window:

1. Select the query group.
2. Select the view and open in Design view.
3. Using the Main menu, select View|Properties.

Figure 14-2 shows the Properties dialog box for the view.

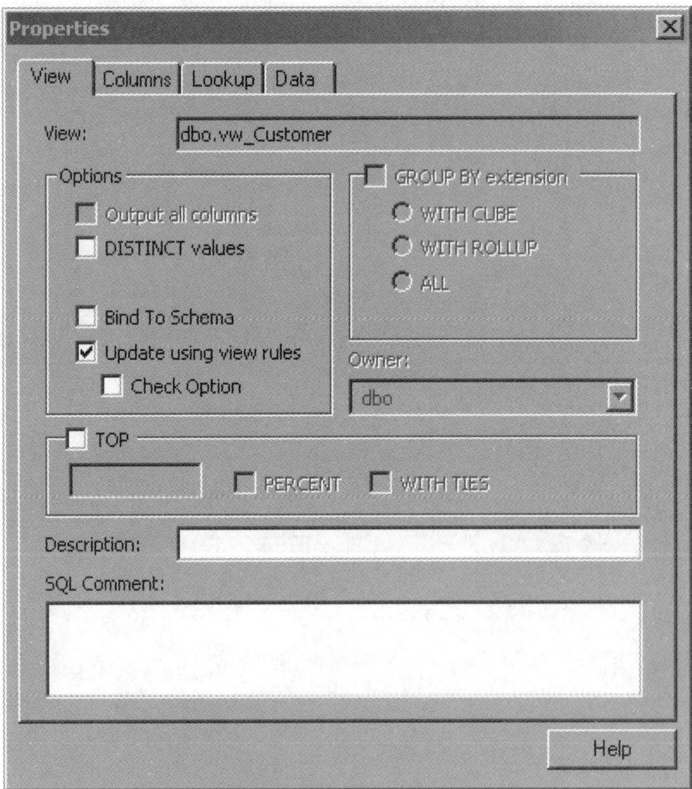

Figure 14-2. View Properties dialog box

4. Check the box "Update using view rules".

5. Close the Properties dialog box.

6. Close and save the view.

7. Exit Northwind and log back in as the previous user.

What are we doing? By default, ADO and OLEDB will try to insert the data to the base table on which the view is based. This is because ADO queries certain information about the data when it is retrieved. By default, SQL Server tells ADO what the base object is, using the table as the base. Of course, the user does not have permission to work with the table, and so the insert fails. In fact, it's impossible to even attempt the insert because the form will not permit you to add data. By changing the option using the Properties dialog box, ADO and OLEDB will use SQL statements that refer to the view rather than the base table for the update. Our user has permission to insert via the view, and so all is well.

Figure 14-3 shows the same form following this action. In this case, notice that the Add New Record button on the navigation bar is now available.

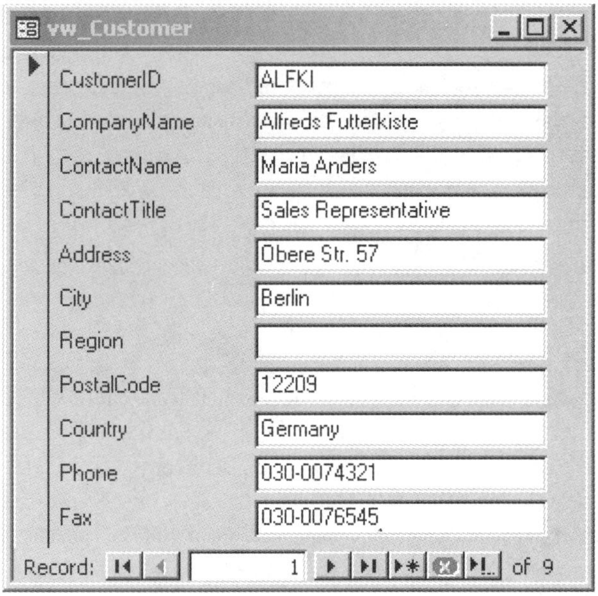

Figure 14-3. Adding a record via the view

> **NOTE** *The Customer table is still not available in the Database window because the user has no direct access to it.*

Let's reexamine the CREATE VIEW statement:

```
CREATE VIEW dbo.vw_Customer
WITH VIEW_METADATA
AS
SELECT dbo.Customers*
FROM dbo.Customers
```

Notice that we have an additional line added to the SQL statement: `WITH VIEW_METADATA`. This is the line that performs all the magic and allows us to insert data via the view. VIEW_METADATA returns information to the client about the view rather than the base tables that the view is based on. This "extra" information permits the client to implement updating of the base tables.

Hiding Complexity to Help the User

Views are a very useful tool for hiding complex joins between tables. Chapter 15 has a simple example of this approach and provides a multitable example. With a view, we can combine several tables and present data to the user as if it existed in a single table. In this way, the user need not understand complex table relationships or SQL join syntax.

Many developers also use a system of active/inactive flags to "delete" records. We can use views to remove "inactive" records from tables before displaying them to the user, which thus eliminates the need for WHERE clauses in SQL statements that access such views. For example, without a view, the users would always need to remember to include a WHERE statement to exclude inactive records:

```
WHERE ACTIVE = True
```

With a view, we can restrict the records to just those active records without the need to either hard-code the WHERE clause or make users remember to include it in any ad hoc queries. Now, when a user requires this data, they can simply construct a simple SELECT statement based on the view without the need for the WHERE clause.

To show how we can hide complexity (and to save on typing), we will use some of the SQL examples from previous chapters and build some simple views.

Many developers also use aggregate queries to summarize data for reporting purposes. The following SQL statement will return all order records that contain more than one order. Chapter 7 provides a detailed explanation of the syntax used in this example.

Using the Northwind example ADP:

1. Select the query group.
2. Click on New on the menu.
3. Select Design View to open Query Builder.
4. Select the Order table and click on Add.
5. Click on the Close button to close the Add Table dialog box.
6. In the Query window, check the OrderDate field to select it.
7. Enter "Count(OrderID)" in the next blank criteria cell.
8. In the Alias cell, enter "TotalOrders".
9. Enter "Min(Freight)" with an alias of "SmallestFreight".
10. Enter "Max(Freight)" with an alias of "LargestFreight".

Note that all we are doing at this point is creating the SQL statement on which the view will be based. This isn't much different from creating a normal view.

> **NOTE** *The Add Table dialog box in Query Builder differs from the one that's normally used. In this case, you are offered a choice of using tables, views, or functions to base the new view on. Views can also be based on existing views or user-defined functions.*

11. In the Criteria cell for the OrderID column, enter ">1".
12. Close and save the query as View_OrderTotals.

Figure 14-4 shows how the window should look when the query has been completed. All three panes in Query Designer are shown.

> **NOTE** *To view all three panes in Query Builder from the Main menu, select View|ShowPanes and ensure that all three options (Diagram, Grid, and SQL) are selected.*

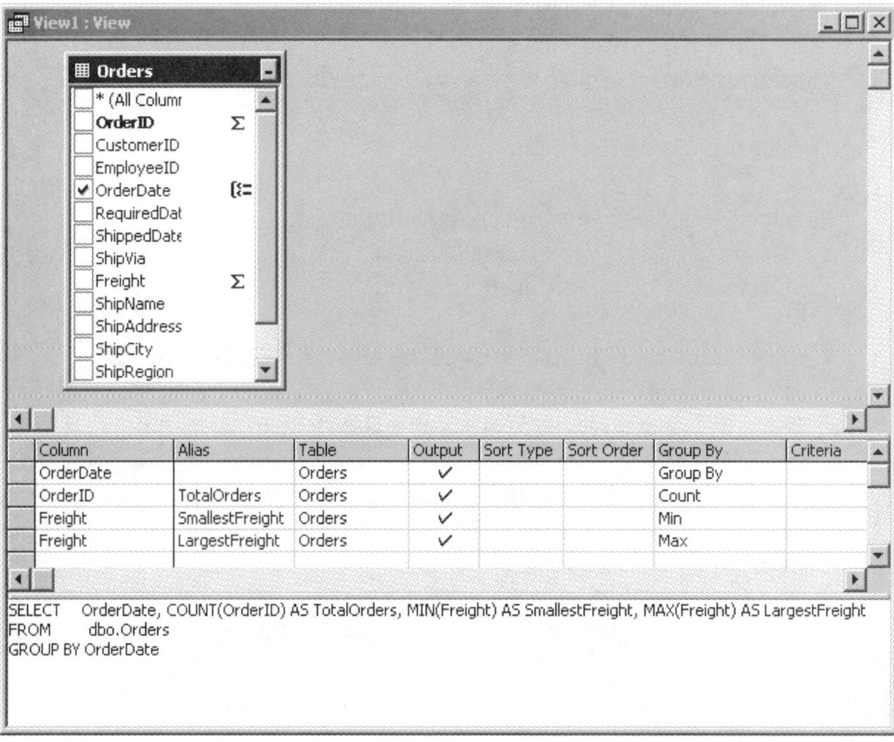

Figure 14-4. Orders view

You won't be able to execute the view prior to saving. As can be seen, all we are doing is creating an SQL SELECT statement. However, what we are really doing is creating the SQL statement (defining the view) for the following SQL Server CREATE VIEW procedure:

```
CREATE VIEW View_OrderTotals
AS
SELECT
OrderDate, COUNT(OrderID) as TotalOrders, Min(Freight)
AS Smallestfreight, Max(Freight) AS LargestFreight
FROM
Orders
GROUP By Orderdate
Having (Count(OrderID) >1)
```

The only change to the SQL statement is the inclusion of the CREATE VIEW instruction to SQL Server.

> **NOTE** *When you open the view again in Access, notice how Access has placed the table owner prefix before the orders table name. In my case, it has been renamed dbo.Orders.*

Using the View

Using the view is as simple as constructing a SELECT statement. Figure 14-5 shows a simple SELECT statement, which returns a specific order, based on the OrderDate. Note that in this case we are creating and executing a stored procedure using the view as if it where a base table. In this case, I have added additional criteria to the stored procedure, as I want to see only those records for which the LargestFreight cost is greater that $40.

The SELECT statement is as follows:

```
SELECT
OrderDate,TotalOrders,SmallestFreight,LargestFreight
FROM
dbo.View_OrderTotals
WHERE
(LargestFreight > 40)
ORDER By OrderDate
```

This example also illustrates one way around the inability to use the ORDER BY clause with views. Simply use ORDER BY in the SELECT statement querying the view. Chapter 15 looks at using the TOP PERCENT clause to facilitate the use of ORDER BY directly with views.

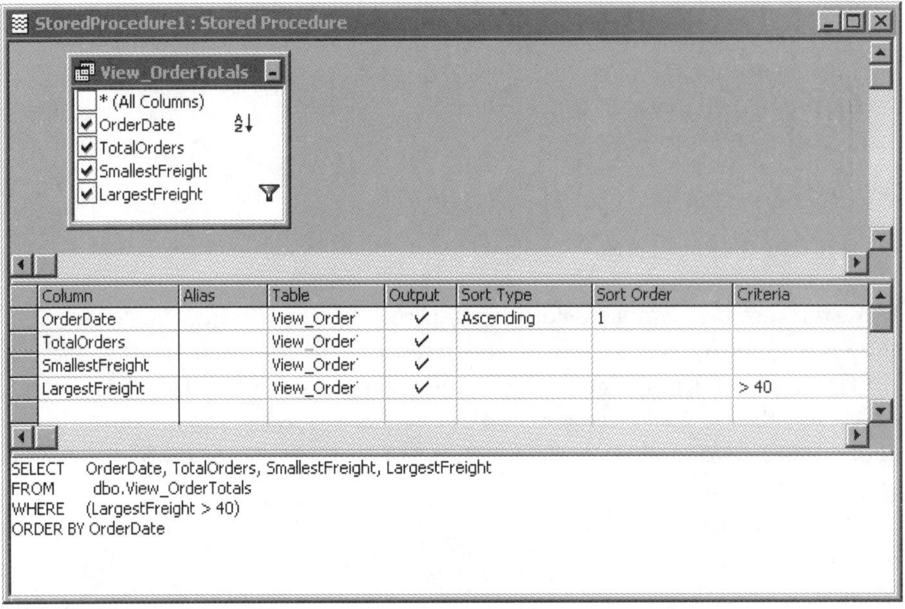

Figure 14-5. SELECT statement

Users can also construct simple SQL statements using the view without having to understand and create aggregate functions like COUNT, MIN, and MAX. For example, to select all the data from the view, simply write:

```
SELECT * FROM View_OrderTotals
```

This will return all records from the view. It's nice and simple.

When we come to use multiple tables, you will really see how views can be used to simplify data access. For example, take the following SQL statement, which returns order details by the employee who placed the order.

```
SELECT
dbo.Employees.FirstName, dbo.Employees.LastName,
dbo.Customers.CompanyName, dbo.Orders.OrderDate, dbo.Orders.RequiredDate
FROM
dbo.Customers INNER JOIN
dbo.Orders ON dbo.Customers.CustomerID = dbo.Orders.CustomerID INNER JOIN
dbo.Employees ON dbo.Orders.EmployeeID = dbo.Employees.EmployeeID
```

To construct this query, the user must have a good grasp of SQL syntax and join notation as well as an understanding of the underlying table relationships.

Look at the next couple of SQL statements:

```
Select * from View_MultipleTables
Select OrderDate,FirstName,LastName from View_MultipleTables
Select CompanyName,OrderDate from View_MultipleTables
```

With these, there's no need to use or understand joins, complicated syntax, or the underlying table structure; this is all handled by the view, View_MultipleTables. One other major benefit of this approach is that all the joins are processed on the server. Only the result of the SELECT statement is passed back to the user.

Views can also be encrypted; in this way, the SQL statements used to create the view can be hidden. However, if you need to amend or re-create the view, you will need to have the original files available. So make sure that you save the definition of the view as a script or text file. Unless you have very good security reasons for encrypting views, we see no real reason for doing so. To encrypt a view, simply add the WITH ENCRYPTION keywords below the CREATE VIEW statement:

```
CREATE VIEW
WITH ENCRYPTION
AS
SQL STATEMENT
```

Reducing Network Traffic

As you may have seen in some of the examples, a view can be used to limit the data passed across the network. Rather than drag all the fields from server to client (where they are filtered), a view permits you to be more selective and filter using the SELECT statements when creating the view. Additional filtering can then be carried out either by the application or by the user.

Indexing Views

New in SQL Server 2000 is the ability to add an index to a view. The index that is created is a clustered index, which is discussed in Chapter 13. One drawback is that indexed views are only utilized in SQL Server Enterprise Edition. When an index is created on a view, the view—rather than being created when called—is maintained as a distinct object on the server, just like any other database object.

There are also some limitations when creating indexed views:

- The view must be created using the SCHEMA BINDING option.

NOTE *Because a view rests on top of a base table, any changes to the base table may invalidate the view. Schema binding will stop any changes to the base table that will cause your view to be invalid. However, this feature may be over written when using SQL Server Enterprise Manager. Schema Binding can be established within Access 2002 by using the Property Dialog box for the view. With the view in Design view, select View|Properties from the Main Access menu. In the View Properties dialog box, check the Bind to Schema checkbox.*

- The view cannot contain references to other views. As with Access queries, it is possible to base a new view on one that already exists. However, you will not be able to index the view if you take this approach, and all tables must be in the same database. It is possible to create a view that accesses tables in different databases. Again, you cannot create an index on this view.

The following list shows functions that cannot be used with an indexed view:

- **COUNT(*)**
- **ROWSET**
- derived table
- self-joins
- **DISTINCT**
- **STDEV**, **VARIANCE**, **AVG**
- float, text, ntext, image columns
- subqueries
- full-text predicates (**CONTAIN**, **FREETEXT**)
- SUM on nullable expression

- **MIN**, **MAX**
- **TOP**
- **OUTER** join
- **UNION**

Creating an Indexed View Using Query Analyzer

The following types of systems are more likely to benefit from indexed views:

- tables with large sets of data
- data warehousing solutions
- OLAP databases
- data mining operations

Creating the Indexed View

The following is the T-SQL script for creating a simple indexed view called vw_CustomersIndex. This script is executed within SQL Server 2000 Query Analyzer.

```
CREATE VIEW vw_CustomersIndex WITH SCHEMABINDING
AS
SELECT
CustomerID,CompanyName,ContactName,ContactTitle
FROM dbo.Customers
GO
CREATE UNIQUE CLUSTERED INDEX CustomerID on vw_CustomersIndex (CUSTOMERID)
```

Note that this is a two-stage process: the first stage is to run the CREATE VIEW statement, and the second stage, which follows the GO keyword, actually creates the index. That is, the view must already exist before we can create the index.

> **NOTE** *You cannot use the GO keyword in Access 2002.*

Figure 14-6 shows the preceding script in SQL Server.

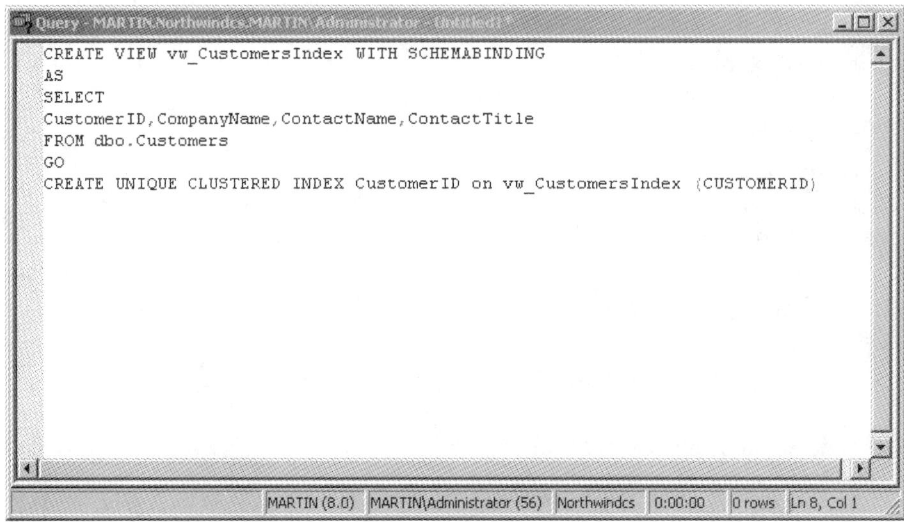

Figure 14-6. T-SQL Create View script

Figure 14-7 shows the partial results running a simple stored procedure, usp_UsingCustomerViewIndex against the view in Access 2002.

usp_UsingCustomerIndex : Stored Procedure

CustomerID	CompanyName	ContactName
ALFKI	Alfreds Futterkiste	Maria Anders
ANATR	Ana Trujillo Emparedados y helados	Ana Trujillo
ANTON	Antonio Moreno Taquería	Antonio Morenc
AROUT	Around the Horn	Thomas Hardy
BERGS	Berglunds snabbköp	Christina Berglu
BLAUS	Blauer See Delikatessen	Hanna Moos
BLONP	Blondel père et fils	Frédérique Cite
BOLID	Bólido Comidas preparadas	Martín Sommer
BONAP	Bon app'	Laurence Lebih
BOTTM	Bottom-Dollar Markets	Elizabeth Linco
BSBEV	B's Beverages	Victoria Ashwo
CACTU	Cactus Comidas para llevar	Patricio Simpsc
CENTC	Centro comercial Moctezuma	Francisco Char
CHOPS	Chop-suey Chinese	Yang Wang
COMMI	Comércio Mineiro	Pedro Afonso
CONSH	Consolidated Holdings	Elizabeth Brow
DRACD	Drachenblut Delikatessen	Sven Ottlieb
DUMON	Du monde entier	Janine Labrune
EASTC	Eastern Connection	Ann Devon
ERNSH	Ernst Handel	Roland Mendel

Record: 1 of 91

Figure 14-7. Results when querying a view

> **NOTE** *You may need to refresh the database before the view is available. Chapter 15 shows how to use ADO to execute stored procedures, which create the same view. Microsoft has published some figures on the MSDN Web site showing the large performance gains that can be achieved using indexed views. The figures can be viewed at* `http://msdn.microsoft.com/library/default.asp?url=/library/en-us/dnsql2k/html/indexedviews1.asp`.

Using Views to Insert Data

So far, we have used views to return data from a single table or to summarize data that is held in multiple tables. In addition, we have seen how to change the properties of a view within Access 2002 to permit a user to insert new records to a table. The process for this insert was fairly simple (once we discovered the View properties). However, inserting data using a view can be a bit harder.

Before actually looking at how this is achieved, we need to look at a couple of T-SQL statements, specifically, triggers.

Triggers

A trigger is a stored procedure that is executed in response to an SQL Server event such as INSERT, DELETE, UPDATE (sound familiar?). For example, when we are doing an insert, we can call a trigger, which can provide additional validation to the data before the changes are actually committed to the table. In addition, the trigger can access two virtual tables: Inserted and Deleted. These virtual tables, which are local to the trigger, contain a picture of the data state before and after the statement causing the triggers to be executed was called. For example, during an insert, the Inserted table contains a copy of the data about to be inserted. During a delete, the Deleted table contains a copy of the data you are about to delete. An update can really be thought of as a delete immediately followed by an insert. The old record is deleted, and a new one with all of the original and/or updated values is put in its place.

The easiest way to understand this process is to use an example. We will update a company record in the Northwind sample database. In the process, a trigger will "fire" (execute) and check the values in the Inserted and Deleted virtual tables. We will then undo the entire process, leaving the Company table intact. To create the trigger with SQL Server 2000 from Query Analyzer:

1. Select File|New.

2. Open the Create Trigger folder in the New dialog box. SQL Server has several template files for common tasks. Figure 14-8 shows the initial screen in the New dialog box.

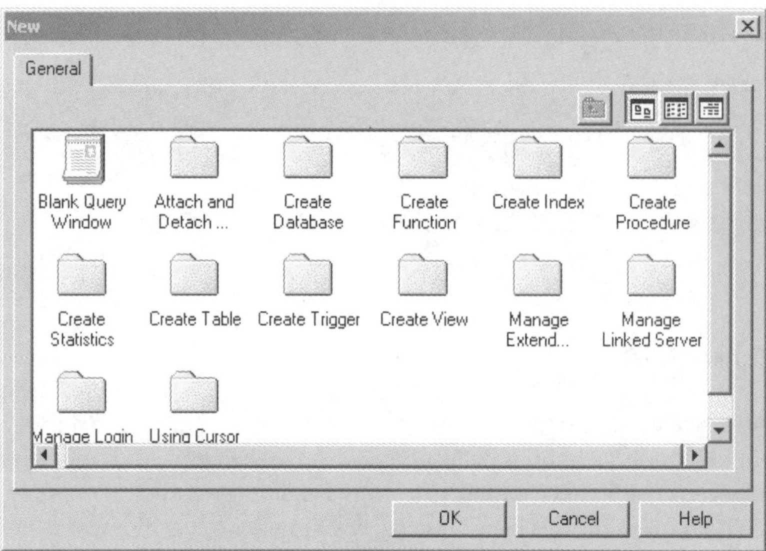

Figure 14-8. Create Trigger Template folder

3. Select Create Trigger Basic template from the template files.

4. Click on OK to close the dialog box. Figure 14-9 shows the template file opened in Query Analyzer.

NOTE: *You can replace the trigger template parameters. From the Main menu, select Edit|Replace Trigger Parameters. This opens the Replace Parameter dialog box. Simply replace the listed parameters with those required for this example. You will still be required to enter the body of the trigger yourself.*

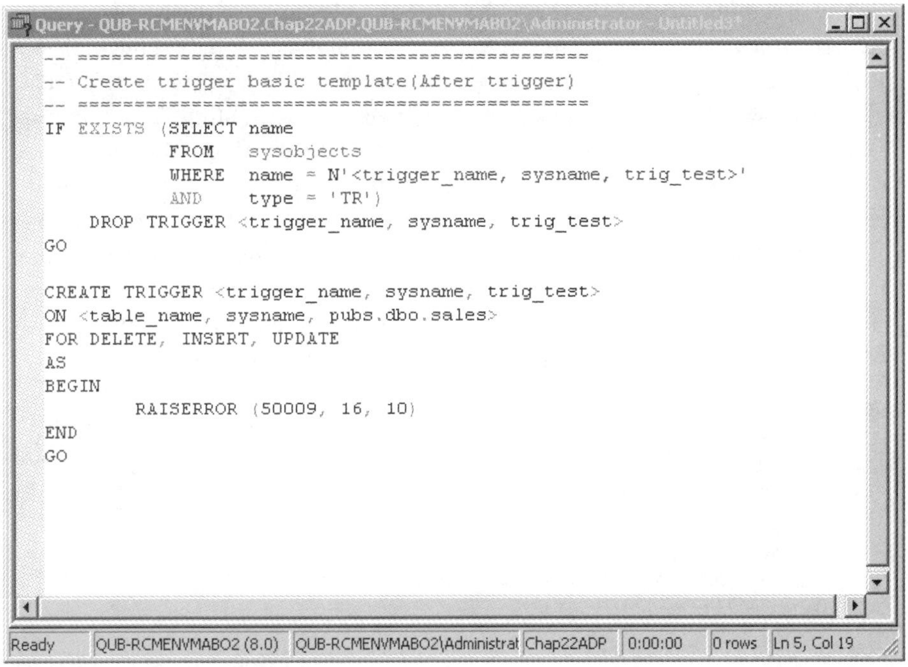

Query - QUB-RCMENVMABO2.Chap22ADP.QUB-RCMENVMABO2\Administrator - Untitled3*

```
-- =============================================
-- Create trigger basic template(After trigger)
-- =============================================
IF EXISTS (SELECT name
           FROM   sysobjects
           WHERE  name = N'<trigger_name, sysname, trig_test>'
           AND    type = 'TR')
    DROP TRIGGER <trigger_name, sysname, trig_test>
GO

CREATE TRIGGER <trigger_name, sysname, trig_test>
ON <table_name, sysname, pubs.dbo.sales>
FOR DELETE, INSERT, UPDATE
AS
BEGIN
        RAISERROR (50009, 16, 10)
END
GO
```

Ready | QUB-RCMENVMABO2 (8.0) | QUB-RCMENVMABO2\Administrat | Chap22ADP | 0:00:00 | 0 rows | Ln 5, Col 19

Figure 14-9. Trigger template

The trigger statement is as follows:

```
IF EXISTS (SELECT name
          FROM   sysobjects
   WHERE  name = N'tr_coname'
 . . . . . . .   AND     type = 'TR')
    DROP TRIGGER tr_coname
GO
CREATE TRIGGER tr_coname ON dbo.Customers
FOR INSERT,UPDATE
AS
BEGIN
Select CompanyName As NameInInserted From inserted
Select CompanyName As NameInDeleted From Deleted
Rollback Transaction
END
GO
Update dbo.Customers
Set CompanyName = 'Martin Reid Changed'
WHERE CustomerID = 'ANATR'
```

The first thing we do is to check the system tables to see if the trigger already exists. If it does, it is dropped (removed from the database). We then begin the CREATE TRIGGER statement by naming the trigger and indicating the table it is attached to. The Begin/End block is used to enclose the two SELECT statements into a transaction. The SELECT statements retrieve the data from the two virtual tables Inserted and Deleted. This statement is purely for illustrative purposes because it is not common practice to include statements that return data to the client using database triggers. The ROLLBACK TRANSACTION statement ensures that the update never actually takes place. The table is returned to its original state when the trigger fires. The UPDATE statement immediately follows the Transaction block. Figure 14-10 shows the results from executing this code.

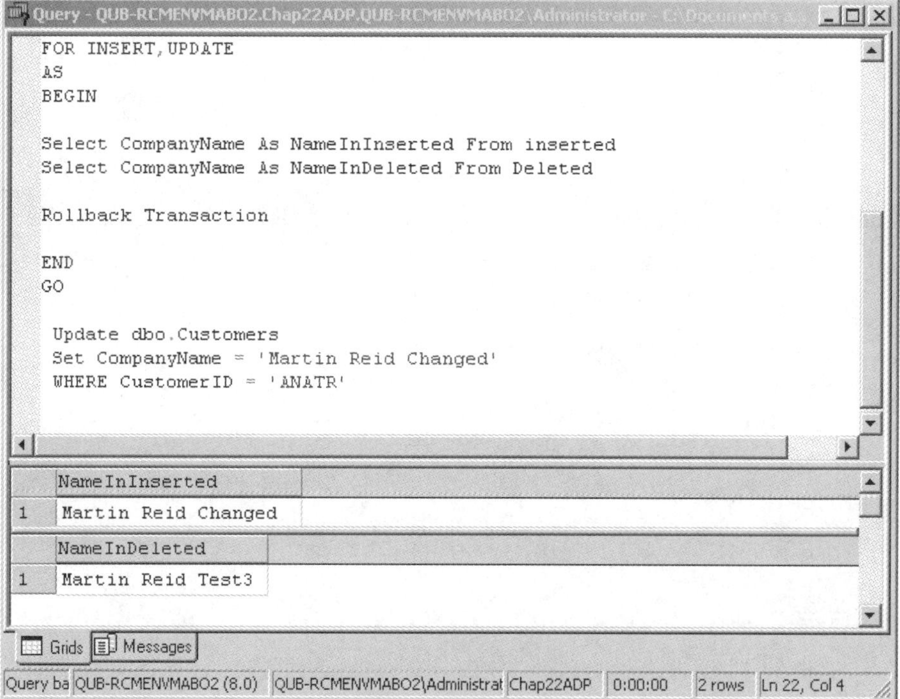

Figure 14-10. Running a trigger

We can also use triggers to check values of individual columns within a table. For example, we can create a trigger to check if a single column, CategoryName, is being updated in the category table. If the column is subject to an update, we can cancel the action. The way we do this is to use the T-SQL **UPDATE()** function (not to be confused with the UPDATE statement that we use to modify data).

```
CREATE TRIGGER tr_category on Categories for UPDATE as
BEGIN
if UPDATE(CategoryName)
begin
Raiserror ('The Category name cannot be Updated', 16, 16)
ROLLBACK
end
END
GO
update dbo.Categories
set CategoryName ='Changed'
where CategoryName = 'Beverages'
```

Figure 14-11 shows the results of running this statement in Query Analyzer.

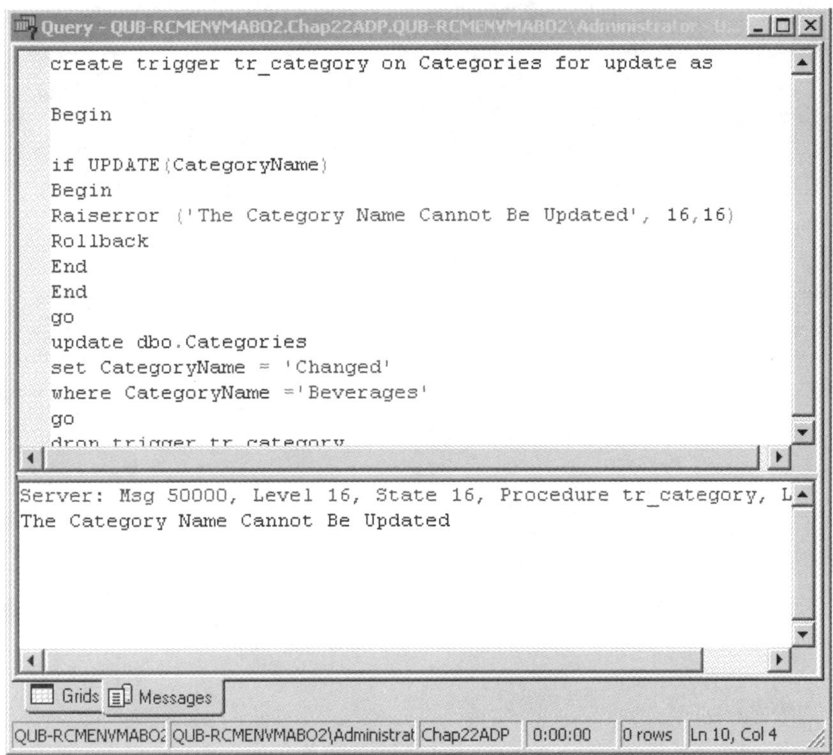

Figure 14-11. Checking column update with triggers

> **NOTE** *This is only a brief overview of triggers. Books Online provides further information on triggers.*

Now what has this to do with views? SQL Server 2000 introduced a new type of trigger: the Instead Of trigger. The name may give its function away, but, rather than executing the code in the INSERT, DELETE, UPDATE statement, the trigger will execute the code within the Instead Of trigger. The data from the original statements is placed into the virtual Inserted or Deleted tables, and we can then reference those values in the Instead Of trigger. Using this method to replace the standard of an Insert statement we can update data through views where normally this is not possible. One thing you need to watch out for using this method to update views is that values for all non-null fields, including Identity Primary Keys, must be provided to the statement. However, it is common practice to simply omit the incrementing value from the statement. SQL Server takes care of the rest.

The concept can be explained using a simple example of a non-updateable view. In this case, we will create a simple view of customers and their total orders. This results in a view that contains a derived column, Total_Orders. This view is usually not updateable. We will then use the view to add a new customer record to the Customer table.

Create the View

The following statement creates a view based on the Customers and Orders tables, vw_CustomerOrders:

```
CREATE VIEW dbo.vw_CustomerOrders
AS
SELECT
dbo.Customers.CompanyName, dbo.Customers.ContactName,
dbo.Customers.Address, dbo.Customers.City,
COUNT(dbo.Orders.OrderID) AS Total_Orders
FROM
dbo.Customers INNER JOIN
dbo.Orders ON dbo.Customers.CustomerID = dbo.Orders.CustomerID
GROUP BY dbo.Customers.CompanyName,
dbo.Customers.ContactName, dbo.Customers.Address, dbo.Customers.City
```

Create the Trigger

The trigger for the preceding view is created in the following manner:

```
CREATE TRIGGER  tr_customer on dbo.vw_CustomerOrders
INSTEAD OF INSERT
AS
BEGIN
```

```
INSERT INTO dbo.Customers
(CustomerID,CompanyName,Address,City)
SELECT CustomerID,CompanyName,Address,City
From INSERTED
END
```

Now, when we carry out an INSERT statement on the view, the code within the Instead Of trigger will be executed rather than the default insert. In this case, the values in the virtual Inserted table are used to carry out the INSERT statement. In this case, all the values with the exception of the Total_Order values are inserted as a new record into the Customers base table.

Finally, using Query Analyzer, create and execute the following INSERT statement:

```
INSERT INTO dbo.vw_CustomerOrders
(CUSTOMERID,CompanyName,ContactName,Address,City)
VALUES
('MREID','MartinReid','MWP Reid','Apress Ltd','Belfast')
```

Figure 14-12 shows the results. One row has been added to the table.

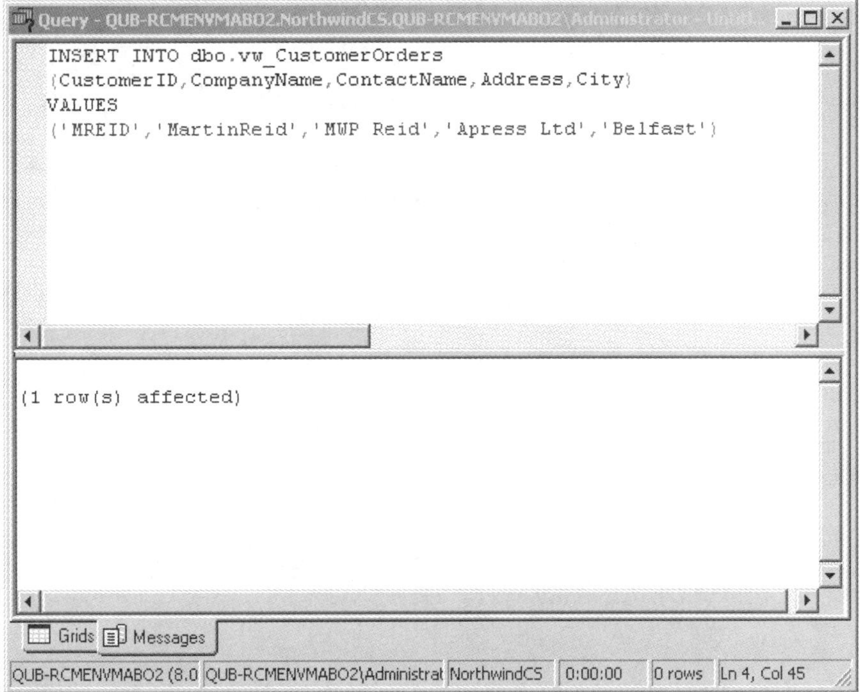

Figure 14-12. Inserting into a non-updateable view

Figure 14-13 shows the newly added row in the customer table within Access 2002.

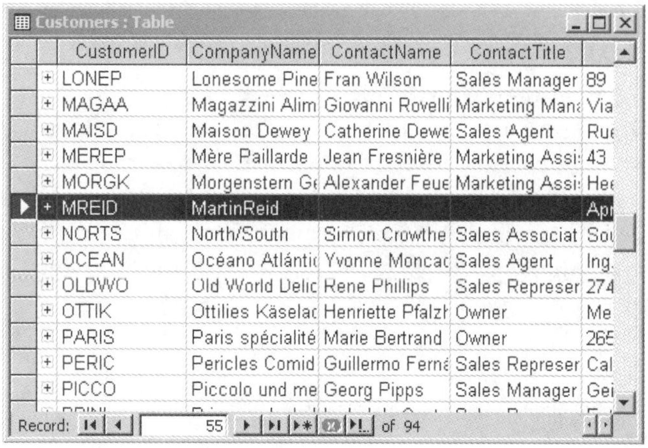

Figure 14-13. New entry in the Customers table

It is possible to create table triggers within the ADP itself, but this is restricted to tables only. To create a trigger on a table, within the database window:

1. Select the table required.
2. Right-click the mouse button.
3. Select Triggers from the shortcut menu.

Figure 14-14 shows the resulting dialog box.

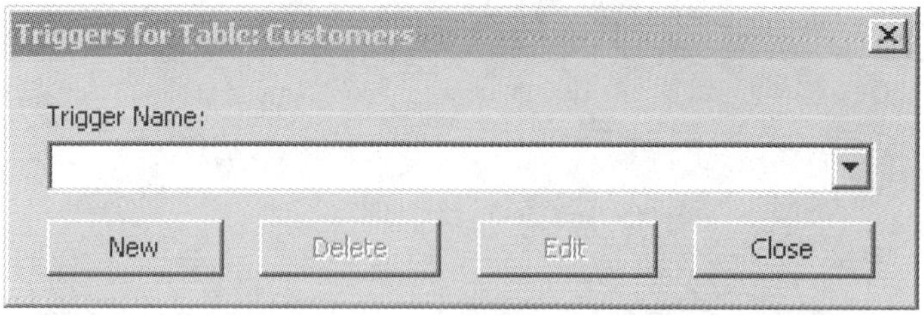

Figure 14-14. The Trigger dialog box in Access 2002

Existing triggers are available using the drop-down list. To create a new trigger, simply click on New.

Figure 14-15 shows the text template file that is used to create a trigger on the Customer table.

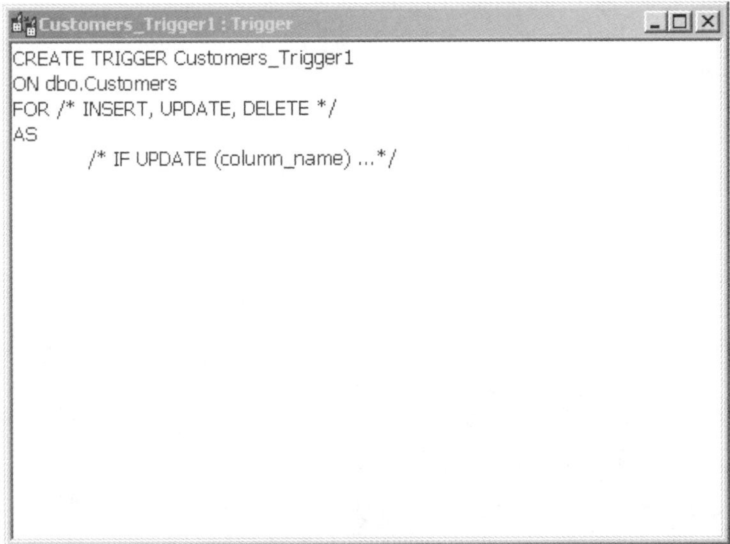

Figure 14-15. Access 2002 table trigger template

Instead Of triggers offer you a way around the limitations of views, particularly if your view includes derived values. As such, they are a powerful addition to the developer's toolbox.

As we have seen, a view provides you with another method of permitting your users to look at data. Rather than permit access to base tables, we can grant access to a view that hides the complexity of the underlying data structures. In these days of sophisticated user tools (such as Oracle Browser and Cognos Impromptu), the more complexity we can remove from our systems the better. We can use the new Instead Of triggers to permit updates using views. Although this has always been possible, the interception feature is new with SQL Server 2000.

I hope this chapter, which served as an introduction to the topic, has also wet your appetite for views. You should look into their use not only to make your own life easier but also to improve the interaction between your users and the database.

CHAPTER 15

SQL Server Structure

SQL Server versus Access 2002

THIS CHAPTER IS AN INTRODUCTION to SQL Server, highlighting some of the main differences between it and MS Access 2002. We will introduce several server topics including T-SQL and the new (to SQL Server 2000) features provided by SQL Server Query Analyzer. A full discussion of these topics is beyond a single chapter, and dozens of books are available, including the following published by Apress Code Centric: *T-SQL Programming with Stored Procedures and Triggers* and *Advanced Transact-SQL for SQL Server 2000.* All references to SQL Server in this and preceding chapters refer to SQL Server 2000.

Comparing Database and Server Properties

A common implementation model used by Access developers is the classic front-end/back-end configuration. The back-end or data tables are placed on a network server, and the front-end application file containing the user interface and other database objects are placed onto the users PC. This can lead to problems including slow data retrieval, corruption of entire databases, and increased coding work by the developer to compensate for this configuration. There is also the problem of issuing changes to the front-end "user application" and the back end.

> **NOTE** *I should also say that many developers on the AccessD Developers List achieve superb processing with the classic Access set up due to good programming practices and "bending" Access to areas where it was not meant to go. Some of the applications the members have running are very interesting. Search the AccessD archive (*`http://www.databaseadvisors.com`*) for "performance" to view the various discussions. Another fine resource for Access developers moving to SQL Server is the Access L List at* `http://peach.ease.lsoft.com/archives/access-l.html`*. Both AccessD and Access L are newsgroups that discuss Microsoft Access databases. AccessD differs from many of the normal Internet groups because it is wholly owned by the membership.*

Developers use several techniques and tricks to overcome this approach, including the widespread use of local tables to store frequently used data.

> **NOTE** *It is not possible to use local tables within an ADP. However, this limit could be overcome by using the ability of Access 2002 to link to other data stores. Using this method, we can use SQL Server Linked Server (link to tables in another SQL Server, ODBC DSN, Oracle, or other data store), or, based on a T-SQL function, link to other data stores including Access, ODBC file DSNs, Excel, text files, and Paradox and Dbase files.*

So what's the main problem with this setup? The problem is that all processing is performed locally on the user's PC, and none on the server. There is also the major concern of multiple processes writing to a single database file. The server acts as a shared storage area for the data files rather than a true client/server; it is in reality simply a file server.

In a large database, retrieving thousands of records can lead to massive network overhead as records are pulled down the wire to your users for local processing, and these users could be using anything from a PII 200 MHz to a P4 1.3GHz machine.

> **NOTE** *For example, if a single query retrieves 1,000 records from a table containing 100,000 records, all 100,000 records are pulled down the wire to the PC to run the query. If this query is popular or serves a common business need and every user has it open, it is not hard to picture the network traffic this one query is causing.*

Once we move on to using Access Data Projects as a front end to SQL Server, we move into a true client/server configuration. In one fell swoop, all processing is moved to the SQL Server database and the remote server. In the same way as a classic MS Access setup, each user is issued with a copy of the ADP or ADE. This move also allows us to take advantage of the general improvements to our applications that are inherent in using a database like SQL Server (such as query processing, stored procedures, and increased security).

> **NOTE** *An ADE is similar to an Access MDE file. Using an ADE prohibits users from "messing" with your code and design. All code modules within an ADE file are compiled and are therefore unreadable. If you do choose to take it, this route ensures that you retain a copy of the original ADP file. You will need it if you need to make any changes to the project.*

One of the other main advantages is the increased stability of SQL Server as a Web database. (We'll discuss this further in Chapter 19.) More and more organizations are requesting that their data is made available either via the Internet or an intranet. SQL Server provides a superb platform for running database information via the Web. SQL Server 2000 also includes new XML features including the ability to pass an SQL statement via a browser URL. Chapter 19 provides an introduction to using Access 2002 via the Web. Access has its uses, but, for a scalable solution, you must use a scalable database, and SQL Server fits the bill. Of course, this all depends on the client or business having the wherewithal to purchase, set up, and maintain an SQL Server installation. For those who do not, there is always MSDE, the cut-down version of SQL Server, but even Access should perform better because it is not "rigged" to reduce performance if more than eight concurrent threads are running. For applications with more than ten users, MS Access and Jet would be the tools I would use. However, if there were a future possibility of Web use and/or SQL Server, then MSDE and ADPs would be the preferred tools. However, some developers are of the opinion that MSDE will outperform Jet for certain applications.

In addition to using ADPs, two other methods are commonly used when working with SQL Server.

> **NOTE** *Linking and Pass-Through queries can be used with relational database systems such as Oracle, unlike ADPs, which are a technology that is unique to Access/SQL Server.*

We can, as in the standard file server approach, just simply link to the server tables using ODBC linked tables. However, ODBC is a technology that is coming to an end. Microsoft will no longer be developing ODBC, and OLEDB is now the recommended approach for data communications. ODBC also has problems of its own that can decrease the performance of your application. For example, all SQL statements must go through several translation processes before it arrives at the server in the correct dialect of SQL.

The other approach to using SQL Server is to use Pass-Through queries. A Pass-Through query is written in the server language and does not need to go through the Jet and ODBC translation process. Pass-Through queries can also be executed via code.

> **NOTE** *ADO is the recommended approach to all programming with Access Data Projects in Access 2002 and indeed all programming that does not involve the Jet database engine. When working with Jet, DAO can still be used. However, many developers—sensing the impending death of DAO and the Jet engine—have already begun migrating existing projects and writing new database projects using SQL Server and ADO as the preferred language for data access.*

Access Data Projects offer many advantages over both linked tables and SQL Pass-Through queries when working with SQL Server, such as:

- SQL Server and many of the server facilities can be accessed directly.
- SQL Server's Diagram tool—a very powerful and useful design tool—can also be accessed.
- Processing is moved onto the server.
- SQL Server security features are far superior to the built-in security of MS Access.
- Batch updates can be created. (Cache changes locally and then is submitted to the server as a batch.)
- Neither Jet nor ODBC are involved in any of the processes.

In effect, you are using MS Access as an application development tool for SQL Server 2000.

So, what are the disadvantages with ADPs?

- Developers will need to learn new processes, such as stored procedures, T-SQL, views, and SQL Server security.
- Existing applications may need to be rewritten if you're moving to SQL Server.
- Developers are restricted to working with SQL Server.
- In regards to backup systems, ADPs require systems that are more complicated than the usual MDB backup because we are now using SQL Server.

In many cases, the Access developer may be the main source of IT skills within a small to medium-sized business, and those of you who are contractors are expected to be all things to the customer. Undoubtedly, moving to SQL Server and ADPs will stretch you of that: there will be new things to learn and on a larger scale, just as there will be different ways of building applications, coding, and SQL.

System Databases

When working with Access, we are used to working with a single MDB file and its system tables. Of course, we also use library files, linked databases, and so forth. But the management of the individual database is usually performed using the system tables. System tables are contained within the MDB file and are normally hidden from the user.

When you move to SQL Server as the back end, you will be dealing with multiple databases and other objects that are used to manage your application. In this section, we will look at some of these databases and provide a brief explanation as to their purpose.

As you'll see, there is a little more to worry about than your single MDB file. Just remember that backup of the following databases is important, as is restricting access to "normal" users.

Master Database

This database contains information on all databases held on SQL Server. This includes information such as user logins, server configuration, data file location, and system stored procedures. We stress that you should always have a current backup of the master database. Just like system tables in Access, you shouldn't work with the master database directly unless you actually know what you are doing. In general, you should not add objects to the master database.

Model Database

The model database is the template database that all new databases are based on. It is useful if you have certain table designs, stored procedures, and so forth that you want to appear in every database that's created. Simply adding them to the model database ensures this.

Tempdb

This database is created when SQL Server starts and is destroyed when the server shuts down. Tempdb is a bit like a scratch pad to which all users have access. It is used to hold temporary tables and stored procedures, and any temporary space required for complex queries.

MSDB

This database stores information on backups and restores. It is important that you do not use this information. For example, if the MSDB is lost, then your backup and restore history data are gone as well. You will have to re-create this data manually. In addition, MSDB also stores information used by SQL Server Agent, including jobs, scheduling alerts, and maintaining information on operators.

Comparing SQL Server and MS Access 2002 Data Types

Another major difference between MS Access 2002 and SQL Server lies in the data types that each uses. You will find that most of the existing Access data types have an equivalent type in SQL Server and that there are some additional types. In addition, SQL Server provides you with a facility to define your own. Table 15-1 shows Access 2002 data types with the corresponding SQL Server 2000 data types.

Table 15-1. Access and SQL Server Data Types

ACCESS	SQL SERVER
Text	char, nchar, varchar, nvarchar
Memo	text, ntext
Byte	tinyint
Integer	smallint
Long Integer	integer
Single	real
Double	float
ReplicationID	uniqueidentifer
Decimal	decimal
Date/Time	smalldate, datetime, timestamp
Currency	smallmoney, money
Autonumber	int (remember to set the identity property to true)
Yes/No	Bit (Yes =1 and No = 0)
OLE Object	image
Hyperlink	None
None	Binary, varbinary

Figure 15-1 shows a page from the Upsizing Wizard report indicating how Access 2002 data types are translated to SQL Server 2000 using the wizard. Upsizing is discussed in Chapter 17 ("Upsizing Directly from Access").

Fields	Microsoft Access	SQL Server
Field Name:	Reference	Reference
Data Type:	Number (Long)	int
Field Name:	NameText	NameText
Data Type:	Text(25)	nvarchar(25)
Field Name:	CommentsMemo	CommentsMemo
Data Type:	Memo	text
Field Name:	DateOfBirth	DateOfBirth
Data Type:	Date/Time	datetime
Field Name:	Salary	Salary
Data Type:	Currency	money
Field Name:	AgeNumberLong	AgeNumberLong
Data Type:	Number (Long)	int
Field Name:	NumberByte	NumberByte
Data Type:	Byte	smallint
Field Name:	NumberInteger	NumberInteger
Data Type:	Number (Integer)	smallint
Field Name:	NumberSingle	NumberSingle
Data Type:	Number (Single)	real
Field Name:	NumberDouble	NumberDouble
Data Type:	Number (Double)	float
Field Name:	NumberDecimal	NumberDecimal
Data Type:	Decimal	decimal
Field Name:	OLEField	OLEField
Data Type:	OLE Object	image

Figure 15-1. Upsizing Wizard report

Transact SQL (T-SQL)

T-SQL is the language used for communication with an SQL Server database. To build professional applications, you should have a sound understanding of this version of SQL. T-SQL is an add-on to standard SQL, and in this section we will look at some general statements to get you started with this powerful language. I have used the term *add-on* because T-SQL provides statements and actions in addition to those common to SQL. This section is not meant to be a resource for T-SQL; rather, it's a starting point. Some useful books are available, and, of course, SQL Server Books Online provide you with a large amount of information on this subject. We will also use this section to introduce stored procedures, but not in any great detail (yet).

You will have to "redo" some major things in your Access SQL before the same scripts will run in SQL Server. For example, the following delimiters are used in SQL Server, and you will be required to amend your Access delimiters to meet this new requirement. Table 15-2 lists some of the most common delimiters you may encounter.

Table 15-2. Comparison of T-SQL Delimiters

DELIMITER	USE
T-SQL Date Delimiter	'
String Delimiter	'
Concatenation	+ - Many Access developers use this already.
Char Wildcard	% - Major source of query failure
Not Equal	!=, <>
Not Less Than	!<, >=
Not Greater Than	!>, <=

Mathematical operators are the same in both versions of SQL. Table 15-3 lists the more common operators.

Table 15-3. Mathematical Operators

OPERATOR	COMMENT
+	Addition
-	Subtraction
*	Multiplication
/	Division
%	Modulo
<	Less than
>	Greater than

SQL Server also supports the following logical operators:

- All
- AND
- BETWEEN
- EXISTS
- IN
- LIKE
- NOT
- OR

A simple example of a T-SQL shell is provided in Access 2002 when you begin to create a new text stored procedure. (We are not concerned with the technical details of stored procedures for the moment because stored procedures are covered in Chapter 16.) Access uses a basic template to assist you with some of the syntax that's required to create a stored procedure. For example, the following is the stored procedure template available from Query Builder in an Access Data Project.

> **NOTE** *The T-SQL color coding used in Access 2000 has been removed in Access 2002. (We have no idea why.) Color coding within code windows is a function that I personally found very useful.*

```
Create Procedure "Samplesp"
/*
   (
            @parameter1 datatype = default value,
            @parameter2 datatype  OUTPUT
)

*/


AS
      /*set NOCOUNT on */
      return
```

- "Create Procedure" (in the first line) are T-SQL keywords. I have overwritten the default SP name (generated by Access) replacing the procedure name with "Samplesp".
- /* and */ are begin and end comment tags. In this case, they comment out the syntax for creating parameters within a stored procedure.
- The AS keyword is always required and precedes your T-SQL statements.
- Set NOCOUNT ON instructs SQL Server not to return a count of the records returned by the stored procedure. Setting NOCOUNT OFF will return a count of the records returned by the stored procedure.

Setting NOCOUNT to OFF can improve the performance of a query over the network, especially when working via ADO. If you don't set NOCOUNT to OFF, you can encounter problems because ADO will return the number of records affected by multistatement stored procedures. This can lead to ADO assuming that your procedure has ended. When working with ADO, it is best to set NOCOUNT OFF and then back to ON just before the last statement in your procedure (the one that actually returns data), so that Access knows how many records are returned and can handle them properly. See SQL Server Books Online for a full listing of SET keywords.

Overview of T-SQL

Being an extension to standard SQL, T-SQL has many features that will be familiar to most Access developers (such as SELECT, INSERT, and UPDATE). In this section, we will look at some of the basic features of the language. We'll first cover most of the SQL required for this section. Chapters 14 and 16 cover stored procedures, functions, and views in greater detail. Let's start with a simple stored procedure containing a SELECT statement. For this example, I will use the Northwind example database that is included with SQL Server.

```
create procedure "EmployeeSalesByCounty"
AS
SELECT Employees.Country, Employees.LastName, Employees.FirstName
FROM Employees
ORDER BY Employees.LastName
```

So, what's so difficult? The only differences are the words *Create Procedure*, the procedure name, and the AS keyword before the SQL statement.

Next is another simple example again using the Northwind Customer table in a stored procedure. Following the stored procedure is the same SQL Select statement created using a standard Access 2002 MDB database for comparison. In this case, we are also using an alias for the CustForename and CustSurname columns and creating a simple inner join with the Contact table.

```
CREATE  PROCEDURE dbo.Customercontacts
AS
SELECT
dbo.tblCustomer.CustForename AS [First Name],
dbo.tblCustomer.CustSurname AS Surname,
dbo.tblcontact.forename AS Forename
FROM
dbo.tblCustomer INNER JOIN dbo.tblContact
ON dbo.tblCustomer.CustomerRef = dbo.tblContact.CustomerRef
```

The standard SQL statement is as follows:

```
SELECT
tblCustomer.CustForename AS [First Name],
 tblCustomer.CustSurname AS Surname,
 tblcontact.forename AS Forename
FROM
tblCustomer INNER JOIN
tblContact ON tblCustomer.CustomerRef
= tblContact.CustomerRef
```

NOTE *One difference that you'll notice is the owner prefix before each table name. With SQL Server, it is possible for two or more individuals to actually create a table with the same name. The only distinction is the table owner prefix. To ensure that we are connected to the correct SQL Server table, a prefix shows the table owner. (In this case, the owner is DBO.) It is recommended that the dbo owner owns all tables. The other small difference is the use of the square brackets in the stored procedure because of the use of the space in the column name. Although Microsoft uses spaces when naming table columns, it is advisable not to do so.*

> **TIP** *An important point to remember when developing Access Data Projects is that during development you will be logged into the server as a sysadmin with full rights on all objects. As a result, you do not need to use the tableowner.tablename format in your SQL. However, when your users come to open forms and reports, it is possible that those users who are not members of a sysadmin role will receive error messages. Prefixing your tablename with the table owner prefix is good practice, and you are encouraged to use it; it just might save you a lot of grief with the users (not to mention recoding time). If you don't use the dbo table prefix, the server will begin looking for the table using the current username as the prefix. For example, if Chris is the user, the server will look for Chris.tablename, then dbo.tablename. When developing Access Data Projects, always create a system role with full rights to SQL Server. Never develop using the default "sa" role.*

Another nice feature in Access 2002 is the Verify SQL Syntax option that's available from the Query Design window. Select Query—Verify SQL Syntax from the drop-down menu. (See Figure 15-2.) This tool will check the syntax of your SQL against the target SQL Server database. In this section, we will confine ourselves to looking at some of the main differences and extensions found in T-SQL.

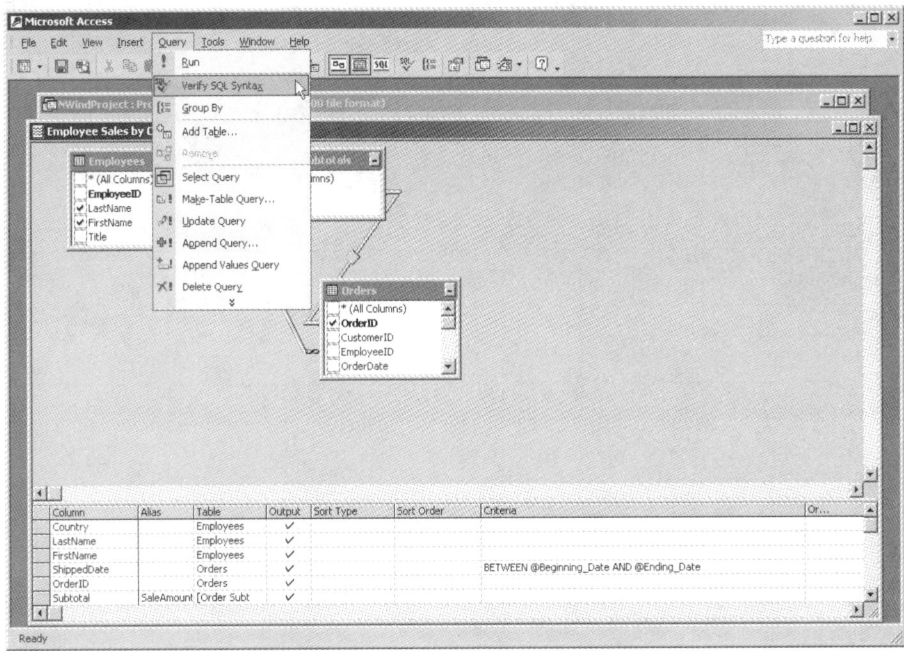

Figure 15-2. Verify SQL syntax

Working with Null Values in T-SQL

Null is not the same as *blank;* rather, Null is used to indicate that a value is missing or unknown. For example, a customer telephone number may be unknown (that is, a Null value). The following SQL statement will return all records with a missing telephone number:

```
SELECT name
FROM company
WHERE
Company.telephone IS NULL
```

Two functions are available when working with Null values and ADPs: ISNULL and NULLIF. The ISNULL function allows you to replace a Null value with something more meaningful. For example, rather than display a blank field, you can output some descriptive text. Figure 15-3 shows a simple stored procedure that selects data from the Northwind Customer table. Note the text "No City Data". This is produced using the ISNULL function to replace the Null City field. To get some data that includes the "No City Data" item, you may need to delete some of the city field data from the table.

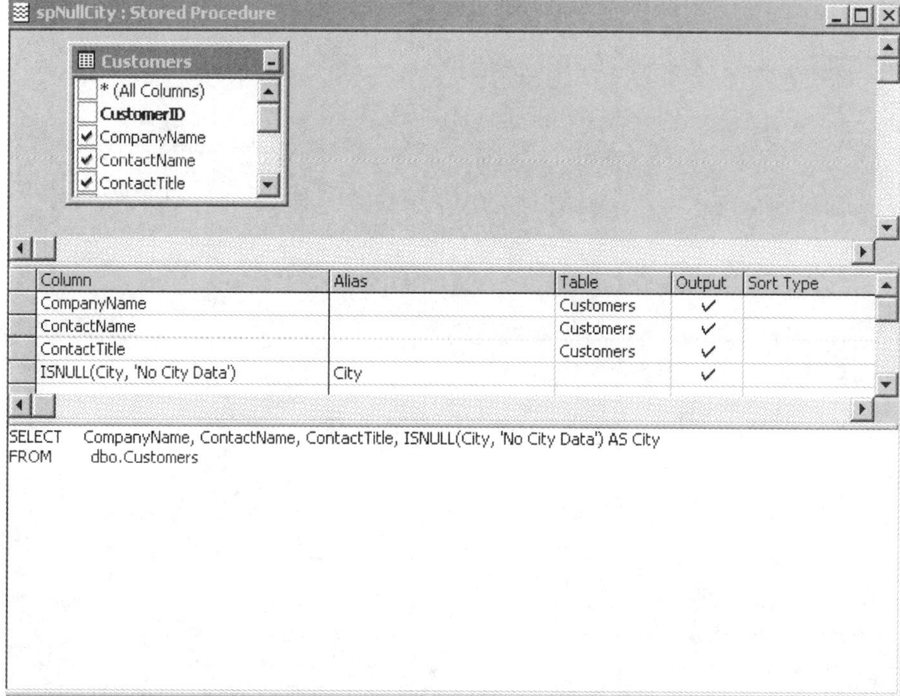

Figure 15-3. Using ISNULL

ISNULL can also be used in aggregate functions to replace missing or null values. For example, Figure 15-4 shows the use of ISNULL and AVG. In this example, I have retrieved some unit prices from the Products table in the Northwind database. With the unit price removed, the average product price is £27.82 using a simple AVG(Unitprice). However, when we use the ISNULL function with the AVG function, the average price changes to £25.29. This is a simple illustration, but it shows some of the problems related to Null values. In reality, it is highly unlikely that you would permit Null values in a Product Price field.

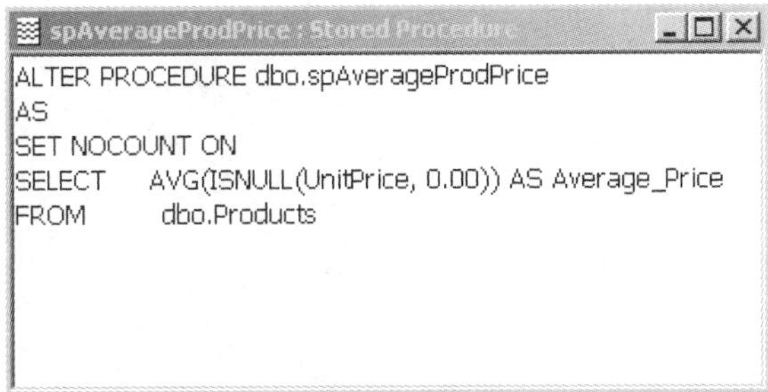
spAverageProdPrice : Stored Procedure
ALTER PROCEDURE dbo.spAverageProdPrice
AS
SET NOCOUNT ON
SELECT AVG(ISNULL(UnitPrice, 0.00)) AS Average_Price
FROM dbo.Products

Figure 15-4. ISNULL and AVG functions

The ISNULL function replaces the VBA function Nz. Watch out for this because it is common to make mistakes in its use.

The NULLIF function is used to replace values with nulls. For example, if the UnitPrice field contained a Zero field, we could use the NULLIF function to convert 0 to Null. This can be very useful because Null values are excluded when using aggregate functions.

Using Control Structures with T-SQL

Just like a standard programming language, T-SQL provides instructions that can be used to control the flow of program instructions, such as:

IF THEN ELSE

BEGIN END

CASE

WHILE

WAITFOR

> **NOTE** *At times, programmers are required to place a delay into program execution. The WAITFOR keyword provides the means to do this in SQL Server. Also note that these keywords are not part of the SQL standards.*

IF THEN ELSE is used in the same way as in VBA with one difference: only one line of code following the statement is executed. If execution of more than one statement is required (you have more than one condition), you must enclose all the statements in the ELSE block with BEGIN and END. The BEGIN and END group your statements into an execution block. Should the IF statement evaluate as FALSE and you have not used BEGIN/END, then the entire block of statement is bypassed.

The syntax for BEGIN/END is:

```
BEGIN
    {
        sql_statement
        | statement_block
    }
END
```

The following example will insert a new record into the Company table. In addition to the columns inserted, we can also use GETDATE() to include the current date

```
CREATE PROCEDURE usp_AddCompany
@CompanyName
@Address1
@Town
AS
BEGIN
    Declase @todaysDate datetime
    SELECT @todaysdate = GetDate() /* returns the current date
    INSERT INTO Company(CompanyName,Address1,Town,Date)
    VALUES(@CompanyName,@Address1,@Town,@todaysdate)
RETURN
END
```

If you are using only a single statement following the IF statement, the BEGIN/END keywords are not required.

CASE

Rather than using CASE to control program execution as is common with VBA, CASE is used in T-SQL to evaluate a list of options and return an alternative value:

```
CASE input_expression
 WHEN when_expression THEN result_Eespression
  [..n]
 [
 ELSE else_result_expression
 ]
END
```

For example:

```
SELECT FirstName, LastName,
   CASE County
      WHEN 'Ant' THEN 'Antrim'
      WHEN 'Fer' THEN 'Fermanagh'
      WHEN 'Tyr' THEN 'Tyrone'
      ELSE County
      END AS County
FROM dbo.Employee
ORDER BY LastName
```

Figure 15-5 shows the results of executing this statement. In the preceding example, the CASE keyword simply replaced the column values with a more descriptive output. It is important to note the ELSE clause. Use of the ELSE clause will catch all columns that do not match the values within the CASE statement. For values other than those referenced using a WHEN/THEN line, the ELSE clause causes the County column as held in the table to be displayed unchanged.

Figure 15-5 shows a simple CASE statement executed in Access 2002. This statement returns the continent of a customer based on the city in which they are located. For instance, "Madrid" will return "Europe".

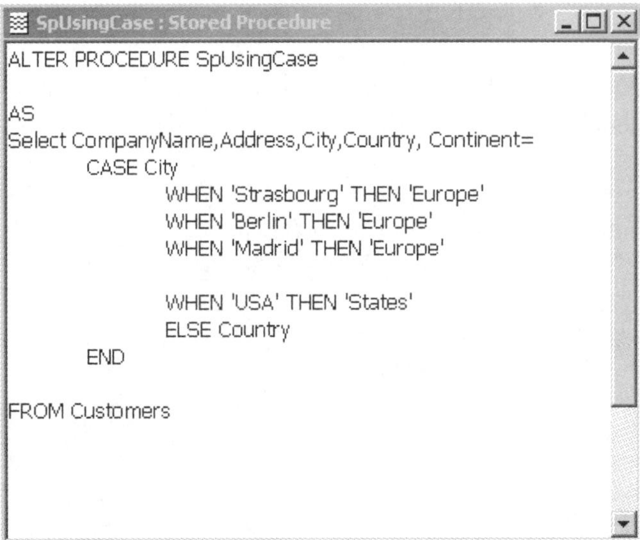
SpUsingCase : Stored Procedure

```
ALTER PROCEDURE SpUsingCase

AS
Select CompanyName,Address,City,Country, Continent=
        CASE City
                WHEN 'Strasbourg' THEN 'Europe'
                WHEN 'Berlin' THEN 'Europe'
                WHEN 'Madrid' THEN 'Europe'

                WHEN 'USA' THEN 'States'
                ELSE Country
        END

FROM Customers
```

Figure 15-5. Access 2002 CASE statement

Figure 15-6 shows the result of running the uspUsingCase stored procedure. Note the two highlighted rows where the Continent field has been changed to "Europe".

SpUsingCase : Stored Procedure

CompanyName	Address	City	Country	Continent
Alfreds Futterkiste	Obere Str. 57		Germany	Germany
Ana Trujillo Emparedados y helados	Avda. de la Cor	México D.F.	Mexico	Mexico
Antonio Moreno TaqueriA	Mataderos 231	México D.F.	Mexico	Mexico
Around the Horn	120 Hanover Sc	Belfast	UK	UK
Berglunds snabbköp	Berguvsvägen {	Stockholm	Sweden	Sweden
Blauer See Delikatessen	Forsterstr. 57	Mannheim	Germany	Germany
Blondel père et fils	24, place Klébe	Strasbourg	France	Europe
Bólido Comidas preparadas	C/ Araquil, 67	Madrid	Spain	Europe
Bon app'	12, rue des Bou	Marseille	France	France
Bottom-Dollar Markets	23 Tsawassen I	Tsawassen	Canada	Canada
Test1	TestAddress	New London	Antrim	Antrim
Cactus Comidas para llevar	Cerrito 333	Buenos Aires	Argentina	Argentina
Centro comercial Moctezuma	Sierras de Grar	México D.F.	Mexico	Mexico
Chop-suey Chinese	Hauptstr. 29	Bern	Switzerland	Switzerland

Record: 7 of 90

Figure 15-6. Output from uspUsingCase

WHILE

The WHILE keyword is used within T-SQL to control looping. It controls the loop while a particular statement or value holds true. Within a loop, the WHILE keyword is controlled with the keywords CONTINUE and BREAK.

BREAK causes an exit from the innermost loop, and CONTINUE causes the loop to continue back at the comparison without executing any more of the statements in the loop. Any statements after the CONTINUE keyword are ignored. Figure 15-7 shows a simple example of a WHILE loop that incorporates all three keywords.

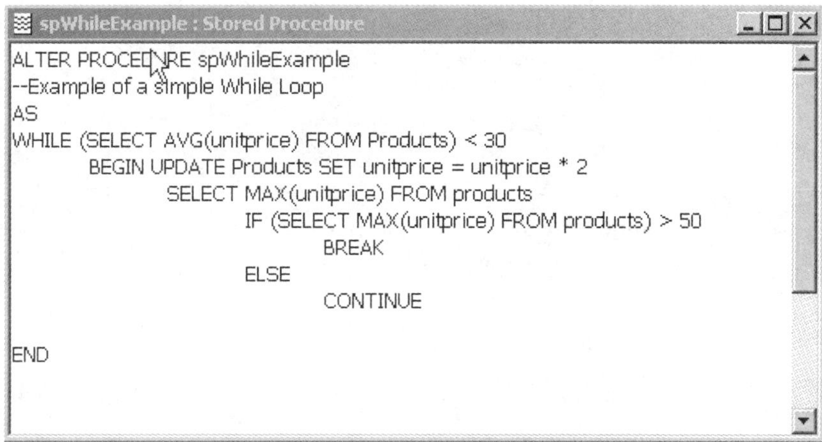

spWhileExample : Stored Procedure
ALTER PROCEDURE spWhileExample
--Example of a simple While Loop
AS
WHILE (SELECT AVG(unitprice) FROM Products) < 30
BEGIN UPDATE Products SET unitprice = unitprice * 2
SELECT MAX(unitprice) FROM products
IF (SELECT MAX(unitprice) FROM products) > 50
BREAK
ELSE
CONTINUE
END

Figure 15-7. Using WHILE

This procedure simply loops through the Products table where the average price is less than £30. When the average price meets the criteria, the unit price is doubled (unitprice=unitprice*2). The process continues until the MAX(unitprice) is greater than £50. The code then exits.

WAITFOR

WAITFOR will pause execution of your SQL statement for a specific time period. For example, the following statement pauses T-SQL for twenty seconds:

```
WAITFOR DELAY '000:00:20'
```

Figure 15-8 shows a simple example that delays for twenty seconds and executes a stored procedure. In this case, the T-SQL is executed using Query Analyzer in SQL Server.

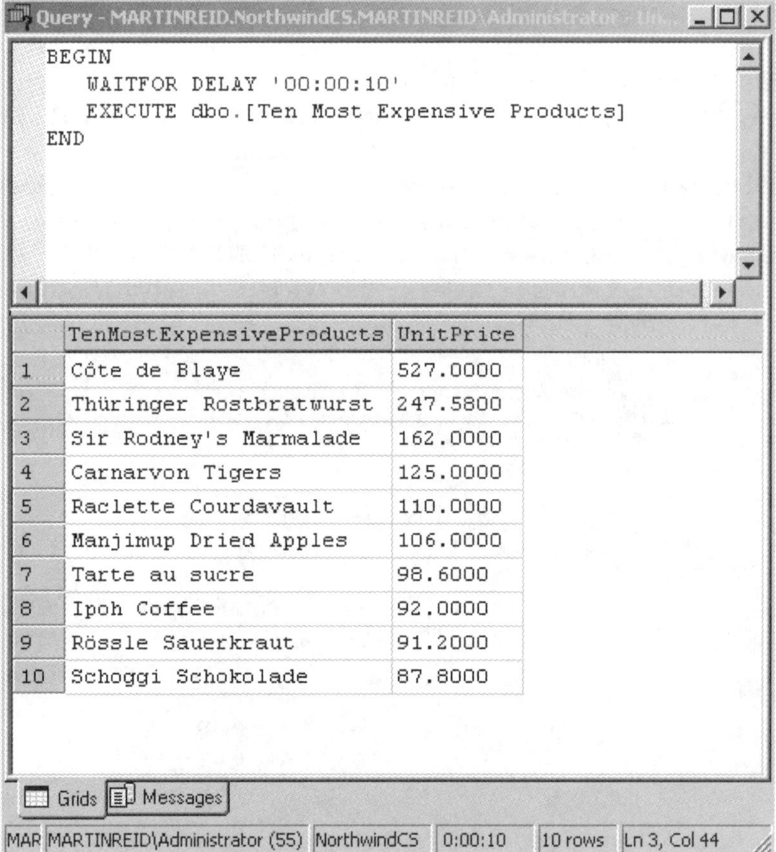

Figure 15-8. WAITFOR

SQL Server Built-in Functions

Many functions are available in SQL Server. Some will already be familiar to you from your work with Access, and others will be new. In this section, we will look at some of the more common built-in functions and introduce user-defined functions.

Functions can be of two types: deterministic functions (which always return the same result any time they are called with a specific set of input values) and nondeterministic functions (which may return different results each time they are called with a specific set of input values).

As you will see, a function such as **GETDATE()** is nondeterministic because it returns a different value each time it is called, that is, the current date. **DATEADD** is deterministic because it always returns the same result for any set of values passed to the three parameters.

Date Functions

SQL Server has many built-in date functions, many of which you will be familiar with.

Several of the SQL date functions match existing date functions within MS Access. We will look at some of the more common functions available.

> **NOTE** *As you know, a date is not simply stored as a date; it also includes a time portion. You will need to be careful with this in SQL Server, and we will look at the date data type in some detail. This will also have an effect on upsizing operations because many upsizing failures center around dates.*

Date functions in SQL Server have several differences from Access. For example, DATEPART works just like its Access equivalent: it returns the required part of a date (the specified date part). Table 15-4 shows a listing of the options available when using the DATEPART function.

> **NOTE** *For those upsizing an existing Access MDB file, the Upsizing wizard will convert all of the listed functions to the T-SQL equivalent.*

Table 15-4. Components of the DATEPART Function

DESCRIPTION	SYNTAX
Year	yyyy
Month	mmm, mm
Quarter	qq, q
Day	dd, d
Week	ww, wk
Hour	hh
Minute	mi, n
Second	ss, s

Table 15-5 lists Access date functions with corresponding SQL Server functions and a simple demonstration of use.

Table 15-5. Access and SQL Server Function Comparison

ACCESS	SQL SERVER	USAGE
Day()	**DATEPART(dd, date)**	SELECT DATEPART (dd, datefield)
Weekday()	**DATEPART(dw, date)**	SELECT DATEPART(dw, datefield)
Month()	**DATEPART(m, date)**	SELECT DATEPART(mm, datefield)
Date()	**Convert GETDATE()**	SELECT CONVERT (varchar, GETDATE(),101)
Now()	**GETDATE()**	SELECT GETDATE()
Month()	**Datepart(mm, datefield)**	SELECT Datepart(mm, GETDATE())

String Functions

Table 15-6 shows a range of string functions that are available when using an Access Data Project.

Table 15-6. T-SQL and Access String Functions

ACCESS	SQL	COMMENTS
UCase	**UPPER(ContactName)**	Converts the target string to uppercase
LCASE	**LOWER(ContactName)**	Returns the target string as lowercase
LTRIM	**LTRIM(Contactname)**	Removes leading spaces from the target string
RTRIM	**RTRIM(ContactName)**	Removes trailing spaces from the target string
LEN	**LEN(ContactName)**	Returns the length of the target string
RIGHT	**RIGHT(ContactName, 6)**	Returns the six characters from the right side of the string
LEFT	**LEFT(ContactName, 4)**	Returns the four characters from the left side of the string
TRIM	N/A	(Use a combination of **Ltrim** and **Rtrim**.)

Figure 15-9 shows a range of string functions created in Access' Query Builder.

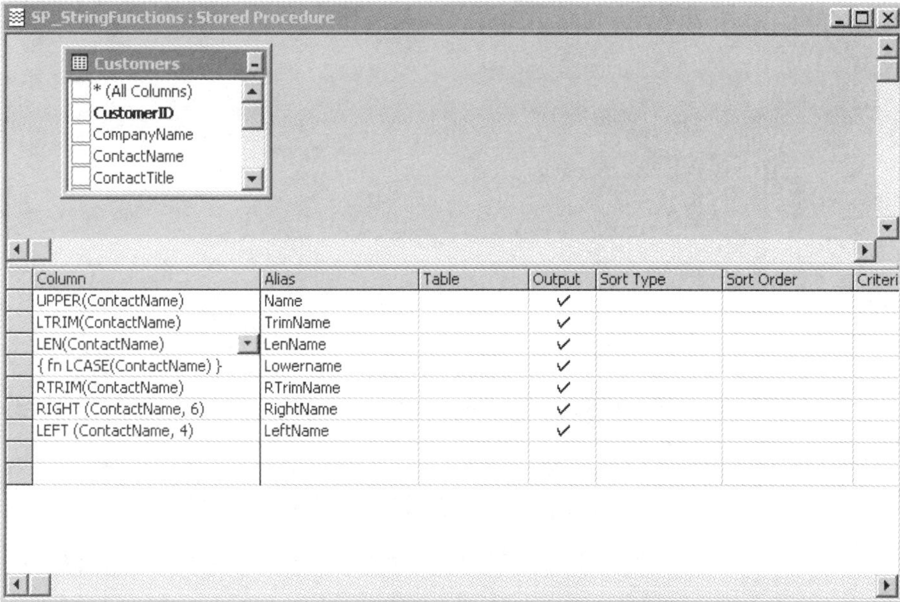

Figure 15-9. Using string functions

Figure 15-10 displays the result of executing this stored procedure.

usp_StringFunctions : Stored Procedure

Name	TrimName	lenName	LowerName	RTrimName	RightName	LeftName
MARIA ANDERS	Maria Anders	12	maria anders	Maria Anders	Anders	Mari
ANA TRUJILLO	Ana Trujillo	12	ana trujillo	Ana Trujillo	ujillo	Ana
ANTONIO MORENO	Antonio Moreno	14	antonio moreno	Antonio Moreno	Moreno	Anto
THOMAS HARDY	Thomas Hardy	12	thomas hardy	Thomas Hardy	Hardy	Thom
CHRISTINA BERGLUND	Christina Berglund	18	christina berglund	Christina Berglund	rglund	Chri
HANNA MOOS	Hanna Moos	10	hanna moos	Hanna Moos	a Moos	Hann
FRÉDÉRIQUE CITEAUX	Frédérique Citeaux	18	frédérique citeaux	Frédérique Citeaux	iteaux	Fréd
MARTÍN SOMMER	Martín Sommer	13	martín sommer	Martín Sommer	Sommer	Mart
LAURENCE LEBIHAN	Laurence Lebihan	16	laurence lebihan	Laurence Lebihan	ebihan	Laur
ELIZABETH LINCOLN	Elizabeth Lincoln	17	elizabeth lincoln	Elizabeth Lincoln	incoln	Eliz
VICTORIA ASHWORTH	Victoria Ashworth	17	victoria ashworth	Victoria Ashworth	hworth	Vict
PATRICIO SIMPSON	Patricio Simpson	16	patricio simpson	Patricio Simpson	impson	Patr
FRANCISCO CHANG	Francisco Chang	15	francisco chang	Francisco Chang	Chang	Fran
YANG WANG	Yang Wang	9	yang wang	Yang Wang	g Wang	Yang
PEDRO AFONSO	Pedro Afonso	12	pedro afonso	Pedro Afonso	Afonso	Pedr
ELIZABETH BROWN	Elizabeth Brown	15	elizabeth brown	Elizabeth Brown	Brown	Eliz
SVEN OTTLIEB	Sven Ottlieb	12	sven ottlieb	Sven Ottlieb	ttlieb	Sven
JANINE LABRUNE	Janine Labrune	14	janine labrune	Janine Labrune	abrune	Jani
ANN DEVON	Ann Devon	9	ann devon	Ann Devon	Devon	Ann
ROLAND MENDEL	Roland Mendel	13	roland mendel	Roland Mendel	Mendel	Rola
ARIA CRUZ	Aria Cruz	9	aria cruz	Aria Cruz	a Cruz	Aria
DIEGO ROEL	Diego Roel	10	diego roel	Diego Roel	o Roel	Dieg
MARTINE RANCÉ	Martine Rancé	13	martine rancé	Martine Rancé	Rancé	Mart
MARIA LARSSON	Maria Larsson	13	maria larsson	Maria Larsson	arsson	Mari
PETER FRANKEN	Peter Franken	13	peter franken	Peter Franken	ranken	Pete
CARINE SCHMITT	Carine Schmitt	14	carine schmitt	Carine Schmitt	chmitt	Cari
PAOLO ACCORTI	Paolo Accorti	13	paolo accorti	Paolo Accorti	ccorti	Paol
LINO RODRIGUEZ	Lino Rodriguez	14	lino rodriguez	Lino Rodriguez	iguez	Lino
EDUARDO SAAVEDRA	Eduardo Saavedra	16	eduardo saavedra	Eduardo Saavedra	avedra	Edua
JOSÉ PEDRO FREYRE	José Pedro Freyre	17	josé pedro freyre	José Pedro Freyre	Freyre	José

Record: 1 of 91

Figure 15-10. Output using string functions

For comparison purposes, Figure 15-11 shows the same stored procedure in SQL Server.

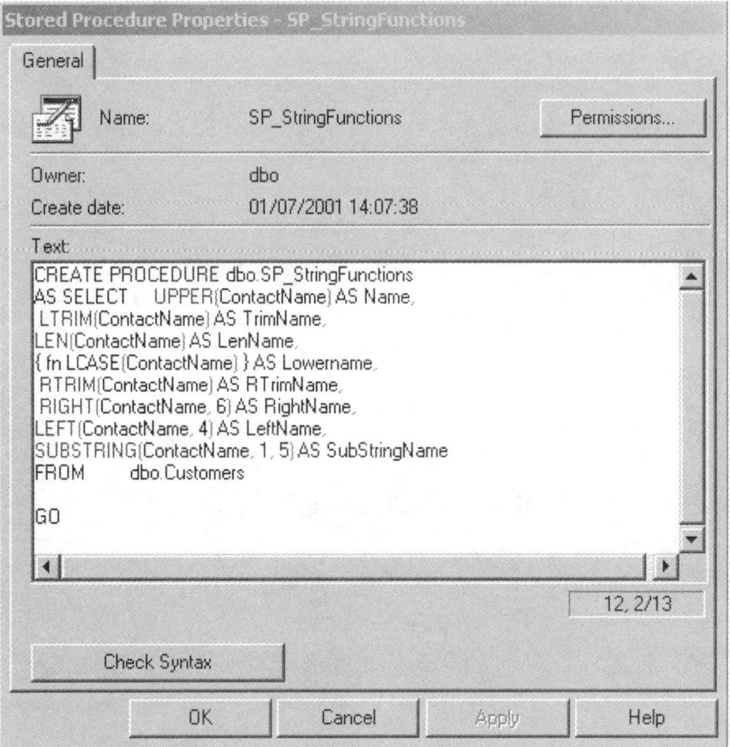

Figure 15-11. String functions using a stored procedure

When working with ADPs, you may (from habit) use an Access function rather than the T-SQL equivalent. For example, entering "Lcase (fieldname)" is not a T-SQL function when used within an ADP. However, Access will permit you to use it within a stored procedure. In this case, the Access function will be translated to its ODBC function equivalent. The syntax of which is:

```
SELECT {fn LCASE(fieldname)} FROM table.
```

Note the addition of the opening brace, the text "fn", and a closing brace. **Lcase** is a valid ODBC function, and Access will convert it to assist you in the migration path to SQL Server. However, you should at all times use the T-SQL syntax for functions. Figure 15-11 includes an example of this behavior with functions. The T-SQL lower function works in much the same way as its Access equivalent. "LOWER(fieldname)" will return the specified fieldname in lowercase.

Working with Dates and the Convert Function

Conversion Functions

Table 15-7 lists the various conversion functions available within SQL Server.

Table 15-7. SQL Server Conversion Functions

ACCESS	SQL SERVER
Ccur(x)	**CONVERT(money,x)**
Cdbl(x)	**CONVERT(float,x)**
Cint(x)	**CONVERT(smallint,x)**
Clng(x)	**CONVERT(int,x)**
Csng(x)	**CONVERT(real,x)**
Cstr(x)	**CONVERT(varchar,x)**
Cvdate(x)	**CONVERT(datetime,x)**

The convert functions will convert one data type to another and are particularly useful when working with date/time data types. They take the following form:

```
CONVERT (datatype,[(length)], expression [, style])
```

The elements of the convert function are broken down and explained in the following list:

- *Datatype:* data type to convert to
- *Length:* length
- *Expression:* valid SQL Server expression (for example, From tablename)
- *Style:* Optional (useful to format date to specific requirements)

You will find the convert function useful when working with date/time data types. In Access, many functions use values or return values of different data types; Access will convert the data types for you. This facility is not available with T-SQL, and you must perform the conversion yourself using the convert function.

For example, Figure 15-12 shows the output from a simple SELECT statement on the NorthwindCS Orders table.

Figure 15-12. Using the convert function

The server returns both date and time because this is the value held in the column

```
1996-07-04 00:00:00.000
```

using the convert function to change the SQL to read

```
SELECT CONVERT(varchar(8), orderdate, 1)from orders
```

Figure 15-13 shows the new output using this convert function to format the date. The function has been executed in SQL Server Query Anayzer.

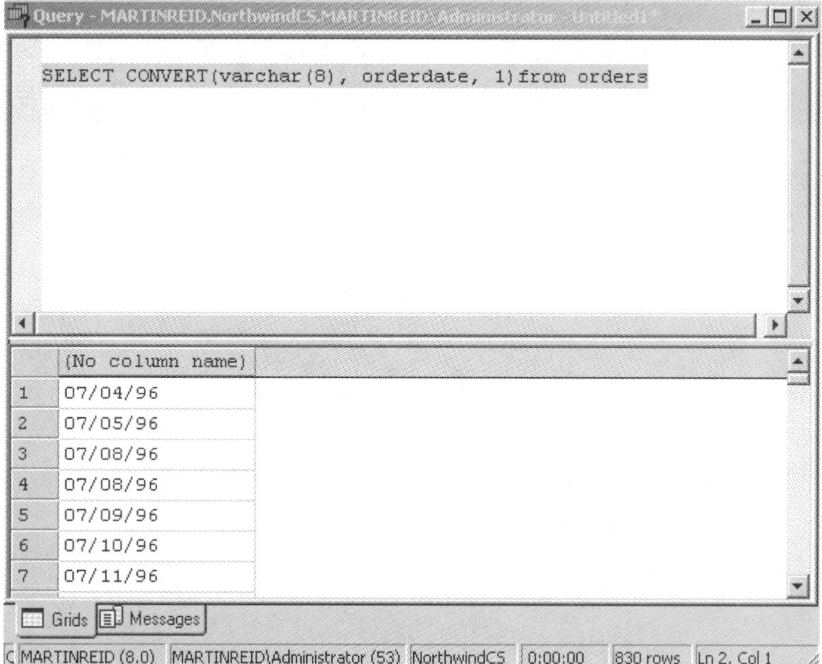

Figure 15-13. Date format using the convert function

> **NOTE** *The result is more presentable as the time portion of the date value has been removed. However, when using dates within Access, it is advisable to use the raw date value and format the control using the control properties. Using functions within forms to convert the date will result in Access* interpreting *the field as a calculated control and thus making the field non-updateable.*

Changing the style component of the convert function, we can reformat the date (in this case, to a UK date format). Figure 15-14 shows the results of changing the style digit from 1 to 3.

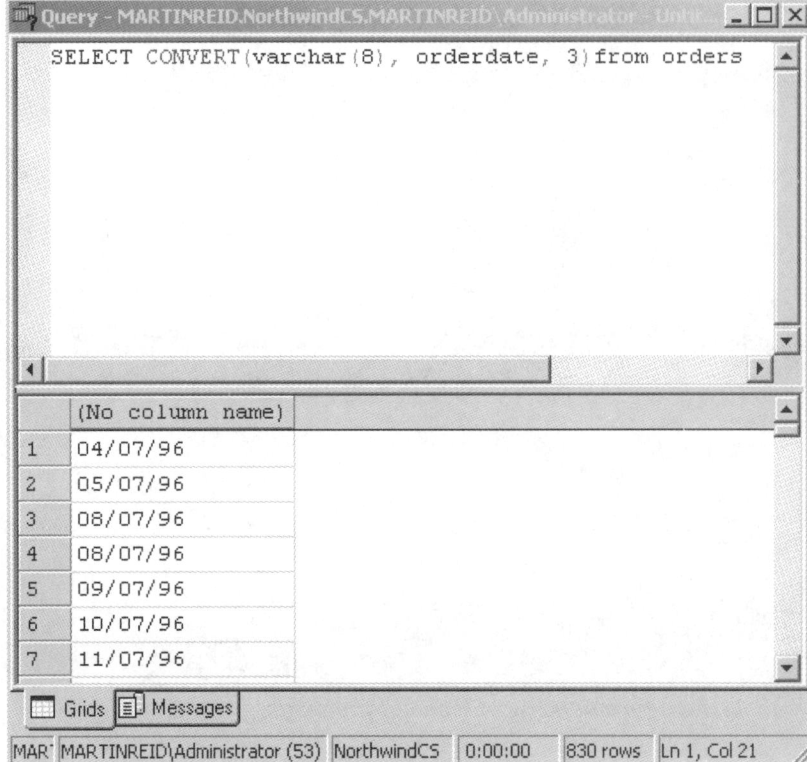

Figure 15-14. Using the convert function to change data output

See Books Online for a full description of the convert function as well as a full list of implicit and explicit data conversions.

For completeness, Figure 15-15 shows the convert function used in Access 2002.

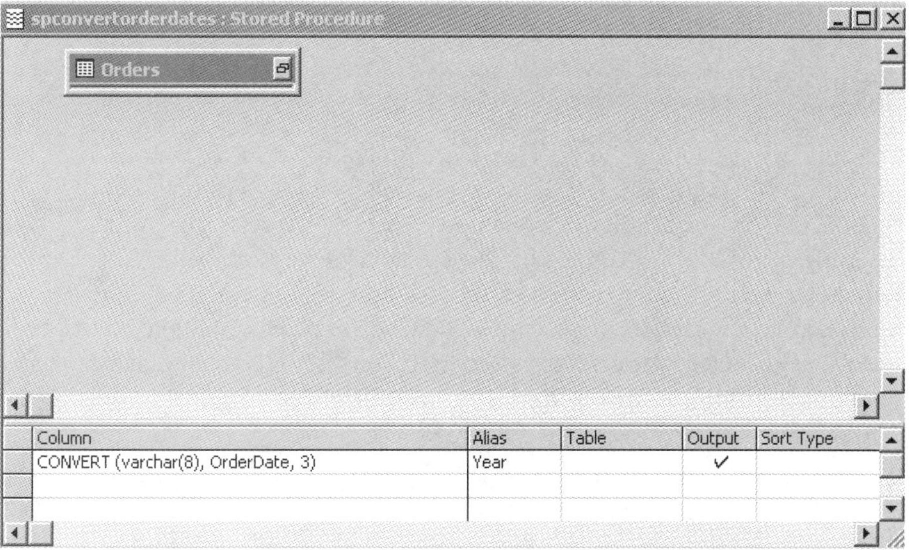

Figure 15-15. The convert function within Access 2002

Mathematical Functions

Table 15-8 shows some common Access functions and their equivalent in SQL Server.

Table 15-8. Common Access Functions and Their SQL Server Equivalents

ACCESS	SQL SERVER
Int(x)	FLOOR(x)
Sgn(x)	SIGN(x)
Rnd(x)	ROUND(x)

SQL Server @@ System Functions

In addition to the prior functions, SQL Server also contains many functions whose purpose it is to return information about the particular instance of the server. Many of these functions are very useful, and some are absolutely necessary to the correct performance of your application. The techie name for these functions is "Niladic," and the non-techie definition is "functions that do not take parameters."

Examples

@@IDENTITY

This function will return the last Identity column entered into a table as the result of an INSERT or a SELECT INTO statement. If there is no Identity column, **@@IDENTITY** returns NULL. For example, Figure 15-17 shows the results of inserting a single record into the Employees table of the Northwind ADP. Remember that this function reports for the entire database, so the value returned may not be the one you expected. If you're doing a multiple insert into more than one table, the identity returned will be that created for the most recent insert. To view this example, you must set NOCOUNT ON. Figure 15-16 shows the syntax of the stored procedure in Access 2002.

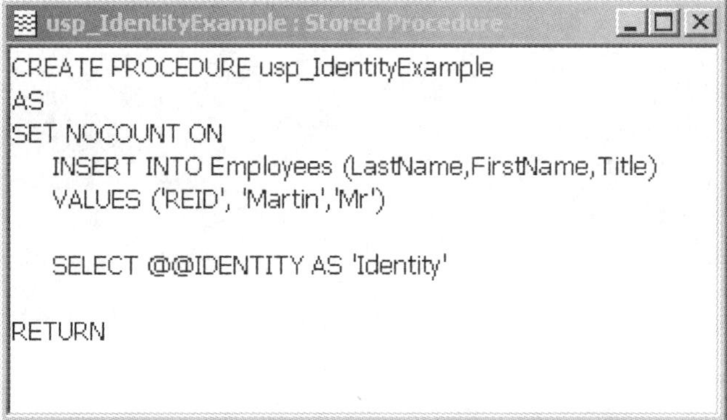

Figure 15-16. Using ***@@IDENTITY***

The result of this stored procedure is shown in Figure 15-17, which displays the Primary Key value from the insert.

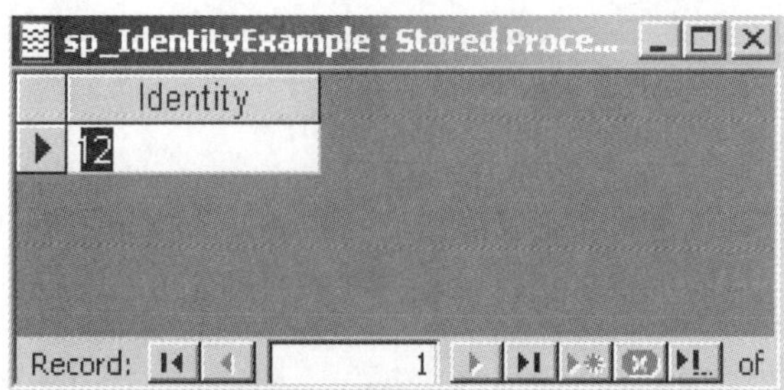

Figure 15-17. Results of using ***@@IDENTITY***

Failure to set the NOCOUNT ON will not inhibit the execution of the statement. In this case, the statement will execute and the record will be inserted, but Access will report with the message shown in Figure 15-18.

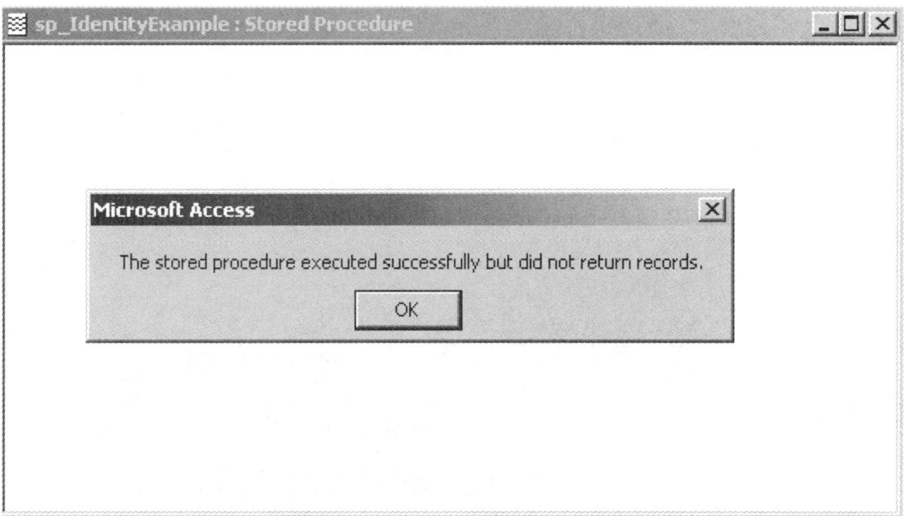

Figure 15-18. Access 2002 response

Another way to return the identity value (and one that is preferred by many SQL Server 2000 developers and recommended by Microsoft) is to use the **SCOPE_IDENTITY()** function. **@@Identity** will return the last Identity column from any insert. **SCOPE_IDENTITY()**, new to SQL Server 2000, does the same thing but—and it's an important *but*—it returns the Identity column from the current scope of the context in which it is called. For example, if you where doing an insert into Table A that contained a trigger to insert a record into Table B, using **@@Identity** would return the value inserted into table B. On the other hand, **SCOPE_IDENTITY** returns the identity from the original INSERT statement, in this case Table A.

SQL Server also introduced another function, **IDENT_CURRENT()**, which will return the Identity column for a specific table irrespective of scope. All three functions are called in the same way.

```
SELECT @@Identity
SELECT SCOPE_IDENTITY()
SELECT IDENT_CURRENT (tablename)
```

@@ERROR

@@ERROR returns the error number for the last T-SQL statement executed. All errors are defined in the sysmessages table within the master database. Figure 15-19 shows some of the content of this table.

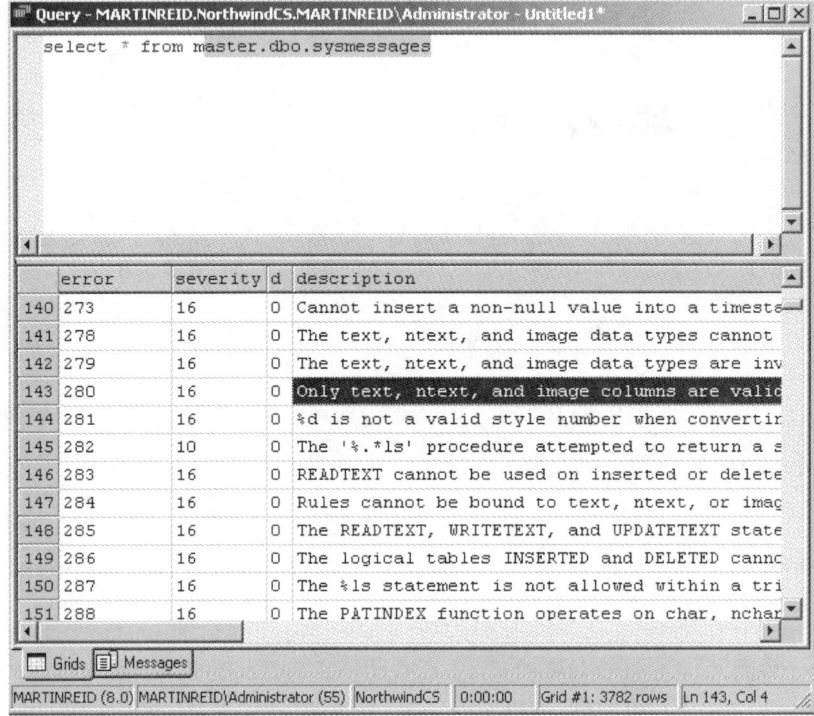

Figure 15-19. The Sysmessages table

@@ERROR can be used with stored procedures as a form of error control. The biggest problem with it is that **@@ERROR** maintains its value only until another SQL statement is executed. It is then replaced. For example, the following code fragment used **@@ERROR** to print a message:

```
IF @@ERROR <>
Print "AN Error Occurred in the statement"
```

We can also use **@@ERROR** to trap specific errors based on the error number.

```
IF @@ERROR = Error Number
Take Action
```

Some General System Functions

@@ROWCOUNT

@@ROWCOUNT will return the number of records affected by a particular SQL statement. For example:

```
UPDATE Customers set Surname = 'Reid'
Where CustomerID ='234'
IF @@ROWCOUNT <> 0
Print 'No Record Updated. Problem'
```

@@SERVERNAME

This one is nice and simple: it returns the name of the server.

```
SELECT @@SERVERNAME
```

@@VERSION

This returns the date and version of the current SQL Server.

> **NOTE** *Books Online contains a full description of all the available system functions.*

Using the Object Browser to Examine Function Syntax

In this section, we will look at SQL Server Object Browser in SQL Query Anaylzer in some detail. However, at this point, it is worth noting that—in addition to access to database objects—the browser gives you access to all the built-in functions within SQL. Functions are classified into groups. Figure 15-20 shows the function tree within Object Browser. The function folders are located below the Common Object folder in the tree. Notice the other folders available within the tree.

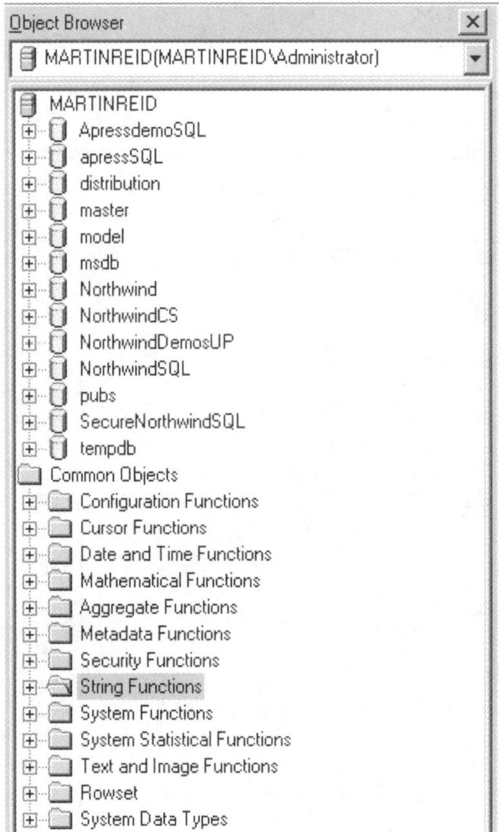

Figure 15-20. The Object Browser function tree

Expanding a folder exposes a function listing, and further expansion of each individual node will show information on the parameters accepted by the specific function. Figure 15-21 shows the date and time function expanded. In this case, I have expanded the **DATEADD** function and further expanded the Parameters folder.

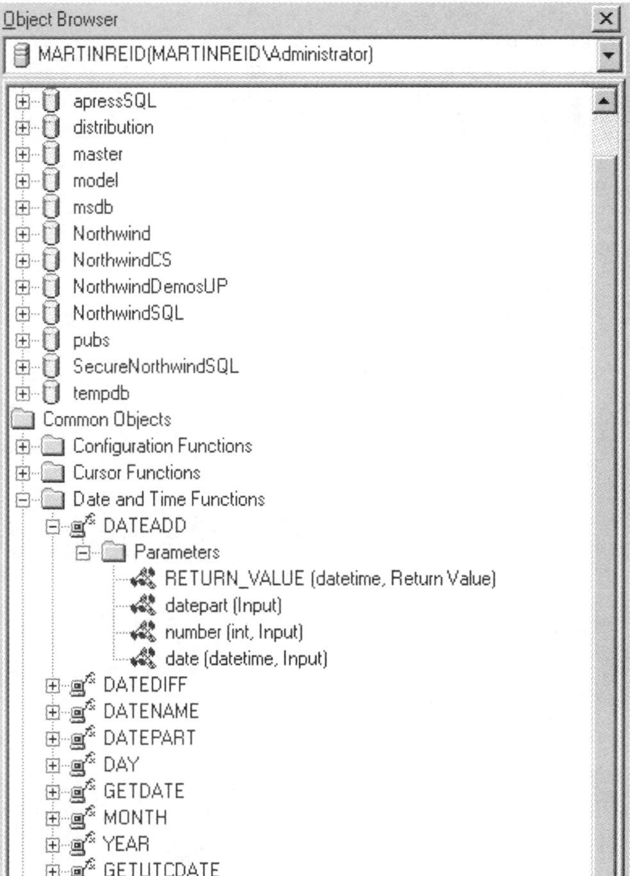

Figure 15-21. Parameters and DateAdd

Holding the mouse over a function name will reveal a tool tip containing a description of the function. (See Figure 15-22.) This can be a quick means of refreshing your memory.

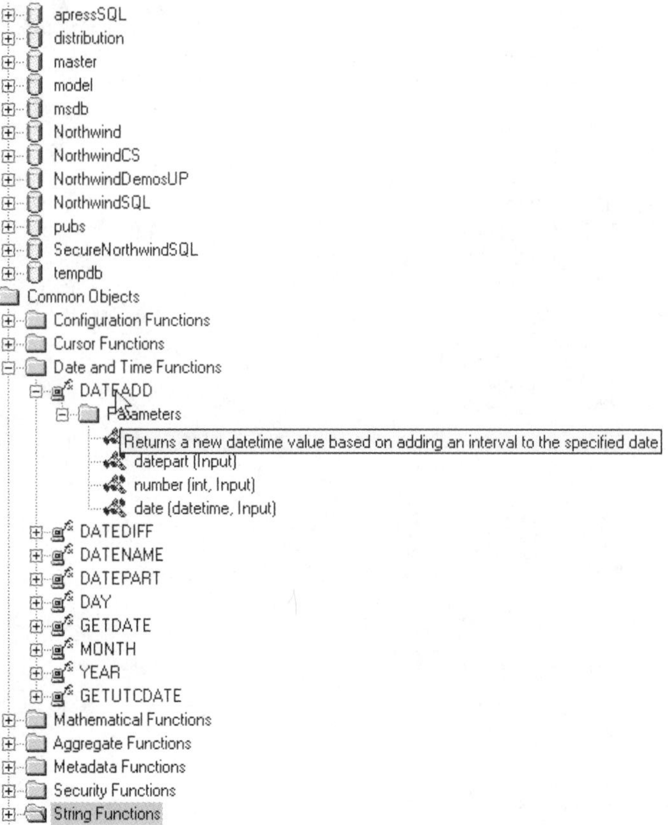

Figure 15-22. Tool tips

Debugging T-SQL

SQL Server also includes a debugger that can prove invaluable when working with stored procedures. To activate the debugger, simply right-click over a stored procedure name in Query Analyzer. Figure 15-23 shows the debugger when opened. Currently, the debugger is not available for function or views.

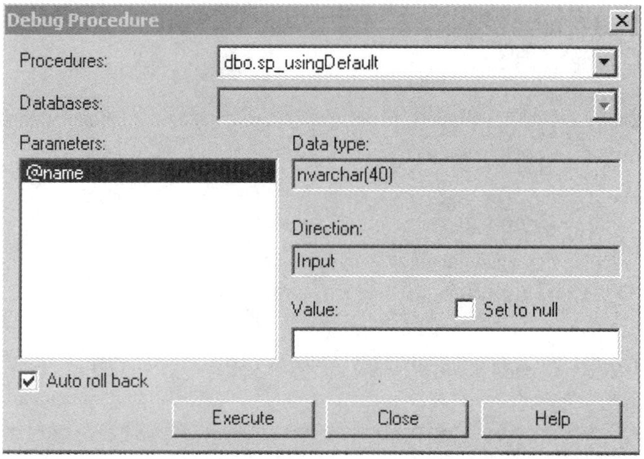

Debug Procedure
Procedures: dbo.sp_usingDefault
Databases:
Parameters: @name
Data type: nvarchar(40)
Direction: Input
Value: Set to null
Auto roll back
Execute Close Help

Figure 15-23. The T-SQL debugger

Figure 15-24 shows the results of executing the T-SQL debugger on a stored procedure called usp_usingDefault. It shows the three panes of the debugger: the top pane shows the procedure currently being debugged, the center pane shows local and global variables, and the bottom pane shows the results of executing the procedure or any error messages returned.

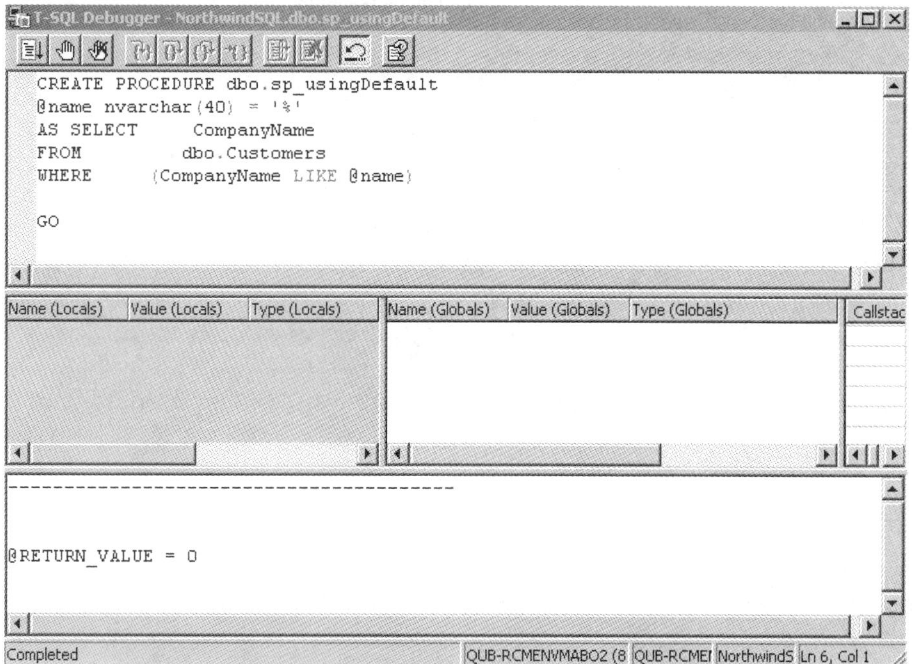

Figure 15-24. T-SQL debugger execution

The following features are available within the Debug Procedure dialog box and in the debugger itself.

- *Procedure*: A drop-down list indicates the currently selected procedure. You may select any stored procedure using this list.
- *Parameters*: Any parameters used by the procedure will be listed.
- *Data Type*: The data type of the parameter is listed.
- *Direction*: This is the parameter of type input or output.
- *Value*: This is the user entry of the parameter. The value can also be set to Null by checking the Set to Null checkbox.
- *Auto Rollback*: Use this to automatically roll back (clear) any changes made to a database object by the stored procedure.
- *Execute*: Use this to run the stored procedure.
- *Step Into*: Use this to execute one statement at a time. (It walks through the program.)
- *Step Out*: If you call another procedure, processing will pass to it. Once it's finished processing, control then returns to the next statement in the procedure being debugged.
- *Run to Cursor*: This executes all statements up to the current cursor position.
- *Restart*: This begins execution again.
- *Stop Debugging*: This halts the debugger.
- *Auto Rollback*: This rolls back all operations carried out by the procedure being debugged.

SQL Server Query Analyzer

One of the most useful tools in SQL Server is Query Analyzer, which is similar to Query Builder in Access. It can be used to create and test T-SQL statements. With the addition of Object Browser, SQL Server 2000 has finally caught up with Access. As useful and as powerful as Object Browser is, you still must have an understanding of SQL and be able to code by hand.

You can use Query Analyzer to:

- Create T-SQL statements interactively.
- Use built-in templates for common database tasks.
- Copy database objects.
- Use the T-SQL debugger.
- Check query performance.
- Find database objects.
- Interact directly with tables for inserts, updates, and deletes.

Query Analyzer

Figure 15-25 shows SQL Server Query Analyzer. As you can see, it is similar to the Access SQL Query Builder, minus the graphical table representation. Unlike as in Access 2002, your statement will be color-coded. SQL keywords such as SELECT will appear in blue, and columns and table names in black.

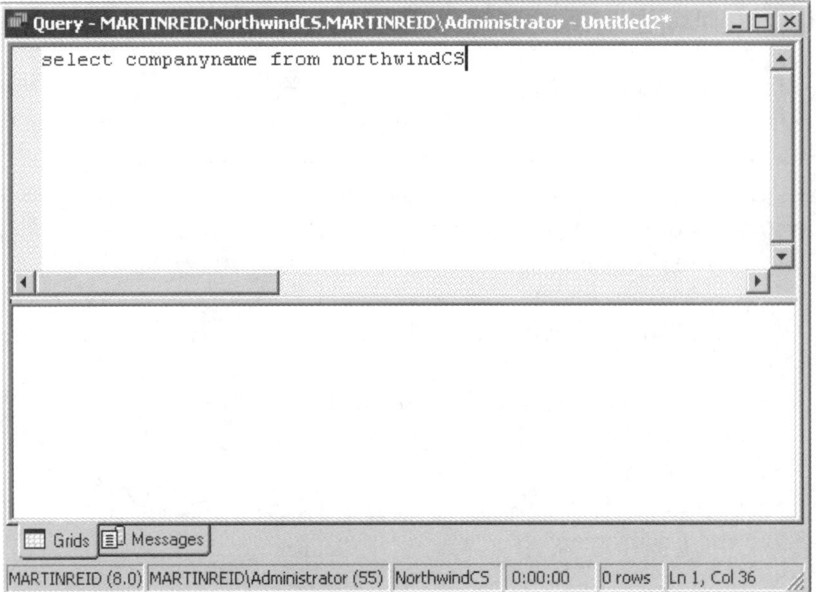

Figure 15-25. SQL Server Query Analyzer

As can be seen in Figure 15-26, the Analyzer window is split into two areas, with the T-SQL statement appearing in the top pane.

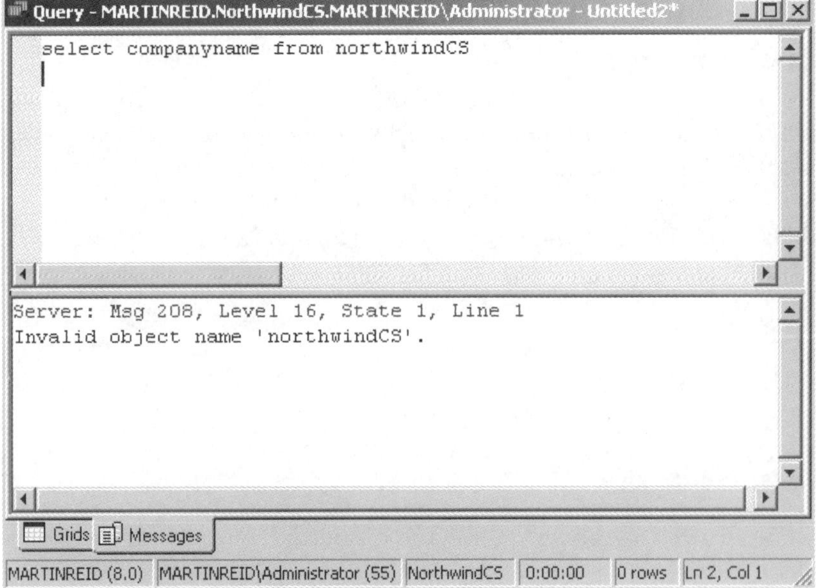

Figure 15-26. Query Analyzer split panes

The result of the T-SQL statement (or, in this case, an error message) appears in the bottom pane. The error message is deliberate to highlight the usefulness of this tool in debugging T-SQL. To determine the position of the error in your code, double-click on the message in the bottom pane. This repositions the cursor to where Query Analyzer has found an error in the top pane. Simply click on the Grid tab to view the records returned by the SQL statement.

Query Analyzer is very useful, as you shall see when we come to upsizing our Access databases. We can use it to validate Access SQL and assist in the conversion to stored procedures.

Object Browser

Object Browser is new to SQL Server, and it provides access to all server objects (tables, views, stored procedures, SQL server functions, and so on). It also assists in creating simple SQL statements, and you can create the following types of statements simply by right-clicking to drag a table to the Query Analyzer top pane and selecting an option from the pop-up menu.

Using Drag and Drop to Create a T-SQL Statement

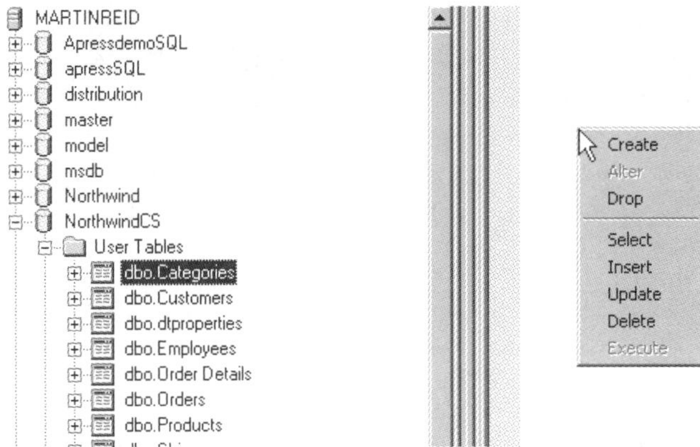

Figure 15-27. The Drag and Drop menu

Using the right mouse button, Query Analyzer allows you to drag and drop objects from Object Browser into a code window. When you drop the object in the code window, a menu appears allowing you to insert some common statements for the object. The following options are available using this method:

- CREATE
- DROP
- INSERT
- DELETE
- SELECT
- UPDATE

For example, right-clicking on the Customers table opens the shortcut menu. Choosing CREATE from the pop-up menu generates the following T-SQL statements. (Some columns have been removed to save space.)

```
/****** Object:  Table [dbo].[Customers]
Script Date: 14/06/2001 22:07:57 ******/
if not exists (select * from dbo.sysobjects where id =
object_id(N'[dbo].[Customers]') and
OBJECTPROPERTY(id, N'IsUserTable') = 1)
 BEGIN
CREATE TABLE [Customers] (
    [CustomerID] [varchar] (5) COLLATE Latin1_General_CI_AS NOT NULL ,
    [CompanyName] [varchar] (40) COLLATE Latin1_General_CI_AS NOT NULL ,
    [ContactName] [varchar] (30) COLLATE Latin1_General_CI_AS NULL ,
    CONSTRAINT [PK_Customers] PRIMARY KEY  CLUSTERED
(
   [CustomerID]
   )  ON [PRIMARY]
   ) ON [PRIMARY]
 END
GO
```

If you choose an Action query (update), the following statement is generated:

```
UPDATE [NorthwindCS].[dbo].[Customers]
SET [CustomerID]=<CustomerID,varchar(5),>,
[CompanyName]=<CompanyName,varchar(40),>,
[ContactName]=<ContactName,varchar(30),>,
[ContactTitle]=<ContactTitle,varchar(30),>,
[Address]=<Address,varchar(60),>, [City]=<City,varchar(15),>,
[Region]=<Region,varchar(15),>,
```

```
[PostalCode]=<PostalCode,varchar(10),>,
[Country]=<Country,varchar(15),>,
[Phone]=<Phone,varchar(24),>,
[Fax]=<Fax,varchar(24),>
WHERE <Search conditions,,>
```

Note the addition of the WHERE clause, which has also been generated. Using the left mouse button permits you to select single tables and columns to create basic statements.

The values (template parameters) within the angle brackets can be replaced. From the Main menu, select Edit|Replace Template Parameters. This opens a dialog box that lists all the parameters within the generated update statement. It is then a simple matter of replacing the generated parameters with something more readable and with the correct syntax. For example, we can replace the generated parameter <CustomerID> with @CustomerID.

> **NOTE** *Be careful using this tool. If you change a single parameter and then click Replace All, you may be in for a lot of typing. The Replace All command will replace the one valid parameter you enter and then remove all other parameters leaving you with a listing looking like:*
>
> ```
> [FieldName]=, [FieldName2]=, etc
> ```
>
> *The same thing happens if you do not add any parameters and click on Replace All: all generated parameters will be removed from the statement. So, before you click on Replace All, make sure that you have added all parameters to the dialog box. In addition, if you reopen the Replace Template Parameters dialog box a second time (after amending a parameter) on the same procedure, no parameters will be listed.*

We can use the same shortcut menus to create any of the other preceding statements.

A useful feature of the generated SQL (once the generated parameters have been replaced) is that it can be cut and pasted into Access 2002 via Query Builder. For example, the previously generated CREATE statement can be copied and pasted into a stored procedure template using Access 2002 and executed from there. Figure 15-28 shows a sample of SQL that has been copied (cut and passed) directly out of SQL Server.

```
CreateCustomerCopy : Stored Procedure
ALTER PROCEDURE CreateCustomerCopy

AS
/****** Object:  Table [dbo].[Customers]    Script Date: 14/06/2001 22:28:11 ******/
if not exists (select * from dbo.sysobjects where id = object_id(N'[dbo].[CustomerCopy]') and OBJECTPROPERTY(id, N'IsUserTable') = 1)
 BEGIN
CREATE TABLE [CustomerCopy] (
	[CustomerID] [varchar] (5) COLLATE Latin1_General_CI_AS NOT NULL ,
	[CompanyName] [varchar] (40) COLLATE Latin1_General_CI_AS NOT NULL ,
	[ContactName] [varchar] (30) COLLATE Latin1_General_CI_AS NULL ,
	[ContactTitle] [varchar] (30) COLLATE Latin1_General_CI_AS NULL ,
	[Address] [varchar] (60) COLLATE Latin1_General_CI_AS NULL ,
	[City] [varchar] (15) COLLATE Latin1_General_CI_AS NULL ,
	[Region] [varchar] (15) COLLATE Latin1_General_CI_AS NULL ,
	[PostalCode] [varchar] (10) COLLATE Latin1_General_CI_AS NULL ,
	[Country] [varchar] (15) COLLATE Latin1_General_CI_AS NULL ,
	[Phone] [varchar] (24) COLLATE Latin1_General_CI_AS NULL ,
	[Fax] [varchar] (24) COLLATE Latin1_General_CI_AS NULL ,
	CONSTRAINT [PK_Customers] PRIMARY KEY  CLUSTERED
	(
		[CustomerID]
	)  ON [PRIMARY]
) ON [PRIMARY]
END
```

Figure 15-28. Cutting and pasting T-SQL

> **TIP** *Remember to delete the word* GO *from the statement before the script can be executed in Access 2002 (ADO error message). GO is a T-SQL keyword that is used to break up different SQL statements and force the execution of any previous statements before the rest of the code is executed. Any statements before GO are treated as a single batch, as are any statements after GO. In addition to this cut-and-paste functionality, this generated code is another useful way to learn T-SQL.*

In this chapter, we have looked at some of the major differences between Access 2002 and SQL Server 2000. We have had a brief introduction to T-SQL and some of the features of SQL Enterprise Manger. In the following chapters, we will look at some of these features in more detail.

CHAPTER 16

Working with Stored Procedures

Working with Objects

THIS CHAPTER LOOKS AT SOME of the more common objects you need to understand when working with Access Data Projects (ADPs) and SQL Server. Stored procedures, functions and views form the cornerstone of much of this interaction. To quote Russell Sinclair, author of *From Access to SQL Server* (Apress): "Stored procedures are a new concept to most Access programmers because there is no equivalent in Access. For this reason, stored procedures are often misused or implemented poorly."

Previous chapters explored the basics of both Jet and Transact SQL (T-SQL), and this chapter examines how T-SQL is used in these server objects. A sample Access project and associated files can be downloaded for this chapter from `http://www.apress.com`.

What Is a Stored Procedure?

A stored procedure is a set of precompiled T-SQL instructions that are stored within the SQL server database. We can also think of stored procedures as similar to Access queries or QueryDef objects; in fact, they are very similar. When working with Access and SQL Server, you need to understand how to create stored procedures and use the procedures supplied with the server.

This chapter examines the basics of stored procedures, user-defined functions, and views. Later, in Chapter 19, in the section about using SQL Server with the Web, we use stored procedures to populate a Web interface. In fact, we'll reuse some of the procedures from our ADP file (thus illustrating the "write once, use several times" theory).

Why Use Stored Procedures?

Stored procedures are used for several reasons that become apparent when we look at their lifecycle. For these examples, we'll use the Northwind sample project included with Access 2002.

When we create a stored procedure, the server checks the T-SQL statements for syntax errors. The name and text of the procedure are stored in two separate system tables: sysobjects and syscomments. (Discussion of system tables is beyond the scope of this book, but a full discussion is available in SQL Server Books Online.)

> **NOTE** *It is possible to refer to objects that do not exist when a procedure is created. However, all objects referred to must exist when the stored procedure is executed.*

SQL reads the stored procedure in a process called *resolution*, during which each object is represented according to its internal SQL Server ID. During resolution, the procedure is reduced to its machine form and in some cases optimized. Once the procedure has been executed for the first time, the server determines the fastest way to get the data and creates an execution plan. The execution plan is then held in the procedure cache.

This execution plan remains in memory for other users who are executing the same procedure. Theoretically, a procedure can remain in the cache for months.

At times you may change table indexes, make major changes to data, or even amend a table structure. Amending a table structure results in an automatic recompile of the stored procedure when next executed. Such changes may cause your stored procedures to become less efficient. (Changing or adding an index is not automatically included in the execution plan.) Should this be the case, it is possible to recompile a stored procedure.

Two methods are commonly used to recompile a stored procedure: the WITH RECOMPILE statement and the system stored procedure sp_recompile.

Using the WITH RECOMPILE statement within the body of your stored procedure causes SQL Server to re-create the execution plan each time the procedure is executed. This option is normally used when the parameters to your stored procedure frequently change and there is little benefit to using a set execution plan. For example, when writing a parameter-based procedure that restricts customers by ZIP code or between a range of ZIP codes. In this case, the parameter changes frequently. There is no advantage to using an execution plan created for another parameter. For example, user A may search for Boston ZIP codes, and user B may search for all customers with LA or Washington ZIP codes.

SQL Server also provides a system stored procedure, sp_recompile, which can be used to recompile a stored procedure. For example,

```
Exec sp_recompile myStored_Procedure
```

recompiles the named procedure.

It is also possible to use a table name as the parameter to sp_recompile. In this case, all stored procedures using the tables are recompiled during their next execution. Using sp_recompile is a useful tool if you need to run a "one-off" recompile.

Stored procedures are also recompiled when SQL Server is restarted and a procedure is executed for the first time following the restart. A third method can be used when executing the procedure: specifying the WITH RECOMPILE option when executing the procedure.

```
Execute Storedprocedure WITH RECOMPILE
```

Stored procedures have many advantages, such as:

- Stored procedures reduce network traffic because we no longer need to send large SQL strings over the network via ActiveX Data Objects (ADO) or Open Database Connectivity(ODBC).

- They execute quickly as all syntax checking, parsing, and compiling have already been performed.

- They are shareable across applications.

- Stored procedures increase security. Users can be granted access to stored procedures rather than the tables that the stored procedures use.

- Stored procedures allow complex business rules to be hidden from users.

- All users use the same stored procedures.

The syntax of a basic stored procedure is fairly simple:

```
CREATE PROCEDURE procedure_name
AS SQL Statements
```

You can include any valid SQL statements, and stored procedures can be executed by using the following syntax:

```
EXECUTE stored_procedure_name
```

or

```
EXEC stored_ procedure_name
```

One of the more useful features of Query Builder in Access 2002—particularly when creating stored procedures, functions, and views—is the ability to split the window into three panes:

- The Table pane displays the tables, views, and functions being used.
- The Criteria pane displays the columns being retrieved, the criteria set, and the sort order of the result set.
- The SQL pane displays the SQL statement being designed. The SQL is created dynamically as you check the column boxes.

Figure 16-1 shows the builder and the three respective panes.

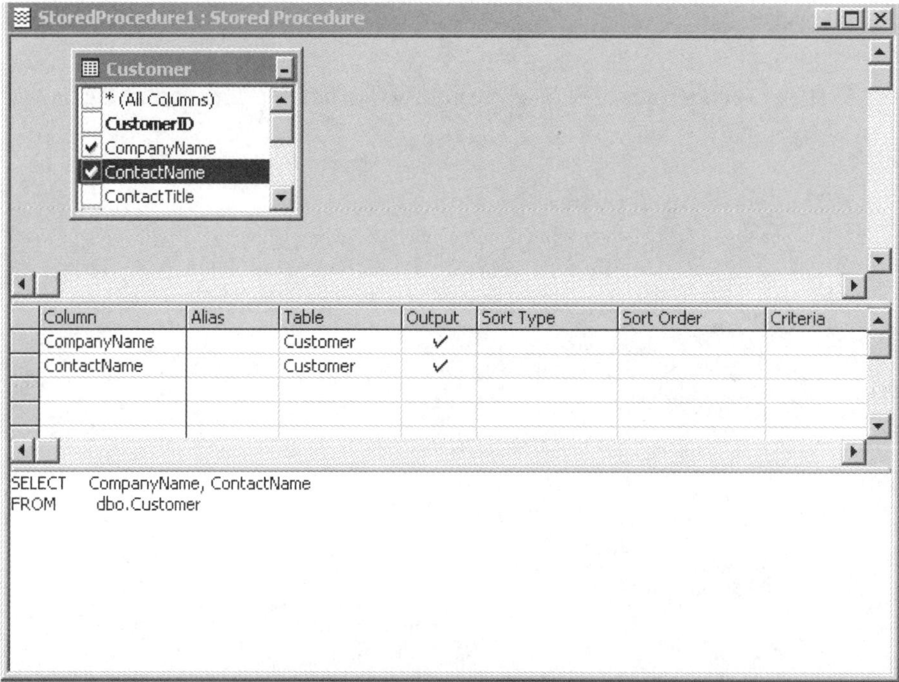

Figure 16-1. Query Builder in split-pane mode showing the Table, Column, and SQL panes

> **NOTE** *Query Builder is a great tool for learning the syntax of T-SQL. The ability to graphically create objects such as stored procedures, functions, and views is new to Access 2002 and saves a lot of two-fingered typing.*

Access users will be familiar with the point-and-click interface used to create queries via this interface. The process to create a stored procedure is identical and much improved in Access 2002.

> **NOTE** *It is useful at times to construct an SQL statement directly within the Query Builder. If you need to do this, simply close the Add Table dialog box without selecting a table. Select View SQL from the main menu to open the stored procedure text template.*

Query Builder in an Access Data Project

In addition to looking at stored procedures, we'll also look at the other options available when using Query Builder in Access 2002 when working with ADPs.

From the database window, select the Query section. Click on the New button to open the Query wizard. You'll immediately notice that the options available via the New Query dialog box have changed from those normally available from the usual Access Query wizard. See Figure 16-2.

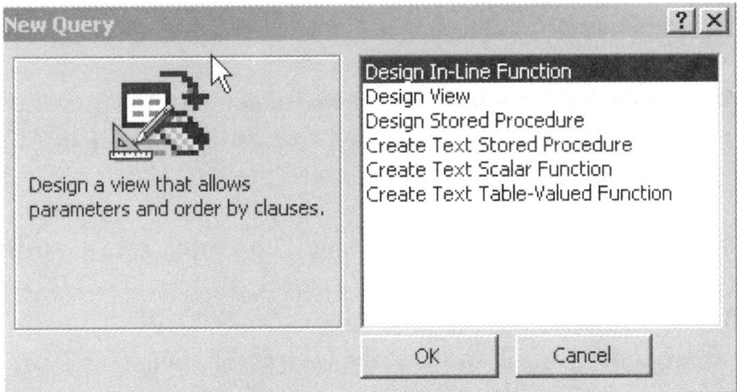

Figure 16-2. The Access 2002 New Query dialog box

> **NOTE** *When working with SQL Server objects (stored procedures, views, and functions), remember that, when using the Query Builder, you'll see only the SQL statement that defines the object. To see the actual CREATE or ALTER statement, you must choose View->SQL using the menu options. This is particularly true when you create the examples in this section. Once a stored procedure has been saved and reopened, you'll see the ALTER keyword rather than the CREATE keyword. Using ALTER saves the developer from having to DROP (delete) an existing procedure before amending it.*

Designing a Stored Procedure

The following examples concentrate on creating stored procedures using Access 2002 and Query Builder. It's also important to have an understanding of how to create stored procedures manually. We'll also briefly look at using SQL Server Enterprise manager to create stored procedures using one of the server wizards.

We have already seen that a stored procedure is simply a collection of precompiled T-SQL statements. The formal syntax is:

```
CREATE PROC [ EDURE ] procedure_name [ ; number ]
        [ { @parameter data_type }
        [ VARYING ] [ = default ] [ OUTPUT ]
        ] [ , . . . n ]
       [ WITH
       { RECOMPILE | ENCRYPTION | RECOMPILE , ENCRYPTION } ]
       [ FOR REPLICATION ]
      AS sql_statement [ . . . n ]
```

When you reexamine the design of a newly created stored procedure, you'll notice that the CREATE procedure has been changed to ALTER. The ALTER keyword is used when amending an existing procedure.

Query Builder in Access 2002 provides you with a basic template to create a stored procedure by hand. Figure 16-3 shows the template. To view this template in the Northwind ADP:

1. In the database window, select the Queries section.
2. Click on the New button.
3. Select the Create Text Stored Procedure option and click on OK.

The stored procedure text template opens.

StoredProcedure1 : Stored Procedure

```
CREATE PROCEDURE "StoredProcedure1"
/*
	(
		@parameter1 datatype = default value,
		@parameter2 datatype OUTPUT
	)
*/
AS
	/* SET NOCOUNT ON */
	RETURN
```

Figure 16-3. The stored procedure text template

To create a simple SELECT stored procedure, enter your SQL statement into the template. First, though, you have to overwrite the text inside the template. Simply select the text using the mouse and press the Delete key to give you a clean template to work with. Figure 16-4 shows the T-SQL stored procedure, ups_AverageProductPrice, that calculates the average product price using the Northwind ADP. The use of the **ISNULL** function is discussed later in this chapter.

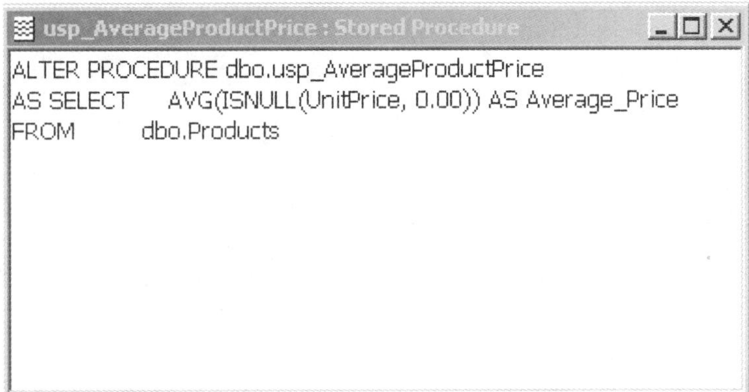
usp_AverageProductPrice : Stored Procedure
ALTER PROCEDURE dbo.usp_AverageProductPrice
AS SELECT AVG(ISNULL(UnitPrice, 0.00)) AS Average_Price
FROM dbo.Products

Figure 16-4. The T-SQL stored procedure to calculate the average product price

By this stage in the book, I think we have flogged SELECT to death, so let's look at a few other SQL statements that are used in stored procedures.

INSERT Stored Procedures

For this example, we are going to create two stored procedures: procedure 1 creates a simple table structure, and procedure 2 is used to insert some records. We'll do this via Access 2002 using Query Builder.

1. In the database window, select the Queries section.

2. Click on the New button.

3. Select Create Text Stored Procedure from the New Query dialog box to open the stored procedure template.

4. Change the default stored procedure name to usp_ExampleCreate. To change the procedure name, overtype the default name following the CREATE PROCEDURE keywords.

5. Enter the following T-SQL statements:

```
CREATE TABLE Contact
(
ContactRef int IDENTITY(1,1) NOT NULL Primary Key,
FirstName varchar(15),
Surname varchar(25),
MiddleName varchar(2),
Address varchar(25),
Region varchar(20)
)
RETURN
```

NOTE *Pay particular attention to the line* `ContactRef int IDENTITY(1,1) NOT NULL Primary Key`*, which creates the primary key. "IDENTITY (1,1)" indicates that the primary key should be an IDENTITY column, with a starting seed of 1 and an increment of 1. Of course, because it is a primary key, it is also set to be NOT NULL. These values are changeable, and you may amend them to suit your requirements. SQL Server automatically creates a clustered index on the primary key. Clustered indexes are discussed in Chapter 13.*

Once you have entered the preceding T-SQL snippet, close and save the stored procedure. Access uses the name entered after the CREATE PROCEDURE statement as the default name when saving the procedure. Create the second procedure to insert some values into the Contact table.

Follow the previous steps to open the stored procedure text template, and enter the following T-SQL statements into the template:

```
INSERT Contact VALUES('Martin', 'Reid', 'MW', 'Apress Ltd','UK')
INSERT Contact VALUES('William', 'Reid', 'R', 'Apress Ltd','UK')
INSERT Contact VALUES('Liam', 'Reid', 'G', 'Apress Ltd','UK')
INSERT Contact VALUES('Sarah','Reid','M','Apress Ltd','UK')
INSERT Contact VALUES('Aine','Reid', 'B', 'Apress Ltd','UK')
```

Save this as usp_InsertContacts.

Let's use some ADO to execute the stored procedures.

Executing a Stored Procedure via ADO

A Note on Connections

Access 2002 offers a new method of connecting to your server database: the AccessConnection. This object is functionally equivalent to the Connection property when used within an ADP. In an ADP, either property returns the following connection string:

```
Provider=Microsoft.Access.OLEDB.10.0;
Persist Security Info=True;
Data Source=YourServer;
User ID=sa;Password="Yourpassword";
Initial Catalog=NorthwindCS;
Data Provider=SQLOLEDB.1
```

However, when working with Jet, each connection property returns a different connection string.

The Connection property returns:

```
Provider=Microsoft.Jet.OLEDB.4.0;
Data Source=
C:\Program Files\Microsoft Office\Office10\Samples\Northwind.mdb
```

and AccessConnection returns:

```
Provider=Microsoft.Access.OLEDB.10.0;
Data Source=C:\Program Files\Microsoft Office\Office10\Samples\Northwind.mdb;
User ID=Admin;
Data Provider=Microsoft.Jet.OLEDB.4.0
```

When using ADO to provide recordsets to forms in Access 2002, Microsoft recommends that you use the AccessConnection property.

You can, if you wish, attach the following code to the On_Click event of a command button. From the database window:

1. Select the Form section.

2. Select Create Form in Design view. This opens a blank form in Design view.

3. Select the Command Button tool from the toolbox. If the toolbox is not available, select View, Toolbox from the main menu. Ensure that the Toolbox wizard is turned off. Click on the Control Wizards (Wand) button to turn the wizard off.

4. With the Command Button tool selected, move the mouse onto the form. The mouse pointer changes to a rectangle with a plus symbol.

5. Hold down the left mouse button and drag out a command button. Name the button CmdCreate. You now need to add the code to the Click event of the Command button.

6. Right-click on the Command button and select Properties.

7. Click on the Event tab (if it's not already defaulted).

8. Click in the On Click Event text box.

9. Open the code builder by clicking on the ellipsis to the right of the On_Click text box and select Code Builder.

10. Enter the following code into the Sub Procedure stub:

```
Private Sub CmdCreate_Click()
Dim Conn as ADODB.Connection
Set Conn = CurrentProject.Accessconnection
Conn.Execute "usp_ExampleCreate"
Conn.Execute "usp_InsertContacts"
Set Conn = Nothing
End Sub
```

11. Close and save the form as frmcreatetables.

12. To execute the code, simply open the form. In Form view, click on the Command button to execute the code.

ADO executes both stored procedures: usp_ExampleCreate to create the table structure, and usp_InsertContacts to populate the table with the data contained in the INSERT statement.

You may notice one problem when you execute the code: the database window does not automatically show the newly created table object. Another problem is also apparent (or will be) if you try to execute the procedure twice: ADO throws an error because the table object already exists on the server.

Refreshing the database window is as simple as pressing the F5 function key or selecting View, Refresh from the main menu. However, a second problem is slightly more difficult to resolve: it involves the use of special views used by SQL Server. System views are held within the master database.

The master database records all system information about the particular installation of SQL Server: user accounts, the data file location for all databases, system settings, and so on. Always—I repeat, *always*—have a backup of the master database. Included within the master database is a set of tables that maintain information on your database objects. The system view INFORMATON_SCHEMA.TABLES selects data from the Sysobjects tables. We use the systems views rather than query the system tables directly because the view is guaranteed to return the same information irrespective of the SQL Server version. Microsoft does not support querying the system tables directly because the tables are subject to change in different versions of SQL Server. In addition, the view contains specific data. Other data items that we do not require have already been filtered out. We are going to use this view to add some control to the above stored procedure.

We need to ensure that the table we are about to create does not already exist within the database. To do this, we can query the INFORMATON_SCHEMA.TABLES view to check if the table already exists. If it does, we can simply exit the stored procedure.

The revised stored procedure (usp_ExampleCreate) is shown below:

```
ALTER PROCEDURE usp_ExampleCreate
AS
IF Exists (select TABLE_NAME from Information_Schema.Tables
                     Where
                     TABLE_NAME = 'Contact')
ELSE
Begin
CREATE TABLE Contact
(
ContactRef int IDENTITY(1,1) NOT NULL Primary Key,
FirstName varchar(15),
Surname varchar(25),
MiddleName varchar(2),
Address varchar(25),
Region varchar(20)
)
End
RETURN
```

The following check has been added to the procedure:

```
IF Exists (select TABLE_NAME from Information_Schema.Tables
                   Where
                   TABLE_NAME = 'Contact')
ELSE
```

The IF EXISTS statement simply checks for a value returned from the SELECT statement. If a value does exist (the Contact table already exists), the procedure exits immediately using the RETURN keyword.

If the table does not exist, the CREATE TABLE statements enclosed between the BEGIN/END pair are executed.

Passing Parameters

Parameters are passed to T-SQL using the syntax of @parametername. Figure 16-5 shows a function amended to accept a single parameter: @CustomerID. The parameter is simply a placeholder to accept input provided by the user or the application. This type of parameter is known as an input parameter, for obvious reasons. Output parameters simply permit you to return a value or values from the procedure.

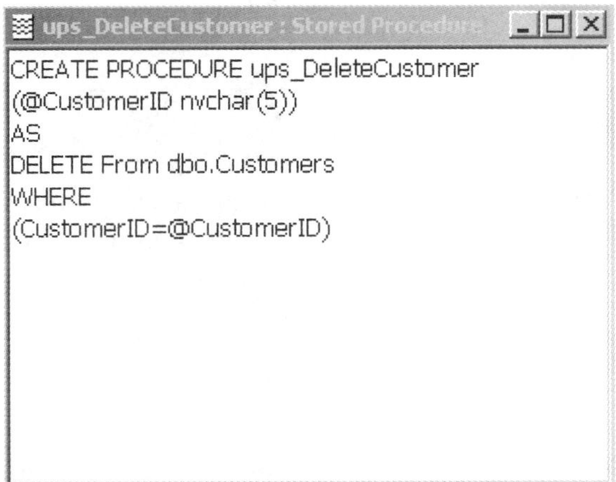

Figure 16-5. A function amended to accept a single parameter

The stored procedure usp_DeleteCustomer accepts a single parameter, CompanyID, and deletes that specific record from the Northwind example ADP. The T-SQL statement is:

```
CREATE PROCEDURE usp_DeleteCustomer
(@CustomerID nvchar(5))
AS
DELETE FROM dbo.Customers
WHERE
(CustomerID=@Customerid)
```

Note that no columns are listed as part of the DELETE statement. For a full discussion of the DELETE keyword, see Chapter 6.

Append

We can also use a stored procedure to achieve the same functionality as a standard Access Append query. The following stored procedure copies all data from the Customer table into a backup table called CustAppend. CustAppend has an identical structure to the Customer table. You could also cut (Ctrl-C) and paste (Ctrl-V) the existing Customer table to create the new CustAppend table if you wanted to copy the table quickly.

```
CREATE PROCEDURE usp_AppendCustomer
AS
INSERT INTO dbo.CustAppend
```

```
SELECT dbo.Customers.*
FROM
dbo.Customers
```

As can be seen at a low level, a stored procedure should not offer many challenges to those of you who are already proficient in Access and SQL. However, don't be fooled. Stored procedures offer many features that we haven't touched upon here, such as transactions, database management, and security.

Design Inline Function

An inline function can be equated to a standard Access parameter query, which accepts a parameter and returns a subset of the data. You can use Query Builder's graphical interface to design the procedure. The resulting function can be used in the FROM clause of an SQL statement as it will return a table of data. We can use only a single SELECT statement within an inline function. Inline functions can use tables, views, and other functions and combine many of the features of stored procedures and views.

> **NOTE** *Inline functions can be used as a replacement for SQL Server temporary tables. As with a standard Access database, we can use temporary tables within SQL Server. Two types of temporary tables are used: local and global. Local temporary tables are created using a single #TableName prefix, and global temporary tables are created using ##TableName prefix. A local temporary table is available to only the session and user procedure that created it. If the user logs out or the procedure ends, the table is lost. Further, multiple users cannot use the same temporary table, but global temporary tables are available to multiple users. However, when the last user exits the table or the procedure ends, the global table is also lost.*

To create an inline function that returns all customers living in London:

1. In the database window, select the Queries section.
2. Click on the New button.
3. Select Design In-Line Function from the New Query dialog box and click on OK.
4. Using the Add Table dialog box, select the Customers table.

5. Click on Add to add the table to the query window.

6. Close the Add Table dialog box.

Figure 16-6 shows how Query Builder should look at this point. (We have yet to indicate the fields required.)

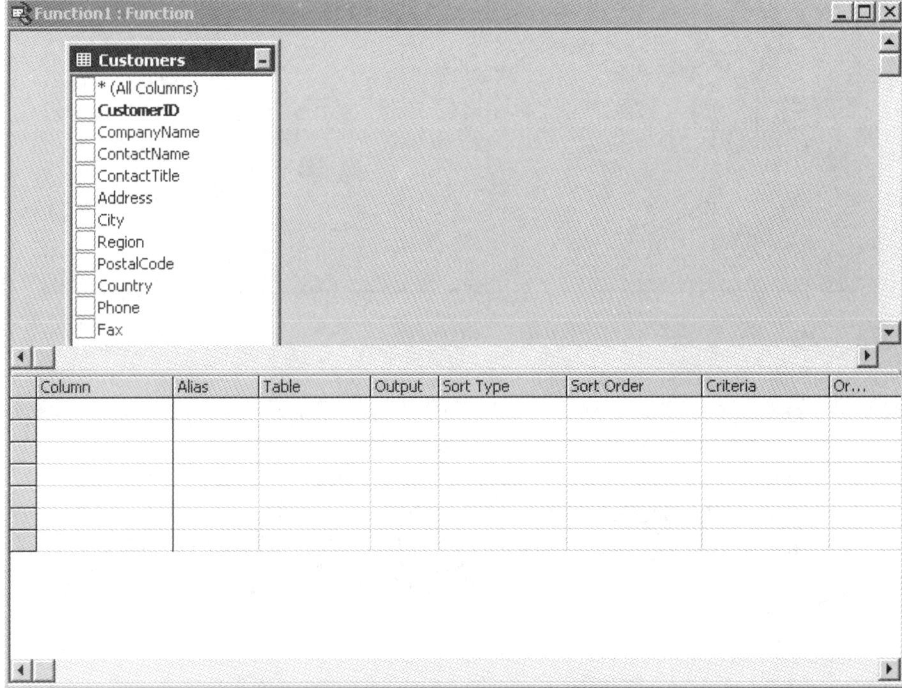

Figure 16-6. Creating an inline function—Customers table

The rest of the procedure is almost identical to creating a parameter query in MS Access 2002.

7. In this case, we use the checkbox to the left of the field name to indicate fields to output in the result (CompanyName, ContactName, ContactTitle, and City).

8. In the criteria cell of the City field row, enter "London".

Note that Query Builder enters an "=" operator, the quotation marks, and the letter *N* in front of the string. (The *N* specifies that the string is in Unicode format). Also note the filter symbol against the City field in the query graphic. Figure 16-7 shows the table containing the filter graphic.

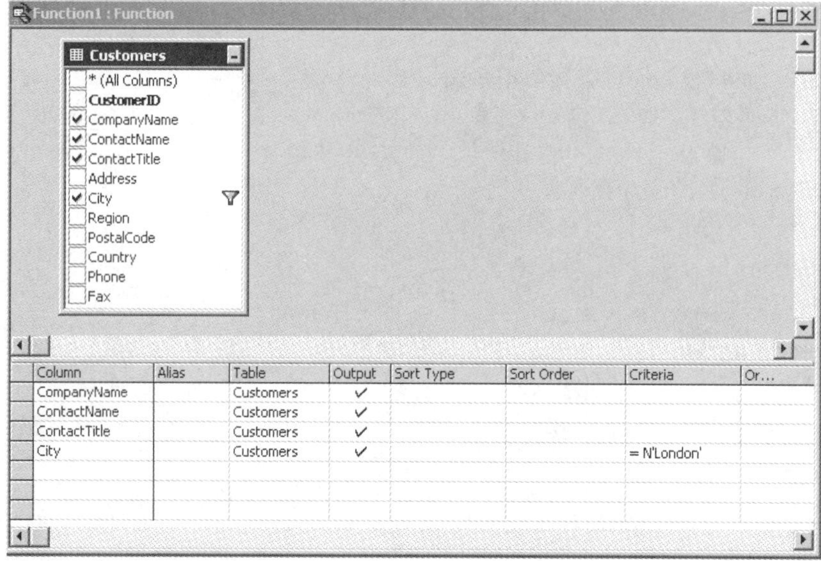

Figure 16-7. Field selection and filter icon

> **NOTE** *Unlike with standard Access queries, you must save the SQL Server function before executing it in Access 2002. If you choose File Save As from the main menu instead of File Save, the save dialog box will have changed from that normally used by Access 2002 when creating functions. Figure 16-8 shows the new options available when using File, Save As to save a function.*

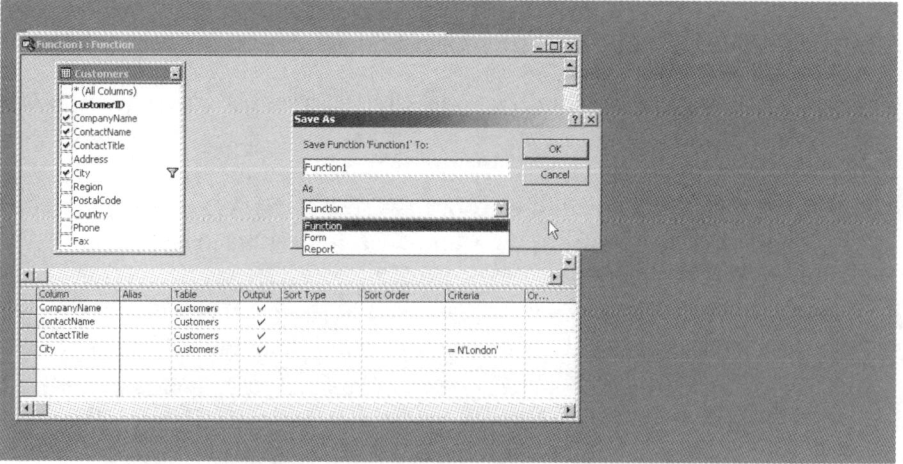

Figure 16-8. Saving a function—the new File Save As options

You may choose to save the function as a function, a form (the function is used as the record source of a form), or a report (the function can be used as the record source of a report).

In this case, we are going to accept the default and save it as a function.

> **NOTE** *If you do try to execute the function prior to saving, you will be prompted to save, but the previous three options won't be available. You will always be prompted to save when you amend a function or stored procedure.*

Enter a name for the function (in this case **fnt_Customertown**) and click on OK. Figure 16-9 shows the results; in this case, six rows are returned.

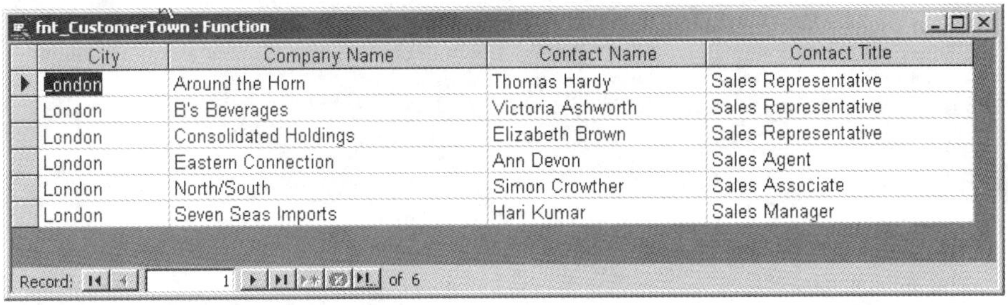

fnt_CustomerTown : Function

City	Company Name	Contact Name	Contact Title
London	Around the Horn	Thomas Hardy	Sales Representative
London	B's Beverages	Victoria Ashworth	Sales Representative
London	Consolidated Holdings	Elizabeth Brown	Sales Representative
London	Eastern Connection	Ann Devon	Sales Agent
London	North/South	Simon Crowther	Sales Associate
London	Seven Seas Imports	Hari Kumar	Sales Manager

Record: 1 of 6

Figure 16-9. Results of executing fnt_Customertown

The syntax for the function is:

```
CREATE FUNCTION dbo.[fnt_CustomerTown]()
RETURNS TABLE
AS
RETURN (SELECT CompanyName, Address, City, PostalCode, Country
FROM   dbo.Customers
WHERE  (City =N 'London'))
```

The really great thing about functions is that they can return data as a table. The second line in the function instructs the procedure to RETURN TABLE.

> **NOTE** *Inline functions can return two types of data—a table or scalar data type—and are much like a VBA function, which returns a value. In the preceding case, the function returns a table. If your function returns a table, you can reference the function in the FROM clause of a SELECT statement.*

For example, using the function we just created, the following SQL statement (which has been created as a stored procedure) can be executed against the function.

```
CREATE PROCEDURE dbo.UseCustomerFunction
AS
SELECT
Companyname, ContactName,City
FROM
dbo.[fnt_CustomerTown]()
Where (ContactName LIKE 'ann%')
```

One record will be returned.

As you may have guessed from the syntax of the function, we can also pass parameters both to and from the function.

For example, consider the following function:

```
CREATE FUNCTION fn_CustomersByCity
(@city nvarchar(10))
RETURNS TABLE
AS
RETURN (SELECT CustomerID,CustomerName
                FROM dbo.Customers
                Where City = @city)
```

The function can be called by the construction of a simple SQL SELECT statement that passed the value 'London' to the function.

```
SELECT * from fnt_CustomersByCity ('London')
```

This returns all records for customers living in London.

Multiple Statement Functions

As we've just seen, the inline table function uses a single SQL SELECT statement to return a table. However, we can also define the columns and data types for the function. When this is the case or we are using multiple expressions, it is referred to as a *multistatement* function. For example, the following function defines a return type of table called @Freight and creates the column and field definition for the table object. To create a multistatement function:

1. In the database window, select the Queries section.

2. Click on the New button.

3. Select Create Text Table-Valued Function from the New Query dialog box. The dialog box opens a function template file.

4. Delete the template text and enter the following function statement:

```
CREATE Function dbo.fnt_Freight (@OrderID Int)
RETURNS @Freight TABLE
(
                OrderDate Datetime,
                TotalOrders Int,
                SmallestFreight money,
                LargestFreight money
)
As
                BEGIN
                Insert @Freight
                Select
                Orderdate,Count(OrderID),Min(Freight),Max(Freight)
                FROM
                Orders
                WHERE OrderID = (@OrderID)
                Group By OrderDate
RETURN
END
```

NOTE *The values from the SELECT statement are inserted into the variable @Freight, thus building the table for the result set.*

When this statement is executed, you will be prompted for an OrderID. Enter OrderID 10248 to run the function. You could simply remove the variable @OrderID and the WHERE clause to return a summary of freight charges for the entire table. The next section discusses passing parameters to functions in more detail.

It is also possible to refer to a function in the query window as if it were a base table. For example, the preceding function has been amended to include the CustomerID column from the Orders table. I have simply copied the existing function into a new template in Access and edited the name and fields: Select,

Query, New, and Create Text Table-Valued Function). In addition, I have removed the parameter and the WHERE clause because I need the **fnt_FreightCustomers ()** function to return all records:

```
CREATE Function dbo.fnt_FreightCustomers ()
RETURNS @FreightCustomers TABLE
(
            OrderDate Datetime,
            TotalOrders Int,
            SmallestFreight money,
            LargestFreight money,
            CustomerID Nvarchar (5)
)
As
BEGIN
             Insert @FreightCustomers
             Select
             orderdate,Count(OrderID),Min(Freight),Max(Freight),CustomerID
             FROM
             Orders
             Group By OrderDate,CustomerID
RETURN
END
```

For this example, we'll use Query Builder in Access 2002 to construct a stored procedure that joins the Customer table to the **fnt_FreightCustomers** function. From the database window:

1. Select Queries.
2. Click on the New button.
3. In the New Query dialog box, select Design Stored Procedure. Query Builder opens with the Add Table dialog box.
4. Select the Customers table.
5. Click on Add.
6. Click on the Functions tab to view existing functions.
7. Select the function we just created: **fnt_FreightCustomers**.

8. Click on Add.

9. Close the Add Table dialog box.

Figure 16-10 shows how your screen should look at this point.

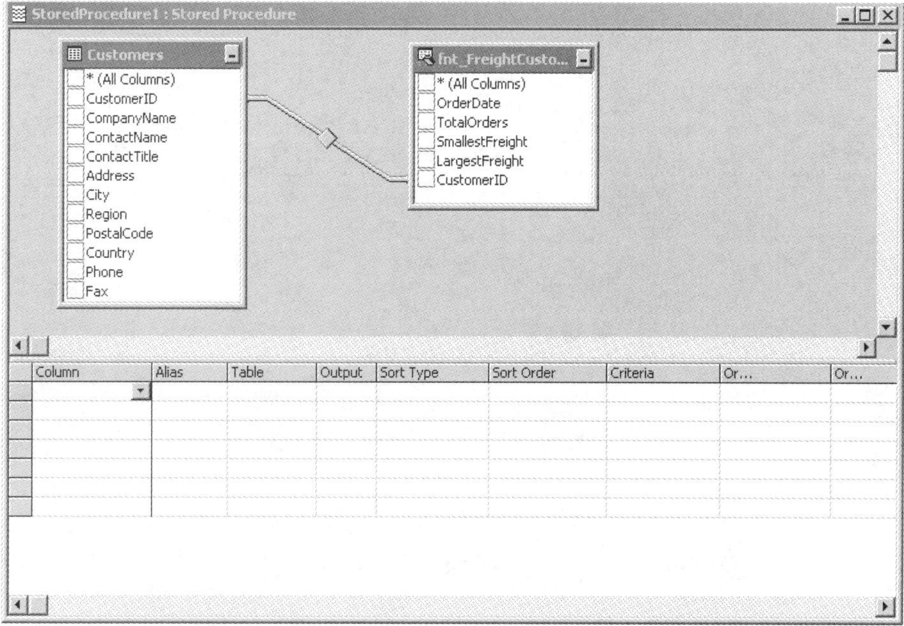

Figure 16-10. Query Builder with both table and function selected

Notice how Access has automatically created the Join between the Customer table and the function.

10. Select (by checking the field name checkbox) the fields you want to retrieve. Ensure you select the CompanyName field.

11. Add "Like A%" to the Criteria cell for CompanyName.

Figure 16-11 shows the query window at this point.

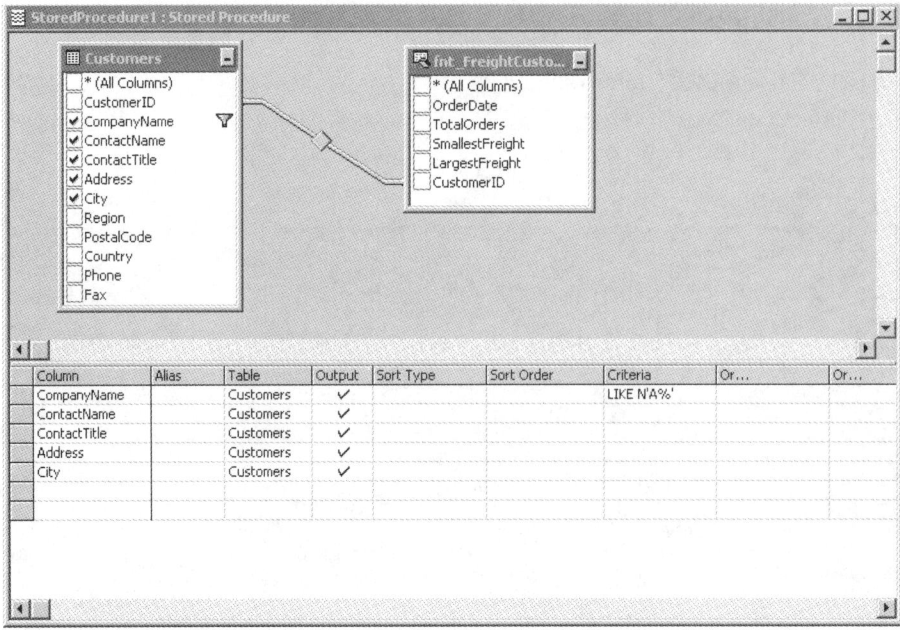

Figure 16-11. Query Builder

12. Execute the stored procedure. (Remember that you will be prompted to save. Save the procedure as usp_CustomersByName.)

The next example returns all records where the order date is between two user-entered values. You can create the function either by typing the text into the function template or using the graphical query builder to construct the SQL statements.

```
CREATE PROCEDURE dbo.ups_functionJoin
(@Enter_Date_From datetime,
@Enter_Date_to datetime)
AS SELECT     dbo.Customers.CompanyName, fnt_FreightCustomers.OrderDate,
fnt_FreightCustomers.TotalOrders,
fnt_FreightCustomers.SmallestFreight,
fnt_FreightCustomers.LargestFreight, fnt_FreightCustomers.CustomerID

FROM      dbo.Customers INNER JOIN
          dbo.fnt_FreightCustomers() fnt_FreightCustomers
          ON dbo.Customers.CustomerID = fnt_FreightCustomers.CustomerID
WHERE
(dbo.Customers.CompanyName LIKE N'A%')
AND
```

```
(fnt_FreightCustomers.OrderDate
BETWEEN @Enter_Date_From AND @Enter_Date_to)
```

When executed, the function prompts you to enter a “from” date and a “to” date.

Defaults and Nulls

Defaults

One advantage of running functions rather than stored procedures in Access 2002 is their use of defaults. When executing a stored procedure or function, the parameter dialog box contains a drop-down list that offers you the choice of two values: Default or Null.

The following stored procedure provides a default value for CompanyName. If the user fails to enter a value in response to the prompt, the default value should ensure that records are returned.

However, when using the same feature in a stored procedure, the result is less predictable. In the following case, a default of ‘%’ is used, so all records are returned. When running this procedure in Access 2002, you are not prompted for input.

```
CREATE PROCEDURE dbo.usp_UsingDefaults
@Name nvarchar(40) = '%'
AS
SELECT
Companyname
FROM
dbo.Customers
Where
(ContactName LIKE @Name)
```

To ensure that you are prompted for a value when using parameters and default values, you must use functions. Create the following function using Access and the Northwind ADP file:

```
CREATE FUNCTION dbo.fn_UsingDefaults
(@name nvarchar(40) = 'London')
RETURNS TABLE
AS
RETURN (SELECT CompanyName
FROM dbo.Customers
Where (City = @name))
```

In this case, if you leave the prompt blank and select Default from the drop-down list, the default value ('London') is used. In this case, all records in which the city is London are retrieved.

> **NOTE** *A very useful feature of functions that accept parameters is that they can be used to hit views. By their nature, views do not accept parameters. Views are discussed in the next section when we look at the next query option: Design view.*

Nulls

As you have seen when executing a parameter stored procedure or function, you are offered two options by Access: defaults and nulls. We have seen how a default value can be used within a function (and ignored by a stored procedure), so now let's look at how nulls are handled. For example, the following fragment of SQL uses a default of NULL if a value isn't entered in response to a prompt. Note that, using the Access 2002 interface, you are still prompted for all the values.

```
@Title nvarchr(30) = NULL
```

The full procedure is:

```
CREATE PROCEDURE usp_InsertEmployee
@LastName nvarchar(20),
@FirstName nvarchar(10),
@Title nvarchar(10) = NULL
AS
INSERT INTO Employees (LastName,FirstName,Title)
VALUES (@LastName,@FirstName,@Title)
RETURN
```

Another way of trapping nulls is to grab them before they get to the procedure (that is, catch them in the user interface).

For example, in a form that captures dates (Date From and Date To), a simple bit of VBA on the click event of a command button could check that the correct data had been entered. (The dates were not null or fell within an acceptable range). In fact, such error trapping should be used.

If a user fails to enter a parameter value, all values are returned. For example, try the following stored procedure in the Access Query Builder. Create a text stored procedure:

```
CREATE Procedure usp_CheckNulls
(@city nvarchar(15))
AS
SELECT CompanyName, ContactName, contactTitle, Address, City
From dbo.Customers
WHERE
(City = @city or
            @city IS NULL)
```

Failing to enter a value for the @city prompt results in all records being returned. You need to be careful when using this on large recordsets.

Parameters and Forms

The following is a standard SQL SELECT statement:

```
SELECT Clients.CompanyName, Clients.Address, Clients.City
FROM Clients
WHERE (((Clients.City)=[EnterCity]))
```

As you can see, when the statement is executed, the user is requested to enter a city. The equivalent stored procedure is:

```
CREATE PROCEDURE dbo.City (@city nvarchar(50))
AS SELECT     CompanyName, Address, City
FROM          dbo.Clients
WHERE      (City = @city)
RETURN
```

Note the differences. A new variable has been created, @city, and, because we are working with a text value, the data type and length have also been provided.

> **NOTE** *It's important to declare the correct data type because the server may not throw an error; it may just fail to return any records.*

The rest of the SQL code is standard. The RETURN keyword is optional but should be used, when possible, as it unconditionally exits the procedure.

Parameter names start with the @ (the "at" symbol) and are always declared before the AS keyword that precedes the SQL statement. This is unlike local variables, which are declared following the AS keyword.

Using a Parameter Stored Procedure to Populate a Form

Using the Input Parameters property of a form, we can use parameter stored procedures within Access 2002. Input parameters are used to pass values to forms and reports. Figure 16-12 shows a form property sheet. The Input Parameters setting is accessed from this dialog box via the Data tab.

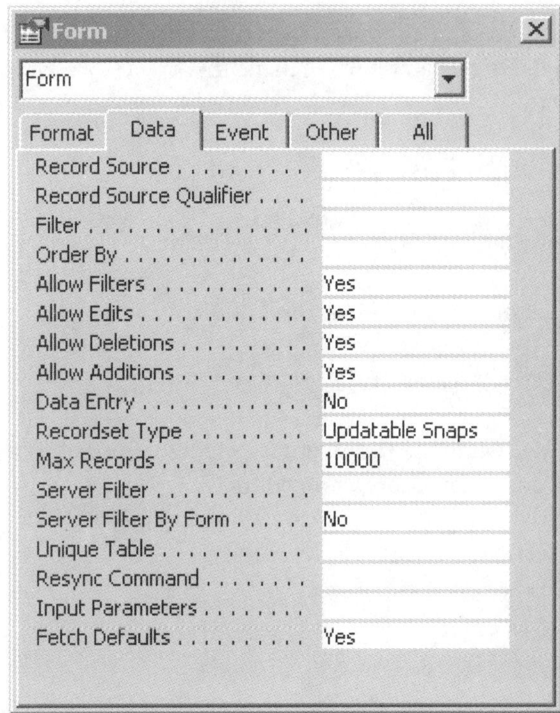

Figure 16-12. Viewing a form's Input Parameter property

We can either hard-code the parameter into the property or pass a parameter (or parameters) to the property via, for example, another form. The use of an unbound form is a popular means of passing values between forms using Access.

Passing from Values to the Input Parameter Using a form

For this example, we require an unbound form to collect input from the user and a bound form. The bound form is the target for the filter and is bound to a stored procedure.

A parameter-based stored procedure will be used as the record source of the bound form. The stored procedure returns all orders placed between two order dates that are input by the user. The dates are entered via the unbound form, which passes them to the stored procedure used as the record source for the bound Customer Orders form.

Step 1. Creating the Stored Procedure

1. From the database window, select the Queries section.
2. Click on the New button.
3. From the New Query dialog box, select Design Stored Procedure.
4. Using Query Builder, create a single stored procedure using the following tables: Customers, Orders, Order Details, and Products.
5. From the Add Table dialog box, double-click on each of these tables to add them to the query design window. You can also select the table and click on the Add button.
6. Close the Add Table dialog box. Click on the Close button.

Table 16-1 shows the fields required for the output.

Table 16-1. Fields Required for Input

TABLE	FIELD
Customers	CompanyName
Orders	OrderDate
Order Details	UnitPrice
Order Details	Quantity
Products	ProductName

A WHERE clause has been added to the SELECT statement. Enter the following statement into the Criteria cell for the OrderDate field to create the WHERE criteria:

```
Between @DateFrom And @DateTo
```

Order the records by CompanyName (ascending) and OrderDate (descending).

Figure 16-13 shows how your query should look at this point. I have also included a Sub Total field using the expression [UnitPrice]*[Quantity] and given this field an alias of "Sub Total". Type the expression into a blank column cell. In the Alias column, type "Sub Total".

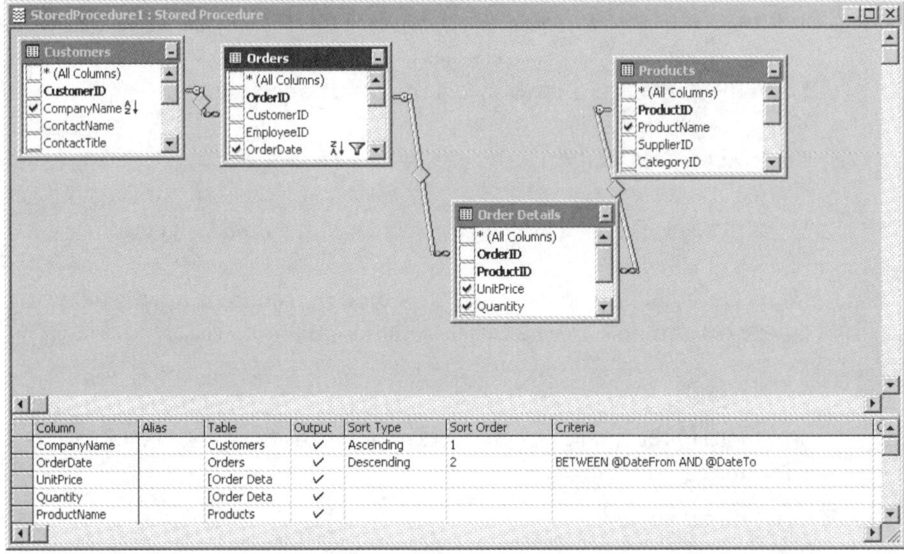

Figure 16-13. Step 1: Creating the stored procedure

Close and save the procedure as usp_parameterpassing.

Step 2. Creating a Bound Form

Create a bound form using usp_parameterpassing as the record source.

1. In the database window, select the Forms section.
2. Click on the New button.
3. Select Autoform, Tabular Form from the New Form dialog box.
4. Select usp_parameterpassing using the drop-down list (in the form wizard) as the record source.

Figure 16-14 shows the forms wizard at this point.

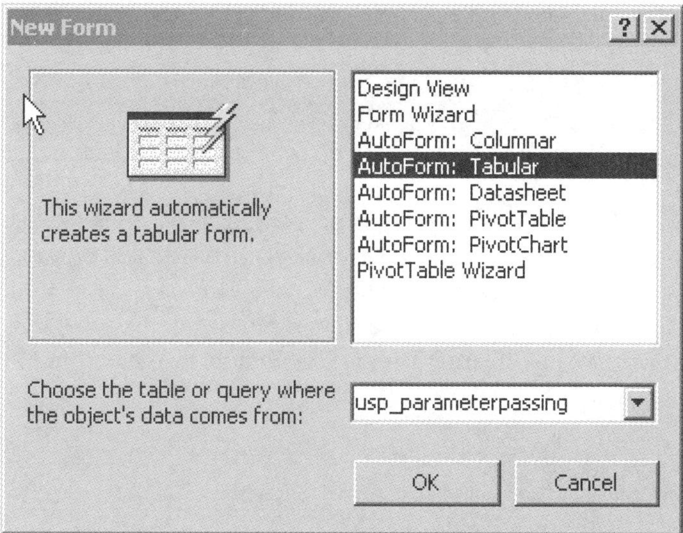

Figure 16-14. The Access 2002 form wizard—creating an auto form

5. Click on OK to generate the form and save it as frmCustomerOrders.

> **NOTE** *When saving the form, you are prompted for the parameter values. Simply leave this blank and click on OK. The form should open with no records. Close the form and accept the save prompts to continue saving the form. You may need to go into forms design to rearrange some of the fields for readability later.*

Step 3. Creating the Unbound Form

Create an unbound form containing two text boxes and a single command button. To create the text boxes for this example, you need to use the form design toolbox.

Name the form objects as follows:

> **NOTE** *To name a text box, click on the box and select View, Properties from the main menu. Select the All tab and enter the name for the object in the Name property. Close the property sheet.*

- txtDateFrom; User will enter the Date From into this object
- txtDateTo; User will enter Date To in this object
- cmdpass; Command button to open frmCustomerOrders.

To create the Command button, in Form Design view, open the form toolbox. Ensure that the Toolbox wizard is active (make sure the Wizard button is depressed), and select the Command Button tool. Draw out the Command button on the form background. The wizard then walks you through a series of steps to open the form we just created. The code generated by the Command Button wizard is shown below:

```
Private Sub cmdpass_Click()
On Error GoTo Err_cmdpass_Click
    Dim stDocName As String
    Dim stLinkCriteria As String
    stDocName = "frmCustomerOrders"
    DoCmd.OpenForm stDocName, , , stLinkCriteria
Exit_cmdpass_Click:
Exit Sub
Err_cmdpass_Click:
    MsgBox Err.Description
    Resume Exit_cmdpass_Click
End Sub
```

Close and save the form as frmPassOrderDates.

At this point, you should have the following objects:

- A stored procedure that accepts two parameters: @DateFrom and @DateTo
- An unbound form containing two text boxes: txtDateFrom and txtDateTo
- A bound form using usp_parameterpassing as the record source: frmCustomerOrders

Step 4. Assigning Values to the Input Parameters

Now, we'll assign the values to the Input Parameters property:

1. Open frmCustomerOrders in Design view. (Click on the form name and then Design in the database window.)

2. From the main menu, select View Properties to open the property sheet for the form.

3. Click on the Data tab of the property sheet.

Note that the Input Parameter property is currently blank. Enter the following values into the Input Parameter cell (all on a single line):

```
@DateFrom Datetime
=[forms]![frmPassOrderDates]![txtDateFrom],@DateTo
Datetime =[forms]![frmPassOrderDates]![txtDateTo]
```

> **NOTE** *The forms parameter should appear on one line. If you right-click on the Input Parameters text box and select Zoom from the shortcut menu, the text box is enlarged, making entry of the parameter easier.*

InputParameter takes the following form:

```
Forms![FORM NAME]![CONTROL NAME]
```

Multiple parameters are separated by a comma.

Figure 16-15 shows the input parameter applied to the Customer Orders form. Right-click on the input parameter and select Zoom to enlarge the text box to make viewing easier.

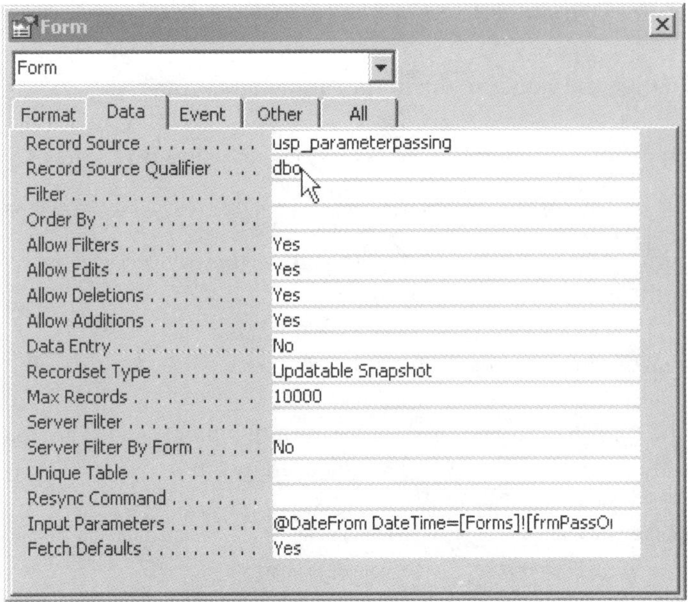

Figure 16-15. Input Parameters in frmCustomerOrders

Figure 16-16 shows both frmPassOrderDates and frmCustomerOrders. A Date From and Date To have been entered into frmPassOrderDates.

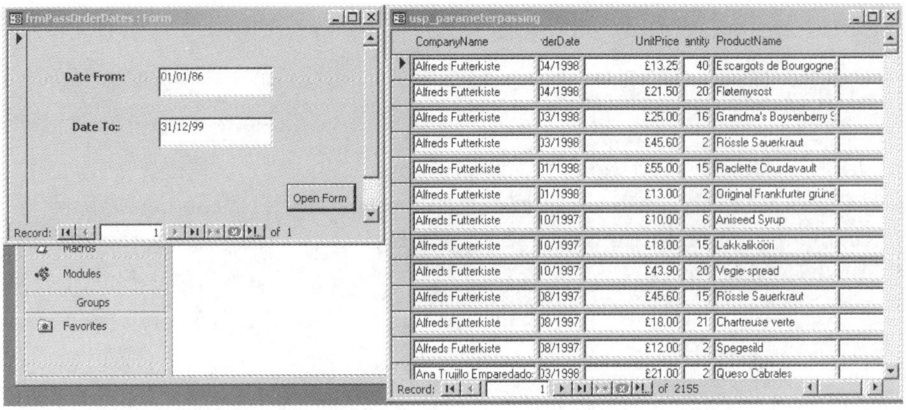

Figure 16-16. The End Result

Another approach is to use a simple SQL statement for the record source. For example, setting the record source to

```
SELECT CompanyName, ContactName, Phone FROM Customers
```

returns all records from the Northwind Customer table. Ninety records are returned, which isn't a great many, but just think if the table had 5,000 customers. This would result in lot of network traffic. Look at the following SQL statement:

```
SELECT CompanyName, ContactName, Phone FROM Customers WHERE (CustomerID = ?)
```

Note the question mark that has been added to the WHERE clause. It acts as a placeholder for a parameter. When the code is executed, you are prompted to enter a CustomerID. Simply enter a value to execute the statement. Figure 16-17 shows the Parameter Input prompt.

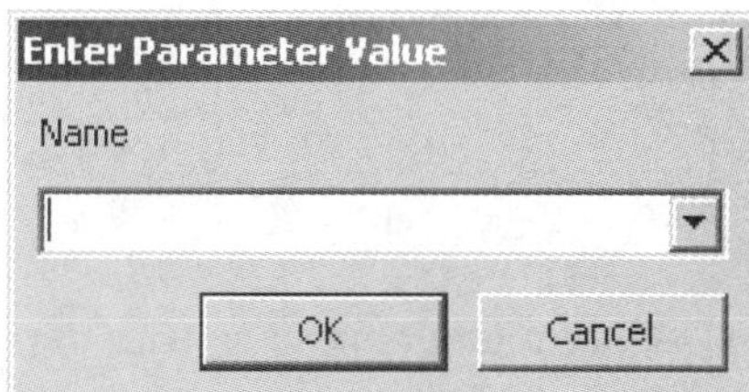

Figure 16-17. The Parameter Input dialog box

Designing Views

We'll now use the Access 2002 Query Builder to create an SQL Server view.

Chapter 14 discusses views in some detail. To recap, a view can be thought of as a virtual table. A view is a window into the data held within a table or tables. As useful as a view is, some things just cannot be done with them:

- Views cannot use the ORDER BY clause unless you add the SQL TOP statement. Use of TOP is discussed in Chapters 14 and 19.
- Views cannot contain INSERT, DELETE, or UPDATE.
- Views cannot be used with DDL statements.
- Views containing aggregate functions cannot be updated.

The SQL statements used to create a view is very similar to that used to create tables and is shown below:

```
CREATE VIEW vw_Customers
AS
Select * from tblcustomer
```

To create the view with Access 2002:

1. In the database window, select the Queries section.
2. Click on the New button.
3. Select Design view from the dialog box and click on OK to open the query design window.
4. In the Add Table dialog box, click on the Customers table and click on Add.
5. Close the Add Table dialog box.
6. To select all columns, check the *All Columns column located at the top of the table graphic.

Figure 16-18 shows Query Builder populated with the Customers table.

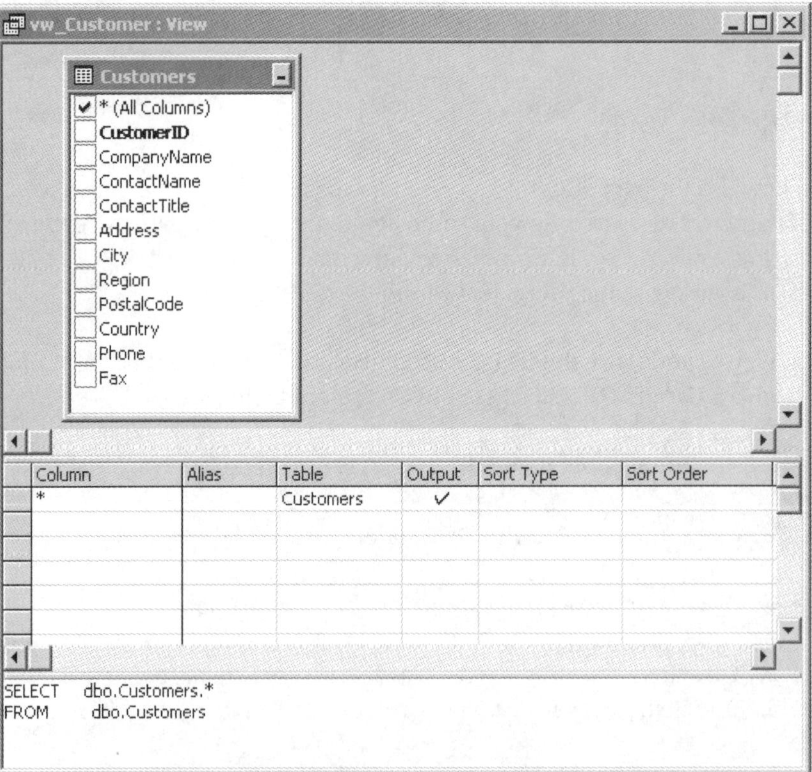

Figure 16-18. Building a view with the Customers table

On this occasion, as can be seen in Figure 16-18, the SQL pane is visible.

> **NOTE** *If you want to view the SQL pane, select View from the main menu, select Panes, and click on View SQL. The SQL pane is a useful learning tool because you can watch the SQL statement being created as you select fields from the table or tables.*

You can see the SQL statement that's used to create the view, and it is a simple SQL SELECT statement. However, when it is viewed from the SQL Server side (or when the SQL is viewed from within Access 2002), the full syntax is seen. Figure 16-19 shows the CREATE VIEW statement as held by SQL Server.

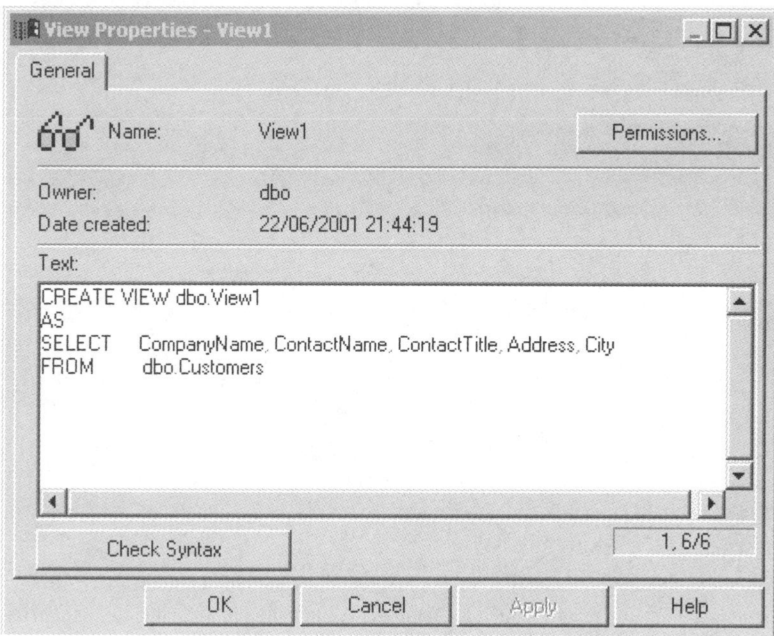

Figure 16-19. The SQL Server 2000 Create View syntax

As can be seen, the SQL statement is included as part of a CREATE VIEW Statement. But let's say that you didn't want all the records; maybe we again want to see only those customers who live in London and order the records by company name. The important bit here is the ORDER BY because views do not support ORDER BY. So can we do this?

The short answer is yes; the long answer is—you guessed it—a bit longer. Before we go into the details, let's create a view that shows the customers in

London ordered by company name. Using the same procedure as before, create the basic view. On this occasion, however, check the individual columns rather than select all columns. In the query window, add 'London' to the Criteria cell. See Figure 16-20.

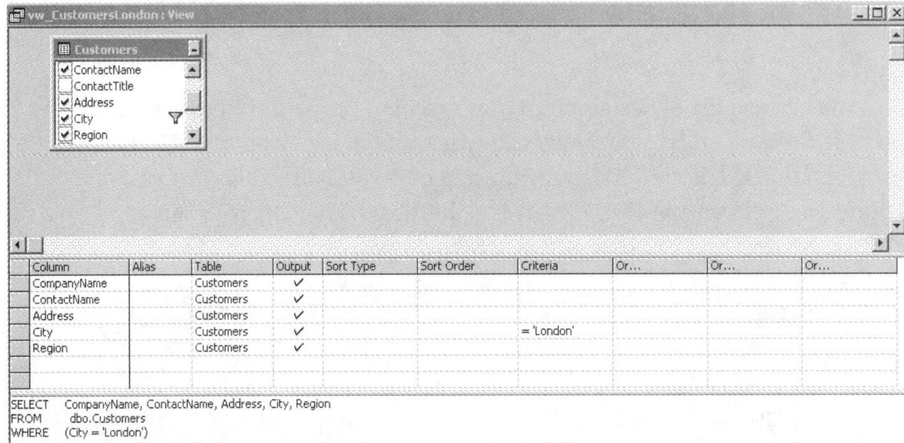

Figure 16-20. Adding the criteria

Note the resulting SQL statement:

```
SELECT      CompanyName, ContactName, Address, City, Region
FROM        dbo.Customers
WHERE       (City = 'London')
```

This simple SQL statement containing a WHERE clause restricts the records to customers in London.

Now, let's return to Design view and order by company name.

Close and save the view and reopen it in Design view. The SQL statements for the view are shown below. Note the changes:

```
SELECT      TOP 100 PERCENT CompanyName, ContactName, Address, City, Region
FROM        dbo.Customers
WHERE       (City = N'London')
ORDER BY    CompanyName
```

The SELECT statement has been modified to accommodate our needing to sort the view. The words "TOP 100 PERCENT" have been added.
What's happened?

To circumvent the SQL standard, which does not permit you to use ORDER BY in a view, the keyword TOP is used. (This may be familiar to Access developers as it is occasionally used in Access queries.)

TOP X PERCENT is used to select the top X percent or top number of whatever you are searching for. In this case, we want all records, so it's the top 100%. Try changing the value 100 to, say, 10 and see what happens. In my case, the result set was restricted to a single row.

> **NOTE** *Beware, if two or more values tie for last place (that is, they are the same), then all but one will be ignored. (For example, if two customer order values are the same—customer A has total orders of $300 and customer B has total orders of $300—then only one value is displayed.)To see all the records, you must add the WITH TIES clause to the TOP statement, for example: TOP 100 PERCENT WITH TIES.*

Figure 16-21 shows the same view syntax as held by SQL Server.

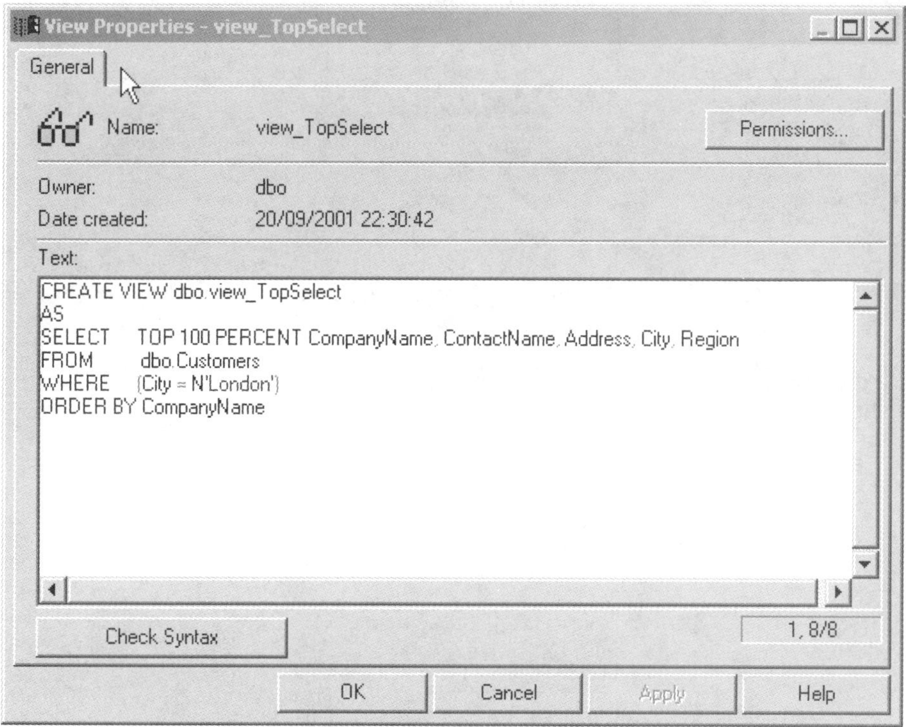

Figure 16-21. The view syntax on SQL Server

Views are also useful to shield users from complex joins between tables. Although this example is not complex, it demonstrates the principle of hiding join complexity.

We will create a single view that retrieves data from the Customers, Orders, and Order Details tables.

Step 1. Creating the View

From the database window:

1. Select the Queries section.

2. Click on the New button.

3. Select Design view from the New Query dialog box.

The Query Builder window opens and you can then select the three tables. Use the checkbox beside the field name to indicate that those fields are required as part of the query output. At this point, your query should resemble Figure 16-22.

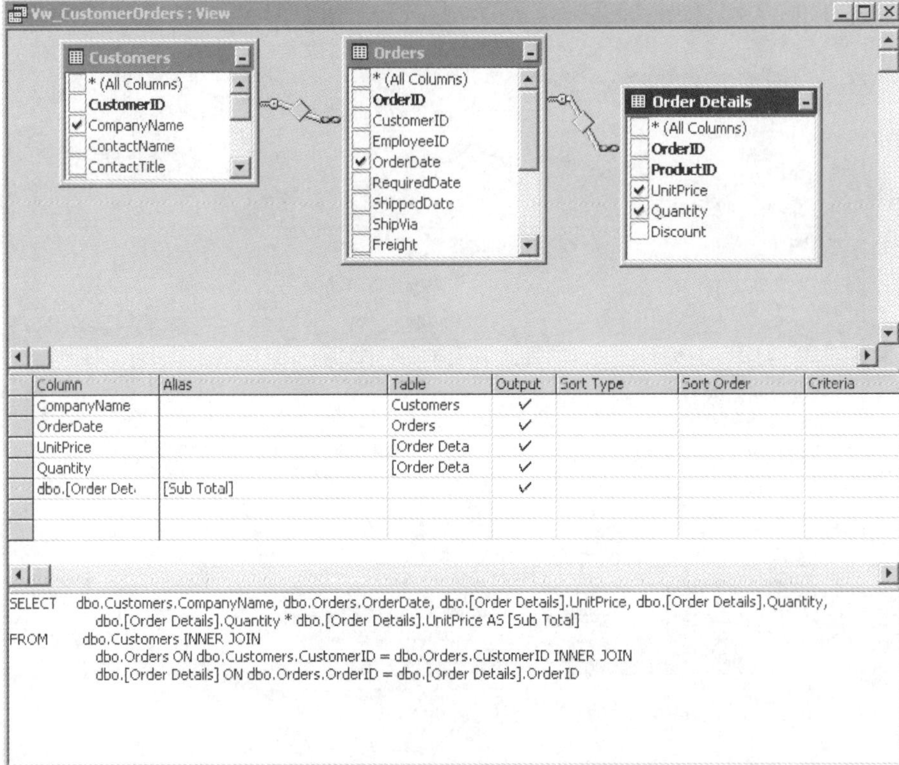

Figure 16-22. The Query Builder window with tables added

Save the view definition as vw_CustomerOrders

NOTE *You can either save the view by using File-> Save, or you will be prompted to save the view upon execution.*

Step 2. Using the View

From the database window, execute Vw_CustomerOrders. Figure 16-23 shows the output.

Vw_CustomerOrders : View

CompanyName	OrderDate	UnitPrice	Quantity	Sub Total
Vins et alcools Chevalier	04/07/1996	£14.00	12	£168.00
Vins et alcools Chevalier	04/07/1996	£9.80	10	£98.00
Vins et alcools Chevalier	04/07/1996	£34.80	5	£174.00
Toms Spezialitäten	05/07/1996	£18.60	9	£167.40
Toms Spezialitäten	05/07/1996	£42.40	40	£1,696.00
Hanari Carnes	08/07/1996	£7.70	10	£77.00
Hanari Carnes	08/07/1996	£42.40	35	£1,484.00
Hanari Carnes	08/07/1996	£16.80	15	£252.00
Victuailles en stock	08/07/1996	£16.80	6	£100.80
Victuailles en stock	08/07/1996	£15.60	15	£234.00
Victuailles en stock	08/07/1996	£16.80	20	£336.00
Suprêmes délices	09/07/1996	£64.80	40	£2,592.00
Suprêmes délices	09/07/1996	£2.00	25	£50.00
Suprêmes délices	09/07/1996	£27.20	40	£1,088.00
Hanari Carnes	10/07/1996	£10.00	20	£200.00

Figure 16-23. Results when running the view

Now close the view. We will now create a simple Select query using the view as our data source. From the database window:

1. Select the Queries section.
2. Click on the New button.
3. From the New Query dialog box, select Design Stored Procedure.
4. In the Add Table dialog box, click on the View tab to view all available database views.

5. Select Vw_CustomerOrders.
6. Click on Add to add the view to the query window.
7. Click on Close to close the Add Table dialog box.
8. Select all the fields available from the view. (Check the box beside each column's name.)

Your stored procedure should look like the one shown in Figure 16-24. All fields have been selected.

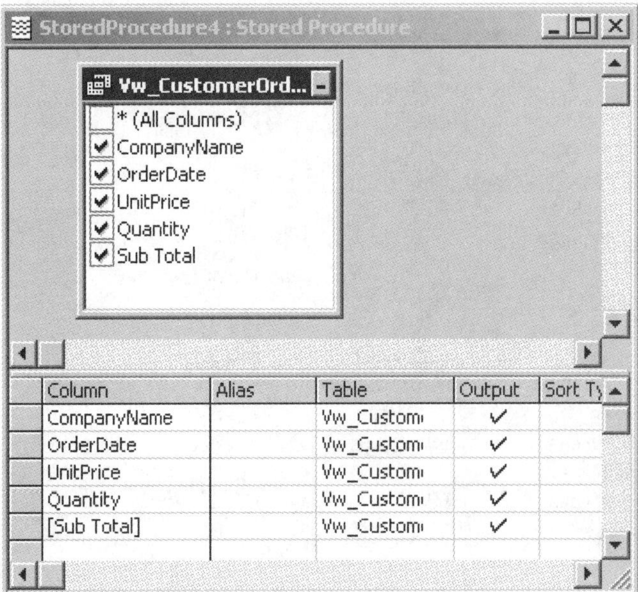

Figure 16-24. Stored procedure using a view

Compare the resulting SQL statement. I think you will agree that your users are very well shielded from the syntax and joins required to retrieve this data.

The following two SQL statements illustrate this point a bit more clearly.

Select from a view:

```
SELECT     CompanyName, OrderDate, UnitPrice, Quantity, [Sub Total]
FROM       dbo.Vw_CustomerOrders
```

Select without the view:

```
SELECT      dbo.Customers.CompanyName, dbo.Orders.OrderDate,
            dbo.[Order Details].UnitPrice, dbo.[Order Details].Quantity,
            dbo.[Order Details].Quantity * dbo.[Order Details].UnitPrice
            AS [Sub Total]
FROM
            dbo.Customers INNER JOIN
            dbo.Orders ON dbo.Customers.CustomerID = dbo.Orders.CustomerID
            INNER JOIN dbo.[Order Details] ON dbo.Orders.OrderID
            =dbo.[Order Details].OrderID
```

It should be apparent just from looking at the two SQL statements which one your users would prefer. Much easier than teaching users about inner and outer joins, no? However, many developers prohibit users from creating their own SQL objects. A view like the one just shown still has a place because there is an increasing use of query tools (Impromptu and Oracle Browser to name two). Users use these tools to perform ad-hoc queries on data structures. The use of views can help to reduce the number and complexity of tables used by such tools.

NOTE *In the previous example, we select all the required fields, but views are also useful for hiding values from users (such as salary details). Thus, you don't need to keep such data in distinct tables. For example, in a salary table, we may have sensitive data that standard users would not be given access to. Those needing access to the salary information could then be given access to the full table or another view containing this sensitive information. By using a view, we can exclude such data, and thus ensuring that your standard user never sees it. In fact, they would be totally unaware that it exists. This brief overview barely scratched the surface of views, and they can be a useful addition to any developer's toolbox and should be investigated further. Chapter 14 looks at views in some detail; included are indexing views and inserting and deleting data using views.*

Chapter 14 also looks at creating a simple view using ADO and the command object.

Dealing with Errors

Error control is vital to your procedures, functions, and views. In Chapter 15, we looked briefly at the @@ERROR system variable. Here, we look at it in a bit more detail. Remember, it is vital that you use error trapping in your code. In many of the examples shown so far, error checking has been omitted. The main idea up to now has been to show you the function of some of the new objects you will face.

As we have seen, @@ERROR defaults to a value of 0 and is repopulated after each statement is executed. As a result, you need to place @@ERROR after each statement executed. Unlike VBA, in which we can use On Error Goto to trap and deal with errors, in T-SQL we must handle them as and when they happen. If you don't, the statements following the error will continue to execute, possibly building up errors that you remain unaware of. The text associated with @@ERROR can be viewed in the sysmessages table in the master database. The following T-SQL statement returns the error, severity, and description when run via SQL Server Query Analyzer.

```
SELECT error,severity,description
FROM
Sysmessages
ORDER BY error
```

For example, to check if an insert was successful, you could check the value of @@ERROR immediately after the statement executed. The following T-SQL statement updates the Northwind Product table:

```
Create Procedure usp_InsertProd
(@ProductName [nvarchar](40),@Unit_Price[Money])
AS
BEGIN
  If @ Unit_Price>100
    BEGIN
    RAISERROR (50001,16,1)
    END
       ELSE
          BEGIN
             BEGIN TRANSACTION
              INSERT INTO dbo.Products
              (ProductName,UnitPrice)
        IF @@ERROR <> 0
    Rollback TRANSACTION
```

```
Else
    COMMIT TRANSACTION
    End
    End
```

Both RAISERROR and the value 50001 are discussed in a bit. In the above case, @@ERROR receives the value of RAISERROR, 50001. As this is greater than 0, the transaction is rolled back (cancelled). The Product table is returned to its state before the procedure was executed. The insert fails.

When executed, the procedure prompts for a value. The input is tested (`IF @Unit_Price > 100`), and, if the value is greater than 100, a custom error message is raised.

> **TIP** *When using RAISERROR to create custom messages in ADO or the Access user interface, the severity must be set to a value of 16 or greater. Severity levels less than 16 are simply warnings; 16 and greater are errors.*

RAISERROR

RAISERROR can return a user-defined error message for debugging purposes. It can replace the Err.Raise statement used by Access developers. The message returned can be a simple string or user defined. It can include an error number, error severity, and state. The error can also be logged in SQL Server's error log and even, if required, the Windows error log.

The syntax of RAISERROR is:

```
RAISERROR ({msg_id |msg_str }{,severity ,state }
   [ ,argument [ ,, . . . n ] ] ))
   [ WITH option [ ,, . . . n ] ]
```

- **Msg_id** is the user-defined error message. The message is stored in the sysmessages table. User-defined errors must have a msg_id greater than 50,000.

- **Msg_str** is the actual error message required. It can be a maximum of 400 characters.

- **Severity**: SQL Server classifies messages in accordance to the severity of the message. Think of the different types of message boxes we can create with Access (Information, Critical, and so on). Levels 0 to 18 can be used by the user, and 19 to 25 can be used by a server role that's fixed by system administrators. Table 16-2 shows some of the severity levels associated with SQL Server errors.

- **State** is used by Microsoft support techs to identify the state of the server at the time the error occurred. It has no meaning to SQL Server.
- **Argument** refers to variables that are used to customize the message.
- In the **WITH option**, three values can be used:
    - **LOG** logs the error to the SQL Server error log and the NT application log.
    - **NOWAIT** sends the message to the client.
    - **SETERROR** sets @@ERROR to the ID for the message, or 50,000.

Table 16-2. SQL Server Error Severity Levels

LEVEL	DESCRIPTION
0–10	Information
11–16	User generated
17–25	Hardware errors – system administrators must be informed

NOTE *Errors with a severity >= 20 cause the connection to be dropped. No message is sent to the client.*

In addition to the error messages already defined in SQL Server, we can define our own by using the sp_addmessages system procedure. In the prior example with usp_InsertProd, we call error 50001. This message was created using sp_addmessage, in the Query Analyzer, as follows:

```
Sp_addmessage @msgnum=50001,
@severity = 10,
@msgtext = 'The Unit Price Must be less than $100'
```

In this way, we can reuse the error number in any number of stored procedures.

PRINT

The print statement works much like the Debug.Print Statement in VBA: we can use it to print variables, statements, and errors when testing code. It is available in the SQL Server Query Analyzer and in ADO when using connections WithEvents. The PRINT statement used in ADO should raise the connection's InfoMessage event. It is not returned as data but as an informational message to the calling application.

> **NOTE** *A detailed discussion of ADO and WithEvents is beyond the scope of this section, but there is an excellent discussion on the limitations of using both PRINT and RAISERROR with ADO in Bill Vaughan's book,* ADO Examples and Best Practice *(Apress).*

For example, the following SELECT statement prints out a message depending on whether the count of customers living in London is greater than 34.

```
BEGIN
  IF (SELECT count(CustomerID)
  FROM dbo.Customers
  WHERE City = 'LONDON')>34
  PRINT ' Lots of Customers in London'
  Else
  PRINT 'Very Few in London'
END
```

SQL Server 2000 Stored Procedure Wizard

On the SQL Server side of things are several methods to create stored procedures: we can hand-code them directly using Query Analyzer; we can use one of the SQL Server wizards to create the procedure for us; and we can create them using Enterprise Manager. This section looks at using the Stored Procedure wizard to create a simple stored procedure for the Northwind ADP.

Running the Wizard

With Enterprise Manager open, click on Tools and select Wizards. Figure 16-25 shows the database wizards available.

1. Expand the Database folder in the Select Wizard dialog box. Click on the + symbol.

2. Select Create Stored Procedure Wizard and click on OK.

NOTE *This is a good opportunity to explore the other wizards available. You might want to run each of them on a test database. They may save you some time.*

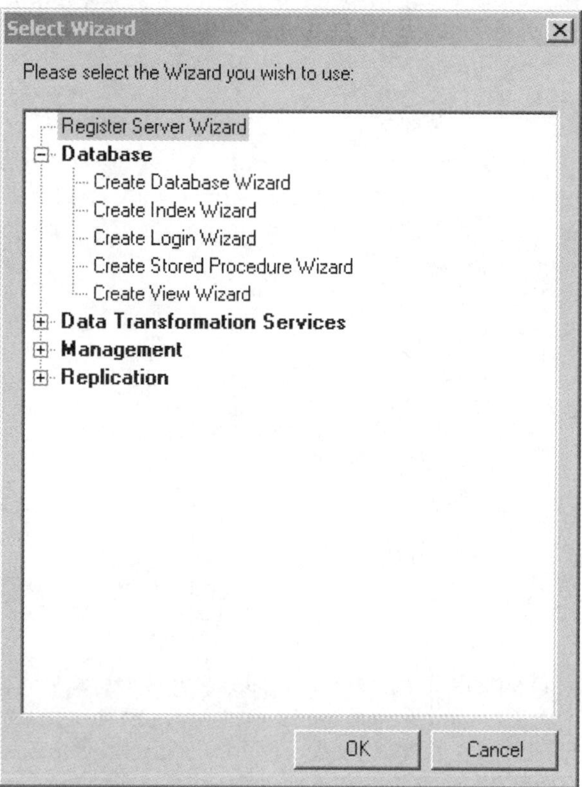

Figure 16-25. Database wizards

Figure 16-26 shows the initial screen of this wizard.

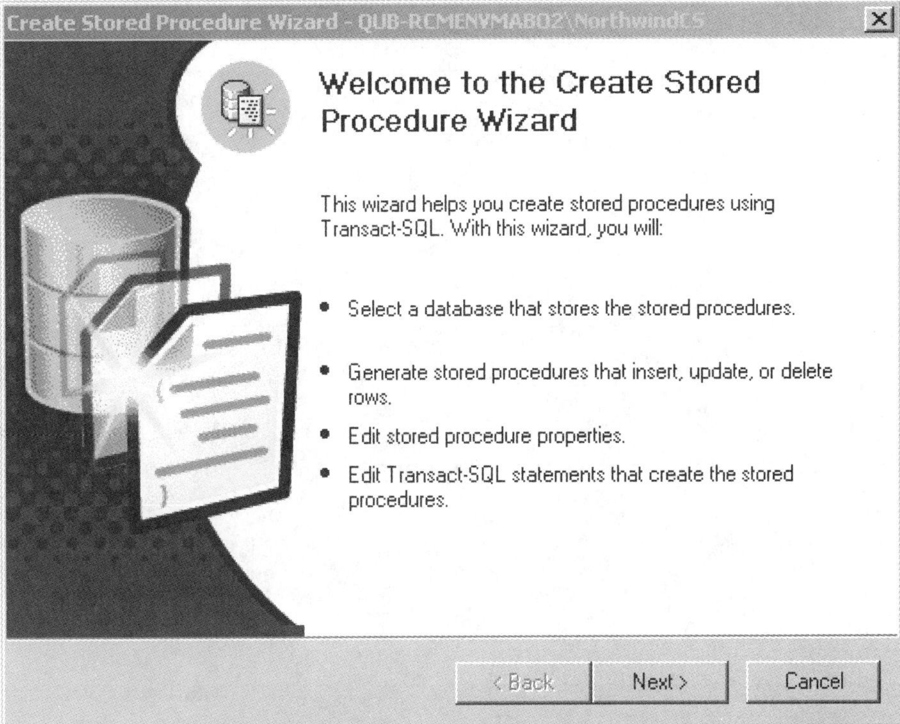

Figure 16-26. The initial screen of the Stored Procedure wizard

3. Click on Next.

4. The second screen requires you to indicate the database you are going to work with. Select the database using the drop-down list See Figure 16-27. Select the Northwind demo database.

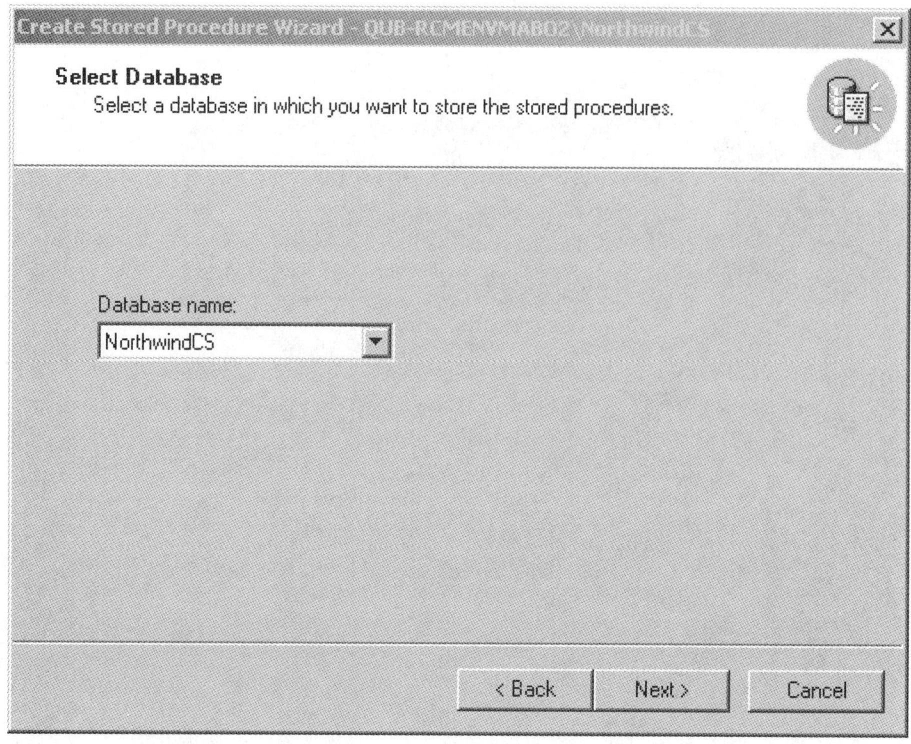

Figure 16-27. Select the database.

5. Click on Next.

Now you will see one of the limitations of the wizard: you are restricted to creating INSERT, DELETE, and UPDATE procedures. However, this still saves you considerable time typing.

Figure 16-28 shows the procedure option screen, which you'll use to select the tables and procedure types.

6. Select the Customers table and check the Insert box.

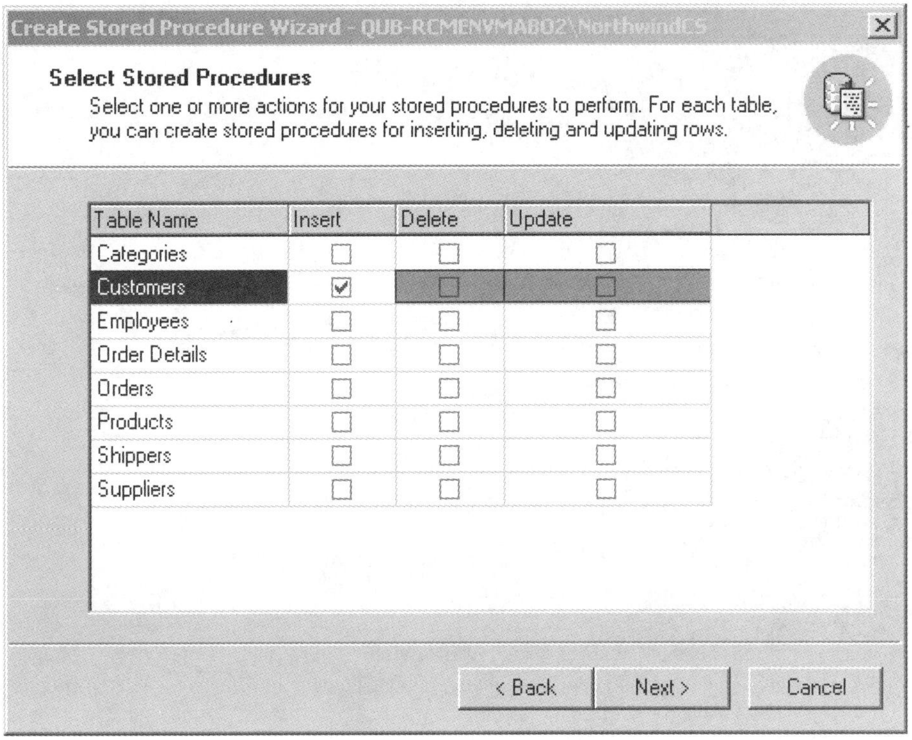

Figure 16-28. Table and procedure choice

7. Click on Next.

The final screen shown in Figure 16-29 provides you with an opportunity to edit the script. It's usually a good idea to change the generated name.

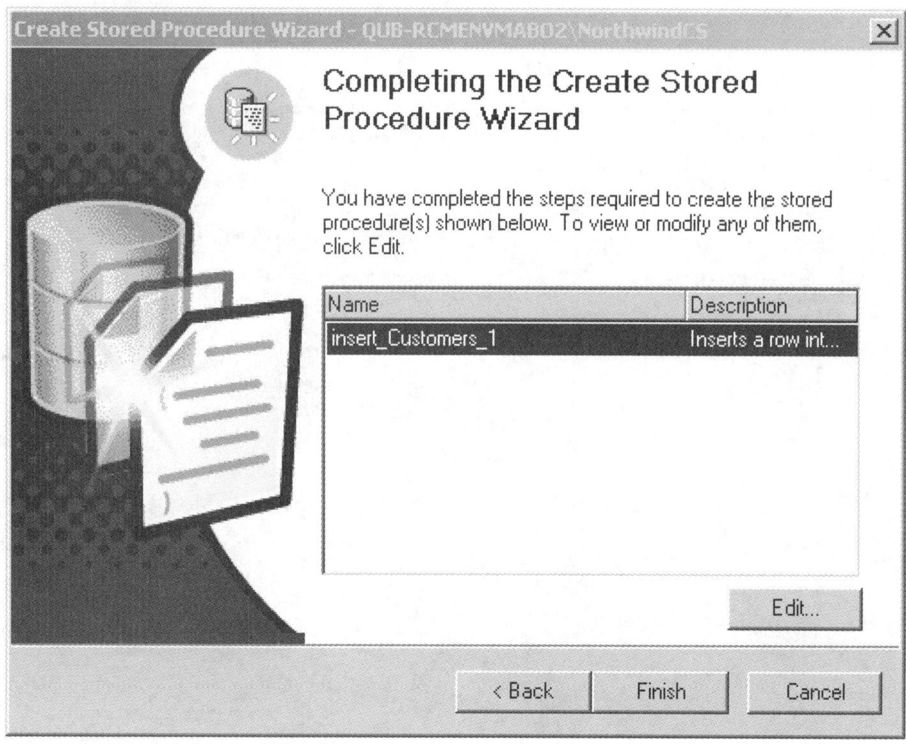

Figure 16-29. Completing the wizard

8. Click on the Edit button.

Figure 16-30 shows the edit procedure screen.

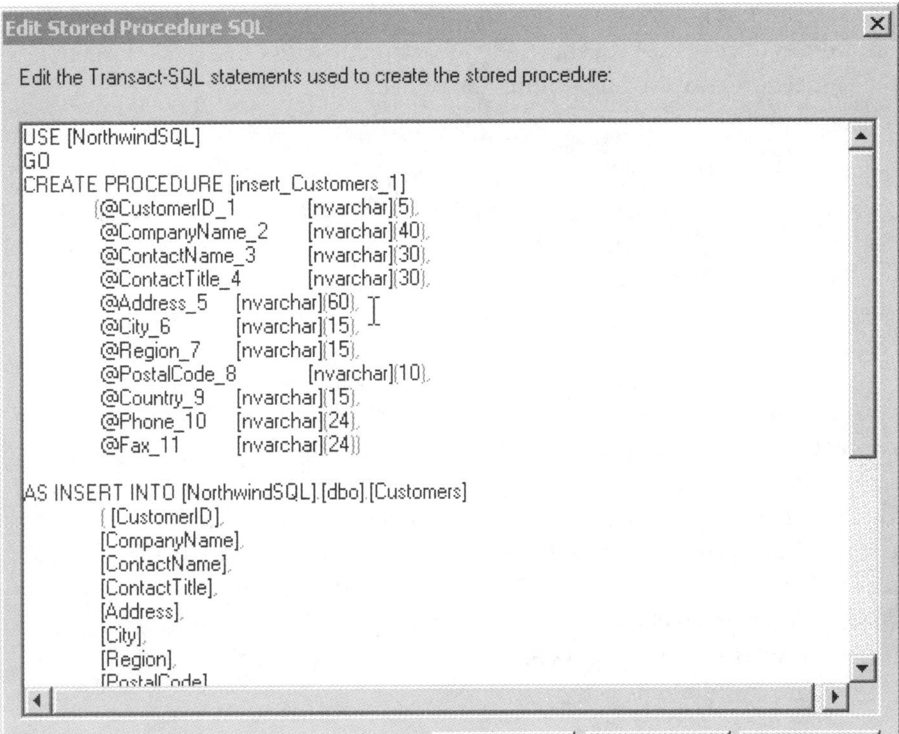

Figure 16-30. The edit procedure screen

9. Click in the name text box and delete the generated name. Change the procedure name to usp_genCustInsert.

> **NOTE** *If you need to remove any of the columns from the script, simply uncheck the box below the select column. Clicking on the Edit T-SQL button opens a window and permits you to directly edit the T-SQL script.*

10. Click on OK when finished.

11. A message confirms that the script has been generated. Click on OK to close the wizard, and you're done.

The script is now available in Enterprise Manager. Click on Stored Procedures to view the procedure. If you're working with an ADP, all the generated procedures are available within the project.

> **NOTE** *The features of the wizard do differ depending on the type of procedure that you're generating. For example, with an UPDATE procedure, you can choose which columns to add to the SET clause and which to add to the WHERE clause.*

The wizard, although not meeting all your needs, does provide help when you need to create INSERT, DELETE, or UPDATE procedures that require a lot of manual keying of column and variable values, particularly if you need to generate several procedures at once.

In this chapter, you had an introduction to functions, views, and stored procedures. I hope you can see how some of your existing skills, particularly in SQL, can be transferred over to Access Data Projects and T-SQL. We also looked at some basic error checking, and you may notice that the error control of T-SQL is just slightly worse than that of VBA.

CHAPTER 17

Upsizing Directly from Access

Taming the Beast

UPSIZING EXISTING ACCESS DATABASES continues to be a major headache for developers moving to SQL Server. As we have seen, Access continues to make strides towards SQL Server, and this version is no exception. It is now easier than ever to work directly with SQL Server from Access, and it can be expected that this process will improve. Access 2 introduced the Upsizing wizard, and Access 2000 included it for the first time as a menu item (but an additional fix had to be downloaded for those using it to upsize to SQL Server 2000). In this chapter, we'll look at the options for upsizing, what to do before upsizing, problems you may face, and which options to choose.

I hope one of the major themes running through this book has been that of professional development techniques, the simple but often overlooked things: no spaces in table and column names, using a proper naming convention for your database objects, choosing the correct data types, using the built-in referential integrity features to control your data, and, most importantly, planning for the future growth and expansion of your database.

> **NOTE** *One important point that should be made is that each upsizing project will be different. This chapter covers the generalities of upsizing. Your own individual requirement may prove to be different.*

One thing should be made clear: the main purpose of the upsizing tools is to deal with your data, that is, tables. Everything else is secondary to the process, and it is generally with everything else that you will have most problems. Upsizing has only one rule: plan everything in advance. Oh, yes, and back up your MDB file before you start anything.

We are also of the opinion that the use of linked tables with SQL Server is the least recommended way to proceed with an upsizing project. We recommend a full move to Access Data Projects (provided that you're working with SQL Server). In this way, you achieve the full benefits of using a large database system while maintaining the Access interface. Access 2002 has made this entire process easier, but some problems still exist in converting. In general, this chapter refers to upsizing to ADPs, but many of the problems are common to whatever method you choose.

How It Can Fall Apart

As we'll see in the following sections, several things can cause upsizing to fail.

Dates

SQL Server and Access 2002 use different date ranges. The start date in SQL Server is 1 Jan 1753 ending at 31 Dec 9999. In Access, we can use a range of dates from 1 Jan 100 to 31 Dec 9999. For example, Figure 17-1 shows an Access-allowable date (01-Apr-100) that was entered by error.

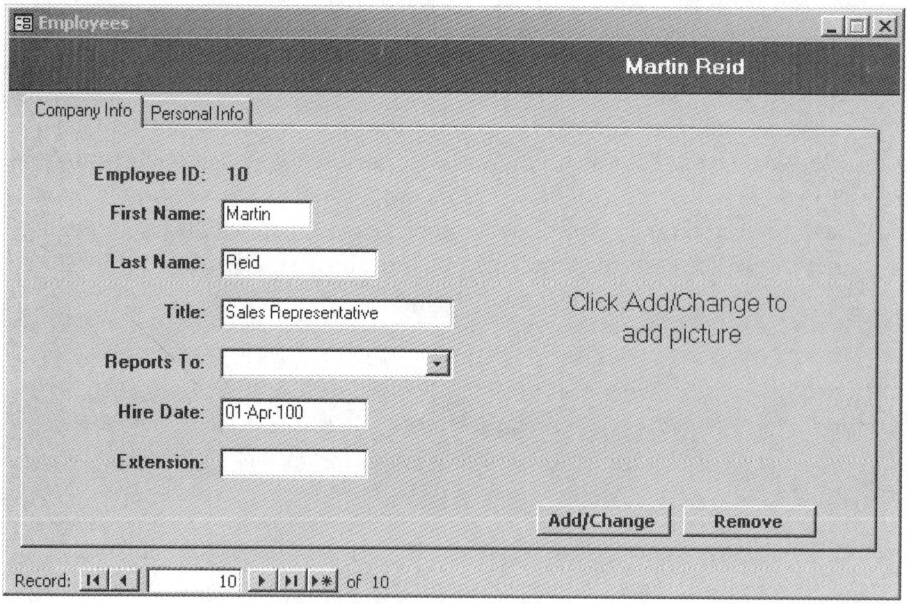

Figure 17-1. An Access valid date

Upsizing the amended Employees table containing the invalid date results in an upsizing failure. Figure 17-2 shows the error contained in the upsizing report.

Errors

Table: Employees

Table was skipped, or export faile

Figure 17-2. Upsizing report fragment

Once the hire date is changed back to an acceptable date (in this case 01-Apr-92), the upsize of the Employees table is successful. See Figure 17-3.

Table: Employees

	Microsoft Access	SQL Server
Table Name:	Employees	Employees
Attached Table Name:		
Aliasing Query:		
Validation Rule:		
	Timestamp field added to SQL Server table.	

Figure 17-3. Valid upsizing report

Many developers embarking on their first upsizing project find most of their problems in date formats.

Unique Constraints

This one should not catch you out: all tables must have a unique constraint or index. If your table does not have a unique constraint or index, the data will be read only when upsized. Of course, this may be exactly what you want. The primary key (unique index) in the EmployeesNoPK table in the sample Northwind database has been removed to illustrate this.

> **NOTE** *To demonstrate some of the features encountered during upsizing, I have modified some of the tables and forms included with the Northwind sample database.*

What's Upsized and What's Not

In this section, we will look at each Access object in turn and discuss how upsizing affects that particular object.

> **NOTE** *You will need at least read/design permissions on the Access database plus appropriate security on SQL Server to enable you to create tables and other objects. If you do not have permissions on some objects, they will be skipped in the upsizing process, and the error will not be logged in the resulting reports. You cannot upsize MDE files.*

Table 17-1 lists some of the basic SQL statements not supported by SQL Server 2000 and those supported by SQL Server 2000 but not by Access.

Table 17-1. Access and SQL Server Statements Support

ACCESS SQL	SQL SERVER 2000 SUPPORT
No Support	Compute, For Browse, Option
Order By	Not in views unless you use the TOP syntax. Chapters 14 and 16 discuss views.
With Owner Access	No support
No Support	Grouping [Column Name]
First	No Support
Last	No Support
Make Table	Create Table
Pivot	No Support
Transform	With Rollup, With Cube
&	+

Queries

When upsizing queries, the wizard will try to deal with all of your queries, and they will be upsized to one of the following server objects:

- SQL Server views
- SQL Server functions
- SQL Server stored procedures

The general idea is to convert your query syntax into comparable SQL Server syntax. Although we can do several things to queries to assist with the upsizing process, the following queries will not upsize:

- Multitable queries wherein the DISTINCTROW property has been set to Yes.
- Crosstab queries
- Pass-Through queries
- DDL queries

These queries must be re-created using SQL Server (lots of fun).

Queries That Reference Form Controls

It is common practice to use form values as parameters to Access queries. For example:

```
SELECT field
FROM table
Where somevalue  =  Forms![formname]![controlName]
```

Because processing is performed locally by Jet, this works okay. Jet is able to evaluate the form control before executing the query. When you move to a client/server configuration, all processing is performed on the server. The server has no way of evaluating the form value, and your query will fail to run. Later in the chapter, Table 17-2 shows the result achieved in upsizing the queries contained in the Northwind database.

The example we will look at here is the Invoices Filter query from Northwind. In this case, it is upsized to a user-defined function. User-defined functions are discussed in Chapter 16. The following function is created:

```
CREATE FUNCTION "Invoices Filter" (@Forms_Orders_OrderID_varChar (255) )
RETURNS TABLE
AS RETURN
SELECT Invoices.*
FROM Invoices
WHERE Invoices.OrderID= (@Forms_Orders_OrderID)
```

We had initially considered using VBA to reuse the invoice file to rewrite the report. However, this is not required. All we have to do is add a WHERE condition to the code that's used to open the invoice report. In this way, we can bypass the additional overhead (although minor) of using the Invoice Filter query. In order to do this, open the Order form in design view. From the Database window:

1. Select the forms group.
2. With the order form selected, click on the Design button.
3. In Design view, click on the Print Invoice button.
4. Right-click on the button and select Properties from the shortcut menu.
5. Select the Event tab in the Property dialog box.

> **NOTE** *There is an existing event procedure in the On Click event of the button.*

6. Click on the button to the right of the On Click Event text box to open the VBA editor at the **Print_Invoice()** procedure. We are going to change one line in the procedure to bypass the Invoices filter and pass the OrderID directly from the form to the invoices report.
7. Change the following line

   ```
   Docmd. OpenReport, "Invoice",acPreview,"Invoice Filter"
   ```

   to read

   ```
   Docmd. OpenReport, "Invoice",acPreview, WhereCondition:="OrderID=" &
   Me!OrderID
   ```

> **NOTE** *The inclusion of the WHERE clause also limits the records returned by SQL Server.*

8. Close and save the procedure.

9. Return to standard Form view and click on the Print Invoice button.

The invoice report will open showing the invoice for the customer record currently displayed on the order form.

The invoice report is based on an SQL Server view. You will be unable to add a parameter to a view. It also is not possible to pass values to the input parameter of a report in Print or Print Preview mode. To pass the value to the report, the report must be in Design view. Using a stored procedure for this report would remove many of these restrictions.

Another way to pass the parameter to the report is to use an SQL statement as the record source for a report. For example:

```
SELECT
OrderDate,RequiredDate,ShippedDate
FROM
dbo.Orders
WHERE
dbo.Orders.OrderID = ?
```

The question mark acts as a parameter placeholder. We can then use the InputParameter property of the report to provide a value to the SQL statement. The following reference is placed into the InputParameter property of the report:

```
OrderID Int =[Forms]![frmOrderID]![OrderID]
```

Another problem that you may encounter when using parameters is using forms-based values in queries. For example, developers often use the following as query parameters to gather data between two dates:

```
Value Between Forms![FormName]![ControlName1] AND Forms![FormName]![ControlName2]
```

If the first thirty characters of the parameters are identical (as they are here), SQL Server will truncate the parameter and your query will fail to upsize. For example, consider the following parameter used in a standard Access query:

```
Between [Forms]![frmThisIsACustomerForm]![Control_1]
AND  [Forms]![frmThisIsACustomerForm]![Control_2]
```

This is quite valid when used in Access 2002. However, it will fail to be upsized. The upsizing report returns the following parameters:

```
Between @[Forms]![frmThisIsACustomerForm] AND
@[Forms]![frmThisIsACustomerForm]
```

Due to the truncation, SQL Server is attempting to create the parameters to the function with the same name. In addition, the reference to the form controls has been removed.

> **NOTE** *When working with Query Builder, you are permitted to enter identical parameter names. However, you will receive only one prompt. That is, if you use the same parameter name for multiple parameters, you will be prompted for only a single value. When using multiple parameters, it makes sense to use different names for each parameter. You will also be permitted to use parameter names up to 128 characters in length.*

A very simple thing that you may stumble on is the use of the asterisk (*) as a wildcard. For example, the Customer Phone List form in the Northwind database no longer works properly when moved into an ADP. When you try to restrict records using the control buttons on the form, a message pops up stating that there are no records for the letter you selected, even though the application should find a match.

The control buttons on the form activate a macro to filter the records by company name. When you click on the "A" button, the companies whose names begin with A are displayed on the form. However, the macro uses the asterisk to create the SQL WHERE clause. The wildcard character in SQL Server is the percentage symbol (%). So, to fix the form, you will need to replace each occurrence of "*" in the macro, Customer Phone List. Once you have made this change, the form works as expected. To amend the macro:

1. Click on the Macro section in the Database window.

2. Select the Customer Phone List macro.

3. Click on the Design button to open the Macro Design window.

4. Click on any of the ApplyFilter values in the Action column.

5. Amend the existing WHERE clause changing the "*" to "%".

6. Repeat this process replacing each instance of "*" with "%".

> **NOTE** *With the Customer Phone List macro selected, you can choose Tools|Macro|Convert Macro to Visual Basic. The Customer Phone List macro will be converted to a VBA function. However, the asterisk is still used as the wildcard, and you must amend the VBA code to contain the percentage symbol so the function works. This may be a faster option because you can then use the Find and Replace option to do a quick change from "*" to "%" in the current procedure. Make sure that you select the current procedure only and choose Find Next in the Replace dialog box to step through the process rather than to replace all occurrences of "*" at once. Select Edit|Replace in the VBA IDE to open the Find/Replace dialog box. When you're finished, close and save the function. You can then replace the Afterupdate event on the Customer Phone List form with a call to the VBA function as opposed to the existing macro.*

Parameter Queries

Parameter queries—that is, those queries that either prompt for a value or receive a value via code—will be upsized to SQL Server inline functions. For example, the following SQL statement selects employee data based on the LastName entered in response to a prompt.

```
SELECT Employee.FirstName, Employee.LastName,
Employee.BirthDate, Employee.HireDate
FROM Employee
WHERE (((Employee.LastName)=[Enter Employee Last Name]))
ORDER BY Employee.HireDate;
```

When this is upsized, the Upsizing wizard will create an SQL Server inline function to provide equivalent functionality. In testing, all parameter queries were upsized as functions. The Access help files state that parameter queries will be upsized as either stored procedures or functions, but we did not find that to be the case. The preceding SQL is upsized to the following inline function.

```
CREATE FUNCTION qryemplastname
(@Enter_Employee_Last_Name varchar (255))
RETURNS TABLE
AS RETURN (SELECT TOP 100 PERCENT Employees.FirstName,
Employees.LastName, Employees.BirthDate, Employees.HireDate
FROM Employees
WHERE (((Employees.LastName)=@Enter_Employee_Last_Name))
ORDER BY Employees.HireDate)
```

It has been suggested by some developers that this is an inappropriate use of inline functions and that stored procedures would have been a more appropriate option. However, at this point, the wizard will convert your parameter queries to inline functions, which are discussed in Chapter 16.

Action Queries

Action queries will be upsized to SQL stored procedures. The following queries are upsized as stored procedures:

- Update
- Delete
- Make Table
- Append

Examples

Lets have a look at how some queries in the Northwind database are upsized when using SQL Server and Access Data Projects. Table 17-2 lists all the query objects in the Northwind database and shows the SQL Server objects that they are changed to when upsized.

Table 17-2. Upsizing results—Access Data Project

ACCESS QUERY	UPSIZED AS ACCESS	QUERY TYPE
Alphabetical List of Products	View	Standard SELECT
Product Sales for 1997	View	Standard SELECT with aggregate functions
Current Product List	User-defined function	SELECT with ORDER BY
Customers and City	Stored procedure	SELECT with UNION
Order Subtotals	View	SELECT with aggregates and GROUP BY
Invoices	View	Complex SQL SELECT
Invoices Filter	User-defined function	SELECT with form-based criteria
Order Details Extended	User-defined function	SELECT with ORDER BY
Employee Sales By County	Not upsized	SELECT with DISTINCTROW
Order Query	View	Simple SELECT
Category Sales for 1998	View	SELECT with aggregate functions
Category Sales for 1997	View	SELECT with aggregate functions
Products Above Average price	User-defined function	SELECT with subquery
Quarterly Orders	View	SELECT with DISTINCT
Quarterly Orders by Product	Not upsized	Crosstab

Note that two queries are ignored: Employee Sales by County and Quarterly Orders by Product.

Employee Sales By County

This query was not upsized because it contains the DISTINCTROW keyword in the SQL statement. SQL Server does not recognize the DISTINCTROW keyword, which is unique to Access. For a discussion of DISTINCTROW, see Chapter 8. DISTINCTROW has no effect when you select a column from each of the tables used in your SELECT statement. You should in almost all cases be able to replace the DISTINCTROW predicate with DISTINCT. This keyword is most commonly seen in SQL statements generated by Access wizards.

> **NOTE** *Replace DISTINCTROW with DISTINCT before running the Upsizing wizard.*

Quarterly Orders by Product

This one is slightly more complicated because it is a Crosstab query. On this occasion, we need to create a more complicated SQL statement to come close to a standard SQL crosstab. We will be using Access 2002 for this example. This example cannot be created via Query Builder, so a bit of typing is required. We will again use the Northwind database for our example.

1. From the Database window, select the Queries section.
2. Click on the New button.
3. Select Design Text Stored Procedure from the New Query dialog box.
4. Click on OK to close the dialog box.
5. Enter the following SQL statement into the Procedure template. Remember to delete the existing template text first.

```
CREATE PROCEDURE usp_CrossTabSales
AS
SELECT     dbo.Customers.CustomerID,
           dbo.Customers.CompanyName,
Sum(Case When Orders.OrderDate between '01-Jan-1996'
 and '31-Dec-1996'  Then UnitPrice Else 0 End)
 as [1997],
Sum(Case When Orders.OrderDate between '01-Jan-1997'
and '31-Dec-1998'  Then UnitPrice Else 0 End)
 as [1998],
Sum(Case When Orders.OrderDate between '01-Jan-1999'
and '31-Dec-2000'  Then UnitPrice Else 0 End)
as [1999]
FROM        dbo.Customers INNER JOIN
```

```
dbo.Orders ON dbo.Customers.CustomerID = dbo.Orders.CustomerID INNER JOIN
          dbo.[Order Details] ON dbo.Orders.OrderID = dbo.[Order
Details].OrderID
Group By      dbo.Customers.CustomerID,
 dbo.Customers.CompanyName
Order By dbo.Customers.CustomerID
```

> **NOTE** *Each CASE statement should appear on a single line within the Procedure template.*

Figure 17-4 shows how your stored procedure should look at this point.

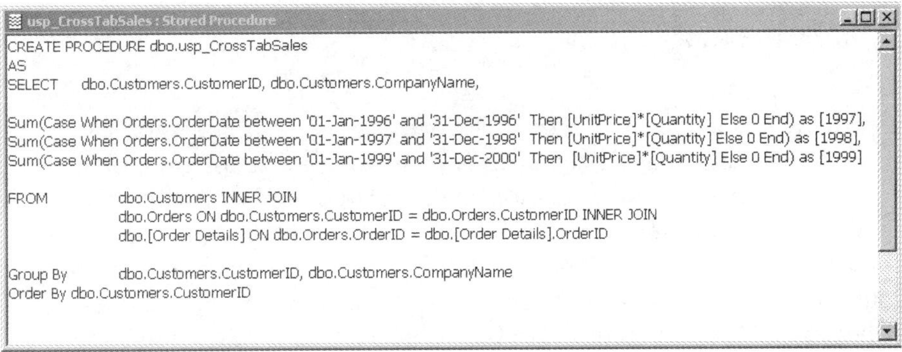

Figure 17-4. Stored procedure text

6. Close and save the stored procedure.

To execute the procedure, select Queries and double-click on the procedure name you just created (ups_CrossTabSales). Figure 17-5 shows the Results window.

usp_CrossTabSales : Stored Procedure

CustomerID	CompanyName	1997	1998	1999
ALFKI	Alfreds Futterkiste	£0.00	£4,596.20	£0.00
ANATR	Ana Trujillo Emparedados y helados	£88.80	£1,314.15	£0.00
ANTON	Antonio Moreno Taquería	£403.20	£7,112.15	£0.00
AROUT	Around the Horn	£1,379.00	£12,427.50	£0.00
BERGS	Berglunds snabbköp	£4,324.40	£22,643.75	£0.00
BLAUS	Blauer See Delikatessen	£0.00	£3,239.80	£0.00
BLONP	Blondel père et fils	£9,986.20	£9,101.80	£0.00
BOLID	Bólido Comidas preparadas	£982.00	£4,315.80	£0.00
BONAP	Bon app'	£4,202.50	£19,648.45	£0.00
BOTTM	Bottom-Dollar Markets	£1,832.80	£20,774.90	£0.00
BSBEV	B's Beverages	£479.40	£5,610.50	£0.00
CACTU	Cactus Comidas para llevar	£0.00	£1,814.80	£0.00
CENTC	Centro comercial Moctezuma	£100.80	£0.00	£0.00
CHOPS	Chop-suey Chinese	£1,799.20	£11,087.10	£0.00
COMMI	Comércio Mineiro	£2,169.00	£1,641.75	£0.00

Record: 1 of 89

Figure 17-5. Query results window

This SQL statement is fairly complex because we are using several statements to re-create what in Access can be done using a wizard. In this example, we are using an SQL Server CASE statement and the Sum function to return the total sales generated for each of the specified years. The CASE statement tests the value of the OrderDate. When it falls between the dates required, the Sum (outside the CASE statement) function is applied to the Unit Price column. Otherwise, a "0" is returned. The column is then returned using the alias name following the AS statement.

Using this example, it is also possible to replace the Sum function with any of the other aggregate functions, such as Min, Max, Average, and so on. Figure 17-6 shows the preceding procedure amended using the Max function to replace Sum.

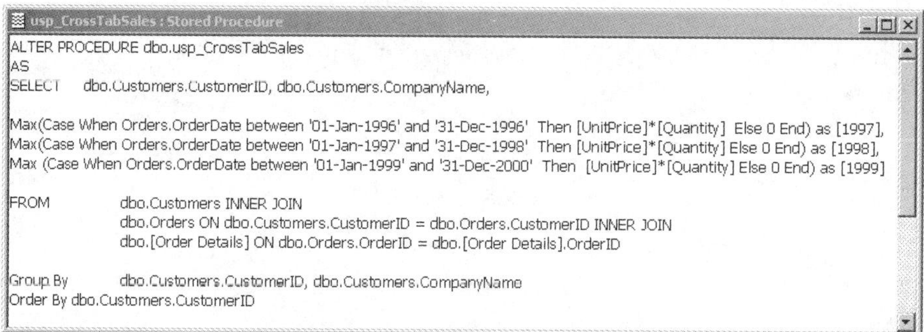

```
ALTER PROCEDURE dbo.usp_CrossTabSales
AS
SELECT     dbo.Customers.CustomerID, dbo.Customers.CompanyName,

Max(Case When Orders.OrderDate between '01-Jan-1996' and '31-Dec-1996'  Then [UnitPrice]*[Quantity]  Else 0 End) as [1997],
Max(Case When Orders.OrderDate between '01-Jan-1997' and '31-Dec-1998'  Then [UnitPrice]*[Quantity] Else 0 End) as [1998],
Max (Case When Orders.OrderDate between '01-Jan-1999' and '31-Dec-2000'  Then  [UnitPrice]*[Quantity] Else 0 End) as [1999]

FROM          dbo.Customers INNER JOIN
              dbo.Orders ON dbo.Customers.CustomerID = dbo.Orders.CustomerID INNER JOIN
              dbo.[Order Details] ON dbo.Orders.OrderID = dbo.[Order Details].OrderID

Group By      dbo.Customers.CustomerID, dbo.Customers.CompanyName
Order By dbo.Customers.CustomerID
```

Figure 17-6. ups_CrossTabSales using the Max function

Queries Containing User-Defined Functions

Queries that contain user-defined functions are not upsized. The wizard is not smart enough to interrogate the database to find the source of such functions. (Perhaps someday it will be.) The following list includes the VBA functions that upsize successfully to SQL Server:

asc()
case()
ccur()
chr()
cint()
clng()
csng()
cstr()
cvdate()
date()
day()
hour()
ime()
int()
left()
mid()
minute()
mod
month()
now()
right()
second()
str()
trim()
weekday()
year()

NOTE *Microsoft whitepapers on upsizing Access 2002 state that functions contained in the WHERE clause of an SQL SELECT statement cannot be upsized. To quote, "If functions of any kind are placed in the WHERE clause the query will not be upsized." However, testing with some of the functions just shown reveal that the wizard will in fact convert some VBA functions to their SQL Server equivalent. For example, the following SQL statement is upsized as an SQL Server function converting the Access* ***Date()*** *function to the SQL Server* ***GetDate()*** *function.*

```
SELECT Customers.CompanyName, Orders.OrderDate
FROM Customers INNER JOIN Orders ON
Customers.ID=Orders.CustomerID
WHERE
Orders.OrderDate = Date()
```

The Upsizing wizard converts this statement to:

```
SELECT dbo.Customers.CompanyName, dbo.Orders.OrderDate
FROM dbo.Customers INNER JOIN dbo.Orders ON
dbo.Customers.ID=dbo.Orders.CustomerID
WHERE
dbo.Orders.OrderDate
=CONVERT(datetime,CONVERT(varchar,GETDATE(),1),1))
```

Another example demonstrates another function that will not upsize: the Access Format function. For example, the following query will result in an upsize failure:

```
SELECT
Orders.OrderID, Format([OrderDate],"Long Date") As DateOrder
FROM
ORDERS
```

Access Forms

Forms should upsize with little problem. All form properties are available within an ADP, and you will see some additional ones, such as Max Records, Server Filter, and Input Parameters.

Max Records

This property specifies the maximum number of records that will be returned by the form. The property can be set either in the form or by using VBA. When the property is set in VBA, we use the form's Max Records property. For example:

```
Me.MaxRecords=100 or
Forms!formname.Maxrecords=100
```

NOTE *If you're using ADO to provide a recordset to a form, the following code fragment shows how to set this property.*

```
Set rst = New ADODB.Recordset
rst.maxrecords = 100
rst.Open "SQL Statement"
```

Server Filter

This property is used to set a subset of a record being displayed. It functions simply as a WHERE clause. This property can be set using the form's property sheet or using VBA code. An important note is that the Server Filter property is ignored if the form's record source is a stored procedure.

```
Me.ServerFilter = "CompanyName Like 'A%'"
Me.Refresh
```

Input Parameters

See Chapter 16 for a thorough discussion of this topic.

Table 17-3 shows the recommended approach when upsizing Access objects. I say *recommended* because each application is different.

Table 17-3. SQL Statements When Upsized

ACCESS OBJECT	UPSIZED AS
Select	Views
Select with Parameter	User-defined function. It has been argued that user-defined functions should not be used to supply data to the client. They should mainly be used within stored procedures. It may have been a matter of expediency by the Access team to use them in this fashion with the Upsizing wizard.
Make Table	SQL Server CREATE TABLE
Update Query	Stored procedure
Delete Query	Stored procedure
Append Query	Stored procedure

Jet Extended Properties

SQL Server 2000 now includes extended properties. As a result, Access Jet extended properties are available when your tables are upsized to SQL Server. Within Access, extended properties are often used to format data for the user (for example, using the Format property on an Access form or report). The following list shows the more popular extended properties that can be upsized:

- Description
- Input Mask
- Decimal Places
- Format
- Caption
- Row Source Type
- Row Source
- Column Heads
- List Rows

- Limit to List
- Column Count
- Column Widths
- List Width

The Upsizing Wizard

So far, we have seen some of the problems associated with upsizing and how the wizard deals with them. In this section, we'll look at running the Upsizing wizard.

Running the Upsizing Wizard

For this example, we will upsize the Northwind database. Remember to back up the database before carrying out any actions. Before beginning the process, also make sure that the Northwind database is open.

To activate the Upsizing wizard:

1. From the Main menu, select Tools|Database Utilities|Upsizing Wizard. Figure 17-7 shows the menu sequence to use to open the Upsizing wizard.

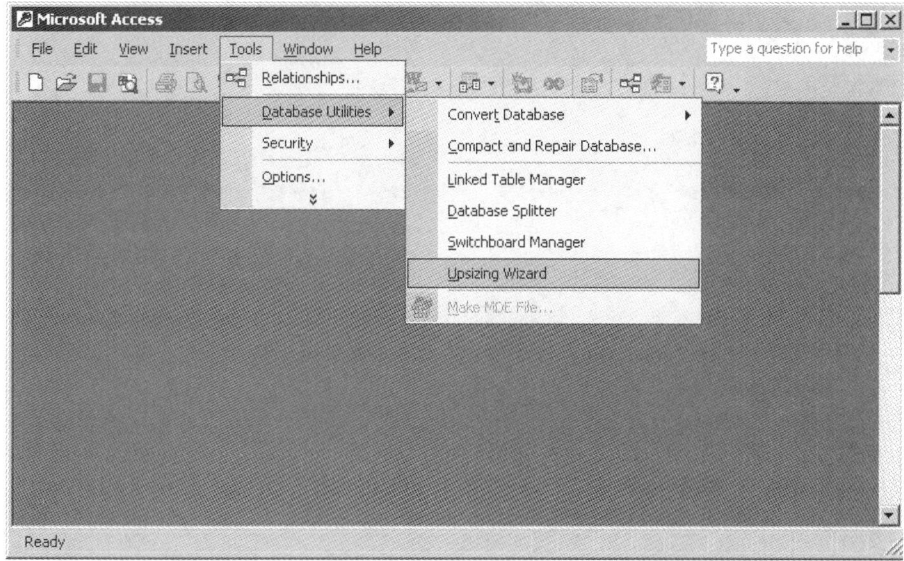

Figure 17-7. Starting the Upsizing wizard

2. The Upsizing wizard starts and presents you with the first of your options:

   - *Use an existing database:* This option will help you to upsize to an existing SQL Server database. If you select it, you will be prompted for an ODBC DSN file data source or a machine data source, or you may choose to create a new data source to the selected SQL Server.

   - *Create new database:* This option will help you create a new SQL Server database using the tables in the existing Access database. Figure 17-8 shows the upsizing wizard.

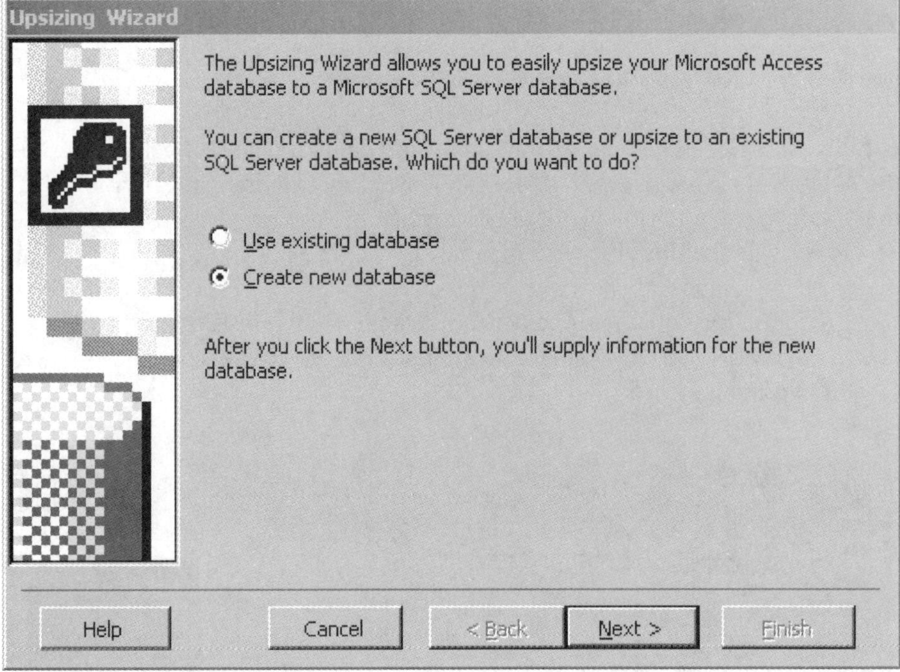

Figure 17-8. The Upsizing wizard

3. Select Create New Database and click on Next.

> **NOTE** *We will use the Create New Database option for this example because with it we can look purely at the results of this upsize without interference from existing database objects.*

The second stage of the wizard will ask you for information about the SQL Server that you're upsizing to and request some login and security information. See Figure 17-9.

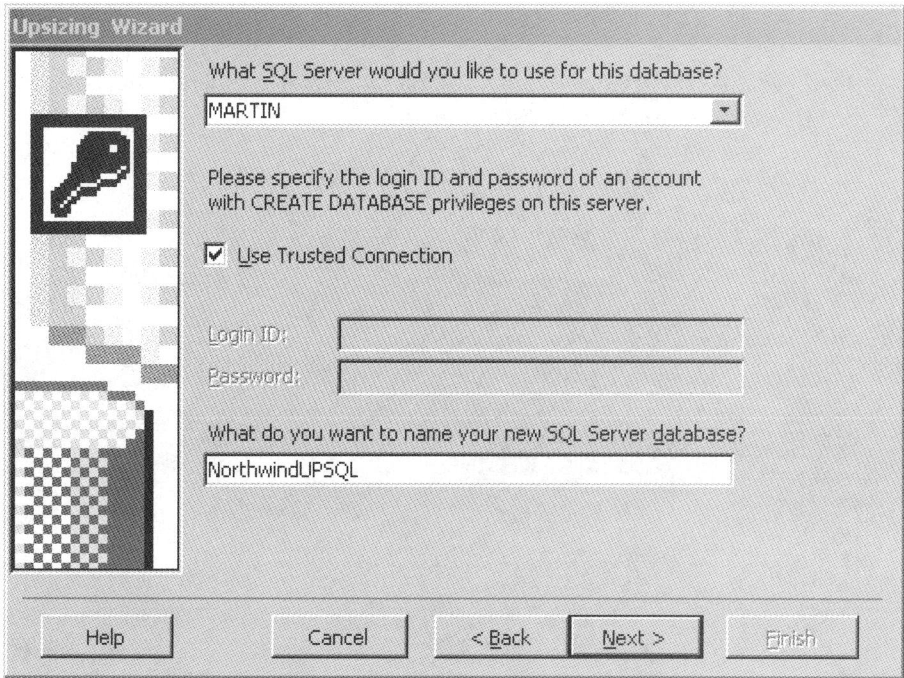

Figure 17-9. Server selection

4. What SQL Server would you like to use? Use the drop-down list to choose your server. All servers that are available to you will be listed in the drop-down list.

5. Please specify the login ID and password with CREATE DATABASE privileges on this server. Enter the required information and click on Next.

NOTE *You must have the Create Database privilege on SQL Server to continue this function. See Chapter 18 for a discussion on security. In my case, I am using a trusted connection with Windows 2000 security, so no further information is required. However, you may be using Mixed Mode authentication; if so, uncheck the Trusted checkbox and enter a username and password with sufficient privileges to create the new database on the server.*

6. What name do you want to use for your new SQL Server database? Simply either accept the default or enter a name for the new server. In this case, I have accepted the default, which is NorthwindSQL. If the database name that you enter already exists on the server, the wizard will amend the name to make it unique (by simply adding an incrementing number to the end of the database name).

7. Click on Next to continue. You will be prompted to indicate the tables to transfer to the server. See Figure 17-10.

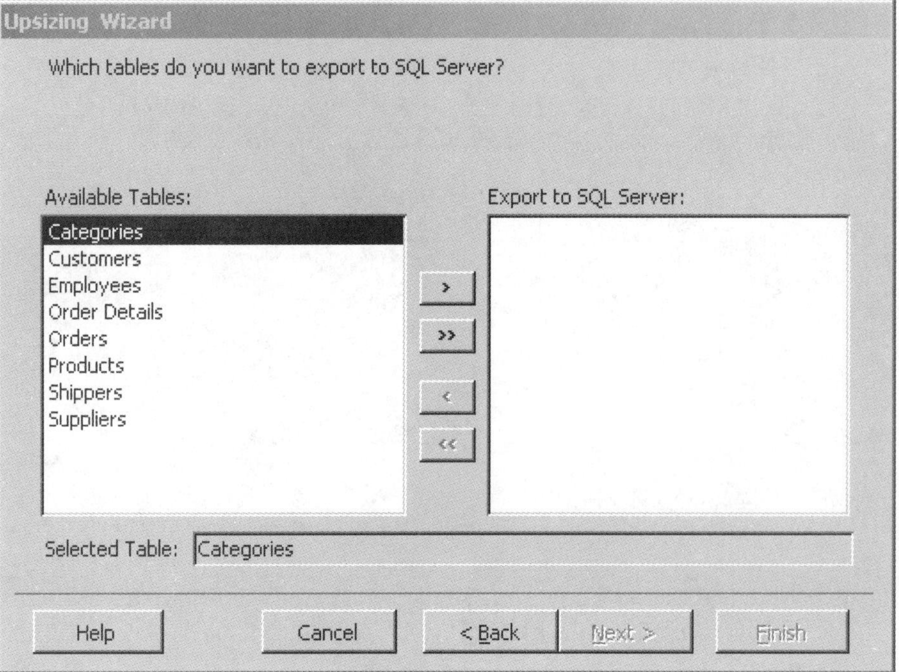

Figure 17-10. Table transfer

In standard Access fashion, you can use the arrow buttons to choose one or more tables to export to SQL Server. In this case, I am going to upsize the entire database (with the exception of the EmployeeNoPK table). Note the grayed text box that indicates the currently selected table. To select all tables at once, click on the double arrow button to move all tables to the selected tables list. Figure 17-11 shows the dialog box with the tables selected. If you are using the downloaded database, remember to remove the EmployeeNoPK table from the listing if it has been selected. Click on Next to proceed.

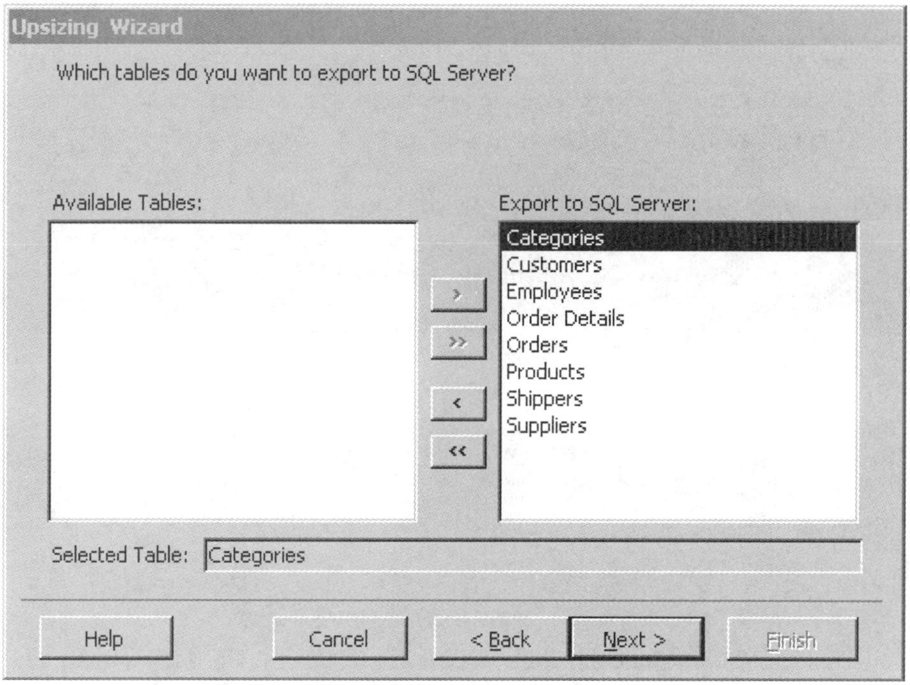

Figure 17-11. Tables selected for upsizing

The next stage in the wizard is one of the most important in the entire process, and so we will look at each option in some detail. Figure 17-12 shows the Properties page.

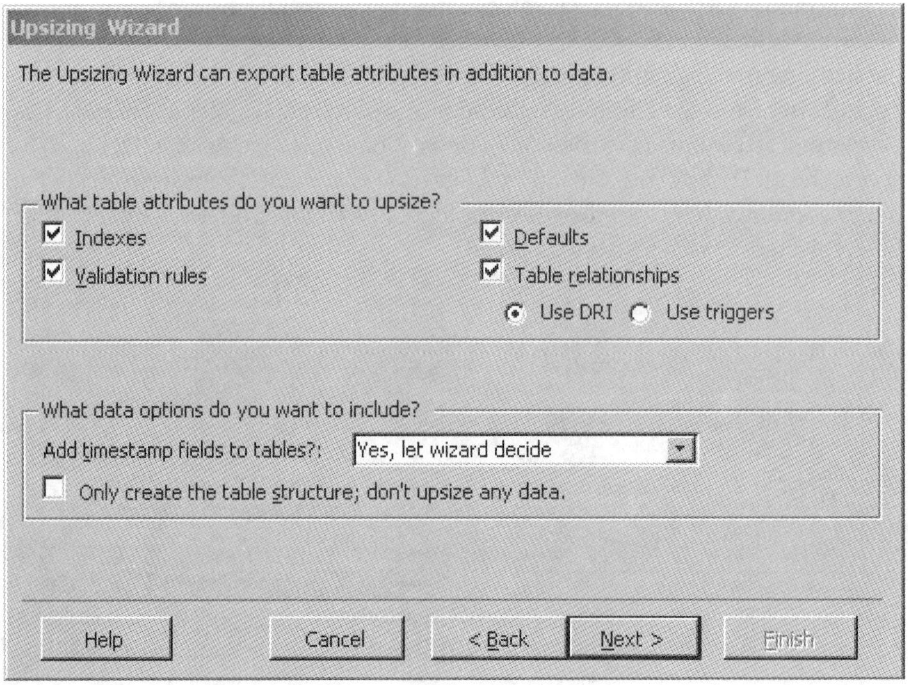

Figure 17-12. Properties page

In addition to the actual tables the wizard can also upsize many of the attributes of your database tables.

Indexes

Indexes are discussed in some detail in Chapter 13, but you need to know some additional things that may affect how the table upsizes to SQL Server.

When you choose the option to upsize indexes, you should understand how this would affect the design of your SQL Server database. Table 17-4 shows how indexes are upsized.

Table 17-4. How Access Indexes Are Upsized

ACCESS INDEX	UPSIZED AS
None	No index added
Yes (Duplicates)	Nonclustered
Yes (No Duplicates)	Unique, nonclustered index
Primary Key	Primary key, nonclustered

> **NOTE** *The wizard does not automatically create cluster primary keys. You must manually set the Clustered property for a primary key using either the Table Design view in Access 2002 or Enterprise Manager.*

A recent discussion arose with some developers who had been using randomly generated Primary Key values. The discussion concerned how the Upsizing wizard handles these particular keys. What happens is that SQL Server creates an additional object. In this case, a trigger is used to maintain the primary key. The following is an example of the trigger created when such a table is upsized:

```
CREATE TRIGGER T_ClientID ON [tble_Client] For INSERT AS
SET NO COUNT ON
DECLARE @randc int, @newc int
SELECT @randc = (SELECT convert(int, rand()*power(2,30)))
SELECT @newc = (SELECT CL_ID FROM inserted)
UPDATE tbl_Client SET CL_ID=@randc WHERE CL_ID =@newc
```

As you may have guessed, SQL Server has no built-in facility to set an INT primary key to generate random numbers. Many Access developers I have spoken to have decided to replace randomly created primary key numbers with incremental autonumbers prior to upsizing.

If you do require random numbers such as those used when replicating, it is possible to replace random autonumbers with Unique Identifier columns. SQL Server provides a means to create this column type, the NEWID function. This datatype can be equated to the Access equivalent (ReplicationID). The unique identifier or GUID (globally unique identifier) can be created via SQL using the CREATE TABLE statement and is globally unique. For example, to create a new table using the unique identifier:

```
CREATE TABLE Employee
(
employeeID uniqueidentifier NOT NULL
     DEFAULT newid()
LastName varchar(25) NOT NULL
FirstName varchar(30) NOT NULL
```

The following stored procedure will insert one record into the Employee table created above using the **NewID()** function to generate the GUID.

```
CREATE PROCEDURE AddEmp
AS
INSERT Employee
(employeeID,LastName,FirstName)
VALUES
(NewID(),'Reid','Patricia')
```

NOTE *If this was created using the Access 2002 interface, you cannot enter data directly into this field, just like the autonumber data type. When data is entered into the table, the database generates the GUID. GUIDs are primarily used for replication, so you have little occasion to use them for standard table design. Using GUIDs as primary keys also has several problems, such as indexes can be slow because a GUID is approximately four times larger than an integer key, data cannot be sorted on a GUID, uniqueness cannot be enforced, and a GUID cannot be used in GROUP BY and Count DISTINCTs.*

Information about table triggers can be accessed by executing a system stored procedure sp_helptrigger. For example,

```
sp_helptrigger tbl_client
```

will return the trigger name and details of the trigger type (that is, if it is an Insert, Update, or Delete trigger). Information on all triggers on the specified table will be returned.

Validation Rules

Many Access developers use table-level validation rules, and the Upsizing wizard is now able to convert your table-level validation rules into SQL Server constraints.

A constraint is simply a rule that applies to data entered into a table. Field validation in Access equals a constraint in SQL SERVER 2000. When creating the constraint, you have the option of validating existing data. Using an example best shows this process.

The Product table in the Northwind database base has a validation rule set on the UnitPrice field. Unit price must be greater than 12. Figure 17-13 shows the constraint created for this rule when the table is upsized to SQL Server 2000.

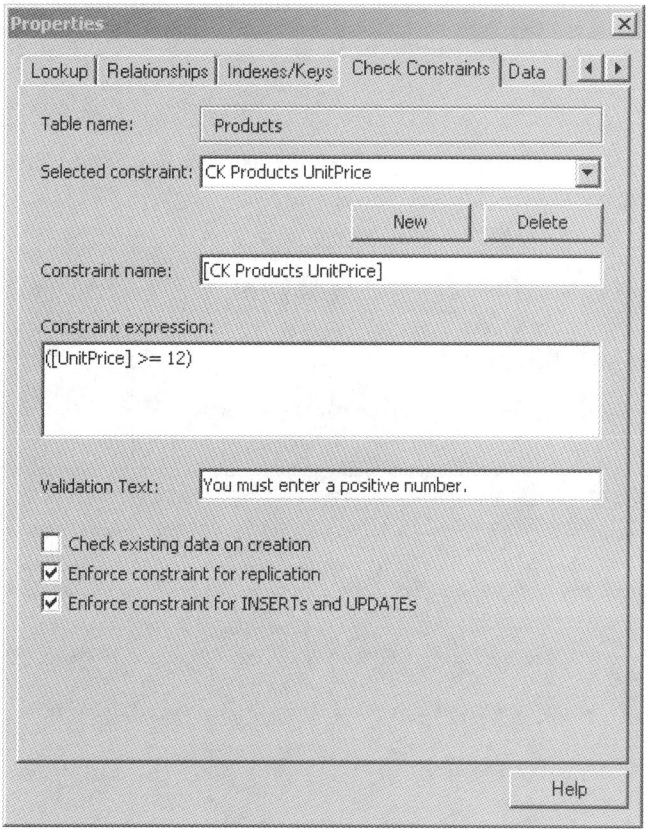

Figure 17-13. Constraints

> **NOTE** *The constraint is named [CK Products UnitPrice], with* CK *indicating that this is a constraint; it is followed by the names of the table and the field.*

Figure 17-14 shows the failure to meet the constraint (entering a unit price of £11) and the resulting error message in Access 2002. The validation text property is not available within SQL Server. In SQL Server, you will get a constraint violation message. Unlike Access (which adds an extended property to the column with the constraint), SQL Server will not carry out work in the background to check the violation against the validation text property.

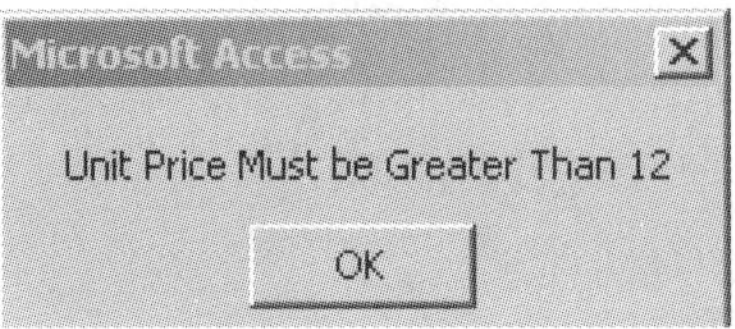

Figure 17-14. Constraint error message

Using a system view, it is possible to list all the constraints that are currently enforced in your application. Figure 17-15 lists all the current constraints in the Northwind application.

ShowConstraints

CONSTRAINT_CATALO(	CONSTRAINT_SCHEMA	CONSTRAINT_NAME	CHECK_CLAUSE
Northwindcs	dbo	CK Employees BirthDate	([BirthDate] < convert(datetime,conve
Northwindcs	dbo	CK Order Details UnitPrice	([UnitPrice] >= 0)
Northwindcs	dbo	CK Order Details Quantity	([Quantity] > 0)
Northwindcs	dbo	CK Order Details Discount	([Discount] >= 0 and [Discount] <= 1)
Northwindcs	dbo	CK Products UnitsInStock	([UnitsInStock] >= 0)
Northwindcs	dbo	CK Products UnitsOnOrder	([UnitsOnOrder] >= 0)
Northwindcs	dbo	CK Products ReorderLevel	([ReorderLevel] >= 0)
Northwindcs	dbo	CK Products UnitPrice	([UnitPrice] >= 12)

Record: 1 of 8

Figure 17-15. Constraint listing in Access 2002

The form in this image (frmdatabaseConstraints) is populated using a stored procedure, which uses a system view to provide the records. The T-SQL for this is very simple:

```
ALTER PROCEDURE  ShowConstraints
AS
SELECT * from
INFORMATION_SCHEMA.CHECK_CONSTRAINTS
```

Defaults

Just as with validation rules, many developers use VBA functions to provide a default value for a field or fields. When upsizing, the wizard will attempt to map these functions into the equivalent T-SQL. Should it fail to do this, the table will be skipped. (We earlier listed a variety of functions that can be upsized.) Standard default values can also be upsized, in this case with more success. For example, it is common to use the **Date()** and **Time()** functions to provide default values. When upsized, your new SQL Server table will retain these values. One difference that you may notice in table design within an ADP is that a drop-down list is provided for the default value. With SQL Server 2000, we can create global default values that can then be used throughout the database via the default drop-down list.

> **NOTE** *Global defaults can be created using Enterprise Manager. With Enterprise Manager open, expand the database tree, expand the tree for the specific database, and right-click over Defaults and choose New Default.*

Table Relationships

SQL Server 2000 is now able to use the Cascade Update and Cascade Delete features that have long been available within Microsoft Access. Previous versions implemented this process via triggers, but SQL Server 2000 can now use these features using declarative referential integrity. (DRI is very similar to the way in which this feature is implemented in Microsoft Access.) Note that triggers provide more flexibility if you need to work with other RDBM systems such as Oracle. Triggers are a common way to enforce referential integrity on many major RDBM systems.

> **NOTE** *Using VBA, we can act in response to events. For example, we can execute VBA in response to the Before_Update event in Access. Triggers behave in a similar manner and are executed or fired in response to an event on SQL Server. See the SQL Server Books Online for a full discussion of triggers.*

It is also important that the data type and field size of your primary/foreign key pairs match. In Access, it is possible to have a primary key set to one size with the foreign key set to another. You will need to ensure that both keys match before you upsize the tables; otherwise, you will have problems when upsizing and using DRI to enforce relationships. It's worth remembering that SQL Server 2000 will not permit you to create this relationship at all.

If this is the case, the tables will be upsized but the relationships won't be. You will have to change the field properties and redo the relationships in SQL Server. For example, Table 1 has a primary key, data type text, and a field size of 20. Table 2 holds the Foreign Key value with a field size of 30. Access will permit you to create the relationship between the Primary and Foreign Key fields. When upsizing this, you will need to amend the Foreign Key field property to 20, matching the value of its primary. Once this has been done, the tables and relationships will upsize. The error message is:

```
[Microsoft][ODBC SQL Server Driver][SQL Server]
Column 'Customers.CustID' is not the same length as
Referencing column 'Orders.CustID' in foreign key 'Orders_FK00'.
```

Timestamps

In addition to the table attributes, this screen also permits you to provide some information to the wizard on how it should handle data. An option is provided to add a Timestamp field to the database tables. Three options are available:

- Yes, let the wizard decide. (This is the default.)
- Always add a timestamp.
- Never add a timestamp.

A timestamp is simply a unique field that is added to your table and updated when data is changed. A Timestamp field cannot be edited by the user. If you do choose to use the default, a timestamp will be added to all tables containing a single, double, memo, or OLE object data type.

> **NOTE** *Timestamps are not the same as a datetime data type; instead, they are binary numbers that are used to indicate the sequence of data changes. In addition, even though the timestamp is a unique number, do not consider using them as primary keys. Just think if a timestamp primary key has foreign keys links. When the primary record is updated, the value of the timestamp changes and the link to the foreign key is lost.*

The final checkbox on this screen allows you to limit the upsize operation to either upsizing your table structure or to include both table structure and data. This option can be useful when you run into upsizing problems. Simply check the box to limit the upsize to table structure to repeat an upsizing job for testing purposes. Once you have finished with the attributes screen, click on Next to continue. The next screen in the wizard requires you to provide some information on the end product of the upsizing process. From this screen, you can choose one of three options:

- Create a new Access Data Project.
- Link SQL Server tables to existing application.
- Do not modify the existing application.

Create a New Access Data Project

Choosing this option will move you completely into the SQL Server world. Selecting it creates a new Access Data Project; in essence, you are now building a front end to an SQL Server database. This option will have the biggest effect on your upsizing strategy as you move from Jet to SQL Server. All tables and data now exist in SQL Server. When you create a full client server setup, remember that the Jet engine is completely removed from the picture. One of the first issues you will need to consider is security, which is discussed in detail in Chapter 18.

> **NOTE** *Access security is not upsized. You must change to SQL Server security. If you have implemented your own security system, you must rebuild it within SQL Server. However, keep in mind that you cannot secure forms, reports, or code in an ADP. (You can however save the ADP as an ADE file thus giving you some control.)*

If choosing this option, you can accept the default path and filename offered by the wizard. Alternately, you can choose your own path using the Browse button. You may also change the ADP name using the File New Database dialog box.

If you chose this option, click on Next to proceed and enter the final screen of the process. From this screen, you can choose to open the new ADP file or remain within the MDB being upsized. Make your selection and click on Finish to begin the upsize to the ADP.

Link SQL Server Tables to Existing Application

This option will migrate your tables to SQL Server in the same way as you would normally set up a standard FE/BE configuration, but using ODBC to link to the tables in the database already specified in the Upsizing wizard. (ODBC is a "dead" technology in the sense that Microsoft will no longer be developing it. OLE DB is now the preferred method for data access.) Once the table is copied onto the server, the local version will be renamed as TableName_Local. Remember that, once your application goes "live," the data held in the local and server tables will begin to differ. One major advantage of this approach is that all of the database objects will remain within the MDB format, with the exception of the tables. One of the major disadvantages to this approach is that some of the processing may be performed on the client rather than on the server. Any SQL statements that are not supported by the server will be passed to Access to deal with, accompanied by all the data required. For example, using an Access-specific function in SQL will result in all data for the tables being queried being passed back to Access for local processing, thus slowing the entire system down.

> **NOTE** *Using this approach, you may see an improvement in the performance of the database, but it is just as likely that you may see performance drop.*

Figure 17-16 shows the Database window when the linking process is finished.

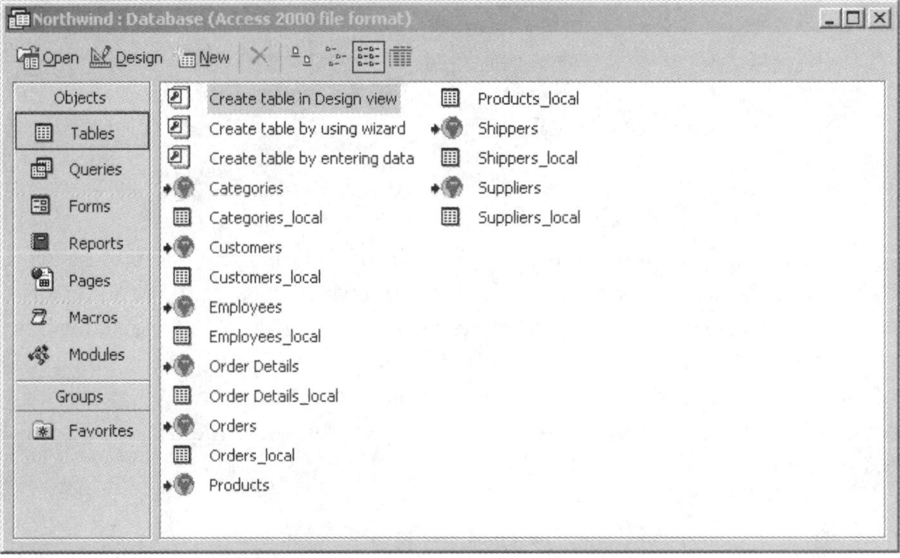

Figure 17-16. The Access 2002 Database window

Notice that a copy of the original tables is retained, and an arrow and a globe symbol indicate the linked tables. All of your Access objects should work as before, including the Crosstab queries.

One of the more useful objects produced by the Upsizing wizard is the upsizing report, which provides you with full details on the entire process. You should print it out as soon as the upsizing process is complete. In addition, a snapshot report is saved in the same folder as the database being upsized.

Wouldn't it be useful if you could run an upsizing report before starting the entire process? Well, you can. Superior Software for Windows provides a wonderful tool that can be used before you upsize the database. It is well worth downloading their SSW Upsizing PRO! product and running it against your database before you do anything else. See `http://www.ssw.com.au/ssw/UpsizingPRO/frmFeature.htm` for more information. SSW Upsizing PRO! will produce an extensive report on the application and provide you with a great deal of help in changing objects to help the actual upsizing process go smoothly. The more assistance you have before getting started the better.

Upsizing with SQL Server—DTS

The Access Upsizing wizard is not the only means of getting your data into SQL Server 2000. We can use data transformation services (DTS) to import our Access data into SQL server. DTS is provided to allow you to gather data from many sources and bring it into SQL server. In addition to importing the data, we can actually transform or change attributes of data, such as columns in MS Access tables. We shall see this as we progress through a DTS import.

DTS, like many features within SQL Server, has filled entire books. In our case, we are going to use it to import the Northwind database into SQL Server. So let's get started. For these examples, I am using Enterprise Manager within SQL Server 2000.

From within Enterprise Manager, select Tools|Data Transformation Services|Import Data. See Figure 17-17.

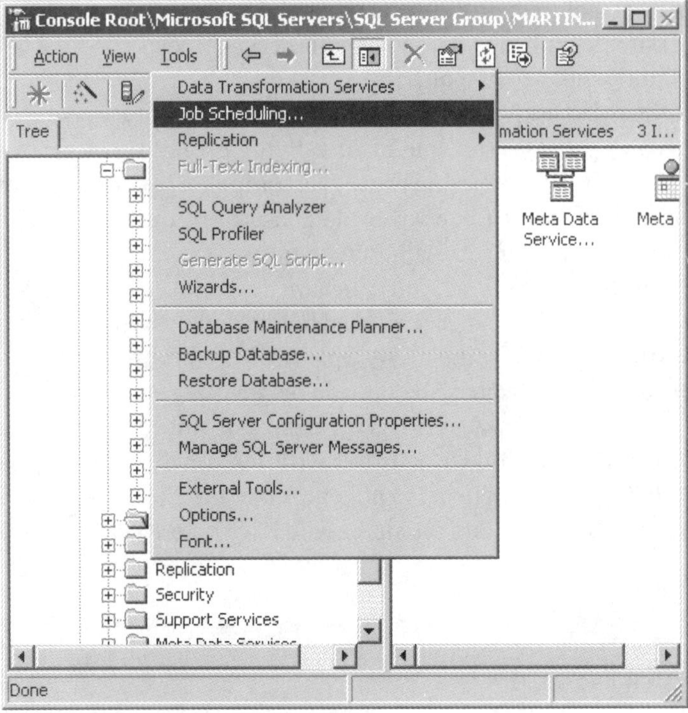

Figure 17-17. Menu for DTS—Import

Guess what? There's a wizard. Figure 17-18 shows its first screen.

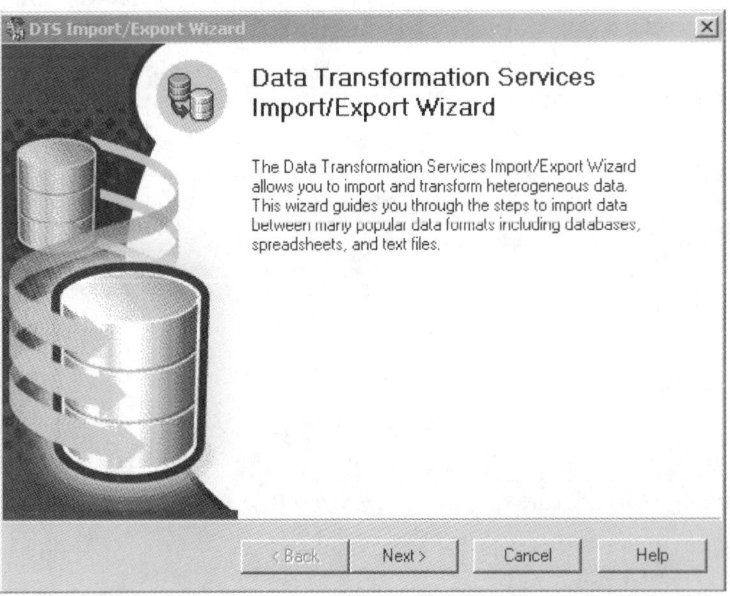

Figure 17-18. DTS Wizard—First screen

Click on Next to view the Choose a Data Source screen, as shown in Figure 17-19.

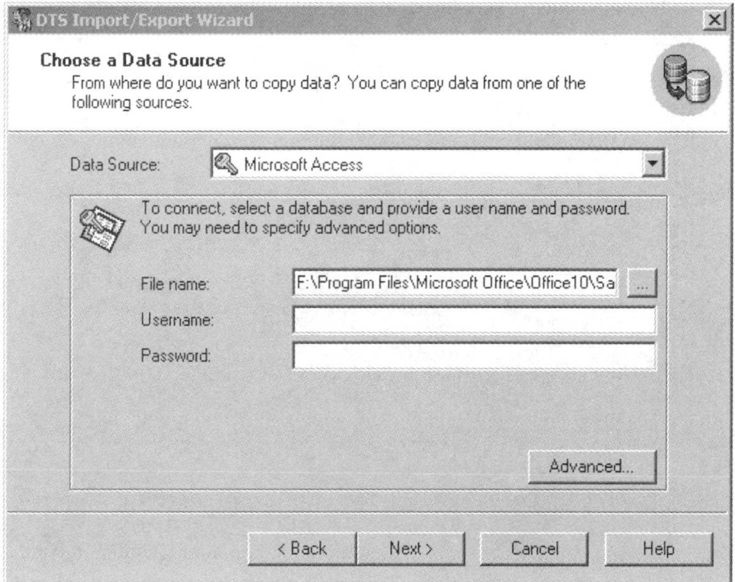

Figure 17-19. DTS Wizard—Second screen

The two options are:

- Select a data source. (Microsoft Access in this case)
- Select a file name (Northwind.mdb in this case)

A username and password is not required. If you are using a secure database, enter the admin username and password. (Note that the path to your database may differ.)

Choose a Destination

This screen of the wizard allows you to enter details about the destination of the data. Figure 17-20 shows the setup for my import. Note that I have chosen to create a new database. Simply select "New" from the database drop-down list. You can of course select an existing database as the destination for the import.

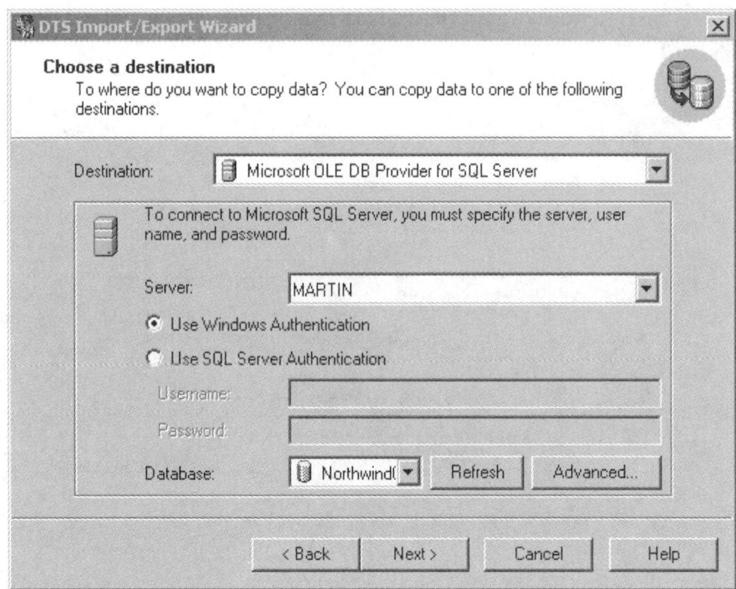

Figure 17-20. Choosing the destination for your imported data

Specify Table Copy or Query

From this screen, we can choose the tables to import or indeed we can construct an SQL query to restrict or be more specific about the data we are going to import. In my case, I am simply going to import the entire database. Figure 17-21 shows the completed screen. Click on Next to proceed.

Figure 17-21. The fourth screen of the DTS wizard

Now, the next screen is where things get interesting because it is where we can actually transform (change) the data being imported. Figure 17-22 shows the screen with the options for selecting the tables to import.

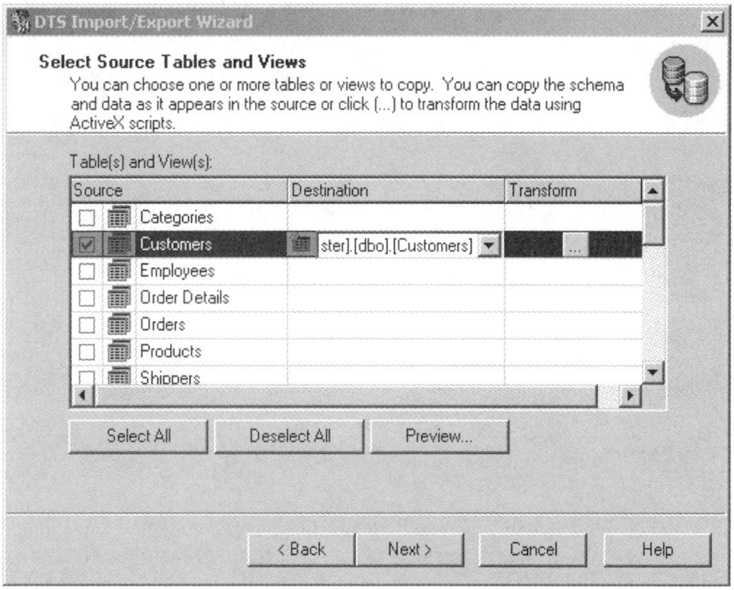

Figure 17-22. Source/destination tables

I have checked a single table, Customers. The Destination column shows the table that this data will be placed into in the new SQL Server database. However, the interesting thing here is the Transform button. Clicking this button opens the screen shown in Figure 17-23.

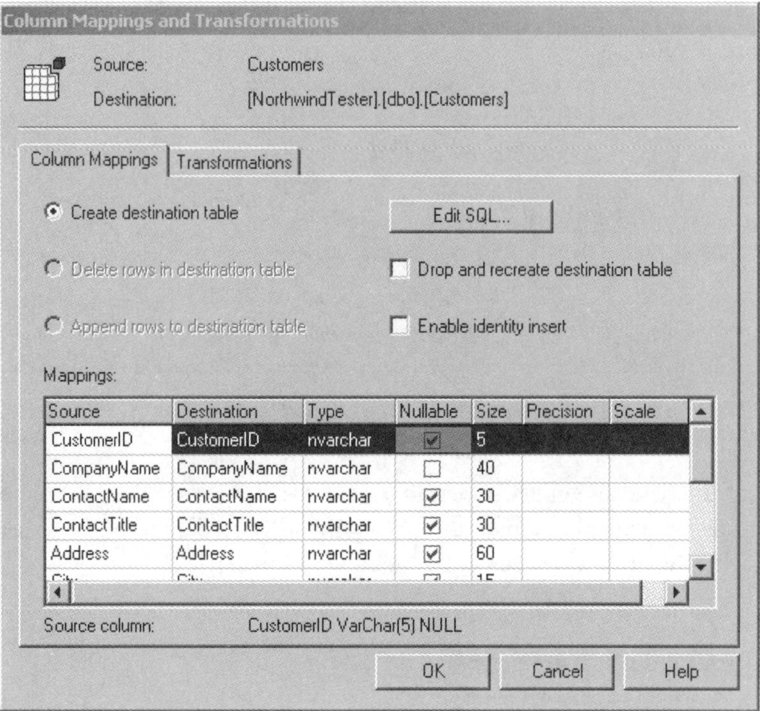

Figure 17-23. Transformations

We have two tabs in this screen: Column Mappings and Transformations. Here we have the opportunity to directly interact with the design of the data being imported. Let's look at each tab in turn.

Column Mappings Tab

Create Destination Table

Because we are creating a new database, no tables are currently in existence. So, not only does this choice make sense, it is in fact the only one available.

Edit SQL

Clicking this button opens a small SQL editor. Here we can see the SQL that will be used to actually create the table and the associated columns. As the screen says, if you do actually change the SQL, you must manually change the mappings on the previous screen. Figure 17-24 shows the editor.

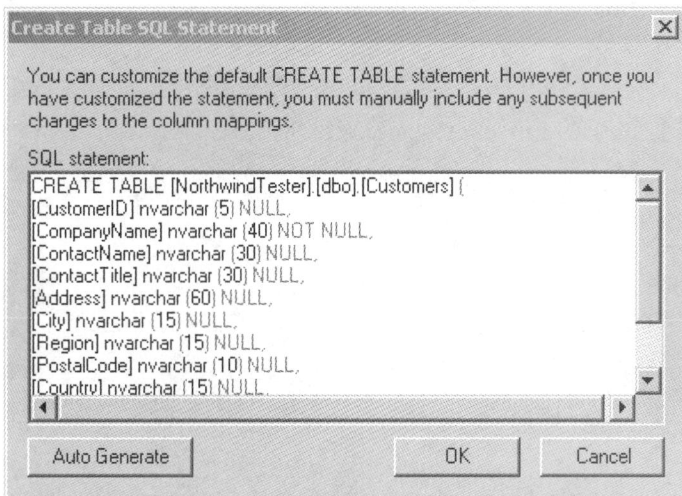

Figure 17-24. The SQL for creating the table

Two options are grayed out in this example: Delete Rows in Destination Table and Append Rows in Destination Table. These will be available when you are importing into an existing table and are fairly self descriptive. We can also drop (delete) an existing table and replace it with a newer version.

> **NOTE** *Notice that the primary key, CustomerID, has not been detected as such. We will manually set the key when we have finished the import. Those readers familiar with SQL Server DDL can modify the SQL CREATE TABLE statement at this point.*

Using this dialog box, you can:

- Change the name of the destination column.
- Change the destination data type.
- Set the column as Null.
- Change the data size.
- Add precision (the number of decimal points that can be stored to the left of a decimal point).
- Enter scale (the maximum number of digits that can be stored to the right of number).

These options give us much more control over how our table data is mapped to SQL Server data types.

Transformation Tab

Two options are offered here: we can simply copy the data to the destination table with no changes or transform it (change) during the transfer process. If you opt for the second option, you can manually amend the transformation script being executed. Figure 17-25 shows the transformation script.

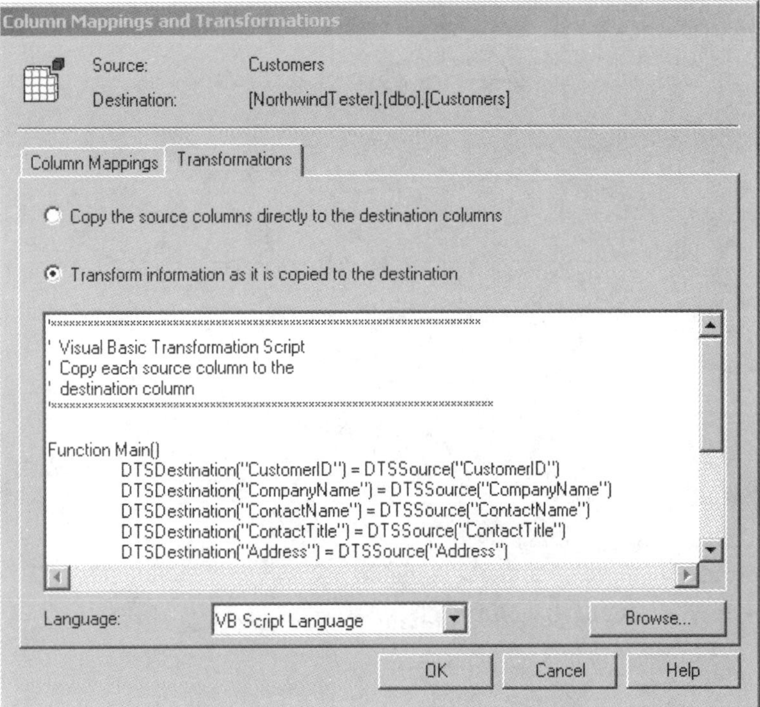

Figure 17-25. Transformation script

We can also change the scripting language that's used. The two options are currently VBScript and Jscript. Additional ActiveX scripting options will be available if they are installed on your machine. Perl is a common addition to this dialog box. It is also possible to use a previously written script. If this is the case, simply select Browse to select the script. Once you have finished with the transformation, close the dialog box and then click on Next in the wizard to open the Save, Schedule, and Replicate Package screen.

This screen, shown in Figure 17-26, allows you to specify some options as to how the actual package is executed by SQL Server.

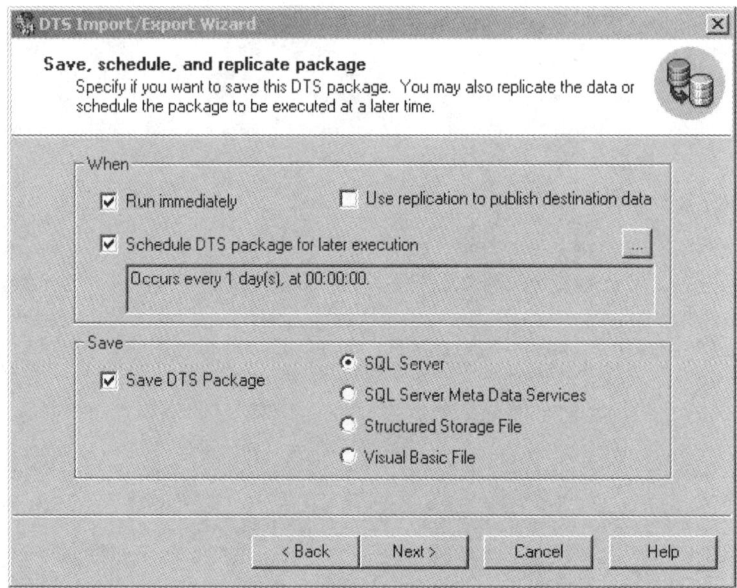

Figure 17-26. The Save, Schedule, and Replicate Package screen

Several options are available:

- *Execute the package immediately:* It is possible to simply execute the package without saving. However, it is usually better to save the package and execute later. If things go wrong, you can amend the package before rerunning.
- *Use replication to publish destination data:* SQL Server can use this as a means to replicate data from the source to the destination. If you do choose this option, the Create Publication wizard will start after the DTS package completes.
- *Schedule the package for later execution:* If you select this option, you can set up the job schedule for this package by clicking on the ellipsis button to the right of the screen. Figure 17-27 shows the screen. The options should be self-explanatory.

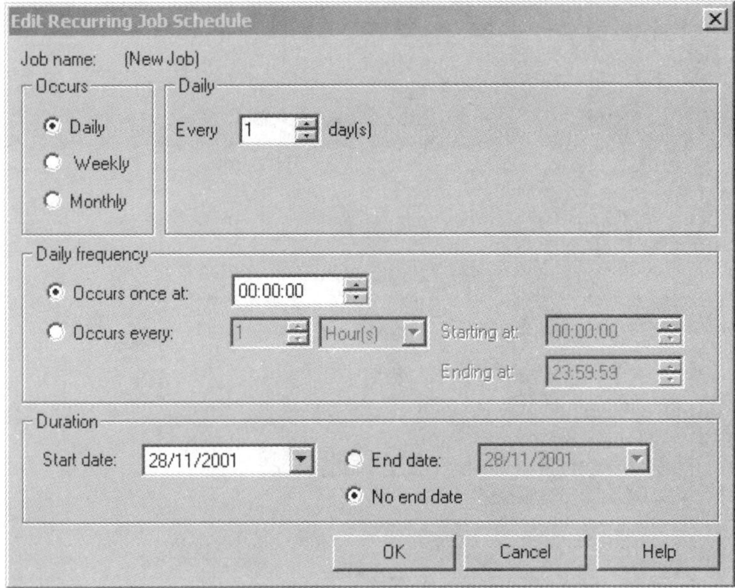

Figure 17-27. Package execution

In addition, you can save the package in one of several places and formats:

- *Save to SQL Server:* The package is stored in the sysdtspackages table in the msdb database.
- *Save it to SQL Server Meta Data Services:* Use this option to track versions of the package and meta data.
- *Save it to a Structured Storage File:* Save the package as a file so that you can copy the file and run it from other locations.
- *Save the package as a Visual Basic file:* It is possible to save the package as a Visual Basic script. You can then amend the package using the Visual Basic development environment.

In this case, I am simply going to save and execute the package now. Ensure that both the Save and Execute checkboxes are checked in the dialog box.

Click on Next to enter the final wizard screen (shown in Figure 17-28). You can scroll though the summary to see the details of how the package will be created and executed.

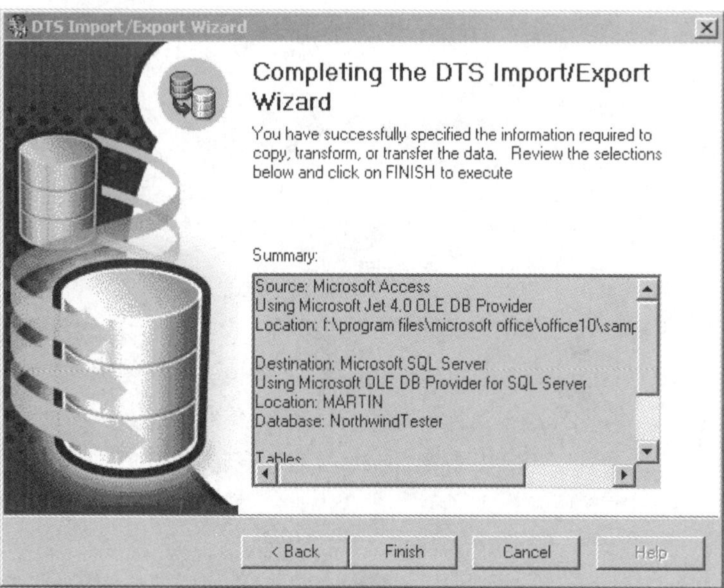

Figure 17-28. The final DTS Wizard screen

Click on Finish. At this point, a dialog box (shown in Figure 17-29) will keep you informed of progress.

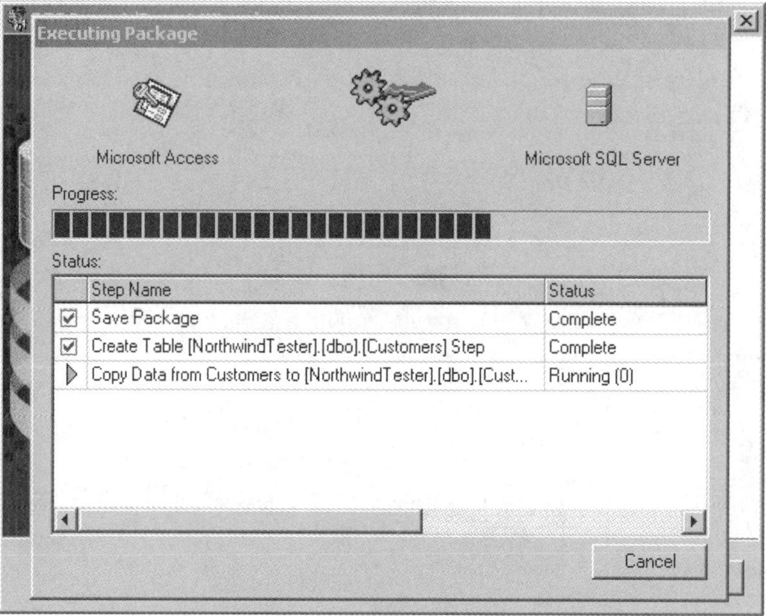

Figure 17-29. Package execution

Once done, you will be given a confirmation screen. Simply click on OK, and you're done.

Once the package is saved, you can view it with Enterprise Manager. I have copied a real database using DTS, and Figure 17-30 shows the package design. Only one table was used for this example because specific data was being examined in an effort to track an upsizing failure.

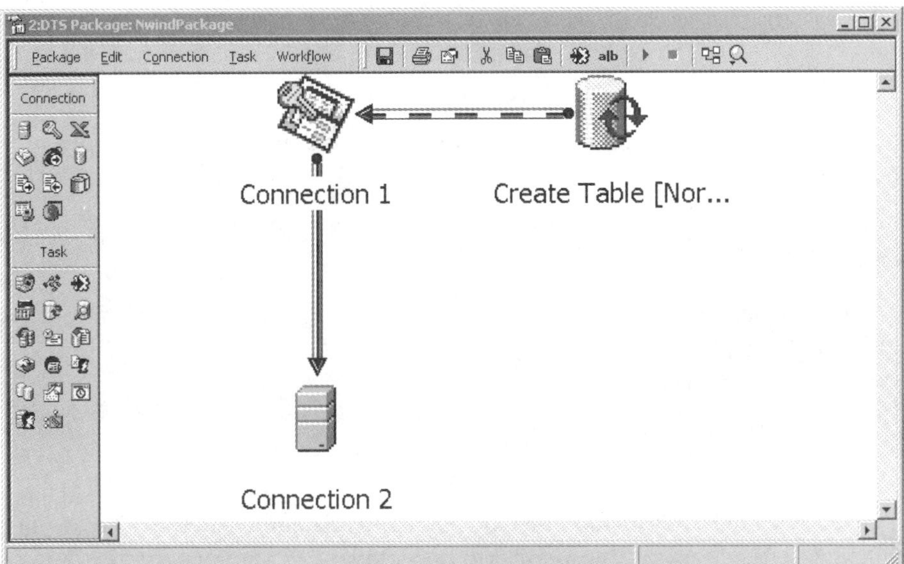

Figure 17-30. DTS package

> **NOTE** *Because this was a real system (a fellow developer, John Colby, provided it one weekend when we were playing with upsizing), I am unable to show the actual data. This particular database failed to upsize using both Access 2000 and Access 2002. Even with DTS, four tables failed to upsize. This was mainly due to problems with Access date fields as discussed previously. DTS was a considerable improvement over the Upsizing wizard.*

As we've seen, the package execution dialog box shows the progress of the execution. Once finished, we get a listing of all tables imported, but another important bit of information we get is a notification of what did not import. In the case of John's database, four tables did not import. Double-clicking a step that failed gives us the details of why the import failed. Figure 17-31 shows this message.

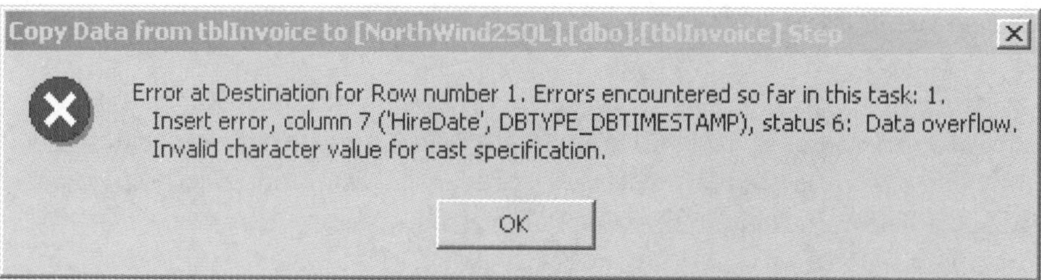

Figure 17-31. DTS table import error

So that's it. You have run the DTS Wizard, and there you have it: a newly upsized SQL Server database. Are we done? You would be so lucky! Now you have to:

- Add the primary keys.
- Create the relationships.
- Enforce referential integrity.
- Rebuild the diagrams.

Oh, yes, one final thing: if you have chosen to include queries in the process, you will find that they are now new tables in the database! (Databases are fun, aren't they?)

In effect, you'll need to re-create the database. DTS has simply imported your data. It's fast, efficient, and useful, but, like the Upsizing wizard, it still leaves you with some manual work. Whatever method you choose, the best advice is to know your data and plan the entire process before you actually hit any keys.

The following list shows some of the things you will need to look for before upsizing your database:

- Dates are going to be a major problem when upsizing. Check to ensure that all dates are within an acceptable range.
- Concatenated foreign keys/primary keys. Tables using more than two fields as the primary key will not be upsized.
- Ensure that primary key/foreign key pairs are the appropriate data type and that the sizes of the data types are identical.
- Ensure that all tables have a unique index.

Following upsizing, check all objects to ensure that there have been no changes and that everything is as it should be. In other words, test it, test it, and test it again.

In this chapter, we looked at some of the issues and (hopefully) resolutions that you will face when upsizing an Access database to SQL Server. We have looked at queries, forms, and reports. We have seen how some of your objects will be upsized to stored procedures, and others to user-defined functions. We have seen two methods for getting your data into SQL Server, and we saw how both require work on your part.

Most importantly, we have seen how you will need to step back and reexamine your skill set before the move to the monster. And the best bit of advice we can give you is to know your application and, when upsizing, to go the whole way and choose Access Data Project. There are more things to learn and more objects to manage, but a whole new world awaits the Access developer.

CHAPTER 18

Security Issues

Working with SQL Server Security and Access Data Projects

SECURITY IS ONE OF THE MAJOR ISSUES facing the Access developer who's moving to SQL Server. For a long time, many developers have fought with the Jet security setup, and recently some assistance has been provided by the built-in security wizards. But, to fully implement SQL Server security, the developer must learn a new security model. Anyone who regularly uses Access security should find this transition fairly straightforward. Although the security issues described here deal with SQL Server 2000 running on Windows 2000 Server, the general issues apply to NT systems as well.

> **NOTE** *Security using a Jet database is handled using a single file, System.mdw, which holds all the information on users and user groups and the access that they have been granted to the database objects. Many Access users are unaware that security is always present but must be turned on by the developer. SQL Books Online provides an excellent resource for security information, and a lot of up-to-date security information can be found at* `http://www.sqlsecurity.com` *and the Microsoft Web site. Out of interest, I checked with a couple of developers to see how easy Access workgroup security could be hacked. One developer managed to open the database and capture all user information in five minutes.*

When installing SQL Server, one of the first options presented to you will be a choice of which security system to install. Figure 18-1 shows the security dialog box. Before you decide which security system to use, you must understand the options and the implications of your choice.

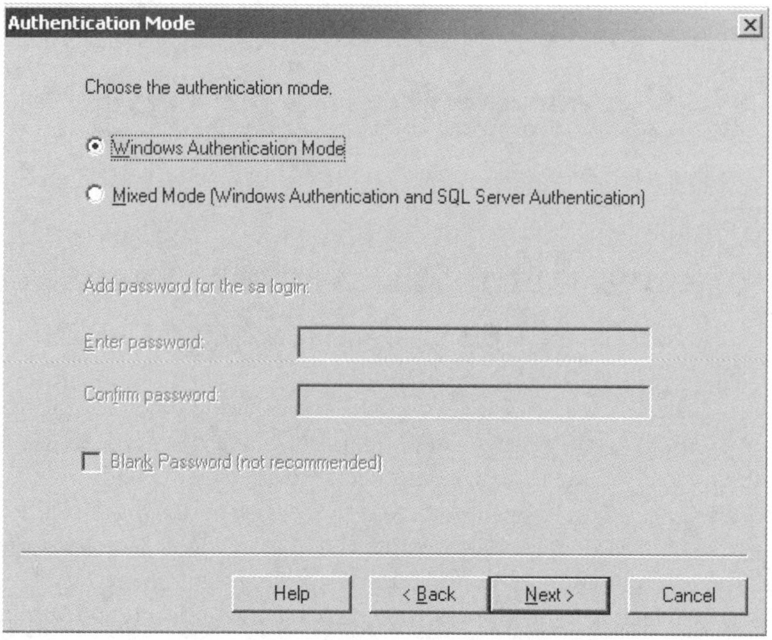

Figure 18-1. Choosing the authentication mode

> **NOTE** *The default is set to Windows authentication mode, which Microsoft recommends as the most secure. (Strange that in other products the default is set to Mixed Mode!) Windows authentication mode is not available to Windows 98/Me users. Remember that your own or someone else's business and data depends on your choices here. Because SQL Server 2000 security is based on the Windows security model, you as a developer should have a sound grasp of this before implementing SQL Server security. It should also be said that network security is usually outside the remit of the database developer, and you often will have little or no access to Active Directory features. It is therefore vital that, if you choose this form of authentication, you work closely with your system administration people.*

Users will be authenticated against their assigned Windows 2000 username and password. The default mode for earlier versions of SQL Server was mixed with a blank password for the sa login. Always assign a complex password to this account.

> **NOTE** *Kerberos is the method that's used to permit Windows 2000 to pass user authentication information between different resources and systems and allow that information to persist. Bear in mind that, to use this protocol, all systems must be using Windows 2000. Of course, in a perfect world, they will! However, in the not-so-perfect real world, this situation is unlikely. If you are in a mixed operating system environment, the Windows option is not available. In most organizations I have been involved with, SQL Security has been the norm.*

Microsoft Access 2000 permitted you to work with SQL Server security directly from within the Access Database window. As you will see in Access 2002, this capability has been removed. I can only assume that the Access team felt that security of an SQL Server installation was too important to be made available within the database window of an Access Data Project. All we can do with Access internally is to change the password for the user who is currently logged in. For the previous examples in this section, I have been working with a trusted connection to SQL Server. In this section, I am going to reconfigure the security and change to Mixed Mode.

SQL Server Security Structure

SQL Server security is based on two levels: logging in to the server and permissions on database objects. It is possible for a user with insufficient privileges to actually log in to the server but be able to do absolutely nothing. The user must be assigned permissions to use a database and the objects within that database. This illustrates the two-phased approach to SQL Server security: granting access to the server and then granting specific access to a database or databases.

The basic setup is to first permit access to the SQL Server hosting the database and then assign permissions to either an individual user or to a user group role within a specific database.

> **NOTE** *The three types of roles are fixed server, user defined, and application. An additional role also exists, the public role, of which all users are members by default. We will look at each type in this section. A role is very similar to a user group in that you can bring users together into groups and assign permissions to the group rather than to individual users. For example, all users within a purchasing office can be added to the purchasing role. Permissions then need to be added only to the purchasing role to enable all members to inherit them. Likewise, any permission removed from the purchasing role will apply to all members of that role.*

We will first look at some of the built-in roles that are available with SQL Server and then discuss user-defined roles.

Fixed Server Roles

Fixed server roles give permissions on the server and are not appropriate for standard users. (Table 18-1 provides an overview of the database roles.) Figure 18-2 shows the actual dialog box within SQL Server. For example, you would not assign a clerical officer to the sysadmin role, or the managing director for that matter! This type of role is server-wide and isn't restricted to a single database (or databases) within the server.

Table 18-1. SQL Server roles

ROLE	DESCRIPTION
Sysadmin	The sysadmin can perform any role within the server. This role is a DBA role and as such is not appropriate for standard users.
Serveradmin	Can configure the server. Again, this is not a role for general users.
Setupadmin	Can work with and manage linked servers, manage setup, and work with replication.
Security Admin	Can work with server security, create users, manage logins, and grant permissions to users to create tables. You do not want a standard user to have this role.
ProcessAdmin	Gives the ability to kill processes.
Dbcreator	Has permissions to create, delete (drop), change, or restore any database.
Diskadmin	Has permissions to work with and manage disk files (for example, managing backups and creating mirrors of the database).
BulkAdmin	Has permissions to perform bulk inserts to the server. This role is new to SQL Server 2000.

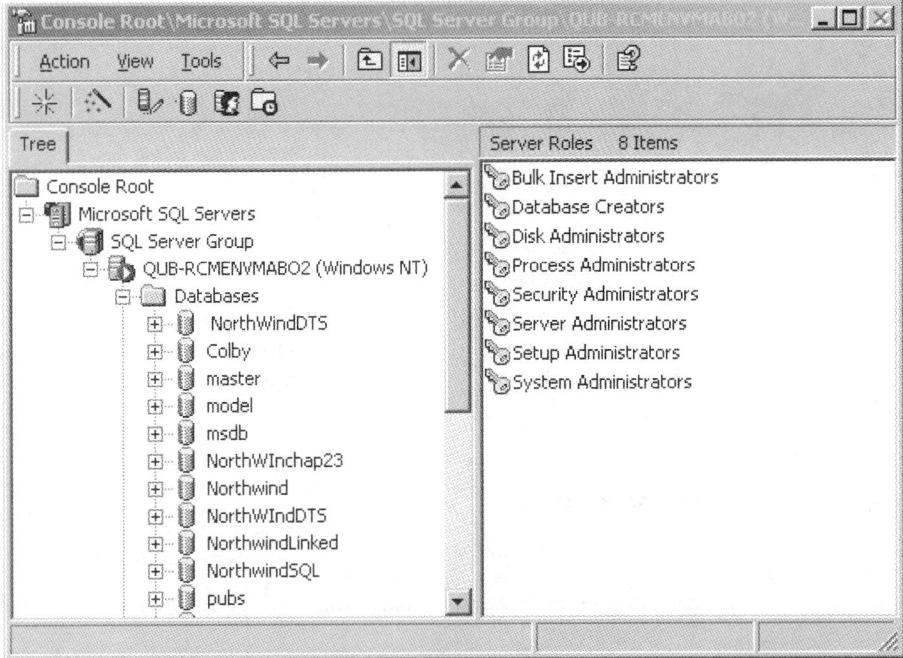

Figure 18-2. Fixed server roles

Fixed Database Roles

Unlike fixed server roles, database roles are specific to a particular database, and they exist in all databases. This type of role cannot be deleted, nor does it have their built-in permissions amended. Access to and permissions on objects are obvious in most instances from the role name. Figure 18-3 shows the roles available within SQL Server, and Table 18-2 defines the roles.

Name	Role Type
public	Standard
db_securityadmin	Standard
db_owner	Standard
db_denydatawriter	Standard
db_denydatareader	Standard
db_ddladmin	Standard
db_datawriter	Standard
db_datareader	Standard
db_backupoperator	Standard
db_accessadmin	Standard
DataPrep	Standard
Clerical	Standard

Figure 18-3. Fixed database roles

Table 18-2. Fixed database roles

ROLE	DESCRIPTION
db_owner	This role "sweeps" together all the permissions of all other database roles and can carry out all owner actions on all database objects. Only the db_owner can assign users to this role. Again, this is not a role that standard users should be assigned.
db_accessadmin	Can manage groups, users, and SQL Server logins but only within the specific database.
db_datareader	Can read data from all tables within the database.
db_datawriter	Can you guess? That's right: this role permits the user to insert, update, and delete from any table within the database. However, an interesting feature of this role is that a member cannot select data from any of the tables.
db_backupoperator	As suggested by the name, this group can back up the database.
db_ddladmin	Members of this role can work with DDL statements to change objects within the database. They cannot use grant, revoke, or deny statements.
db_securityadmin	Can manage permissions on objects, object ownership, and database roles in the database.

Manage Role, Membership and Other Object Permissions within the Database

Figure 18-4 shows a view (within SQL Server Enterprise Manager) of the user dialog box with the database roles available. Also note the checkmark against the NorthwindCS database indicating that this user has access to only the named database. All other database access checks are blank. This user is also by default a member of the public role, and this permission cannot be removed. See the following section for a discussion of the public role.

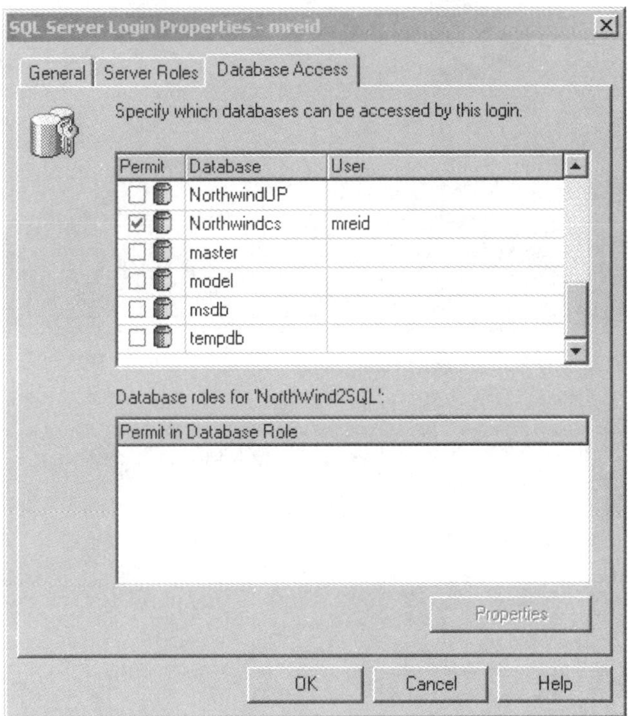

Figure 18-4. Database roles

Figure 18-5 shows the facilities that are available under the General tab of the Login Properties dialog box. This is used to create the user login, and the password for this login is also assigned here. In this case, I have chosen to use SQL Server authentication rather than Windows 2000 authentication.

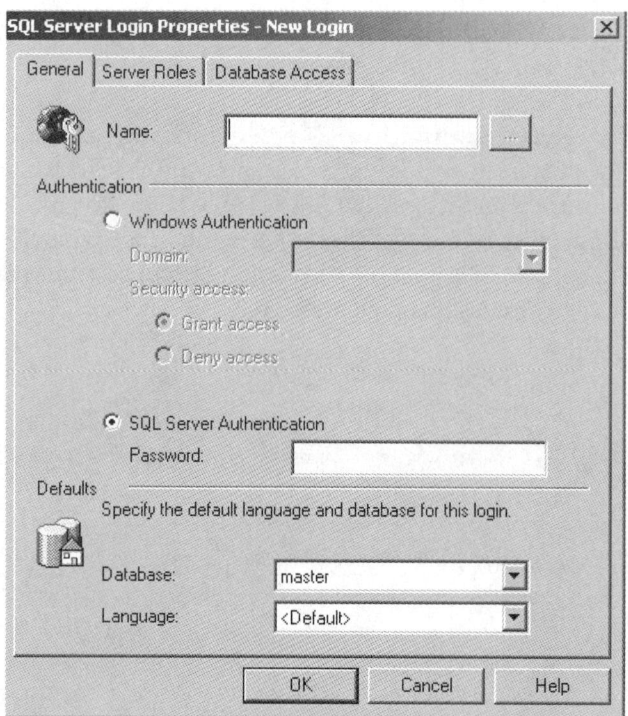

Figure 18-5. General tab—Login Properties dialog box

Figure 18-6 displays the built-in server roles available for this user.

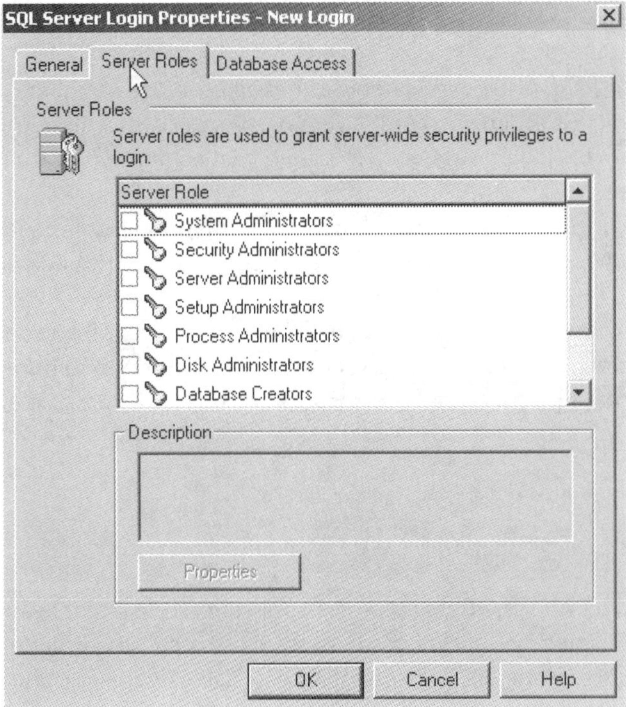

Figure 18-6. Server roles

Once you have entered all the options required to create the user, simply click on OK. You will then be prompted to confirm the password. See Figure 18-7. Reenter the password and click on OK.

Figure 18-7. Password confirmation

> **NOTE** *If the password does not match, you will be prompted to reenter it.*

The Public Role

The public role exists in every database, and all users are members of the public role by default. Although you cannot remove this role, you can remove all permissions from it. (In large systems, it is likely that all permissions will be removed from this role.)

The public role, however, may have a place in a small system. Rather than create your own roles, you could grant permissions to the public role on your objects.

The public role may also be useful if your users all require a common permission; for example, you could grant the Select permission to public while denying all other permissions. Users would automatically have Select permission on objects.

The Application Role

We shall touch upon one final role—the application role—that I would expect to gain in significance. You should also expect to see increased functionality in future releases of both SQL Server and Access ADPs. In this case, rather than users having permissions on databases and objects, we can grant permissions to an application, such as MS Access or Excel. Currently, you cannot manipulate application roles via ADPs or ADO, but you can use Visual Basic (and ADO together) or the built-in SQL Server Query Tools.

As we can see, the various fixed database roles are very similar to fixed server roles. The main difference is that server roles work with the entire server environment whereas database roles are specific to a single database.

User-Defined Roles

In addition to using the fixed roles within SQL Server, you can define your own. For example, let's say that in our purchasing office we have a staff member who is filling a temporary role. We could just assign him or her to the purchasing group, but then they would have the same permissions as all permanent members of staff and this may not be the best solution. How do we get around this? We create a temporary purchasing role with reduced permissions on the database and its objects, and we assign to that role those permissions that are required by the temporary staff member.

For example, an organization I was employed by hired a temporary worker to update company data. They would not be permitted to work with any other data or table within the database. Rather than assign them to an existing role with full permissions on all tables, it was a fairly simple process to create a new role and assign permissions on only the company table.

Ownership Chains

Another area of security you will need to understand is that of ownership chains. For example, User A owns Table B and grants Select privilege to User C. User C could in theory create a view based on the table and grant permissions on the view to User D. User D can now see the data in Table B. This may not be desirable. In this circumstance, you now have a broken ownership chain.

SQL Server handles this for you. When User D attempts to use the view, the underlying table permissions are checked back to those given at the beginning by User A. Because User D does not have access to the table, User D is therefore unable to use the view. User D would either have to be given permission to the original table or the new view.

Creating the Login

We will now create a login for a user called LiamLiamReid with a password of LiamLiamReid and assign him a db_datareader database role (read-only).

First, let's create Liam:

1. Open your server.

2. Open the Security node. Figure 18-8 shows the Security node expanded.

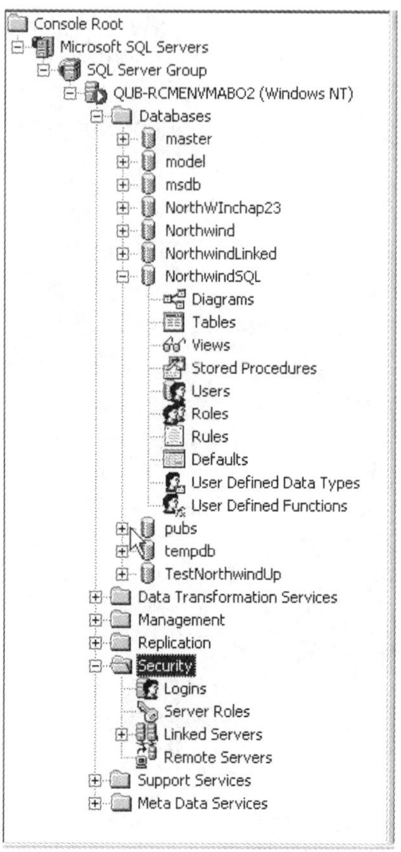

Figure 18-8. Security node

3. Right-click on Logins.

4. Select New Login from the shortcut menu. (See Figure 18-9.) You can also choose New Login from the Tools menu. The Login Properties dialog box will open. (See Figure 18-10.)

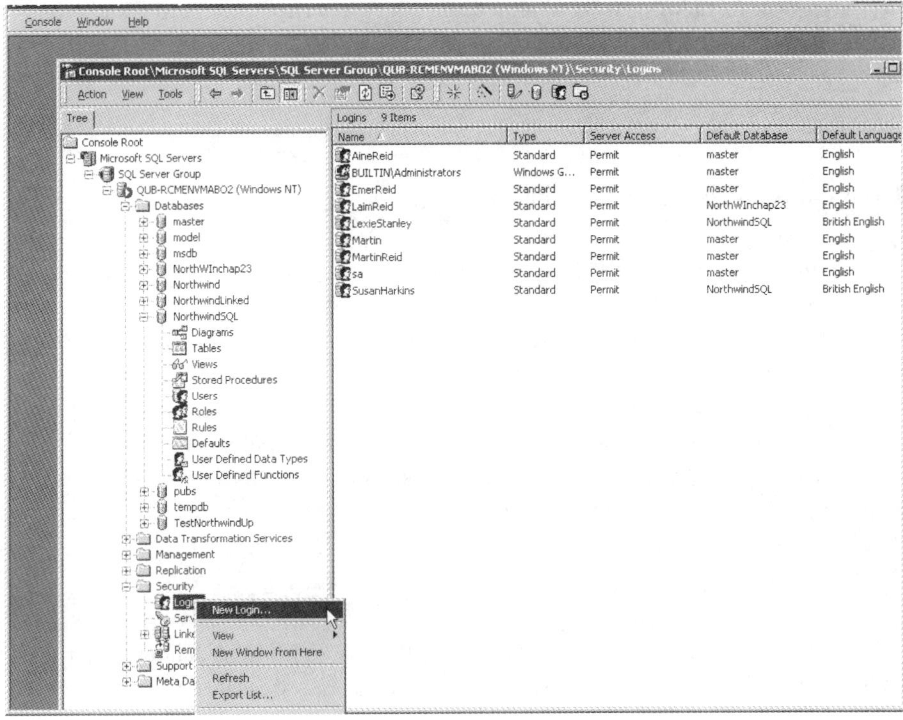

Figure 18-9. New Login menu

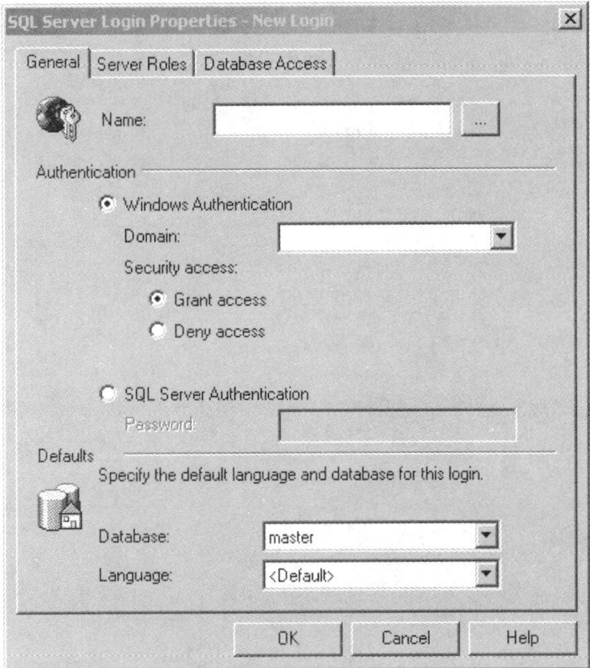

Figure 18-10. Login Properties dialog box

Let's look at the options available under the General, Roles, and Database Access tabs.

General

The options under the General tab are as follows:

- *Name:* Login name for this user. Enter LiamReid (or a name of your choice).
- *Authentication:* You have two options now—Windows or SQL Server authentication. Click on the radio button for SQL Server Authentication and enter a password for the user. As usual with passwords, if you write it down, take care and store it in a secure location. I have lost count of the times I have seen usernames and passwords tacked to the office wall! In this case, the password is LiamReid.

Roles

Using this dialog box, we can also assign the user to a server role. However, this isn't required for this user because we are simply going to assign him to a fixed database role.

Figure 18-11 shows the Server Roles dialog box.

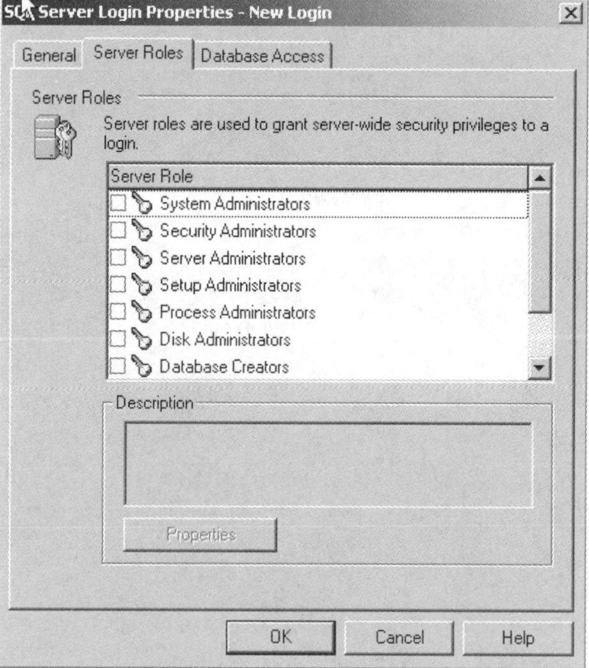

Figure 18-11. Server Roles dialog box

Database Access

Under this tab, we can assign permission to specific databases and to a database role. To permit access to the NorthwindSQL database, check the box beside the database name. To assign a database role, simply check the box beside the role(s) required when the appropriate database is selected.

Figure 18-12 shows the permissions that are granted to user LiamReid. In addition to the public role, he has been set up as a db_datareader.

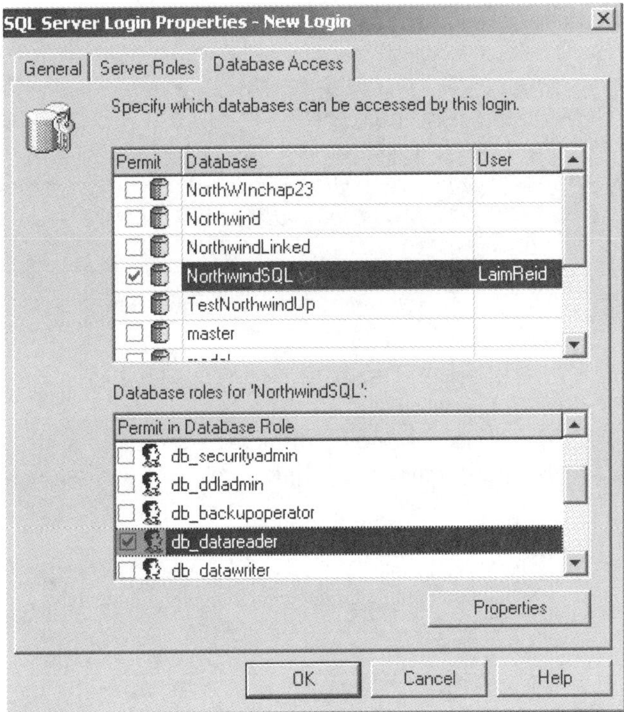

Figure 18-12. Database permissions

Note that the process changes slightly when we are assigning a user to a specific user-defined role. (However, if we are assigning the user to a role that has already been created, then the process is identical.) We shall see how this is accomplished shortly. For this example, the preceding process is sufficient.

> **NOTE** *Using the Properties dialog screen (available when we click on the Properties button), we can add existing users to the same role. Do not follow these username and password conventions in your own systems. They are for illustrative purposes only. All passwords should be strong; when possible, they also can be encrypted (such as the password used for an application role). Otherwise, login passwords are encrypted and stored within the SQL Server 2000 system tables.*

Click on OK when you're finished to save the changes. The new login should now appear in the login window listed with your existing login names.

> **NOTE** *If you do happen to forget to change the authentication from Windows to SQL Server authentication, you will get an error message, particularly if the username is not a valid Windows username. If this happens, change the authentication mode to SQL Server and continue.*

Consequences in the Access Data Project

The first change you will see is when opening the Northwind ADP: you will be prompted for a password. Figure 18-13 shows the password dialog box.

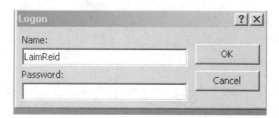

Figure 18-13. ADP password prompt

Access 2002 prompts you for the password. The username is maintained in the ADP connection file.

The second major change you will see is in the Database window: all tables will now contain the name of the table's owner (in this case, tablename followed by the owner's name in brackets). Figure 18-14 shows the Database window.

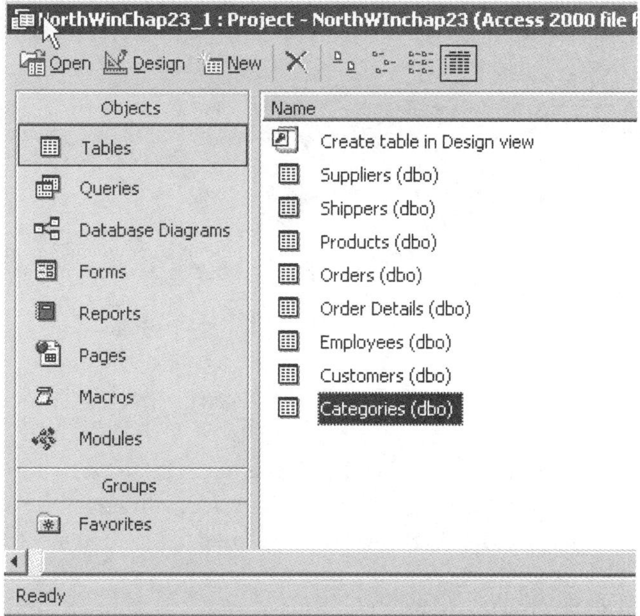

Figure 18-14. Database window

The major difference arises when Liam tries to change a record in any of the tables. Figure 18-15 shows the response from the server. It's cryptic but understandable.

Figure 18-15. Error message

What happens then can be a bit of a pain. Because the user does not have Update permissions, we get a circle of error messages if he insists in continuing. Notice the only button available on the error message dialog box is "OK".

So Liam clicks on OK. He clicks on the table again, and once again the same error message is returned. The only way out of the trap via the user interface is to choose Edit|Undo Current Field/Record from the main menu (`Ctrl+Z`)

Even if Liam closes the table following the error message, he will still receive an additional message, as shown in Figure 18-16.

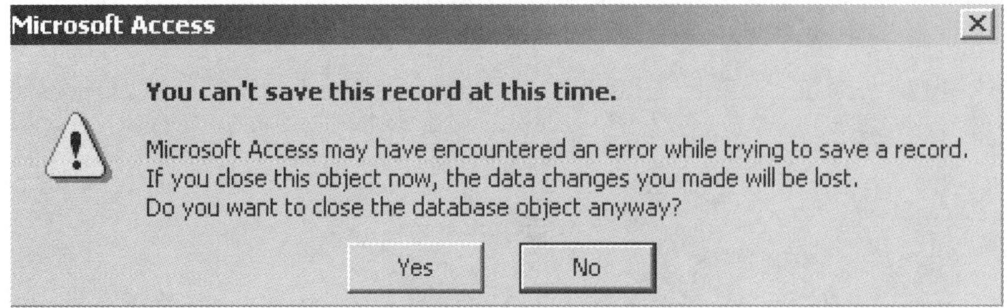

Figure 18-16. Error—No Insert/Amend Permissions

Clicking on No in response to this message starts the entire process over again.

It's highly unlikely that you will have a single user in the database. SQL Server can support hundreds of users, and one way to cope with large numbers of users is to create database roles. Table 18-3 shows a small listing of users for the Northwind ADP. We will use this table to create the users and roles for our system. Security, like everything else with databases, should be planned beforehand.

Table 18-3. User Groups

USER GROUP	TABLE	PERMISSION
Data Prep	All	Insert
Clerical	All	Insert and Amend
Middle Management	All	Read Only

This is a very simple setup designed to show you the basics of creating groups and users. Your own system will be more complex, but remember that there is no substitute for planning. Table 18-4 shows the users within each group. By the way, this is a family business.

Table 18-4. Groups and Users

GROUP	USERS
Data Prep	Liam Reid, Aine Reid, Emer Reid, Maeve Reid
Clerical	Martin Reid, Susan Harkins, Lexie Stanley
Middle Management	Patricia Reid (The Boss)

Creating the User Logins

Create a login for each of the aforementioned users. Follow the previous steps that we used to create the user Liam. Grant database access to only the Northwind database (or a database of your choice).

Once the users have been created, we will create the three roles:

- Data Prep
- Clerical
- Middle Management

Creating the Database Roles

Using SQL Server Enterprise Manager, select the NorthwindSQL Server database in the database tree and expand it. Figure 18-17 shows the expanded folder tree.

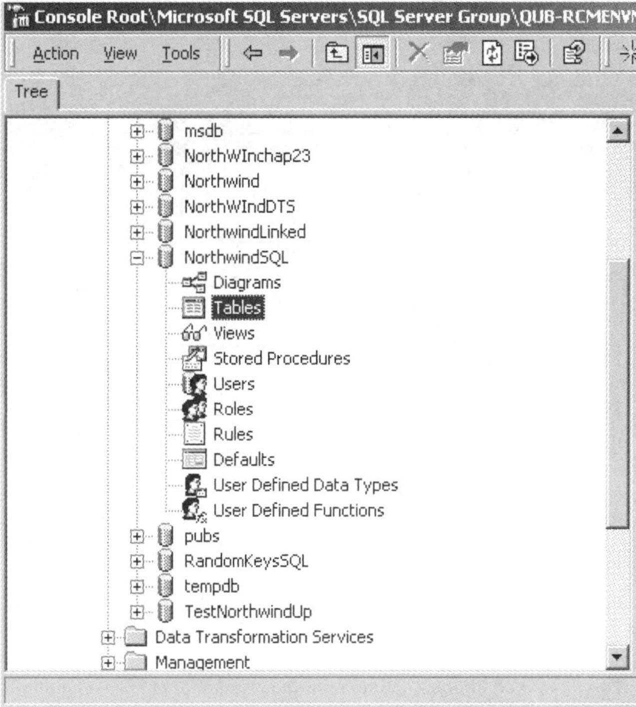

Figure 18-17. Northwind database tree

Select Roles|New Database Roles from the tree. Figure 18-18 shows the resulting dialog box.

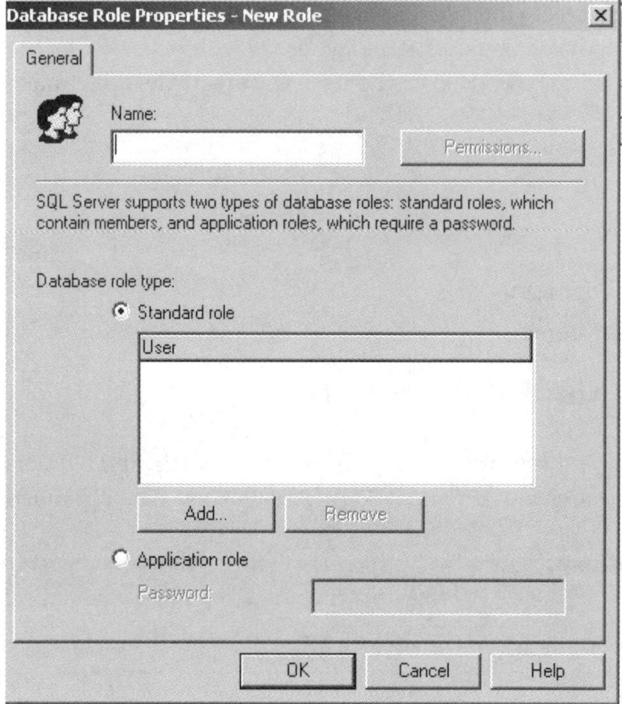

Figure 18-18. New Role dialog box

Enter the first role (Data Prep). Note that currently the user list is blank. We will not add users to the role at this point. Users will be added shortly. Click on OK to close the dialog box. Users within this role will have insert permissions of all tables in the Northwind database.

With the Northwind tree expanded, click on the Roles node to view a listing of all current roles available. Figure 18-19 shows the right-hand pane at this point.

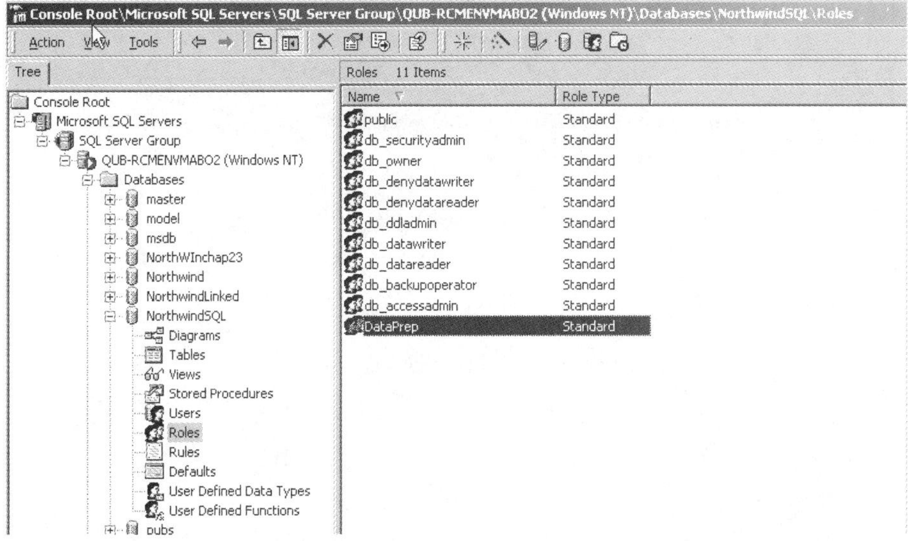

Figure 18-19. Current database roles

Note our Data Prep role at the bottom of the list. Double-click on the Data Prep role to open the Properties dialog box. See Figure 18-20.

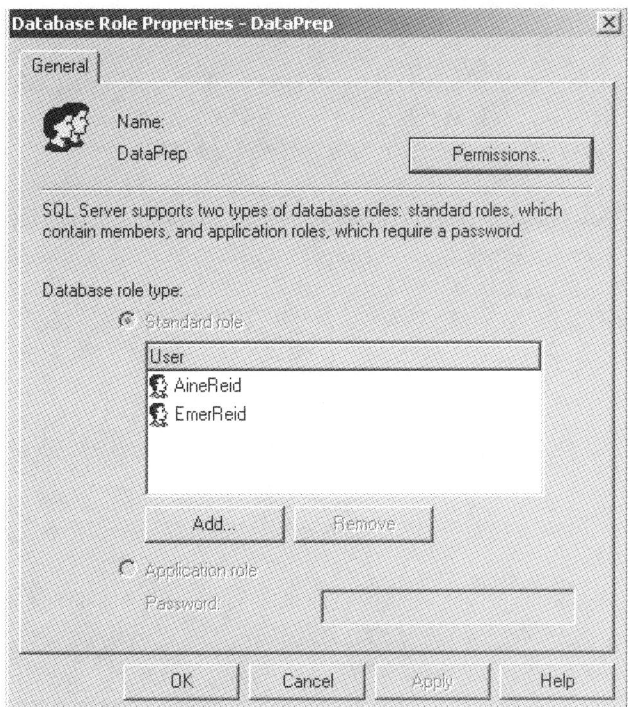

Figure 18-20. Properties dialog box

Click on the Permission button to open an additional property dialog box. Figure 18-21 shows the permissions view of the dialog box.

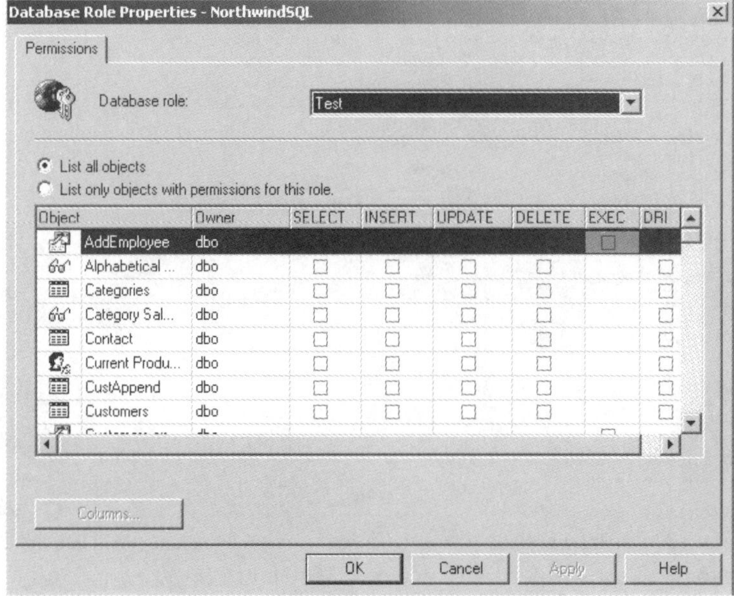

Figure 18-21. Role permissions

All objects in the database will be visible (tables, stored procedures, functions, and so on). It is at this point that we assign permissions on each object to the new role. Our Data Prep role will be responsible for inserting data only. So, we will grant SELECT on each table. Again, the process is simply a matter of checking the box located below the Insert heading for each table. Figure 18-22 shows the permissions granted at this point, and Table 18-5 shows the permissions that are available.

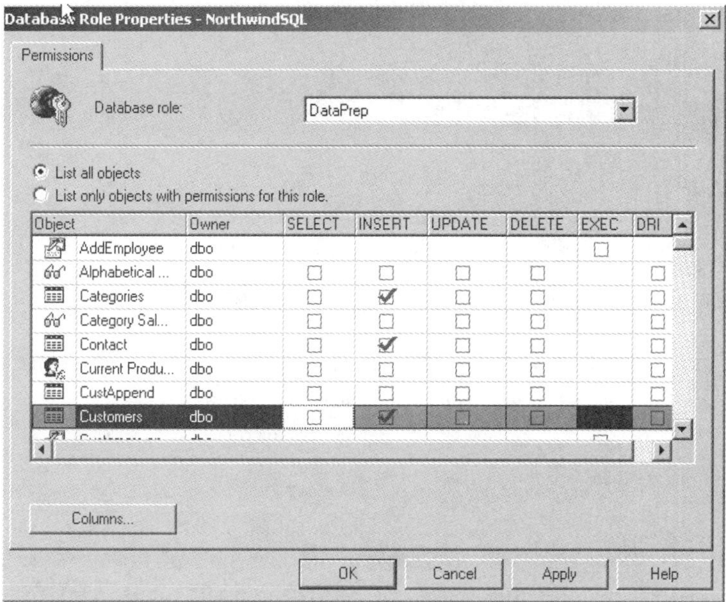

Figure 18-22. Current permissions

Table 18-5. Permissions available

PERMISSION	COMMENT
SELECT	Permits the user to run SELECT statements against the data
INSERT	Permits a user to insert data to the table
UPDATE	Permits a user to update existing data
DELETE	Permits a user to delete data
EXECUTE	Permits a user to issue execute commands for stored procedures

The role has been granted permission to insert to the tables only. No additional permissions have been given.

Once permissions have been assigned to the role, we will add our users. Clicking on OK when done returns you to the dialog box. From there, we can assign users to the role.

Click on the ADD button. Figure 18-23 shows the Add Role Members dialog box. Here, you will see a list of users created within the Northwind database.

Figure 18-23. Add Role Members dialog box

We can select one user at a time, or hold down the shift key and click to select multiple users. Select the new users you just created and click on OK. To deselect a user, simply click on the username.

Figure 18-24 shows how the database role properties should look. (Note that you may have more or fewer users assigned to the role.)

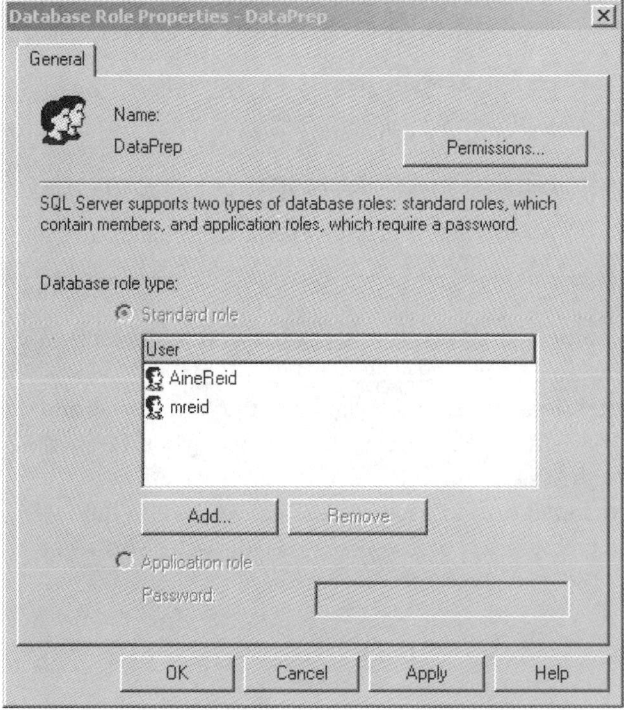

Figure 18-24. Database role properties

Click on OK to close the dialog box.

Viewing the Results in Access 2002

I have logged into the Northwind ADP as AineReid. Figure 18-25 shows the password dialog box for this user.

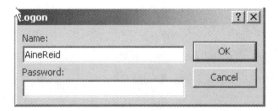

Figure 18-25. ADP password dialog box

Entering the correct password opens the application.

But where are the tables? Oops! Although we have granted our user Insert permission on the tables, we forgot to add Select permissions. Without Select, the user can't see anything. We need to return to Enterprise Manager and add Select permission to the Data Prep role.

Figure 18-26 shows the properties dialog box when this has been done.

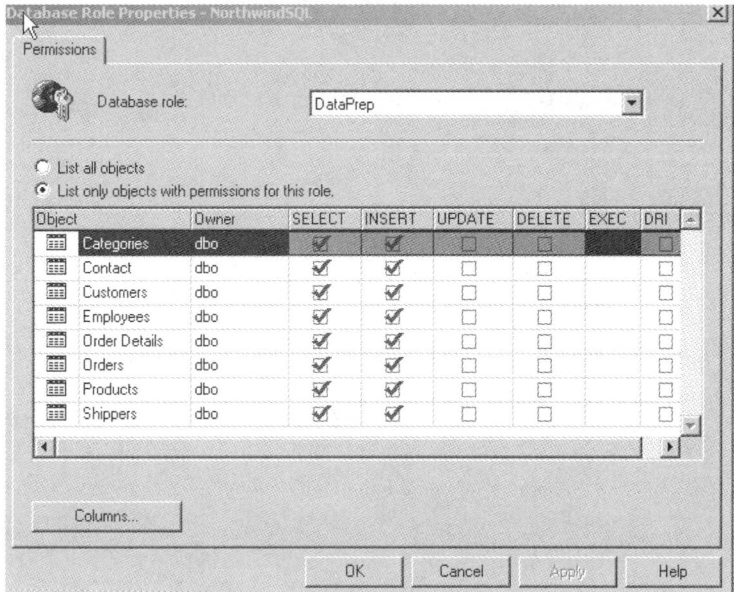

Figure 18-26. Adding Select and Insert permissions

> **NOTE** *The nice thing about this process is that we can handle all the user permissions by using the role. All users assigned to that role inherit permissions assigned to the role. Remember that the users also inherit the public role and its associated permissions.*

Now, when you're logged into your ADP, you should be able to see all records in all tables, but the only additional activity you perform is the insertion of new records. Of course, you will also be able to view existing records due to the inclusion of the Select permission.

Creating the Clerical Role

The permissions to be given to this role are Insert and Update, and this user will be permitted to insert new records and update existing records.

If you haven't already done so, create a login for each user and assign permission to the NorthwindSQL database:

- Create a new database role as before. Name it Clerical.
- Create the users (Martin Reid, Susan Harkins, and Lexie Stanley).
- Assign the users to the Clerical role.
- Assign Select, Insert, Update to all database tables.

Figure 18-27 shows the permissions for this role.

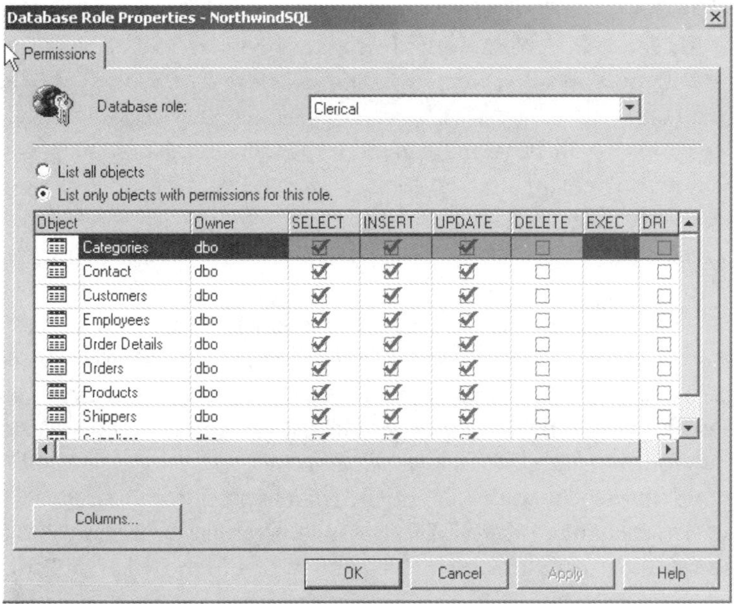

Figure 18-27. Clerical permissions

Figure 18-28 shows the users assigned to the Clerical role.

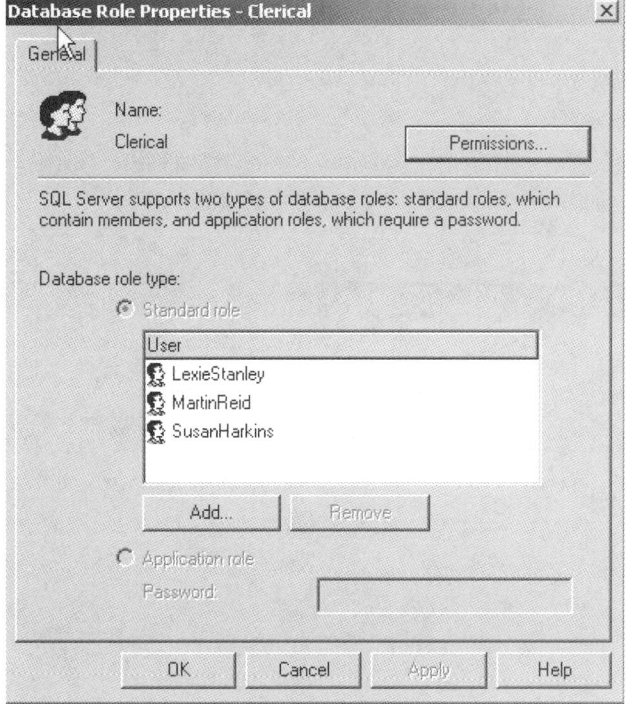

Figure 18-28. Clerical role users

Log in to the Northwind ADP as one of the newly created users. Remember that you will need the username and the password. When logged in as a member of the Clerical role, you will have permission to Select, Insert, and Update data. Try it out.

Before we look at the final management role, have a look at the Query window in your ADP. There are no stored procedures, views, or functions showing. Why? Because we haven't given permission on any of those objects to the roles created.

Check out reports. Run the customers label report. You will get an error message because the report has lost its record source. Why? Because it is looking for a record source called dbo.customers. When the report was created, the record source used was the standard Access table name. The Customers table now uses its SQL Server two-part name: dbo.Customers. When you change the record source to the correct table name, it will work as before.

Try to do the same with the alphabetical list of products. Open the report in Design view. Notice that the record source is set to a stored procedure. You do not have access to the procedure under the login used, and the report fails to run. However, the user can go into report design, change the record source, and save the changes. The same holds for forms. We will look at creating an ADE to resolve part of this problem later.

> **NOTE** *These changes are possible because the role the user is assigned to has been given permissions on the underlying tables. In addition, the forms and reports are Access objects and as such are unaffected by the security you have just set up using SQL Server.*

Logged in as the same user, open the Northwind form "Orders". In this case, you will also get an error as shown in Figure 18-29.

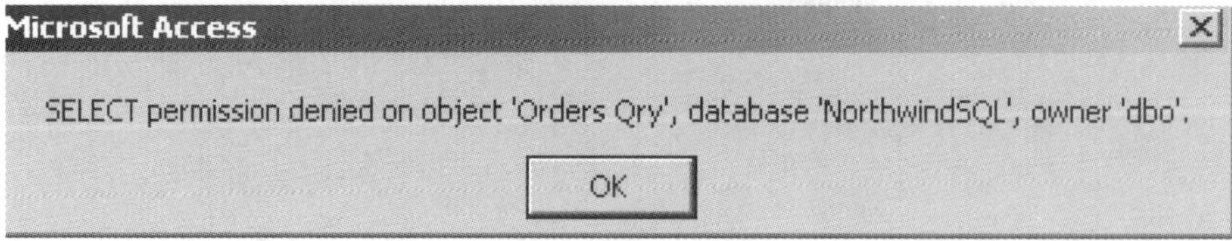

Figure 18-29. ADP error

This is because we have failed to give the role any permission on the underlying stored procedure "Orders Qry", which is used to populate the form.

We will leave it as a simple exercise for you to assign the appropriate permissions.

Middle Management Role

We will now create the Middle Management role, which will be a read-only role. In this case, we will simply create the user login and assign it to the database role db_datareader. This role contains one user, Patricia Reid (my wife). Patricia has read-only access to all tables.

I will not go into details here because the process has already been covered. In general, the steps are as follows:

1. Open the Server Security folder.
2. Create the server login for Patricia Reid.
3. Set the default database to NorthwindSQL.
4. Specify the Northwind as the database that this role has access to.
5. Add the user to the db_datareader fixed database role.

Now let's create the role:

6. Open the Role tab in the NorthwindSQL database tree.
7. Right-click and select New Database Role.
8. Enter a name for the role (Middle Management).
9. Click the Add User button to select the user from the user list.
10. Click on OK to close the Add Role Members dialog box.
11. Click on OK to close the database role properties and save your changes.

Test your new user in the Northwind Access Data Project.

Windows Integrated Security

This is the recommended security model for SQL Server; however, it is of little use if your organization doesn't use Windows server technology. If that is the case, then you are restricted to the preceding security model. For this section, I have used Windows 2000 Advanced Server.

> **NOTE** *Management of Windows Active Directory and users is not a simple process. You are advised to either read up on the subject or buy your network admins a nice bottle. This chapter is not meant to provide you with instructions on Active Directory or user security management. It merely illustrates the basic principles behind using Windows security.*

We are going to re-create the security model but this time using Windows. Bear in mind that you may not have the same level of access to the server to permit you to do this. It is important that you develop a sound working relationship with your network admins.

The following three user groups have been created using Windows 2000 Advanced Server at the operating system level (Control Panel|Administrative Tools|Computer Management):

- *WindowsDP:* Equates to our Data Prep role
- *WinClerical:* Equates to our Clerical role
- *WinManagement:* Equates to our Middle Management role

Creating the Groups

1. Expand the Local Users and Groups menu in the tree.
2. Double-click on the Groups folder to open it. Figure 18-30 shows the Groups folder when open.

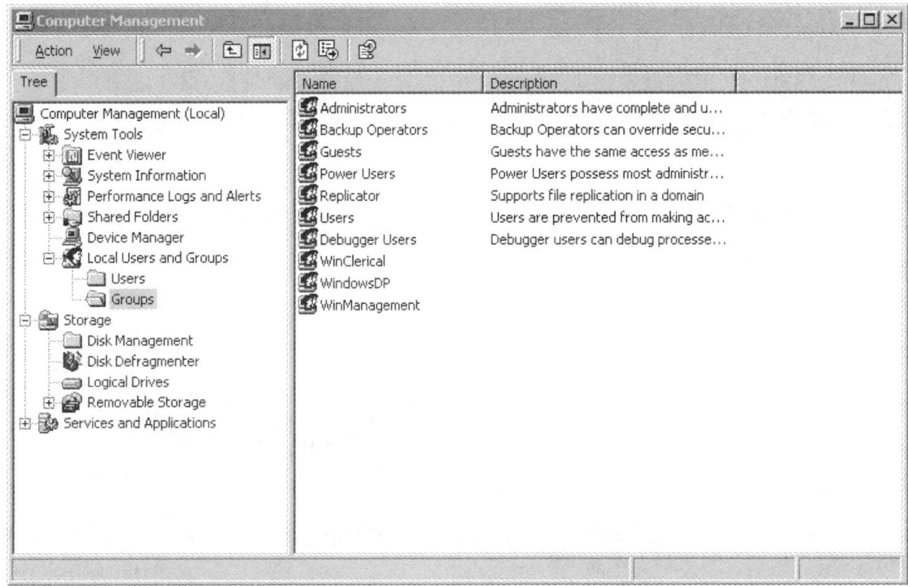

Figure 18-30. Group folder

3. Right-click anywhere within the right-hand window pane and select New Group from the shortcut menu. See Figure 18-31.

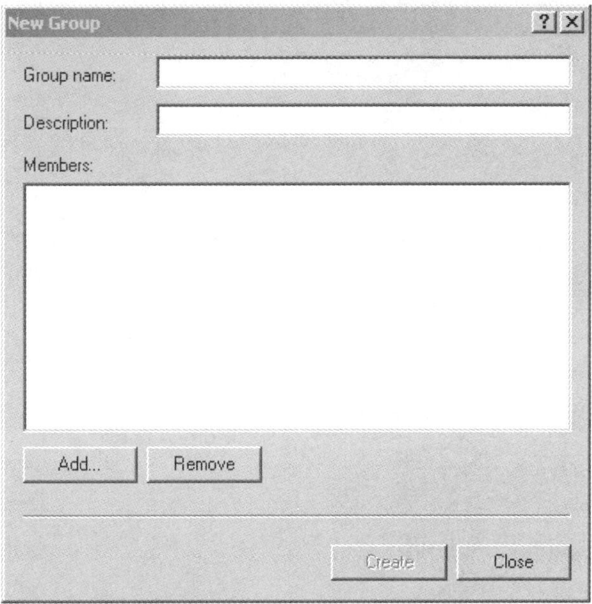

Figure 18-31. New Group dialog box

This dialog box can be used to add preexisting users to a group.

4. Complete the first two fields: Group Name and Description. (Enter a group name from the previous list.)

> **NOTE** *We will create the users soon. You could in fact have set up the users first and then simply added them to the newly created group.*

5. Click on the Create button.

Continue and create the additional Windows groups, and close the dialog box when you are done. Figure 18-32 shows the right-hand pane in the dialog box once the three groups have been created.

Name	Description
Administrators	Administrators have complete and u...
Backup Operators	Backup Operators can override secu...
Guests	Guests have the same access as me...
Power Users	Power Users possess most administr...
Replicator	Supports file replication in a domain
Users	Users are prevented from making ac...
Debugger Users	Debugger users can debug processe...
WinClerical	
WindowsDP	
WinManagement	

Figure 18-32. New groups

Creating the Users

1. With the Local Users and Groups dialog box open, select Users.

2. Right-click and select New User.

3. Enter the following details:

   - username: AineReid
   - full name: Aine Reid
   - password: AineReid

4. Uncheck the “User must change password at next login” option.

5. Click on Create. Figure 18-33 shows how the dialog box looks when completed.

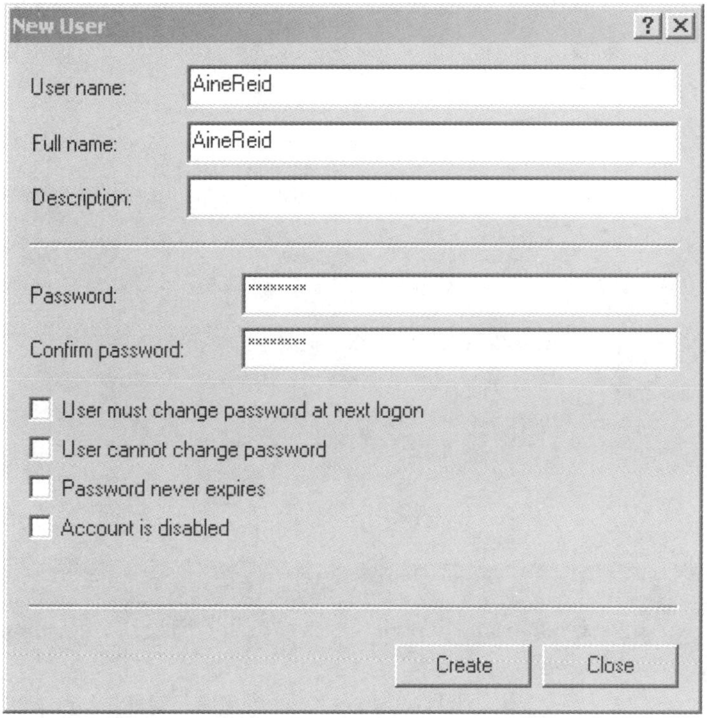

Figure 18-33. Creation of the users

If the procedure has been successful, the user will be created and the screen will be blank, ready for the next user. Create additional users as required and add them to the appropriate groups created earlier.

> **NOTE** *To add the user, double-click the group name to open the Group properties. Click on the Add button. Select the required user from the Select User or Groups dialog box and click on Add.*

Figure 18-34 shows the group with a user added.

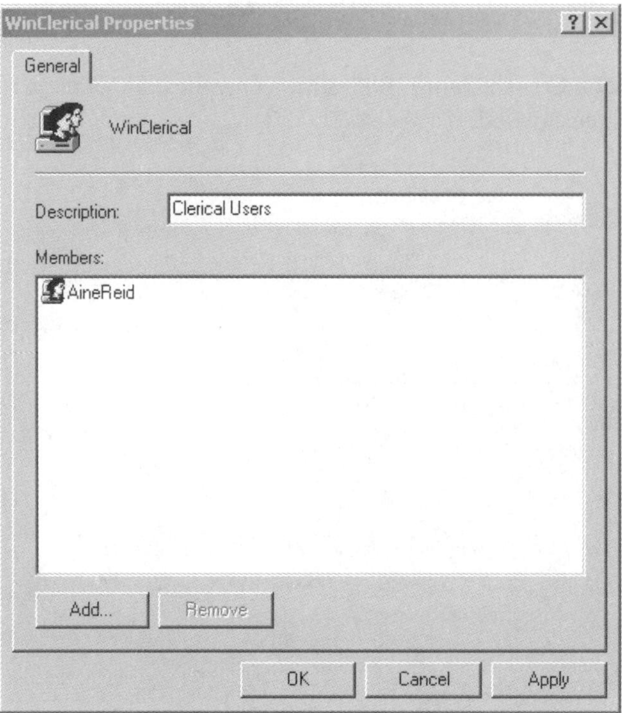

Figure 18-34. User added to Windows group

Now we need to make sure SQL Server is actually using Windows integrated security:

1. Open Enterprise Manager.
2. Select your server from the server tree.
3. Right-click and select Properties from the short cut menu.
4. Click on the Security tab to view the current setup.
5. Set the authentication to Windows Only.
6. Click on OK to save the changes.
7. Accept the prompt to restart the server and click on Yes.

Figure 18-35 shows the setup for Windows security.

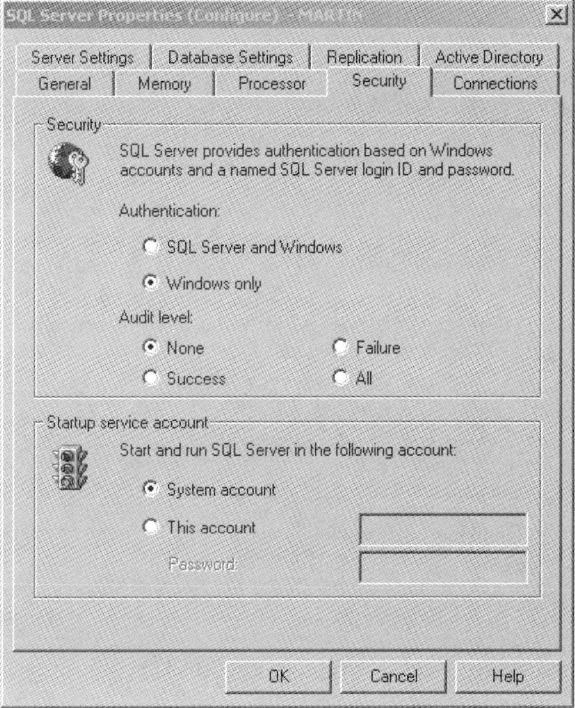

Figure 18-35. Windows security setup

Now that the Windows accounts and users have been created and SQL Server authentication has been changed to Windows Only, you must now permit access to SQL Server 2000. To add the user AineReid to SQL Server, from within Enterprise Manager:

1. Open the SQL Server group.

2. Expand the Security folder.

3. Right-click on the Logins option and select New Login from the shortcut menu. The SQL Server Login Properties dialog box will open. (The earlier Figure 18-10 shows the dialog box.) On this occasion, rather than simply typing the login name into the Name text box, we can view a listing of existing Windows users.

4. To the right of the Name text box, click on the button containing the ellipsis. Figure 18-36 shows the new dialog box with our recently added groups and user visible.

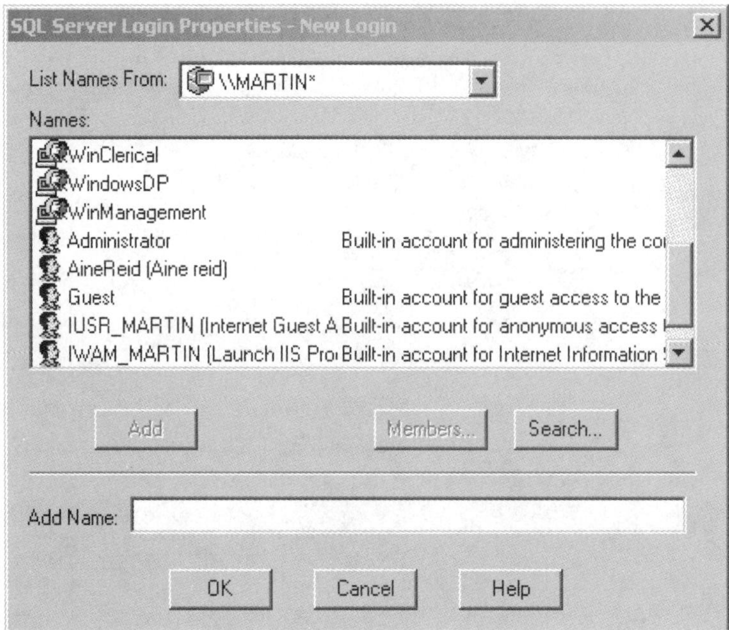

Figure 18-36. Login properties—Windows 2000 users

The dialog box will list all users and groups from the local Windows account.

5. Select or accept the group name in the List Names from Group drop-down menu.

6. Scroll down the list of available names. All the groups created plus the user "AineReid" will be listed.

7. Select AineReid and click on Add.

8. Note that the name is added to the Add Name text box as MARTIN\AineReid. The Windows account will differ on your machine.

9. Select the default database for this user using the database drop-down list.

10. Click on OK to finish adding the Windows account. Figure 18-37 shows the SQL Server Login Properties dialog box with the new login account created.

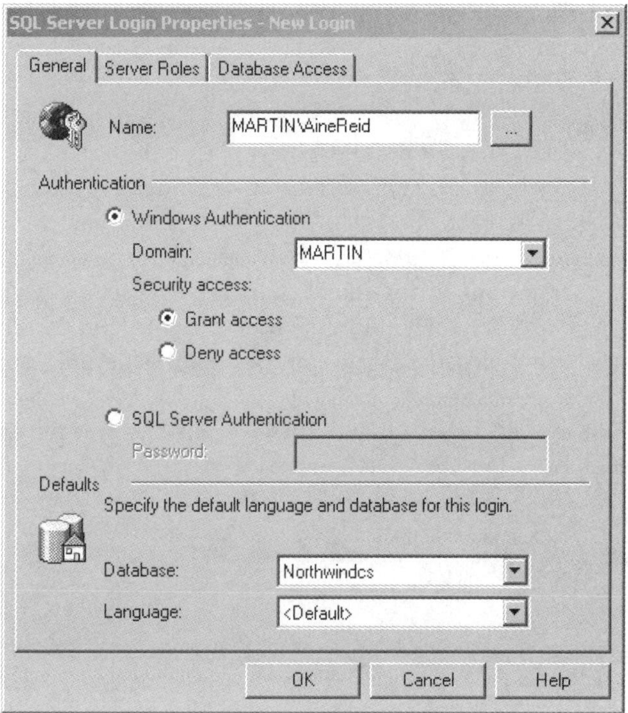

Figure 18-37. Windows user account added

11. Click on OK to close the Server Login Properties dialog box.

We can then assign permission to our user for the database selected at step 9:

1. Expand the default database. (In my case, it is the NorthwindCS demonstration file.) Failure to enter a default database can result in the user having access to the master database, which is something you do not want.

2. Double-click on the Users icon.

3. Your new user will now appear in the Users pane (right-hand side of the window).

4. Right-click on the user name to open the Database User Properties dialog box. By default, the user is already assigned to the public role.

5. Click on the Permissions button. (The earlier Figure 18-21 shows the dialog box.)

6. Grant the appropriate permissions for the user in the Permissions grid.

7. Click on OK to finish.

You have now assigned your first Windows user to the database. But, what if you have 500 users who are members of the same group? Do you repeat this process 500 times, once for each user? Of course you don't. Rather than assign permissions to Windows users individually, we assign the permissions to the group that the users belong to. Instead of adding a new user login, we can select a Windows group. We grant login permissions to the group (in the same way as for an individual user) and then assign specific database permissions to the group, just as we do for a user.

Figure 18-38 shows the permissions dialog box again. This time we are adding permissions to the MARTIN\WinClerical group.

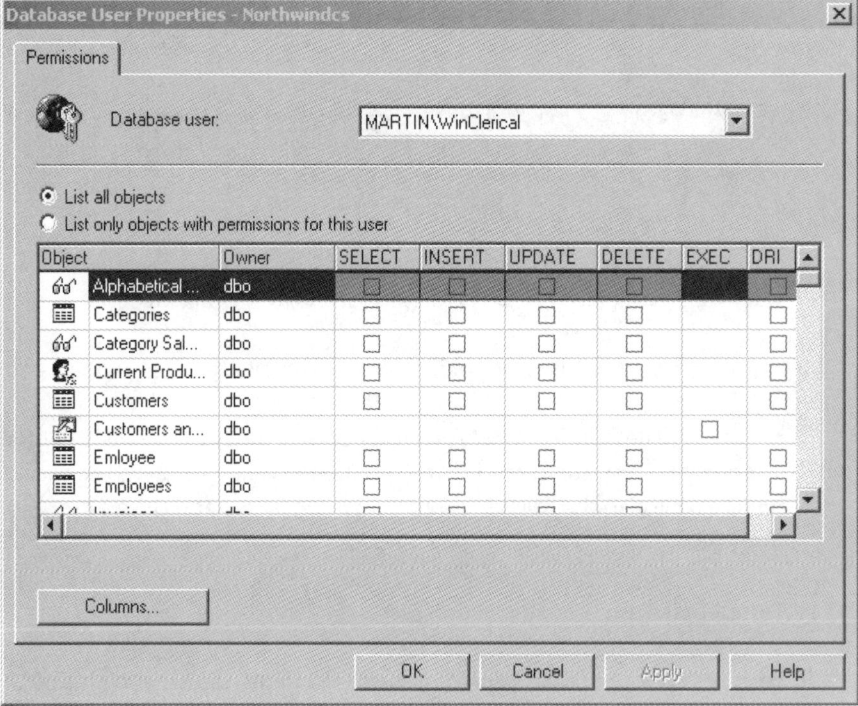

Figure 18-38. Assigning object permissions to a Windows group

NOTE *To test the users we just created, you need to exit Windows and log in as one of them.*

As you can see, creating logins, users, and roles is the "easy" part of the process. The difficult part is planning the security system: not only do you have to assign users to roles, but you must then assign permission on all the database objects: tables, stored procedures, functions, and views. The use of groups can speed up this process as permissions can be assigned to groups and will therefore apply to all the group members.

Security and T-SQL

T-SQL provides you with several different ways to work with users and their permissions on objects. We will look briefly at the required statements. Chapter 11 also includes a discussion on these statements: GRANT, DENY, and REVOKE.

GRANT

The GRANT statement permits a user to work with a database or with specific objects in that database. For example,

```
GRANT SELECT
ON Customers
To LiamReid
```

will give multiple permissions to the Customer table to our user Liam Reid. We can also grant permissions to multiple users and objects in a single statement. For example:

```
GRANT INSERT, UPDATE, DELETE
ON Customers
To LiamReid, AineReid, PatriciaReid
```

In addition to granting rights to take action on objects, we can grant permissions to:

- create a database
- create a function
- create a procedure
- create a table

- create a view
- back up a database
- back up a log

The following permissions can be granted on specific objects:

- Select
- Insert
- Delete
- Update
- Execute
- DRI

> **NOTE** *It is also possible to grant permissions to specific columns within a table. If specific columns are not provided, the permissions default to all columns within the table.*

The full syntax of GRANT is:

```
GRANT
    { ALL [ PRIVILEGES ] | permission [ , . . . n ] }
    {
        [ ( column [ , . . . n ] ) ] ON { table | view }
        | ON { table | view } [ ( column [ , . . . n ] ) ]
        | ON { stored_procedure | extended_procedure }
        | ON { user_defined_function }
    }
TO security_account [ , . . . n ]
[ WITH GRANT OPTION ]
[ AS { group | role } ]
```

DENY

As implied by the name, the DENY statement will restrict how a user interacts with objects. DENY can be used with the preceding list of users. For example:

```
DENY INSERT, UPDATE, DELETE
ON Customers
To LiamReid,AineReid,PatriciaReid
```

This statement will reverse the earlier GRANT statement for the specified users.

> **NOTE** *If you use DENY to remove permission and then add the user to a group that has the specific permission, the permission remains denied.*

The full syntax of DENY is:

```
DENY
    { ALL [ PRIVILEGES ] | permission [ , . . . n ] }
    {
        [ ( column [ , . . . n ] ) ] ON { table | view }
        | ON { table | view } [ ( column [ , . . . n ] ) ]
        | ON { stored_procedure | extended_procedure }
        | ON { user_defined_function }
    }
TO security_account [ , . . . n ]
[ CASCADE ]
```

REVOKE

The REVOKE statement revokes an assigned permission, as in:

```
REVOKE CREATE TABLE FROM Martin
```

We can also revoke permissions from multiple users:

```
REVOKE SELECT ON TABLE  FROM USER
REVOKE CREATE TABLE FROM USER ROLE
```

The full syntax for the REVOKE statement is:

```
REVOKE [ GRANT OPTION FOR ]
    { ALL [ PRIVILEGES ] | permission [ , . . . n ] }
    {
        [ ( column [ , . . . n ] ) ] ON { table | view }
        | ON { table | view } [ ( column [ , . . . n ] ) ]
        | ON { stored_procedure | extended_procedure }
        | ON { user_defined_function }
    }
{ TO | FROM }
    security_account [ , . . . n ]
[ CASCADE ]
[ AS { group | role } ]
```

Although this chapter deals with security from the SQL Server side of things, there is also one other action we can take to help secure access to our data and (on this occasion) our codebase and nonserver objects (such as forms and reports). We can save the Access Data Project as an ADE file. Saving your ADP file in this way means that all VBA code is compiled and removed from the project. In addition, users cannot:

- view or change forms, reports, modules in Design view
- change references to the object libraries
- import forms, reports, or modules

There are a couple of problems with ADE files and Access 2002. The main one is that the Make ADE File command may not be available from the Tools menu. To create an ADE file in Access 2002, the database (MDB or ADP) file must be in the Access 2002 file format. Access 2002 permits (and in fact defaults to) the Access 2000 file format when creating new databases or projects. You can change this by selecting Tools|Options from the Main menu. Click on the Advanced tab and change the default file format to Access 2002.

To save your database to the Access 2002 format, select Tools|Convert Database|To Access 2002 File Format from the Main menu.

Once your file is in the new format, the Make ADE command is available from the Tools menu. To save your database as an ADE file:

- Back up the database.
- With the database open, select Tools|Database Utilities|Make ADE File.
- In the Save ADE AS dialog box, select a location for the file, enter the filename, and click on Save. Open the ADE file. Note that you can no longer view forms, reports, data access pages, and modules in Design view. You can, however, look at the design of stored procedures, functions, views, and database diagrams. This is of course dependent on the permissions assigned to the user account accessing the project file.

NOTE *To my knowledge, hacking an ADE file (and particularly the modules) has so far proved impossible. It is therefore a useful tool for standard MDBs to protect your VBA code.*

This chapter has introduced you to SQL Server security. I stress the word *introduced* because SQL Server security should be understood in detail. Although it has many features in common with Access, there are many distinct differences. Windows security is a totally different ball game altogether.

We have seen that there are several ways to manage security and different levels of security. Security can be managed via Enterprise Manager or via T-SQL. For your general information, you should know that one important means of administrating the server—SQL Distributed Management Objects (SQLDMO)—has been omitted because it is outside the scope of this book. It is worth reading up on SQLDMO using Books Online or the MSDN Web site. SQLDMO provides you with an object model to all SQL Server objects.

CHAPTER 19

SQL Server Meets the Web

Becoming a Spider

WELL, WE HAD TO INCLUDE a chapter on the Web. No self-respecting database book can omit one. In this chapter, we will be looking at how to provide access to your newly upsized data via the Internet. The first part of this chapter will look at using Access 2002, and the second will examine using the same technologies with SQL Server 2000. However, some general comments (HTML and XML) and syntax apply equally to both.

We will look at XML: what it is, how to use it with Access 2002, and how to set SQL Server 2000 up to use it. We will also look at active server pages (ASP) and data access pages. All examples are displayed using Microsoft Internet Explorer 5. Again, like other sections in this second part of the book, all of these topics have filled complete books. I hope that what you see here will help in your understanding of the technology and demonstrate some of the promise yet to come.

Without a doubt, one of the major advances in technology has been the Internet. Using Web technologies, we can build a single interface to data and make it available, independent of platform, to users all over the world. With the advent of XML, we can transport data between systems again irrespective of platform. Just think of the possibilities: instead of having to update many user interfaces, we simply update a template file and instantly all our users see the changes. We can export data as XML for SQL Server and read it into Oracle. There is no doubt that XML is the future of data transfer, and you should use the opportunity provided by Access 2002 to get to grips with the technology.

Before we look at the specific technologies, let's have a quick overview of some of the more common requirements to show not only data but also standard text on a Web page.

Hypertext Markup Language

HTML, the language of the Internet, consists of a series of code statements known as *tags*. For example, the following tag instructs the browser to show the text "This is Bold" as bold:

```
<b> This is Bold </b>
```

Tags surround the text: <B> TEXT </B>. This is a tag pair, and it is good practice to always use tags in pairs.

Notice the opening tag, <B>, and the closing tag, </B>. The text within a tag pair will have the rules of that tag applied to it. In this case, the text appears in the browser as in a bold font. A good understanding of HTML is required before you start working with database output. HTML underpins almost all the current Web technologies, and, as you will see, both XML and ASP use a similar tagging technique.

Tags in HTML

HTML tags have both elements and attributes. For example, the following is used in our table example later:

```
<font color="#CC0066">Example of a Simple HTML Table</font>
```

The element is *font*, the attribute of the element is *color*, and the value of the attribute is *#CC0066* (hex red). Bear in mind that almost all HTML elements have multiple attributes. We will see some of this terminology repeated when we look at XML.

I will not go into great detail here but instead state again that you should find a good book or tutorial and study HTML. Learn to construct pages using Notepad. Don't worry about using generators like Microsoft Visual Studio, Microsoft FrontPage, Macromedia Ultradev, and Macromedia Dreamweaver just yet. Understand the tagging, learn how it works, and it will pay off when you begin to open your databases to the Web. Table 19-1 defines some of the HTML tags that we'll use in the following examples.

Table 19-1. HTML Tags

TAG	COMMENT
<HTML>	Begins your document and encloses all other tags.
<HEADING>	Contains other tags that define the header of the document.
<TITLE>	Contained within the <HEADING> tag. This is the document title as displayed by the browser.
</HEAD>	Closing tag to end the heading section.
<BODY>	The main content of the document. All other tags are enclosed within the body tag. In the following example, we can see additional attributes to the tag that set the background and text color of the page.
<FONT>	Instructs the browser which font to use to describe the text it encloses.
<TABLE>	Beginning of the table construction. Note the attributes including the Border attribute, which is set to 1. Setting this to 0 instructs the browser to hide the border.
<TR>	Begins a single row in the table.
<TD>	Begins the cell construction within the table.
</TD>	Ends the cell construction. Notice that this tag is repeated for each cell in the row.
</TR>	End of a single row in the table.
</TABLE>	Ends the table construction.
</BODY>	Ends the body section.
</HTML>	Ends the HTML file.

As can be seen, HTML is not an overly complex tagging language, but it is vital that you master it before working with it via code and XML. We will look at some of the more common tags you will need to understand basic HTML, and particularly those used to construct HTML tables. Like any construction in HTML, tables are created using tags. However, in this case, we need a set of tags that together create the table. The following example shows a simple table created using HTML. (I cheated and used an editor.)

```
<html>
<head>
<title>Table Example</title>
</head>
<body bgcolor="#FFFFFF" text="#000000">
<font color="#CC0066">Example of a Simple HTML Table</font>
<table width="64%" border="1">
  <tr>
    <td><font color="#000000">Column 1</font></td>
    <td><font color="#000000">Column 2</font></td>
    <td><font color="#000000">Column 3</font></td>
  </tr>
  <tr>
    <td>Table Cell</td>
    <td>Table Cell</td>
    <td>Table Cell</td>
  </tr>
  <tr>
    <td>Table Cell</td>
    <td>Table Cell</td>
    <td>Table Cell</td>
  </tr>
</table>
</body>
</html>
```

One of the initial ideas behind the Internet was to separate content from appearance. This process has been blurred because HTML provides many tags (such as the <B> for bold text) that have nothing to do with content but are specifically designed to control the appearance of the content. For example, the following fragment of HTML contains one line of content and several formatting instructions to the browser. The instructions tell the browser how we want the content displayed.

```
<html>
<head>
<title>Page Title</title>
```

```
</head>
<body bgcolor="#FFFFFF" text="#000000">
<h1><font face="Times New Roman, Times,
 serif" size="6" color="#CC3333"><b>I am a single red line </b>
</font> </h1>
</body>
</html>
```

Within the HTML code are instructions on:

- the Font to use (Times New Roman, Times, serif)
- the text size (6)
- the color of the text #CC3333 (hex for red)
- bold text (<B>, </B> tags)
- the heading (<H1>, </H1> tag)

As you can begin to see, a large amount of information is contained on the average Web page that has nothing to do with the content of the actual page. Each page is completely self-contained with its own content plus formatting instructions. In many cases, you will see hundreds of lines of HTML used for formatting, which is far more than the actual content.

Just think if we wanted to change all our document headings (<H1>) tags to, say, blue, size 3, left aligned. We would have to manually edit every page on our Web site, which may be thousands of pages. This is an impossible job. So, what can we do about this? One method currently used is known as *cascading stylesheets* (or *CSS*). They are individual files that contain formatting instructions for HTML pages. When we create a page, we can attach it to a CSS file from which it picks up its formatting instructions.

In this way, if we need to amend a text format or a particular style, it is simply a matter of changing the CSS file to have the changes proliferated down to every file attached to it. When we add in HTML template files (those files containing common header and footers), we can build Web pages, which require a minimum of management. An excellent use of CSS can be seen in many of the Microsoft Web sites including the Access 2002 pages. For example, the following HTML file is attached to a cascading stylesheet, which controls the various formatting options. Notice that the HTML file on this occasion contains no formatting information. Figure 19-1 shows the HTML file as seen in Internet Explorer.

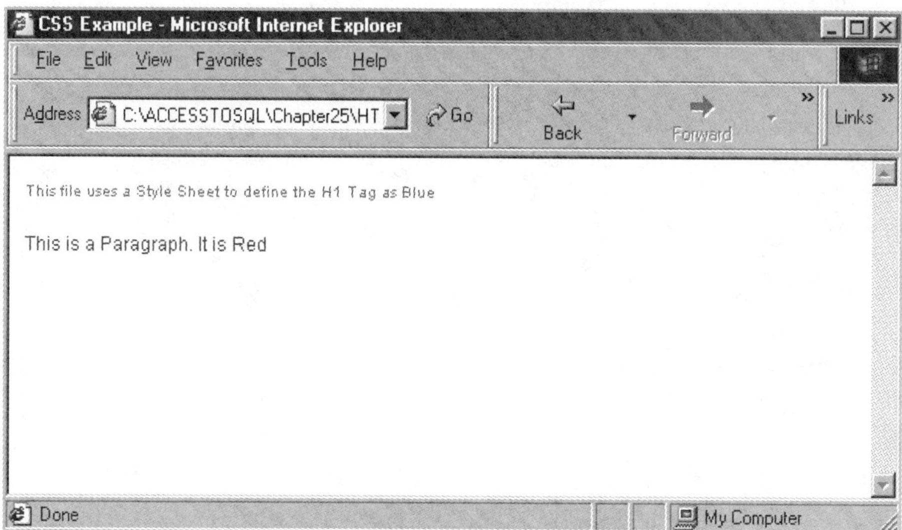

Figure 19-1. Using cascading stylesheets

The source HTML for this file is:

```
<html>
<head>
<title>CSS Example</title>
<link rel="stylesheet" href="apress" type="text/css">
</head>
<h1>This file uses a Style Sheet to define the H1 Tag as Blue</h1>
<p>This is a Paragraph. It is Red</p>
</body>
</html>
```

The line `<link rel="stylesheet" href="apress" type="text/css">` references our external stylesheet.

The contents of the CSS file are:

```
h1 {  font-family: Arial, Helvetica, sans-serif; font-size:
10px; font-style: normal; font-weight: normal; color: #0099FF}
p {  font-family: Arial, Helvetica, sans-serif; font-size: 12px;
color: #CC0033}
```

Using the CSS file, we can now control the formatting of as many HTML files as we care to attach it to. This is a simple example, and I have added only two formatting options (<h1> heading 1 and <p> paragraph), but I think you should get the general idea. Now we have a means of separating content and appearance.

XML also uses Extensible Stylesheet Language (XSL), which is a type of CSS to assist in the presentation of the page. XSL is very similar in concept to CSS and is in fact based on the CSS specification. The full specification to XSL can be viewed at `http://www.w3.org/TR/xsl`. XSL deals with the presentation of XML files in the same way that CSS deals with the presentation of HTML. XSL defines how the XML file will be presented via the browser.

Before looking at XML in detail, let's look at some of the main differences between HTML and XML.

- Tags used in XML are very similar to those used in HTML but with some significant differences.
- Like HTML, we have an opening and closing tag. Unlike HTML, you must have an opening and a closing tag.
- Tags in XML are case sensitive. For example, <TAG> and <tag> represent two completely different things.
- XML is not concerned with presentation but with the data and how to describe that data. This is the most distinct and important difference.

> **NOTE** *XML by itself does absolutely nothing. For it to be used, we need additional scripting and software. The most popular browsers have built-in software that allows them to parse XML (Internet Explorer 5 and above and, to a lesser extent, Netscape Navigator versions 5 and below).*

XML: The Future of Data Transfer?

Unlike HTML, with XML we can actually define our own tags. So, if I want a tag called <AineReid>, I simply define it. We will look at how to define our own tags later when we look at the document type definition (DTD), which is a formal description of a particular type of document.

Another important principle—and one that is vital you understand—is that of elements and the children of elements. For example, if I want to use XML to describe a house, I could have an element called *house*, and the house element can consist of other elements such as type, rooms, garden, and so forth. These can be known as the *children* of the house element. To present this with XML, I could construct a simple file:

```
<House>
<Type>Detached</Type>
<Rooms>6</Rooms>
<Garden>Yes</Garden>
<Drive>Yes</Drive>
</House>
```

Notice that the file contains no information informing the browser how the information is to be presented. Without this presentational information, a browser such as Internet Explorer (5 or above) will apply a default formatting file. The formatting file is very similar to a CSS file and is known as an XSLT file. This default formatting results in the "tree view" appearance that is common to raw XML files. Notice that we have no formatting information in the XML file at all.

> **NOTE** *Some requirements of XML have been omitted from this example to keep it simple.*

Notice that an opening tag (<house>) and a closing tag (</house>) surround the entire XML file. This is one of the rules of XML. This tag is known as the root element and all other elements extent from the root element.

Within the browser, the XML parser maps your elements into a tree structure. Note that the file itself is not changed in any way. Manipulation of the file is carried out in memory. In this way, we can use the same XML file and transform it in many different ways. Figure 19-2 shows the house file displayed in Internet Explorer using the browser default formatting.

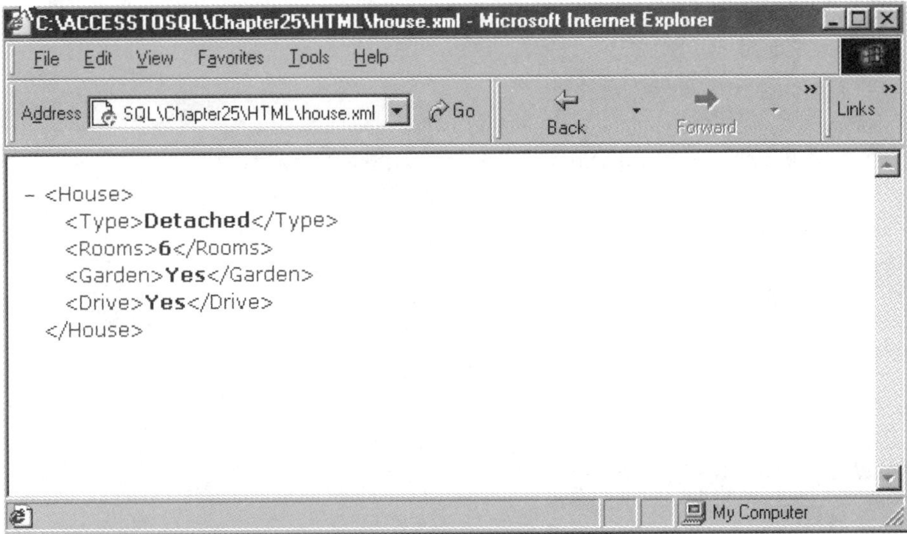

Figure 19-2. House.xml with Internet Explorer

So What's So Good about XML?

XML has many benefits. The following list describes its major advantages.

- XML is cross platform. An XML document can be used on Windows, Unix, and Macintosh operating systems.
- XML can be stored in a database.
- XML is an open standard.
- XML is widely used.
- XML is designed to run via the Web.
- Many tool vendors are now incorporating XML (C++, C#, VB.Net).
- XML permits different systems to interact.

How Is XML Being Used?

XML also has many uses, such as:

- on the Web (naturally) to publish interactive documents
- to extract and insert data to RDBM systems
- to publish to cellular phones, pagers, and mobile communication devices
- for business-to-business data exchange

How Do We Use XML?

XML is basically a structured text file that, when processed by an XML parser, can be used to present data within a Web browser. Just like HTML, XML consists of tags. In this case, however, you are not restricted to the tags that compose the language: you can create and define your own. Let's have a look at a simple XML file produced by Access 2002.

> **NOTE** *For the moment, these examples produce static data, and there is no live connection to the database. We will look at producing "live" data later. It is also worth pointing out here that this is version 1.0 technology, so don't expect magic.*

For this example, I am going to amend the Current Product List function in an Access ADP. The only purpose in doing so is to reduce the amount of data that's displayed on the Web page. In my case, I have simply copied and pasted the existing function from the Database window. (Click on the function and use `Ctrl+C` to copy and then `Ctrl+V` to paste.) The function has been renamed fntProductXML, and the following criteria has been added:

```
WHERE (ProductName Like 'A%' or ProductName Like 'B%')
```

Restricting the records to only two keeps the XML file small and uncomplicated while we dissect it. Don't worry; we will look at more-complicated examples later.

To create the XML file using Access 2002 is simply a matter of exporting the function as XML. Well, not really; several options are actually involved when exporting. The options chosen depend on how you want to present the data via XML and if you also need to export the schema of the database object, but let's give it a go.

Like everything in Access, we can export a file in a number of ways. We can select File|Export or right-click on the object to export. I like using the mouse button.

Right-click on our new function, fntProductXML, and select Export from the shortcut menu. A standard Windows File Save As dialog box opens asking for a filename and location. For these examples, I simply created a new folder, XMLFiles.

Select the option to save the file as an XML document, and click on Export. A new dialog box, Export XML, will open. Figure 19-3 shows the initial dialog screen.

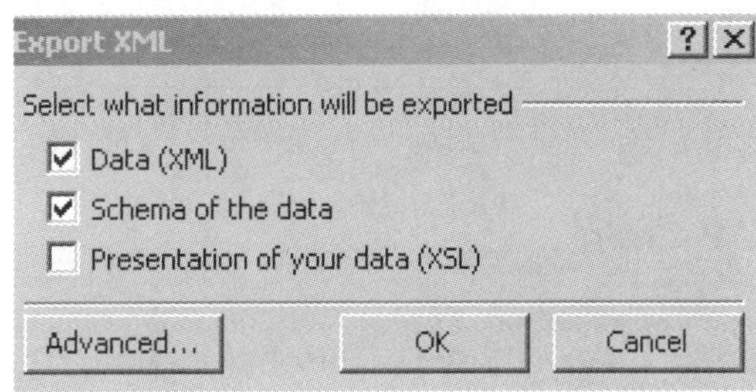

Figure 19-3. Exporting to XML

Now we get to some of the complicated stuff. Three options are available, two of which are selected by default. In the next sections, we will look at each detail.

Data (XML)

This option will export your data as a raw XML file, Figure 19-4 shows how it is presented in Microsoft Explorer.

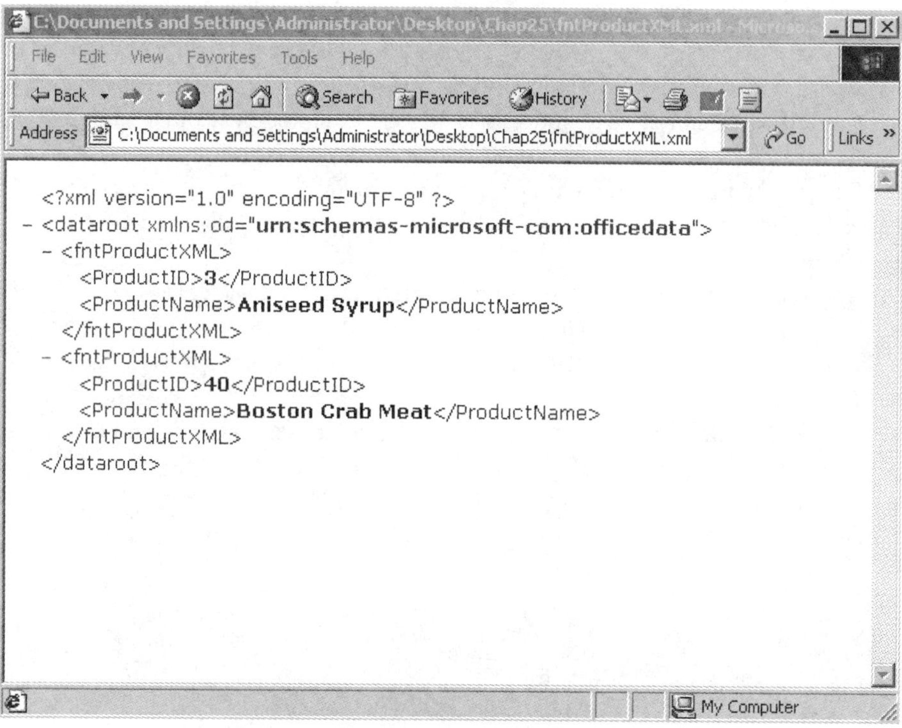

Figure 19-4. Raw XML Export

Notice the minus sign (–) to the left of the object names. This works very much like the folders in Windows. A plus sign (+) indicates that there are additional nodes, and you can expand the nodes by clicking on the plus sign. The minus sign collapses the node. It's all very much like the tree view control in Access. Following is the full XML file we used previously:

```
<?XML version="1.0" encoding="UTF-8" ?>
<dataroot XMLns:od="urn:schemas-microsoft-com:officedata">
<fntProductXML>
<ProductID>3</ProductID>
<ProductName>Aniseed Syrup</ProductName>
</fntProductXML>
<fntProductXML>
<ProductID>40</ProductID>
<ProductName>Boston Crab Meat</ProductName>
</fntProductXML>
</dataroot>
```

Let's take it apart.

Table 19-2. Access XML File

STATEMENT	COMMENT
<?XML version="1.0" encoding="UTF-8" ?>	Version of XML being used. UTF refers to the character set supported by the browsers.
<dataroot XMLns:od ="urn:schemas-microsoft-com:officedata">	Document root level. All other elements are children of this root level.
<fntProductXML>	Product element.
<ProductID>3</ProductID>	Child element of product. Product ID.
<ProductName>	Child element. Product name.
</fntProductXML>	Closing the product element.
</dataroot>	Closing the root element.

Notice that the opening and closing tags for the child elements are repeated for each child element of the document root. For example, to add another child element, simply type the following into the XML file:

```
<fntProductXML>
  <ProductID>50</ProductID>
  <ProductName>Irish Stew</ProductName>
</fntProductXML>
```

> **NOTE** *Make sure that this is entered after the closing </fntProductXML> tag and the ending </dataroot> tag.*

The preceding XML document is said to be *well formed,* in that it meets all the rules for XML syntax:

- It contains a root element.
- All elements are children of the root element.
- All elements are correctly paired.
- The element name in a start tag and an end tag are the same.
- Attribute names are used only once within the same element.

Let's export it again. Right-click on the function, fntProductXML. Enter Products2 for the file name, and save as file type XML. This time ensure that all the options are selected. (See Figure 19-5.) Click on OK.

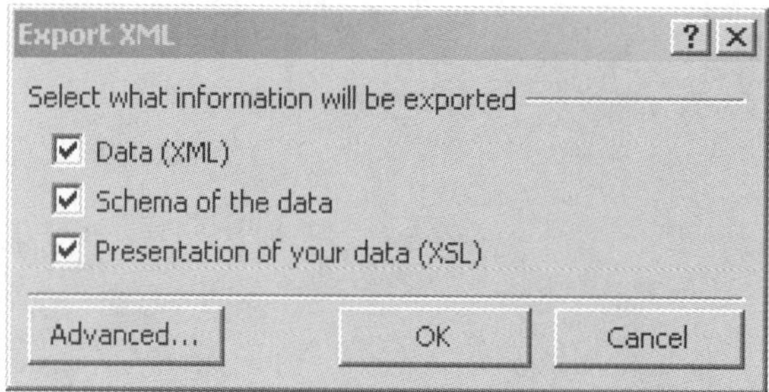

Figure 19-5. XML options

Note that several files are created this time (XML, HTML, and two new file types: XSD and XSL):

- Products2.html
- Products2.xml
- Products2.xsd
- Products2.xsl

What's going on? Before answering that question, let's look at the output. Figure 19-6 shows Products2.html in Internet Explorer. This time we are not opening the XSL file directly; instead, we are opening a standard HTML file.

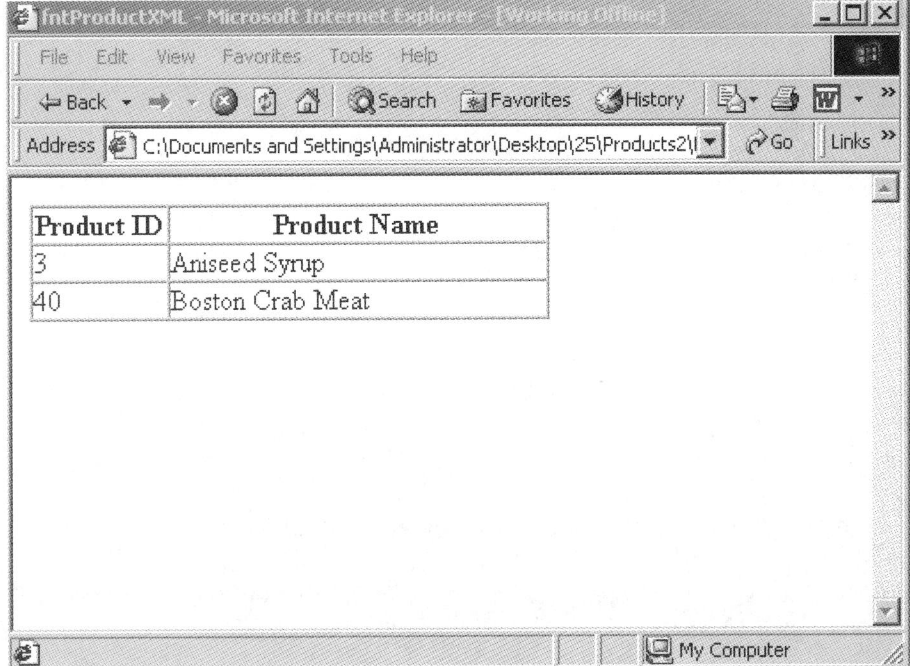

Figure 19-6. Products2.html in Internet Explorer

This looks a bit more like your usual HTML file, and that's exactly what it is. Using a combination of files, we can now "override" the built-in stylesheet used by Explorer and replace it with one generated by Access 2002.

In the next sections, we'll look at each of the files that were generated this time.

Products2.HTML

This appears to be a standard HTML page, but, as you will see, it actually contains little HTML. What it does contain is some script that actually loads the XML file into the browser. The script is:

```
<HTML XMLns:signature="urn:schemas-microsoft-com:office:access">
<HEAD>
<META HTTP-EQUIV="Content-Type" CONTENT="text/html;charset=UTF-8"/>
</HEAD>
<SCRIPT event=onload for=window>
  objData = new ActiveXObject("MSXML.DOMDocument");
  objData.async = false;
```

```
  objData.load("Products2.XML");
  if (objData.parseError.errorCode != 0)
    alert(objData.parseError.reason);

  objStyle = new ActiveXObject("MSXML.DOMDocument");
  objStyle.async = false;
  objStyle.load("Products2.xsl");
  if (objStyle.parseError.errorCode != 0)
    alert(objStyle.parseError.reason);

  document.open("text/html","replace");
  document.write(objData.transformNode(objStyle));
</SCRIPT>
</HTML>
```

This script, held within the HTML file, simply checks that the XML file parses correctly; if it does, it's loaded into the browser. But an additional file, Products2.xsl, is also loaded. Again, the script checks that this file also parses correctly before loading.

> **NOTE** *Both the XML and the XSL file are loaded into the browser, and TransformNode (a Microsoft extension to the W3C Document Object Model) is used to format the content using the XSL stylesheet and write it out into the HTML file. (XSL stylesheets will be discussed shortly.)*

Products2.XSL

This is a new file type. XSL is used to format or transform our XML file, producing the output seen in Figure 19-7. Because the XSL file produced by Access 2002 is quite long, it is not shown here in its total. Several of the functions have been omitted to save space. (To view the file, simply open the XSL file in Notepad when you have exported some data.)

```
<?XML version="1.0"?>
<xsl:stylesheet XMLns:xsl="http://www.w3.org/TR/WD-xsl" language="vbscript">
<xsl:template match="/">
<HTML>
<HEAD>
<META HTTP-EQUIV="Content-Type" CONTENT="text/html;charset=UTF-8" />
<TITLE>
```

```
fntProductXML
</TITLE>
<STYLE TYPE="text/css">
</STYLE>
</HEAD>
<BODY link="#0000ff" vlink="#800080">
<TABLE BORDER="1" BGCOLOR="#ffffff" CELLSPACING="0" CELLPADDING="0"><TBODY>

<xsl:for-each select="/dataroot/fntProductXML">
<xsl:eval>AppendNodeIndex(me)</xsl:eval>
</xsl:for-each>
<xsl:for-each select="/dataroot/fntProductXML">
<xsl:eval>CacheCurrentNode(me)</xsl:eval>
<xsl:if expr="OnFirstNode">
<TR><TH style="width: 2.01cm">
Product ID
</TH>
<TH style="width: 5.661cm">
Product Name
</TH>
</TR>
</xsl:if>
<TR><TD>
<xsl:eval no-entities="true">
Format(GetValue("ProductID", 3),"" ,"")</xsl:eval>
</TD>
<TD>
<xsl:eval no-entities="true">
Format(GetValue("ProductName", 202),"" ,"")</xsl:eval>
</TD>
</TR>
<xsl:if expr="OnLastNode">
</xsl:if>
<xsl:eval>NextNode()</xsl:eval>
</xsl:for-each>
</TBODY></TABLE>
</BODY>
</HTML>
<xsl:script>
<![CDATA[
```

Functions have been removed:

```
]]>
</xsl:Script>
</xsl:template>
</xsl:stylesheet>
```

This is quite an extensive file, and we will look at only those areas that we have not yet covered. When the browser loads an XML file into memory, it also looks for a reference to an XSL file. If one is found, the XSL parser applies it to the XML file. As before, if no XSL file is found, a browser such as Internet Explorer will use a default file to format the output. Basically, the XSL file searches the tree of XML data for matches to format. Let's break down the preceding file:

```
<xsl:stylesheet XMLns:xsl="http://www.w3.org/TR/WD-xsl" language="vbscript">
```

This line simply tells the XML parser that this is a stylesheet. The next section took me a while to get a grip on it:

```
XMLns:xsl=http://www.w3.org/TR/WD-xsl
```

This line defines a namespace.

> **NOTE** *The current recommended namespace is* `www.w3.org/TR/XSL/Transform`. *Internet Explorer uses the namespace above because the W3 namespace was incomplete at the time of release. A namespace puts your XML or XSL into context. Because we can use the same tag name, it is important that they can be uniquely identified in the context of the XML file. In this way, we can have the same named element but can refer to it uniquely. The namespace is simply used as a unique resource for our XML elements. It follows, therefore, that we could use the same XSL tag, but because it refers to different namespaces it can be treated uniquely with each tag having a different context with its own namespace. The concept of a namespace is also used in both ADO and ASP .NET. So, it is worth your while spending some time understanding their use with Access.*

Now comes our first real bit of XSL:

```
<xsl:template match="/">
```

This line is used to indicate the particular part of the input file that the XSL template should be applied to. In this case, the XSL file will begin at the document root. ("/ " indicates the root node of the input file.)

> **NOTE** *This is not strictly XSL. The language we are seeing is something called XPath, which allows you to refer to specific elements within an XML document by specifying a location path. For a full discussion on Xpath, see* `http://www.w3.org/TR/xpath`.

The next few lines are basic HTML that will be used in our final document:

```
<HTML>
<HEAD>
<META HTTP-EQUIV="Content-Type" CONTENT="text/html;charset=UTF-8" />
<TITLE>
Example of XML from Access 2002
</TITLE>
<STYLE TYPE="text/css">
</STYLE>
</HEAD>
<BODY link="#0000ff" vlink="#800080">
<TABLE BORDER="1" BGCOLOR="#ffffff" CELLSPACING="0" CELLPADDING="0"><TBODY>
```

> **NOTE** *Notice that I have changed the title of the document from fntProduct to something more descriptive.*

I have not included the remaining HTML tags, but you should see that they are used to format our output from the XSL file into a standard HTML table. The real work in this file is performed by the following code fragment, which loops through the XML file preparing it for output. Note that the functions used have been omitted from the example to save space.

```
<xsl:for-each select="/dataroot/fntProductXML">
<xsl:eval>AppendNodeIndex(me)</xsl:eval>
</xsl:for-each>
<xsl:for-each select="/dataroot/fntProductXML">
<xsl:eval>CacheCurrentNode(me)</xsl:eval>
<xsl:if expr="OnFirstNode">
```

Products2.xsd

In addition to exporting the actual data, we can also export the schema as XML. This is the function of the Products2.xsd file. We can export the schema and then distribute it to others to assist in helping them to provide data as XML that meets our schema. The following code shows the schema of the data used by Products2.xml:

```
<?XML version="1.0" encoding="UTF-8"?>
<xsd:schema XMLns:xsd=
"http://www.w3.org/2000/10/XMLSchema" XMLns:od=
"urn:schemas-microsoft-com:officedata">
<xsd:element name="dataroot">
<xsd:complexType>
<xsd:choice maxOccurs="unbounded">
<xsd:element ref="fntProductXML"/>
</xsd:choice>
</xsd:complexType>
</xsd:element>
<xsd:element name="fntProductXML">
<xsd:annotation>
<xsd:appinfo/>
</xsd:annotation>
<xsd:complexType>
<xsd:sequence>
<xsd:element name="ProductID"
od:jetType="autonumber" od:sqlSType="int"
od:autoUnique="yes"
od:nonNullable="yes">
<xsd:simpleType>
<xsd:restriction base="xsd:integer"/>
</xsd:simpleType>
</xsd:element>
<xsd:element name="ProductName"
od:jetType="text" od:sqlSType="nvarchar"
od:nonNullable="yes">
<xsd:simpleType>
<xsd:restriction base="xsd:string">
<xsd:maxLength value="40"/>
</xsd:restriction>
</xsd:simpleType>
</xsd:element>
</xsd:sequence>
```

```
</xsd:complexType>
</xsd:element>
</xsd:schema>
```

You can see that each data element is defined. For example,

```
<xsd:element name="ProductName" od:jetType="text" od:sqlSType="nvarchar"
od:nonNullable="yes">
```

defines the Product Name element.

Using Access 2002 to Export Schema

To export the schema of the Customers table in the Northwind ADP:

1. Right-click on the Customers table and choose Export.
2. In the Export table dialog box, name the file CustomersSchema.
3. Select Save as Type, XML Documents.
4. In the Export XML dialog box, ensure that Schema of Data is checked and click Advanced. Figure 19-7 shows the advanced options.

> **NOTE** *Once you open the advanced dialog screen, you cannot return to the first screen the export dialog.*

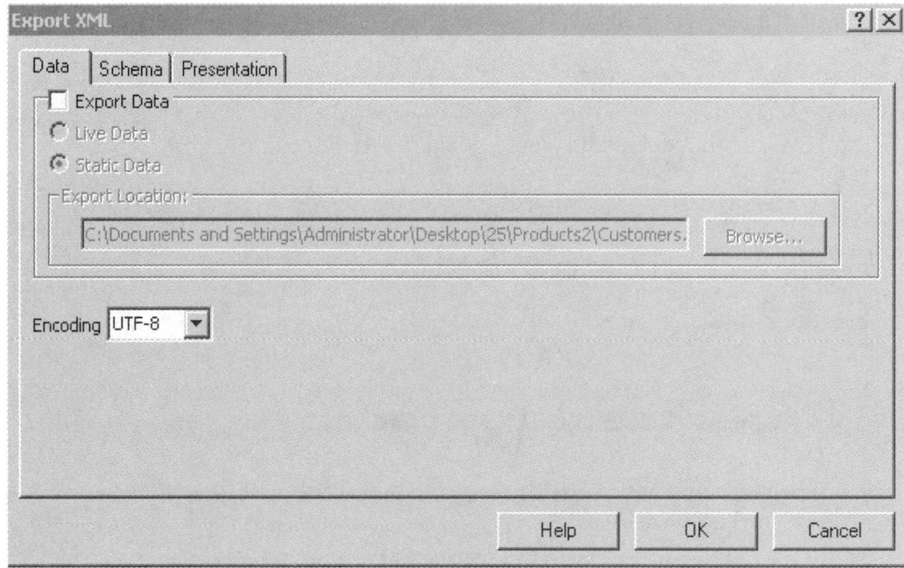

Figure 19-7. Advanced options when exporting to XML

5. Check Export Data. Confirm that the path for the file export is correct and click on the Schema tab. When exporting the schema, we can include primary key and indexes, embed the schema in the XML document, or create a separate file. In this case, we are going to create a separate file.

6. Click the Create Separate Schema Document radio button.

7. Confirm the location of the folder for the document using the Browse button.

8. Click on OK to save. Figure 19-8 shows the Advanced dialog box when all options have been completed.

9. Click on OK to finish and save the document.

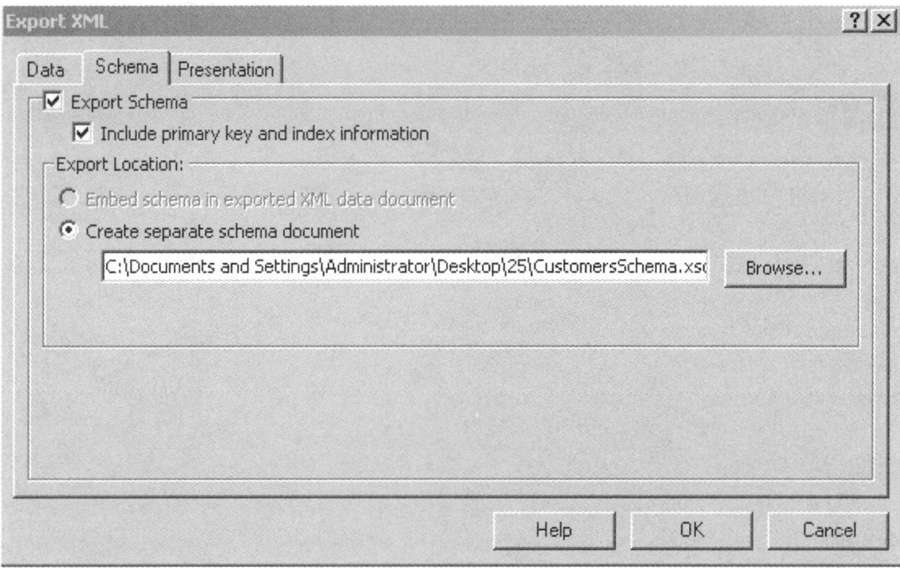

Figure 19-8. Advanced schema dialog box

Again, quite a large file is produced, and it has been edited to save space. The following code fragment shows part of the schema file just created. As can we can see, on this occasion we have details on indexes as well as the actual data.

```
<?XML version="1.0" encoding="UTF-8"?>
<xsd:schema XMLns:xsd=
"http://www.w3.org/2000/10/XMLSchema"
XMLns:od="urn:schemas-microsoft-com:officedata">
<xsd:element name="dataroot">
<xsd:complexType>
<xsd:choice maxOccurs="unbounded">
<xsd:element ref="Customers"/>
</xsd:choice>
</xsd:complexType>
</xsd:element>
<xsd:element name="Customers">
<xsd:annotation>
<xsd:appinfo>
<od:index index-name="aaaaaCustomers_PK"
index-key="CustomerID " primary="yes"
unique="yes" clustered="no"/>
<od:index index-name="City" index-key="City "
primary="no" unique="no" clustered="no"/>
```

```
<od:index index-name="CompanyName"
index-key="CompanyName " primary="no"
unique="no" clustered="no"/>
<od:index index-name="PostalCode"
index-key="PostalCode " primary="no"
unique="no" clustered="no"/>
<od:index index-name="Region"
index-key="Region " primary="no" unique="no"
clustered="no"/>
</xsd:appinfo>
</xsd:annotation>
<xsd:complexType>
<xsd:sequence>
<xsd:element name="CustomerID"
od:jetType="text" od:sqlSType="nvarchar"
od:nonNullable="yes">
<xsd:simpleType>
```

> **TIP** *Out of interest, I imported the CustomersSchema.xsd using the Northwind ADP. Once it's completed, I have an exact copy of the company table in SQL Server 2000, right down to the indexes. This is a very simple means of passing a table definition around.*

In this way, not only can we send an XML data file to another organization, but we can include the table or database schema as well. This will assist in "reassembling" the file in another system. For instance, we know that there are several indexes. The line

```
<od:index index-name="CompanyName" index-key="CompanyName " primary="no"
unique="no" clustered="no"/>
```

defines the index, the field used, whether it's a primary key, and the index type (in this case, a nonclustered index on the CompanyName field).

We can also use ADO to generate an XML file. The generated files differ slightly from those created using the built-in export methods. For example, the following ADO will export a table to a local XML data file.

```
Sub CreateXML()
    Dim cnn As ADODB.Connection
    Dim rst As ADODB.Recordset
    Set cnn = New ADODB.Connection
```

```
    With cnn
        .Provider = "Microsoft.Jet.OLEDB.4.0"
        .ConnectionString = "Data Source=C:\Book\ContactManagement.mdb"
        .Open
    End With
    Set rst = New ADODB.Recordset
    With rst
        Set .ActiveConnection = cnn
        .Source = "SELECT FirstName, LastName, Address FROM Contacts"
        .CursorLocation = adUseServer
        .CursorType = adOpenForwardOnly
        .LockType = adLockReadOnly
        .Open
        .Save "C:\Book\Contacts.XML", adPersistXML
        .Close
    End With
    cnn.Close
    Set rst = Nothing
    Set cnn = Nothing
End Sub
```

Copy this code into a new module in either an existing Access Database or a new blank database and execute in the intermediate window. (Type "CreateXML" and click on Enter.)

> **NOTE** *The code uses the Contact Management database created by the Create Database wizard. The database path and the file save path may be different, so check where the database is and amend the appropriate lines.*

Figure 19-9 shows the resulting XML file in Internet Explorer.

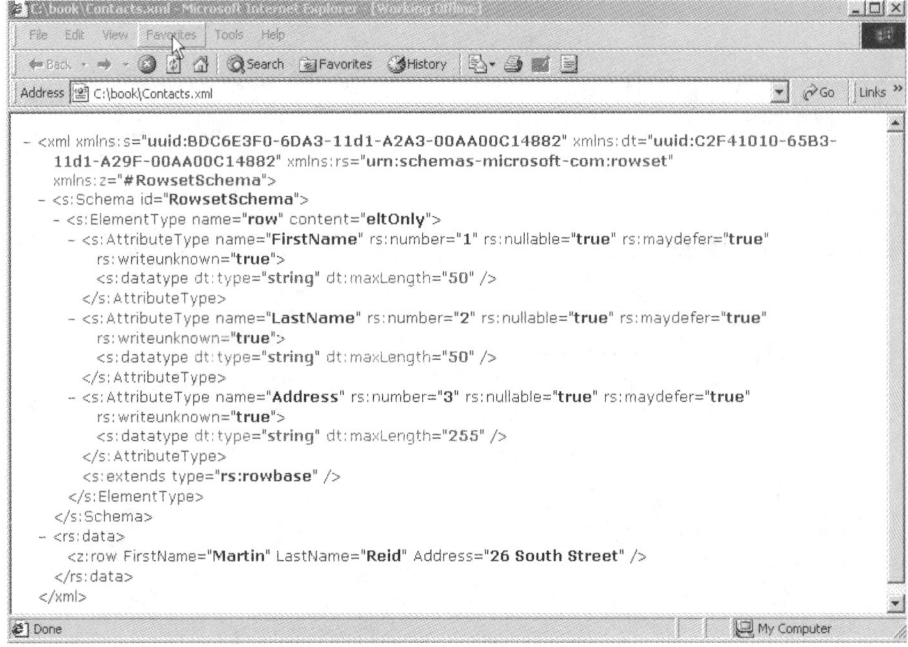


```
- <xml xmlns:s="uuid:BDC6E3F0-6DA3-11d1-A2A3-00AA00C14882" xmlns:dt="uuid:C2F41010-65B3-
  11d1-A29F-00AA00C14882" xmlns:rs="urn:schemas-microsoft-com:rowset"
  xmlns:z="#RowsetSchema">
 - <s:Schema id="RowsetSchema">
  - <s:ElementType name="row" content="eltOnly">
   - <s:AttributeType name="FirstName" rs:number="1" rs:nullable="true" rs:maydefer="true"
      rs:writeunknown="true">
      <s:datatype dt:type="string" dt:maxLength="50" />
    </s:AttributeType>
   - <s:AttributeType name="LastName" rs:number="2" rs:nullable="true" rs:maydefer="true"
      rs:writeunknown="true">
      <s:datatype dt:type="string" dt:maxLength="50" />
    </s:AttributeType>
   - <s:AttributeType name="Address" rs:number="3" rs:nullable="true" rs:maydefer="true"
      rs:writeunknown="true">
      <s:datatype dt:type="string" dt:maxLength="255" />
    </s:AttributeType>
    <s:extends type="rs:rowbase" />
   </s:ElementType>
  </s:Schema>
 - <rs:data>
   <z:row FirstName="Martin" LastName="Reid" Address="26 South Street" />
  </rs:data>
 </xml>
```

Figure 19-9. XML created using ADO

Compare the XML produced using ADO and that created using Access' file export methods. Two distinct types of XML are created, and you may not notice the differences until you try to import the ADO XML into a database. Two major differences are that ADO uses a different XML namespace than does Access-generated XML, and that ADO also includes the schema of the table as part of the XML file. Access cannot use the namespace created by ADO. Importing the preceding XML file results in the error shown in Figure 19-10.

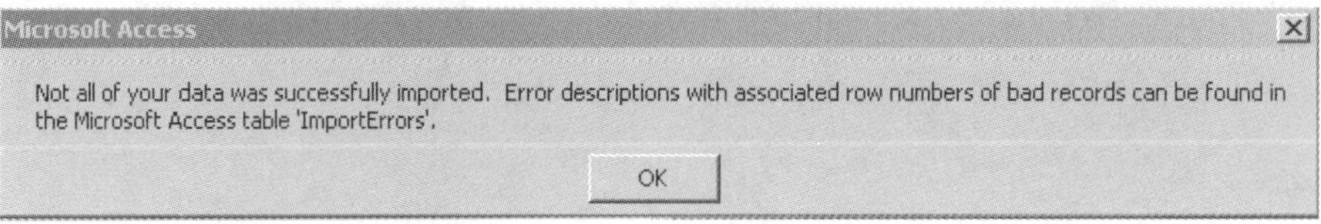

Figure 19-10. ADO XML import error

You may also notice that, instead of having a single contact table, you will have four tables, including the Import Errors table. Figure 19-11 shows the Database window following a failed import of ADO-generated XML.

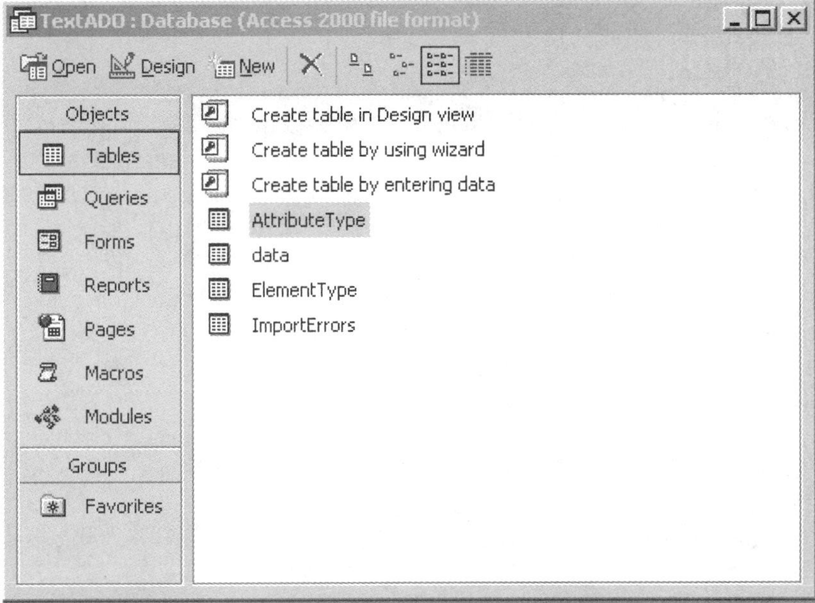

Figure 19-11. Tables created following ADO XML import

If we had simply exported the Contacts table as XML using Access 2002 and reimported it, we would have ended up with a duplicate of the existing contact table. So what went wrong?

Access 2002 exports a special type of XML, called *element-centric* XML. ADO creates *attribute-centric* XML. In attribute-centric XML, all data is represented in the XML elements, whereas element-centric XML returns data and subdata as elements and subelements.

For example, ADO returns the following row for the data:

```
<z:row FirstName='Martin' Lastname ='Reid' Address='26 South Street'/>
```

A straight export from Access 2002 returns the following format:

```
<FirstName>Martin</Firstname>
<LastName>Reid</>
```

As you can see, the files have two different structures. Access 2002 cannot handle the import of ADO XML without first transforming it using XSLT into the proper structure.

This has been a very cursory glimpse at XML. XML is a complex language, and Microsoft (being Microsoft) has added to the specification with a new version of XML, ReportML.

ReportML

ReportML is a language created by Microsoft that is specific to Access databases. It is used to describe forms, reports, or data access pages in XML. ReportML is used to save the object definition, and it can then be used to create a data access page. Just like XML, ReportML uses a set of tags to describe the data. With ReportML, Microsoft has included two stylesheets: ReportML2DAP and ReportML2.html (located in C:\Programfiles\Microsoft Office\Office 10\AccessWeb). Reports2DAP is used to transform Report2ML to data access pages, and ReportML2.html is used to actually create the HTML Web page.

Using the Contact Management database again, we will export a report to XML:

1. Select Alphabetical Contact Listing Report.
2. Right-click and select Export from the menu.
3. Select XML as the file type. Access 2002 will present a default filename in the File Name text box. You can overwrite this name if you wish. The Export XML dialog box will open.
4. Click on OK to accept the default export of data only.

Figure 19-12 shows the resulting report in Internet Explorer. As you can see, this is an exact copy of the Access report. Bear in mind that this is a fairly simple report layout.

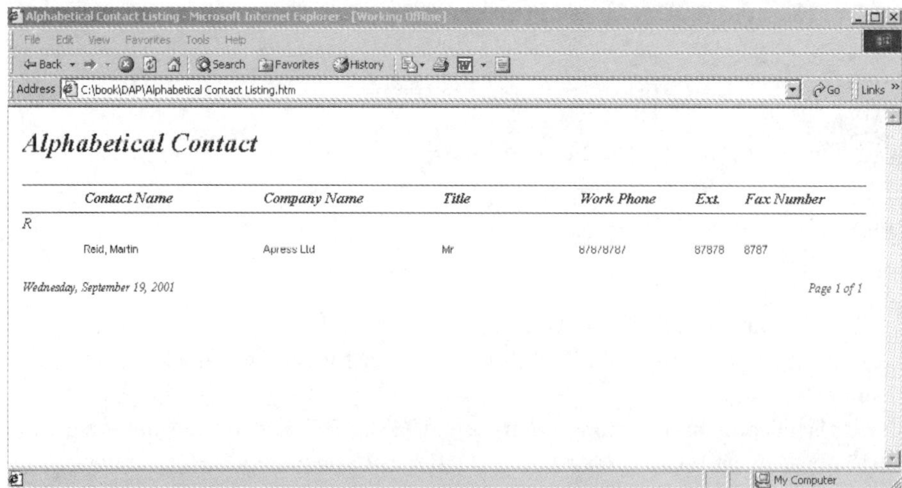

Figure 19-12. Access report to XML

> **NOTE** *Because this file contains the connection string to the database, it is a simple procedure to transfer the folder onto a Web server. Note that subreports will not export at all (which again reflects the version 1.0 status of this technology).*

Data Access Pages

This is another Microsoft technology, but it's fairly useless if you (like me) work somewhere with every browser under the sun. However, in an environment in which you can control the browser in use (such as making sure that all users are running IE5 and above), you may find a use for this technology in the intranet scene.

> **NOTE** *I mainly use Macromedia Ultradev 4 for all Web work, including working with databases. It is my opinion that, as a development environment, Ultradev is superior to Microsoft FrontPage. The HTML editor alone is superb. I find this tool to be one of the best available and would recommend its use particularly for RAD. The editor is particularly useful for the occasions when generated code is not sufficient. In truth, all the sites I have worked on use ASP rather than DAPs for all interaction with the database back end. This is mainly due to the requirement for IE5 with DAPs.*

A DAP is simply an Access form that has been reformatted and made available via a Web browser. It is a combination of DHTML, ActiveX, and at times XML. DAPs in Access 2000 were considered version 1.0 technology. This is no longer true in Access 2002 because they have been much improved.

The easiest way to come to grips with DAPs is to get straight to building one. We will use the Northwind.mdb file for this example. Life is easier all around if you develop your DAP directly on a Web server. I am using IIS5 for these examples, but Personal Web Server will suffice. Remember to store the database outside the Web root files. If you don't, someone will download it.

> **NOTE** *When working with Access 2000 DAP files in 2002, you cannot open the DAP in Design view in Access 2000 unless you have the Microsoft Office XP Web components installed. Access will display a warning message to this effect if you're working with the Access 2000 file format in Access 2002.*

For this example, we are going to create a simple page that will show data from the Northwind shippers page. Rather than use the Page wizard, we will create the entire page by hand. In this way, you will get a good feel for how the pages are constructed and for the tools available in Access 2002.

1. Click on the Pages section in the Database window.

2. Double-click on Create Data Access Page in Design view to open the Page Design screen. This is substantially different from the Forms Design screen. Figure 19-13 shows the new design screens.

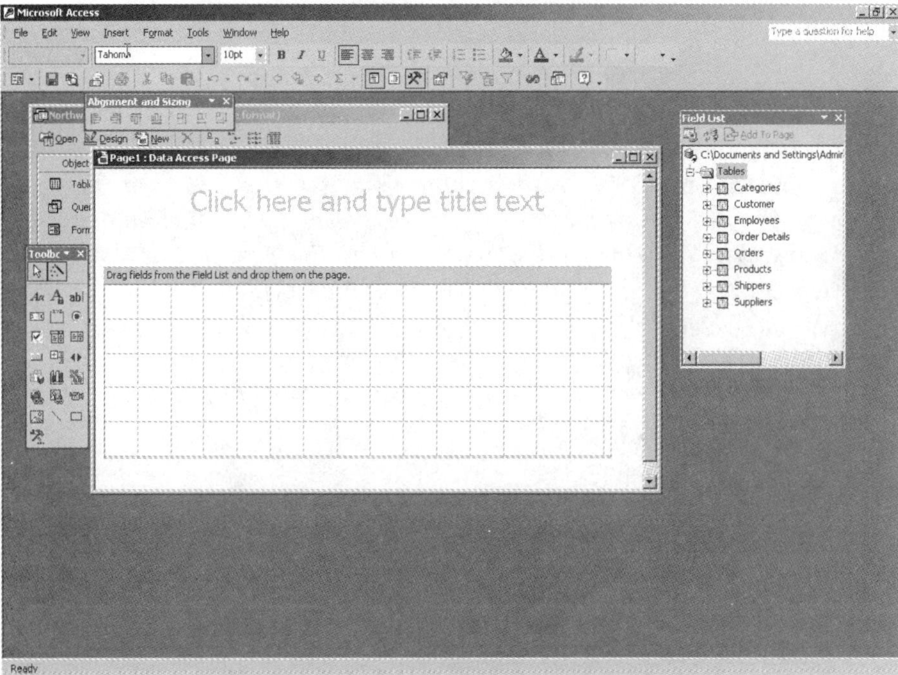

Figure 19-13. Data access page—Form Design environment

Let's look at the components:

- *Toolbox*: This is similar to the toolbox used with standard form design. In this case, though, we can use some additional controls. Figure 19-14 shows a view of the available buttons. The objects shown on the toolbox can be removed, and additional tools can be added. Objects are added to the form by clicking an object and drawing it out on the form background. To view this menu option, select the Toolbar Options arrow (next to the Toolbox close symbol), select Add or Remove buttons, and then select Toolbox. This will open the additional menu shown in Figure 19-14.

Figure 19-14. DAP toolbox objects

- *Field list*: I really like this. The field list provides you with a graphical list of all tables in the database. Not only that, but expanding the tree for a table also shows you the related tables. We can further expand a table to look at the fields. To place a field onto the form design background, simply drag and drop it. (Click on a field and drag it to the form design background.) Figure 19-15 shows the field list, expanded for the Suppliers table. Note the Related Tables folder. When expanded, this folder shows the tables related to the Shippers table. We then have access to the fields for the related tables as well. This would be a wonderful addition to the standard Access Forms Designer. Maybe in the next version!

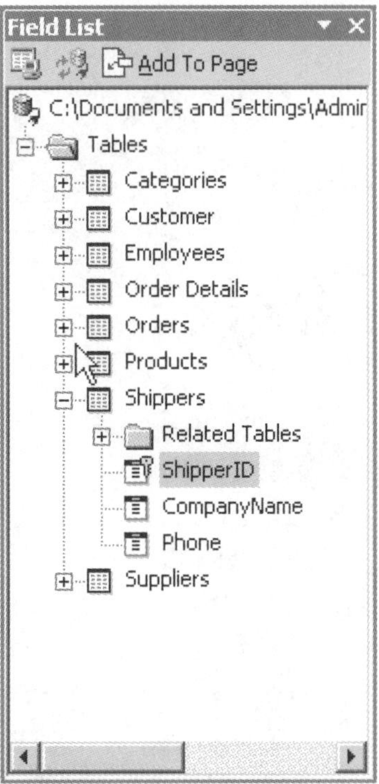

Figure 19-15. DAP Field List window

> **NOTE** *The Field List window also gives you access to the connection properties for the page. Click on the Data Link Field icon below the words* Field List *in the window title. This opens the connection properties for the DAP. If you find the Design window to be too cluttered, you can close the field list and toolbox screens until you require them. To reopen them, simply select View Field List or View Toolbox from the Main menu.*

- *Alignment and sizing*: This is another toolbox, but it provides you with a shortcut to the various alignment tools used within DAPs.

3. Close the Field List and Toolbox windows.

4. Add the text "Suppliers Demo DAP" to the form. (Click on the placeholder text "Click here and type Title text" and overtype it.) As with a standard Access form, we need to assign the record source for the form.

5. Click the mouse anywhere in the section (grid) of the form. Right-click and select Section Properties from the shortcut menu to open the section properties. This is very similar to our usual form property sheet. Figure 19-16 shows the section property sheet.

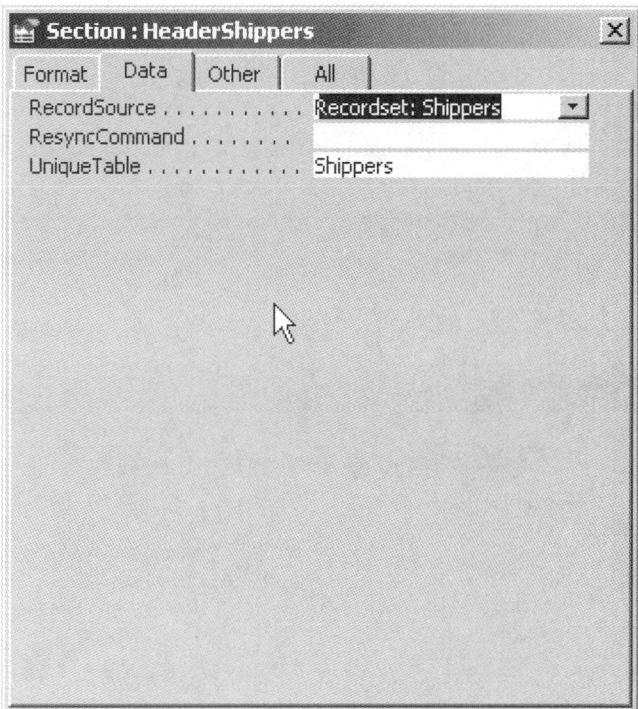

Figure 19-16. DAP section property sheet showing the data properties

> **NOTE** *Clicking on any object while the property sheet is open will reveal the properties for that particular object.*

6. Click on the Data tab, and, from the record source drop-down list, select Shippers Table. Note that a navigation bar is automatically added to the form.

7. Click View Field List. We will add the Shippers fields to the form.

8. In the Field List window, expand the Shippers tree. Click on the plus sign beside the Shippers table icon.

9. Drag and drop the CompanyName, Phone, and the ShipperID fields onto the Section background. Double-clicking a field name also places it into the form.

> **NOTE** *Once the objects are placed onto the form (descriptive label and a text box), double-clicking the object opens its property sheet. Form fields can be positioned, resized, and formatted in the same way as standard Access form objects. Right-click on any object to open a shortcut menu. If preferred, you can double-click the object to work with the property sheet.*

Figure 19-17 shows our DAP at this point.

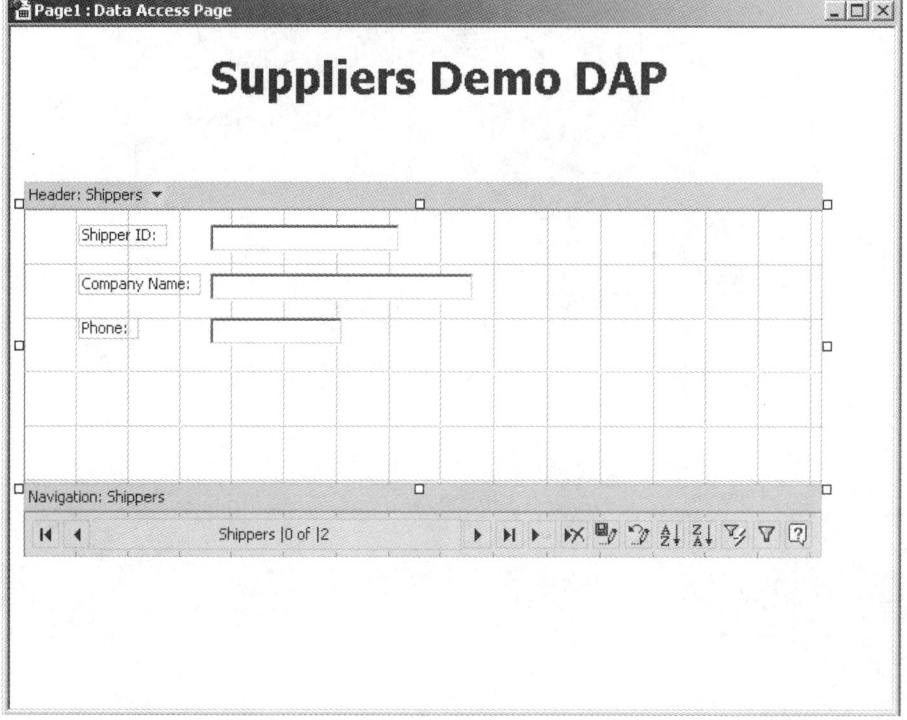

Figure 19-17. DAP containing Shipper fields

At the moment, this is all that is required to create the page.

10. On the Main menu, click on File|Save.

11. Select a folder to save the DAP into.

12. Name the page "ShippersDAP".

13. Click on Save.

NOTE *The page is not saved with your database. Instead, a shortcut to the page is maintained in the Database window. You may also be prompted to use the folder you select as the default for DAP pages. In this case, select Yes to close the message dialog box. An additional warning may be given about the connection string. For the moment, though, simply click on OK. We will look at this shortly.*

14. Close the DAP.

15. Open the page inside Access 2002. Figure 19-18 shows the Shippers page opened in Access. Click on the Pages section and then double-click the Shippers page to open it.

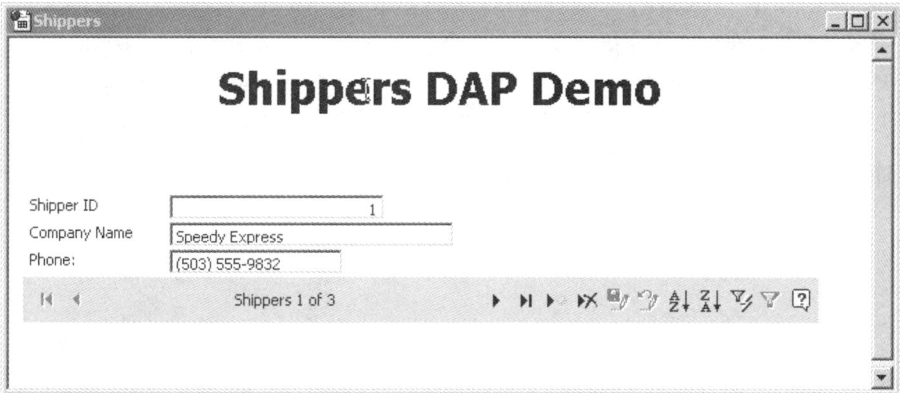

Figure 19-18. Shippers DAP in Access 2002

As can be seen, the page contains a text box for each of the database fields and a navigation bar. Let's have a look at the navigation bar. Figure 19-19 shows the full bar.

Figure 19-19. DAP navigation bar

We can use the navigation bar to:

- scroll the records
- add new records
- delete records
- save changes to the records
- undo edits
- filter by selection
- view help

In the form's Design view, we can remove any or all of the navigation bar buttons. Figure 19-20 shows the navigation bar and the shortcut menu used to add or remove buttons. Right-click on the navigation bar and click on Navigation Buttons to open the button submenu. Simply uncheck any of the button checkboxes to remove the button from the navigation bar.

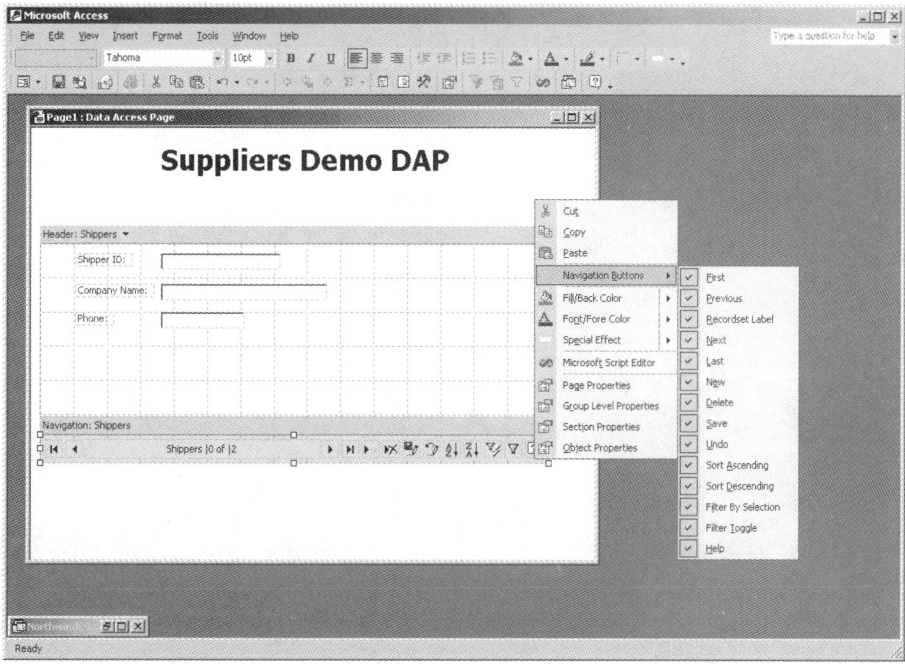

Figure 19-20. Navigation bar

Let's try a Master Detail form. For this example, we will use the Customer and Order tables. This is where things really start to change with DAPs as opposed to standard Access forms. We are going to use the standard DAP page and include the Customer table. In addition, we are going to add a pivot to the page. The PivotTable will be used to show the orders placed by the selected customer. In effect, we are using the PivotTable control to duplicate a standard Access master Detail form. Another advantage to using a PivotTable is that it can connect to data stores other than Access or SQL Server.

> **NOTE** *The PivotTable portion of our page is an ActiveX Office Web component (which is installed with Office XP). To use the Web components in Access 2002, you must have Internet Explorer 5 or higher installed. Users who wish to view these pages must also have the Web components installed. Users can also download and use the components without having Office XP. (Users without Office XP installed on their computers can view the control but cannot interact with it.)*

Before going into the details of how to construct the form, look at Figure 19-21, which shows the form in Access 2002.

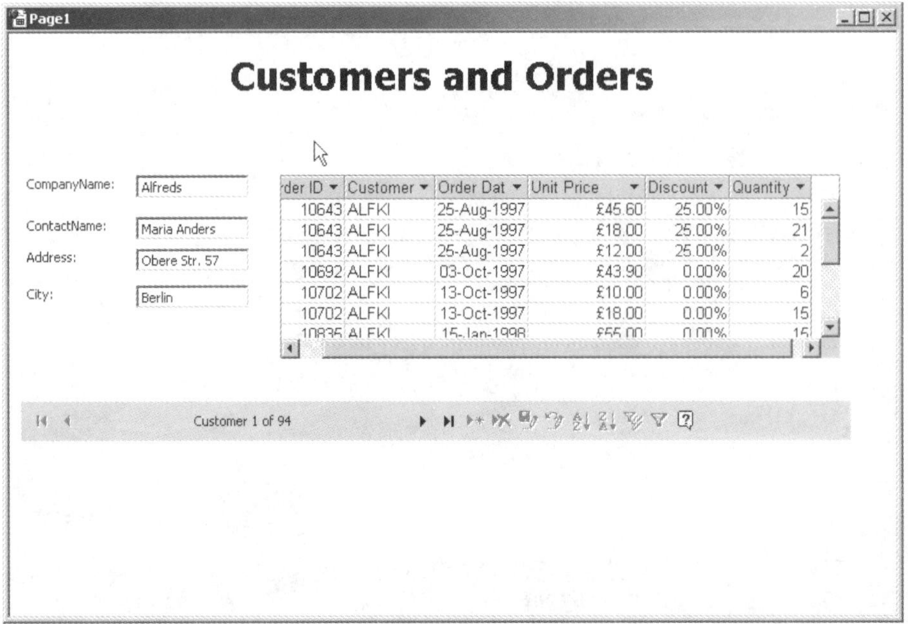

Figure 19-21. DAP with ActiveX PivotTable control

> **NOTE** *The technology behind this page is impressive, but the usefulness of the page is open to question and discussion (given the browser limitations and the required download of the Web components). Also, the design features differ depending on the version of Internet Explorer you have installed. For example, you cannot select multiple controls in Design view if you have Internet Explorer 5. Pages may also perform slower in Internet Explorer 5 than in version 6.*

Let's create the form:

1. Select the Pages section in the Database window.
2. Click on Create Data Access Page by Using Wizard.
3. Select the Customer table in the Table/Queries drop-down list.
4. From the available fields, select CustomerID, CompanyName, ContactName, ContactTitle, Address, and City.
5. Click on Next.

6. Click on Next in the Grouping page. (We do not want to add grouping this time.)

7. Click on Next without adding a sort order.

8. Enter a title for the page: "Customer Orders".

9. Click on the radio button next to "Modify the page's design".

10. Click on Finish to leave the DAP in Design view. We will need to resize the grid section of the form.

11. Click the section grid. Notice the handles (squares) that appear around the selected section.

12. Select a handle (square) and drag to resize the section. Now we'll add the PivotTable.

13. Select View Field List from the Main menu (if it is not already showing).

14. Ensure that Wizard mode is enabled (by clicking on the Control Wizards item in the control list if it is not already highlighted).

15. In the Field list, click on the plus sign beside the Orders table to expand the tree.

16. Select the OrderID field and drag it onto the grid section. The Layout wizard will open. Figure 19-22 shows the first stage in the wizard.

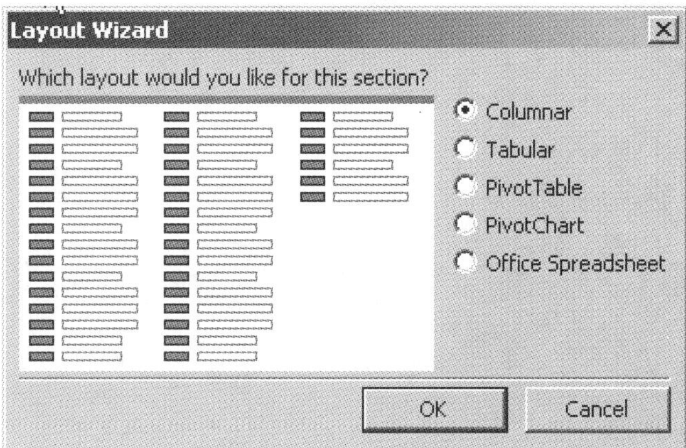

Figure 19-22. Layout wizard—Screen 1

Two of the options are similar to those normally used in forms: Columnar and Tabular. The next three are new, however: PivotTable, PivotChart, and Office Spreadsheet. In this case, choose PivotTable.

17. Click on the radio button beside PivotTable.

18. Click on OK. Figure 19-23 shows the final screen with the PivotTable selected.

Figure 19-23. The Layout wizard—Screen 2

Access may pick up the table relationship for you. If not, the screen shown in Figure 19-24 will be displayed. This is used to build the relationships between the tables chosen (in this case, Orders and Customers). Figure 19-24 shows the Relationship wizard with our relationships created. Use the drop-down lists to select the fields in the relationships: Orders.CustomerID and Customer.CustomerID.

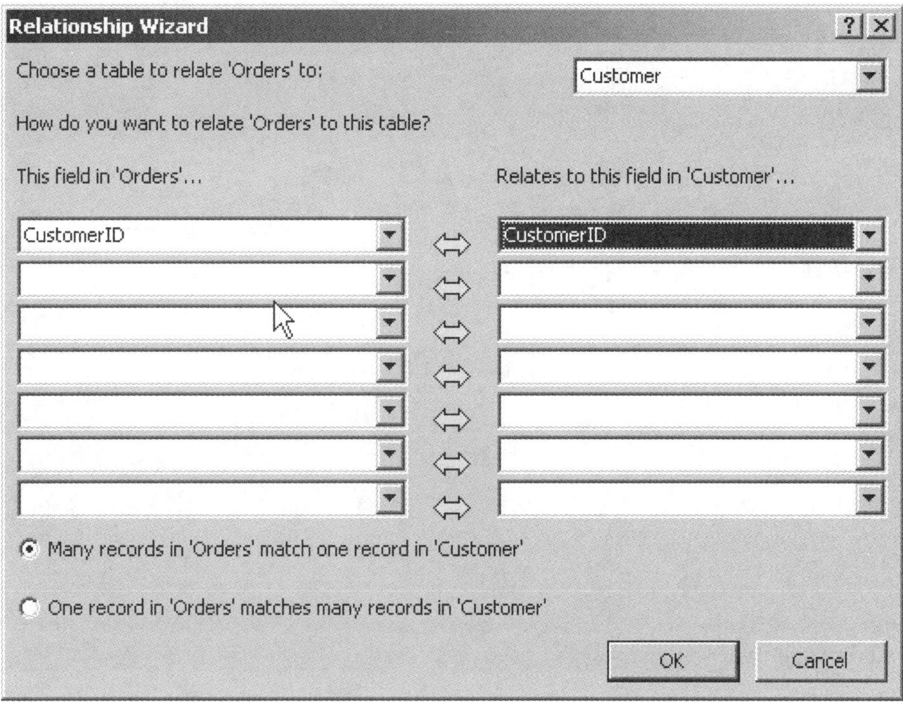

Figure 19-24. DAP Relationship wizard

19. Set the relationships and click on OK. Figure 19-25 shows our DAP with the PivotTable control added.

20. Expand the Order Details tree. (Click on the plus symbol beside the tablename.)

21. Drag and drop the UnitPrice, Quantity, and Discount fields onto the PivotTable control.

22. Close and save the page as CustomerOrders.

And that's it. You have created your first complex form. It contains a link to the database and a fairly sophisticated ActiveX control. I am sure you will agree that we did this with very little mental effort on our part.

So, what does it all look like on the Web? Figure 19-25 shows our customer and order page displayed in Internet Explorer. I have also added the product name from the Product table and some data from the Order Details table to the PivotTable. Expand the Order Details and Products tables and drag and drop the required fields onto the PivotTable. Try it and see how it looks.

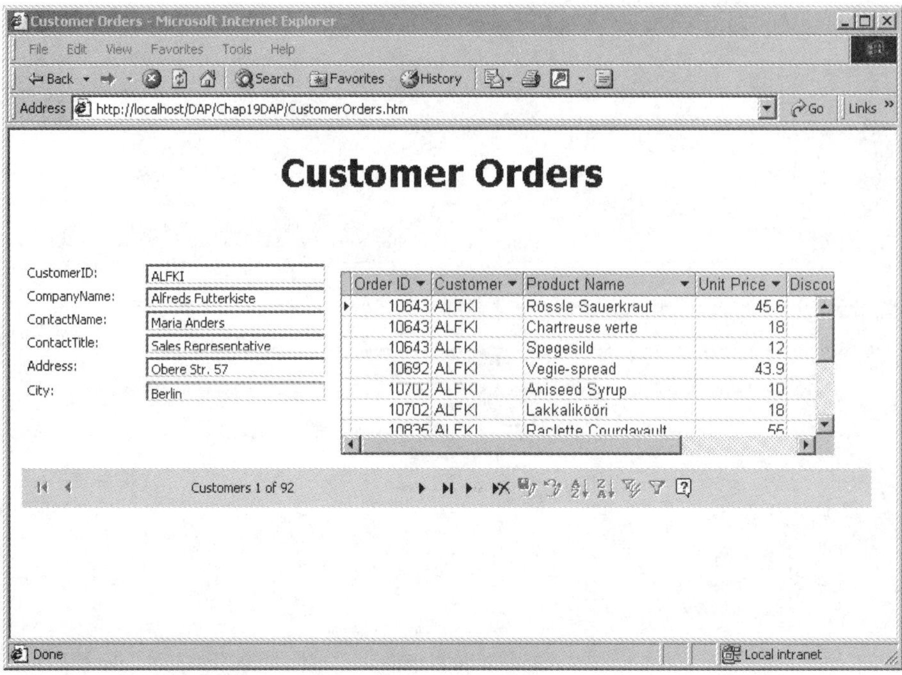

Figure 19-25. Customers and orders on the Web

Some Odds and Ends

Remember, if the Web components are installed you have an interactive PivotTable. For example, click on the arrow beside the OrderID column heading in the PivotTable. Figure 19-26 shows the listing that opens. We can deselect orders displayed by unchecking any of the checkboxes beside the OrderID.

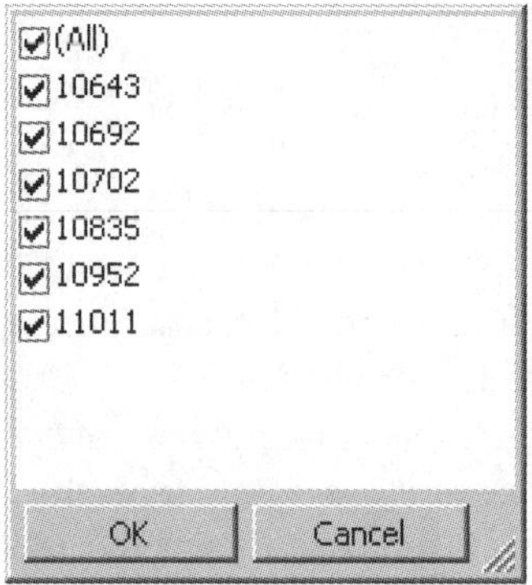

Figure 19-26. PivotTable order numbers

We can use the same process with all of the fields displayed in the PivotTable. We can add fields to the PivotTable, provided we selected them when we were designing the form. Right-click on the PivotTable and select Field List from the shortcut menu. Figure 19-27 shows the Field List dialog box.

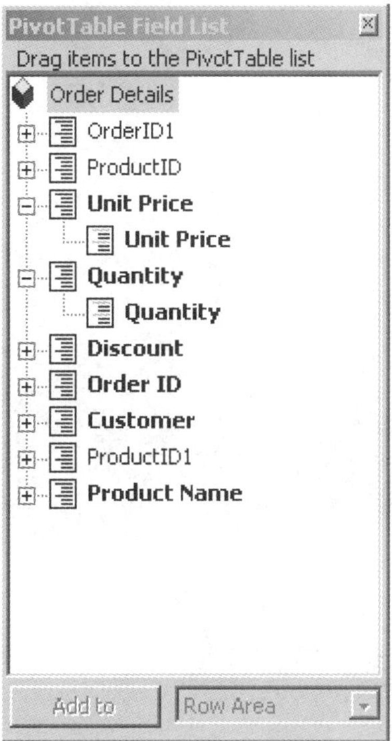

Figure 19-27. The PivotTable Field List dialog box in Internet Explorer

Simply select a field and drag it onto the PivotTable. You can also remove a field from the table by right-clicking on the control and choosing Remove Field from the shortcut menu. Out of interest, try to change one of the Unit Price fields. It's updateable, just as the Quantity and Discount fields are. Note that the OrderID and product name (if you added it) are not updated.

We can also get the PivotTable to calculate a total of the Unit Price column in the browser:

1. Select the Unit Price column by clicking on the column heading. The selected column will then appear with a light blue background.

2. Right-click and select Autocalc from the menu. Figure 19-28 shows the menu in Internet Explorer.

3. Select Sum to add a total of the Unit Price column to the PivotTable.

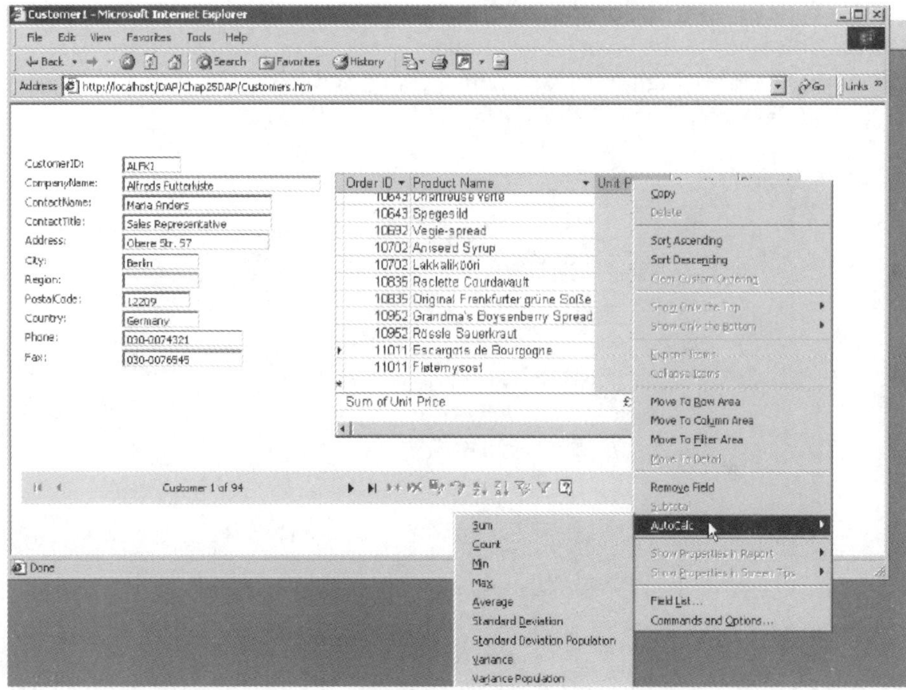

Figure 19-28. Summing the Unit Price column

Although the PivotTable permits users to update the data, this isn't a great idea. A PivotTable can present data in many different ways, and you as the developer have very little control over how the user will interact with it. It is highly recommended that you disable all updating of the records. Figure 19-29 shows the Command and Options screen with the Properties tab open. The Protection tab is available only in Design view of the page. Using this dialog box, we can "shut down" many of the features by which users interact with the PivotTable.

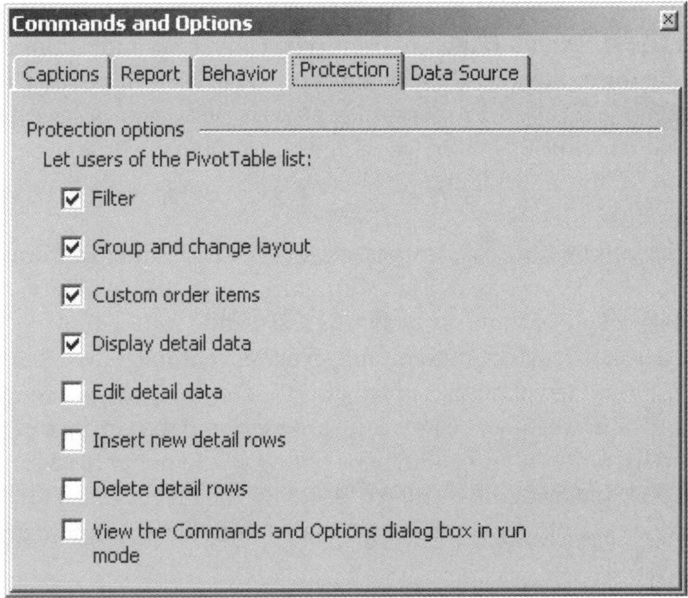

Figure 19-29. Command and Options—Securing the PivotTable

To secure the PivotTable:

1. In Page design, right-click on the PivotTable.
2. Select Command and Options from the shortcut menu.
3. Click on the Protection tab, and uncheck the following options:
    - Edit detail data
    - Insert new detail rows
    - Delete new detail rows
    - View the Command and Options dialog box in Run mode
4. Close and save the changes to the page.

Access 2002 also allows you to save directly to a DAP of tables, queries, and forms. Simply select the object and use File|Save As.

Results with tables and forms are not impressive other than for simple objects. For example, saving the Employee form as a DAP means that we lose the photograph, and the memo field (Notes) is unreadable because it is created as a standard HTML text box rather than a text box with rows and columns. This would permit the entire record to be seen. Forms are even worse, and, again, other than simple forms, the process may prove to be a waste of time. However, some samples are provided with Access 2002 (including the Employees form), which show that the equivalent functionality is achievable with some programming knowledge.

Overall, although DAPs are impressive in some cases (mainly from a technology point of view), I see no real place for them as yet in the land of the spider. The source code of a DAP is daunting to say the least, and I would think that even those of you with extensive programming experience would have a hard time understanding and recoding the source directly. They may have a role to play in an environment in which you control the browsers and the versions of Office that the staff and users are running. But, personally, I would prefer to use standard HTML and ASP, and, with the coming of ASP.NET, the process used for getting similar (and in my opinion better) functionality from these technologies far outweighs the use of DAPs with Access 2002.

Active Server Pages and Access 2002

ASP has been around for a long time and is the favored method of many Access developers for database access via the Web. We can publish our Access data to the Web in either of two main ways: as static files or interactive files.

> **NOTE** *For database connection, we can use system DSNs (data source names) and ODBC, or we can use OLEDB, which is the preferred method for working with database connections via the Web. For our first few examples, we will use ODBC and DSNs, and then we'll move on to using OLEDB to connect to the database.*

Static Data

Publishing static data (a table, report, or query) is very straightforward. The major problem is that it is static. For example, if we were to save a table as HTML and add records to the table, our HTML page does not get automatically updated. You would have to rerun the export or File Save As procedure to re-create the file. We can also use ADO to output data as static HTML. For example, the following script will output the Employee table to HTML. Table 19-3 shows the arguments available with the OutputTo method.

> **NOTE** *OutputTo is not restricted to use with HTML; it can output your data to different formats including text. Docmd is used in VBA to carry out commands that are normally created by using macros.*

Table 19-3. Access OutputTo Arguments

ARGUMENT	COMMENT
Object Type	The object type containing the data we want to export (such as table, query, or report).
Object Name	Name of the object.
Format	HTML, Text, ASP, Excel, RTF, or XML.
File	The file to contain the output. Make sure you include the full path.
Auto Start	If yes, the application associated with the output format will start.
Template File	For Web pages, we can specify a template file.

For example, to output the Employee table as an HTML file, we could create the following procedure:

```
Sub OutEmployeeAsHTML
DoCmd.OutputTo actable, "Customer", "HTML", "C:\employee.html"
, True, "", 0
End Sub
```

Figure 19-30 shows the section of the output of this procedure in Internet Explorer.

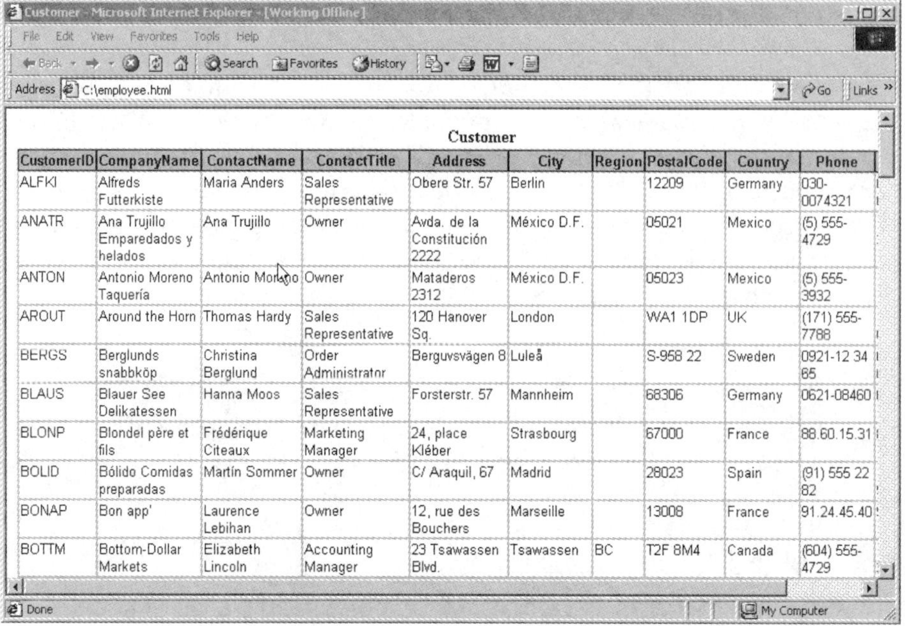

Customer

CustomerID	CompanyName	ContactName	ContactTitle	Address	City	Region	PostalCode	Country	Phone
ALFKI	Alfreds Futterkiste	Maria Anders	Sales Representative	Obere Str. 57	Berlin		12209	Germany	030-0074321
ANATR	Ana Trujillo Emparedados y helados	Ana Trujillo	Owner	Avda. de la Constitución 2222	México D.F.		05021	Mexico	(5) 555-4729
ANTON	Antonio Moreno Taquería	Antonio Moreno	Owner	Mataderos 2312	México D.F.		05023	Mexico	(5) 555-3932
AROUT	Around the Horn	Thomas Hardy	Sales Representative	120 Hanover Sq.	London		WA1 1DP	UK	(171) 555-7788
BERGS	Berglunds snabbköp	Christina Berglund	Order Administrator	Berguvsvägen 8	Luleå		S-958 22	Sweden	0921-12 34 65
BLAUS	Blauer See Delikatessen	Hanna Moos	Sales Representative	Forsterstr. 57	Mannheim		68306	Germany	0621-08460
BLONP	Blondel père et fils	Frédérique Citeaux	Marketing Manager	24, place Kléber	Strasbourg		67000	France	88.60.15.31
BOLID	Bólido Comidas preparadas	Martín Sommer	Owner	C/ Araquil, 67	Madrid		28023	Spain	(91) 555 22 82
BONAP	Bon app'	Laurence Lebihan	Owner	12, rue des Bouchers	Marseille		13008	France	91.24.45.40
BOTTM	Bottom-Dollar Markets	Elizabeth Lincoln	Accounting Manager	23 Tsawassen Blvd.	Tsawassen	BC	T2F 8M4	Canada	(604) 555-4729

Figure 19-30. Outputting the Employee table as HTML

NOTE *Of course, you could simply select the Employee table in the Database window and select File|Export from the Main menu and select HTML Documents from the Save As dialog box.*

Static pages have their uses, though. For instance, there is no point in creating a full ASP application if your data changes once a year.

NOTE *For all of these examples, I am using IIS5 and Internet Explorer 6. In addition, I am saving all files directly to a local folder on the Web server. In the real world, it is likely that you will develop pages locally and then move the completed files onto the production server.*

However, most developers are faced with bigger projects that require a degree of interactivity. For our first example, we will use an ODBC DSN connection. I have created a system DSN on the Web server called "nwind". This DSN points to a copy of the Northwind database on the Web server. To create your first ASP file:

1. Select the Employees table in the Database window.

2. Select File|Export from the Main menu.

3. In the Export Table dialog box, navigate to a folder on the Web server.

4. Select Microsoft Active Server Pages using the Save As list.

5. Enter the filename "EmployeeTable." Figure 19-31 shows the dialog box at this point.

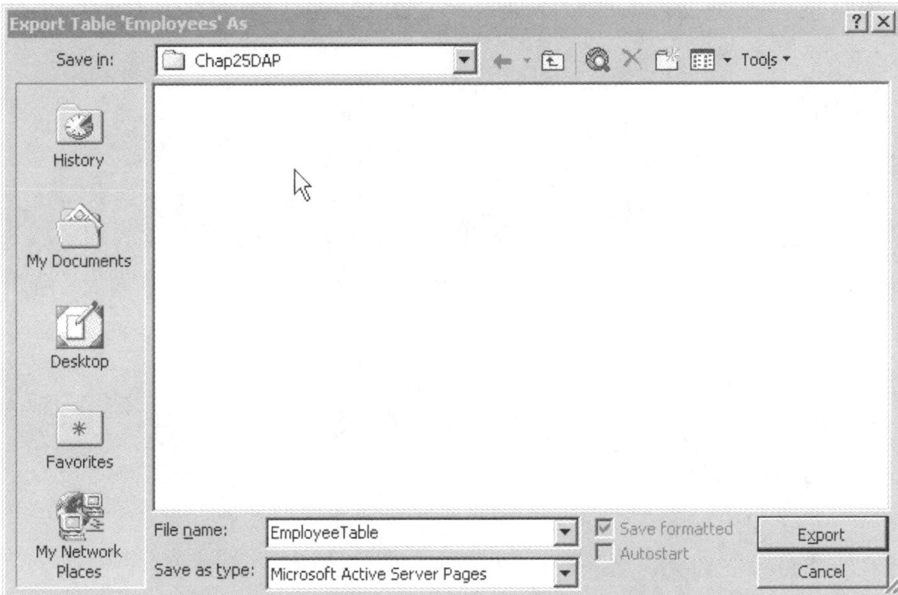

Figure 19-31. The first step when creating the ASP file

6. Click on Export.

7. Now, to complete the output options, all that is required is that you enter the DSN name "nwind" and click on OK.

That's it. You've built your first ASP page.

Now open Internet Explorer and navigate to your newly created page. However, this time you must enter the full URL into the browser. In my case, the URL is `http://localhost/DAP/Chap25DAP/EmployeeTable.asp`. Figure 19-32 shows the table in the browser. It's not very impressive, is it?

> **NOTE** *If you look at the source (choose View|Source in Internet Explorer), you may notice that the Web server returns only HTML to the browser. All code is executed on the server.*

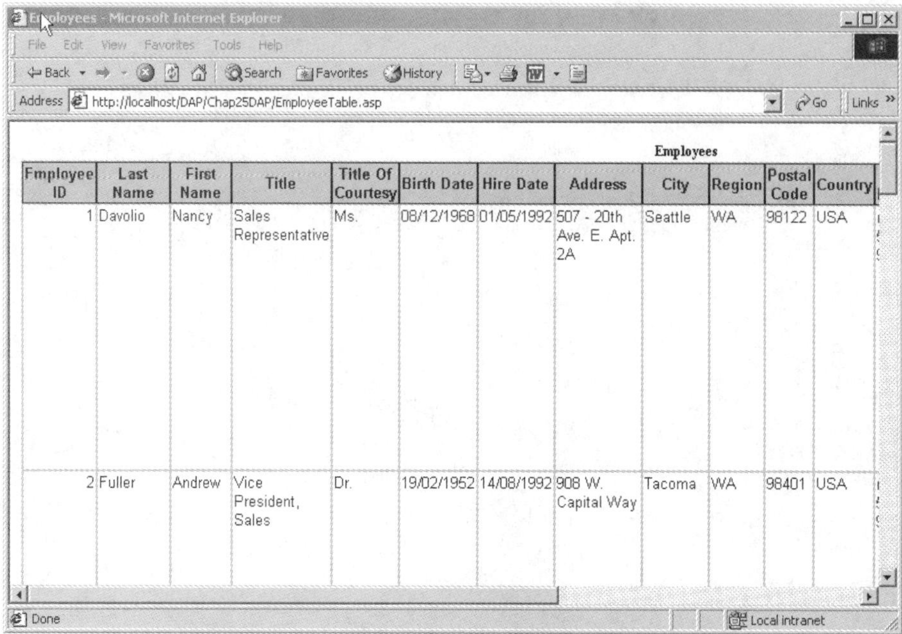

Figure 19-32. EmployeeTable.asp in Internet Explorer

Let's look at another example. This time I have created a Parameter query that requests the user to enter an employee name. I am going to export this as an ASP file to a Web server folder. The syntax for the parameter is:

```
Like [Enter Employee Name]&"*"
```

I am using the Access wildcard "*" to return all records that meet the criteria. In this way, the user doesn't need to know the full employee name when requesting the record. Follow the previous steps to export the file as ASP. On this occasion, select the query in the Database window rather than a table.

The SQL for the query is:

```
SELECT [FirstName]&" "&[LastName] AS Name
Employees.Address,Employees.City,Employees.region
FROM Employees
WHERE
Employees.LastName like [Enter Employee Last Name]&"*";
```

However, because this is a Parameter query, you will be prompted to enter the employee's last name during the export. Simply click on OK in response to the prompt to continue to export the files as ASP.

On this occasion, Access will create two files, the first of which is a simple HTML form. (A form is a common method used to pass parameters to ASP scripts.) The HTML for qryEmployeeASP.html is:

```
<HTML>
<HEAD>
<TITLE>qryEmployeeASP</TITLE>
<BODY>
<FORM METHOD  ="GET" ACTION]"qryEMPLOYEEASP>ASP">
[Enter Employee Name] <INPUT TYPE ="TEXT" NAME = "[Enter Employee Last
Name]"><P>
<INPUT TYPE = "Submit"VALUE = "Run Query">
</FORM>
</BODY>
</HTML>
```

This HTML file "collects" the value entered into the form field "[Enter Employee Name]" and passes it to the ASP script on the server. The ASP script that processes this value is:

```
<HTML>
<HEAD>
<META HTTP-EQUIV="Content-Type" CONTENT="text/html;charset=windows-1252">
<TITLE>qryEmployeeASP</TITLE>
</HEAD>
<BODY>
<%
If IsObject(Session("nwind_conn")) Then
    Set conn = Session("nwind_conn")
Else
    Set conn = Server.CreateObject("ADODB.Connection")
    conn.open "nwind","",""
    Set Session("??nwind_conn") = conn
End If
%>
<%
If IsObject(Session("qryEmployeeASP_rs")) Then
    Set rs = Session("qryEmployeeASP_rs")
Else
sql = "SELECT [FirstName] & "" "" & [LastName]
```

```
AS Name, Employees.Address, Employees.City,
Employees.Region  FROM Employees
WHERE (((Employees.LastName) Like "
& Request.QueryString("[Enter Employee Last Name]")
 & " & ""*""))   "
Set rs = Server.CreateObject("ADODB.Recordset")
rs.Open sql, conn, 3, 3
End If
%>
<TABLE BORDER=1 BGCOLOR=#ffffff CELLSPACING=0>
<FONT FACE="Arial" COLOR=#000000><CAPTION>
<B>qryEmployeeASP</B></CAPTION></FONT>

<THEAD>
<TR>
<TH BGCOLOR=#c0c0c0 BORDERCOLOR=#000000 >
<FONT style=FONT-SIZE:10pt FACE="Arial"
COLOR=#000000>Name</FONT></TH>
<TH BGCOLOR=#c0c0c0 BORDERCOLOR=#000000 >
<FONT style=FONT-SIZE:10pt
FACE="Arial" COLOR=#000000>Address</FONT></TH>
<TH BGCOLOR=#c0c0c0 BORDERCOLOR=#000000 >
<FONT style=FONT-SIZE:10pt
FACE="Arial" COLOR=#000000>City</FONT></TH>
<TH BGCOLOR=#c0c0c0 BORDERCOLOR=#000000 >
<FONT style=FONT-SIZE:10pt
FACE="Arial" COLOR=#000000>Region</FONT></TH>

</TR>
</THEAD>
<TBODY>
<%
On Error Resume Next
rs.MoveFirst
do while Not rs.eof
 %>
<TR VALIGN=TOP>
<TD BORDERCOLOR=#c0c0c0 >
<FONT style=FONT-SIZE:10pt FACE="Arial"
COLOR=#000000><%=Server.HTMLEncode(rs.Fields("Name").Value)%>
<BR></FONT></TD>
<TD BORDERCOLOR=#c0c0c0 >
<FONT style=FONT-SIZE:10pt FACE="Arial"
```

```
COLOR=#000000><%=Server.HTMLEncode(rs.Fields("Address").Value)%>
<BR></FONT></TD>
<TD BORDERCOLOR=#c0c0c0 >
<FONT style=FONT-SIZE:10pt FACE="Arial"
COLOR=#000000><%=Server.HTMLEncode(rs.Fields("City").Value)%>
<BR></FONT></TD>
<TD BORDERCOLOR=#c0c0c0 >
<FONT style=FONT-SIZE:10pt FACE="Arial"
COLOR=#000000><%=Server.HTMLEncode(rs.Fields("Region").Value)%>
<BR></FONT></TD>

</TR>
<%
rs.MoveNext
loop%>
</TBODY>
<TFOOT></TFOOT>
</TABLE>
</BODY>
</HTML>
```

The important part of the script (for the moment) is the SQL statement:

```
sql = "SELECT [FirstName] & "" "" & [LastName] AS Name,
Employees.Address, Employees.City, Employees.Region
FROM Employees  WHERE (((Employees.LastName) Like
" & Request.QueryString("[Enter Employee Last Name]") & " & ""*"")
```

Note the following section in the WHERE clause:

```
WHERE (((Employees.LastName) Like
 " & Request.QueryString("[Enter Employee Last Name]") & " & ""*"")
```

The value from the form is passed to the SQL statement and is used to restrict the records returned. Figure 19-33 shows the HTML file in Internet Explorer.

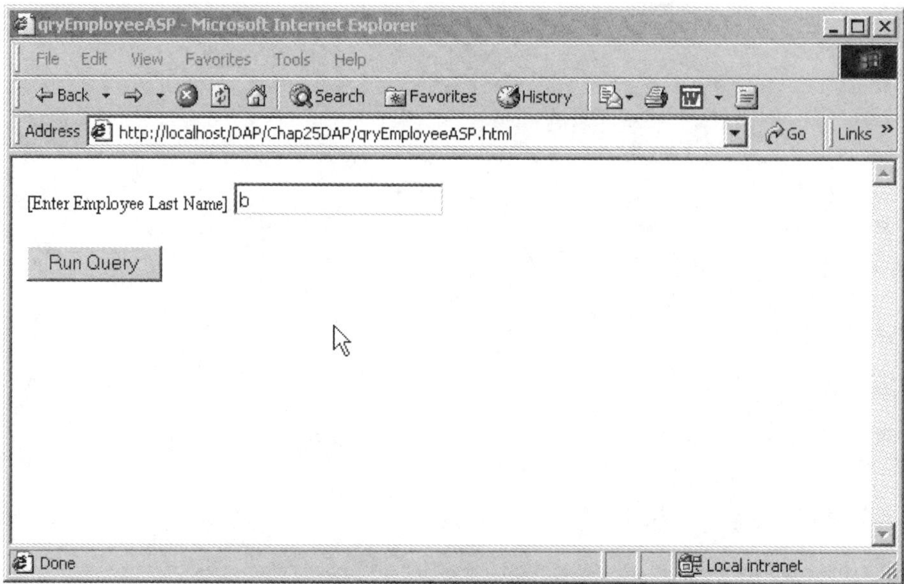

Figure 19-33. qryEmployeeASP.html in Internet Explorer

Enter some text (for example, "b") into the text box, and click on the Run Query button. Did all go well? No? The error you just encountered has been around in Access and ASP from the first time it was possible to export files as ASP, and it is still not fixed. So, to get the ASP script to work, you must manually open the file in Notepad and change the WHERE clause. Remember our wildcard character "*"? To get the script to work, it must be changed to "%", which is the standard SQL wildcard. (Remember that ASP is using ADO to communicate with the database.)

Change the previous WHERE clause to:

```
WHERE (((Employees.LastName) Like
'" & Request.QueryString("[Enter Employee Last Name]") & "%' ))"
```

Open qryEmployeeASP.html in the browser and enter "b". Figure 19-34 shows the output now that the WHERE clause has been amended.

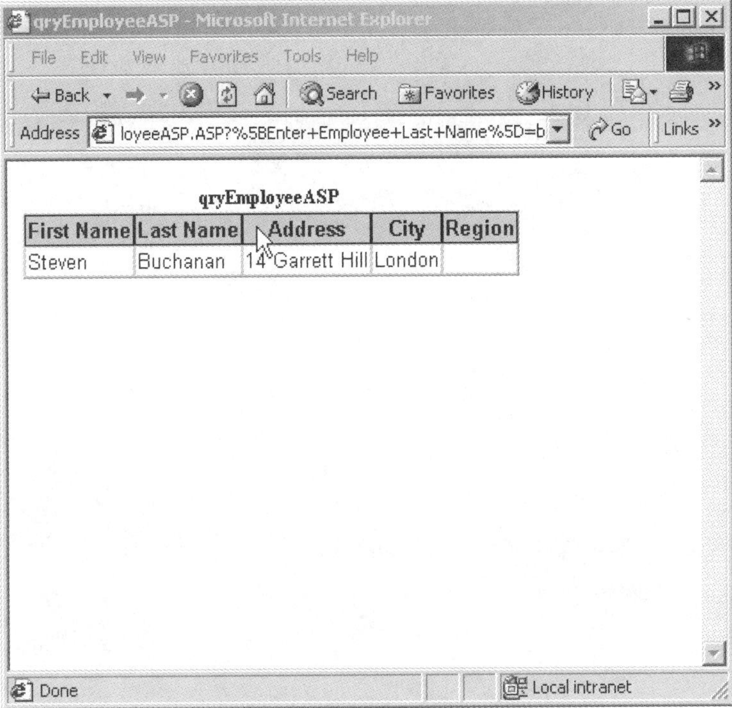

Figure 19-34. Amended employee script in Internet Explorer

We can improve the look of the Web page by touching up the HTML. Changes are made solely to the HTML portions of the ASP file, and there have been no changes to the actual ASP script. Figure 19-35 shows the employee page (qryEmployeeASP.asp) with the changes.

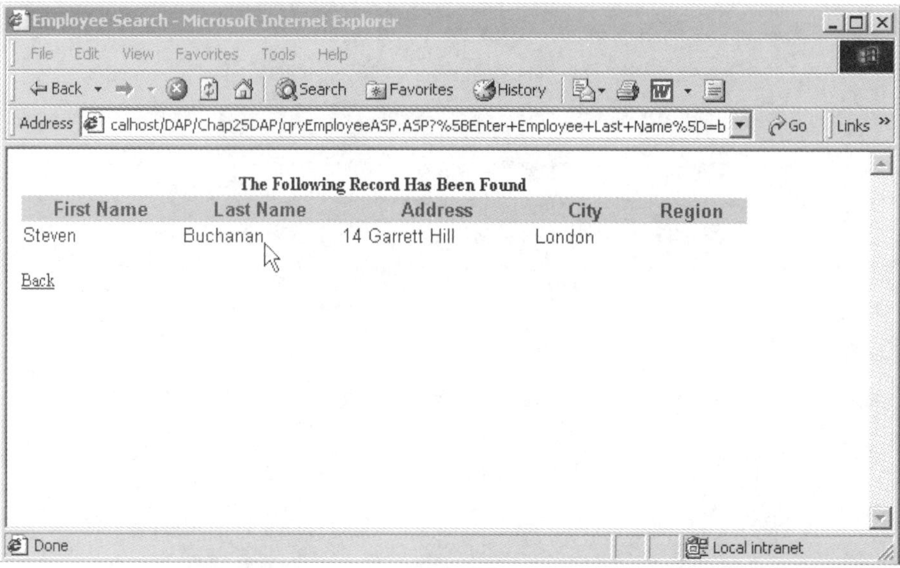

Figure 19-35. Reformatted output

Adding a New Employee

We can use much the same procedure to add a new Employee record to the table. This time, we will create the HTML page and the ASP page by hand using Notepad (or your favorite HTML editor). As before, we will need two files: UpdateEmployees.html and AddEmployee.asp.

The HTML form is used to collect the values that are then passed to the ASP script. On this occasion, I have used a HTML table to hold the various form objects. Tables are a common method used to control the layout of form objects in HTML. Table 19-4 shows the form objects used for this example, and Figure 19-36 shows the form in Internet Explorer.

Table 19-4. HTML Form Objects

OBJECT	NAME	COMMENT
Form	frmemp	This is the actual HTML form used.
Text Box	txtFirstName	Text box used to enter the employee's first name.
Text Box	txtLastName	Text box used to enter the employee's last name.
Text Box	txtTitle	Text box Used to enter the employee's title.
Text Box	txtAddress	Text box Used to enter the employee's address.
Text Box	txtNotes	Text box Used to enter any notes about the employee.

> **NOTE** *I have omitted some fields because this example is only to demonstrate one method used to add a record. One field not included is the EmployeeID. This is an autonumber primary key and will be added by the database upon insert. It is common to add Autonumber fields to the form and then find out you cannot actually insert one.*

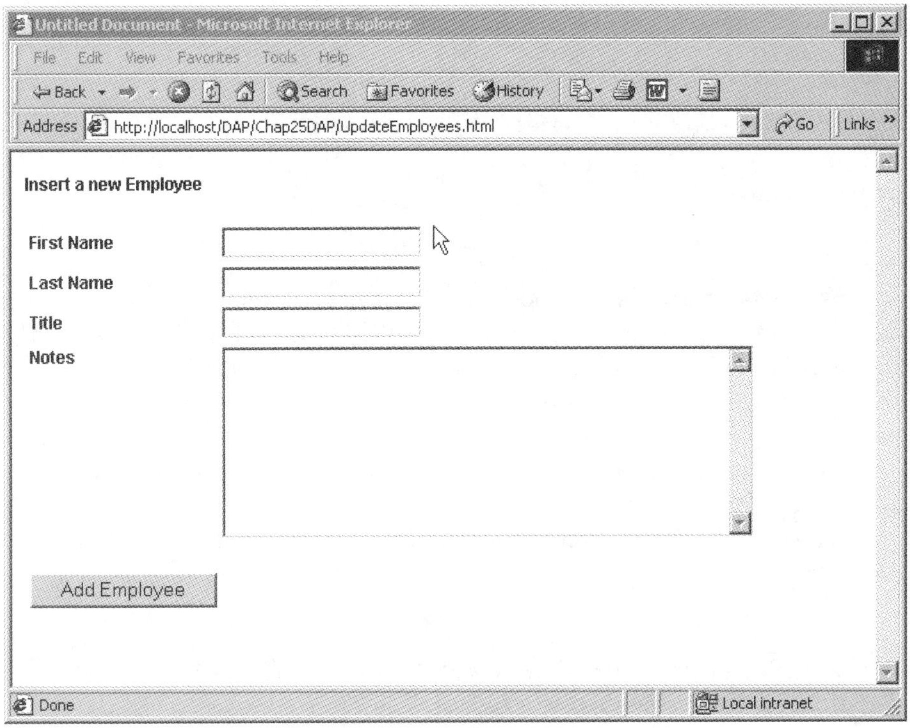

Figure 19-36. UpdateEmployees.html

The code for the processing script is shown next. This is a very simple approach to inserting the data to the table. For the moment, no error checking is performed.

```
<%
Dim FirstName
Dim LastName
Dim Title
Dim Address
Dim Notes
```

```
Dim cn
FirstName = request.form("txtFirstName")
LastName = request.form("txtLastName")
Title = request.form("txtTitle")
Address = request.form("txtAddress")
Notes = request.form("txtNotes")
Set cn = Server.CreateObject("ADODB.Connection")
cn.Open "nwind"
sql = "Insert into Employees (LastName,FirstName,Title,Address,Notes)"
sql = sql & " values('" & LastName & "' , '" & FirstName & "' , '" & Title & "'
, '" & Address & "' , '" & Notes & "' )"
cn.Execute(sql)
Response.write "One Record Inserted Into the Employee Table"
cn.Close
Set cn = nothing
%>
```

Save the file into the same folder as the employee HTML file. In the browser, load the HTML page, using the full URL. In my case, the URL is `http://localhost/DAP?Chap25DAP/UpDateEmployees.html`. Complete the form and click on the Add Employee button. Make sure that you complete all the form fields because, at this point, we do not have any error checking in place.

Open the Employees table in the Northwind database to view the newly inserted record.

Some things in the previous code may be new to you. Table 19-5 defines some of the new items.

> **NOTE** *In the preceding ASP, we take the form values and pass them into variables. This makes it easier to create the INSERT statement. I also name the form fields in a similar way as the database fields but prefixed with "txt". Again, this makes them easy to identify.*

Table 19-5. HTML Form Values

ITEM	COMMENT
Request	Takes the values passed by the Action attribute of the form.
POST	Ensures that the values are not visible in the browser URL when we submit them to our script. Using GET will pass the values via the URL. The POST method also permits us to send large amounts of text to the server as opposed to GET.
Response	Passes a server response back to the browser.

In the previous scripts, we have been using ODBC and DSNs. However, ODBC is getting to be outdated. As focus shifts from accessing databases to accessing data stores (that is, data held anywhere), most developers will now use OLEDB to get at data. OLEDB is the future of data access with Microsoft technologies and is the recommended method now used to connect to databases and other data stores.

To use OLEDB connections with the preceding script, we need to change a couple of lines, most notably those that refer to the DSN "nwind".

> **NOTE** *Remember, if you have used ADO connection objects, you will see very little, if any, difference in the connection objects used with ASP. The connection is required to naturally establish a link to the data, maintain that link, and eventually release the resource.*

We are going to change the code

```
cn.Open "nwind"
```

to read as follows:

```
cn.Open "Provider=Microsoft.Jet.OLEDB.4.0;" & _
"Data Source=C:\Inetpub\wwwroot\DAP\Northwind.mdb;" & _
"User Id=admin;" & _
"Password=;"
```

> **NOTE** *The script should work as before. One of the more common errors when first using this syntax is incorrectly entering the path to the database. For ease of use, I have placed the database into the same folder as the ASP pages. But you shouldn't do this: make sure that your database is outside the Web root and in a secured folder.*

On this occasion, we have placed the full path to the database into the connection. We can deal with this in other ways, and we will look at them shortly. It has also been reported that the following syntax may speed up the ASP script. Simply change the connection code to read as follows. In this case, we pass the path to a variable that is then appended to the open property of the connection. Although we can't confirm this, it does make your connection string easier to read (and type).

```
Dim cn, DataLocation
DataLocation = "C:\Inetpub\wwwroot\DAP\Northwind.mdb"
Set cn = Server.CreateObject("ADODB.Connection")
Cn.Open "PROVIDER=MICROSOFT.JET.OLEDB.4.0;DATA SOURCE=" &
DataLocation
```

Figure 19-37 shows all the OLEDB providers available on my system. To view the providers in Microsoft Access:

1. Select About Microsoft Access from the Help menu.
2. Click on the System Information button.
3. Expand the Office 10 Applications folder.
4. Expand the Microsoft Office 10 Environment folder.
5. Open the OLEDB Providers folder.

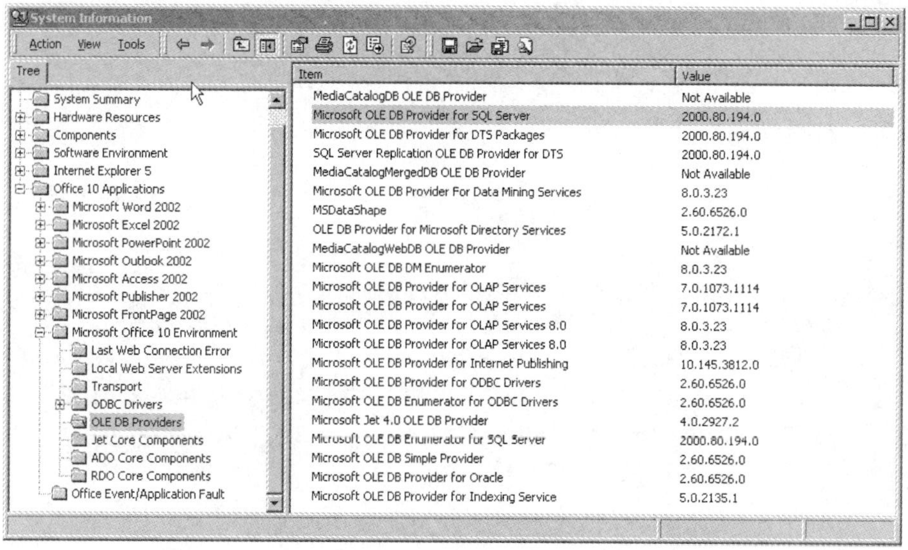

Figure 19-37. OLEDB providers available in Office 10

There is another approach to inserting a record to our employee table: rather than executing the SQL string, why not simply execute a query in Access, pass it some parameters, and thus insert the record? The next example does just that. I have created a simple Insert query using Access 2002. The SQL for the query is:

```
INSERT INTO Employees( LastName,FirstName,TitlemAddress)
VALUES ([PrmLastName],[PrmFirstName],[PrmTitle],[PrmAddress]
```

To create the query in Access, from the Database window:

1. Select the Queries group.
2. Click on the New button.
3. Select Design view from the New Query dialog box.
4. Click on OK.
5. Close the Add Table dialog box without selecting a table.
6. Click on View|SQL View from the Main menu.
7. Enter the previous SQL statement into the SQL pane.
8. Close and save the query as InsertEmployee.

Now we need to create the ASP file, which is fairly simple and is very like the one we have already seen.

Create the following file using Notepad:

```
<%
cn.Open "Provider=Microsoft.Jet.OLEDB.4.0;" & _
"Data Source=C:\Inetpub\wwwroot\DAP\Northwind.mdb;"
 & _ "User Id=admin;" & _
"Password=;"
cn.Execute "exec InsertEmployee 'Reid', 'Patricia' ' 'Mr' , 'Apress USA'"
cn.close
set cn=Nothing
%>
```

Save the file as Insert_Query.asp.

Open the query in Internet Explorer (using the full URL to the file). No records will be returned when you execute the script. Loading the file in the browser executes the ASP file. Open the employee table in Access to see the newly added record. One major advantage to this approach is that we no longer have to construct and send complex SQL strings over the network. If the SQL statement in the query changes, rather than open ASP scripts and recode, we simply change the query or stored procedure.

TIP *A useful tip is to create an Include file that contains the details of the connection. For example, with the previous file, we could remove the connection completely and place it into a file on its own. When we wanted to use the connection, we can refer to the Include file and reference it in a single line:*

```
<!- #Include file = connectionfile.inc-->.
```

Now we can reference the connection without having to retype all that text.

The following code fragment uses the Include file containing a connection called "cn". We then execute a simple SQL SELECT statement against the connection to return a recordset.

```
<! - #Include file = connectionfile.inc-->.
<%
DIM SQLstr, rst
Set rst = Server.CreateObject("ADODB.Recordset")
SQLstr = "SELECT FirstName FROM Customer"
Set  rst = cn.execute(SQLstr)

Do While not rst.EOF
Response.Write rst("FirstName")
rst.MoveNext
Loop
%>
```

TIP *The Do Loop simply moves through our recordset. Until we reach the end of file, MoveNext takes us to the next record in the recordset.*

Using Access 2002 and other versions of Access is a good method of teaching yourself about various technologies that are used to pass information from databases to users via the Internet. However, the real game is played with SQL Server 2000. SQL Server 2000 can use both XML, ASP and, of course, PHP.

In our final section, we will look at using SQL to produce XML within SQL Server 2000.

SQL Server provides an extension to the SQL SELECT statement that is used to produce XML: the FOR XML clause. Table 19-5 explains the arguments available when using the FOR XML statement with SQL:

```
FOR XML
[RAW | AUTO | EXPLICIT]
[,XMLData]
[, ELEMENTS]
[, BINARY BASE64]
```

Table 19-5. XML Arguments

CLAUSE	COMMENT
FOR XML	Informs SQL Server that the query results are for XML.
RAW	Each row in the result set becomes an XML element.
AUTO	Multitable queries become nested sets of XML elements.
EXPLICIT	The query will contain information on the shape of the XML tree to be created. Provides more control over the result set.
XMLDATA	Includes the document type definition (DTD) in the generated XML.
ELEMENTS	Column values are returned as elements.
Binary BASE64	Binary data returned is encoded using base64 encoding.

Constructing the SQL statement is basically the usual SELECT statement followed by the FOR XML AUTO statement. For example:

```
SELECT CustomerName,Address
FROM
Customers
FOR XML AUTO
```

Before proceeding, we will configure SQL Server for XML use with IIS and Internet Explorer. We will then look at the different output provided by the FOR XML statement, executing queries via the URL, and executing stored procedures via the URL. We'll close by offering some warnings about these methods of interaction.

Configuring SQL Server for XML and HTTP Query

From the Start menu:

1. Select Programs|Microsoft SQL Server|Configure SQL XML Support in IIS.

2. Expand the server.

3. Click on the default Web site.

4. Right-click and select New|Virtual Directory. Figure 19-38 shows the Virtual Directory Management snap-in at this point.

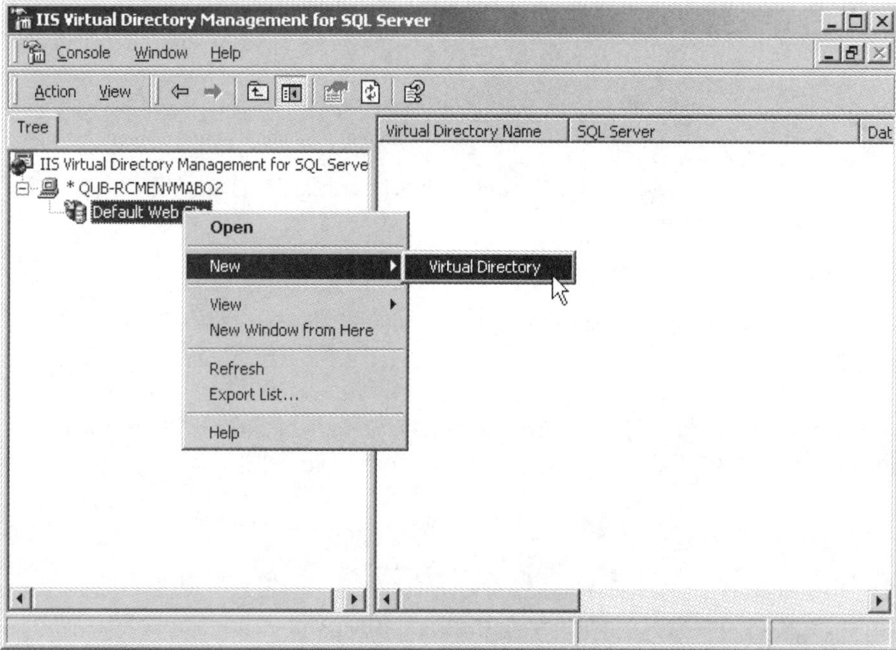

Figure 19-38. Setting up a virtual directory

The New Virtual Directory Properties dialog will open. Figure 19-39 shows the dialog box.

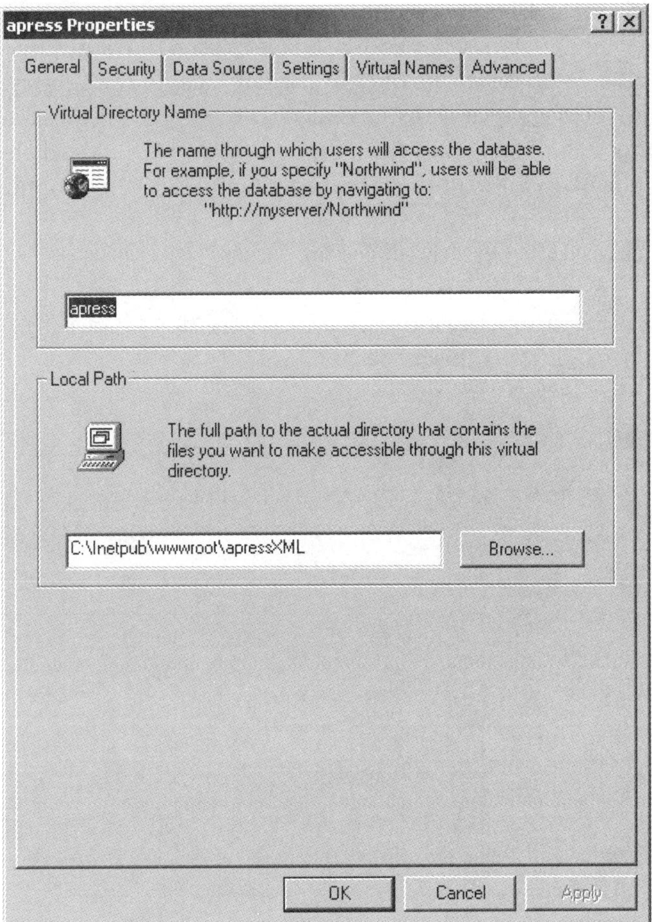

Figure 19-39. New virtual directory properties

5. Under the General tab, enter a name for the virtual directory.

In addition to the virtual directory, you will also need a physical directory on the Web server. In my case, the folder is C:\Inetpub\wwwroot\apressXML. You can use the Browse button under the General tab to navigate to the appropriate folder.

6. Click on the Security tab. You can choose either Windows authentication or SQL Server security. In my case, I have chosen to use SQL Server security and have entered the username and password for a system administrator. You will be prompted to reenter the password.

7. Click on the Data Source tab. You can select an SQL Server to use and set the default database for access. I have chosen the local server, and the default database will be the NorthwindCS demo file. Be very careful of your choice here and ensure that you do not select either the master or temporary database. Click on the Setting tab within the dialog box and set the Allow URL Queries and Allow Template Queries option.

8. Click on OK to close the dialog box.

9. Close the Virtual Directory snap-in. Figure 19-40 shows the Management snap-in following this process.

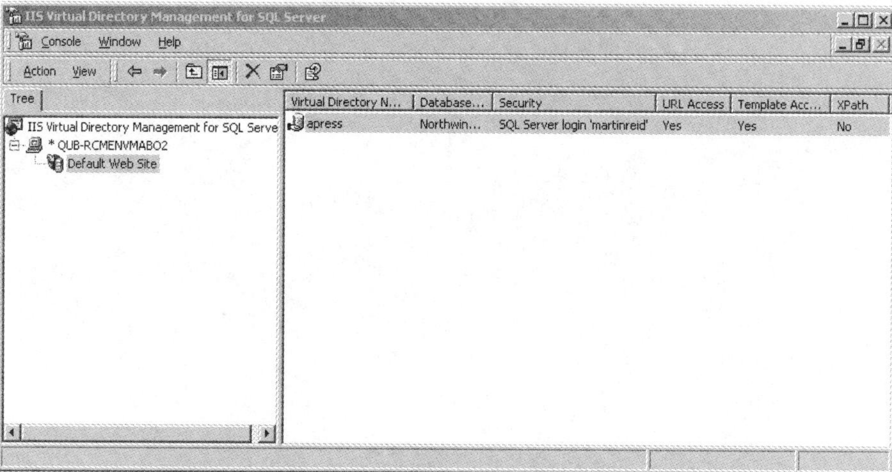

Figure 19-40. Virtual directory management

Figure 19-41 shows the results of executing an SQL statement in the URL. Open Internet Explorer and enter the following URL into the browser. Make sure that you enter it without spaces and directly into the location box. Remember to change the names of the folders and whatever else to reflect your own setup.

```
http://localhost/apress/?sql=SELECT+CustomerName+FROM+
Customers+FOR+XML+RAW&root=root
```

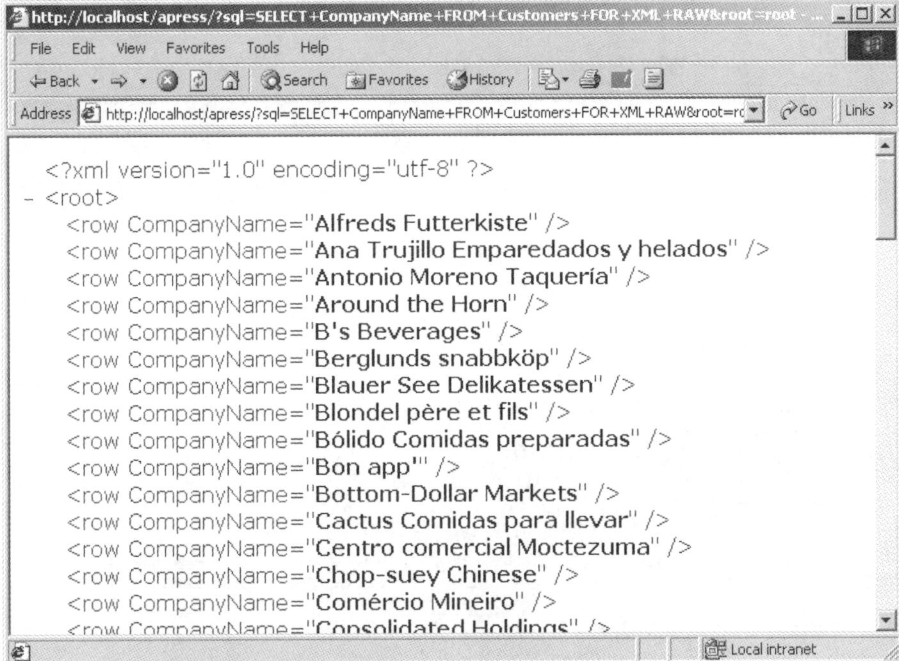

Figure 19-41. Executing SQL via a browser URL

This statement uses the RAW argument. Let's change this to AUTO and see the results. They're not very different.

The next example queries the Customer and Order tables via the URL. The SQL statement is entered directly into the browser. Figure 19-42 shows the results. On this occasion, the page of XML that's returned is a bit more interactive. We can select a customer and view their order within the browser.

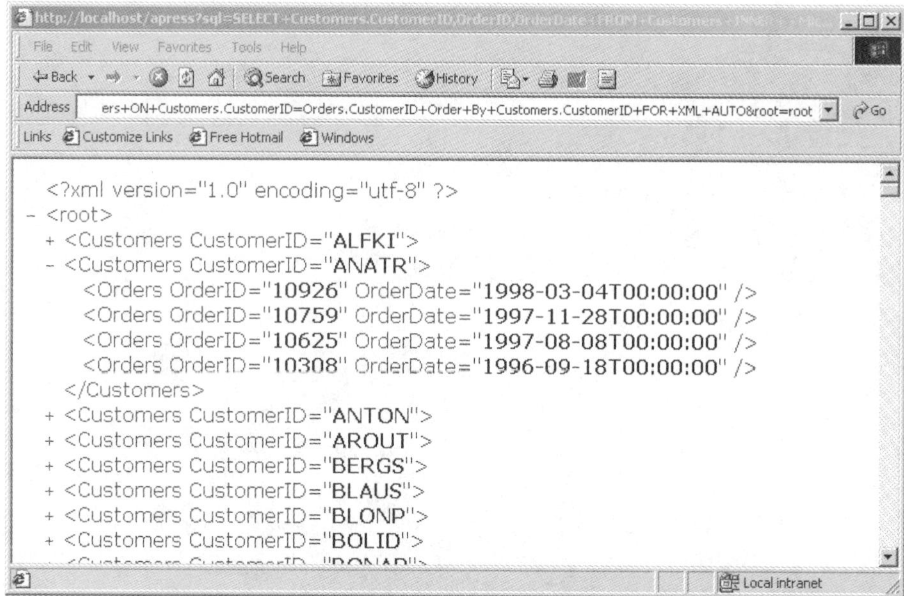

Figure 19-42. Customer orders via XML

As can be seen, I have expanded the orders for CustomerID "ALFKI". Four orders are retrieved and displayed.

We can also use this method to execute stored procedures (and herein lies the danger). Duplicating the previous example, create a simple stored procedure that returns customer and order data. In my case, I have named the procedure usp_CustOrders. Remember to place the FOR XML keywords as the last line in the procedure. The stored procedure can be created in Access 2002 and the FOR XML line added manually in the design grid.

To execute this procedure via a browser URL, enter the following address, replacing the procedure name with your own:

```
http://localhost/apress?sql=EXECUTE+ups_CustOrders&root=root
```

Figure 19-43 shows the result.

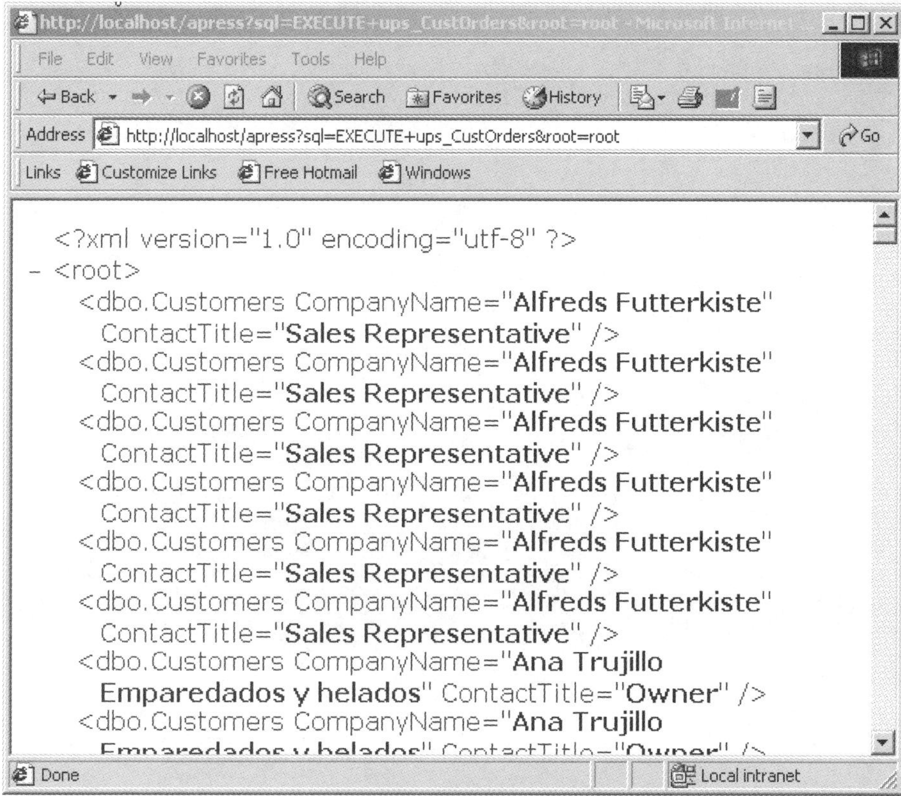

Figure 19-43. Executing a stored procedure via the URL

Being honest, this type of approach reminds me of data access pages in Access. From a technological viewpoint, it is impressive and fun. But would I let users execute queries and stored procedures via a Web URL? Not in this life! The ability to execute SQL and stored procedures in particular via a URL opens up the server to additional security requirements and hacking attempts.

In this chapter, we introduced you to XML, some HTML, and basic active server pages. Along the way, we looked at data access pages in Access 2002. Without a doubt, the Internet and Internet access to your data will form the future of computing and in particular will affect the relational database. No single chapter can provide you with all the necessary information on this subject. We can only introduce the subject, provide a few pointers, and show you how some of the technology works by demonstrating some of its features. You can investigate this technology further. Many Web sites contain articles and code examples, such as `www.msdn.microsoft.com` and, in our opinion, two of the oldest and best ASP sites: `www.learnasp.com` and `www.4guysfromrolla.com`.

APPENDIX A

More SQL Solutions to Common Problems

Problem 1: Begin a Label Report at Any Label on the Sheet

MOST LABEL RUNS leave unused labels on the last sheet. The following technique will start a label run at a specific label position, so you can use those partially used sheets. The components are a form, a temporary table, and a label report. You'll use the form to identify the position of the first available label. Then, an event procedure will populate the temporary table with blank rows, with one blank row for each missing label. The number of blank rows is determined by the value you enter. If you enter a value of 3 (meaning that the first label is in the third label position), the procedure will add two blank rows. Next, the procedure appends the label data below the blank rows. The report doesn't care that the rows are empty; the positions are still filled in the label report. Each blank row represents a blank label, pushing the actual data down to the first label. This technique doesn't accommodate missing labels between the first and last label.

Example: tblOne, frmOne, and rptOne

Solution 1: SELECT, DELETE, and INSERT INTO

To create the temporary table:

1. In the Database window, select the table that contains the data you're printing.
2. Press `Ctrl+C` to copy the table to the clipboard.
3. Press `Ctrl+V` to paste a copy of the table. In the Paste Table As dialog box, enter a name for the dummy table. (We'll be working with tblOne.) Select the Structure Only option button in the Paste Options section, and click on OK.

4. Open tblOne and delete any primary key. Don't delete the fields; just delete the primary key.

5. Review the Indexed and Required properties for each field and make sure that each is set to No.

6. Save the table.

To create the form:

1. Open a new, unbound form in Design view.

2. Insert a text box and enter an appropriate label caption.

3. Name the text box txtBlankRows.

4. Insert two command buttons, side by side.

5. Name them cmdPrint and cmdCancel and set their Caption properties to Print and Cancel, respectively.

6. Click on the Code button on the Form Design toolbar to launch the Visual Basic Editor.

7. In the form's module, enter the following event procedures:

```
Private Sub cmdPrint_Click()
Dim rst As New ADODB.Recordset
Dim bytCounter As Byte
Dim bytBlanks As Byte
On Error GoTo errHandler
bytBlanks = Forms!frmOne!txtBlankRows.Value
DoCmd.SetWarnings False
DoCmd.RunSQL "DELETE FROM nameoftemporarytable"
Set rst.ActiveConnection = CurrentProject.Connection
rst.Open "SELECT * FROM nameoftemporarytable ", , _
    adOpenDynamic, adLockOptimistic
For bytCounter = 2 To bytBlanks
    rst.AddNew
    rst.Update
Next
rst.Close
Set rst = Nothing
```

```
DoCmd.RunSQL "INSERT INTO nameoftemporarytable " _
    & "SELECT * FROM datatable"
DoCmd.SetWarnings True
DoCmd.OpenReport "nameoflabelreport", acViewPreview
Exit Sub
errHandler:
MsgBox "Please enter a valid label number"
DoCmd.SetWarnings True
End Sub

Private Sub cmdCancel_Click()
DoCmd.Close acForm, "nameofform", acSaveNo
End Sub
```

8. Save the form. The example form is named frmOne.

Because the label report will be unique to your application, we won't build one. The example file uses a label report named rptOne, based on the Customers table in Northwind.

Before running the report, insert your label sheets into the printer. Be sure to position the partially used sheet as the first sheet. Then, open the form (frmOne) and enter the position of the first existing label. (For instance, if two labels were missing, you'd enter the value 3, and, if six labels were missing, you'd enter the value 7.) Then, click on the Print button, and the event procedure prints the report.

Problem 2: Finding the Second-Highest or -Lowest Value in a Group

Querying for the second-highest or second-lowest value in a table is easy, and it requires two queries. First, you identify the data source and the fields you want to see in the results. Then, you set the sort order, ascending for the highest and descending for the lowest. Then, set the Top Values property to 2 so that the query returns only the highest and second-highest or the lowest and second-lowest values, depending on the sort order. Base the second query on the first query, set the Top Values property to 1, and reverse the sort order. This technique is complicated when you need to return the second-highest or second-lowest value in a group, and the solution again requires two queries.

Example: qryOneFirstQuery, qryTwoSecondQuery

Solution 2: GROUP BY

To create the first query:

1. Base a Totals query on the data source. Be careful to use only those fields that identify each group. To manually define a Totals query, choose Totals from the View menu in the Query Design toolbar. Specify the Max aggregate in the grouping value's total cell, or, in the SQL window, add a GROUP BY clause in the form:

   ```
   SELECT groupedfield, Max(valuefield) AS name
   FROM table
   GROUP BY groupedfield
   ```

   where *groupedfield* represents the field(s) by which you're grouping, *valuefield* is the field with the values you're sorting in order of largest to smallest, *name* is the alias column name for *valuefield,* and *table* is the data source.

2. Save the query using an appropriate name. Our example query is qryTwoFirstQuery.

3. Base a second query on your data source and add the first query (qryOneFirstQuery) to it. Open the SQL window and use an SQL statement in the form

   ```
   SELECT dsgroupedfield, qrygroupedfield, Max(dsvaluefield) AS name
   FROM ds LEFT JOIN query ON (dsvaluefield = name) AND (dsgroupedfield =
     qrygroupedfield)
   GROUP BY dsgroupedfield, qrygroupedfield
   HAVING qrygroupedfield Is Null
   ```

   where *dsgroupedfield* is the grouped field in the data source, *qrygroupedfield* is the grouped field in the first query, *ds* is the data source, and *query* is the first query. Or, create the query manually by following steps 4 through 9.

4. Create a relationship for the grouped fields and the value fields between the data source and the query. Remember, the value field's name will probably be different in the query.

5. Add both grouped fields to the query (from the data source and the query). Also add the value field from the data source.

6. Make the query a Totals query by choosing Totals from the View menu.

7. Change the value field's Totals aggregate from Group By to Max.

8. Add the criteria Is Null to the query's (qryTwoFirstQuery) group field.

9. Save the query. We saved the example file as qryTwoSecondQuery. To see the results, run qryTwoSecondQuery.

These instructions return a list of the second-highest product for each order in the Order Details table. Simply change the Max aggregate to the Min aggregate in both queries.

Problem 3: Adding a Summary Row to a Query

We often see totals in a form or report, but you can also view totals in a query. This technique is more limited than the form or report solutions, but it's extremely easy: simply use a Union query to append a single row of aggregate functions to a SELECT query. The number of columns for each SELECT must match.

Example: qryThree

Solution 3: Union Query

To create the Union query:

1. Base a query on the data source.

2. Add the appropriate fields to the query.

3. Open the SQL window and add to the existing SELECT statement a UNION clause in the form

   ```
   UNION
   SELECT agg(fld1), agg(fld2), . . .
   FROM ds
   ```

   where *agg* is one of the aggregate functions, *fldx* represents a field from the original SELECT clause, and *ds* is the data source.

4. Save the query. The example file is named qryThree. The totals row will appear as the first or last row in the query's results, depending on how it sorts.

Each field in the original Select query must be represented in the Union query, either by entering an aggregate function, a delimited string, or a zero-length string (""). For instance, the following statement displays the string "Averages" in the first column, and the result of aggregate functions in the remaining columns:

```
SELECT OrderID, UnitPrice, Quantity, Discount
FROM [Order Details]
UNION
SELECT 'Averages', Avg(UnitPrice), Avg(Quantity), Avg( Discount)
FROM [Order Details]
```

If you use "" to represent the first column, Jet would sort the averaged row first in the resultset:

```
SELECT OrderID, UnitPrice, Quantity, Discount
FROM [Order Details]
UNION
SELECT "", Avg(UnitPrice), Avg(Quantity), Avg(Discount)
FROM [Order Details]
```

Problem 4: Returning Alternating Rows

Returning alternating rows—either oddly or evenly numbered—is a simple task if your table includes an AutoNumber field. The solution uses the MOD operator and sequential values in an AutoNumber field.

Example: qryFourEven, qryFourOdd

Solution 4: MOD Operator

To return a table of oddly numbered records, use a statement in the form

```
SELECT fldlist
FROM tbl
WHERE AutoNumberfield Mod 2<>0
```

To return a table of even-numbered records, use a statement in the form

```
SELECT fldlist
FROM tbl
WHERE AutoNumberfield Mod 2=0
```

If no AutoNumber field exists, you can temporarily add one using the ALTER TABLE statement in the following form:

```
ALTER TABLE tbl
ADD COLUMN fldname AUTOINCREMENT
```

Run one of these preceding statements and then delete the temporary AutoNumber field using the DROP COLUMN clause in the form

```
ALTER TABLE table
DROP COLUMN fldname
```

Problem 5: Producing a Random Sort

There's no way to create a truly random sort in Access, but you can return a seemingly random set. They won't really be randomly selected, but it will seem that they are, and for most tasks, this will be adequate. The solution requires that you use the **Rnd()** function to return a random value for each record, and then sort by those values. Because the random values will have no connection to each record, the sorted results will seem to produce a random collection of records. You can then use the TOP predicate to reduce the result set to a specific number of records.

Example: qryFive

Solution 5: TOP predicate and the Rnd() function

To produce a random sort, use a statement in the form:

```
SELECT TOP x fldlist, Rnd(value) AS RanSort
FROM table
ORDER BY Rnd(value)
```

where *x* is the number of records you want to return and *value* is a literal value or a numeric field.

The **Rnd()** function returns a value between 0 and 1, and that value will be the next random value in a sequence, determined by *value:*

- When *value* is greater than 0, **Rnd()** returns the next random value in sequence.
- When *value* equals 0, **Rnd()** returns the most recently generated value.
- When *value* is less than 0, **Rnd()** returns the same value.

One limitation is that Access always resets the seed value to the same value each time you launch. If you need a completely random sort each time, you need to execute the **Randomize()** function before running the query.

You may notice that Jet doesn't appear to sort the records correctly, and that's correct. The reason is that the query actually calls the **Rnd()** function twice, so the values that you see and the values that Jet sorts by aren't even the same. However, in the context of our solution, it makes no difference. You're not using the random values for anything other than to sort, in an effort to mix up your records in a seemingly random manner. Which set of random values Jet actually sorts by makes no difference to the solution.

Problem 6: Counting Specific Entries

You can use the **Count()** function to return a number of records using the syntax:

```
Count(*)
```

But, used in this way, **Count()** returns the total number of records in your data source. Counting a specific number of entries requires that you add a WHERE clause.

Example: qrySix

Solution 6: Count() and WHERE clause

To count the number of specific entries, use a statement in the form

```
SELECT Count(*) AS alias
FROM table
WHERE condition
```

For instance, to return the number of orders from the Order Details table in the Northwind database that have a Unit Price value greater than 20, you'd use the following statement:

```
SELECT Count(*) AS Total
FROM [Order Details]
WHERE [Order Details].UnitPrice > 20
```

Problem 7: Counting Unique Values

A Totals query (or view) will group records by different values. You can include aggregate functions in a Totals query to learn more about these groups: you can total all the values in each group, you can learn the maximum or minimum value in each group, and you can even count the number of records in each group. Returning the number of unique values in a group is a bit different. For instance, let's suppose that you want to group a table by dates and then count the number of unique items entered for each date. This isn't the same as returning the number of records for each date. A subquery is the easiest solution in this situation.

Example: qrySeven

Solution 7: A Subquery

To count the number of unique items in a group, use a statement in the following form:

```
SELECT grpfield1, Count(grpfield2) AS alias
FROM (SELECT grpfield1, grpfield2
FROM table
GROUP BY grpfield1, grpfield2)
GROUP BY grpfield2
```

Let's compare the results of this query to a Totals query. Let's suppose that March 1, 2001, has three entries. The entry "red" occurs twice, and the entry "blue" occurs just once. An aggregate Count for this group (March 1, 2001) will return the value 3 because this group has three records. However, the subquery will return 2 because there are only two unique entries: red and blue.

Problem 8: Finding Unique Values

Problem 7 and its solution deal with counting the number of unique values in a group. Sometimes you may need to find each unique value, and that can also be accomplished using a Totals query and the Count aggregate. In this case, the query will return actual entries and not a count of those entries. But, this time, the query will return just one record for each unique entry, and that result will depend on the fields you include in the query.

Example: qryEight

Solution 8: A Totals Query and the Count Aggregate

To return unique entries in a group, use a statement in the following form:

```
SELECT grpfield1, grpfield2, Count(grpfield2) AS alias
FROM table
GROUP BY grpfield1, grpfield2
HAVING Count(grpfield2)=1
```

Keep in mind that each field you add to the group changes the group. As such, this query will return different values for different groups. A table that contains three groups based on dates and different values for each group will return a different unique value than will a query based on the same table but including only the date field or the data field.

Problem 9: Displaying Optional Data in a List Control

Chapter 5 shows you how to use an SQL statement as the Row Source setting for a list control (list box or combo box). To display data in a list or combo box, you'd use an SQL statement in the form

```
SELECT DISTINCTROW fldlist
FROM table
```

as the control's Row Source property.

Sometimes you may want to display something other than the actual items in a table, and SQL can help here as well. For instance, let's suppose that a table contains a Yes/No field, but, instead of showing Yes or No in a column, you want to display some other qualifier, such as Active and Inactive, Old and New, or In and Out. Adding an **Iif()** function to the SQL statement solves this problem.

Example: frmNine

Solution 9: Add an Iif() Function to the SQL Statement

Because the Yes/No field equates to True and False, the **Iif()** function easily handles this problem. Use an SQL statement as the control's Row Source property, in the form

```
SELECT fld1, fld2, . . . , IIf([yesnofld]=True,"truestring","falsestring") AS alias
FROM table
```

where *fld1*, *fld2*, . . . are the different fields you want to display and *yesnofield* identifies the Yes/No field for which you want to display optional data. The example form frmNine displays the ProductID and ProductName fields from the Products table. In addition, a third column (Status) displays either the string "Discontinued" or "Active," based on that record's Yes/No entry in the Discontinued field. That control's Row Source property is:

```
SELECT Products.ProductID, Products.ProductName,
IIf([Discontinued]=True,"Discontinued","Active") AS Status
FROM Products
```

Problem 10: Custom Sort for Controls

You learned in Chapter 5 how to sort a recordset using the ORDER BY clause, but you can also use this clause to sort a control's list: simply add it to the control's Row Source SQL statement. If you combine the ORDER BY clause with VBA code, you can offer sort choices to your users. In other words, instead of facing a predetermined sort order, the user can click a choice and sort the list as needed.

Example: frmTen

Solution 10: VBA and ORDER BY

The only condition that this technique supposes is that a control's list has more than one column. After creating and populating the control, add an option frame and insert an option button for each column in the control. Label the option frame and each option button accordingly. (Each option button should correspond to one of the control's columns.) Then, use the following procedure to reset the list control's Row Source property, and make the appropriate adjustments to the ORDER BY clause appropriately:

```
Private Sub framecontrol_BeforeUpdate(Cancel As Integer)
Dim strSQL As String
Dim strSort As String
Select Case framecontrol
    Case 1
        strSort = fld1
    Case 2
        strSort = fld2
    Case 3
        strSort = fld3
End Select
strSQL = "SELECT fld1, fld2, " _
    & "IIf([Discontinued]=True," & """truestring""" & "," & """falsestring""" & _
    & "") AS alias FROM table ORDER BY "
strSQL = strSQL & strSort
Debug.Print strSQL
lstcontrol.RowSource = strSQL
End Sub
```

This particular procedure assumes that the control has three columns, but that's not necessary. You can adjust the Select Case statement as needed. The user simply selects the appropriate option button to resort the contents of the control by the selected option. The example form frmTen allows you to sort its list control by each column.

APPENDIX B

An Introduction to Using ADO and ADOX with SQL

Visual Basic for Applications (VBA) is the programming engine behind Microsoft Office and all its applications, but it isn't the only library available. In fact, a great deal of your programming tasks can be handled more efficiently using SQL. However, not all of SQL's functionality is accessible via Access' SQL window. Some extensions are available only through code, and that's where the data object libraries come in handy.

Microsoft ActiveX Data Objects Library (ADO)

ADO is a library of objects that represent the structure of your database and its data. In other words, ADO gives you easy access to the tables and queries in a database. In addition, you can use ADO to manipulate data. In Access, the Microsoft ActiveX Data Objects (ADO) Library is probably used as much if not more than VBA.

In hierarchical terms, ADO is a high-performance interface to OLEDB, a system-level interface. That's about as clear as mud, isn't it? In simpler terms, OLEDB is a technology that allows you to interact with all data, regardless of its location, format, or type. Think of it as a universal data snatcher.

A typical client/server setup has a database management system (DBMS) engine, an SQL engine, a transaction manager, a cursor engine, data, business rules, and so on. OLEDB allows all of these components to talk to one another. This magic is made possible by data providers that directly interface between an application and the native data (Access in our case). Next in line is the service provider, which interacts between the application and the data providers, and this is where SQL enters our sights. For our purposes, ADO service providers give us access to SQL extensions that we can't access any other way. And these extensions often make short work of an otherwise laborious task.

The ADO Object Model

The top dog in the ADO object model, shown in Figure B-1, is the Connection object. The Connection object creates a connection to a data provider; it's the actual link to your data. This could mean opening an actual connection to a server or simply identifying the database that contains the data you need. You never need a translator; the Connection object takes care of all that for you. The Command object replaces DAO's torturous QueryDef objects. The Recordset object is similar to its DAO counterpart. (There are differences, but the object itself isn't new.) The Record object is similar, conceptually, to a one-record Recordset object; but it always represents only one row of data. The Stream object represents a stream of binary data or text, such as data or email files. We'll concentrate on the Connection and Command objects because these are the two you'll be using to access SQL extensions.

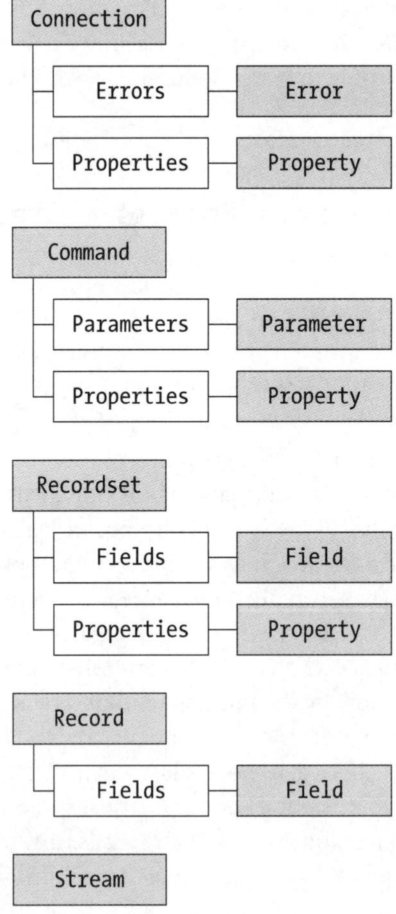

Figure B-1. The ADO 2.7 object model has five objects. (© 2001 Microsoft Corporation. Reprinted with permission from Microsoft Corporation.)

Opening a Connection

The first step to using ADO is to establish a connection to a data source using one of the following methods:

- Use the Open method of the Connection object to establish a connection to an external source.
- Use the Connection property to establish the current database as the connection's data source, which works with a Connection or Command object.

The methods available when using a connection include:

- *BeginTrans:* Begins a new transaction
- *Cancel:* Cancels the call to a method
- *Close:* Closes a connection
- *CommitTrans:* Saves and end the current transaction
- *Execute:* Executes the named query, SQL statement, or stored procedure
- *Open:* Opens the connection to the data source
- *OpenSchema:* Returns information about the database schema
- *RollbackTrans:* Cancels any changes made within the transaction

To establish a connection using the Open method and the ConnectionString property, use the following form:

```
cnn.Open connectionstring, userid, password, options
```

where *cnn* represents a Connection object, *connectionstring* is a string that identifies the connection, *userid* is a string that identifies the user, *password* is a string that identifies the password (when the source is password protected), and *options* determine whether the connection returns synchronously or asynchronously.

The *connectionstring* argument consists of a series of *argument = value* components separated by a colon character. The five valid settings are reviewed in Table B-1.

Table B-1. Settings for the Open Method's connectionstring Argument

ARGUMENT	DESCRIPTION
Provider	Specifies the connection's provider (for a list of providers, see Table B-2)
File Name	Specifies a provider-specific file
Remote Provider	Specifies a provider when opening a client-side connection (remote data service only)
Remote Server	Specifies the path name of the server to use when opening a client-side connection (remote data service only)
URL	Specifies the connection string as an absolute URL, which identifies a resource, such as a file or directory

Table B-2. ADO Providers

PROVIDER	PROVIDER STRING
Access	Microsoft.Jet.OLEDB.4.0
SQL Server	SQLOLEDB
Oracle	MSDAORA
ODBC	MSDASQL
Index Server	MSIDXS
Active Directory Service	ADSDSOObject

Armed with this information, you can quickly open a connection to most data sources. For example, let's suppose that you want to open a connection to a local Access database. In this case, your code might resemble:

```
Dim cnn As ADODB.Connection
Set cnn = New ADODB.Connection
cnn.Open "Provider=Microsoft.Jet.OLEDB.4.0;Data Source=C:\Program " _
  & "Files\Microsoft Office\Office\Samples\Northwind.mdb;"
```

This code would open a connection to the sample database, Northwind.mdb, on your local system. Once you're connected, you can use the Execute method to execute most SQL statements in the form

```
cnn.Execute(SQLstatement, recordcount, textorstored)
```

where *recordcount* and *textorstored* are optional arguments. (The SQL statement would specify any extensions.) Many of the examples throughout the book use the Connection object and the Execute method to get the job done, often replacing laborious VBA code to complete the same task.

For more in-depth coverage of ADO's objects, properties, methods, and events, read the *ADO Programmer's Guide* online at `http://msdn.microsoft.com/library/default.asp?url=/library/en-us/ado270/htm/mdobjstream.asp`.

> **NOTE** *Connection strings don't have to be long and complicated. After assigning a data source name (DSN) to a data source, a connection string may be as simple as:*
>
> ```
> cnn.Open = "DSN=datasourcename"
> ```
>
> *The defaults are assumed in this statement.*

It is also possible to connect to a secured Access database. You must provide the path to the MDW file that's used to store the workgroup security information. For example, the following code establishes a connection to a secured copy of the Northwind database, in which *yoursystemfile* represents the name of your MDW workgroup file:

```
Dim cnn As New ADODB.Connection
cnn.Open "Provider=Microsoft.Jet.OLEDB.4.0;" & _
    "Data Source=c:\Program Files\Microsoft Office\Office\Samples\" & _
    "Northwind.mdb;" & _
    "Jet OLEDB:System Database=yoursystemfile.mdw;", "admin", ""
```

The Command object is probably used more frequently in projects (ADP files) than Access MDB files, but both SQL Desktop and Access support the Command object. If an MDB file has the potential to be upsized, the Command object is usually the better choice over the Connection object. One big advantage is that the Command object accepts parameters. And the Command object has a few more properties, which we've listed in Table B-3, than does the Connection property.

Table B-3. Command Object Properties

PROPERTY	DESCRIPTION
Name	An optional argument, but we recommend you use it. If the Command object is executing a stored procedure, the Name property must match the name of the stored procedure. Set this property before setting the ActiveConnection property.
CommandText	Generally, a stored procedure, an SQL statement, table name, or a URL where data can be found.
CommandType	A constant that defines the type of command you're processing. Table B-4 lists those constants.
ActiveConnection	Defines the data source. You can use a Connection object of a simple connection string.
Prepared	Precompiles ad hoc queries.
CommandTimeout	Determines how long to wait while executing a command before terminating the action and returning an error.

Table B-4. CommandType Constants

CONSTANT	DESCRIPTION
adCmdUnspecified	Doesn't specify the type of query.
adCmdText	The CommandText string is a simple SQL command string.
adCmdTable	The CommandText string is the name of a table.
adCmdStoredProc	The CommandText string is a stored procedure.
adCmdUnknown	The default type, forcing ADO to guess.
adCmdFile	The CommandText string is the name of a file-based recordset.
adCmdTableDirect	The CommandText string is a table name, only used with Jet 4.0 databases and providers. You may find it unnecessary to be this specific because adCmdTable usually works just fine.

". . . when you use Connection.Execute you are creating and then destroying a virtual Command object to do the actual work. The advantages to using an explicit Command object:

1. If you're going to execute multiple SQL strings, there is a moderate speed boost to creating the object once and just altering its properties, rather than creating and destroying it.

2. If you create an explicit Command object, you can set properties that are not available through Connection.Execute. For example, you can use Command.Prepared to compile the Command (useful if you're going to execute it more than once), or (if you're using SQL Server) specify a value for Command.Properties ("XSL") to apply an XSL transformation to the results of a query.

Mike Gunderloy, Lark Group, Inc., (`http://www.larkfarm.com`*)*

Listing B-1 shows the typical method for declaring and executing a Command object. This procedure is fairly generic because you can pass the SELECT statement via the text argument. You could also pass the CommandType setting, making the procedure even more flexible. To populate a recordset, use the procedure shown in Listing B-2.

Listing B-1. Command Object

```
Function CmdObject(text As String)
    Dim cmd As ADODB.Command
    Set cmd = New ADODB.Command
    With cmd
        Set .ActiveConnection = CurrentProject.Connection
       .CommandType = adCmdText
        .CommandText = text
        .Execute
    End With
    Set cmd = Nothing
End Function
```

Listing B-2. Recordset Object

```
Function CmdObjectRst(text As String)
    Dim cmd As ADODB.Command
    Dim rst As ADODB.Recordset
    Set cmd = New ADODB.Command
    Set rst = New ADODB.Recordset
    With cmd
        .ActiveConnection = CurrentProject.Connection
        .CommandType = adCmdText
        .CommandText = text
        Set rst = .Execute
    End With
    Set cmd = Nothing
End Function
```

The Connection Property

You'll use the Connection property to set or return a reference for the Connection object. Use the form

```
object.Connection
```

where *object* is either CurrentProject or CodeProject. The CurrentProject object refers to the current MDB or ADP file, and the CodeProject object is a bit more complicated and you probably won't use it as often. It refers to the code database object when you are creating add-ins for Access. The active database is the CurrentProject, and the add-in database is the CodeProject. We're introducing this property to you because it provides a quick method for establishing a connection to the current project. Simply use the following syntax:

```
Dim cnn As ADODB.Connection
Set cnn = CurrentProject.Connection
```

This shortcut allows you to bypass all the provider and data source information that's necessary when connecting to an external data source. We use this method throughout the book in most of our procedure examples in which a connection is required. It is also possible to shorten the code required to open a recordset using the following code:

```
Dim rst as ADODB.Recordset
Set rst = New ADODB.Recordset
rst.open "Employees", CurrentProject.Connection
```

ADO also permits us to work directly with data. We can use the AddNew method to add a record to an existing recordset. The only condition is that you must call the Update method to actually add the new record to the table, as shown here:

```
With rst
      .AddNew
       .Fields("FieldOne") = "New Text"
       .Fields("FieldTwo") = "New Text"
       .Fields("FieldThree") = "New Text"
       .Update
End With
```

This notation is very formal, and field names can be referred to using the syntax:

```
![FieldName]
```

For example, in the preceding example, we could change the field line to read:

```
!FieldOne = "New Text"
```

It is also possible to actually test if the recordset supports the capability to add new records using the Supports property. For example, the preceding statement could be enclosed in an IF statement block which tests this property:

```
IF rst.Supports(adAddNew) Then
    'Run the Code
Else
    'Do something
End if
```

We can also use ADO to update existing data. Note that, when you move to another record following the update, the changes are saved. Be careful of this if you are new to ADO. This is unlike DAO, in which the update had to be explicitly called and used with the Edit method. The Edit method does not exist in ADO.

> **NOTE** *Updating data is best performed using SQL statements (or, if using SQL Server, stored procedures). This example is provided for illustration only.*

The main problem you might have when using ADO to update records is to identify the record to update. In the following example, we will (in keeping with the book's topic) use an SQL string to filter the recordset:

```
Function ADO_Update()
  Dim rst As ADODB.Recordset
  Dim sql as String
  Set rst = New ADODB.Recordset
  sql = "SELECT * FROM Customers WHERE CustomerID = 'AROUT'"
  rst.Open sql,Currentproject.Connection, adOpenKeyset, adLockOptimistic
  With rst
    !CompanyName = "Martin"
    !ContactName= "Martin Reid"
```

```
    !ContactTitle = "Mr"
    .Update
  End With
  rst.Close
End Function
```

The update could be cancelled by calling the CancelUpdate method in the following form. However, if your code has previously called the Update method, then further calls to this method will fail:

```
rst.CancelUpdate
```

> **NOTE** *adLockOptimistic opens an updateable recordset. Record locks are not placed until an attempt is made to actually save the update.*

Microsoft ADO Extensions for DDL and Security (ADOX)

As we have already stated, some things you cannot do directly with SQL and they can be carried out only via code. ADO is used mostly for data manipulation. To work with database objects more easily, Microsoft provides an additional library named Microsoft ADO Extensions for DDL and Security (ADOX), which allows you to work directly with database schema and security. The AppendixB.mdb file (which can be downloaded from `http://www.apress.com`) contains a form that will allow you to run the initial samples shown.

> **NOTE** *Before you try any of these examples, ensure that you have set references to ADO 2.X and ADOX for DDL and Security. We won't attempt to discuss ADOX in depth because numerous resources are available. One of the best resources is of course the Microsoft page at* `http://www.msdn.Microsoft.com`. *Search for ADOX and ADO.*

The ADOX Object Model

Figure B-2 shows the library's object model. The Catalog object contains details about the schema of a database, and the catalog acts as a container for all table, procedure, and view collections. In addition, it also holds the collection used to manipulate security, users, and groups. The ability to manipulate objects within the catalog depends to a large extent on the data provider. Some providers do not support changing schema information. For example, we could not use ADOX to create an SQL Server database because properties for existing tables will be read only and users and groups are not supported. We can add objects to the catalog and remove them. We can open the catalog by setting a connection to the CurrentProject, and a new catalog may be created using the Create method. We will briefly look at the Table object (following). However, a full review of these objects is beyond the scope of this section. For the most part, you won't use ADOX *with* SQL, but perhaps *instead* of SQL.

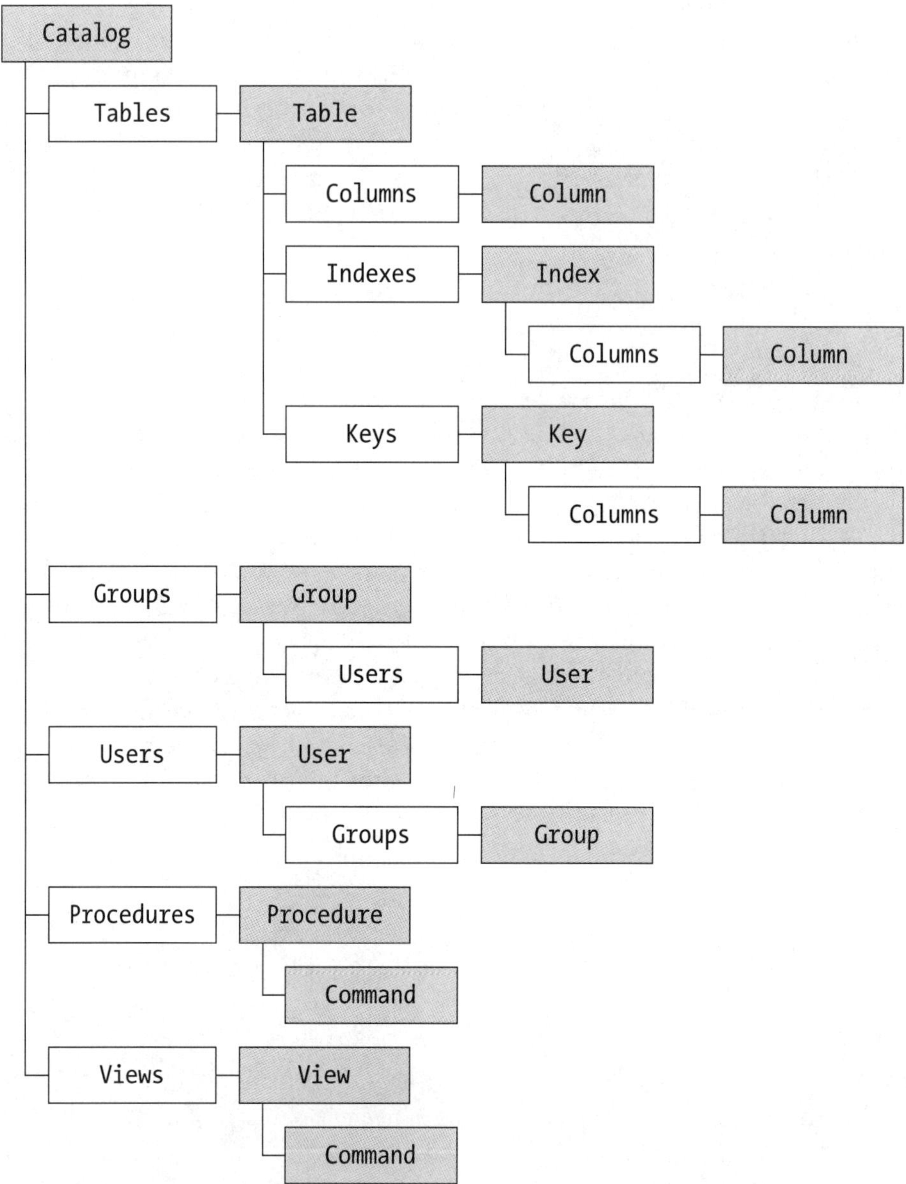

Figure B-2. The ADOX Catalog object contains tables, procedures, and view collections. (© 2001 Microsoft Corporation. Reprinted with permission from Microsoft Corporation.)

The Tables collection contains all the Table objects for the named catalog. We can add a new table using the Append method, check existing tables using the Item property, and delete tables using the Delete method. In addition, the Table object also provides access to the properties of a table, keys, indexes, and columns. Using the properties and collections of the Table object, we can:

- Identify a table using the Name property.
- Discover a table's type (User, System, or Global Temporary) using the Type property.
- Examine or add items to the Columns collection using the Column property.
- Append a column using the Append method.

ADOX offers you another option when creating and redefining database objects. For example, to create a database we could simply execute the following ADOX code:

```
Dim cat As ADOX.Catalog
Set cat = New ADOX.Catalog
cat.Create "Provider = Microsoft.Jet.OLEDB.4.0;Data Source=" _
     & "C:\Apress\Apress.mdb"
Set cat = Nothing
```

This code fragment will create a new database called Apress.mdb in the folder C:\Apress. If the database already exists, the code returns error number –2147217897, which can be trapped using a statement in the form:

```
IF Err.Number = -2147217897 Then
Take some Action
```

> **NOTE** *While writing the above code, I could not get it to work. I spent a considerable amount of time looking at references, DLL files, and searching the Web for answers. But I simply could not get it to run. It turns out that I had made a simple spelling mistake in the Create method's Provider string. The moral of the story is don't look for the hard answer first. Check the code, check the spelling, and then look for the hard answer if the simple check doesn't turn up a solution.*

We are using the top-level object in the ADOX object model, the Catalog object. Each Catalog object refers to a single database, and the Catalog object contains the Tables, Views, Procedures, Groups and Users collections.

The following ADOX code will add a new table to the collection and create several fields. The following code has been added to the click event of a button on a form:

```
Private Sub cbo_addTable_Click()
    Dim Cat As ADOX.Catalog
    Dim tblCustomer As ADOX.Table
    Dim Conn As ADODB.Connection
    Set Conn = New ADODB.Connection
    Conn.Open "Provider = Microsoft.Jet.OLEDB.4.0;Data Source" _
              & " = F:\Chapter8\Apress.mdb"
    Set tblCustomer = New ADOX.Table
    Set Cat = New ADOX.Catalog
    Set Cat.ActiveConnection = Conn
    tblCustomer.Name = "tblCustomer"
    With tblCustomer.Columns
        .Append "CustomerID", adInteger
        .Append "CustomerName", adVarWChar, 35
        .Append "CustAddress", adVarWChar, 35
        .Append "CustTown", adVarWChar, 20
        .Append "CustZipCode", adVarWChar, 12
    End With
    With Cat.Tables
        .Append tblCustomer
        .Refresh
    End With
End Sub
```

This code uses the Catalog object. Note that we also set a connection to the database named Apress.mdb, so Jet knows to which catalog to add the Table object. First, we identified the new Table object as tblCustomer. Once the table is created, you can then append columns to the Table object's Columns collection. In the preceding case, we are appending several columns to tblCustomer. Note the data types that are used, particularly the Unicode as adVarWchar for the text fields. (Unicode is used with Access 2000 and above.) Table 8-2 below lists the ADOX data types and their Access 2002 equivalent. Finally, we append the table to the catalog and refresh the database to make the table visible. One simple problem remains with the preceding code, however: if you execute the example twice, Access will return an error the second time because the table already exists. To deal with this, simply add the line

```
Cat.Tables.Delete "tblCustomer"
```

following the Set Connection statement. If the table does not exist, we will still receive an error.

In addition to using ADOX to add new tables to the database, we can also use it to list existing tables. The following procedure will list all the tables within the current database in a small message box:

```
Private Sub cboViewTables_Click()
    Dim strlisttables as String
    Dim Cat as ADOX.Catalog
    Dim tbl as ADOX.Table
        Set Cat = New ADOX.Catalog
        Cat.ActiveConnection = CurrentProject.AccessConnection
          For Each tbl in Cat.Tables
          strlisttables = strlisttables & vbCrLf & tbl.Name
          Next tbl
     Msgbox strlisttables
End Sub
```

On this occasion, we can use the CurrentProject connection to refer to the appropriate catalog. You may also notice that system tables are included in the message. If you don't need to view the system tables, add the following IF statement after the initial For loop:

```
If tbl.Type <> "TABLE" Then
   strlisttables = strlisttables & vbCrLf & tbl.Name
End If
```

By checking the Type property, we can ensure that only the user tables are listed in the message box.

> **WARNING** *You need to be careful of the connection used. It appears that AccessConnection can't be used to create indexes or primary keys.*

If you examine tblCustomer, you'll notice that we haven't defined a primary key. In the following example, we amend the CustomerID field to act as the table's primary key (make sure that you have the Apress.mdb demonstration file open):

```
Private Sub CboIndex_Click()
    Dim cat As New ADOX.Catalog
    Dim tbl As ADOX.Table
    Dim IndNew As New ADOX.Index
    cat.ActiveConnection = CurrentProject.Connection
```

```
        Set tbl = cat.Tables("tblCustomer")
        Set IndNew = New ADOX.Index
          With IndNew
         . Name = "NewIndex"
         . PrimaryKey = True
         . Unique = True
          End With
    IndNew.Columns.Append ("CustomerID")
    tbl.Indexes.Append IndNew
End Sub
```

The data type of the preceding primary key is set at Number. We can also use ADOX to create an AutoNumber data type, which Access developers often use as a primary key. To do so, we must set the appropriate column property. For example:

```
.Item ("Column_Name").Properties("AutoIncrement") = True
```

It is also possible to manipulate the autonumber seed and increment values using this method. For example, we could add the following code fragment to the prior sample:

```
.properties("Seed") =CLng(15)
.properties("Increment") =CLng(15)
```

This code will start the autonumber with a seed value of 15, incrementing the autonumber by 15 as records are added. The CLng simply ensures that the value we are using (15) is a long data type as required by this setting.

In addition to working with tables, ADOX can also be used to create and amend queries. To work with queries, we can use the Views collection. To add, delete, or amend existing views, we work with the ADO Command object. In this next example, we will use ADOX to create a simple query based on our customer table that we created earlier. The following procedure will create a new query in the ADOX database file that's available for download for this appendix.

```
Dim cmd as New ADODB.Command
Dim cat as New ADOX.Catalog
Cat.ActiveConnection=CurrentProject.Connection
cmd.CommandText = "Select CustomerName,CustAddress,CustTown From
tblCustomer"
cat.Views.Append "qryCustomerDetails", cmd
```

The new query will now be available within the Database window, and you can then use it as normal.

> **NOTE** *The connection can also point to another Access database. For example changing the connection to*
>
> ```
> Cat.ActiveConnection =
> "Provider=Microsoft.Jet.OLEDB.4.0;" _
> & "Data Source=c:\Folder\Database;"
> ```
>
> *will permit you to create the query in the database specified by the path.*

Deleting a query is just as easy, so be careful. The following code will delete from the database the query qryCustomerDetails we just created:

```
Dim cat as New ADOX.Catalog
Cat.Activeconnection=CurrentProject.Connection
Cat.Views.Delete "qryCustomerDetails"
```

ADOX can also be used to work with database security. However, many Access developers find that using JET 4 and SQL makes the process of creating users and managing security easier. In this way, we can (for example) use SQL to create a new user account:

```
CREATE USER username Password pid
```

where *pid* is used to uniquely identify the user across workgroups.
The equivalent ADOX code to create this user is:

```
Dim cat = New ADOX.Catalog
cat.ActiveConnection = CurrentProject.Connection
cat.users.Append "AineReid", "Martin"
Set cat = Nothing"
```

Note that, in this case, we do not set a *pid* value, which ADOX sets automatically.

> **TIP** *Be very careful when working with security via code but especially when working directly with JET because no warnings are issued and you may find the database locked even to you! Make sure that you read and understand the Access security model before you start messing with it.*

This very brief section on ADOX introduces you to a powerful technique that can be used to manipulate your database schema and objects via code. We have given you a mere taste of ADOX, and many areas have not been covered. But what you have seen should encourage you to research and experiment with these powerful techniques.

Index

Symbols

A

D

T

U